Treading Through:

45 Years of Philippine Dance

Treading Through:
45 Years of Philippine Dance

Basilio Esteban S. Villaruz

The University of the Philippines Press
Diliman, Quezon City

and

Philippine Folklife Museum Foundation
San Francisco, California, USA

THE UNIVERSITY OF THE PHILIPPINES PRESS
E. de los Santos St., UP Campus, Diliman, Quezon City 1101
Tel. No.: 9253243 / Telefax No.: 9282558
e-mail: press@up.edu.ph

and

Philippine Folklife Museum Foundation
San Francisco, California, USA

Book Design by Zenaida N. Ebalan

ISBN 978-971-542-509-4

Printed in the Philippines by EC-tec Commercial

to my mother

Ester de los Santos Villaruz

Contents

Foreword

To write a foreword to the present volume is a task that I should not have acquiesced to undertake. Going through its content under time pressure, one immediately realizes that its originally conceived title *Look, Talk Dance* is quite deceivingly simple for what the volume really is. As it turned out, the book is a supreme challenge to one's literacy and imagination to properly introduce and capture in just a few words and paragraphs myriads of things that dance as it unfolded in the Philippines in the last forty-five years has engendered, at least in the mind and pen of the author Basilio Esteban "Steve" Villaruz. While one can easily identify its voluminous content as the compendium of the lifetime papers, lectures, and reviews written by Steve, the book itself is one of those rare publications that either defy categorization or at best create its own reading category. The information on dance in the context of its practice, concept and popular understanding in the Philippines is simply encyclopedic in scope, transcending the boundaries of art criticism and journalism and traversing the thresholds of dance ethnology, dance history, philosophy, literature, anthropology, sociology, musicology, and the humanities. At the end of the day, one can also conclude that the book is a biographical dissertation of the author's own personal life of dance. In a way approximating his unobtrusive and modest persona, he has managed to so subtly interface his own not-so-modest contributions with the entire dance scenario that he has impressively "choreographed." Everything that Steve Villaruz has written are not pure theory or interpretative fantasy (though one could mistake the incredibly rich documentation as something close to a cosmic chimera) but his very own empirical ventures and experiences either as a subjective executor or an involved, sensitized observer.

On the other hand, in spite of its multidimensional and multilayered content and substance, the entire volume is anything but difficult or taxing for any reader to ingest. It is a printed material that can either stimulate the intellectual and academic genomes of an earnest scholar or feed the curious and unsophisticated cravings of an eclectic aficionado. I would easily attribute this not only to the author's fine literary grounding but much more to his virtuosic and articulate expertise in the art of dance. It is only a dancer and an accomplished conjurer of motion who can successfully imbue the intellectual, philosophical and aesthetic discourse with such engaging fluidity and candor that can easily transport the reader through the labyrinthian depths and luxuriant spaces of the dance world without being subjected to the overbearing language of present-day scholarship.

Whether it is from the vantage point of history or stylistics, as in the accounts on Philippine ballet's French connection or the dance diaspora in the Philippines through the years, the extent and volume of data that Steve has collected are simply staggering. One gets the impression that the author literally did not leave a single stone unturned as far as dance in the Philippines is concerned. I am almost sure that one will find in the present volume every name and personality—whether of great or little significance, entire repertoires properly categorized and stylistically classified, events vividly chronicled, companies, schools, studios, other publications, and the thousand and one miscellanea related to both Philippine dance and the dance world. What is also amazing in uncovering this cornucopia of dance knowledge is that it was accomplished and communicated not by way of recovering dead files of forgotten lore but by retelling them as though each event is of recent vintage, occurring within the temporal ambitus of the author's and reader's contemporary life. Steve has evoked and vivified the memories of Ricardo Cassell, Anita Kane, Lubov Adameit, Kay Williams, and Mara Selheim, international icons responsible in varying degrees to the establishment and evolution of ballet in the Philippines, as well as the local inheritors of the ballet patrimony in such celebrated names as Remedios "Totoy" de Oteyza, Felicitas Layag Radaic, Eddie Elejar, Julie Borromeo, and several others. The illustrious sixties are relived with the founding of the

Hariraya Ballet and the Dance Theatre Philippines, two companies that directly linked Philippine ballet to such international figures as Poul Gnatt, Sulamith Messerer, Erik Bruhn, and August Bournonville. (I would not have known these names were it not for this book.) In short, the present volume could easily be the most comprehensive publication on dance in the Philippines to date, not in the form of a lexicon or dictionary, but in extended and well-chiseled essays and a host of critical and highly attractive vignettes memorializing in living images specific occasions and events as well as tributes to dance personalities and their achievements in the last forty-five years. In a few instances, the essay format changes into direct transcription of interviews, as those with Edna Vida and Cecile Sicangco.

It is to be noted that his tributes to Philippine dance personalities are contextualized by gender distinction, unequivocally revealing with candid frankness, the chasm that separates the female and male dancers in the eyes of Filipino society. While the author is not wanting in giving due significance and recognition to the historical and artistic contributions of such pioneering icons as Leonor Orosa Goquingco, Francisca Reyes Aquino, de Oteyza, Tina Santos, Alice Reyes, and other women of vision in Philippine dance, Steve has rightly championed the almost heroic self-immolation and dedicated idealism of the Filipino male dancer who not only faced the social ostracism connected to being a Filipino male dancer but also achieved excellence in their chosen medium of artistic expression. Thus, the author's colloquy on the likes of Tony Llacer, Eddie Elejar, Nonoy Froilan, Tony Fabella, and others, carries its own distinctive gravity and impact on the sympathetic reader, especially considering that the author himself has proudly kept his share of both the bane and the glory of Philippine danseurship.

More than providing a semi-definitive source of information on personalities, landmark events and philosophical truisms in the realm of Philippine dance, the essays in the present volume collectively create a broader view of an art form whose formal concept evolved as an integral part of an artistic heritage from Europe and western civilization at large. In the context of the Filipinos' search and erstwhile invention of a national and self-identity out of disparate ethnicities and differentiated historico-cultural traditions, the author has advanced the phenomenon of dance as another prism which could effect some degree of discernment of what could possibly be a or the Filipino psyche as well as a Filipino's sense of humanism. A view of the uniqueness of the Filipino dance perspective may be accessed in the author's deliberation on dance as ritual, dance as both craft and a way of life—its function as an occupational, spiritual, transformative and transcendental instrument in human communication as well as its utilization of space in theater and in real life. As a reflection of human behavior and conduct, dance likewise reflects social institutions in structures concretized and materialized in the human body as it moves in harmony with its own spatial environment. His in-depth account of the Subanen *buklog* clearly illustrates the larger role of dance in social and community life in the Philippine setting. In this ritual, the bounded definitions of the art of dance become subsumed by the collectivity of human volition and the use of multi-directional space, that are involved in the process of creating local expressive productions of breath-taking magnitude.

Such a scenario provides the author with a contextual framework by which to comment (this time as a true critic) with his wonted metaphoric subtlety, on the state of artistic integrity and freedom in Philippine contemporary dance. Using space as a point of trajectory, he cites the role of small spaces and stages in giving birth to creative adventures and almost adoringly exalts the artistic struggles of non-mainstream artists like Myra Beltran, Luis Layag, Paul Morales, and the young Ernest Hojilla, a product of the UP College of Music Dance Program, itself born out of idealism and unfettered vision. Without much trepidation on possibly antagonizing his own journalistic milieu, the author expressed his reservation on how these small spaces are lamentably "shunned by critics and neglected by media.". In contrast, large open spaces have become the instruments of "political and commercial agendas" as exemplified by the proliferation of dance festivals and extravagant spectacles of curious intent and para-artistic motivations. He further critiques the current general apathy of present-day audiences and producers on unknown creative explorations and the commodification of an otherwise potent Filipino imagination in order to cater to the unimaginative mass. In this particular discourse which actually occupies the opening section of the book captioned "Carving Out Spaces for Identity," the author has made a rather bold assertion of his recognition of the value of the young, the independent, the sensitive, the perceptive, and the enlightened though-unheralded practitioners of the art of dance. These observations are by no means groundless as Steve's dance career (defined by groundbreaking endeavors and achievements as the first Filipino choreologist, chief designer and implementor of the UP College of Music dance program, dance critic, scholar, theorists, pedagogue, choreographer and dance artist) serves as the very epitome of his own advocacy.

Finally, the space metaphor can aptly summarize the total contributions of this book, in that no matter how they are portrayed and perceived as to their impact in the Philippine dance world, each and every person, aspect, production, and event is given its own legitimated space somewhere in the four-hundred plus pages of this book. As earlier cited in this writing, these have been documented in larger historical and even global contexts (as the age of space exploration led by Yuri Gagarin and Neil Armstrong vis-á-vis the political experimentation of Ferdinand Marcos) and transforming them into timeless ingredients in the totality of Filipino life and culture. Much a reflection of Steve's singular and self-imposed mission as the Philippine's premier dance scribe, the book likewise is an embodiment of what dance is—motion in space, where the pages provide the spaces for everything that dance in the Philippines has undergone, generated, and has become. It touches and highlights practically everything under the sun—culture, society, history, politics, economics, gender, religion, education and pedagogy, research, literature, theater, and music to a degree. With the theory and practice of dance serving as the fulcrum and binding force in the present discourse, the world that surrounds and revolves around it as presented in *Treading Through: 45 Years of Philippine Dance* has suddenly become boundless.

Ramón P. Santos, Ph.D.
December 29, 2005

Acknowledgments

When you've lived a rewardingly variegated life, you have so much and so many to thank for encouragement and influences.

One notable point is that much of these folks and friends are women. Many women have been so supportive of my career. This starts with my mother, Ester de los Santos Villaruz who never discouraged my involvement in dance despite the long-lasting opposition of my father. (My father's negative attitude the more reinforced my determination, like a dancer's foot against the resistant floor to keep a balance. In fact, because of him, I came to choreograph *The Rebels* to music by Leos Janacek inspired by the story of the prodigal son, but keeping the thematic cycle of authority-rebellion left open.)

It was also my mother who gave me the arts; she would sing or whistle over her sewing machine, or read romances from where I took off elsewhere. Two stories go: 1) as a young girl, she would escape washing dishes by running off to our barrio's bailes, and 2) when she was pregnant with me, she always dreamt she was dancing. Add to that my elder sister Edna Villaruz Bergara who was a singer, always the lead in our church choir, and our youngest Cecilia Villaruz Cua who also went to dance.

My first ballet teacher in Bacolod, Elsie Uytiepo Torrejon, offered me free tuition after my father refused to pay anymore for my lessons or buy new ballet shoes (so that I made my own by hand or with my mother's sewing machine, breaking many needles). Later, her brother Pancho Uytiepo endorsed me to Remedios "Totoy" de Oteyza for a scholarship in Manila.

In Iloilo where I had my first job as literature teacher, I had a most supportive musical director for our CPU Student Ballet in Elora Garcia

Jordan. Nanay Loring was our organist in the university church; she sustained an intellectual discussion in a provincial setting. Our university president, Joseph T. Howard, became an informal patron for the productions of my ballet group on campus. He initiated an Academic Arts Festival which then helped launch my serious choreographic career out there. At the same time, we had the likes of Edith Albaladejo Dizon and Majella Caipang Palacios to make that campus busy with inspired productions.

Another woman in Felicitas "Tita" Layag Radaic took me in as teacher and choreographer after I left Ballet Philippines (then the CCP Dance Company, earlier the Alice Reyes and Modern Dance Company). Even before that, she and Julie Borromeo, with Eddie Elejar, Tony Llacer and El Gabriel spruced up my technique to more presentable level. When I came back from my study in London in 1980, Tita offered me the artistic direction (her own position) of Dance Theatre Philippines.

Soon after, Cora Dioquino sought me out in the St. Theresa College (Quezon City) studio of Tita to help set up the dance degree program in the UP College of Music, under the deanship of Ramon Santos. It was a return to Diliman where I had taught English under such assiduous chair like Concepcion Dadufalza. Before that and while in Iloilo, I had a penpal in then ex-UP Josefina Constantino, now Sis. Susana Jose, who continued to guide me (after a course in Far Eastern University). She also went on to write the libretto for Lucrecia "King" Kasilag's operatorio *The Spiritual Canticle* based on St. John of the Cross, on Christ and His Bride, the Church, which I choreographed. Her and my other theologian friends' influence must have inspired me to do *The Rebels*, *The Resurrection of Lazarus* (to Messaien) and Ryan Cayabyab's *Misa (Filipina)* which had the martyrdom of a Marcial Bonifacio ending in Christ's own sacrifice.

My most supportive editors were Ester Dipasupil of *Manila Times* and *Manila Standard*, and Thelma Sioson San Juan of *Manila Chronicle*. Their publications I now heartily acknowledge. Earlier, there were Angel Lobaton in Bacolod's *Negros Clarion* and N.V.M. Gonzalez at *Weekly Nation*. Running the Ballet Federation of the Philippines' newsletter *Sayaw Silanganan* gave me focus as dance writer and editor. My editors at the CCP publications I have acknowledged in the introduction, topped by

Nic Tiongson's indefatigable scholarly drive. (Ethnic materials in my writing I owe much to Ramon Obusan.) That perhaps enabled me to edit the 1998 proceedings of the Philippine International Dance Conference, coming out as *Dance in Revolution, Revolution in Dance* volume. There are two UP publications to be acknowledged, from *Diliman Review* and College of Arts and Letters with Commission on Higher Education.

Herewith, I must apologize for some quotations that I can no longer trace specifically.

Many conferences, seminars and workshops enabled me to write some of the papers in this volume, mostly those run by World Dance Alliance in the Philippines, Hong Kong, Malaysia, Indonesia, Japan, India, Korea, Philadelphia, Dusseldorf; Philippine Studies Association and the Sangandaan 2003 conference; Association for Asian Studies; Dalubhasaan ng Edukasyon sa Sining at Kultura (DESK); Francisca Reyes Aquino Memorial Foundation; and for presentations at University of Michigan and University of California-Riverside.

Doubtlessly, my travel and study grants through the Asian Cultural Council, British Council, Goethe Institute, SPAFA-SEAMEO, (past) USSR Ministry of Culture, International Theatre Institute-Japan, Japan Foundation and the National Commission for Culture and the Arts (and its Dangal Haraya for a life-achievement in dance) have also strengthened not only my dance background but also my resolve to stick to dance scholarship.

Through thick and thin, the challenge my dancers at Dance Theatre Philippines, UP Dance Company and the UP dance majors (a few now writing their theses), and my general education students in dance in the university keep my focus and energy in dance inculcation and education—a life-long but inspired task that I hope will be followed by them.

Finally, this book would not have been possible without the nudges from two women, Ruth Pison and Jing Pantoja Hidalgo, former UP Press director.

Introduction:
Body Biting a Biscuit

We are what we eat.

At a summer workshop in Baguio in May 2004, I got a pack of waffle biscuit from Zamboanga. This came from Johar Bahru (Malaysia) with Arabic and Chinese scripts, calling what I bite into as biskut coklat. Its trademark is even more global, "Apollo: Boy Boy." What a good lot to bite and decipher!

The biscuit was chocolate-coated, wrapped in colors orange-yellow-red plastic, and among its ingredients were palm kernel fat, sugar, cocoa, soya and vanilla. Some of these are what were hungered for from the East that started old-time colonialism. Or today's WTO. (Food as culture and culture is so political!)

This little pack dramatizes the difference in diet—at least in packaging—between "down" there and "up" here, between the so-called North and South divide in global ascendancy and economy. Here in Manila I get Hershey or Cadbury from the North or "abroad."

I have not been to Zamboanga City since the 60s (and Dipolog since the 90s) where Dance Theatre Philippines performed with tansan caps for admission. (We repeated this at the Araneta Coliseum, filling it to the rafters, when bottled drink—and jeepney fare—was just ten centavos, and lunch at Little Quiapo was a peso.) If I remember right, it was at a Jesuit school where we performed. But we also went out to the Badjao shore. To be surprised by calendar pictures of one of us up a sari-sari store. Tina Santos was also then modelling high-fashion gowns together with Chona Recto Kasten, Toni Serrano and her own ballet teacher Joji Felix Velarde. (She is one of our loveliest but forgotten ballerinas, the first I saw in a first ballet performance I ever saw in a Bacolod moviehouse.) In many ways that incident was a show of north-over-south hegemony.

What further dramatizes this for me today is that in origin I am neither "here" nor "there." I am a Visayan provinciano, belonging to the low-economic middle, neither au courant to the fashionable Existentialism of mid-20th century nor to Islamism except in a course in history of Spain and my father's (then affordable) *Life International* issues. There, in that middle, I was evangelized by long-predetermined territorial distribution decided on by American missions.

So that much of my life adjusted to the shifts and subleties of differences, diachronically and synchronically delineating conceptual and affinial loyalties and confusions. Or stomach upsets.

To begin with, I negotiated Hiligaynon, Tagalog (how Pilipino was then called and taught) and English in school, and in college majored in English and History. (Furthered in Asian Studies, Comparative Literature and Benesh movement notation later.) All along I was getting free tuition in King Louis XIV-descended art of ballet from a Luva Adameit-descended Elsie Uytiepo Torrejon in Bacolod. While doing graduate work and teaching assistantship in UP, I also did some dancing until a UP-Rockefeller scholarship allowed me more time to steal away! Soon I traded school-teaching for Terpsichore.

Somehow I progressed on, not exactly as a great dancer then but as an obsessed choreographer and later artistic director. Those kinds of job were of different texting systems, publicly displayed on stage, amid the petty politics of dancers. (And later of hegemonic dominance of influential companies, a reflection of our other kinds of group-dynamics.) To adequately survive, I was also teaching dance in Manila, Mandaluyong, Makati and Malabon—long distances to negotiate by pedestrian and choreographed steps.

A sustaining supporter of my generation's choreographic drive was engineer-photograph Rudy Vidad. His phenomenal recorded music collection and his magnanimity oiled much our dance compositions, allowing us to know and use obscure contemporary composers.

Then I went on to study the text-bound "reading and writing" of dance in a movement notation system in London. (Which we now demand as added-literacy for UP dance majors in the College of Music. Unfortunately, it is a thing which has never taken off elsewhere here, because dancers and dance teachers in the Philippines prefer the cumbersome word-oriented "movement notation" which communicates insularly but not to the rest of the world.) While out there, I wrote home (to a different college) proposing a dance degree program I had long contemplated.

From the academe to stage and back to academe, I designed a technical and theoretical degree in dance in UP with Ramon Santos and Cora Dioquino. From knowing the dance in the body, I got back into "dancing dance" in different measures or "feet," in embodying movement in verbs, and in pinning down in thought what's fleeting on the ground or up in the air.

I have many to thank for giving me lots of practice. Back in Bacolod, I started reviewing performances for Angel Lobaton's *Negros Clarion*. In my three-year teaching job in Iloilo, my chair published me while our university president (Joseph T. Howard) helped me realize my first serious choreographic writings on campus. While doing graduate work and to sustain myself, I wrote for each issue of Cubao's *Weekly Nation* without fail for two years. At first N.V.M. Gonzalez supervised my output; he also introduced me to mainstream newspaper life in Sta. Cruz, to his violin maker nearby, and hired me for the secretariat of the first UP writers' workshop in Los Baños. For the Araneta-owned weekly, I dared review all (similar to what Morli Dharam, Rosalinda Orosa, Rodrigo Perez III were doing): music, dance, plays, the visual arts, even films.

I must have gained some credibility, because I went on to Alex Hufana's *Pamana*, Pablo Tariman's *Arts Monthly*, Bien Lumbrera's *Kultura* and editing an issue of *Ani*, all for the Cultural Center of the Philippines; column-writing for *Manila Times* and *Manila Standard*; reviewing for *Manila Bulletin* and *Manila Chronicle*; contributing for free to *Business Day* and *Today*. During the Ballet Federation of the Philippines days in the 70s, I edited (and at the start cut the stencils) of its bi-monthly newsletters, *Sayaw Silanganan*. Nicanor Tiongson entrusted to me the fifth (dance) volume of

The CCP Encyclopedia of Philippine Art as writer and editor, and two prize-winning scripts for dance documentaries (directed by Ramon Obusan) in the *Tuklas Sining* series. (For these I got the Congress on Research in Dance—CORD—award for outstanding contribution to dance research in 2003.)

Moreover, foreign publications in Hong Kong, Singapore, Korea, Japan, Germany and the United States solicited articles from me. Several articles in this book come from these publications, as well as papers read in conferences, national and international, sponsored by the World Dance Alliance.

Through the years I negotiated through various texts and contexts: choreographic and literary, songs and sonatas, the Bible and the Mass, Jose Rizal and Thomas Mann, the dancing body and the social body. Some of these I can only give the reader glimpses of, but reference shall be made to what is Philippine dance, its operation in creation, performance, and reception, with the complex dynamics of our society in mind.

That biskut coklat from Zamboanga signals and signifies what has gotten into me and more. It stands for what attracts me, what I have to adjust to, admit—or reject: of much that I have bitten into, that now you can also taste in this collection and recollection of some forty-plus years, since I first danced in our elementary school's first-prize rigodon/rigaudon in our town plaza in Talisay.

When I bite into the biscuit, I sense something more than the taste and the ingredients; I am confronted by the mix, like the digested hybridity in Hommi Bhabha or the adaptation of Indian theatre to the modern world in Rustom Barucha. This is how we view our contemporary body, speaking in various tongues (languages and media, disciplines and contexts, times and spaces); of the divisions within and without us which we try to unify: the life context. It's biology and psychology, anatomy and philosophy, past and.present; the varying geographies, ideologies, economic directions charted and still to chart.

This book goes through my (and hopefully yours by empathy, about dance) various digestive processes in my artistic and cultural education. I was born through the body (changing in age, training and adaptation) and ideas that were learned and unlearned, between reason and belief, techniques and sometimes trance. This book is about my dance education as it is about what I see in our training, dissemination and reception of the art. Sections are divided according to basic aspects in order to understand dance. Separation does not mean compartments; they are on the whole related and shed light on each other. In this way, it is as a reader for dance that I have meant this book to serve, which I believe is a first to be put together locally.

My further reason in putting together the book is to hopefully modify the climate in our thinking and practice in the arts. What is sad is that sometimes we grow into arrogance, into monolithic notions in an ever-changing world, undergoing transformations of generations, redefining localizations and identities. From the kinesthetic wisdom of dance, I hope we keep our balance or common sense as we tread on in our cultural history. I always liked Doris Humphrey's description of dance as heightened, stylized walk as the arc between two deaths—the dynamic transfer between the standing and the fallen which are the stillnesses.

Dance never expires. It is all of the balances and off-balances that communicate life, or art that symbolizes life. Just as well, dynamic thinking is such: a static resolve poised like a flying arrow aiming for acclaim. Thinking (and reading, writing about it) is just like dancing, biting into something mixed, betwixt many arts and parts, that makes sense to one, to some or to all of us.

BASILIO ESTEBAN S. VILLARUZ
Quezon City, 2006

Carving Out Spaces for Identity

A fight over territorial space is so much more than a defense to keep self, family, and tribe. It is holding on to a heritage, a system of beliefs and behavior, and an assurance of a future beyond the self.

Indigenous struggles have led to rebellions and revolutions, as seen in Europe (for example, the reassertion of identities in the former Yugoslavia), the successful and still simmering struggles in Indonesia (East Timor and Aceh), and the long-standing claims for autonomy of the Moro in our own shores.

At the same time, migrations break down physical and psychological borders. Filipinos who leave home are now citizens of the world, even if their hearts are still tied to the Philippines. For everyone, stories and histories, travel and technology have opened eyes and ears to human rights and protective laws, enabling each to claim both physical and spiritual homes wherever and whenever he or she is.

These changing landscapes of loyalties may now threaten the long-defended notion of nation. Even globalization can be reversed in autochthonous assertions, an issue now much more projected by the media. The media has two- or multi-pronged uses and effects; it can strengthen or subvert solidarities. At no time in history has society, national or international, been more exposed to assent or dissent, particularly in the context of fluid political and cultural shifts.

In the arts, to consolidate national influence, old and new hegemonies have built royal institutions or more contemporaneous cultural centers. Funding for the arts is ruled over by councils and commissions that can solidify into bureaucracies that are urban counterparts to old tribal hierarchies. Claims to democratic governance can be negated by political enclaves and patronage policies. What is "democratic" can be so defined, determined, and dispensed by those who are dominant in number, perpetuity, and ideology. For example, the Philippines under the Marcoses was far ahead of Hong Kong, Singapore, and Malaysia in instituting a cultural center to imitate royal theaters and museums in Europe, or the Lincoln and Kennedy Centers in the United States, validating and perpetuating Eurocentric heritage and nostalgia.

We were all so grateful for and gratified by our Cultural Center of the Philippines, only to realize that it accommodates only a few, perhaps just a favored few. Those included are happy to assert their self-proclaimed "flagship" identities. Those excluded continue to seek their spaces in municipalities and provinces—if these are at all hospitable to the arts and not invested solely in more populist and political ameliorative programs. It took a long time to legislate on (still limited) local autonomy, a substitute for outright federalism which seems to be a feared form of governance. So many more artistic initiatives (not always noticed and ignored by all-too-few critics) are often private, even arising in poor communities. This problem of visibility and identity are well discussed in *Choreographing Difference* by Ann Cooper Albright (1997) and *Butting Out* by Ananya Chatterjea (2004) that covers class, color, gender, and marginality.

Two contemporaneous but contrasting spaces that have come to design and assert their own concepts, genres, and actualities are the open streets and the studio-size places. These spaces are the subject of this investigation.

On the Street Where We Live

A traditional space that has recently pluralized in municipal uses is the street. Where previously it had been the territory of saints and church-related feasts as seen in processions, the street has more increasingly been the site of industrial, touristic, and cultural projections. Sadly, much of these have become so popular as contemporary projects to the neglect of such traditional practices as the *daigon*, *panuluyan*, and *pastores de belen*.

Even such religious genres as the *ati-atihan* in Aklan and the *sinulog* in Cebu have been swept over by secular, political, and commercial color. Invented counterparts of the sinulog are Camiguin's lanzones festival, where people wave branches instead of the Santo Niño image, and San Carlos's (Negros Occidental) *pintaflores* (body-painting in floral designs). Newly spawned ones like the *dinagyang* in Iloilo and the *masskara* in Bacolod have been accused of having no "authentic" basis. Mindanaoans flock to the hyped-up January feast in Cebu to compete in the choreographed narration of the conversion (into Christianity) story dressed in their Manobo, Maranaw, or T'boli extravagance. Or sail to Manila to join a newer Aliwan competition for the biggest of prizes ever in the contemporary genre of street-dance contest. Municipalities find excuses in domestic industry or revived legends to stage-manage more feasts, as demonstrated in the flowers in Baguio (*panagbenga*), pandan plants in Mapandan, lanterns in San Fernando (Pampanga), shoes in Marikina, or *tinapa* in Lemery (Batangas).

But who and how is an outsider to question the making of new "traditions" under new situations and dispensations? (I suspect that the invitation of an "independent" jury from outside a community is also window-dressing and a means for a sought-after validation from an "advanced" center as Metro Manila.) Accusations about the lack of authenticity forget the communal rise of folklore, often hidden in a past and anonymity (attributed to a tribe or people). On the other hand, modern art forms like painting and the novel (also called "fiction," a very unsettling term) have long established their own conventions and critical parameters.

If you look at the street scenes of Breughel and Goya, the masques, the *commedia dell'arte*, the funerals in Bali and our own *comedia/moro-moro* and *moriones*, these have always been outdoor activities. Out in the open, customs are made anytime by a group of people, perhaps to celebrate a saint or hero, lore or lure. In our time, customs are also used to sell a product, a political leadership (as European monarchs did), or a media outfit that can rake in many advertisements.

What I find interesting is the rise of new choreographers (plus designers and directors) for this genre. Many of them first learned their trade in school and field presentations, some simply aping what they see on television (not aware of the illusory but restricted studio space of the medium). Often, they are accused of having no "craft" and no sense of sophistication. (The reverse is interesting because staged choreography started off with the so-called proto-theater forms as rituals and processions.) These choreographers' kind of space is made of ground and sky, open to loud bands or whatever needs amplification, with dancers deployed in a non-proscenium manner and without pause, as there are no exits in between. In the former presentation of the sinulog outside of Cebu's sports complex, choreographies could be viewed from varied angles.

Moreover, the audience itself can be as mobile. When the old Dance Theatre Philippines took on the Ballet at the (Rizal) Park seasons, they accepted the flux of their audience, the coming and going of the viewing public during the performance. The old Luneta crowd had been there since the open-air concerts during the Spanish and American regimes, the latter raising the constabulary band that went all the way to National Artist Col. Antonino Buenaventura and his successors.

The roots and aesthetics of this new genre of choreographic presentation in the streets still have to be justly accessed, especially in the context of social semiotics and expressional phenomena. Academicians and proscenium-stage choreographers judging this genre may have to examine their own reception in terms of the social necessities that brought it about.

Speaking in Intimate Spaces

In contrast to large spaces, we now have studio spaces in Metro Manila. (There may be others in the regions, but I have not been to many, only to one or two. I also remember that Agnes Locsin started choreography in the dance studio of her mother and in Ateneo de Davao. I myself started choreography in a small physical education gym of Central Philippine University in Iloilo.) Artists who left established dance companies now come to terms with their relocated selves in confined spaces and as small-time entrepreneurs balancing art and economics (which Nicanor Tiongson says can evolve into the aesthetics of poverty, much experienced by many theater groups).

Now, in their new roles, these artists follow their mentors' steps in setting up a school or dance studio where they can continue their craft and calling, and engage in the inevitable task of training young dancers to perpetuate their art. They are not always supported by boards of trustees or corporate subsidies.

Those who have stuck to their calling as serious dancers manage to carve out new sounds and shapes to maintain their authenticity as creative artists. I remember Manolo Rosado who flitted from studio to studio in Metro Manila to teach and realize his choreographies, even just for studio recitals. Rosalia Merino Santos nursed our modern dance in a small studio at Far Eastern University while running the better-known FEU Folk Dance Troupe. Still oriented to stage presentations, partly because we had no studios of our own, Luis Layag's Dancers of Mercury and my Movement Men/Manila operated through pick-up productions or under the auspices of private schools. Our time raised a number of other choreographers for this kind of managing, often for then fashionable musicals and religious schools' commemorative celebrations.

Today, in the forefront of studio presentations is Myra Beltran with her Dance Forum, first inspired by her collaboration with Enrico Labayen from San Francisco. (The US has a long tradition of solo artists and small modern dance companies, as in the reformist New Dance in the sixties of Judson Church and the environs of Soho, and the rest of Manhattan today.) Often sharing her space on West Avenue, Quezon City is Chameleon Dance Company of Jojo and Ida Lucila, and now of Raul Alcoseba. From this space, Beltran consistently espouses the cause of independent (of establishment structure and agenda) dancers, often collaborating with musical and visual artists. Her own kind of work sustains serious pieces (including writing her own narratives, scenarios, and public espousals) and sincerity of purpose worked out with other dancers and choreographers. She has also allied herself with feminist causes, but not of the restrictive kind. She has worked with and presented all kinds of artists, of different genders and class colors.

For their part, the Lucilas have helped out dancers and choreographers without elitist backgrounds, giving them opportunities to present themselves and to be given serious public consideration in Metro Manila and on tours. In their midst, they have nurtured such unconventional choreographers as Raul Aldecoa, perhaps our only butoh-like dance-maker who spins his creations out solely from his own imagination.

Also in Quezon City is the Airdance studio on Quezon Avenue, where three ex-Ballet Philippines choreographers (like the Lucilas and many others) present not only their own works but those of their own young members and other groups (such as Ernest Mandap who now has his own group in France, after dancing with Jeune Ballet de France and Claude Brumachon company). Paul Morales, a theater major from UP (and alumnus of Transitions of London's Laban Center) is deliberately introspective or ironic in his pieces. These he can alter through the witty juxtaposition of content and musical styles. In contrast is the forceful impact of Dwight Rodrigazo, as in his prize-winning *Los Indios Bravos*, seen in spectacular stage construction or in well-woven textures of a solo presentation. A third is Christine Maranan Novales, a dance major from UP who can write out strange sketches as in the solo *Ernest*, which has the oddest of ballerinas (a male), both agile and awkward.

A discovery in Airdance's midst is Avel Bautista, whose craftsmanship seems to be always sure, and his telling compelling in its weaving in of shapes and relations. He has one of the surest hands in the group, and unassumingly so.

Once all in one group called E-Dance, colleague Gerard Mercado carries on the identity from the Pasig end. I have seen only a few of his pieces; they are obviously with serious intent, a perspective that perhaps he learned from Agnes Locsin, who made him a protagonist in her ballets for Ballet Philippines.

Another leader in this genre is Juan Jay Cruz. Also a UP theater major and a prize-winning playwright, he dares bare both body and soul in most of his solo pieces. He gets inside himself to courageously share a conviction, sometimes starting off with a personal or social ritual, or plunging into a seemingly spontaneous outburst of energy and time-space exploration. He is not bound by any accustomed technique but he can be marvelous in knitting and unknitting movements in sly constructions. Aside from his Malate studio, associate Cruz with a cubicle of a gallery at the old Marikina Shoe Fair shops in Cubao, and you see how space shapes him and how he shapes space. He is not as public an advocate like Beltran, but his being candid and gay in his presentations prevents anyone from missing who he is and what his dances are like.

Often seen in these artists' company are two young ladies of dance, Donna Miranda and Nina Habulan. They are both still carving out their specific identities, but their focused intentions or directions are already worthy of respect. They adapt well to various dimensions and shapes of space to resonate personal or confessional inclinations.

This was a recent surprise with Elena Laniog, who performed with these two ladies at the narrow Green Papaya. She worked with the wall to evoke a dialogue. Her other solo, *Isa*, done for the Asia Pacific Arts Forum in Taipei, was more spacious but still drawn from and inner motivation. With Herbert Alvarez, also of UP, Laniog fleshed out a deconstructed *Petrouchka* as *Pedro Kusinero*, which they both reset in Subic and infused with a caustic postcolonial commentary. In her recent more showy and virile *Warrior Women* many may miss a critique of phallocentric society in the use of a *bahag* (g-string) manipulated by two dancers on pointes and the piercing female voice from Pinikpikan. (As of this writing, she is scheduled to premiere a piece for the Asia Young Choreographers Project of the Jih Sun Foundation for Education in Taiwan.)

A colleague of theirs in UP is Ernest Hojilla. He is adept in devising movements, such as for the UP Concert Chorus where he is a resident choreographer. He may have to tighten his management of both content and construction to arrive at more credible, creditable works. What is also striking is his accompanying gift as designer (sets and costumes), something that reminds me of Luis Layag. This we can see in Hojilla's striking configurations in *Enigma* (to the music of Ramón Santos), and in *Noche Despues Mariposas*, *Didgeridoo Incantations*, and *Holocausts Forever*, all to the riveting music of Erik Santos.

Both Laniog and Hojilla have worked with Flordeliza Fernandez of the UP Dance Company. A prize-winning choreographer, Fernandez can be entrancing in a minimalist work as *Of Death and Resurrection* (to the music of Josefino Toledo), or assertive in a woman's statement, as in *Femina*. Her translation of *Les Noces* into *Ang Kasal* captures both the Nijinsky original's sketching of marital relations and the puissant air of the Cordilleras. Working with her in Diliman as artistic associate, I've always marveled at Fernandez's focus and facility in making dances. Unfortunately, she has migrated to Canada.

At the Cultural Center's Tanghalang Batute and Tanghalang Aurelio Tolentino, a black box and a small theater, respectively, we have seen tantalizing works by Alden Lugnasin. A choreographer whose cleverness is evident in the way he comments on dance images and manipulates space and properties, sometimes infusing them with poignant social commentaries (as seen in a work he did after a visit to postwar Cambodia), Lugnasin has the potential of being a major choreographer in the Ballet Philippines (BP) context. Other dancers in the company have revealed surprising viewpoints and constructs in an exposition of confined dances in corners of CCP's Main Gallery, something that harked back to the more seminal days of the company with Alice Reyes and the center's summer workshops. Many of its first members are the well-known choreographers of today, including Antonio Fabella, Gener Caringal, and Denisa Reyes. Today at the CCP Nicanor Abelardo (main) stage, BP has to appeal and sell itself to a big crowd, restricting its own experimentation and going big and plush as a Petipa classic or glossy as a commodified venture. Somehow and sometimes it reminds itself of its past as a seabed of adventurous choreographies and choreographers.

That adventurousness was born out of small spaces and stages, even for earlier dance companies, and continues in today's economics of culture where artists have to live in studio spaces to survive as creative (Myra Beltran says "independent") artists. These spaces call for different ways of crafting and staging dances and of choosing themes, less for all-dressed-up spectacles than for personal statements and smaller-scale yet complex, intricate constructions or ideas. These spaces also call for a different public response, more immediate and intimate, thus eliciting a different kind of critical evaluation.

A group in Koronadal has arrived at such evaluation. Led by Noel Garovillo, the Kahayag Community Dance and Theater Company may have learned from the old success of Dagyaw Theater and Dance Company of La Paz, Iloilo, especially with Agnes Locsin's *Hinilawod.* (This is a contemporary ballet springing from an understanding of a Panay epic but not a specific folkloric depiction that aspires for "authenticity.") While enjoying local government backing, the Kahayag met its own identity crisis when they started asking, "Do we espouse our ethnic neighbors' culture while we forget our present selves?"

No matter how much they revel in the colorful and musical traditions of the T'bolis around them, their members are descendants of migrants to Mindanao. Not only was the question about their own identity, but also about their right to represent the T'boli, who were identified with them because of their location in South Cotabato, in their performances and tours. They had to confront the questions of cultural appropriation and empowerment: it was important for the T'bolis to be able to represent themselves and for the group not to fake their convictions. Today, the members of Kahayag aspire to work out their own identity as migrants and young artists in a contemporary world. They want to speak about their own conflicts, causes, and celebrations. This is born out of respect for their ethnic hosts and the necessity to speak for themselves.

Thus, Kahayag avoids easy success from exoticism, but is bravely going the hard way of finding and projecting their own circumstances and identities. (An exemplary ethnographic study about the threatened cultures in Mindanao was done by Albert Alejo in his *Generating Energies in Mount Apo: Cultural Politics in a Contested Environment,* Ateneo de Manila University Press, 2000.)

Big and Small Spaces

Unfortunately, this kind of thinking that has evolved in humbler spaces is hardly attended to by most critics and neglected by the media, for they are more interested in popular personalities and classifiable cultures. The media themselves seem to be more interested in running and selling their own "shows" rather than attending to the birth of new artists and perhaps discovering them at their workplaces.

Also, street-dance groups gain attention for their ranks or prizes in competitions rather than for their role in the evolution of a contemporary folklore in dance. They easily become instruments in political, promotional, or commercial agenda. They are viewed less as laboratories of cultural expressions than as products to prove a municipality's or a market's stage management of a state/product image. The support they receive is both tendentious and intermittent, a showcase of prestige and power rather than a genuine effort to nurture culture in general.

Whether big and open, or small and enclosed, our contemporary spaces for dance realign our sights and insights. There for us to look at and live in, and they ask us examine ourselves both as artists and audience, calling us perhaps to revalue and revalidate our notions of what such spaces are for. They also invite us to reconsider what happens in and what emerges from such realms, promising us a better understanding of the art of dance and the lives we lead together in a cultural landscape.

What Is Dance

The Exact, Exacting, and Exciting Task of Dance Scholarship and the Model of a Dance Globe

I.

The drive to dance is strong in our culture. The research of scholars such as National Artist Francisca Reyes Aquino only confirms the vitality and sophistication of Philippine dance. It is therefore somewhat disconcerting, though not surprising, when the cultural function of dance is not always fairly and justly understood. People often consider it solely within the context of an exotic, esoteric, religious, or secular ritual. It is a thing of beauty that lasts only a few hours. It is a performance meant to prettify an occasion, an excuse for an extravaganza to raise funds, or a marvel in the theater enjoyed by privileged few who can afford it.

Even in the academe, dance is seen as a welcome yet inessential element of education. It is not taken as seriously as the visual arts, drama, literature, and music. Very few educators truly understand the nonverbal and communicative nature of dance, its cultural, political, and economic functions. Dance is often considered the least literate of the arts because the academe has been so rooted in modes of thinking that are either verbal or mathematical.

The development of film has been instrumental in the development of dance scholarship and instruction. It has allowed communication about dance to go beyond the verbal. Film does not exactly duplicate the full dimensions and dynamics of a live performance, yet it at least makes the performance accessible to a wider audience. Film does not do full justice to dance, but like music notation and recording which also have their limitations, at least the film gives an intimation and an invitation to the full appreciation and evaluation of the dance.

Granted, there are limitations to watching dance on film. It records the what, where, when, and who of a performance, and it certainly captures movement, but it does not communicate the full kinetic appeal of dance. The medium tends to rive sound and color, the participants, and somehow, the patterns. Lacking depth, it intimates the scale and scope of movement, the shape and form of the choreography. Complemented by a notation system that takes into consideration the volumes, directions, and trajectories, planes and dynamics of the human body in relation to time and space, film becomes a more precise and perceptive medium with which to study dance.

We have come to depend on a comprehensive film and a perceptive notation to give us the steps, gestures, patterns, and dynamics of a dance, but this dependence should challenge us to know the qualities and eccentricities of dance more. In the past, we could exculpate our shortcomings as scholars of dance by the very ephemeral nature and the difficult-to-observe dimensions of the art form. Today, a performance can be played and replayed on film, analyzed and compared in notation, so that the obvious and even the subtleties can be detected and articulated. This permits our dance scholarship to go deeper and to surpass the scholarship produced without the aid of film and notation.

I believe the late National Artist Aquino has left us with the challenge to steer forward and help amplify the dance research and scholarship to which she dedicated her life and career. As dance is increasingly appreciated and studied worldwide, and as the tools for its analysis are made more and more available to us, our task as scholars of dance becomes easier and harder at the same time.

This first series of lectures and demonstrations on folk dance* intends to shed light on our attitudes and conceptions regarding the nature and methods of our scholarship. This is just the beginning. Much is expected

---

* Held by the Francisca Reyes Aquino Memorial Foundation in Metro Manila, Cebu, and Cagayan de Oro.

of us teachers and researchers on dance as we continue our work in this field. I think we can create a climate for the respectable recognition of dance in the academe and in our society. It is appreciated, but not enough, and sometimes for the wrong reasons. It is given value, but only as a temporary diversion from the more important matters that govern our lives as Filipinos rather than a defining element of Filipino culture. After all, if dance were truly, fully respected, school administrations would recognize its interdisciplinary values and functions, and would not scrimp on resources for dance programs.

II.

Let me proceed to synthesize what has been said by those who spoke ahead of me and incorporate these ideas into my own discussion.

It is important to note that the theme of the series confronts the problem of moral recovery in our society. I don't think this simply has to do with rudimentary specifications regarding our morality. I think it has to do with reminding ourselves of the overall moral dimension in our culture—Christian or Moslem, tribal or urban. It has to do with how dance cultivates precision and discipline, camaraderie and solidarity, articulation and eloquence. These are the very ideas we hope to communicate to our students, their parents, our authorities, and our society in general; these are the ideas about dance that they will all take seriously in their studies and lives, in their decision and administration.

The details of dance, as applied in the performance of the Samal-Tausug *Pangalay* and of the *Birginia* and its variants in Ibanag, Ilocano, and Palawan contexts, were well-analyzed and demonstrated by both Ligaya Fernando Amilbangsa and Sally Datoc. We need this kind of intensive and comparative focus in Philippine dance scholarship.

Their talk and demonstration about the anthropological and ethnological aspects of dance, its traditions and transformations in our society, its identities and qualities in specific times and places, were all dealt with according to the factors that make the dance—in movement, in forms, in time and space, which in larger terms are the movements and institutions in our society or the historical details and the physical and ideational geography of our people.

III.

My synthesis takes the form of what I call the Dance Globe. It is actually a flat circle, but it is suggestive enough of the roundness needed in this preliminary summary. It isn't like the very attractive spatial icosahedron of the great dance teacher and theoretician Rudolf von Laban, but for today it will suffice.

The Dance Globe has a cross whose four points represent the four main aspects that formulate dance. The two points held together by the horizontal line signify the materials and ideas that allow dance to exist: movement and structure. Dance manifests itself in movement through time and space, takes shape in the human body and the surroundings with which it interacts, and experiments with modulation in tempo, rhythm, and dynamics. It is necessary for the mind to formulate the dance: it can only be moldable, memorable, appreciable, and understandable if it achieves a form, a structural formulation. By its structure, it is recognizable, repeatable, and analyzable. Otherwise, it is lost in pure spontaneous expression, a kind of spontaneous combustion through movement. Dance structures vary from dance to dance, in style and in genre.

The two points held together by the vertical line represent society and meaning. As dance aesthetician Graham McFee says, dance is embedded in society, in its functions in society. Even if dance is appreciated only for its formal values, it only becomes meaningful in the context of its culture, its people's lives, values, and needs. Society is like the ground on which dance takes root.

Every society has its own traditional practices which make possible the execution and institutionalization of dance. Tradition always partakes of infusions that make it grow. The watering and fertilizing of the ground result in social and cultural transformations. These are hard to observe, but they do happen. It is the task of serious dance scholarship to specify social and cultural transformations that govern dance. Generalizations are dangerous because bogus and sweeping claims can mislead a whole nation, especially one like ours that is struggling with the concepts of identity and nationhood.

From this social ground springs meaning. This passes through the horizontal plane that holds the instrument of dance, the human body in movement, and the ideational or thinking part of the dance, which gives it form or structure. Essential to the journey toward meaning is the process of conceptualization, which both the creator and the viewer of the dance must undergo. In society, both creator and spectator are actually jointly and simultaneously caught up in the temporal execution and revelation of the dance. Dance needs conceiving to come into existence, and this is made possible by institutions like society. Thus, we arrive at the meaning of the dance, and its meaning may be multiple, multifaceted, and multifunctional. It is really hard to speak of what a dance means, but if we consider its roots in society in relation to its physical manifestation and by way of its conceptualization, then we may arrive at a meaning.

In the transept of this cross is the big entity I call the Arts. It is there because dance is completed by the other arts in terms of accompaniment, costuming, designing, structuring, and telling. The other arts themselves are also rooted in society and are influenced by dance as a unique form which they cannot duplicate.

The points representing movement, structure, society (for which the word function can be readily substituted), and meaning are held together by four curves. These four curves I've drawn as connecting arrows.

Between the points that signify society or function and movement is the Curve of Expression. This pertains to the emotive aspect of the dance, which through time has come out in specific styles, schools, or techniques. Technique is functional only as a means of expression; otherwise, it is pure mechanism. Consequently, classic dance (in folk or ballet) is different in style and technique from the plainly folkloric or modern dance. These styles and techniques have been defined through codifications, which might admit innovation through contributions of individuals or a group of people. Expression is a big psychological term, but when specified in style and technique, it is analyzable. When new, of course, analysis is not that easy to do.

Between the points that signify movement and meaning is the Curve of the Imagination, under which fall the concepts of fantasy and intellect. Imagination is usually thought of as intuitive, but it can only be "caught"

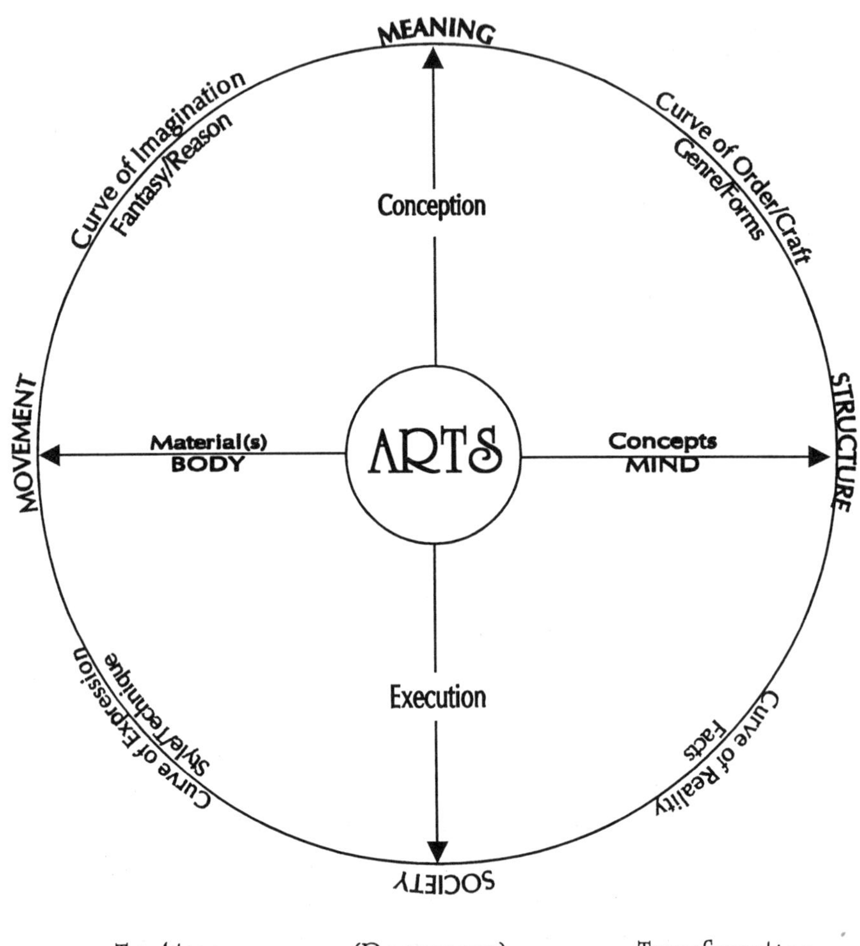

Tradition ⟶ (Resources) ⟶ Transformation

if intelligence or reasoning is applied. Imagination is also inventiveness, so that it is also tied to new styles, techniques, inspirations, and discoveries in making dance. But it is not enough to be inventive; imagination is also controlled by the meaningfulness of an idea and the formulation of movement in a context—of both dance and the occasion, of the participants and the culture.

Between the points that signify meaning and structure is the Curve of Order or Craftsmanship. This is often thought of as the rational side of art-making; thus, it is quite opposite of the imagination curve (which does not, however, rule out intelligence). Order is manifested in art, and genres are accepted recognizable formulations made through time. For example, folk dance is a genre different from ballet. Genre is a type of dancing; it does not merely refer to style and technique, which are included in yet do not fully constitute the criteria for determining a type of dance. Genre can also refer to a story or abstract dance, folkloric or balletic, as distinguished from the styles of classical, romantic, or modern ballet. Thus, the Curve of Order is entwined with the idea of form or structure.

Finally, between the points that signify structure and society (or function) is the Curve of Reality. The curve represents facts of life: what we consider real, like nature and history, and systems of beliefs. We understand nature and beliefs to have structures or rules of their own. Facts of nature and of life are subjects of imitative and occupational dances, as well as ritual and martial dances. Social practices are also manifested in our initiation and courtship dances, and social and theatrical dances. The circle is made complete by pointing to society or the function of dance in a culture. The Curve of Reality completes the circle that illustrates the Dance Globe.

By plotting this globe, I hope I have summarized the main points of previous lectures and provided an aide-memoire in the study of dance. This globe not only highlights the aspects of movement and structure, of meaning and society as crucial determinants in dance study and research; it also calls attention to the contextual formulations in which we study them. The globe also considers the inner and outer supporting forces of expression, imagination, order, and reality. The core is the composite general called the Arts, which influence and are influenced by both dance and society.

I have not considered the communicative nature of dance because it is a given. Especially in the context of these aspects, factors, or forces, dance inevitably becomes a means of communication. It is a kind of speech, although not a verbal one. It can be part of a verbal expression when paired, for example, with a song or chorus, but its basic material of body in movement emphasizes its nonverbal nature. The musicologist John Blacking emphasized this nature in his study or music and dance. While this nature makes it difficult to prove the intellectual seriousness of the dance art or manifestation, it is also the source of dance's uniqueness, making it irreplaceable by any other culture form.

Yet it has also made dance scholarship difficult. It is the task of dance scholarship to intimate and articulate the richness of dance, the creative influence it has on our lives and culture, and the variety of its meanings so that dance becomes a respectable force in any society. As Blacking said, dance constitutes "a primary modeling system for thought and action" in a culture.

Then by its practice and its prestige, we might not even have to worry about moral values. Dance is a value, a contributor to the moral and political order of any society.

Francisca Reyes Aquino Memorial Foundation
Manila
1993

A Critic in an Asian Cultural Context

The Philippines has a long tradition of protest throughout the long governance of Spain. There were intermittent or sustained pockets of resistance or rebellion by Filipinos. (They were then called Indios; *Filipino* was applied to a Spaniard born in the islands.) These continued into the tricky start of the American takeover, but could not last long. The Americans had more encompassing authority and adroitness throughout the islands, more advanced military and artillery machinery (finally subduing the independent-minded Muslim Filipinos in the south), and a more persuasive cultural and educational system. Filipinos also engaged in resistance as guerrillas during the Japanese occupation while waiting for the promised but protracted return of Gen. Douglas MacArthur and his United States forces.

These active forms of protest were also sustained through literature and theater. When the educated Filipinos were finally empowered to understand the motives and overwhelming structures of Spanish rule (Spain did not want to truly and widely educate the natives), they launched a propaganda movement in Spain. The ilustrados were brilliant thinkers, writers, and propagandists for the representation of the Philippines in the Spanish Cortes. At home, they and the long-repressed peasants formed more organized and rationalized reformist or revolutionary forces—La Liga Filipina and the Katipunan. During the American and Japanese periods, theatrical presentations like the Tagalog zarzuelas (from the original Spanish form) and the indigenized vaudevilles took potshots at the foreign imperial authorities through delivered lines and actions, as well as through costumes.

Traditionally, both Philippine politics and the Philippine press have always been critical, even confrontational. To this day, Philippine politics is rife with dissensions and discords, and political parties are hardly forged based on principles. In Southeast Asia, the Philippine press has been the freest, except at the height of the Marcos years in the seventies. (Marcos's control was worn away in the eighties, especially after the assassination of Benigno Aquino, Jr. in 1983.)

Yet the general culture of the Filipinos has, at the same time, been conciliatory. Up in the mountains of Luzon—where head-hunting is part of the old inter-tribal conflicts—they hold the *budong*, where differences are reconciled and a peace pact is forged. In the lowlands, cooperation in the spirit of the *bayanihan* (to demonstrate helpfulness or togetherness in an endeavor) is a communal practice. There is also closeness among peers called *pakikisama* (to stand by a friend) or *malasakit* (to empathize, sympathize even, under extreme situation, *sakit* meaning pain or illness). Filipinos may be short on patience, but overall, they are quite tolerant.

Furthermore, Filipinos share a psychological complex with the other Asians with regards to the importance of "face" or *hiya* (shame). To lose it (*walang hiya*) is more than just embarrassment, while to lack it (also *walang hiya*) is to be utterly shameless, even ruthless. This *hiya* might be simply carried as a social mask, but more deeply it is a matter of personal, familial, or national pride. This ranges from the purely egotistical to the strongly regional (both unifying and divisive) and finally, to national self-regard or self-respect.

The Filipino is a very sensitive fellow, easy to hurt or offend, although he also has a broad sense of humor. But this sensitivity can also be expressed in reverse by deferring most self-effacingly (or even so submissively) to a respected authority or guest. When extended to a foreigner, this is perhaps one reason for the assiduous native hospitality, where hosts are willing to give up the one bed in the house for their guest. (In tribal homes, there might be no such fixture but rather a choice space or mat.) This is also one reason why local and national authorities can exploit the loyalties and properties of the ever-deferring "natives"—as Marcos did on a sustained and broad scale.

This is also one reason why overcentralization has dominated Philippine families, institutions, and regional and national structures. In terms of formal governance, this was first imposed by Western-style administration from the Spanish to the American colonial times, in an effort to subdue and administer a geographically (with more than 7,000 islands) and culturally diverse country. This kind of governance continues to this day, only now initially alleviated by the newly instituted local autonomy law, which hopefully will work.

In terms of cultural policies, this centrist governance has dominated and determined both Filipino consciousness and systems. Cultural pronouncements and designations stem from the top, mostly emanating from Malacañang Palace (the Filipino White House and former residence of the Spanish governor-general). That is why Imelda Romualdez Marcos, in her time as First Lady and Metro Manila governor, was a crucial policymaker, as exemplified by the Cultural Center of the Philippines, which she built (initially with American funds and benefit-initiatives from some Filipino artists, whom she later ignored). This of late has been modified by the Center's new administrators and rectified by the National Commission on Culture and Arts (NCCA), although there is still much to say about the NCCA's own bureaucratic structure and procedures.

Where does the Filipino critic stand in this great overarching cultural and political context? He seems such a puny fellow amid elusive giants and structural windmills. How dare he go against these form and forces, when he is as much part of this society? When he is also sometimes involved in organizational setup and decision-making?

Unlike the Western critic who is traditionally and generally free, for one, because of a more viable income which indicates respect for the writer—the Filipino critic combines jobs and roles to survive, whether by teaching, directing, advising, and even by writing commissions from the very institutions he may be critical about. No critic in any art or discipline can survive just as a critic in the Philippines.

Moreover, written discourse had always been a Western form, only adopted by the Filipino propagandists in Europe or America, then at home, in the late nineteenth and twentieth centuries. The few who live on writing are full-time journalists, excluding the critics.

To be a critic in the Philippines is to be both dexterous and dubious. Many Filipino fictionists and dramatists are also critics. Most writers in English have been trained to be teachers of literature and literary scholars, which are fields they might have entered out of their interest in writing fiction, an endeavor that cannot be considered a source of income. Playwrights may also be theater directors and actors closely involved in the theater craft.

Most of the very few dance critics were once dancers, choreographers, artistic directors, or all three. Writers on dance who have not had dancing experience are usually not very respected. (Is this related to the guru standing in Asian art and life?)

Thus, dance critics in the Philippines are closely involved in the practice of the dance profession. As choreographers and directors, they have had to produce and bargain for bookings and funding (often at a minimum). As a result, this may cast a shadow what should be independent critical writing, but this so far has been the scenario. One, a National Artist in dance, is Leonor Orosa Goquingco, choreographer and artistic director. She was a dancer and a drama major from Columbia University. Another is a well-known ballerina and a dance teacher who has trained a few of the most outstanding dancers of the Philippines. Today, Felicitas Layag Radaic is a choreographer and artistic director, and has a master's degree in Spanish from the University of Madrid. Another was never a professional, but she trained long in dance and earned her master's degree in mass communication in San Francisco through a video-dance production.

I myself danced for many years with two professional dance companies, choreographed for them and many other groups, served as ballet master and artistic director, and continue to be a professor in dance and movement notation for the dance degree program of the University of the Philippines. An English and history major, I have also taught English and literature before dancing full-time. I have written extensively on dance (beyond criticism) and have won three awards for video-scripts on dance documentation, two of which are from France. I have also been chairman and am still an executive board member of the Dance Committee of the grant-giving NCCA.

Thus these four present-day critics are deeply involved in the field of dance. The collegial (but sometimes also contentious) climate in Philippine culture has allowed for tolerating or remaining contented with this situation. There might be unsaid reservations about their vested interest in the field, but they are the ones the Philippine newspapers want and choose to hire. Most of them never applied for such jobs and were asked out of respect for their practical and professional achievements.

How objective can they be in their judgment?

It can be appreciated that most of these dance critics are aware of the progress and problems of the dance in the country. As they broadly consider the newfound professional status of dance and dancers, they can be generally sympathetic. Since they know dance inside and out, from both sides of the proscenium or performance-space (some doing field-research in the folkloric), they are aware of the larger social context of dance. They are well versed in the resources of the art, the craft of theatrical dance, and the technique of the dancer. They view dance from various, if not all, angles. Respected as experts, their editors mostly leave them to write on what or whom they wish.

They are also well traveled; they might have even toured abroad with their own companies and trained with teachers in Asia, America, and Europe in ballet, modern dance, folk dance, drama, and/or music.

Lastly, they have had direct dealings with cultural or artistic administrators as grantees or consultants, or have been commissioned for their choreography or writing. Thus, their critical writing might be brought to question when considered in the context of Western-style integrity. But then again, the situation is so because there are limited funds for artistic endeavors (or funds have been limited to a chosen few), and no one can pursue a career as a full-time critic. (Given the choice and finances, some of them might prefer choreographic duties to critical writing. But writing on dance also has its missionary aspects—to propagate and disseminate their art.)

Furthermore, because of financial and other limitations, critics can cover presentations mostly located at main and central places and involving named artists and established works. As they are paid only a token fee for their contribution, they cannot afford to cover regional (meaning provincial, without that word's derogatory implication) events. But in time, they also get accustomed to writing about artists in the urban centers most of the time.

On the other hand, because of limited and centralized promulgations and funding, hardly any initiatives come from municipal and provincial artists and governments. There are minimal presentations on the fringes. Provincial artists may have to get a nod from Metro Manila to secure acknowledgment from their own local government. Hopefully, the NCCA will soon change this by virtue of a more extensive and equitable grant-giving system.

But that still does not assure conscientious care and allocation from municipal and provincial governments. Regionally, it would be nothing short of a miracle should a congressman (or national senator) use his a portion of his discretionary or pork barrel fund for the arts. There are so few philanthropists interested in the arts. Erratic corporate or commercial sponsorship is a result of a inadequate understanding about the function of the arts in society.

As a consequence, all these have kept critical coverage limited and focused on only a few artists. Provincial artists are doubly disadvantaged. The call for critics in the newspapers is at a minimum. (One well-known young drama critic in Metro Manila has in fact returned to his province.) Again, these reflect the limiting and limited centrist leadership in the Philippine setting.

As a further consequence, these have also restricted innovation in dance. Courting support, provincial dance artists may even gear their presentations toward acknowledged standards and proven styles. Critics themselves get accustomed to write about the same subjects. (When abroad, most also seek out established places and companies. They have minimal experience of the postmodern.) Add to these the collegial attitude and the nonconfrontational atmosphere and you get conservative tastes and conservative writing.*

Yet as mentioned at the beginning of this essay, Filipinos have also been rebellious, and in fact can be informally and openly critical. Word-of-mouth can often stir a following, but only after a span of time. (Most performances only last a weekend or two; critiques may however be published long after the events.) But at the same time, because of a prevailing culture of conciliation, much of the reservations might not see print. (Recently there were confrontational exchanges between youthful and older critics, the former arguing from current cultural studies, the latter questioning the newly positioned questioners. These arguments remain unresolved.) Officials can also exercise a mild or informal mode of collegial censorship through *pakikisama* or *pakiusap* (to talk to, or out of a plan or position).

At the 1993 Japan Asia Dance Event conference, which was organized in the name of the Asian Pacific Dance Alliance (now renamed the World Dance Alliance-Pacific-Asia Center) in Tokyo last July, the critic Hakudai Yamano asked whether Asians should really follow Western critical practice and standards.

Considering that Asians have their own complexes (as already explained from a Philippine viewpoint), their own classical and traditional dances that have features that do not conform to Western aesthetics (and cultural contexts), should there be a need to come up with new criteria

* The relation between the centralization of governance and the consequent limitation in choreographic practice and critical writing may appear exaggerated. Filipinos are generally prolific in dancing and the country has hundreds of diverse folk dances. This creativity is reflective of the geography, the ethnic and regional differences, and the prevailing tolerance in social life (and in governmental enforcement, to the point of vicious license). Elsewhere I have emphasized prodigality and creativity in the people's folk expressions that date back to precolonial times. Colonial control by centralization is still evident in the enforced cedulas (identification and taxation certificates) from the Spanish period that are paid for on top of regular tax filed, and used as one among several means of identification, including: tax identification number, election or voter's certificate, employment and social security identifications, passport, identification cards for licenses, etc.

for an Asian approach to criticism? Yamano favored much the descriptive emphasis in criticism raised in response by Susan Street from Australia.

For my part, I raised the issue of approaching contemporary Asian works that have been infused with or have utilized traditional and ethnic elements and features, and are therefore not necessarily subject to established aesthetics or critical analysis. How does one view very ritualistic presentations? How does one evaluate movements and themes that are close to communal celebrations and occupations and cannot be viewed from a proscenium or other more formal perspectives?

Are the cultural reasons and contexts for the dancing to be considered in a so-called aesthetic evaluation? May criticism itself reflect the values of a society? A study of critical writing in the Philippines could prove enlightening about the relationship or dynamics between theory and practice, living and writing in a society. (To start, it must be said that there has been some daring criticism. Has this proven useful and transformative of Philippine art-making?)

Yamano's suggestion to veer away from the abstract absolutes and distanced viewpoints in Western approaches needs to be looked into with patience. Will any Asian critical practice arise in isolation? Will it in fact enrich universal critical perception?

World Dance Alliance-Asia Pacific
Kuala Lumpur, 1994

The Filipino Soul in Dance

What is dance for Filipinos? What is the soul of the Filipino? Although dancing is universal, it is important to ask these questions because the manifestations of dance are diverse and particular, and these are reasons for its richness and magic.

Philippine dance is composed of what we generally call the folklore—the dances of the people. They are as follows:

a) those that propitiate the spirits—our *diwatas* (spirits) and *anitos* (ancestors)—by the power of the *babaylan* or shamans;

b) those that are imitative of animal life or activities, like hunting, fishing, and planting, as well as mock-war dances;

c) those meant for socializing and celebrating, whether for courtship, communal harmony, or political hierarchy, from courtship to ceremonies;

d) those that we have inherited from our colonial masters like the Spanish and the Americans, most of which are for social purposes and meant to preserve social amenities and protocols; and

e) those mentioned above—whether religious and secular—that have now been arrogated by tourism programs for both cultural and economic ends.

We may also include what we simply refer to as theatrical dance, which was a product of evolving and revolutionary forces in society, such as ballet and modern dance, jazz and tap dance, which have become staples of our theatrical consumption.

What is the soul? In our own terms, it is the *kaluluwa*. Simply, it is the spirit or essence of ourselves. Perhaps the definition must stay simple because the soul is unseen but felt, is hard to capture. We see body and soul as a typical dichotomy, but we know that they are not separable, as in body-and-soul or body-soul. Today's consciousness of the body—enhanced and enforced by Eastern beliefs and practices like yoga and tai chi, the bharata natyam dance and the trance-state of a dancing babaylan—widens our consciousness itself, our soul-states.

The soul is what is inside, our *loob*. It can range from empathy or *malasakit* to our sense of worship or *samba*. It is only understood when seen in or brought out by the body. So the soul is felt or practiced *sa labas*. What's inside—the motive, the passion, or the idea—is projected outside via movement and as expressed through task or dance.

The soul is not a static essence. We are in constant search of the soul, and our encounters with it come in stages, in conflicts, and complexities. The lives of saints are excellent examples of such journeys. No wonder *The Dark Night of the Soul* of St. John of the Cross has inspired many choreographers, including myself.

Like in dance, the soul is always active and in flight.

What's found—in stages and finality—is the achieved or defined soul. In personal and national terms, we call this identity.

Thus we can think of dance from phenomenological and epistemological perspectives. Phenomenologically, it is what is danced or done, and I have already enumerated the kinds of dances that the Filipinos do. But we cannot divorce discussion of these from their functions, meanings, or souls.

For example, in our shamanistic dances, the human spirit communicates with the divine. Both babaylan and his followers stage a ritual to achieve this. They prepare a special place, as in the *buklog* of the Subanon (a bouncing platform way above ground), or a swing and an altar as in the *pagdiwata* (ritual to the spirits) of the Tagbanwa. In both cases, they also prepare wine and food, of which they believe the spirits will partake. This ritual is both spiritual and physical; it may even have industrial and political implications. In Philippine society, the priest or babaylan in Christian or animistic functions still exerts pervasive influence.

Then there are the imitative and occupational dances that reflect nature and nurture in our society. Depending on the locale or labor, these dances are diverse and ingenious in their manifestations. They embody the power of both abstraction and stylization in Philippine art and life. Some say that they also have magical efficacies in that imitation brings about the real. In other words, people render their hunting, fishing, and planting in dance in order to rehearse and realize the real hunt and harvest. They may believe that these are more than fun but can actually be magically effective as their curative dances.

On the other hand, the people of the Cordilleras or Marawi perform their choreographic enactment of combat to ensure of victory in war. Similarly, we seek a religious blessing or cure when we join the sinulog or ati-atihan in honor of the Santo Niño, or seek a husband or child when we join the pandanggo in Obando.

Through dance we forge social solidarity. We do our courtship through dance—from the La Jota to the lambada, the kuratcha to the chacha. We even ape these dances in our political jousts.

Significantly, we were colonized not only through tracts and preaching but also through processions and dances. Our religious *turumba* (supposedly to trip) matches the habanera and rhumba. The Spaniards knew our choreographic proclivity so that even priests used dance to convert us. As for the Americans, the Thomasites came not only with their books but also with their so-called Big Apple.

As we can see we are not only converted through the mind but also through the body.

By virtue of our ingenuity, we modified these dances to suit our climate and quality of movement. Sally Ann Ness studied the sinulog of Cebu and discussed how Filipinos move, why they move the way they do, for what purpose, and with what inventiveness. Today's Philippine folk dance groups simply show, too, how we have somehow reversed our colonial experience by "colonializing" the European dances by altering them according to our own qualities and purposes. Colonial domination has been changed through choreographic transformation.

We see this transformation in our theatrical dances. After doing our *Giselle* and *Swan Like*, we create our own ballets or deconstruct the classics. The technique (like the Spanish and English languages) has been used to express our own choreographic literature, using myths and legends, historical and contemporary subjects. The Filipino soul can still be seen through these imported choreographic dresses.

What does dance do for a society? It gives expression to the pulse and impulses of a people. It is a journey toward the Filipino soul and identity.

Often enough, we think that only literature and the visual arts so concretely show this soul or identity. What can be more concrete than the Filipino body itself, a body that is in motion, living out its agitation and aspiration?

Because it is ephemeral, the dance has not been thought of as social document. Today's movement notation systems, photography, and films now belie this neglect, especially in the academe.

Those of us teaching the Humanities courses need to enlarge the vision and resources of our educational institutions. Beyond the verbal text, we have the choreographic text that also captures the human imagination and embodies a cultural identity. Of course it is harder to "think dance," or think of dance in ways other than through accustomed verbal means—because the body-in-soul, or soul-in-body is actually elusive and not yet well studied in the academe. If ever it is studied, it is often studied only as physical education, as recreation and not as the creative art itself. Dance still has to be reckoned with as an educational tool and a method of cultural construction.

The educational system still has to study dance as a phenomenological and epistemological subject. It is in the Humanities where we begin to instill the idea of serious art, a realization of the imagination and identity—of the Filipino soul.

Philippine Normal University
Manila
1997

Philippine Ethnic Dance in the 21st Century: An Urgent Call (Katutubong Sayaw Pilipino sa Siglo 21: Isang Panawagan)

All art begins as action—in the act of writing,[1] of speaking, of painting, of curing or molding, of cranking a camera, or thumbing a violin or guitar. But all these acts disappear into a finished work: a book, a script, a score, a recording, a picture, or a sculpture. For performers like the actor, musician, and dancer, the art is lived in its being played or performed. But unlike the actor and musician who will have a printout of the author's intention or articulation in the form of a script or score, the dancer's performance is unwritten, not to be lived out in exactly the same way again.

It is thus understandable why the katutubong sayaw Pilipino or Philippine ethnic dance is a problematic concept by nature. As an art form, dance is transient and temporal, born at its moment of dying. Lamenting our native script's disappearance through time, and language being translated in people's lives, we prove that we continue to puzzle over culture's ephemeral nature of existence. That is why dance continues to be treated in the academe as an ephemeron and is only truly rescued today by phenomenological study, such as the physical education programs of recent years.

The reason for this is easy to pin down. High priority is given to the material evidence of an art, something that puts dance at a great disadvantage. What is dance? And where is it? Is the dance that we see today, like the Ifugao courtship dance *talip*, the same dance we saw a few years ago? How much has it changed in form, in context, and in intention? Has it continued to be for courtship or is it now for the purpose of tourism? Are the reasons for the dance's existence today and the changes it has undergone as legitimate as in the past?

These questions point to the fact of the nature of dance as an art. And it is because of this nature that we distrust dance. We cannot pin it down. Our penchant for bookish definitions and categorization do not fit the vagrant and phenomenological elements of dance.

Now imagine how much more difficult it is to deal with a particular type of dance such as the katutubong sayaw Pilipino.

Most of these dances are beyond understanding for many of us. We watch a katutubong sayaw on one or two occasions and form an understanding of it without truly knowing the dance. We also can't bring the dance with us—unlike pots and mats, sculpture and furniture—as proof of its existence. And because the katutubong sayaw has evolved through time, conditioned as it is by the changing social milieu, what we may see, point at, deduce from, is never the same. Dance is never the same.

Furthermore, few go into the faithful recording of these dances, which is another problem that *sayaw* (or *sa-ut*, which can also refer to a war dance) faces. Sixty years after Francisca Reyes Tolentino (later Aquino), there is still no one of her stature and with her wise strategies in education who has given credence and respectability to the study of the katutubong sayaw. In her book, Maria Montessori spoke of how a real scientist or artist (and therefore teacher) makes many sacrifices to do his/her work. And yet the same scientist or artist does not recognize such deeds as sacrifices because he loves what he is doing.[2] There have been many dance researchers who have done field work, but in the end they do it for a thesis, a performance, or a promotion. I do not discount the works of Libertad Villanueva Fajardo or Jovita Sison Friese, of Ligaya Fernando Amilbangsa or Ramon Obusan. What I grieve over is the fact that they are so few.

Many of our researchers are also satisfied with notation and collection. They fail to analyze, much less contextualize their findings. I myself have not done this at length, as my area is dance theater (one of the few field researches I have done will be dealt with later). For both these areas of dance—the folkloric and the theatrical—the methods of cultural preservation are still primitive.

I consider video documentation a primitive form of cultural preservation because it does not document dance faithfully. It leaves out the dimensions of actual performance and distorts shapes and space (flattening levels, angles, directions). In the end, analyzing a videotaped dance performance requires assiduous (or reckless) work at interpretation. A video is really only useful for someone who had actually seen the dance performed. It is not a reliable medium for a proper and comprehensive analysis. Yet, most people seem to be happy with using video to preserve and study dance.

Many are also happy with the most developed system of movement notation as a way of documenting dance. But it doesn't solve everything. It is unable to record many things such as color, the dancer's interpretation—save for maybe a noted version or stylistic difference—and actual time and space, despite measurements for time, continuity or accents and spatial relations, and the approximations of width and depth. But at least dance notation allows for analysis, and particularly for dance theater, the terms that allow for some kind of definitive edition. Proof of notation's credibility as a form of dance documentation is that in countries like England, it is required for a dance work to be copyrighted.

Beyond documentation is the problem of performing the katutubong sayaw. How much of what we see now has been changed? How does the occasion of the dance's staging (for tourists, for government officials who might want suppressed grime and blood) change the way it's performed? How much are the form and function of a katutubong sayaw changed when performed by a school or a folk dance group? There are also more complex questions about the study of the katutubong sayaw. For example, who owns the katutubong sayaw? The troupe that brings it abroad and wins raves? These questions bring to the fore problems of cultural appropriation.

The problems of documentation and performance are subsumed by the basic problem of dance's nature—no two performances of it are alike. As such, the relevant question is: what will make them recognizable as dance? Whether as a document or as performance, there is a degree of fidelity to which an act or art may be rendered again. And despite the aforementioned societal changes that affect the form and function of dance, this is still true. It is here that what becomes important is who determines the changes that will be considered acceptable.

In the repeated performance of the katutubong sayaw, these changes are often determined by cosmopolites like us rather than by the folk who danced it in the original. These people did not only dance the katutubong sayaw; they lived it as a matter of course based on the season, urged by social, political, and economic necessity, as called for by a momentous occasion such as a birth, a coming of age, a wedding or a death. To the katutubo, the dance is integral to their life cycle and celebration. To most of us who deem its present form acceptable, it is simply for show.

In an essay on the katutubong sayaw that I wrote with Ramon Obusan entitled *Sayaw: An Essay on Philippine Ethnic Dance* (Cultural Center of the Philippines 1992), we introduce a number of rituals and dances in the life of the katutubo by tracing the segments of their life cycle and viewing them in relation to corresponding practices or dances.[3] A *Tuklas Sining* film corresponds to the essay and illustrates these dances in their musical, social, and environmental settings. For this paper, I will focus on the ritual dance (*buklog*) as an example of a *katutubong sayaw Pilipino* that has suffered the problems mentioned thus far. I would like to discuss the buklog because aside from the few occasions that I've seen the dance performed in Dipolog, I have observed with greater enthusiasm this dance as ritual.

The Subanon Buklog

The significance of the buklog to the Subanons is proven by the fact that they can spend a whole year preparing for both its structure and its performance. This is not to say that there are no other Subanon dances. In 1995, while in Dipolog, I saw other dances being performed during a buklog occasion. But the buklog is unlike others because it is less individual and more communal, less imagistic (except for the circular formation) and more spiritual. While I saw a shaman (*balian*) dancing indoors in honor of the dead, the buklog is done outdoors.

For the *Tuklas Sining* film, Obusan was able to document a good, big buklog structure and ritual. The one I saw, on the other hand, was held in the city of Dipolog as part of promoting the city itself. The buklog was performed after a parade that wound through the few streets of Dipolog and ended at a sports-cultural complex, and after a dance contest of the many commercialized folk dances, speeches of government officials, and a "cultural show."

Beyond the particularity of the context of this staging, the buklog structure and ritual dancing that I saw was unlike those that I read about in books—far from it. This buklog was performed beside a supposed Subanon house and on a buklog structure that wasn't very high. And yet, there was sincerity in the structure and performance. There was no pretension in the staging of this buklog. Everything in attendance to that buklog event—the *kulintang* playing, the food and wine, the corner altar, effigies and clothes stacked together, the Subanon costuming—created the proper ambiance for the proceedings.

The group who staged the buklog was from Sindangan and led by their timuay and balian Datu Agdina Bacong Andus, who was sixty-five years old in 1995. Datu Andus's father has been described as legendary—a timuay and balian who braved the stormy sea. Datu Andus himself was gentle, with a reticent wife with whom he had sixteen children. He finished high school and earned an elementary teacher's certificate but taught for only three years. He then spent thirty-one years at the treasurer's office in Sindangan and proudly spoke of how he joined Admiral Espaldon's floating exposition for one month.

According to Datu Andus, the buklog is held for three reasons: 1) to heal someone who is ill in the form of a pledge or vow (*pana-ad*); 2) to rid them of gangan (or *dimalas* in Visayan, i.e., ill-fortune) before farming starts or to assure them of a good harvest; and 3) to commemorate the dead floating up in the skies (*langit*) who, after a year, may be released into heaven to join the *magbabaya* (*gino-o* or god). Ernie Andus, a teacher in Sindangan and a nephew of the elder Datu Andus, confirmed that the buklog is indeed held to help heal the sick. Meanwhile, according to Nenita Bermudez Lacaya, who grew up among the Subanons and was an organizer of the Dipolog City buklog event, the ritual is also held for thanksgiving.

Heavy preparation is called for by the buklog. Two months before the *gampang*, the ritual (*dulang*) is prepared. Datu Andus used the term sulampong, although this may just be a facet of the dulang, or vice versa. For the dulang, permission is obtained to cut trees for building the buklog structure. According to Datu Andus, there must be a total of sixty-four trees, including the pestle-pole and log-mortar.

The gampang is held at the end or beginning of the year, when they offer propitiatory gifts to the spirits or deities so that they may send away the bad ones. They send a toy boat down the river and offer 360 eggs. The *gatud* (or *hatud* in Visayan, perhaps, a send off) is also celebrated to tell the gods of the forthcoming buklog. Here, gifts are also offered. Another term used for this ritual is *canao*; perhaps also *kanu* as mentioned by Maranan in the *CCP Encyclopedia*.[4]

When a house is built for rituals beside the actual buklog structure, the gintrigal (or *intrigo* in Visayan/Spanish) is also celebrated. The house built beside the buklog that I saw in Dipolog had three-sided windows, plus a porch by its entrance. The house itself is an offering, along with everything inside it—the altar, effigies, clothes, wine, and food.

In building the buklog structure itself, the place is first blessed to rid it of demons. Stalks or poles with small altars are strung together. The buklog itself must be built in a day; otherwise an adverse event may befall to those who have built it. The buklog that I saw in Dipolog was six feet high, complete with a dug hole in which sat jars covered with a log that acted as mortar. Directly above it was a pestle that would drop and rise when the dancers on the buklog floor danced from above. The floor was made of bamboo tied together with rattan, without the use of nails. Barriers were built around the four sides of the structure, with some space for a stepladder.

The event I witnessed in Dipolog was for the dead, with the ritual (*pilata*) held inside the house. Here, the eight-shelved altar *pangamu* was built, as well as the seven-tiered altar called *balay-balay*. On the pangamu, eight chickens were offered, while on the balay-balay (also called *sulambi*), seven were offered. On the third altar, the *pinulaw*, which bore the dead person's clothes, one chicken was offered. On the other hand, new clothes were offered to the balay-balay.[5]

Other than the buklog structure, the preparation of food for the ritual is also important and meticulous. The process of preparing food for the buklog is called *ginaman*. Aside from the number of chickens offered and brought to the altars, if I understood correctly, four chickens and four hard-boiled eggs are always offered for the *sigakad*; eight eggs are offered to the pangamu, and seven eggs for the sulambi. A cut from the roasted pig's (the lechon's) neck is offered to the dead. For the buklog that I saw, the roasted pigs had eggs strung around their necks. In the middle of the floor were a jar of wine or softdrinks and rice, of which the guests could partake.

Like the structure and the preparations for the ritual, the attendant performance for the buklog is complex as well. Aside from the incantations and dancing before the corner altar or pinulaw, there was much dancing in the rest of the house. These dances were in fact courtship or wedding dances, accompanied by gongs and a set of kulintang. Couples took turns dancing on the floor. According to Datu Andus, the dancing is dependent on the kind of music that is played. Among the dances he mentioned were the courtship dances *dumadal*, *linukbaklukbak*, and *dinimpadayan*, and the fighting dance (perhaps the *soten* we know of).

The dancing on the buklog structure itself is fun for the whole community. The dancers hold hands or each other's waists and do crisscross steps while moving in a counterclockwise formation. The dancers' movements sideways and forward-backward in a diagonal towards the right are compounded by the bouncing floor.

According to the Subanon epic *Keg Sumba neg Sandayo*,[6] the Subanon hero Sandayo rose up to the heavens with his relatives after a wedding where he helped secure dowries for his cousins. With its rhythmic energy and the atmosphere of ecstasy it creates, the buklog may be seen to suggest this transported experience of Sandayo. While it may seem to be a simple dance, the preparation that went into the buklog builds up the community's anticipation and leads to a feeling of fulfillment in the act of coming together for the ritual.

The buklog, in the end, also characterizes the close-knit communities of Subanon society. Tracing one circle in a dictated rhythm that everyone follows, the *buklog* endures beyond its spiritual bases. The pounding of the pestle on the mortar is supposedly the people's common call to the gods, but this sound also drives them to keep on going, energizing them when they are tired, and making them responsible for the rhythm that they themselves create.

Conclusion

The contemporaneity of the katutubong sayaw endures not only in autochthonous practice but also in its influence on today's dance theater, as seen in examples ranging from the seminal *Trend: Return to Native* of Leonor Orosa Goquingco to the recent works of Denisa Reyes in *For the Gods* (on *dugso*), Agnes Locsin in *Bagobo*, and Tony Fabella in *Buklog*. But because of what has been termed as progress in the form of globalization, the katutubong sayaw may drastically change or die due to forces beyond the control of those who do and enjoy them. As artists and scholars, there is something we can do. With our hearts and minds, as a form of retrieval, we can take that one step toward truly studying, understanding, and documenting the katutubong sayaw.

This reminds me of another dance for which the Subanon is famous: the *sinalimba*. I have never seen it save for one instance when a group from Mindanao used it in a folk musical called *Sinalimba*. The dance uses a swing on which three to four persons jump, balance, and jump off without losing control. The sinalimba for the Subanon is supposed to be a symbolic vessel for launching into an adventure.

As children, we have all felt the thrill of swinging up and down. It's a transcendent feeling that allows us to forget the mundane, as we lose ourselves in the rhythm of going up and down, in the wind, and in the dramatic beating of our heart—our total being. I believe that the buklog creates this feeling for us as well. Its rhythm, created by everyone involved, allows for utter abandonment. A taste of ecstasy is reached through the act of dance, and there is that unexpected surge of energy in the act of abandonment. And in the buklog these emotions are very much a product the whole community's effort.

With dances like these—and to certain degrees and differences the other dances we abandon ourselves to, from ballroom to ballet—people will have a hard time letting go of the act of performance. And when urged by both social and spiritual forces, the people won't be able to help but dance on. Thus, despite its temporal nature, the experience of dance seems to have no terminal regulation (especially in ethnic dance, where there are no specified counts or set figures to conform to). Although I said earlier that one dance can never be performed in the same way again, it remains the same in the way it engages the senses and creates experiences of abandon. Ideally, the folk dance should not succumb to the trends it has been subjected to in the process of acculturation. And yet it endures in its seeming simplicity while being always complex and deep in its social and spiritual dimensions. What both the buklog and sinalimba in fact point out is that the katutubong sayaw Pilipino is not only a way of sensing life; it is also a philosophy. It is more than just a matter of doing, but a way of living. And in saving the katutubong sayaw ng Pilipino, we are in the end, also concerned with saving not just our bodies, but our souls as well.

Dalubhasaan ng Edukasyon sa Sining at Kultura
University of the Philippines
2000

Notes

1. See James Clifford and George Marcus, eds., *Writing Culture: The Poetics and Politics of Ethnography* (Berkeley/Los Angeles: University of California Press, 1986). Also see Marcus and Michael M. J. Fisher, *Anthropology as Cultural Critique: An Experimental Movement in the Human Sciences*. (Chicago/London: University of Chicago Press, 1986).

2. Maria Montessori, *The Discovery of the Child.* Trans. M. Joseph Costelloe. (New York: Ballantine Books, 1972).

3. Basilio Esteban S. Villaruz and Ramon Obusan. *Sayaw: An Essay on Philippine Ethnic Dance*. (Manila: Cultural Center of the Philippines, 1992).

4. E.B. Maranan, "Subanon," *CCP Encyclopedia of Philippine Art*, ed. Nicanor Tiongson (Manila: Cultural Center of the Philippines, 1994): 282-95.

5. The *CCP Encyclopedia of the Philippines* (Vol. II) quotes Charles O. Frake who notes thirty types of altars. Also see Charles O. Frake, *Language and Cultural Description* (Stanford: Stanford University Press, 1980). It has five chapters on the Subanon.

6. "Keg Sumba neg Sandayo," *Kinaadman*, Vol. V (1982), 259-426.

An Odyssey into Authenticity: A Choreographer and His Society

> You and I, when we argue, are made in each other. For when I understand what you understand, I become your understanding, and am made in you.
>
> —John Scotus Erigena

What is the material of a choreographer? In its malleable form, it is basically movement—the raw and basic manifestation of life, from the atom to single-celled animals, from man to his inventions. To transform it into art, the choreographer has to bring movement into focus, into a form. By selection, stylization, and synthesis, the choreographer is able to bring to movement his personal vision and concretize his concept of public taste.

To put it succinctly, the choreographer's art is determined and defined by a combination of his personal vision and his art as the public's domain.

Today, I am not so much interested in explaining the choreographer's creative process—his method of selection, stylization, and synthesis[1]—as much as I am in clarifying the possible tensions that exist between the two factors that determine the quality and outcome of his craft: his intention, idea or vision, and the social nature or appeal of his art.

The Choreographer as Artist

As an artist, the choreographer must start off with an idea or a tale that must be told through movement. This may be produced through the simplest, most transparent, and pure movement-to-music concept; it can also be brought to life in the dramatic portrayal of mood- or story-ballet. In whatever guise, the choreographer is displaying himself—his being, his wit, his depth, and his taste—through the movements of dance.

The artist's personal self cannot be divorced from the life that is lived, the everyday body that is inhabited, the habits that create style, the surprises that delight, and the fears that are fled from. This artist's life is thought about and felt within, and it is shaped by and released into society. Even in pure abstraction, the choreographer exhibits personal and artistic strengths and weaknesses. A witty allusion or an ironic put-down may be made about known art works or life situations, but what is certain is that regardless of whether it is immediately obvious to the audience or not, this choreographer is making a statement.

Whenever the late Remedios de Oteyza staged a ballet, she objectified her feelings toward and understanding of the music of Grieg, Tchaikovsky, or Cornejo. The detached perspective she employed was belied by a propensity for deployed beautiful bodies, clever choreographic architecture, and seriousness with time-textures. These were elements of life that preoccupied her, and as these composers appealed to her ear, she collaborated with them and established a historical or contemporary relationship. Whether she succeeded or not in rendering this in dance, by going through the process she could agree with Havelock Ellis in saying that dancing is "no mere translation or abstraction from life" but life itself.[2]

At the other end of the spectrum is the treatment of dance as a narrative, a story. Definite characters are brought together and legendary, historical, or fictional situations enacted. Recognizably lifelike, the tale is at turns rendered realistically or stylistically.

In the Philippines, mythical stories, as exemplified by the tale of the first man and woman, have been rendered in dance a number of times. So have historical events, such as Alice Reyes's *Rajah Sulayman* and *Itim Asu* or in Basilio's *La Lampara*, which is about Jose Rizal. Fictional inspirations also abound, as with Leonor Orosa Goquingco's *Noli Dance Suite*, Corazon Generoso Iñigo's *Sisa*, Alice Reyes's *Amada*, and Eddie Elejar's *Kapinangan*. Attempts have been made at working with generic life-situations, as in Felicitas L. Radaic's *The Prey*, about a woman and some humanoids; Tony Fabella's *Batuque*, an initiation rite; Fabella's *Siklo*, about evolution and devolution, and Basilio's *Between Sky and Sea*, an abstraction from Thomas Mann's philosophical book, *A Death in Venice*. All these dances, while different from each other, portray some form of reality and an aspect of the psychology of its people. Each one also makes a statement of some kind.

But more importantly, this makes clear the fact that the choreographer's interactions with life are manifested in dance with some peculiarities and from a certain perspective. Through the choreographer's commitment to art, these are all laid bare.

A recent example of this is my experience when I choreographed *Testament* to Bela Bartok's *Third Piano Concerto*, his last known composition. When I decided on my central theme of alienation for the dance, having heard the adagio while still in London, Bartok's life was unknown to me. Later, I read that he was a patriotic Hungarian who was forced to leave his country by the opposition. At a certain point, he arrived at what he called the real keynote of his life and music: "the concept of the brotherhood of peoples—brotherhood in spite of every war, every dissension."[3]

I, on other hand, as choreographer of *Testament*, arrived at a crossroad between creating pure abstraction and a generic statement about life. I felt as though I was going through two processes: one of de Oteyza who adored Balanchine, the supreme abstractionist in the world today; and another of Leonor Orosa Goquingco, whose dramatic impulse is strong. I myself felt no need to dress up my feelings in naturalistic designs; even if at the core of the ballet is a personal alienation from my own society. The dancers were dressed simply in basic black practice clothes.

Whether the audience sensed the intensity of my alienation in the central sole of dejection (second movement) or not, I wanted to show a strong personal feeling. Prior to it, I presented in the opening section called "Prolegomena" two things: 1) an ideal and lofty vision (*pas de trois*); and 2) an earthly and eye-level horizon (*pas de deux* with *corps de ballet*). And to reassure my audience, and perhaps myself, after the alienation sole, I continued with a predominantly symmetrical *pas de quatre* to depict harmony, calling it "Of the Same Feather." Then, through a climactic allegro finale, with dancers deployed variously, I concluded with the central protagonist in a powerful lift, as though aspiring or hoping with desperate hands. This allegro I called "Ode."

The Choreographer and the Public

How does the choreographer appeal to the public? How is public appeal created? How interested is the choreographer in society, with a consciousness of the public and the personal stakes in public life?

That the choreographer deals with joys and fears, with lifelike situations, with generic statements about existence, is proof of a form of social interest and consciousness. A choreographer is, after all, part of a society and an advocate or critic of its values. The public sometimes forgets to recognize these manifestations of the choreographer's choices, especially in spectacular dance. In fact, the choreographer can push for changes or reforms as critic of society's values.

It is not surprising that the public is less discerning of the choreographer's statements. More often than not, a choreographer is called to celebrate the customs and traditions of our society. Our folk life is full of celebrations in music and dance, in rituals and recitations, and these become psychic reenactments of our history and our race. Folkloric choreographers and, to cite a fine example, Leonor Orosa Goquingco have found their métier and expressive fullness in what Orosa Goquingco has called our life, legend, and lore in dance, *Filipinescas*. Intended or not, the theme also asserts a healthy reaction to our colonial experience and the uncontrolled entry of imported technology and culture into our every day. It also spells out for us, with some mythic magic, the basic truths of life that may be unchanged by novelties and innovations in the commercial and international age.

But there are two sides to this coin of reenacting celebrations. These can also become too ornate and too extravagant—financially and otherwise—and thus a distraction, keeping us from clearly seeing what life is today. These celebrations may be done in excess. And here lies my second point.

In Soviet Russia, modern experimentation in dance used to be strongly discouraged, and the people only had an overdose of the pretty Petipa classics such as *Swan Lake*, *The Sleeping Beauty*, and *The Nutcracker*, which were all products of a former age of glory. In Red China, on the other hand, only "revolutionary ballets" like *The Red Detachment of Women* and *The White-Haired Girl* were tolerated. Pure aesthetics and social comments that opposed state policies were banned. Today, in Red China there is a counter-reaction to this trend set by the former cultural revolutionists. Someone has viewed the communist policy on art as a paradox: "The communist countries take art very seriously and consequently they mistrust it."[4]

However, there is the view that if "the dictates of the state" are in favor of justice and fairness, it may not be altogether evil. State participation in the affairs of the arts is, after all, necessary in our time. According to John Kenneth Galbraith, only the state can balance the dominance of "the planning system" that prevails in the industrial state, by promoting aesthetic goals that are in obvious conflict with it.

> Aesthetic goals contest the claims of power lines over landscape, of power development over natural streams or national parks, of highways over urban open spaces, strip mining over virgin mountainsides, modern shopping centers over ancient squares and high-speed air travel over tranquility below.[5]

Galbraith also points out the creation of the conflict between the urge to organize and the individuality of the artist whose "aesthetic dimension" is "beyond the reach of the planning system." But he is quick to add that "the role of the state on the aesthetic dimension is not merely protective; it is also affirmative." He exemplifies this most concretely with architecture and urban and environmental design, which only the state can adequately encourage, regulate, and subsidize.[6]

Precautions about these state affirmations must be made, however, as Herbert Marcuse warns that even in a democracy, "domination has its aesthetics, and democratic domination has its democratic aesthetics."[7] In spite of the fact that we witness the reduction in state subsidies for the arts in Great Britain under the Thatcher administration and another is feared in the United States under the Reagan administration, it is not fruitless to ask how much should a state grant for technology and how much for the arts. Industry and the arts are, after all, interrelated. Technology has made artistic venues and facilities efficient and numerous. The media have enlarged the outreach of the arts and they have helped in creating the keen responses to it. But theorist Theodore Roszak has voiced the alarm over a possible imbalance which Galbraith has already noted. Roszak warns us of "how remote we can become from the resources of our daily life" which results in our growing "hopelessly stupid about our relation with the natural environment."[8] Marvin Harris echoes the warning when he speaks of a "relentless deterioration of the conditions of production" implicit in technological advances because of the exploitation of natural resources.[9]

I am constantly reminded of this everytime a rehearsal is interrupted or cut short by a brownout. And during my first long visit abroad, what struck me most was the great wastefulness in the Western world and its hankering for Asian spiritual values.[10] Because of, or despite, progress, it is still possible to arrive at "the great periods of art ... in which insight operates inside a system of accepted ideas,"[11] as in the times of the Greeks and the Elizabethans? How can this happen when improved living conditions, faster means of travel, and administrative centralization result in both the dissemination of diverse cultures and the reduction of these into modified or urbanized forms?

If and when the state is allowed to dominate, will alternative statements or moves be allowed and even aided? Or will artistic conformity—to tourist-oriented and diplomatically sound images, or to centralized and monopolistic administration—be enforced? Will art be "the armchair in which the State sits for its own pleasure,"[12] like the indulgent Emperor in his new clothes?

Fear in state domination over art is well founded. In Great Britain, in order to provide alternatives and to avoid a monopoly, an Arts Council was instituted instead of a Ministry of Culture. An M. P. in the House of Commons warned in 1959 against "the risk of control of the arts" based on the German and Italian experience before the war and the Russian one after.[13] In 1966, Lord Goodman, who became chairman of the council, said of both the Ministry and Council:

> I think it would be difficult for a Minister not to impose his own cultural notions, this I think is absolutely fatal. What we the Arts Council have always tried to do is not to seek to lay down an artistic policy, but to seek to lay down a sensible and organized use of money. Dictation of an artistic policy would I think be an unavoidable consequence of a Minister of Culture and if not an unavoidable consequence a constant risk.[14]

In Germany, on the other hand, state and municipal theaters are subsidized, and these are composed of various complexes—from the opera and ballet stage to the dramatic and other multipurpose little theaters. Aside from these, there are also land theaters and touring theaters, most of which are supported, partially or in full, by public funds. Artists are provided, too, with several securities.[15]

Whether it is a government-led body or not, it is important to see if within an organized program for the arts, artists are actually allowed to contribute their ideas, to speak on how to gain support and how responsibilities may be shared. This is currently being done through artists' panels for the National Endowment for the Arts in the United States.

To avoid the inconveniences wrought by "managing practical arrangements" for the artists and their intractable artistic and personal lives, it is important to see if the tractable ones are the lucky recipients of consultative power and actual subsidy. It is also important that the social minority be given the chance to "make its views become that of the majority"—a system in a democracy as idealized and defined by John Dewey.[16]

Is this august body aware of any of these warnings and alternatives, and what's to be done about them?

The third point I would like to make about the choreographer and his public was suggested by Dewey's declaration. There is a trend to succumb to the so-called popularization of the arts in order to give a semblance of artistic success. To a certain extent, popular works and famous personalities should be seen. They broaden our outlook and improve our so-called universal standards. But these should not be attempted at a scale and with an energy that debilitates the life or undermines the growth of original ideas and native talents. I've had the opportunity to be warned by an artistic director about "artistic compromises" in order to survive as a performing company.

American Ballet Theater realized it was the final straw when the company went on strike after finding out that a handsome contract was offered to still another defecting Russian star, Godunov. Earlier, Cynthia Gregory, an American ballerina of equal stature, had protested the predominance of foreign elements by her series of resignations. But today, a Russian himself, Mikhail Baryshnikov, has inaugurated a new deal by highlighting the best dancers even from the *corps de ballet.*

Arthur Miller once put it this way: "I think that more Americans than not concede that an artist and his importance in proportion to his ability to make money with what he creates, for our measure of value is closely attuned to its acceptance by the majority."[17] Somebody else asserts the fact that "the recognition of an artist arrives via the market is the clearest evidence of his alienation in Western societies."[18] A serious artist could be prevented from realizing his true potential and talent because of what Arnold Toynbee has called a "spiritual standardization" that is the price of affluence.[19]

Because of this urge to succeed, we may be missing the chance to make a real and meaningful contribution to the One World of Dance. I am not an out-and-out nationalist in art, but I look and aspire for works that are derived from the "authentic self" of the artist, from the true center of his experience, and relevant to the needs of his society. Works that are from a truly cultured man.[20]

For example, I may not be popular in this advocacy, but I find the Bournonville classics in ballet to be closer to our life than the Petipa classics which are peopled by Western nobility. The Bournonville ballets with their common talk are also closer to the Orosa Goquingco ballets. But, of course, the superpowers have preconditioned our tastes, including my own, and our diet, filled with international ballets, is one that is a bit imbalanced. Does that have any relation to the fact that no Orosa

Goquingco ballet is alive today? And if it has happened to her and her contemporaries, what prevents it from happening to anyone of us? Why is it that most of our dance heritage is adumbrated and native needs and resources pale beside Western influences and demands?[21]

The Choreographer as Filipino

In the latest of a six-part series for the *Evening Express* on "The Quest for Filipino Choreography," I asked what makes a Filipino ballet and who assures the future of the dance here or in any part of the world. Why is a Western classic patronized over a Filipino work? What is the chance that the Asian psyche can give birth to an outlook or orientation that will help strengthen the impact of the One World of Dance beside the claims of other human aspirations? If I said that Modern Dance is the best form to adapt indigenous cultural resources and that therein lies its stylistic value and creative approach in an Asian context, why is it that it would rather be called ballet?[22] Perhaps the future of dance lies in the artistic collaboration between the composers and the choreographers, when they both explore the same psyche, strive for related and cogent forms, appeal for undiscovered avenues.[23] Meanwhile, history has shown that great ballets are born where there is an Adam, a Delibes, a Tchaikovsky, a Glazounov, a Stravinsky, etc.

There is a universal trend to use ready music, but sometimes it also lends itself to what a Swedish critic termed as "international choreographic merchandising."[24] It is an easy way out, a ready inspiration. Indeed, many ballets have been created that way, including mine, but number is no criterion. I have reason to suspect that it is because of their commissioned music that Martha Graham and Merce Cunningham (with his "independent" musical accompaniment) are more respected; and that perhaps Balanchine, because of Stravinsky, will overshadow Ashton who has less original scores for his ballets.

In this same essay, I claimed that the heart of Philippine dance lies in the Filipino choreographers, and their lives as artists depend on the survival of their companies—most of which remain inadequately unaided, if aided at all. Even if they live abroad, they live out essentially Filipino lives. They cannot escape their being, which no costuming can dissemble. Thus, if a nation wishes to claim for itself works of art as true and meaningful cultural treasures, it must invest in its artists. And the investment should be broad and equitable. I concluded in that essay that

> As talent is numerous and genius so rare, the only chance a country can take for its stake in its cultural future is to encourage many of the willing and of the able; i.e., to create the climate for such geniuses to grow. There is no other way; even science cannot predict its own creative giants.[25]

To arrive at the particular point I want to make here, I've answered several personal questions that may be read in light of my harpings at the already described artist-in-society syndrome.

How did I arrive at a ballet like *Testament* with its theme of alienation? In another ballet, *Tropical Tapestry*, why did I resort to using a Spanish composer, a French, and an Italian to realize a Luzon-Visayas-Mindanao panorama? Why have I had one ballet with a Filipino composer in *La Lampara* (which critics didn't like or understand)? Why did I leave the prestigious Cultural Center of the Philippines Dance Company and opt for a struggling Dance Theatre Philippines? How come most of the critics I can quote about my ballets are foreign ones? On the other hand, why do I keep on promoting Philippine dance mainly in foreign periodicals? Today, I see no reason to drastically revise an essay I wrote quite presumptuously on "the state of the Philippine dance" for a New York quarterly in 1977.[26]

Why?

Indeed, the generalizations I've asserted need to haunt me as well if I am who I claim to be: a choreographer, an artist, contributing his life and his works to his society. Have I realized my potential and tested both my capacities and limitations in good measure?

Have I lived the dance of life at all?

I speak for and direct these questions to others like myself.

Diliman Review
1982

Notes

1. The choreographer selects from his experience and according to his needs. His styles are conditioned by his training and imagination; the elements he has chosen—the music, the designs, the story, the theme, the movements, etc.—are synthesized by his intelligence and taste.

2. See Villaruz, "The Dancing Dolls Are Still, but Only for Totoy," *Sayaw Silanganan*, vol. III, no. 4. July 1978, 4-5. Society is a conglomeration of movements, too, which is why we call a campaign a movement. From the events in earthly societies and environment to the planetary galaxy we can speak of some universal or cosmic movements.

3. Lajos Lesznai, *Bartok*, 57.

4. Michel Ragon, "The Artist and Society," *Art and Confrontation*, 32. A problem in the rest of Southeast Asia is the tendency to keep a traditional form "authentic." Kapila Vatsayayan voiced this about Indian dance where for the dance enthusiasts—performer and audience—a problem is "to retain the vitality within the tradition without stultifying the art." Vatsayayan, "The Sahrdaya—The Initiated Spectator" in van Tuyl, *Anthology of Impulse*, 115.

5. John Kenneth Galbraith, *The New Industrial State*, 315.

6. Galbraith, 317-18.

7. Herbert Marcuse, *One Dimensional Man*, 64.

8. Theodore Roszak, *Where the Wasteland Ends*, 12.

9. Marvin Harris, *Cannibals and Kings*, 195.

10. In this universally noisy and wasteful race, how do we attain the true essense of leisure—necessary for the enjoyment of the arts—that is found in what Josef Pieper termed as silence, "the prerequisite of the apprehension of reality?" *Vide* Josef Pieper, *Leisure, the Basic of Culture.*

11. A. Boyce Gibson, *Muse and Thinker*, 126.

12. Alain Jouffroy, "What's to be done about Art?" *Art and Confrontation*, 178.

E. M. Forster, "What I Believe" in Ned E. Hoopes and Richard Peck, eds., *Edge of Awareness*. In the same anthology, Winston Churchill quotes John Keats: "Without a measureless and perpetual uncertainty, the drama of human life would be destroyed," and Keats goes on to say himself: "An adventure must be defined as an undertaking whose end it is impossible to know." Keats, "On Running Away" in Hoopes and Peck, 23.

This is somehow echoed by Mary Wigman about a dance: "Every created work is always no more than a step in the way to perfection, but can never be perfection itself." Wigman, *The Language of Dance*, 14.

In a Nietzschean paradox, Jean Cassou says that "the negative side of all art is a necessary concomitant of its positive side"—an Asian yin and yang. *Art and Confrontation*, 17.

13. Roland Bell, quoted in Janet Minihan, *The Nationalization of Culture*, 244.

14. Sean Day-Lewis, interview with Lord Goodman, quoted by Bell in Minihan, 245-46.

15. Werner Schulze-Reimpell, *Development and Structure of the Theatre in the Federal Republic of Germany*, 10-13. See Karla Fohrbeck and Andreas J. Wiesand, "The Social Status of the Artist in the Federal Republic of Germany."

16. Harold Taylor, "The Arts in America," *Dance Magazine*, November 1965, 38.

17. Arthur Miller, "The Playwright and the Atomic World," in Robert W. Corrigan, ed., *Theater in the Twentieth Century*, 33.

18. Raymonde Moulin, "Living without Selling," *Art and Confrontation*, 126.

19. "Contemporary Western advertising business has made a fine art out of taking advantage of human silliness." Toynbee, "Why I Dislike Western Civilization," in Hoopes and Peck, eds., *Edge of Awareness*, 83.

20. Martha Graham once said that no artist is ahead of his time. He is his time. Still the best definition of culture is Alfred North Whitehead's: "Culture is activity of thought, and receptiveness to beauty and humane feeling. Scraps of information have nothing to do with it. A merely informed man is the most useless bore on God's earth. What we should aim at producing are men who possess both culture and expert knowledge in some special direction. Their expert knowledge will give them the ground to start from, and their culture will lead them as deep as philosophy and as high as art. We have to remember that the valuable intellectual development is self-development ..." Whitehead, *The Aims of Education*, 13.

21. See Leonardo N. Mercado, *Applied Filipino Philosophy*, and Villaruz, "A Turning Point for the Filipino Dancer and His Dancing," *Sayaw Silanganan*, December 1978, 28-32.

22. Even Martha Graham has succumbed to the use of the term; whereas, before she called her dances "plays." Franziska Boas questions "the wisdom of modern dancers in turning back to the ballet-form when they find themselves without a large following for newer, less stylized forms. These dancers are giving up in midstream. Instead of widening their communities of support by attracting more of the people whose new experiences and interests might help them to understand new symbols in movement, they are turning back to mere artifices of movement, instead of progressing toward true meaning and expression. Thus they are trying to prolong the life of a style in dance whose symbolism are drawn from and directed

to only one of the groups in our culture." Boas, *The Function of Dance in Human Society*, 2.

In my *Evening Express* series, I also mentioned that the Western repertoire is still an inner source for choreographers, and that dance needs an outside impetus, like music, to further its life.

23. In terms of physical avenues, Eric Bentley has pointed that "the milieu of the radical theatre today is the church, the schoolroom the loft, the cellar, the meeting hall, the storefront, and of course the street." Bentley, *Theatre of War*, 412-14.

24. Report from Stockholm by Erik Naslund, *Dance News*, April 1981, 8. Naslud also quoted a British critic who called Glen Tetley and Hans van Manen as "the Marks and Spencer of the ballet world."

25. Villaruz, "The Quest for Filipino Choreography, *Evening Express*, January 28, 1981, 8.

26. Villaruz, "The State of Dance in the Philippines Today," *Eddy About Dance*, Winter, 1977, 31-38.

Where Is Philippine Dance

Sailing in Two Streams: Language and the Body-Politic of Philippine Dance

For someone who comes from the backwoods—who can at first see clearly, if not always objectively—Manila is still the center of things. Going to Manila is both enticing and distressing. Enticing, because it is the site of technological advancement and the speed and sophistication it affects. In the province, there is a feeling of confinement, but also of being carefree. In the metropolis, there is too much to see with too little time. This is when Manila becomes distressing, as the speed and sophistication are difficult to cope with, and there is a need to guard against being swallowed up and losing one's identity. As a stranger in the city, much is asked for one to be accommodated. There's a need to know who's who and what's what in the city, and how things work. In the process of understanding it, one can get lost in the city—at a high price. The stranger is always far behind, and is in a hurry, only to find that there is no self to look at anymore; the city has rendered it awkward, incompetent, ignorant. The only thing to do is to start all over again.

And yet I believe that this stranger in a strange city must have had something. He has danced, and danced about something. He believes in what he's done; and he has done what he believed in. He has gotten around despite his ignorance, and he still has potential that the cosmopolites can monkey around with.

All along he has been sailing in the two streams of his new and old selves, between an old technique and a new one. With exhilaration and exhaustion, he smiles on in a characteristically Filipino fashion.

Language as the articulation of these two streams—these two selves—is possibly the most important thing in this process. Language in its broadest sense is a way of rendering and a way of conveying. It articulates the manner of movements and the movement of manners. It also speaks of the gigantic system of cultural manifestation as Levi-Strauss sees it. The realm of language encompasses not only choreographic means or body-language, but also kinship and political relations, customs and rites of the people, historical encounters and cultural influences. In its linguistic sense, it is Saussure's *langue* or generalized synchronic means, and not the *parole* or specific diachronic mode.

Simply put, as language allows for the articulation of these two streams, it also speaks of the state of theatrical dance in the Philippines. And why exactly it stays where it is.

Accommodation and Kinship in Language

Smile the Filipinos did when they imbibed the *rigaudon* and changed it to the *rigodon*, the *cachucha* and transformed it to *kuratsa*. *Valse* became *balse* and got corrupted with the polka into *polka-bal*. *Jotas* were regionalized all over the country; they became a *creole* or *indio* Catalan.

Native dancing retreated to the hills and mountains. It had no choice, not only because of the invasion, but also because the environment had changed due to ecological exploitation. The reasons for indigenous dancing could also only be found in the more pristine places.

For those who stayed behind in the lowlands, they went through the process of conversion. And yet, much of their devotion was a kind of transference. That is why the rites of All Souls' Day or of Holy Week are so indigenous to the people, even if the honored personages are now Biblical or apocryphal.

Those who accommodated the foreigners also assimilated the foreigners' way of life. On the whole, European government and European customs were successfully imposed despite sporadic resistance throughout the Spanish regime. Three hundred years of this regime and their acculturation changed the dancing of the people not just around the seat of government but also in the towns and barrios that had any church/plaza. For, in fact, it was the Church that ascertained Spanish imperialism in the lives of the people.

Recent scholarship claims that even native rebellion was patterned after the religious sentiments that Jesus, Mary, and Joseph inspired. Reynaldo Ileto asserts that the *pasyon*—which was not only about the trial, crucifixion, and resurrection of Christ, but also about Paradise of Eden or the Hereafter—clothed the ideology behind the people's movement for liberation.

The Sagrada Familia is also a clue to the people's brotherhood or society—*katipunan*—and their aspiration for enlightenment and happiness. The kinship system in the Philippines is very deeply entrenched, signified by a time when there was a Mary and/or Jose, even Jesus, in almost everyone's name—a form of liberal christening that often surprises foreigners about the country. This extended family system also sustains the Filipino in the face of psychological, economic, and political stresses. One can be a rightist but be tolerant of a leftist uncle or cousin. In the same manner, this kinship system promotes personal progress. A destitute distant cousin won't be turned away, while a lucky half-brother (as is the case with Juan Ponce Enrile) or half-sister can become a source of influence. This may further be extended to adoptive relations in the case of godfathers and godmothers, godbrothers and godsisters, or the "Tito" and "Tita," who become adopted avuncular and other relations by way of close friendships or coincidental circumstances. You don't need to know influential people; instead, you can resort to someone who is their relation, or even just their *kumpare* or *kumare* (fellow-godparents at a baptismal or wedding). Levi-Strauss himself says that while these are not objective justifications, they nonetheless arbitrarily operate.

Thus, even if rites and relations are later used against them, these are still accommodated into Filipino culture because of the course of events. This accommodation, of course, will later be questioned by Western notions of integrity and fair play, through for example, the accusation of *balimbing*—turncoat, fence-sitter, or chameleon—but in the long run, *pakikisama* (comradeship) and *pakisuyo* (emotional appeal) ease and erase conflicts. A perfect example of this is the theater scene in

Manila where, despite competition, there is a lot of helping out—the movement of talents, costumes, and properties among different groups, the lending of expertise and services. This, in the end, also creates the complex, if convoluted, but workable communication system of Manila.

This flexibility with relationships was a major factor in the EDSA Revolution of 1986, where appeals to friends' and relatives' *pagkatao* (humanity) and *pagkamakabayan* (national allegiance) operated. The hospitable nature of the Filipino also operates here as only the guardedly affluent and the completely westernized are beyond traditional hospitality.

Language, Culture, and Resistance

While notoriously faddish, Filipinos are actually resistant to change. When they accommodate some form of change, they only outwardly do so; inwardly, they still hold the same beliefs and reasoning. They wittingly copy or poke fun at foreign personages and titles, as the structures they present are characteristically local or regional.

And so when Filipinos acquired American English, this came to be heard and framed in native locution and construction. Books may require a grammarian's rules, but when the natives speak they do it their way—in *Taglish*. In former times, only very few spoke Spanish because the authorities did not really want the natives to be knowledgeable. Speaking Spanish was a kind of peninsular (of the Spanish peninsula-born) birthright. But out in Zamboanga or Cavite until of late, the natives spoke Spanish their own way, with utter disregard for grammatical rules.

The native way of speaking is heavy with the use of affixes, for which exist native rules. The people even use affixes on foreign words. Throughout the country, there are numerous ethnolinguistic groups that make up nearly ninety dialects. This Babel makes national integration difficult and up to this time the issue of the national language is cause for heated debate.

Most educated Filipinos speak two or three tongues, English and/or Spanish, and Tagalog (or Pilipino), together with their regional language. As these tongues are preconditioned by their cultures, only few take real pains to master any of these languages. This is why acculturation is never complete nor completed; accommodating a little of each language and culture has been the easy way out.

Filipinos are comfortable speaking two or three languages. Yet they never really "think" in English or Spanish so that up to this day the majority of students may read a lot, but they don't really grasp the content of and culture behind what they read. Oral communication has become more efficient—something that is loosely and unconsciously indulged in. Stanley Karnow in his book, *In Our Image: America's Empire in the Philippines*, speaks of Manila as a city without secrets, and adds that "from the president to the lowest official (circa 1959), everyone was easily accessible and often exhaustingly garrulous." As a result, Manila "was a reporter's paradise" (360).

Lately, there has been a concerted move to use the national language—Pilipino—as a sole medium of instruction, particularly in the University of the Philippines. Called such since the Marcos years, Pilipino has increasingly been used in the writing of serious prose and poetry. There have also been requests to continue conducting TV talk shows in Pilipino. Obviously allied with these calls to use the national language as a medium of instruction is the intensified nationalist movement fighting for the abolition of the US military bases in the Philippines. While these military bases may only be situated in a few strategic places in the country, they are symbols of the sustained colonial ties of the country with America. The phasing out of the bases will undoubtedly have great cultural repercussions on the Philippines.

But what will continue to be the consistent source of cultural influence from America will be the Filipinos who now live there. As many as they are, these Filipinos will continue to make significant American culture and the English language in the Philippines. Add to this the technological advancements that have had a great impact on Filipino lives, bringing in that which is American and in English.

Language and the Articulation of Philippine Ballet

Dance itself is a medium. It is a nonverbal medium which communicates not only its contents but also its technical bases and stylistic conventions. In Manila, the ballet is still a favored dance offering of the elite. The very term "ballet" has a currency that is also used to accommodate modern dance, and sometimes even jazz forms. The term "ballet" mainly means dance or a theatrical presentation in dance, but outside the Philippines, it is used strictly to apply to *danse d'ecole* or classical ballet and its contemporary manifestations.

The usage of the term "ballet" in this country is liberal and is mostly a reflection of the accommodating nature of Philippine society; however, it also suppresses the usage of the term modern dance, and the practice itself of ballet has overshadowed the idiom and technique that it asserts. For good or bad, a specific audience for modern dance has not been developed. While this problem with terms has been favorable to ballet, there are choreographers like Denisa Reyes and Agnes Locsin who want to stress the stylistic distinction of modern dance. And they are not alone.

Currently, there are companies like the American Ballet Theater that have been very open to modern dance choreographers. There are types of bodies with range and training that can shuttle from one technique or style to another. There are also bodies, psyches, and preferences which have a specific bent or limitation, and by choice or capability, these dancers concentrate on only one form of dancing.

Among Filipinos, there is a proclivity for acquiring various techniques and styles. As they are receptive to various tongues, so are they receptive to various idioms and styles of dancing. Folk dance companies in the Philippines accommodate almost all possible examples of regional and foreign-influenced dances. The range is so wide in scope that it is a tribute to the Filipino dancer for having the ability to cope.

Most of the time, Filipinos are not the specialists. They love to know, dabble in, and develop in various directions, taking on numerous and various posts and positions in institutions and communities, with calling cards that are crammed with varied designations. Their taste is very cosmopolitan, notwithstanding some biases here and there. These biases are in part dictated by: 1) their regional diversity, 2) their historical or colonial past, 3) their receptivity to outside influences and personages,

4) their psychological ability to cope as caused by economic and/or political situations, and 5) their innate curiosity, which may lead to intellectual acumen or pernicious gossip.

In theatrical dance, it was the European social dances that the Filipinos acquired since the Spanish times. These underwent regional or native changes and variations, as some of these dances were presented as bailes on stage, much like the way the preclassic dances composed the ballets in the Europe of old. The Italian Maestro Appiani had his own Compañia Infantil de Baile that performed regularly in Manila until his return to Europe. This was later paralleled by the teaching of and productions by such foreigners as the Austrian Trudl Dubsky in European modern dance (which she called ballet), the New Zealander Anita M. Kane (born in the Philippines), and the American Ricardo Cassell in ballet. Their institutions did not survive their departures to the America, but they left significant residual effects.

And then there were those who lived and died in the Philippines, like Madam Luva Adameit, supposedly a Polish-Russian who claimed membership in the Anna Pavlova company, and Remedios de Oteyza, a Philippine-born Spanish citizen, who devoted most of her life to teaching and choreography of ballet in Manila. After Dubsky (Mrs. Zipper) and another Viennese Kathe Hauser, modern dance was reintroduced by Rosalia Merino Santos (a baby ballerina of Adameit) and Manolo Rosado. Merino Santos gave formal and consistent instruction at the Far Eastern University, where she set up an experimental group.

It took many years before modern dance was again reasserted by Alice Reyes in the most prestigious theater in the country, the Cultural Center of the Philippines's Abelardo Hall. But Reyes herself has confessed that she had to make compromises. Among these, I suspect, is the billing of "modern dance" as "ballet." When Reyes's first company was born, it specifically meant to concentrate on modern dance, and to tour locally and internationally as the Alice Reyes and Modern Dance Company. It wanted to be a separate company that would be distinct from the CCP Dance Workshop and Company (even if composed of the same core members). Later though, the Alice Reyes and Modern

Dance Company was absorbed by the CCP Dance Company or Ballet Philippines, with the oneness in name indicating a merging of styles and a simultaneity of techniques. Today, the original distinction between the two dance companies isn't clear anymore—not even to the Ballet Philippines members.

Jazz is another imported idiom that continues to be popular in the field of entertainment, although there was a time when the use of the term would refer to a form that was considered to be of higher quality. Today there are about two to three groups that deal exclusively with jazz as a serious theatrical form, and they are easily accommodated into ballet or modern dance festivals.

All these prove that like the stranger in the city who needs to deal with two selves, and like the Filipino who has undergone colonization and acculturation, the Filipino dancer speaks in various languages or idioms, techniques, or styles. As much as the folk dancer has to deliver many regional and cultural modes, the theatrical dancer has to train and dance in ballet or modern dance, even jazz, and sometimes adapt to or adopt an ethnic or folkloric orientation or style. In modern dance, a choreographer may utilize this latter orientation. Certainly, the exposure and deftness at all these dance forms have enriched the practice of dance in the Philippine scene.

The Philippines also has exceptional dancers who express themselves only in classical ballet or modern dance techniques. Among these are ballerinas Maniya Barredo and Tina Santos who have graced Atlanta Ballet and San Francisco Ballet, respectively. Anna Valladolid is now a young ballerina in Munich, dancing in both ballet classics and contemporary ballets. For two years, Lisa Macuja was a member of the Kirov Ballet, concentrating on the Soviet ballet style. Since her return to Manila, she has danced modern pieces by Norman Walker and Denisa Reyes—on pointes. Elizabeth Boxes of the Alvin Alley American Dance Theater is described in an issue of *Dance Magazine* to have "strong classical technique" and whose "reserve allows movement to speak for itself." Modern dancer Alice Reyes bills herself as a ballerina even if she never danced on pointe in her professional life.

This rundown of Filipino ballerinas who have been part of dance companies in different parts of the world attests to the fact that the Philippine rendering of ballet is more eclectic. The term *ballet* has come to be uniquely used to refer to any kind of theatrical dancing, as choreographers all over the country accommodate the particular technical levels and cultural traits of dancers and dances from the regions.

Living with the Two Streams in Dance: A Conclusion

The two streams in my title is a simplification of the complications choreographers and dancers deal with in practicing dance in the Philippines. Limitation in time and space has not allowed me to investigate their modes of expression and communication in more detailed and semiotic terms. These approaches, of course, need to be focused on, as Susan Leigh Foster has started to do by *Reading Dancing: Bodies and Subjects in Contemporary American Dance.*

It is important to note that two things are important here. The first is the identification of the issue of two streams in Philippine dance based on the "languages" or techniques and styles, traditions, and accommodations that are manifested in the art. Having raised the issue, there is now a need for another imperative: coming to terms with this phenomenon in the context of the cultural or social milieu and conventions briefly described at the beginning of this paper.

Because of economic reasons, Philippine theatrical dance is biased for ballet, with the middle to upper classes as its patrons. With the fall of Marcos, even the Ballet at the (Rizal) Park by Dance Theatre Philippines, which was meant for ordinary strollers and pedestrians, was discontinued by the National Parks Department Committee. Another area that needs to be looked into is the politics in Philippine dance, which affects both content (for example, rituals in the Philippines are tied to religious and/ or political elements and forces) and the shaping of the practice of the art in society.

The eclectic nature of Philippine dance and the social dynamics in Philippine life may be paralleled. Philippine dance is what it is today because of social and political events. There are a number of ballets that are of a clear political orientation, while some are inspired by historical events and forces, as well as commentaries on social situations. Folk elements have gradually crept into dance theater, at first in the awkward stylizations of Adameit or the balletic posturings of Kane's *Maria Makiling* (1930s). Folk spirit is much more authentically captured in the modern dance idiom, and there are now choreographers like the young Denisa Reyes and Agnes Locsin who have adapted not only folkloric elements in form, but also folk spirit's obvious or implied essence.

As far as development is concerned, much may be said about why Philippine dance went in the direction that it has, or why it has gone in several directions instead of toward a more hegemonic center. Physically and psychologically, there is a plurality of practice, despite the desired approval from the Manila as center, which would guarantee a following. In reality, the "double-entendre" of the term *ballet* in the Philippine context accommodates both classical and modern dance and enables the art to succeed in a very stratified and diversified society.

Thus, today's artistic developments, particularly in dance, stem from the economic, political, and cultural life of the people, and through the various strata of society. As a cultural manifestation, dance does not only reflect Filipino life; it also brings light and form to that very life. After all, the significance of creating art—of articulating and expressing, feeling and forming—is to deepen and enlarge the very act and process of living, of reflecting, and of receiving, toward affecting values and fulfillment in the very society that brings art about. By dancing, we also speak. By speaking, we not only create a manifestation but also realize the body-politic of the Filipinos.

Hong Kong Academy for Performing Arts
Hong Kong
1990

Twice a Stepchild in Cinderella's Satin Slippers: Dance in the Philippines during the American Period

In a recent brief on Philippine ballet history, I included the ballet *Cinderella*. Now, I find the need to explain myself. I did not see a problem with including this particular ballet because while the story is foreign, so is the art itself of ballet, with foreign roots and its use of French as universal terminology. Also, ballet is an art in the Philippines that has to deal with a prevailing problem of *pointes* shoes.

Invented during the Romantic period in Europe, the modern pointes shoes now (in 1983) cost anywhere from P300 to P400 a pair, depending on its make. With careful use each pair can last a week, after which it is only fit for the garbage can. There are no good substitutes for the imported shoes because we do not have the kind of craftsmanship to create perfect pairs of these. Some of the foreign-made ones aren't even durable in the Philippines as the paste used on the blocks softens easily under the tropical heat. Thus, our ballerinas are always beset with the problem of scarcity, cost, and tax on these shoes. There have been periodic moves to make them tax-exempt like musical instruments and sporting balls, but authorities haven't considered these shoes important enough.

Ballet, of course, can be danced with unblocked shoes, but the dance has been technically and aesthetically perfected with the use of these pointes shoes. Invented to create the illusion of lightness, of gravity defiance, of the wisp-like wilis and dream world of Theophile Gautier, any ballerina has to be aware of these shoes' context. A device against which Isadora Duncan rebelled (among many others, including the confining corsets of nineteenth century ballet costumes), these shoes are now equated with toughness and agility as well as modern sharpness and speed that have allowed ballet's range to evolve and develop.

Meanwhile, another art form that arrived in the Philippines during the American period was a European-descended story, a Cinderella (to be renamed Cofradia with Gloria Romero, Superstar with Nora Aunor, or Goldmedalist with Yoko Morishita). This may be seen, along with other dance styles, to have come into the country through a second stepmother after Europe—America. In fact, it may even have come from a success-oriented Fairy Godmother who tried to fit our dancer's feet into some kind of golden, satin, or dollar-priced slippers.

And yet, even our second stepmothers, the Americans, struggled to fit into those European-style shoes, and it took them a long time to become graceful on the tips of their toes. They were worshippers of Fanny Elssler and Anna Pavlova, both romantic virtuosos of the art. It took the hard work of American ballerinas in their homeland to convince them that they could do it, with people like Augusta Maywood, who danced from Philadelphia to Paris and Vienna; Mary Anne Lee, the first American Giselle; and George Washington Smith, the first American Albrecht. In 1866 though, even the long-running ballet *Black Crook* at Niblo's Garden in New York had to employ the Italian dancers Bonfanti and Sangalli as box office guarantees. This was also true in St. Petersburg, where the Italians were the acknowledged masters of the form. In the United States today, you get a Russian defector who also happens to be a ballet dancer, and that assures a sold-out show despite an Afghanistan or the Korean Airline shootout.

In the Philippines, we have yet to feel comfortable in those shoes that are now being made in New York, London, Paris, Moscow, Tokyo, and Beijing. Ballet has indeed come to be involved in international trade and politics. Meanwhile, our third world ballerina struggles to prove herself to be as good an Odette-Odile as Plisetskaya or Makarova, as pure a Princess Aurora as Fonteyn or Gregory, or as touching a Juliet as Ulanova or Haydee. Unlike the ballerinas of the late George Balanchine, our danseuses seem to mainly aim for that kind of "international" standard or image. It's no different from wanting to meet the requirements of the World Bank, or from keeping the US Military Bases for geopolitical security.

The point of this essay is to look at dance during the American period in the Philippines, the effects of which psychologically and politically continue today as proven by the cost of and lack of support for the art. This also means looking beyond ballet and toward other social dances and theatrical forms.

Most of my facts are based on a survey of the first five years of the American period from 1898. So far I have focused on only one newspaper, the *American Manila Times*. Information on the 1920s and 1930s is scant but more accessible, given printed materials and interviews. Certain distinctive careers of the time helped in putting together the events up to World War II. Hartendorp's *Philippine Magazine* has proven indispensable, with his own biases pushing him to interview artists from the West. Raymondo Bañas's sketchy summation of the indigenous and Spanish-based theatrical forms as comprehensively covered by the Spanish periodicals, has also proven to be useful.

Between Colonizers: A Transition in Dance

While the Spanish period brought the comedia and the zarzuela to the Philippines, the Americans brought in vaudeville and ballet, along with the cinema. The Spanish theater forms continued to spread throughout the country, flourishing in various provincial towns. The zarzuela lived on in the Spanish language through famous companies like Ratia and Carvajal, and in Tagalog through the companies of Reyes, Poblete, Soto, and Ilagan. As Doreen Fernandez has documented the zarzuela in Ilonggo, it also flourished in the province of Cebu, with well-known names such as Buenaventura Rodriguez and Florentino Borromeo, who wrote and produced zarzuelas, Manuel Velez, who composed, and Eulalia "Lalyang" Hernandez, who was a famous actress. These plays, both imported from Spain and written by Filipinos, continued to be performed around the country.

Circuses and operas were popular forms from the Spaniards as well. Although not always complete in form, the opera in the Philippines was important enough for Bañas to call the country, primarily Manila, the "Italy of the Orient." At the end of the century, the advertised theaters were the Zorilla Grand Opera House, Teatro Filipino, Teatro Paz (which came to be renamed the Orpheum), the Alhambra, Teatro Libertad, Cosmopolitan Theater, and sometimes, the National Cycle Track, with an amphitheater for a circus. One of the last sites for opera was the Manila Grand Opera House. Cristina Laconico-Buenaventura's listing of Philippine theaters from 1846 to 1896 has proven here to be most useful.

The zarzuela, circus, and opera were not theatrical forms that did not always require a lot of dancing. On the other hand, the comedia, a story that always has the confrontation between the Christians and the Moslems, in its stylized form is almost a dance. It lifts the imagination up on its toes, so to speak (something I experienced myself when I co-choreographed with Alice Reyes the combat-dances for *Principe Baldovino* in 1971, which was directed by Rolando Tinio at the Cultural Center of the Philippines). Although the zarzuela did include some dancing, it was not on the scale of the production numbers in the modern musical comedies, and of course, actresses then could also sing and dance.

There was one personality who became famous as a dancer in theater during this time: Patrocinio Tagaroma, described by Laconico-Buenaventura as "beauteous and graceful." Retana praised Tagaroma for her tango and can-can and said "Tan lindas piemas!" Later, during the American period, her own daughter, Patrocinio Carvajal, was called by the poet Flavio Zaragosa Cano as a protégé of "Diosa de Baile." There was also Praxedes "Yeyeng" Fernandez, who was a "precocious singer and dancer of ten" when she trained with La Raguer and Alejandro Cubero. By 1880, the zarzuela became notorious for introducing the can-can along with the so-called liberal ideas from Europe.

Dance during the period from 1846 to 1896 as discussed by Laconico-Buenaventura was supposed to have been greatly influenced by Maestro Appiani, an Italian teacher from Madrid. He taught social dances like the *gavotte*, *schottishe*, *redowa*, and his shows ran up to twenty or thirty performances—something that has yet to be matched by the "choreographic shows" today. These Spanish dances must have continued to be popular beyond the Spanish period, as well-known dancers like Anita and Emilia performed these with the American vaudeville artists of the American period. Together with an artillery band, juggling, tumbling, boxing, acrobatics, and a glee club singing, there was Spanish dancing in a bill of fare at Teatro Filipino with dancers named Teresa, Planella, Malgrosa, and Juan Panadei. The Spanish Francisca Nabalo was famous for her "flea" dance. The Agita Sisters were billed as "a clever Spanish trio."

In the week that Emilio Aguinaldo was captured by Brig. Gen. Fred Funston, Teatro Paz advertised a benefit for actress Victoria Saez, with the aforementioned Anita and Emilia, the "Franco-Spanish dancers," to take place that Sunday. Soon after, at the National Cycle Track, the Harmston's Circus gave a benefit for the "famous terpsichorean artistes Frezagonda."

Audiences became familiar with musical excerpts from Delibes's ballet *Coppelia* as much as with operas by Verdi, Gounod, Rossini, Bellini, or Bizet. A German waltz was supposed to have been "essayed by the natives" (musicians) for the first time [*sic*] during a concert in Luneta—a regular event then—by the Sixth Artillery Band led by Carl Mindt who respected Filipino musicianship. An essay, "Filipino Native Character," in the October 5, 1899 issue of the *Manila Times* mentioned the native "balitao" as an "extremely graceful" dance. The composer Jose Estella created the valses of that time. On the other hand, by 1900, Cuban dancing was condemned by a George Kerman as "immodest dance."

There were dancing clubs and societies, social dancing schools (like that of a Mrs. Baker, which was advertised), and grand balls at the Oriente Hotel at the turn of the century. Even the Chinese had grand balls held by rich businessmen like the Palancas. Ragtime was the musical craze and cakewalk the staple dance for production numbers. The "Two-step" and "Comique" were announced for a Caloocan band concert, arranged by Loving.

As Americans became theater's primary patrons, English plays started to invade the scene, together with what was called "mimicry" and "pantomime." There were even so-called impersonators. American soldiers patronized American or Colored Minstrels as they were hungry for theatricals "from home." Plays like *The Mascot, The Geisha, Runaway Girl, Belle from New York,* and *Charley's Aunt* were staged by visiting troupes from the start of American rule in the Philippines. An Amateur Dramatic

Society was organized around the time war was declared in the Transvaal in 1899; another one was formed when there was a raging fear of the bubonic plague in 1900.

The Vaudeville and Ballet: America in the Philippines

According to Winthrop Palmer, the term vaudeville either comes from *voix de ville* for street song, or *chansons de vaux de vire* for popular topical or satirical drinking songs from Normandy. The latter was supposed to have been created by a fifteenth century literary society, and by the late seventeenth century, Boileau used the term vaudeville for ballads of this kind. By the next century, the term entered theater vocabulary to pertain to performers of mime, song, and dance. In the United States, "variety and entertainment" was initially used before the Civil War. By the middle of the nineteenth century, "concert saloons" replaced minstrel shows. Vaudeville was popular—something that Douglas Gilbert himself asserts in his history of the American vaudeville when he said that "the backbone of American vaudeville was low comedy."

But what does low comedy have to do with anything? According to Palmer, low comedy has been essential from Aristophanes to Shakespeare to Moliere. To wit,

> a theatre child, low comedy must learn many disciplines—precision, polish, timing, and many techniques, such as juggling, mime, ballad singing, dancing, and acrobatics. The techniques were not an end in themselves. They were a preparation for putting across low comedy's message. That message was (and is) a satirical view of the life of the times in popular language, gesture, and movement. (p. 12)

From Tony Pastor, Palmer brings us to Gene Kelly and Jerome Robbins; great artists like Sarah Bernhardt acted and Anna Pavlova danced on vaudeville stages or in music halls in England. Outside of the opera houses in Russia, Italy, France, or England, that was the only way to survive as a performing artist in the West.

It is not surprising then, that the vaudeville in Manila was crowded with American and Australian dancers who came to do clog dancing, buck-and-wing dancing, and the so-called skirt dance. The latter dance was once described by Elizabeth Kendall as "a whole new genre ... a cross between jigs and clogs and the formal pseudo-ballet steps of spectacles." A notice in Teatro Paz in May 1901 (as seen in the *Manila Times*) mentioned that a skirt dance by Georgie Gould was cancelled "as the electric current which connected with the colored lights was cut off."

There were many types of eccentric, grotesque, and acrobatic dancing during this period. In 1900, a Miss Ada Delroy, billed as "the world's greatest dancer," portrayed the heroine She in *The Fire of Life* at the Zorilla. It was reportedly a "terpsichorean sensation." This reminds us of the famous Loie Fuller, the American toast of Paris, a contemporary and rival of Isadora Duncan. A contemporary description of Delroy was like a notice for Fuller:

> An exceedingly graceful dancer ... she held the audience spellbound during her realistic impersonation of "She," a terpsichorean creation adapted from Rider Haggard's novel. She manipulated countless yards of silk with great deftness, and a wonder effect is produced by the cooperation of the limelight. (MT, May 26, 1900, 1)

Another famous contemporary performer was the girl Emily Lucifer who was a member of a vaudeville family. She was well loved by the audience and continued to stay even after a benefit for her, which was a kind of gala or farewell.

And then there was the famous group of young performers, the Lilliputians, who for a time in 1901 ruled the Zorilla. As far as my research has shown, they were the first to have done the so-called ballet numbers during the American period. "Ballet girls" did pieces called *Amber*, *Housemaids*, and *Seaweed Ballet.* Daphne Trott and Mary Pollard did a "fascination" dance, Edie Pebble did a "pas seul," while a "devil dance" by Mimmie Tropping and Ivy Trott was encored. They later added a *Widow's Ballet* and a *Pierrot Ballet.* This Australian troupe even invaded the United States. In the same year, a Japanese Infantile Company opened at Teatro Oriental in Santa Cruz and they concluded with a "Japanese ballet."

The year 1902 brought in the circus troupe, Baroufski's Imperial Russian Circus, to the National Cycle Track. They advertised twenty-five "ballet beauties" as part of the company entourage. They danced pantomimes about the Boer War, and those like *The Sea Robbers* and *Faust*. These pantomimes were "a mammoth production" often about life in Russia and Poland. The journalistic style of these dances matched that of the vaudeville, and

> the lovers of lingerie, pink tights and shapely anatomy with really pretty faces were not disappointed when the nightly ballet and pantomime numbers were given. (MT, February 18, 1902)

Similar to the circus were the Barnes and Cogill-Sutton companies at the Zorilla, which were "the best that have been given in Manila since many moons" (MT, February 1, 1902). At the Teatro Rizal, Ceferino Soliven's theatrical company staged Spanish plays, and at La Paz Theatre there was the raid on a rehearsal of a play by "the notorious Isabelo de los Reyes" under the "ever wakeful eye of Chief Curry." Among those arrested was orchestra leader and composer Estella.

By April of 1902, Estella was leading the Rizal Orchestra at the La Paz Theatre in a benefit. That month, general amnesty was declared and Aguinaldo was released, although the newspapers *Volcano* and *Freedom* were suppressed. A curious piece of news in May was about a Mr. Bradford K. Daniels of the Department of Education advocating for teaching in "Tagalog" rather than in English. Meanwhile, in the United States, a Rev. Dr. George F. Pentecost of the Presbyterian Alliance spoke so lowly of the "half-civilized people," with some who were "barbarous" and are in the practice of "slavery." A year after, a Senator Teller compared the Filipinos to Europeans and said that they were "as well able to govern themselves."

While King Alfonso XIII was ascending the throne in Spain, Senator Spillman was teaching "a combination of two-step, three-step, Manila waltz, and a hundred yard foot-race … termed the 'new' Virginia Reel." In the mountains, James E. Smith was introducing mixed dancing to the "Igorotes" by way of the waltz. More dances were set to come into the Philippines as faster national and international transportation began to be developed. Reynaldo G. Alejandro noted in *Philippine Dance* that

> of American influences are dances such as *Ba-Ingles* (*Baile Ingles* or English Dances from Ilocos region), *Lanceros* (from the American square dance "Lancers"), *Birginia* (from "Virginia Reel"), and *Escopitan,* a dance from Negros Occidental which is comparable in its general pattern to the American square dance.
>
> The Fox Trot, Swing, Castle Walk, Lindy Hop, Big Apple, and Tango, among others, were to be seen in social gatherings such as coronation balls and traditional fiestas, and at various dance halls such as the Sta. Ana Cabaret (at the time billed as the world's largest). [p. 53]

In 1929, John Maynard serialized his impressions of the vaudeville in Manila for *Philippine Magazine*. He first named their counterparts in the United States like Fanny Brice, Grace la Rue, Chic Sales, Sophie Tucker, and Joey Brown. He called John C. Cowper the "dean of the Philippine variety show." Cowper's first venture was at the Paz Theatre with an all-European vaudeville in 1911. He lost in the venture and worked for the famous jazz pianist Borromeo Lou. He also reformed the Lux company and produced shows at the Rivoli (later Tivoli) and the Savoy Nifties.

Another personality to whom Maynard gave special mention was Buster Dunson, "a clever and versatile dancer" at the Savoy who also trained girls like the Garcia Sisters, Flo and Modesta. Dunson also designed costumes. There was also Catalina or Katy de la Cruz, who was "the greatest favorite of Manila variety" and was called "the Sophie Tucker of the Philippines." Aside from the others Maynard mentioned who were mainly singers like Toy-Toy, Leonora Reyes, Elizabeth "Dimples" Cooper, Vitang Escobar, and Nazarina Farias, who sang with the stranded Mario Padovani from Genoa and Chicago, there were also the singer-dancers Helen and Lucy Martin, Anita Fiori from Budapest, Carmen "Miami" Salvador, with her "hula wiggle that is entirely unequalled by any other local performer," and again the Garcia sisters. The latter performed with Dunson, and they became the "three-cornered combination [that was] the best dancing act Manila has ever had." Of the Filipino vaudeville dancers in general, Maynard concluded that

> there is a dainty nymph-like grace and beauty about those tiny Malay figures possessed by no other race in the world. They are quick to learn their routine, and are natural dancers. (306-07)

Making Dance Our Own

Even such institutions as the Manila Grand Opera House, reconstructed as a more viable venue in 1902, welcomed the bodabil (as vaudeville came to be translated). It was here that the First Philippine Assembly was convened in 1907 and three world-famous stars performed.

In 1922, Anna Pavlova performed in the Manila Grand Opera House at a time when it is assumed that ballet of some sort must have already been taught. Here is an excerpt from a memoir of one of her partners, Algeranoff, on their performance in Manila:

> We arrived in Manila. There we had a very gay social life, and barely reasonable box-office success in an artistic desert. Several of the girls received proposals, although none of them left the Philippines engaged. Some of the Poles were deeply shocked that the girls occasionally went out without chaperones—was it possible, I wondered, in 1922, that people could have such old-fashioned ideas? I remember with horror the matinees when we danced in torrid heat in our thick peasant costumes and wore ourselves out in front of practically no audience, for Madame did not dance at all in those early evening performances. In Manila we spent our time bathing in a warm sea, playing polo and feeling grateful that hotels and meals were not as expensive as in Japan. We also went to a wild St. Andrew's Night Ball, complete with bagpipes and eightsome reels. Of course we could only take part in sober one-step and occasional waltzes, because it would have been so easy to get our ankles kicked, our toes trodden on or even worse …
>
> Pavlova was invited to see the best of the local dancing schools. She came back very cheerful and we thought she must have discovered an infant genius. But not at all.
>
> "It was very sweet," she said, "all work very hard, you ask arabesque, they all do attitude! But very sweet." (p. 87)

(If Pavlova were to see her own people perform today, she'd be surprised that their arabesques are a la attitude!)

It was also at the Manila Grand Opera House that the Denishawn company performed five times in 1926. The company was led by Ruth

St. Denis and Ted Shawn, and included Doris Humphrey and Charles Weidman who were to be innovators of American Modern Dance. They brought back to the Orient, even as far as India, their Orient-inspired dances. It is interesting to note that today, our very own Elizabeth Roxas and Maxie Luna, a nephew of Leonor Orosa Goquingco, perform some of the Denishawn dances for the Joyce Trisler company in America. Meanwhile, Shawn himself went all the way up to the Mountain Province to see our indigenous dances. Alejandro's article, "Stopover: Manila, 1926," in *Sayaw Silanganan ng 1976-1977* had this to tell:

> Shawn found that "the native dances are dying out from general practice in Manila, being kept alive by schools and clubs." He observed several dances such as Surtido, Cariñosa, Rigaudon, Balitao, and others performed at the residence of Victoria Lopez (now Araneta) and at the Philippine Women's College (now Philippine Women's University). He met Francisca Reyes (now Aquino) who was at that time the director of Physical Education ... and was able to see Ms. Reyes' manuscript on Philippine dance which was later on published by Silver-Burdette as *Philippine National Dances* (1946). He gathered secondhand information on Muslim dancing from a certain Col. Langhorne, one of General Wood's military advisers and went to Camp John Hay in Baguio with General Wood to observe tribal dancing of the Igorots, Bontocs, Ifugaos, Kalingas, and Apayaos ... "we went to a natural area in the hills and there saw dancing in the most violent contrast to the anemic and unoriginal dancing of the (Christian) Filipinos." Shawn recorded his impressions of Philippine dance in a descriptive article "Dancing in the Isles of Fear" (*The Dance Magazine*, February 1927).

Earlier than these now acknowledged legendary figures of dance, Paul Nijinsky (not known to be related to the famous Vaslav but claiming to be with the Imperial Russian ballet) came to Manila in 1915 and performed for the benefit of the Belgian Red Cross. He performed again the following year at the Manila Hotel. His repertoire used music by Chopin, Saint-Saens, Grieg, Wieniawsky, and Schubert, with costumes done by Leon Bakst and dancing done on bare feet. He was assisted by "the best local talents" that Pavlova was later to see.

In the 1920s, there were well-known teachers like Kay Williams, who had a school in Ermita and among whose pupils was the diva

Mercedes Matias-Santiago; and Katrina Makarova, from the Imperial Russian Ballet who was a teacher to Anita M. Kane. More significant was the presence of Madam Lubov "Luva" Adameit, of Polish extraction, who started her Cosmopolitan Ballet and Dancing School in 1927. She claimed to have been a member of the Pavlova company. Remedios V. Piñon says Adameit was a graduate of the Malinowski School of Ballet and Free Art in Kiev. She put "Planting Rice" and "Cariñosa" on pointes, and contrived a "Maria Clara" number, perhaps the first ballet teacher-choreographer to merge ballet technique with native dancing. She also used a lot of Orient-inspired Western music in her annual recitals that had Egyptian, Persian, Chinese, or Indian numbers. Among her pupils were the late Remedios de Oteyza, National Artist Leonor Orosa Goquingco, Pacita Madrigal, Rosalia Merino, Fe Sala, Inday Gaston, Elsie Uytiepo, and Esperanza de los Santos, who later named her school the Adameit Ballet School. Several of these students became the true cornerstones of Philippine ballet.

Two Russians, Olga Dontsoff and Vladimir Bolsky, also set up schools that were short-lived. They also taught "aesthetic dancing" at the University of the Philippines, a dance that must have been allied with the Central European expressionistic modern dance that was brought to us in the 1930s by Kaethe Hauser and Trudl Dubsky. Both Viennese, Hauser and Dubsky started a movement in the Philippines that culminated with Mary Wigman and Harald Kreutzberg in Europe and Gertrud Bodenwieser in Australia.

In the Philippines, Hauser taught our Spanish-Filipino Manolo Rosado who later proceeded to study with Ted Shawn in Jacob's Pillow, Massachusetts, and who danced with Marienela de Montijo in Spain and with Magda Briones in Mexico. At one time Rosado was a director of dance at the University of the East and taught or made dances for the studios of de Oteyza and Julie Borromeo. Dubsky, meanwhile, came here to marry the Manila Symphony Orchestra director Dr. Herbert Zipper. She founded the Manila Ballet Moderne which had annual shows from 1939, reviews of which appeared in *Philippine Magazine*. She was noted for her *Iron Foundry* performed to Mossolov for its machine-like precision, *Polovetsky Dances* to Borodin, *Peer Gynt Suite* to Grieg, *Pictures at an Exhibition* to Mussorgsky, and *L'Arlesienne Suite* to Bizet. After migrating to the United States in 1946, Dubsky periodically returned to the Philippines and repeated her earlier successes like *A Midsummer Night's Dream*, even producing *Carmen* in Tagalog and a Charlie Brown ballet. Among the Filipinos she influenced were Benny Villanueva, Remedios Villanueva Piñon, Corazon Generoso Iñigo, Ricardo Reyes, and Lucio Sandoval.

During this period of the 1930s, the Metropolitan Theatre (inaugurated in December 1931) was in full operation, and many performances were done there. While not perfect, it was a great improvement on the Manila Grand Opera House. Much later, during the Japanese Occupation, the Volunteer Social Aid Committee (VSAC) started hosting concerts and operas in the Metropolitan Theatre. It was there that de Oteyza, Chloe Cruz (Romulo), Cecile Yulo (Locsin), and Josefina Sabater earned their merits as mature ballerinas. Paul Szilard, a Hungarian and now New York impresario, choreographed for the theater, and Lucio Sandoval created the dances for *Rigoletto*. While still living in the country through the 1950s, Szilard also staged stylized folk dances with his Philippine Art Theatre.

Meanwhile, it was also in 1939 that the Manila Carnival, established as a place where a lot of entertainment could be brought together, became cause for debate. Since 1908, attendance continued to be phenomenal in the carnival which was credited to the "Father of the Manila Carnival," Col. George Langhorne, and which made the carnival an annual cause for jubilation. But in 1939, the government backed-out of its official duties to the carnival, a place where our most notable first-generation choreographers like de Oteyza attempted their first dances. Defending the cause of the carnival in 1939, A. V. H. Hartendorp wrote:

> Jugglers and magicians, tight-rope walkers, high-divers, and bare-back riders, tumblers and contortionists, giants, dwarfs, and fat ladies, clowns and pantaloons, chorus girls and hula-hula dancers; gypsies, fortune-tellers, and phrenologists, trained animals, two-headed calves, puppet-shows, merry-go-rounds, ferris wheels, and skating rinks, sparkling, beautiful eyes behind black dominoes, dancing, romance, lights, music, noise, pop-corn and peanuts—who is the man, unburied, who is so dead that he can fail to respond to such things, if only once

> a year? And then there are the children. Ask them whether they want the carnival. (February 1939, p. 67)

Earlier, in 1934, Anita Kane founded her own school with Janet Miles. A student of Katrina Makarova and of Martha Thalberg, Norma Gould, and Ernest Belcher in the United States, Kane was born to New Zealanders but grew up in Camarines Norte. She was one of those who saw dancers like Pavlova in many dance stories, causing her to be obsessed with dancing. She studied medicine in the United States, but came to be the teacher of present-day leaders in Philippine dance like Tony Llacer, Julie Borromeo, and Felicitas L. Radaic. She introduced the Royal Academy of Dancing syllabi in her school and produced the first full-evening ballet with a Filipino theme and to Filipino music, *Maria Makiling* (with a score by Ramon Tapales). Kane also did *Reconstruction*, an abstract ballet about post-WW II set to a score by Marcelino Carluen, as well as other adaptations of local themes, as in *Inulan sa Pista*, a vignette, and *Sweepstakes, Mahjong*, and *La Mer*, set to western music. Her influence is now recognized to be pervasive not only because of her Kane and Panama companies, which toured the remotest parts of the country and followed later by efforts of Radaic and Fe Sala Villarica in Cebu, but also because she introduced the significance of dance to such artists as playwright Severino Montano, composer Eliseo Pajaro, essayist I.V. Mallari, and folk dancers Ricardo Reyes and Lucio Sandoval.

De Oteyza, a student of Adameit, became the neoclassicist of her generation. Furthering her studies with Szilard, Preobrajenska, and other luminaries in Europe, she composed ballets to the piano concertos of Grieg and Tchaikovsky, the rhapsodies of Rachmaninoff and Gershwin, and to a few Filipino compositions. Popularly known as Totoy, she also had her de Oteyza Manila Ballet and Hariraya Ballet companies, and later closely collaborated with Inday Gaston Mañosa. Her dancers include Maribel Aboitiz, Joji Felix, Sony Lopez, Vella Damian, Effie Nañas, Nida Onglengco, Eddie Elejar, Cesar Mendoza, Jamin Alcoriza, Jun Dalit, Eric Cruz, Rene Dimacali, and Basilio who all have made their mark in the ballet scene.

Leonor Orosa Goquingco, also from the Adameit school, is a phenomenon in local dance. She furthered her studies abroad not only in dance but also in dramatics. Even before her early attempts to do dance in Iloilo with Lilia Lopez (Jison), she was already doing dances in the Visayas. Adameit supposedly said, "Leonor, you will take my place." As early as 1939, she did *Circling the Globe*, which had a sequence that took place in a European concentration camp. From then onward, she progressed to *The Elements* (Hilarion Rubio), *Trend: Return to Native*, and other native-inspired dances that culminated in the *Noli Dance Suite* and *Filipinescas*. The latter, a full-evening program about Philippine life, legend, and lore rendered in dance, was seen worldwide through her Filipinescas company. Mainly credited for using folk themes and dances in her ballets, Orosa-Goquingco was lauded by Nick Joaquin for her so-called stylization of dance:

> Kikay Reyes (Mrs. Aquino) took the folk dances out of the sticks and into the schools. Leonor Orosa took it out of the schools and into the theater. (Quijano de Manila, "Dances of the Cross," *Philippines Free Press*, April 1, 1961, p. 37.)

A baby ballerina when she was still studying with Adameit, Rosalia Merino Santos went on to major in modern dance in Wisconsin, in the process later encountering European dance artists like Kurt Jooss. Returning to Manila, she founded the FEU Experimental Dance Troupe and brought to Manila the best lecture-demonstration on dance hereabouts and experimentations with folk themes, including a rendering of the story of Alejandro Roces entitled *Of Cocks and Kings* (Kasilag). Reviewing the latter for *The Manila Times* in 1958, Morli Dharam wrote:

> The dance drama based on the legend revealed fertile possibilities of this dance style—its dynamism, its tendency for oblique expression, its rich overtones for symbolism and many-layered meanings.
>
> In that manner, the legend becomes a true dance-drama, evoking the universal sentiments of love and hate and avarice and horror and awe but all within a unique Philippine context—a contribution from us to the world's treasury of dance dramas. (December 20, p. 8)

Reviving the Folk in Dance: Francisca Reyes

According to Regino and Carmen Ylanan, as early as 1922, the revival of Philippine folk dances was already initiated by Francisca Reyes when she became a student assistant in the Department of Physical Education at the University of the Philippines. In 1927, UP President Jorge C. Bocobo sent Reyes out to the provinces to collect folk dances, which were presented at the Philippine carnival. From 1934 to 1938, Reyes, along with Ramon Tolentino and Antonino Buenaventura, ventured to the provinces, this time under the auspices of the President's Advisory Committee on Dances and Songs. They encountered all sorts of problems with transportation and with trying to get people into the "proper mood" for dance, as Celia Olivar Bocobo puts it. As the end result of all the research, the UP Folk Song and Dance Club, now known as the Filipiniana Dance Troupe, was formed. Numerous books on dance reconstructions, which have become bibles for folk dancers, were also produced.

Reyes's influence is widespread because so many people were involved in her projects; even to the present day, the Philippine Folk Dance Society is still involved in these. The pioneering work of Reyes has brought to us today the various institutions in dance like the Bayanihan Folk Arts Center and the Bayanihan Philippine Dance Company, the Baranggay Folk Dance Troupe, the UP Filipiniana, several other university-based folk groups, and the theatrically oriented Filipinescas of Orosa-Goquingco. The national debt to Reyes, first married to Tolentino and then to Aquino, is priceless. UP President Bocobo is also credited for having supported dance at a time when much of its folk forms were disappearing as the country evolved towards modernization.

Reliving the American Past: Present Problems in Dance

The problems we face in dance today are no different from those encountered by Francisca Reyes. And we're not only talking about the folk and ethnic dances.

The vaudeville age is no more and we can at best only pay tribute to Atang de la Rama and Katy de la Cruz out of nostalgia, and maybe out of a sincere appreciation for their having sustained a theatrical art that links us to the past and affects today's artistry. Without de la Rama's and de la Cruz's nightly efforts, theatrical forms associated with vaudeville—music, mimicry, acting, and dancing—could have dwindled and fewer artists would have followed in their footsteps. I myself grew with the cinema that starred Fred Astaire and Gene Kelly, Marge and Gower Champion, Vera Ellen and Cyd Charisse, before I discovered Galina Ulanova and Margot Fonteyn. Out in the provinces I could only read about Orosa, Kane, and de Oteyza, that I was in awe when I met or studied with them. But often enough, we claim originality and fail to acknowledge our debts to earlier, if smaller, attempts than ours. And then there are those later attempts expanded by more stages and more media exposure, which could create the shift to classic dances that make Astaire or Kelly less fantastic or elitist. Even Kane and de Oteyza become less prestigious after some classes in New York or London.

Furthermore, we tend to prefer an Augusta Maywood in Paris (or Maniya Barredo in Atlanta) to a Mary Anne Lee in the backwoods of Pennyslvania (or Ester Rimpos in Manila). Reasons are both financial and artistic. Financial, because only few can survive as dance artists in this country; i.e., to earn one's keep through dancing. Artistic, because we would rather earn merit as a princess of Petipa or a ballerina of Balanchine than as an inspiration to a local choreographer. This also translates to music, when a Tchaikovsky piece is deemed superior to a Molina. After all, even Americans had to earn accreditations in Europe, down to the music hall artist Josephine Baker who conquered Paris. Loie Fuller and Isadora Duncan gained renown outside of their country. But they did more. They also invented their dances, and they were not worried that they were unlike Pavlova or Karsavina. To a great extent Balanchine owed his ballerinas his fame for they did not cry to be Odette-Odiles or Auroras; instead they courageously danced his dances, from the successes to the failures. Locally, we badly need to honor our own dancers and choreographers so that they be further encouraged to do their own projects.

We also have lost almost beyond retrieval the works of the first generation choreographers like de Oteyza, Orosa Goquingco, Merino, and Kane. When the various modes of filming started invading the performance of dance, choreographers became very wary of plagiarism (despite the fact that piracy is virtually beyond the control of puny laws in our copycat land). Retrieval also entails money, time, and the right people to technically restage or record them. Movement notation is slow, but it is increasingly recognized as important not only as a recording device but also as a system of analysis, even in Asia. An awareness of our heritage of dances, on stage and in scores and films, is essential so that the art form can continue to undergo revolutions and revivals (as opposed to advancement or development). Thus, regardless of whether these works will be performed again or not, the effort and willingness to record our dances, past and present, must continue.

It is also most unfortunate that the so-called modern dance, whether European or American, has not really taken solid root in our land. I do not mean just the technique of modern dance (and there are several). According to Selma Jeanne Cohen, modern dance is primarily a point of view. That point of view is the desire to reexamine the nature of the dance, to go back to its roots if necessary, and to explore the possibilities inspired or motivated by past or present climates. Even if the modern dance by Martha Graham, Eric Hawkins, or Merce Cunningham was influenced by Oriental style or thought, there should be more to the merging of techniques than just our way of life and physique. We should be more original and create something that would subsequently be the Filipino choreographers' contribution to the world of dance. There is, after all, something in the intuitive part of the creative process that will help us "rest" on tradition or "rebound" from it (i.e., to understand today based on the resources of yesterday). This is part of the creative impulse in modern dance, something that is limited in classical ballet because of its stricter range and Western aesthetics, despite its Oriental inspirations (*bayaderes* and *peris* as characters, the designs of Bakst and Goncharova, or some flexed hands and feet). Ballet remains to be primarily viable when it sticks to its centuries-old standards of performance that shows a near-perfect technique in dancing and a spectacle as performance. On the other hand, when unshod, modern dance is closer to our folk life and dances.

Finally, there's the problem with our audience—sometimes our dancers. As a choreographer, I have met resistance from my own dancers and patrons regarding ideas or dances I feel so strongly about but which are not sweet, safe, or sellable in an age of consumerism, which disregards imagination while dictating that which is "best" or "advanced" (which in turn is usually "imported"). This undoubtedly limits the choices I make. Temporal and elusive as the art I practice is, I have to compete with the hallowed aesthetics established by the French, Russians, or Americans, or earn their stamp of approval, and stage the project in the one and only Cultural Center which has been elevated to the stature of a national pinnacle. Anyone who wants to sell a ticket knows this.

We cannot deny that our colonial past has everything to do with this present state of dance. As a people, we are twice stepchildren—first of Spain and second of America. Even in dance, we've seen that the Westerners have trained us—as they did in language and education, in government, trade, and industry. But like the American artists who had to liberate themselves from an obsession with and subservience to European culture, we have found the need to assert our own style and sensibility. These may not altogether exclude foreign ideas and techniques—because everything is utilized by transformation if not by outright imitation—but creatively, these foreign influences should be processed or renewed. Perhaps not so self-consciously by the so-called and generic filter we name "Filipino," which is itself indefinable, but by each individual and liberated artist making choices, and by his society appreciating and supporting his art.

Diamond Jubilee Lecture
University of the Philippines
1983

A Turning Point for Dance and the Filipino Dancer

The Ballet Federation of the Philippines was borne of the First National Ballet Festival of 1976, a project conceived by its chairpersons to showcase dancing in the Philippines. It aimed to project a plurality in dance practice in the country, and to give senior dance groups the chance to perform on stage. The festival was also meant to be a vehicle to honor those who had contributed much to the building of the art of ballet in the Philippines. If anything, the festival proved that more than one man or woman is needed to do this. I have often quoted theologian and critic Nathan A. Scoot, Jr. on this point:

> that the modern theatre has indeed been very greatly impoverished of many genuinely gifted playwrights of minor rank. For it is probably the case that our sense of the liveliness of a given form is far more dependent on its engaging a large number of interesting artists of minor stature than on the relatively small number of major figures who may be working in its medium. If there is no large efflorescence of activity, of the sort that becomes possible when a host of significant artists of minor scope are exploring the possibilities of a particular medium, then we do not have a sense of that medium's possessing vivaciousness and richness of interest.[1]

With all these goals, it was hoped that dance artists in the Philippines would find a common ideology that allowed for unity in diversity, something that would strengthen their sense of community and develop a tolerance for their differences. As I said in last year's *Philippine Dance Annual*, we can only be singular by being plural.[2]

---

[1] Nathan Scott, Jr., *Man in the Modern Theatre* (Richmond: John Knox Press, 1965) 9-10.

[2] See "Plural to Be Singular: The Festival Aims," *Sayaw Silanganan ng 1976-77.*

Despite the lack of unity, there is currently reason for celebration (although inconvenient for those who have no booking prowess). The CCP Theater is hard to book these days—proof that more dances are being staged. It is unfortunate though, that should a performance be staged somewhere else, the patronage is not the same, which is why the status of the formerly prestigious Philamlife Auditorium and of Meralco Theater has suffered. In the latter's case in particular, it's not a very encouraging sign for artistic life in San Juan, Quezon City, and Pasig. The audiences in these areas seem to be resisting the urge to go to the Meralco Theater, though it's not really inconvenient to get there, save for participants who need to commute by bus to watch presentations. Audiences also don't like the Folk Arts Theater because of the heat and mosquitoes, although of course the globe-trotting patrons can stand the cold in European outdoor places of exhibition. This bias for what is seen as "classy" is related to what Father Leonard N. Mercado says about the Filipino middle and upper classes and rich artistic practitioners. In *Applied Filipino Philosophy*, he says succinctly:

> when this elite tries its artistic expression, it is natural that its models as well as aspirations are Western. The Filipino Beethoven, the Filipino Frank Lloyd Wright, the Filipino Picasso—these are its goals. With this bias, what the elite produces are often Western imitations that do not relate to their countrymen.[3]

These well-entrenched cliques in Philippine culture don't encourage the growth of groups that show the plurality of dance in this country. There is a college-based hegemony in Manila, and associations just end up keeping to themselves. Thus, should a dance artist have no chance to belong to the existing cliques, the only choice is to turn somewhere else, a move that easily results in alienation.

In the United Kingdom, the growth of groups is testament to the need for alternatives. It is no longer enough to just have the Royal Ballet; Rambert Ballet has always been there. The London Contemporary Dance

---

[3] Leonardo N. Mercado, *Applied Filipino Philosophy* (Tacloban: Divine Word University, 1977) 11.

Theater also rose,[4] while regional growth was encouraged in Manchester, Glasgow, and Cork. Germany and Soviet Russia are the best examples of subsidized plurality, while the United States has been spawning companies all over the country, typified by the dizzying diversity in New York. In this city, the Metropolitan Opera House accommodates both American Ballet Theater (ABT) and the Martha Graham Dance Company; it also hosts the National Ballet of Canada. The Kennedy Center in Washington, DC has ABT and the Jeffrey Ballet as its resident companies.[5]

Tied to the growth and encouragement of plurality in Philippine dance and its groups is the growth of Filipino choreographers as artists. I insist that the original works by Filipino choreographers be upheld. Hopefully relevant to our needs, there is no need for these works to "look Pinoy" as these are universal themes and forms that reaffirm the Philippine context. (For instance, I do not apologize for the use of Rodrigo and Vivaldi in my *Philippine Tapestry*, although I have some reservations about the use of Barber in the Visayan section.)

Not that nothing has been done for the Filipino choreographer. Prior to the CCP Dance Company, Dance Theatre Philippines (DTP) encouraged the growth of Filipino choreographers, which produced some enduring works by Eddie Elejar, Julie Borromeo, and Felicitas L. Radaic. Luis Layag also first established himself in DTP. Hariraya Ballet Company tried to encourage the Filipino choreographer as well when it hired Reynaldo G. Alejandro, Roberto Caballero, and Cesar Mendoza to diversify its all de Oteyza repertory. Ballet Philippines showcases this idea of variety.

But the institution that has succeeded most in this direction is still the CCP Dance School and Company.[6] Through the direction of Alice Reyes, choreographers like Tony Fabella, Gener Caringal, Effie Nañas, Denise Garcia, and Edna Vida gained expert craftsmanship and realized their perhaps unknown choreographic potential. Those of us who started

---

[4] Unfortunately, this has long been dissolved.

[5] True in the year this was written; today ABT tours nationally, while Jeffrey Ballet has settled in Chicago.

[6] Now Ballet Philippines.

out in the provinces, like Fe Sala Villarica of Cebu, Lydia M. Gaston of Bacolod, Agnes Locsin of Davao, Lucy Jumawan of Dumaguete and myself, were fortunate to have started there before being subjected to so-called cosmopolitan taste.

After the refreshing impact of modern dance brought about by Alice Reyes in the early 1970, and the extensive outreach program of the Philippine Educational Theater Association around that time (which was preceded by Wilfredo Ma. Guerrero's Mobile Theater and Severino Montano's Arena Theater), the most vital theatrical development has been the recent rise of community theaters in separate and unpretentious areas all over Metro Manila, as well as the integrative experiments of such groups as the Kombayoka in Marawi City.

The CCP Dance Company's emphasis on native works by Filipinos (which are not necessarily on native themes) has encouraged the growth of local aesthetics against which we may measure our own accomplishments. The experimental works (limited in extent because of its opera-house sized residence and patronage) point to the exploitation of indigenous styles; although it is possible that these experiments may open the way to uncharted routes that will characterize what in the future will be called Filipino dance.

The need for this system of aesthetic valuation is obvious, and no apologies are needed. The fact is, the Asian arts possess their own standards, set by Asian living conditions and traditions. The West simply has to accept us for what we are, our styles and tastes, as they do when they witness a rite in Bali, a Noh performance in Japan, an opera in Taiwan. Despite our low opinion of the current Red Chinese troupes,[7] they have made their mark in the West as no other Asian company has. The needs they've recognized have shaped and authenticated their works of art. This is the kind of conviction we need. We need to feel confident about what we can offer and hold up against the rest of the world. This confidence and this art can only arise out of the context of our national life, formed out of native experience in the Philippines. With this, even expatriates will be able to recognize the true significance and relevance

---

[7] I refer to the Cultural Revolution period in China.

of their work in their homeland. This is the turning point that will make them compatible with their countrymen.

Of course modern dance has it easier than ballet, since the former adjusts better to natural, folkloric styles. It is also frequently the case that ballet companies produce fewer choreographers than modern dance companies. But like our experience with Western politics, religion, education, and languages, we just have to suffer a sea of change before we can make ballet authentically ours. This is not to deny the universal history of the art form and the use of the classics for local consumption, but we need to realize that these will never be the source of our sincerest expression or of our international fame.

To drive home the point of this essay for the current leaders of the Philippine dance scene, let me quote Father R. Mercado:

> It is not our intention to belittle the elite. In general the elite suffer from identity crisis through no fault of their own since they are the victims of a westernized educational system. If the elite artists want to contribute something of value, they have to consider their national patrimony and return to the aspirations of the common *tao*. In other words, the rest of the world wants the Filipinos to be themselves. But if the Filipino artists continue to aspire after Western models, they will continue to be second-rate artists, having less than original to offer.[8]

The elite have a role in nation building. The middle class and the intelligentsia have traditionally served as leaders of revolutionary reform movements. Rizal and the other Filipino members of the anti-Spanish Propaganda Movement were Spanish-trained, and yet they became the leaders of the people. The masses need brains and leaders to represent their aspirations. The Filipino elite have to rediscover their identity and in doing so contribute positively to the country's growth and well-being.

In 1975, I witnessed a black opera group from South Africa in Aberdeen, Scotland. They performed a section from *La Traviata*, complete with wigs and buckled shoes. We just couldn't suspend enough disbelief

---

[8] Mercado, 14.

to accept an illusion that couldn't come across convincingly. And these were matters that went beyond skin-deep. Another example of this is in architecture when skyscrapers and plush suburbia aren't the best for the country's business of tourism. The fact is, it is by what is inherent, by what has been shaped by our history, by what is demanded by our people and their needs, that our presentations, performances—our art—will become convincingly true.

We, after all, need to convince ourselves first and our public second, in both life and in art.

Biased for Ballet: Patronage, Stratification, and Compromise in Philippine Dance

It has become commonplace to decry the loss or lack of an audience for dance, a complaint that's usually heard about ballet in the theaters. This paper simply wants to point out the social context within which ballet in the Philippines survives. In the future, a more comprehensive study should be done on dance in general, and look at its broader implications.

Philippine Ballet's First Students and Teachers

The Philippines saw ballet at the turn of the century. It was seen then as spectacle, something that was not to be viewed on its own. It took time before ballet was allowed to be part of the musical theater, the vaudeville or the circus. The "ballet girls" of the children's troupe called Lilliputians arrived from Australia to grace the Zorilla in 1901 in sections with the "ballet girls" entitled *Amber, Housemaids, Seaweed Ballet, Widow Ballet*, and *Pierrot Ballet*. In the same year, the Japanese Infantile Company arrived at Teatro Oriental in Santa Cruz with a "Japanese Ballet." In 1902, the Baroufski Imperial Russian Circus had its own twenty-five "ballet beauties" dancing the pantomimic ballets *The Sea Robbers*, *Faust*, and another about the Boer War at the National Cycle Track. These were performed around Avenida Rizal, where the future Manila Grand Opera House (MGOH) was to rise. It's possible that other visiting circus troupes (like the Barnes and Cogill-Sutton companies) might have had their own ballet dancers.

Famous artists also arrived in Manila, like the questionable Paul Nijinsky who claimed ascendancy from the Imperial Russian Ballet in

St. Petersburg but whose name seems to be an anomaly. He came in 1915 and 1916 for the Belgian Red Cross and Manila Hotel, claiming designs by Leon Bakst of the Diaghilev Ballets Russes. Appreciably, he exhibited musical reforms in dance initiated by Isadora Duncan and Michel Folkine, as he danced to Chopin, Saint-Saens, Grieg, Wieniawski, and Schubert.

In 1922, Anna Pavlova danced with her company at the MGOH, with performances by her in the evenings. She visited local ballet schools, where she was charmed but not convinced by the pupils' standards. One local girl she inspired was Anita Kane, who then sought out Katrina Makarova to be her teacher. Similarly, Fe Sala Villarica of Cebu also sought to get Russian Mara Selheim as teacher. Among the other teachers of that time were Olga Dontsov, Vladimir Bolsky, the English Kay Williams, and the Spanish-American Carmen Mcleod. Williams was teacher to soprano Mercedes Matias Santiago while Mcleod taught choreographer Chuchi Hernandez.

But it was the teacher Lubov or Luva Adameit who stayed long enough in the country to establish her Cosmopolitan Ballet and Dancing School with her manager G. Leibovitz and pianist Ivan Sitnik. She claimed ascendancy from the Malinowski School of Ballet and Free Art in Kiev and membership in the Pavlova company. It was in her school that the larger roots of ballet in the Philippines were planted. Her good crop of students included National Artist Leonor Orosa Goquingco, Remedios "Totoy" de Oteyza, Rosalia Merino Santos, Ma. Luisa "Inday" Gaston Mañosa, Chloe Cruz Romulo, Joji Felix Velarde, Pacita Madrigal, Fely Franquelli, Esperanza Santos, and Elsie Uytiepo Torrejon. According to Orosa Goquingco, Adameit had real imagination, even wanting to put *Cariñosa* and *Planting Rice* on pointes. Using today's theoretical terms, this was like seeing the "Other" in a kind of choreographic ethnology.

Rather than talk about Adameit's stand and thoughts on dance, I would like to speak of what we ourselves did with this foreign art form that is ballet. I shall limit the discussion to the aforementioned pupils in order to make this brief. My teacher Uytiepo Torrejon in Bacolod and Santos (who named her own school in Adameit's honor) in Manila continued the career of teaching after studying ballet. Gaston Mañosa,

Cruz Romulo, and Felix Velarde also did so after they lived out their dancing days with distinction. Our first Giselle, Madrigal, set up a school of her own in collaboration with the American Ricardo Cassell, who himself prepared the way for the professionalization of dance in the country. Franquelli became one of our first international performers, touring the world with a repertoire derived from Madame Adameit and gaining rave reviews in America and Europe with her "jeune femme d'allure distinguee, a la silhouette elegante; le visage joli."

The baby ballerina Merino Santos also taught ballet but later fully turned to modern dance and folk dance. Meanwhile, inspired by classical music in various forms, de Oteyza specialized in abstract ballets and was the most Balanchinian of our early choreographers. Orosa Goquingco also drew from the germ Madame Adameit planted and espoused the infusion of folkloric style and literature into ballet. She charted the return-to-the-native movement and pointed the way for today's "neo-Filipino" and "neo-ethnic" formulations in dance. Orosa Goquingco's seminal works blossomed into the full-length evening ballet *Filipinescas: Philippine Life, Legend and Lore in Dance* (1961).

Dance as a Site of Power: Women Lead

From the abovementioned list, we can already deduce that it was the women who were the leaders of Philippine dance. They were our first outstanding choreographers and directors in dance. Because, save for a few exceptions, women were always identified with dance, it became stereotypical to speak of women and dance synonymously. This has made society less tolerant of male dancers and has kept their number at a minimum. To date no single male has been adjudged a National Artist in dance. Of late though, men have become artistic directors, yet they are always backed by a bevy of female supporters made up of a combination of "ballet mothers," ex-dancers, rabid admirers of the dance (who may feel at home with the predominantly homosexual directors), or the ballerinas, who wish to be served by male choreographers because they will receive fair if not equal treatment, than if they are choreographed by a woman and they end up becoming rivals.[1]

This predominant female leadership and patronage in dance seems to contradict the patriarchal hegemony in Philippine society. It is an acknowledged fact that women have such important and strong roles in Philippine domestic and social life. Sociologists, and recently Niels Mulder, observe how mothers play the moral and orderly core in the nuclear family system.[2] The supposed shamanistic tradition that was and is pervasively female is perhaps representative of the sexual divide in religious devotion today: the women have become more ardent (and in the past more subject to priestly seduction, typified by Maria Clara and her mother in Jose Rizal's novel), and the men have become more nominal (and promiscuous outside of the sanctified family). In the same folk tradition, there was carried on a kind of political rivalry between the religious (shaman) and the secular (the datu) leaders.[3] Herminia Menez discusses the different issues that deal with separate male-female realms.[4]

With the same kind of gender divide in the more secular realm of the arts, particularly in the non-folkloric and Western modes, female leaders on the cultural front have more fervor and the wiles to woo male bankers, merchants, and industrialists to give the arts financial support. Perhaps the criticized but accepted double standard in Filipino gendered relations has allowed the female *culturati* to prevail upon rich men to part with their money for the cause of music or dance. In the long run though, these women remain subservient and at the mercy of the men on whom they are dependent to sustain their work and prolong their projects in the arts. In the end, the woman's vulnerable position of having to ask for support simply reflects the predetermined and limited scope within which they can carry on their cause. Sadly, this also results in artistic work that is meant to please bourgeoisie taste and values.

Let's not forget that there have also been women of power (who may have gone up because of their menfolk or other powerful women) who have themselves been manipulative. We can always cite as an example Imelda Romualdez Marcos, to whom many of us still chant tributes of gratitude for the Cultural Center of the Philippines (1969) and other cultural edifices and projects. I risk being tactless by saying that it also took a long time for the CCP's first artistic director to warm up to other dance companies, and it was only in 1983 that she finally accommodated the Festival Four group (Hariraya Ballet, Dance Theatre Philippines, Dance Concert Company, and Manila Metropolis Ballet) at the CCP main stage. These groups would later on formed the core of Philippine Ballet Theater. Earlier, in the latter half of the 1970s, it was the CCP-delegated leadership of Teodoro Hilado at the Folk Arts Theater that proved hospitable to these groups and other members of the Ballet Federation of the Philippines. National Artist Lucrecia R. Kasilag was among the female leaders who sustained the hegemonic prioritization of the Bayanihan Philippine Dance Company since the late 1950s. Its acknowledged artistic director was Jose Lardizabal, its musical director was Kasilag, and its choreographer was Lucrecia R. Urtula. Last April, the Bayanihan was declared the first national folk dance company, and become the first state cultural company.

The Bayanihan's contemporary groups were also led by women: National Artist Orosa Goquingco for the Filipinescas, Paz Cielo Belmonte for the Baranggay Folk Dance Troupe, Corazon Generoso Iñigo and then Rosalia Merino Santos for the Far Eastern University. Much later came Ramon Obusan, who now typifies the new male leader in the folk dance field.

Women also mostly monopolized the leadership of ballet schools and companies, which may primarily be because they were the socially acceptable teachers of dance (as in the Catholic schools run by nuns). De Oteyza and Mañosa at Hariraya, and Julie Borromeo, Tita Radaic, and Eddie Elejar at Dance Theatre Philippines, led the first professional dance groups in 1968. Ballet Philippines had yet to come out in 1970, as initiated by Alice Reyes; she later shared the group's leadership with Elejar (and future foreign guest choreographers). Meanwhile, Dance Theatre came to be led by Basilio, but he always had Radaic behind him, in the same way that Vella Damian was behind Eric Cruz at the Dance Concert Company, or Lisa Macuja at Ballet Manila.

As already intimated, the predominance of women in dance leadership is telling of the surface and subliminal gender politics in the realm of the Philippine performing arts. These women still have to plead their cause to the male (or the powerful female) leaders in economy and politics. This was the case in Edgar Degas's time, when he documented the ballerinas on stage and backstage in the Foyer de la Danse at the Paris Opera—these are the very same pictures we have viewed through rose-tinted glasses. Because of cases such as these, the path dance has had to take is one of compromise between artistic integrity and bourgeois taste. To a certain extent this is the one commonality that has been sustained throughout Philippine dance, and the kind of context and representation the ballet stage builds upon. In her book *Dancing Women*, Sally Banes discusses the predetermined role of women in society in matrimonial, gender, sexual, and political relationships.[5]

The Audience and Patronage of Ballet

As ballet dancers, choreographers, and scholars dealt with the economics and politics of its creation, it also came to be identified with a specific audience. The modern dance pioneers Kaethe Hauser and Trudl Dubsky Zipper, both Viennese, helped build this audience. They called their works modern ballet rather than ausdruckstanz as these were called in Europe. Dubsky Zipper was, a dancer of Gertrude Bodenweiser, who later pioneered in Australia.) By tradition, there were two basic audiences in the Philippines. One was the audience that followed the shadow plays called *carillo*, the moro-moro or comedia, and the passion plays (*cenaculo*) outdoors. People could watch most of these productions for free, sponsored as they were by the church or community. Stages were improvised, while certain ritual forms like the pastores, sinulog, and subli included dances that were done in honor of saints and their holidays. These plays functioned as supplements to the Masses held inside the monumental Catholic churches of that time, while other types of "performances" and enactments were also done inside the church.

Meanwhile, there were other forms such as the zarzuela and the opera which were performed indoors and had paid admission. It was the Compania Infantil de Baile of the Italian maestro Appiani that performed in constructed theaters during the Spanish period. It was during this century that the stage show from which the vaudeville evolved was performed in the combined stage and movie house. Improvised stages were also set up for provincial tours for movie stars in skits and musical numbers.

But even during this time, ballet was distinct; it mainly catered to the upper class. Its staging and aesthetics aspired for the conventions of the proscenium stage from which the courtly halls and ballrooms evolved. The primary perspective here is distance, with a clear division between the performers and the audience. In the end, ballet only survived because it was under the patronage of the royal courts. Later, when they started being staged in the opera houses, ballet began to be promoted by impresarios.

These point to the fact that commercial currency is essential to ballet's survival. The commercialization of popular theater has nothing to do with it; even now, ballet only continues to survive through subsidies from rich patrons, corporate houses, and state sponsorship. In fact, ballet isolates itself from the popular (although for a time it had to be performed with vaudeville or musical theater to survive), typified by being housed in places such as the opera house of yesterday and the cultural centers of today. We of course understand that the training of a ballet dancer requires this special isolation. Ballet has rigorous requirements in technique and style, repertoire and production that can only be attained through special nurturing and individual realization.

All the abovementioned factors have kept ballet from having an audience that may include the lower classes. While some dancers are from the lower class, they "improve their lot" through dance, in the same way that the poor ballet girls survived during Edgar Degas's time. Meanwhile, our own showgirls of the past at the MGOH or at Clover Theater are now equivalent to the Filipino *japayukis* in Japan today.

Not that there has been a conscious effort to limit ballet's audience to the upper classes. When Alice Reyes started Ballet Philippines (as Alice Reyes and Modern Dance Company in 1970), it was not according to this concept of an audience, although she was courting an audience that could only be served by the aesthetics and organization of ballet.

Ironically, in its first inception as a modern dance company, Ballet Philippines was mostly made up of ballet dancers who came from Dance Theatre Philippines—a confessed supporter of Orosa Goquingco's projects of Filipinization and contemporaneity, unlike the classically entrenched Hariraya Ballet Company.

It is no surprise then that modern dance remained an enclave, while the rest of Manila and the country were peppered with ballet schools. Earlier, exponents of modern dance had to resort to strategies for popularization. To overcome its "modern look," the group of Dubsky Zipper started being called Manila Ballet Moderne. Carmen Adevoso Ferrer stayed in the schools to inculcate modern dance technique. Rosalia Merino Santos had the eyrie of Far Eastern University to keep her modern group going; sadly, it never gained the same kind of prominence as other ballet and folk dance companies. Manolo Rosado who studied with Ruth St. Denis, Ted Shawn, and the European modern dance masters was a noble and profound dancer essaying roles like Judas and Don Quixote; as a modern dancer though, he never matched his stature as a classical Spanish bailarino.

Meanwhile, in the process of developing her company, Reyes had to surrender to the demand of the ballet-inclined audience. While staging modern dances, she had to promote the company in ballet with its standard war-horses (first started with local choreographers in a composite *The Nutcracker* Act II) and sought the collaboration of the most noted danseur, Eddie Elejar. She made the CCP Dance Company popular with such rock opera ballets as *Tommy*, *Tales of the Manuvu*, and *Rama Hari*, and found that it was classical ballet that had a more consistent following, no matter the standards used in its reproduction.

Reyes's sister Denisa also wanted to form a modern dance group when she returned from New York, but there was no means of supporting such an enterprise and she had to agree to directing Ballet Philippines instead. Within the compass of the company's mixture of ballet and modern dance, Denisa created works that showed the scope of her expertise in the modern dance form; classicism was obviously not her medium. Similarly, Denisa's successor Agnes Locsin fared tentatively with glossy versions of so-called ballet, but earned her real merit as a modern dance choreographer in her neo-ethnic orientation.

Social Stratification and Choreographic Implications

I believe that today we do not have a choreographer who is steeped in the choreographic tradition of ballet. Instead we have become versatile at merging styles and approaches, as in the case of Orosa Goquingco's success during her time. We do not have a choreographer with the stature of the late Choo San Gob of Singapore or of William Forsythe in the field of ballet reconstruction; nor do we have someone who has the same popular success as Matthew Bourne with his *Swan Lake* and *Cinderella* as performed by his Adventure in Moving Pictures company.

Ballet creation has a special focus that our local traditions do not truly allow. And yet our larger audience for dance is primarily for ballet. Whereas Filipino ingenuity rests in the fusion of forms and styles, it is something that the audience does not always appreciate; in fact, the audience for this kind of presentation is becoming scarce.

This same audience, however, still puts out money for classical ballets that are not even popular in Europe anymore. Always looking to the United States for our own artistic standards—and with the United States having a prolonged nostalgia for Imperial Europe both in cultural taste and political dispensations—we have come to prioritize these classical ballets as well. Thus, a greater number of patrons of dance are of the same social class as the balletomanes and ballet students.

Who are these balletomanes? These are people from the upper classes who, in the past, were led by the Legardas and the Valdezes. Today, some are listed as members of the boards of trustees of various ballet companies. A few of them can't even stand watching barefoot dancing; they can only appreciate the ideal ballerinas doing pleasant choreographic symmetries. No Filipino has dared deconstruct *Giselle* or *Sleeping Beauty*, as Mats Ek, Peter Schaufuss, or the Harlem Dance Theater have done abroad.[6] An exception is the UP Dance Company, which recently transformed *Giselle* into *Higanti*, and rendered social class conflict with babaylanes as wilis.

For the most part though, we are comforted by the accepted and acclaimed foreign taste in dance, which has undoubtedly stunted the growth of dance in general and of the ballet in particular. Despite the transformations our native choreographers have done, Philippine dance continues to exist as though we have never heard of Diaghilev's reforms early in the century. This impresario's choreographic, musical, and scenic revolutions have obviously failed to flower fully in the Philippines. It is not surprising then that at present we still want our Coralli and Perrot, our Petipa and Ivanov, our Odette-Odile and Princess Aurora of the past century.

The abovementioned system of patronage limits the audience of dance. For the most part, it has continued to be the rich patrons, corporate sponsors (which will only help prestigious dance companies), funding institutions (which have of late defined "merit" as "world class" based on Western forms),[7] and the upper classes that send their little girls to ballet schools. This kind of patronage is reflective of a social stratification that favors those at the top. In Philippine society, those of the upper classes still exercise dominance in economy and politics, in culture planning and social recognition. They also help direct and shape dance, among other arts, by the extent of their patronage. In choosing to help only the prestigious forms of dance, they've limited dance appreciation and innovation in terms of its functional aspects and forms. This is why there is very little alternative dance in the country, and there aren't enough differences among the dances that we see. This is unlike the great variety of dances in our folkloric arts which are nurtured by the grassroots. There is also very little of local crossbreeding that may allow for a more fertile ground for dance creation. As a result, even the ballet stage is bereft of developed choreographers stimulated by these differences and crossbreeding.

The few good choreographers we have are from my generation and the generation immediately after it; this younger generation is made to appear as minor or peripheral choreographers. An example of this is Myra Beltran, an enterprising woman who is not always well supported by funding institutions despite a good number of presentations. Beltran is one of those who have remained isolated and distinct from the patronage system that exists in dance, and as such is unable to exert a larger influence. Solo artists are also normally not prominent in the country, unlike those Filipinos who practice dance abroad. This is not surprising when one considers the fact that the requirements of the ballet stage and its patrons do not encourage the development of new choreographers. Some of those who have shown daring, like Enrico

Labayen, Hazel Sabas, Kristin Jackson, and Raul Alcoseba, have either gone abroad or have left dance altogether.

In like manner, the ballet stage also does not attract the young audience whose lifestyle is now removed from the eighteenth and nineteenth centuries' classicism that ballet patrons in the Philippines prioritize. Although pandering to this generation's taste, as in what the Joffrey Ballet did and still does, may cheapen ballet, there is a need to appeal to this kind of audience whose concerns are different from their elders who hold the pocketbooks. Even if the youth today are being given more money in the form of allowance, they still do not attend ballet performances because it doesn't interest them. When Alice Reyes tried to court this audience with her rock opera ballets, she attracted them for a while. But where are those ballets now? That Ballet Philippines no longer presents much of her works just might be an indication of its inability to hold an audience captive.

Today we still deify dancing on pointes,[8] the foreign classical repertoire, the pyrotechnics of the virtuosi ballerinas, and the antiquated mime-speech (that is obscure to the public, especially the youth). Yes, we still tantalize the audience, but only for a while. On the whole, ballet dancing is but a diversion, whether for the rich man or the provincial girl who chances upon it. It is also only a partial building up of dance, disregarding as it does its full usefulness and meaningfulness for everyone.

In the end, ballet in the Philippines becomes but a reflection and a reinforcement of the social and economic divide that exists in the country. This kind of "ballet for the gods" also unwittingly speaks of the problems of social justice in the Philippines.

Dance in Revolution, Revolution in Dance:
1998 Philippine International Dance Conference.
Manila: World Dance Alliance, Philippines
1999, 46-51.

Notes

1. For related aspects on gay artists/performers in the Philippines see the essays of Martin Manalansan and Fenella Cannel in Vicente Rafael's *Discrepant Histories*, Mark Johnson's *Beauty and Power*, and the writings of J. Neil Garcia.

2. See Niels Mulder's *Inside Philippine Society*.

3. This is the theme of the dance-drama *Ang Babaylan* based on the epical story of Datu Sumakwel and the shaman Bangotbanwa, written by Edward Defensor, choreographed by Basilio, and set to music by Arlene Chongson and Taga-Aton Band.

4. See Hermina Menez's *Explorations in Philippine Folklore*, especially "Female Warriors in Philippine Oral Epics" and "The Shaman and the Warrior in Isneg Society."

5. See Sally Banes's *Dancing Women: Female Bodies on Stage*.

6. Locally, Denisa Reyes spawned her own versions of *The Firebird* and *Rite of Spring*. These were innovative works in Fokine and Nijinsky's time. Recently, Filipina choreographer Hazel Sabas staged her own *Firebird* for Memphis Ballet. UP Dance Company has deconstructed *Cinderella* (Prokofiev), and is scheduled to do the same with *The Nutcracker*, both by student choreographers with libretti by Basilio.

7. Thelma Sioson San Juan, "How NCCA Can Survive the Laya-Padilla Row," *Philippine Daily Inquirer* June 8,1998, p. E1-2.

8. Many feminists have said that the encased foot of the ballerina (like the bound foot of the rich Chinese wives) is something that is critical, not only of the upper class, but also of patriarchal dominance. But they also neglect to relate all these to the male dancer's experience—he who has to hoist loftily the ballerinas, who often gets blamed for slips in partnering, whose career is even more short-lived because of the great physical demands, etc.—in the overall interest to denigrate ballet as a display to please or stimulate the so-called male gaze. Male dancers are also mostly from the lower class and are discriminated against by their parents and peers, especially in the Philippines.

Catalabutte's Equivocal Calls to Manille: The French-Filipino Connection in Dance[1]

A recent article on the last presidential cabinet reshuffle in the *Sunday Times Magazine* (January 21, 1990) reverts to the use of the old term *rigodon* as the "exchanging places and partners" to parallel "the practice of swapping positions among bureaucrats." It went on to say, "it's not the graciousness of the moves but the superficiality of the changes in the government—as though done only for entertainment—that explains the sarcastic use of that label."[2]

My own title refers to the master of ceremonies in the ballet *The Sleeping Beauty* (*La Belle au Bois Dormant*) whose list of guests to the christening of Princess Aurora misses out on the vengeful fairy Carabosse. For the slight, Carabosse casts the spell of sleep on the princess. As far as dance is concerned, there were some attempted kisses.

From Rigaudon To Rigodon

The *Rigodon de Honor* used to be an extravagant high point for the Kahirup Club of the Visayas, a time and place for displaying their expensive ternos done by Valera, Moreno, or Farrales, along with their jewels that are familiar to Guy de Maupassant. Among the surviving social dances now considered folk in our storehouse of national dances, the *Rigodon* stands as typical of the *Quadrille*.

The name *Rigodon* itself suggests its own superficiality. It is originally the *Rigaudon* in duple-time, and sometimes appears as the *Hornpipe* or the sailor's *Rigaudon* that is referred to in Oscar Wilde's "Ballad of Reading Goal." According Louis Horst, the great musical director of Martha

Graham, the writer Wilde chose this very image "of a hanged criminal dancing a *Rigoodon* of death with his heels upon the empty air" in order to contrast the light character of the dance with the somber death in the ballad.[3]

Catalabutte: The French-Filipino Connection

Horst's masterful sourcebook quotes Johann Mattheson (*Der Vollkommene Capellmeister*, 1739) about the *Rigaudon*: "this melody, to my judgment, is one of the most agreeable. Its individuality springs from a somewhat frivolous pleasantry. The *Rigaudon* was often used by Italians as a closing chorus in dramatic works; by the French for the singing of particular odes and pleasing ariettas." The parallelism with the superficiality of a cabinet shuffle is not merely operating on sarcasm after all.[4]

The *Rigaudon* is also supposedly from Provence and Languedoc, "sung and danced to the rhythmic accompaniment of the tambourine." Some authorities think the name came from a famous ballet master of Marseilles, Rigaud, who brought it to Paris during the reign of Louis XIII (1601-43). Mattheson says that the name came from the Italian *rigo*, meaning river or stream. An old song from Provence goes:

> Let us go to Bordeaux
> My little Jeannette,
> Let us go to Bordeaux
> While the weather is nice.
> There we shall eat an omelette,
> And there we shall dance a rigaudon.[5]

The *Rigodon* is also one of the dances stressed in the choreographic art of Maestro Appiani, as so well dwelled on by Juan Atayde in his series, *The Theaters of Manila*.[6]

Another *Quadrille* Atayde mentions is the *Gavotte*, along with the Polish *Crakovienne*, the Romanian *Redowa*, and the Scottish *Schottische*. Also in duple time, it is sometimes called the Breton, and was originally a peasant dance like the *Rigaudon*. It is attributed to southeastern France, from a place named Gap where the natives are called the Gavots.

The *Rigodon* may have also been derived from the *Branles* or *Brauls*, which was briefly dealt with by Thoinot Arbeau (the priest Jehan Tabourot) in his book *Orchesography* that documents pre-classic dances. After it was introduced into the French court in 1500, its kissing and capering were tamed into formalities and stateliness. Yet it maintained its gaiety, and Mattheson thinks it evokes the emotion of "mountain folk jumping about on the hills with their Gavottes."[7]

One of Anna Pavlova's famous dances was the *Gavotte*, and no one knows if she might have danced it during her visit in Manila in 1922. Definitely, it was used by choreographers like Gardel, Vestris, and Little, and by composers like Rameau, Handel, and Telemann; in our time, Prokofiev and Schoenberg have used it as well.

The third *Quadrille* is the *Minuet.* Francisca Reyes Aquino included this in her book *Foreign Folk Dances* (1948) and she describes it as "a very stately, graceful and dignified dance depicting the grandeur and magnificence of the court of Louis XV. In dance, it polished up 'courtesy, ceremony and chivalry.'"[8] By virtue of its courtly prominence, it was the dance of dances. Yet Horst considers it "the least interesting of all the old dance forms (due to its highly artificial and rococo character); nevertheless, it attained the greatest popularity and degree of importance over all the other dance forms."[9] Horst continues: "it expressed more completely than any other dance the artificial behaviorism of the 18th century"; and "its short, mincing and dainty steps graphically and choreographically register for us the decline of the great French court, until it was engulfed by the French Revolution."[10] The dance lasted into the nineteenth century, when its place was taken over by the waltz, which was at first considered scandalous. But for 150 years it was "the Queen of Dances" and all except one Mozart symphonies had minuets.

Although an Italian, Appiani must have been well versed in the French dances. After all, the codifications of the language of dance happened in French, and Atayde even used a technical term, *batiment,* that meant a beating of legs in the academic vocabulary. Appiani made dancing in Manila a school and a profession. He was not just satisfied with teaching these dances for the ballroom in "this country of proverbial hospitality, where the love for dance is proverbial."[11] Appiani taught in order to form a children's ballet called the Compania Infantil de Baile, which made its debut on the large stage of Binondo. From there it went to the more native theater in Tondo, and finally to the small one in the Sibacon district. There he did not just make dances but he plotted them into dramatic acts, for *El Cornetin y la Grizeta* or *El Paso Stirio*. The scenery was supposed to have been done by Lozano, and it lasted from twenty to thirty successive performances, unlike what at best were three nights for the opera.

Unfortunately, Maestro Appiani returned to Europe. Atayde last saw him directing "a large dance company" in Granada, "where the celebrated Pitteri, who was called Queen of the Wind, was idolized." But Appiani left his students who "emerged the masters who are at present the comic, lyric and choreographic artist of Philippine theater."[12] Cristina Laconico Buenaventura speculates that one of them, Mariano Farrell, presented choreographic shows "on condition that the shows would not offend sound morals."[13] Impresario Zacarias Deplace also presented dance, gymnastics, and acrobatics at the Teatro de Variedades.[14]

The other French *Quadrilles* were in the form of the *Pasakat* (*Pas de Quatre*) from Laguna, the *Alcamfor* (a minuet) from the Tagalogs, the *Pupuri* (Potpourri) and *Los Bailes de Ayer* in Tarlac, and the *Rodoba* (*Rotuenge*) in Mindoro. Many Spanish dances were also popular in those times in France, like the *Cachucha* (*Katsutsa*), the Fandango (*Pandanggo*), the *Jota,* and the *Zapateado* (*Pateado*). Throughout the Philippines, these dances found regional expressions so that many variations exist today.

A number of these dances were performed in the staging of zarzuelas, which were not just being done in Manila but also in all the colonized parts of the country. Like the moro-moro or comedia, these also started to be made and performed in the native tongues, with famous actresses Patrocinio Tagaroma, Patrocinio Carvajal, and Praxedes "Yeyeng" Fernandez also dancing in them.[15]

As there is mention of the can-can, the practice of this boisterous and scandalous French dance indicates that Manila was in step with the decadence in Parisian music halls. It also tells us why there were warnings against the choreographic shows of Farrell—many a can-can must have spiced up a number of zarzuelas and variety shows.[16]

But the variety show that came to the fore more than any other was the vaudeville. Once more this was French in origin, from "either *voix de ville*, street song, or *chansons de vaux de vire*, popular topical or satirical drinking songs" in the fifteenth century Normandy. In 1674, the term vaudeville was used by Boileau to describe a ballad in couplet form.[17] Later, it began to apply to both performances in pantomime and song and dance on the streets and country fairs, as an alternative to the monopoly of the Comedia Francaise or state theater, which was a theater close to the people but possible only in music halls and clubs or social centers.[18] Loie Fuller danced under these circumstances, and it indeed helped in keeping the standard of popular theater up.

Under the Americans, Manila had bands, jugglers, tumblers, acrobats, boxers, singers, and dancers, such as Teresa, Planella, Malgrosa, and Juan Panadei, the Agita Sisters, the famous terpsichorean artists Sisters Frezagonda, and Francisca Nabalo, who was known for her "flea dance."[19] This last dance must have been the type made famous by the American Loie Fuller in Paris, with her innovative lighting and use of shadows and mirrors to highlight her magnified skirt dances. It was through the creation of these illusions on stage that this contemporary of Isadora Duncan was able to make famous her fire, serpentine, and floral dances. The *Dictionary of Modern Ballet* states that "she might have been born to illustrate Mallarme's paradox that *la danse n'est pas une femme qui danse* because she is not a woman but a metaphor returning aspects of human form, sword, chalice of flower."[20] Fuller's kind of French-endorsed dancing came with a Georgie Gould or an Ada Delroy who visited Manila at the turn of the century. The latter billed herself as "the world's greatest dancer" and a "terpsichorean sensation."[21]

Enter the Ballet

It seems that most of the French influences on Philippine dance have been indirect, taking an Italian Appiani or the American vaudeville artists to popularize French aspects and types of dance. There must have been, however, many French men and ladies who danced the *Rigodon* or *Minuet*, or at least witnessed them with nostalgia such as Paul de la Gironiere, Rene Jouglet, or the Duc D'Alençon. The last mentions how "the natives executed diverse dances more or less languorous, which they call(ed) *bolero, fandango and mollares.*" D'Alençon goes on to mention how in Bauang, Batangas, there is a dance that parallels the practice of the pages at the Cathedral of Seville called the *Sieses*; the waving of banners he described might have descended to our *Bati*, which is religious and mostly danced by the young.[22]

In the same manner, ballet was brought to Manila by way of nationalities other than the French. Although the first great ballet masters and dancers were really Italians, it was the French who institutionalized the ballet, with King Louis XIV and the Academic Royale de Danse coming together for it and its music. Ballet's codification also came to be French so that today all ballet dancers around the world may count in their own tongues, but like in the classic Latin Roman Catholic Mass, the ballet steps are chanted in French.

From my limited readings, among the first ballet dancers were the itinerant Lilliputians (the names suggests another children ballet), the Japanese Infantile Company, and the imperial Russian circus of Baroufski. They brought the more stylized ballet to this country at the turn of the century; Maestro Appiani could very well have done so, but perhaps in the more pre-classic forms. The older court and mythological ballets were not danced on pointes, but certainly they did the *Gavottes* and *Minuets*.

A personage unknown in world histories but recorded in our periodicals came to the Philippines in 1915 and 1917 sporting the name Nijinsky. There are only two famous Nijinskys, Vaslav and his sister Bronislava, and then there's their brother Stanislav, who went mad ahead of the famous Vaslav. This one Paul Nijinsky even attributed his costuming to Leon Bakst, but perhaps he was really just passing himself off as an alumnus of the Tsar's imperial theaters.

More honest-to-goodness was, of course, Anna Pavlova, who came in 1922 and inspired numerous young girls (one of them Anita Kane), like she did in the rest of the world. Her supposed company dancer, Luva Adameit, established the most important Cosmopolitan School of Ballet and Dancing in Manla in 1927. For a long time, there was no visiting Frenchman to contribute to our local ballet.

Subsequently, in the 1960s, there were French troupes that visited the Philippines. Before then, we knew of French ballet only by way of the tuition of de Oteyza and her pupils like Maribel Aboitiz and Eddie Elejar in Paris, and by way of the choreographies of Roland Petit in films for Leslie Caron or his wife Renee Jeanmaire. Petit's name echoes that of one lieutenant of the *Trinidad* in the Party of Magellan in 1521. Supposedly, there were about fifteen Frenchmen in Magellan's party, including chaplain Bernard Calmette. The only possible survivor was a carpenter called Richard.[23]

Roland Petit, who is now the artistic director of ballet in Marseilles, became a noted choreographer after he left the Paris Opera and formed his Ballets des Champs-Elysees and later Ballets de Paris. Many will remember Leslie Caron dancing on a cake in *The Glass Slippers* and a prior scene of a kitchen ballet, and again Caron with Fred Astaire in *Daddy Long Legs*. And then there was Renee Jeanmaire in the all-ballet film *Black Tights* (with French title *Un-deux-trois-quatre*), and again with Danny Kaye in *Hans Christian Andersen*.

Petit's later company came in 1964 to the Rizal Theater with a performance that starred his wife Renee Jeanmaire or Zizi, partnered with Felix Blaszka. For ballet mistress they had Francoise Adret, whose choreography for Le Ballet Theatre Contemporain was seen ten years after in 1974 at the Cultural Center of the Philippines.

Zizi's cherished appeal of being "witty, elegant, seductive, assured and intensely French" as in her famous *Carmen*[24] was also noted by *The Manila Times* critic Morli Dharam as a "saucy characterization laced with the spice of sex." The presentation was reviewed as "a variety show—an extravaganza … performing music hall turns, visual gags, music hall songs, parodies, production numbers—all designed to ravish the eye." Dharam goes on to say that the "numbers are staged with an eye to visual wit. An imaginative humor informs the show. The ambience is light, chic, effervescent, in short, Parisian."[25] It included that which is typical of Petit's "wonderful sense of theater and his impeccable feeling for style"[26] that put him in good steed beside the pretentious and long-winded heaviness of the Lifar ballets[27] against which he rebelled.

Another dancer who has been seen on special ballet films is Maurice Bejart, who is unforgettable in his seductive ballet set to Ravel's *Bolero*. But forgettable was his *Songs of a Wayfarer* (to Mahler), which Rudolf Nureyev did in Manila with Johnny Eliasen in 1977. Perhaps the dancing of our Augustus Damian (and lately a Parungao) in his company in Brussels and now in Lausanne will contribute towards influencing his later ballets in Manila.[28]

Prior to Petit's revue-troupe in 1964, the earlier French company that came to Manila was the Theater D'Art du Ballet, which performed in the old UP Theater in 1959 under the auspices of the late impresario Alfredo Lozano. Their repertoire was mostly Michel Fokine's: *Les Sylphides* (as romanticized by Diaghilev in Paris from the Russian-styled *Chopiniana*), *Le Carnaval*, *Les Elfes*, *Le Spectre de la Rose*, *Islamey*, *Adventures of Arlequin*, and *Igrouchki* or *The Russian Dolls* to Rimsky-Korsakov.

More evidently French were Janine Charrat's *Danseuses d' Opera* to music by Ivan Semenov, and by way of its music Leonide Massine's *Ballade* to Faure with a Greek story of Daphne. Although it was apparently based in Paris and it employed French dancers (it has a Yoguslav in Nicolas Petrov for example, who later became director for the Pittsburgh Ballet Theater where Odon Sabarre briefly trained), the company was headed by an American of Hungarian-Armenian extraction, Evelyn Courmand, who renamed herself Anna Galina.

Dharam reviewed these works and said that they possess "old world grace" and "continental finesse, a lightness of approach and a subtlety in communication."[29] On the other hand, Rosalinda & Orosa observed that they were "rather dated" (after seeing the New York City Ballet in Quezon City in 1958), and the dancers were "not being very outstanding" yet "refreshingly lacking in sophistication with child-like grace and abandon."[30]

This same company returned in 1965 at the Rizal Theater, still under the artistic direction of Tatiana Piankova and the musical direction of Nicolas Kopeikine. The 1959 performance was to the Manila Symphony Orchestra, the 1965 visit to the Quezon City Philharmonic Orchestra as prepared by Ramon Tapales. This time they were under the aegis of Rafael Zulueta's International Relations, Inc. Galina, who apparently owned the company, headed it again, this time with the Polish Bogdan Bolder as her partner. To be noted were Roy Tobias who used to be with the New York City Ballet, and Hirojumi Inoue, a Japanese. Its repertoire included *Marguerite Gautier—La Dame Aux Camelias*, choreographed by William Dollar to the music by Verdi (other than *La Traviata*) and designs by George Wakhevitch. In 1977, Margot Fonteyn and Rudolf Nureyev were to dance Sir Frederic Ashton's *Marguerite and Armand* (to Liszt) in Manila, and Dance Concert Company staged *Camille* by Eric Cruz to new music by Jeffrey Ching.[31]

There were also the stars of the French ballet at the Philamlife Auditorium, under the impresarios Alfredo Lozano and Claude Giraud.[32] In the small group were the esteemed Liane Dayde and Michael Renault of the Paris Opera, Rosella Hightower and Andre Prokovsky of the Ballet du Marquis de Cuevas, and three danseuses, Vreny Verina, Josyane Consoli, and Maryse Thavenon. They all danced to piano transcriptions played by Jean Michael-Damase. They offered two programs on the tiny Philamlife stage, including Serge Lifar's *Suite en Blanc* (to Edouard Lalo), *Aubade* (to Poulenc), *Romeo and Juliet* (to Tchaikovsky), and *Entre Deux Rondes* (to Samuel Rousseau). Vintage were *Suite Romantique* by Aveline after Fokine, the *La Peri* excerpt by Hightower after Jean Coralli, the classic "Black Swan" and the *Don Quixote* pas de deux, and *Pas de Quatre* by Dolin after Jules Perrot.

The last-mentioned ballet was witnessed earlier in Manila when the Alexandra Danilova group brought it in 1955. Mocelyn Larkin danced it with three other Filipinas, Maribel Aboitiz, Elizabeth Guasch, and Joji Felix. This recreation of the remarkable Jules Perrot vehicle for the ballerinas in 1845 by Taglioni, Ceirito, Grisi, and Grahn—has since been danced here by Dance Theatre Philippines (restaged by Robin Haig) and Ballet Philippines (restaged by William Morgan). Visiting troupes like the Junior Ballet Celeste (in a version by Benjamin Villanueva Reyes), and French, Russian, and Estonian companies have also performed it here. Along with *Giselle*, this is the classic French ballet that continues to be done in Manila today, although in Dolin and/or Kieth Lester's reconstruction.

Giselle (1841) was first done here in 1950 by Pacita Madrigal and Benny Villanueva (the same Villanueva Reyes today) at the Far Eastern University, as staged by the American Ricardo Cassell. Later, Anita Kane presented it with either Felicitas Layag or Maureen Tiongco as her alternating Giselles. In 1964, it was done by Maribel Aboitiz and Eddie Elejar at the old UP Theater, restaged by Sony Lopez Gonzalez. Since then, it has been done and redone many times, all the way to having Natalia Makarova and Yoko Morishita, plus Russian, English, and French contingents, and with our own Maniya Barredo, Anna Villadolid, Lisa Macuja, and Toni Lopez Gonzalez. Of all ballets, *Giselle* has been performed in the Philippines the most, and ironically, it was the Russian Diaghilev who brought back this French classic (by Coralli and Perrot) to Paris after many years of dormancy in France. Here, it was an American (Cassell) who first staged *Giselle*.

When Le Grand Ballet Classique de France visited in 1965 at the Rizal Theater, the company brought along this much-loved ballet, with Liane Dayde and Nina Vyroubova alternating as Giselle, Juan Giuliano (of Opera Comique), and Michael Bruel (of Marseilles Opera Ballet and the National Ballet in Washington, DC) as Duke Albrecht, and Maina Gielgud (now artistic director of the Australian Ballet) as Myrtha, the Queen of the Wilis.

The Le Grand Ballet Classique de France also brought along *Pas de Quatre* again (with Gielgud as Taglioni, Dayde as Cerrito, Vyroubova as Grisi, and Janin Monin as Grahn), and *Entre Deux Rondes* by Lifar. William Dollar was again represented by *Constantia* to Chopin; his *The Combat* was also done here by the New York City Ballet, of which Remedios de Oteyza later made her own version. Vyroubova danced *La Morte du Cygne*, Pavlova's immortal role that was seen with the legend in Manila in 1922. More decidedly French was Michael Descombey's *The Painter and His Model* to music by Georges Auric and libretto by Boris Kochno (who was associated with Diaghilev, and later with Petit and Jean Cocteau). Another was *Les Forains*, which made a name for Petit in 1945, but this time attributed to Christian Foye, with designs by Christian Berard and music by Henri Sauguet.

It was a fairly large company, performing three different programs. Anthony Morli (the same Morli Dharam) of *The Manila Times* wrote of them as "a strong company, one whose performance always shone with the clear bright light of superior execution" and which "fabric of the performance was shot through with the pure gold of fine technique and dance musicianship." Lifar's *Noir et Blanc* he described as a "coruscating number, flashing with feats of agility and grace," and *Les Forains* (The Show People) as made of "bitter-sweet vignettes."[33]

In 1969, the same company returned with Dayde but without Vyroubova, at the Cultural Center of the Philippines for its inaugural season. It had another sprinkling of well-known names like Tessa Beaumont, Monique Janota, Josette Clavier, Georges Goviloff, Milenko Banovic, Jean Pierre Mortal, Jean Golovieff, Michel Nunes, and Jean-Claude Ruiz. This time, the Lifar ballets were *Noir et Blanc* and *Entre Deux Rondes* again. Aside from these, nothing was really memorable except *La Morte du Cygne* again and, perhaps by way of credits, *Delibiana* by Leo Staats.

This reminds me of the first visit of Marcel Marceau to the CCP in 1970, and of the Berlin Opera Ballet in 1973 with the very French ballet *Coppelia* to music by Leo Delibes, scenario by Charles Nuitter, and choreography by Arthur Saint-Leon, which today has been changed much by Marius Petipa. This same ballet was first produced here in full for the Ballet Federation of the Philippines by William Morgan in 1976 at the Folk Arts Theater and the Meralco Theater. Irene Sabas alternated with Josette Salang as Swanilda, Benjie Toledo with Luther Perez as Frantz, and Morgan and Tony Fabella as Dr. Coppelius.

The next French troupe to come to Manila was Ballet Theatre Contemporain from Angers. It was a troupe noted more for its scenic designs than for its choreographies. And yet it had advanced choreographic taste in the works of John Butler, Dirk Sanders, Rene Goliard, and Francoise Adret, whose *Requiem* was set to the avant-garde music by the Hungarian Ligeti. Leonor Orosa Goquingco, writing for *Bulletin Today*, described this ballet as "eerie and novel, and the juxtaposition of colors produced a surreal effect; the ballet demonstrated the strong musicality of the choreographer and her fertile imagination."

Orosa Goquingco summed up the group to have had "freedom of approach, of spirit, and the pursuit of artistic expression."[34]

Still another company was Jeune Ballet de France-Cote D'Azur, which came in 1977 to the CCP. It was really a pick-up company directed by the British Petrus Bosman, headed by South African ballerina Diana Cawley and her husband Georges Teplitsky. Orosa Goquingco wrote again in *Bulletin Today* that they "may not be the most spectacular group in the world, but they charmed the audience with their youth, vitality and neat execution."[35] Their mixed bill again included *Pas de Quatre* and the dances from the final act of Bournonville's *Napoli* with the *Flower Festival in Genzano pas de deux* (which is characteristic of the old French school) from the classics. Otherwise, there were also the contemporary French touches to Erik Satie's music for Ashton's *Monotomes I and II*, Debussy's for Jack Carter's *Dans La Chaleur du Soleil*, and Jacques Ibert's for Derek Deane's *Valse Excentrique*. But all these choreographers were English, along with John Cranko and Robert North.

The Theatre du Silence also came in 1977, which shall be the last French troupe to visit before Bagouet Dance Company in 1989, twelve years later. By then, it was the only truly avant-garde company to come from France, and according to La Rochelle, the company was founded by Jacques Garnier and Birgette Lefevre. As noted by the critic Vilma Santiago Felipe, their music ranged from Bach, Handel, Cimarosa, and transcribed Mozart to avant-garde and pop like Philippe Besombes and Morton Feldman. She thought of the performance as "a theatrical experience in the contemporary vein steeped with meanings and ideas uncommonly expressed."[36] On my part, I observed in *Sayaw Silanganan* that there was a "serene celerity that seemed to have urged everyone inwardly, outwardly, quietly" in a Cunningham piece, *Summerspace*. I noted how "invigorating were the non-sequiturs brought about on stage by Theatre du Silence."[37] From the titles and credits, we can glean the clues; *Le Cordon Infernal*, *Leda* (to poetry), *Portrait* to Alban Berg and *Pas De Deux* to Anton Webern by Garnier; *Ceci et Cela* to Besombes and *Instantanement* to John Cage by Leferve; *Avalance* to Bach and Cite Veron to voices of the dancers by Lar Lubovitch; and *Summerspace* to Feldman by Merce Cunningham, which could not hold Santiago Felipe's attention.

Manila could not hold much of last year's Bagouet company, too. The avant-gardism which stems from Cunningham and Carolyn Carlson is remote from the Filipino experience. Bagouet's full-evening *Les Petites de Berlin* was novel in all aspects of music (by Gilles Grand), designs (by William Wilson and Dominique Fabreque), and choreography (by Bagouet and his dancers), but these were too removed and abstract for domestic appreciation. Yet it was something that needed to be admitted in order to keep pace with the universal modern dance trends.

Filipino-French Ballets

For local practitioners of the dance, contemporary French attachments are found in many a folkloric group's tours of Paris and the rest of France. The Bayanihan Philippine Dance Company was awarded First Prize in Paris's Theatre des Nations festival in 1959, a year after their acclaim in the Universal Exposition in Brussels; they have also had Claude Giraud as their faithful impresario in Europe. The defunct Far Eastern University Folk Dance Troupe also visited Paris in 1959 at the Sarah Bernhardt Theater for the same festival. The University of the Philippines Filipiniana Dance Company scored a success in 1978 in a festival in Dijon, and the Leyte Kalipayan Dance Company followed suit in 1980.

Aside from tasting the French in dishes and wine, in fashion and in films (like Gene Kelly's *An American in Paris* with Leslie Caron *Les Girls* or *Can-Can*), the local productions of *Giselle* and *Coppelia*, and occasionally of *La Fille Mal Gardee* (1789) and *Sylvia*, remind us of the music of Adolphe Adam and Leo Delibes, and the choreographies of Jean Coralli and Jules Perrot, of Arthur St. Leon and of Jean Dauberval. Of course, the master of the classical style was still a Frenchman, Marius Petipa, and he rewarded us with an idealization of the court of Louis XIV with *The Sleeping Beauty*, which was based on Charles Perrault's fairy tales. *Cinderella* is also a much-used story for the ballet, first rendered here by William Morgan in 1971 (to Prokofiev) and later by Alice Reyes in 1981 (to Tchaikovsky).

More contemporary are local treatments like *Carmen* (also a popular opera in Manila, sung by our divas like Conching Rosal—even in Tagalog version—and Conchita Gaston), rendered by Eric Cruz, Rene Dimacali,

Eddie Elejar, and Alice Reyes. Another is *Camille*, which has been rendered in Filipino film and in ballet by Cruz to Ching's original music. Because of the late Remedios de Oteyza's training in Paris (among them with Olga Preobrajenska), she had some choreographic influences from the neoclassicism of Lifar and Balanchine.

De Oteyza's students Maribel Aboitiz and Eddie Elejar briefly danced in Europe, and Elejar himself took same classes in Paris under the old master teachers. He sometimes evidently shows French chic in his ballets. Perhaps Tony Fabella's interest in massive and popular effects could be attributed to the same influence from Maurice Bejart, as the shocking effects of his in *La Verité* and *Batuque* are more European than American.

The use of French music is quite rare locally. From the more contemporary repertoire, Alice Reyes has used Darius Milhaud in *The Emperor's New Clothes* in 1970 (Lifar has his own *Le Rol Nu* to Hans Christian Andersen in 1936), Fabella has Michael Columbier in *Orpheus Descending* (1973), and Effie Nañas has Jean Françaix in *Variations D'Amour*. Guest choreographers like Norman Walker used Marius Constant in *Season of Flight* (1972), Gray Veredon used Maurice Ravel in *Daphnis and Chloe and Pan* (1979), and Alfred Rodrigues used Claude Debussy in *Ile des Sirénes* (1982).

Many of the senior teachers and choreographers in Manila must have used at one time or another Jacques Offenbach's *Gaite Parisienne* or *Orpheus in the Underworld*, Ravel's *Mother Goose Suite*, Charles Gounod's ballet music for *Faust*, and even Jules Massenet, as Fabella does in *Love like the Moon... the inconstant Moon*, a captivating duet with Anna Villadolid and Luther Perez. Emmanuel Chabrier's *Bourree Fantasque* by Balanchine was performed here in 1958 by the New York City Ballet.

From the Diaghilev to Jean Borlin (Swedish) and Petit (in Paris), there has been much use of French music, like turning to Debussy for *L'Apress Midi d'un Faun* based on Mallarme, or courting Francis Poulenc for *Les Biches*, Georges Auric for *Les Facheux* and *Les Matelots*, Darius Milhaud for *Le Train Bleau* (now being revived), *La Creation du Monde* and *L'Homme et son Desir* (libretto by Paul Claudel), Henri Dutilleux for *Le Loup*, Henri Sauguet for *Les Forains*, Erik Satie for *Parade* and *Relache*, and much later

Charles Koechlin for *Shadowplay* by Anthony Tudor, based on Kipling's *The Jungle Book.*[38]

Locally though, we only have very few attempts at using these composers. I do remember the unsuccessful use of Ravel's *Bolero* by de Oteyza, and I've seen it done by the visiting Luisillo Spanish company and by the Holiday on Ice, both at the Araneta Coliseum. Last year I choreographed the "Ondine" section from Ravel's *Gaspard de la Nuit* for Lisa Macuja, with Raul Sunico at the piano. I have also danced in Robin Haig's *La Valse* for Dance Theatre Philippines.

I must confess that of all local choreographers, I have used the French composers the most. My first French composer was Claude Debussy, whose "Nuages" from *Nocturnes* I used for a study on alienation in *Rooms*, done for the CPU Student Ballet in 1965 in Iloilo. I used the complete *Nocturnes* for a ritualistic ballet with Jungian underpinnings in *Id*, which was set in the world of the Pintados. This was for Dance Theatre Philippines in 1981. Strange but sublime is the music of Oliver Messiaen, which I used for *The Resurrection of Lazarus* in 1971 for the CCP Summer Dance Workshop. My friend Rudy Vidad and I guiltily cut him up and pasted him again together for cuts and repeats, but his music remained a wonderful, glorious piece to help manage an unusual modern ballet that used a sinking and rising orchestra pit. I heard it used again in New York for a run of Jean Genet's *Lady of the Flowers* production by the British mime-choreographer, Lindsay Kemp. I then used Gabriel Faure's *Pelleas et Melisande* for *Royal Sonnets* (1972) that was based on Shakespeare's poems and their supposed personages. Balanchine used it, too, for a section of his *Jewels*. Fanciful and brief was Poulenc's Flute and Piano *Sonata for Paean to Pavlova* (1982). Briefer yet is Camille Saint-Saens "My heart at Thy Sweet Voice" from *Samson and Delilah* for a passionate *pas de deux*. Fancier is a spoof on male vanity with Cleo Laine and James Galway in Satie's *Gymnopodie no. 1*, which I called "Me, me, me" in the collective *Scrapbook* ballet. For many years now, I've been contemplating a ballet on the *Songs of the Auvergene* transcribed by Canteloube de Malaret. Last year I restaged Leo Delibes *Coppelia* for Philippine Ballet Theater.

What all these amount to is still small. Despite our fascination with Perrault's Cinderella and *Sleeping Princess*, or Dior and Lacroix, the French influence on the dance in this country is very minimal if not insignificant. More dancers and choreographers have been exposed to the American, British, German, and perhaps even Russian scenes. Where earlier the Filipinos were much taken by the *Minuets* and the *Rigodons*, and in the Fifties with Zizi or Leslie in many a Petit film, today there is very little heard or seen of French dance in Manila. As already mentioned, it took twelve years for Bagouet's company to follow Theatre du Silence, and it took Marceau eighteen years to return (from 1970 to 1988 and 1989) to Manila. *C'est dommage*!

A Valery to Impart

But one thing that dancers around the world instinctively have in common is an attitude about dance, the living out of the art in Paul Valery's terms.

Valery talks of dancing from the ecstatic point of view, dealing with Curt Sachs in his *World History of Dance* (but not leaving it there alone). We can very well observe ritual dances and how they are obscure to us but functional to the people they serve, how their priests and followers seem to be lost in intoxication but how these dances are meant to give peace, cleansing, and inspiration to a society. Valery describes the dancers to be like Rilke's Spanish dancer, like a flame that "is visibly sustained by the intense consumption of a superior energy." I further quote:

> This person who is dancing encloses herself as it were in a time that she engenders, a time consisting entirely of immediate energy, of nothing that can last. She is the unstable element, she squanders instability, she goes beyond the impossible and overdoes the improbable, and by denying state or being, she creates in men's minds the idea of another, exceptional state—a state that is all action, a permanence built up and consolidated by an incessant effort, comparable to the vibrant pose of a bumblebee or moth exploring the calyx of a flower, charged with motor energy, sustained in virtual immobility by the incredibly swift beat of its wings.[39]

Valery compares this to Baudelaire's "lights that serve no useful purpose," and I also sense some Nietzchean paradox of destruction and creation. Valery also aligns dance with poetry which is "action" or "verbal dance." The dance has to detach itself from stability and to consume itself in the act of its own making. It is so much like life at the same time that it stresses the temporality of life itself. This is perhaps the very wisdom the art of dance contributes to mankind and history. Dancers anywhere in the world are the most poorly paid of performing artists, but because of their art's all-consuming and time-consuming demands, they who love this art just have to abandon the practicalities and advantages of safety and security.

Dancers seem to be uncaring of tomorrow. They even starve themselves to stay trim. They seem to think (and Valery speaks of the thinking process as one of deepest significance in the "utility from the useless") that all things of the flesh (and dancers deal with the body most directly) and material baggage aren't really needed in their work and life. For after all, they are the work they produce, their bodies the very shape and rhythm of their art, and their art the most ephemeral of human expressions.

Modern movements in the visual arts often aspire for this temporality, making grass instead of canvas, making air and water instead of wood and stone. Valery speaks of this time-space impermanence, or of virtual powers as Suzanne Langer puts it[40] that leaves art-making under the threat of dissolution and always beyond teleology. According to Valery, "for many great artists a work is never finished."

Great choreographers know this by instinct. Balanchine adapted or revised his work according to who was dancing and how he was hearing or seeing a piece anew. Cunningham allows chance to rule his works and sets and resets them to fit new spaces and new bodies. Dancers are not afraid of change; everyday their bodies tell them they are getting into a different shape, feeling an altered weather, growing another day older. As they work for balance, they feel the imbalance; as they work for order, they pass through, run through, leap through a moment "broken free from its usual states of balance." Yet they cling to dance, a symbol for life, tenaciously.

Moreover, dancers cope with life like poets. Our age of prose seems unable to keep our lives peaceful and fulfilled. Prose which runs faster but in multiples of words can't seem to match the economy of poetry's few words and broken lines. The art of the dance is like such. By the very physical frugality of its exponents, by the very temporality of its mode, the dance calls for attention to be brought back to the bare bones of existence—the body.

As the spirit moves it, as breath and blood push and propel it, as exhaustion stills it—for a while, the dance exhibits the basic life which is the body. But dance is the body in action, and by moving, Valery suggests that this body is no longer in just a material world, but by action is "transposed into a world, into a kind of *space-time*, which is no longer quite the same as that of everyday life." Adding that it is an "art derived from life itself," or as the psychologists Havelock Ellis puts it, "life itself," the dance offers its impractical wisdom to the material world. It requires devotion like that of a yogi or a priest, a master or a mystic. It is devotion to the elegant and the refined, even as the dance exhibits all the excesses of locomotion or the wildness of a body dissolving in action: it is devotion to order and to rhythm, even as it disappears into space and time, in a story's rise and fall, in its very own ephemerality that brings the most memorable ecstasy.

In the end, it is Valery's lucid thoughts that remain as our most vital and visible French connection. His is the spiritual kiss that awakens any artist or lover of the arts, and puts Catalabutte's protocol or equivocation away.

1991 Manila International Dance Conference,
Cultural Center of the Philippines and
Asia Pacific Dance Alliance

Notes

1. The masters of Russian Ballet could very well have been Italians, but it was the Frenchman Charles Didelot who became "the Father of Russian Ballet." He was followed by Jules Perrot, Arthur St. Leon, and the master classicist of them all, Marius Petipa. Since then, there has been no acclaimed French Master of their proportion, with Roland Petit and Maurice Beiart only laying claim to minor fame today. In return, it was a Russian, Serge Lifar, who put French institutions back on the map as an important source of ballet.

2. Arnold Molina Azurin, "The President's Dilemma: The Stalemate between her Official Family and Close-in Kibitzers," *Sunday Times Magazine* Jan. 21, 1990 p. 4.

3. Louis Horst, *Pre-Classic Dance Forms* (New York: Dance Horizons, 1972), p. 90.

4. The *Rigaudon* was indeed a light dance that was not always included in the standard Dance Suite form. Some composers did not even distinguish it carefully from the *Bourree* (with two eighth-note up-beat), which was supposedly merged with the Gavotte to produce the hybrid form of the *Rigaudon* and, rightly, a four-part *Bourree*, according to Mattheson.

5. Horst, p. 87.

6. Translated by Conception Rosales and Doreen Fernandez for *Philippine Studies*, vol. 30; 1st and 2nd quarters, 1982. The series first appeared in the weekly *La Illustracion Filipina*, August 21, 1892 to September 7, 1893. Subsequently referred to as Atayde in PS pagination.

7. In Horst, p. 75. Also see Thoinot Arbeau's *Orchesography* trans. by Mary Stewart Evans (New York: Dover Publications, Inc., 1967).

8. Francisca Reyes Aquino, *Foreign Folk Dances* (Manila: Floro P. Agustin, 1948), p. 57.

9. Horst, p. 62.

10. Horst, p. 63.

11. Atayde, p. 63.

12. Atayde, p. 83.

13. Cristina Laconico-Buenaventura, "The Theaters of Manila: 1846-1896," *Philippine Studies*, vol. 27, 1st quarter, 1979, p. 22.

14. Laconico-Buenaventura, p. 23.

15. Raymondo C. Bañas, *Pilipino Music and Theater* (Quezon City: Manlapaz Publishing Company, 1975), p. 197.

16. Peter Buckman in *Let's Dance—Social, Ballroom and Folk Dancing* (New York/ London: Paddington Press, Ltd., 1978) theorizes that there was an erotic fertility dance in southern Britanny where the women lifted their skirts and kicked their legs up, which might have begun the can-can.

17. Winthrop Palmer, Theatrical Dancing in America' (New York: A. S. Barnes and Company, 1978), p. 11. Also see Frederick Brown's *Theater Revolution and the Culture of the French Stage* (New York: The Viking Press, 1980).

18. Palmer, p. 12

19. Basilio Esteban S. Villaruz, "Twice a Stepchild—Cinderella Fits Satin SLIPPERS: Dance in the Philippines during the American Regime." An unpublished paper read for the Diamond Jubilee Lecture, University of the Philippines, 1983.

20. Francis Gadan, Robert Maillard and Selma Jeanne Cohen, eds., *Dictionary of Modern Ballet* (New York: Tudor Publishing Company, 1959), p. 155.

21. *The Manila Times*, May 26, 1900, p. l.

22. Duc D'Alencon, *Luzon and Mindanao*, trans. by E. Aguilar Cruz (Manila National Historical Institute, 1986), p. 32. The so-called Duc D'Alencon was one of those travelers who reached Mindanao. The French were interested in acquiring a place in the south, at least Sulu or Basilan. See Carmen Guerrero Nakpil's *The Philippines and the Filipinos* (Quezon City: A Vessel Book Vibal Publishing House, 1977). pp. 162-64. Also see—on the Sieses—William Ridgeway's *The Drama and Dramatic Dances of Non-European Races in Appendix on the Origin of Greek Comedy* (New York/London: Benjamin Blom, 1964). Paul P. de la Gironiere refers to some dancing in his *Adventures of a Frenchman in the Philippines* (Manila: Burke-Miailhe Publications, 1972).

23. Denis Nardin, France and the Philippines (Manila: National Historical Institute, 1989), trans. by Maria Theresa J. Cruz, p. l.

24. Fernau Hall and Mike Davis, *The World of Ballet and Dance* (London: Hamlyn, 1972), p. 93.

25. Morli Dharam, *The Manila Times*, March 21, 1964.

26. Mary Clarke and Clement Crisp, *The History of Dance* (London: Orbis Publishing, 1981), p. 201.

27. Hall and Davis, p. 92.

28. Spire Pitou in *The Paris Opera—An Encyclopedia: Genesis and Glory*. 1671-1715 (Westport/London: Greenwood Press, 1983) writes: "Fokine exerted a strong influence during his time through his large authorship consisting of more than 50 ballets, some of which have become near classics, if not classics. Also, he is remembered as a guiding force in the art of ballet on account of his convictions about gesturing, miming, and dancing as balletic function." pp. 111-112.

29. Dharam, *The Manila Times*, January 10, 1959.

30. Rosalinda L. Orosa, *The Manila Chronicle*, January 10, 1959.

31. The other works from Theater D'Art du Ballet included were *Rendezvous* by Roy Tobias set to Emil Waldteufel (a French composer), *Trilogy* by Edward Caton to Rachmaninoff's *2nd Piano Concerto*, *Serenade* by Bulder to KarLowic, and Dollar's *Simple Symphony* to Britten and Francesca do Rimini to Tchaikovsky. Repeated from the last visit were Fokine's *Les Sylphides*, *Spectre*, and *Adventures of Arlequin*.

32. Claude Giraud was the impresario of the Bayanihan and other Filipino troupes in Europe. He is the husband of the ballerina Liane Dayde.

33. Anthony Morli, *The Manila Times*, June 7, 1965. Of the dancers, Morli described Dayde as a Giselle with "simple sincerity" and her technique approaches near-dazzling quality" and her mime of "an accomplished actress." (MT, June 6, 1965) On the other hand, Anita Kane of *Manila Bulletin* (June 7, 1965) was ecstatic over Vyroubova. Her Giselle was observed as from "a dancer with intelligence, grace, musicality, dramatic power, lyricism, all brought together with refinement to reveal a great artist. To talk of technique is superfluous when you think of Nina Vyroubova; she is mistress of her craft and performs with her whole being discarding any movement that detracts from the interpretation—it is the mastery of simplicity that marks truly great dancers." Vyroubova echoed these qualities in *Constantia* ballet where she "shone with inner light that qualifies a perfectly out jewel" and in *La Morte de Cygne* where she gave "a shimmering poignant performance that gently turned back the pages of time to the night we saw Pavlova."

34. Leonor Orosa Goguingco, *Bulletin Today*, March 21, 1974.

35. Orosa Goquingco, *Bulletin Today*, April 6, 1977.

36. Vilma Santiago Felipe, *Bulletin Today*, November 8, 1977.

37. Villaruz, *Sayaw Silanganan*, vol. 111, no. 1 January 1978. p. 7.

38. See David Drew's close study of these composers in "Modern French Music" in Howard Hartog's (ed.) *European Music in the Twentieth Century* (Middlesex: Penguin Books, 1961), pp. 252-310.

39. Paul Valery, "The Philosophy of the Dance" in the author's *Aesthetics*, trans. by Ralph Manheim (Princeton University Press, 1964); included in Cobbett Steinberg's (ed.) *The Dance Anthology* (New York: New American Library, 1980), and in Roger Copeland and Marshall Cohen's *What is Dancer* (Oxford/New York: Oxford University Press, 1983).

40. Suzanne R. Langer, "The Dynamic Image: Some Philosophical Reflections on Dance" in her *Problems of Art*. (New York: Charles Scribner's Sons, 1957).

A book that explores dance from the phenomenological point of view (taking off from Jean-Paul Sartre's *Being and Nothingness* and Maurice Merleau-Ponty's *Phenomenologie de la Perception*) is Maxine Sheet's *The Phenomenology of Dance* (Madison/ Milwaukee: University of Wisconsin Press, 1966).

This was followed by her (Maxine Sheets-Johnstone) *Illuminating Dance Philosophical Explorations* Lewisburg: Bucknell University Press, 1984) where she edits a collection not only on phenomenology but also on semiotics of dance. Semiotics of dance is also extensively explored by Susan Leigh Foster in her *Reading Dance: Bodies and Subjects in Contemporary American Dance* (Berkeley: University of California Press, 1986).

Ballet in the Non-West:
Dance Theatre Philippines as a Pirouette Off-Center

Worldwide, social scientists now look back at the 1960s, trying to find its true meaning in order to figure out what went wrong on the way to the 1980s and 1990s.

The 1960s were optimistic years despite the threat of a nuclear conflict and the devastation of World War II more than a decade earlier. Internationally, a fair-haired young man in the person of John F. Kennedy led a world power and captured the imagination of a restless world increasingly being peopled by the youth. He and his wife Jackie were deemed exemplary despite the rumblings about the Vietnam War and the fight for Black Civil Rights. In 1963, when Kennedy was assassinated, it spoke of social excesses, and leadership shifted back to the older generation. Thus, men like Nikita Khrushchev, Charles de Gaulle, and Mao Zedong led their own countries, although there were still newer and uncompromising young men like Fidel Castro, Che Guevarra, and Nelson Mandela, and women like Sirimavò Bandaranaike and Golda Meir.

It was also in the 1960s that we heard rock 'n' roll, which peaked with Elvis Presley, swung with the Beatles, revised *Romeo and Juliet* in Bernstein's *West Side Story*, and saw the end of the beatniks. This led to the rip-roaring Woodstock concerts, with artists and audiences tripping on drugs. Benjamin Britten wrote the sublime *War Requiem* (1962) to commemorate the restoration of the Coventry Cathedral that had been destroyed by German bombs. He added the poems of Wilfred Owen, with Abraham still sacrificing Isaac despite the warnings of God, to underline man's continued murder of his kind. In Washington DC, writers like Norman Mailer and Robert Lowell led marches to the Pentagon in protest of the Vietnam War.

The celestial spheres rang with successes. Launched from behind the Iron Curtain and the West were the first men in space: Yuri Gagarin followed by John Glenn, and the famous walk on the moon by Neil Armstrong in 1969. Stanley Kubrick warned of a nuclear holocaust in *Dr. Strangelove* and enchanted audiences with the sci-fi movie *2001: A Space Odyssey*.

There were other man-made miracles, such as lung and heart transplants, as well as the use of laser light and nuclear energy. Introduced were oral contraceptives (1955), incubator babies (1969), and the declaration that psychic problems are not diseases (1962). Confrontations continued on stage, as in Peter Weiss's *Marat/Sade,* in books like Solzhenitzen's *A Day in the Life*, and on film in *Who's Afraid of Virginia Woolf* (from the Broadway stage), between husband and wife Richard Burton and Elizabeth Taylor.

As for sexual liberation there was *The Boys in the Band*; in dance, there was the rise of the megastars in Rudolf Nureyev, after his defection in 1961 from the old Soviet Union, and in Dame Margot Fonteyn of the British Empire (both were even caught in a drug-den in San Francisco). There was also the surprisingly fresh but familiar pop art of Roy Lichtenstein, Robert Rauschenberg, Jaspers Johns, Andy Warhol, and David Hockney.

In the Philippines, there was the young and dynamic Ferdinand Edralin Marcos of 1965, the first person to be reelected President. He and his fair lady Imelda Romualdez, later called the "steel butterfly," created a contemporized myth of *Malakas at Maganda* (Strong and Beautiful), as they aspired to be the Asian archipelago's very own JFK and Jackie O. Later on, the President and his First Lady also projected themselves as European royalty, symbolizing political and cultural eminence, if not hegemony.

What Was There of Ballet?

Before this decade closed, the first two Philippine professional ballet companies rose to ambitiously join the rest of the world. To attend to their births, one had a famous dancer in Poul Gnatt and the other a Russian ballerina in Sulamith Messerer. The first was a distinguished contemporary of the greatest *danseur noble* of our century, Erik Bruhn of the Royal Danish Ballet and London's Metropolitan Ballet; later Gnatt founded the Royal New Zealand Ballet. The second was sister to the legendary virtuoso, acclaimed ballet master and People's Artist, Asaf Messerer.

Ahead by a few months, Hariraya Ballet (then called Dance Company) had its debut at the Rizal Theater in 1968. After the small but much-used stage at the Far Eastern University Auditorium of the '50s, Rizal became the theater in Metro Manila where companies from London, Paris, New York, and Melbourne performed. In July, on the same stage, Hariraya's debut was followed by an equal claim to professionalism by Dance Theatre Philippines.[1] For Dance Theatre's debut, Gnatt set an international repertoire, with pieces such as his own *The Miraculous Mandarin* (to Bartok), *Peter and the Wolf* (to Prokofiev), *Prismatic Variations* (to Haydn-Brahms) with choreographer Russell Kerr, and *The Flower Festival at Genzano pas de deux* leading to the *tarantella* from *Napoli* as finale. This was the first time August Bournonville was ever seen in the Philippines.

A strict disciplinarian and a practical showman, Gnatt also set up a lecture-demonstration that became the CORE (Cultural Out-Reach in Education) program of the company. Dance Theatre brought CORE to schools as a way of maintaining the dancers with a meager weekly allowance, and to develop an audience for dance even in far-flung provinces. Unlike Hariraya, which had an initial private subsidy (then unheard of in the Philippines), Dance Theatre sustained its dancers by also using some of them for a weekly TV show to back up the popular singer Pilita Corrales, with jazz choreography by Julie Borromeo. The latter was one of the three founders and officers of the company, together with Felicitas Layag-Radaic and Eddie Elejar. The company was run like a cooperative, with each member voting in major decisions. This system made for internal mumblings and rumblings, but it also ascertained everyone's commitment. It was like a loose commune, which was popular at the time. A stellar dancer like Tina Santos (later principal dancer with Harkness and San Francisco Ballets) was just a regular member of Dance Theatre, even with the advantageous public relations hype as a TV, stage, and modeling personality. As far south as Zamboanga on tour, Santos was recognized as a model-calendar girl; she is the predecessor of today's Lisa Macuja as far as being the media's personality for classical dance is concerned.

In the Dance Theatre, dancers had Philippine ballet history in common. Borromeo and Elejar were trained by Ricardo Cassell, a distinguished American pioneer in Manila after World War II. They, along with Radaic, all danced for Anita Kane's school or company at one time or another. Kane was a New Zealander raised in the Philippines, and she toured her own group most extensively during her time, a move that was later duplicated by her pupil Fe Sala Villarica of Cebu in the Visayas, and then by Dance Theatre itself. Kane was a pupil of a Russian expatriate Katrina Makarova from the Russian Revolution and was one of the few who helped establish ballet in the Philippines, together with Lubov Adameit, Kay Williams, and Mara Selheim.

Elejar also had another teacher in Remedios "Totoy" de Oteyza. She was a pupil of Preobrajenska, Egorova, and other noted teachers in Paris and Madrid, and of the Hungarian expatriate in Manila, Paul Szilard, who became a noted New York impresario. Elejar himself studied with Preobrajenska, Volkart, Plucis, Taft, and Bejart in Europe. He toured Spain and the rest of Europe with his scintillating partner Maribel Aboitiz, and was also partner to most of the leading ballerinas in the Philippines like Santos, Borromeo, Radaic in Dance Theatre, Joji Felix Velarde, Indav Gaston Mañosa, and the modern dancer Alice Reyes. While studying at the University of Madrid, Radaic also trained with and danced for ex-Ballets Russes dancer Valentina Kaschuba and, like Elejar, the ex-Royal Danish Ballet Karen Marie Taft; in Paris, Elejar also danced with Zenia Tinpolitov. Both Radaic and Elejar studied at the school of Marie

Rambert in London. Borromeo herself studied mainly with Vladimir Dokoudovsky at Ballet Arts in New York, and also specialized in jazz and musical comedy. It was at her Dance Arts Studio in Mandaluyong City where Dance Theatre was first based.

Other dancers came from various backgrounds, from Metro Manila and the provinces, while some studied abroad. Often dancing with the company after Gnatt left were the next ballet masters from New York and Los Angeles, both close colleagues of Borromeo at the Cassell and Kane schools. Tony Llacer and Israel "El" Gabriel both danced in Broadway musicals and taught in Eugene Loring's school in Los Angeles.[2]

The longer part of Dance Theatre's history was made possible by Layag Radaic. Coming home from Spain, Paris, and London, she established her private school at the St. Theresa's College campuses in Manila and Quezon City. Married to a Yugoslav, she raised a daughter Sophia, who later became a member of Dance Theatre and of the Royal New Zealand Ballet. Layag Radaic is also elder sister to two other Layag dancers and choreographers, Lucy and Luis, both pupils of Kane.

After a company debacle in 1969 and a year of inactivity, Layag Radaic valiantly revived Dance Theatre in 1971. She was able to temporarily draw many former Dance Theatre dancers from the Reyes and Elejar company at the Cultural Center of the Philippines (CCP). She presented a new program at the new and well-appointed Meralco Theater in Pasig City; she was also able to draw new works from Basilio and herself, and revivals from Llacer and Elejar. After that, she forged talents in her own RAD-based school for the company, or borrowed from less active groups. With her admirable ability at persuasion and her perspicacity, Radaic convinced the influential journalist and chairman of the National Parks Development Committee, Teodoro F. Valencia, to initiate the Ballet at the Park Sunday series in Luneta (Rizal Park), which lasted for more than twelve years. She was able to draw her brother Luis and Basilio, both formerly with Ballet Philippines at the CCP and of the first Dance Theatre, to again work with the company. Later, she even raised new dancers who achieved greater renown, even in companies abroad.

As Dance Theatre moved from St. Theresa's College (1971-1984) to the University of the Philippines (1984-1989), it continued to train and provide experienced dancers for the Rizal Park performances. In between, it had two full seasons formally subscribed at the Meralco Theater from 1981 to 1983. Here, Dance Theatre ran three programs per year, most of them premieres from notable Filipino choreographers. The company also periodically joined the musical seasons of the Puerta Real Evenings in Intramuros, and in the 1980s, it was invited (along with other groups, among them Hariraya) to perform in concert programs at the CCP, when it opened its doors to groups other than Ballet Philippines.

Fruitful in the Fringes

It was in the 1970s when Dance Theatre had very little exposure at the nationally recognized center, but was most active and well known for performances at Rizal Park and briefly, for the Ballet Federation of the Philippines's annual festivals and special full-evening productions (1976-1979). Aside from dancing before school and park audiences, Dance Theatre visited Britain twice (1975 and 1979). Becoming more active in the 1980s, it served the different campuses of the University of the Philippines throughout the islands, save for Mindanao. When the company had its two seasons at the Meralco Theater, its dancers blossomed in technique and expressiveness enough to be coveted by Ballet Philippines. Its then pubescent ballerinas became the best of the company's roster for fifteen years. To this day, Anna Villadolid and Lisa Macuja remain the two top rating ballerinas of the Philippines, along with a third in Toni Lopez Gonzalez, who dances with Ballet Philippines and Washington Ballet.

Aided by the RAD examinations to keep her dancers on their toes, plus the regular monthly or fortnightly park and other performances, Layag Radaic thoroughly prepared her pupils. When Macuja, Villadolid, Irene Sabas, Sophia Radaic, and Mary Anne Santamaria had scholarships abroad, they immediately went into the penultimate or final year of the prestigious state schools. Layag Radaic was herself helped at one time or another by Basilio, William Morgan, and Sonia Domingo as ballet masters.

All three Layags—Layag Radaic, her sister, and her brother—became dance leaders in the Philippines. Before her brother Luis moved to Heidelberg and Wuppertal (with Pina Bausch) as dancer-choreographer, he worked with Dance Theatre and Ballet Philippines, creating avant-garde pieces. Basilio succeeded her as artistic director for seven years. Soon after his directorship in 1980, Basilio started the dance degree program at the UP College of Music, and with Layag Radaic's initiative, this program led to the residency of Dance Theatre in the College. During his term, Basilio produced the majority of works for the company; Domingo meanwhile was not only ballet mistress but also re-stager of local and international dance pieces. A pupil of and assistant to Ruth French, she became a senior lecturer at the College and now runs her own studio, Dance Centre Philippines. Domingo is also the Philippine organizer for the Royal Academy of Dancing.

Reaping a Repertoire

Immediately after its first international repertoire, Dance Theatre started to produce works by Filipino choreographers, premiering an all-Filipino program with works by Borromeo, Elejar, Layag Radaic, and Luis Layag set to all-Filipino musical compositions. Borromeo took the European-influenced social dances of the Filipinos, Layag Radaic caught the native sense of broad humor in a *pas de trois*, and Elejar translated a Maguindanao epic and set it to the avant-garde but ethnic-based music of Jose Maceda. Also avant-garde was Luis Layag's visual piece, which was set to Nonon Padilla's new music.

Borromeo and Layag Radaic followed these up with two other Filipino works. Radaic's *Tanan* has endured as a little comedy classic, like a capsulized *La Fille Mal Gardee*, while Elejar offered a Japanese dramatic work about doomed lovers to music by Edgar Varese, entitled *Gates of Hell*. With *In the Beginning*, Tony Llacer had lyric evocation to Villalobos's music for a soprano, while with *La Valse*, a guest Australian ballerina Robin Haig created a fetching Ravel ballet.

A historic landmark was the first three-act ballet in the Philippines, *Mir-i-nisa*, based on a short story by National Artist Jose Garcia Villa, and jointly choreographed by Borromeo and Layag-Radaic to new music by Eliseo Pajaro. This was part of the inaugural season of the CCP in 1969, when dancers from Cebu, the Bayanihan, and the Folklorico Filipino companies augmented the company. It made for an impressive spectacle, with the debuts of young dancers Mary Anne Garcia and Nini Gener in the title roles, paired with the rivals in the story, Odon Sabarre and Tony Fabella. Choreographers Borromeo and Layag Radaic, with Elejar and Tina Santos, also took stellar parts in the ballet.

After that big performances though, and because of some leadership problems, the company lay low. No other invitation was forthcoming from the CCP, as after 1970 the CCP's annual ballet commissions, which was previously open to other groups, became exclusive to the CCP Dance Company which we now know as Ballet Philippines.[3]

In 1971, Layag-Radaic reactivated the Dance Theatre company. Launching it anew at the Meralco Theater, she premiered another Pajaro ballet based on a short story by National Artist Nick Joaquin entitled *May Day Eve*. Basilio meanwhile premiered his first significant work in Metro Manila, *The Rebels*, which is the first local Janacek ballet. It was based on the story of the prodigal son but made cyclic through its theme of devolved authority from the father. By then, Dance Theatre could only occasionally do productions at the CCP, among which were Layag Radaic's arresting piece on the humanoids, *The Prey*, to music by Rosalina Abejo, Basilio's exploration of the four classic elements to J.S. Bach, and Luis Layag's playful, witty, and hip ballet to Lennon, McCartney, and Rifkin, called *They Came Jorkin In*.

Another visit from Robin Haig in 1974 brought fresh input to the Philippine repertoire with her *Pas de Quatre* after Anton Dolm and the *adagio* from her *Triptych* to Mozart. These were all launched at the new University of the East Theater in Manila. In 1975, Layag Radaic brought the company to a moving festival that covered Aberdeen, London, Cardiff, and other Scottish towns and cities. The program included her Japanese-inspired ballet to music by Lucrecia Kasilag, her Igorot story-ballet *Nan-*

Pangkat, Basilio's now little classic *Mosque Baroque* to Vivaldi, the now lost *Between Sky and Sea* to Mahler after Thomas Mann's *A Death in Venice*, and two short works from Fabella.

After this tour, senior dancers moved to Ballet Philippines, and the company carried on at the park. But in 1978, with the return of Irene Sabas from the Royal Ballet School in London, Dance Theatre became more active again. To his *Mosque Baroque*, Basilio added two other sections to complete *Tropical Tapestry*, with additional music by Samuel Barber (later replaced by a new section on the creation of *Malakas at Maganda* to Ruben Federizon) and Joaquin Rodrigo. In 1978, the company visited Hong Kong for a shared program. In 1979, Borromeo did her 1968 *Zagalas de Manila* again, while Layag-Radaic made another comedy ballet. That year the company went on another successful trip to London and Aberdeen, visiting other Scottish performance centers. In 1980, a new work was added to their repertoire with Basilio's *Testament* (to the third piano concerto of Bela Bartok), premiered at the Asian Arts Festival in Hong Kong.

It was a landmark year (1981), as it was the start of Dance Theatre's two full and valiant seasons at the Meralco Theater. Between 1981 and 1983, and between Rizal Park and the said theater, the company premiered thirty-six pieces, twenty-four of which were commissioned by the company. No other Philippine company had done that much in two years' time. Significant among the works of this time were *Limang Dipa* (In Five Measures) by Fabella, set to music sung, arranged and composed by Ryan Cayabyab, which became a Filipino classic for young dancers; *Masks* by Elejar to innovative music by Ramon Santos and based on a poem by Virginia Moreno about a girl, her lover, brother, and father; *Love Like the Moon, the Inconstant Moon* by Fabella, a series of three love *pas de deux* to Massenet's elegiac arias or melodies with the lovely Anna Villadolid (now a ballerina with the Bavarian National Ballet) and Luther Perez; *Tarantella* and *Tchaikovsky pas de deux* both from Balanchine; and the winsome duet *Poeme* by Gary Wahl to Fibich. Others were William Morgan's *Herodias* to Richard Strauss, *Vermilion Scarf* (an abstracted *Othello* quartet) by Gener Caringal to the Beatles on orchestra, Borromeo's jazzy *Strands of Time,* and Radaic's *La Innamorata* to Chopin.

Among Basilio's works, of considerable worth were *Id* to Debussy, taking both psychic and ethnic angles; *Sweet Warfare* to Stravinsky, with its gamesome treatment of the contest between the sexes; *Paean to Pavlova pas de quatre* to Poulenc's flute and piano sonata; *Tchaikovsky Fantasy*, which dealt with the abstracted triangular relationship among the composer, his wife Antonina, and his patroness Von Meck.[4] In 1984, Basilio staged *Misa Filipina* to Cayabyab's short Mass (which Basilio first essayed for the UP Concert Chorus's international tour). In the religious ballet, he introduced the historic assassination of Ninoy Aquino in 1983, where a Man-in-White (in the modern bush-jacket often worn by Aquino) became a kind of national sacrifice and universal Christ-figure. From its premiere at Puerto Real with improvised costumes, it moved to the altar of the Manila Cathedral, witnessed by His Eminence Cardinal Jaime Sin and the then non-presidential aspirant Corazon C. Aquino. Today it is still performed by the UP Dance Company. Another one of Basilio's enduring works from 1984 is *Exultations* to Nicanor Abelardo's well-developed *Sinfonietta*. This is about the changing relationships among three couples and was inspired by Emily Dickinson's work on overwhelming love; Philippine Ballet Theater later acquired this work. After Basilio left the Dance Theatre directorship in 1987, he still staged Fokine's *Les Sylphides* for the company.

Nineteen eighty-five saw the discovery of a promising choreographer in Regina Debuque, a leading dancer in Dance Theatre. Set to Claude Boiling, her *Play It As The Wind* was surprisingly good for an untested choreographer. Debuque later joined Ballet Philippines but now has no professional dance association. Later, in 1988, Layag Radaic and Sonia Domingo restaged Dance Theatre's first full-evening classic in *Giselle* with Macuja (already a ballerina of Philippine Ballet Theater and a former principal dancer with the Kirov Ballet) and Nonoy Froilan from Ballet Philippines as guest artists. Later, they both staged the same production for Philippine Ballet Theater as a tribute to Layag-Radaic's teacher Anita Kane, who once made her essay the title-role. In this production, Macuja was partnered with Vivencio Samblaceño.

In 1989, Dance Theatre ended a cycle with a new version of *Mir-i-nisa*, again with Borromeo and Layag Radaic. As in its 1969 premiere ten years before, this Pajaro ballet was once more staged at the Center. It had a fresh ballerina in Mylene Saldaña, who briefly became a dancer with Philippine Ballet Theatre and later an apprentice with Atlanta Ballet.

Appraisal of Achievements

Youthfulness and drive were characteristic of the first Dance Theatre and its very democratic spirit. In the 1960s, National Artist Nick Joaquin called them "Julie Borromeo's Jet Set Dancers." They spawned the most creative choreographic works in the latter part of the decade. In the 1970s and 1980s, with or without pay, members choreographed based on what inspired them, and worked on both native themes and contemporary times. Borromeo and Layag Radaic found real fame as ballet choreographers with their Filipino works. Elejar was a noted internationalist despite some native derivations; he used the twentieth century music of Maceda, Varese, and Santos.[5]

Fabella exploited the youthful members of the second and third turnovers in his playful and witty Bach ballet and his inventive sketches of Filipino street scenes in *Limang Dipa*.[6] Among Llacer's works, the most memorable were his Villalobos ballet and its atmosphere of life or love's beginning, and his diverting *Les Patineurs* to Meyerbeer. The Australian Haig had enduring contributions to Philippine ballet with her version of the Romantic Ballet *Pas de Quatre* and her adagio to Mozart's now famous Elvira Madigan theme. Both works lasted well into Dance Theatre's final years. With his *Herodias*, the Scottish Morgan worked out a dramatic ballet for Mary Anne Santamaria and Sophia Radaic, but this did not go beyond a production.

Borromeo's European-derived social dances turned into a ballet in *Zagalas de Manila* to music by Julio Nakpil and endured with a second version in the 1970s; it also went to England, Scotland, Hong Kong, and did the rounds locally as well. Layag Radaic's own comedy ballets never failed to entertain and capture the Filipino's broad sense of humor in *Oy Akin Yan* and *Tanan*, both to Juan Silos, Jr. Her starkly dramatic *The Prey* had arresting moves and mood, while her ethnic-inspired *Nan-Pangkat* worked toward a striking climactic end.

Awkward as it may seem to say so, I, Basilio, contributed the most to Dance Theatre's repertoire in my more than ten years as dancer, choreographer, ballet master, and artistic director. I was lucky to have had a good debut as choreographer in the company with my Janacek (*The Rebels*) ballet in 1971. My *Mosque Baroque* (in the *Tropical Tapestry* suite) to Vivaldi was deemed a happy merger of East and West in Scotland and is still performed by other companies. Not as well-appreciated is my Debussy (*Three Nocturnes*) ballet (which I perhaps perversely called *Id*), which ritualized a transformation of a novice into a *pintado* or painted member of a Visayan community—all rendered in ballet. I also enjoyed working to Carl Reinecke's harp concerto for a Boticelli-inspired ballet with its allusions to the Virgin (Mary) visited by three angels, the Three Graces, and Mercury. Pun and fun were the spirit of my own Stravinsky ballet (to *Dumbarton Oaks*) on a contest between the sexes in *Sweet Warfare*.

What have endured beyond Dance Theatre are my Bartok ballet *Testament* that dwelled abstractly on the feeling of alienation and my Nicanor Abelardo *Exultations*; both were absorbed by Philippine Ballet Theater's repertoire. *Paean to Pavlova* and *Misa Filipina*, meanwhile, moved to the UP Dance Company. More than my other fully Filipino ballets (*Sa Baybayon* or By the Sea, *Muling Pagsilang* or The Rebirth, etc.), *Misa* has had the most exposure. For the company, I composed a total of forty ballets, from solos to ensembles.

Dance Theatre's repertoire was wide in scope. Aside from some excerpted and complete classics, it also acquired contemporary works from Gnatt, Kerr, Haig, and Morgan. Their repertoire included national and international subjects and styles, in the works of Filipino choreographers, several of which explored psychological, historical, mythical-epical, fictional, and pure-dance musical themes. After National Artist Leonor Orosa Goquingco and Anita Kane, Dance Theatre pursued native themes, which was later followed by Ballet Philippines and other companies. It thus charted routes for those after it.

Dance Theatre also raised a good number of dancers who not only led the company at home but who also found artistic legitimacy in companies in England, Germany, Belgium, Spain, Russia, the United States, Canada, New Zealand, and Hong Kong. Most of them even became principal dancers or soloists, including Hazel Sabas (later also of Ballet Philippines), who became the first Filipino to be an artistic director of a foreign ballet company (in Lubbock, Texas) and is now ballet mistress with Memphis Chamber Ballet.

Dance Theatre's Place

Unfortunately, Dance Theatre was always sidelined by Ballet Philippines. While older, it was never given a real place at the then (1960s-1980s) only national artistic funding agency, the CCP. In 1969, Hariraya, like Dance Theatre, also hoped for subsidy. But neither got any substantial or residential privilege, except for the first two years' ballet commissions. Thereafter, these commissions devolved fully and only to Ballet Philippines, then called the Alice Reyes and Modern Dance Company, which was later legitimized as the CCP Dance Company.

Dance Theatre and Hariraya's choreographers were consistently invited to choreograph for Ballet Philippines, but their works were never taken into its repertoire and were shelved after their premieres. Dance Theatre's foreign tours were closely monitored by the authority of the Center (who also took part in the decision of the Music Promotion Foundation, which was then the only institution that subsidized trips and scholarships abroad, something that folk dance companies, some of them now disbanded for lack of real encouragement, would fight over).

National and international exposure were focused on the only resident company at the CCP, abetted and aided by foreign embassies and foundations that sometimes sought the Mrs. Imelda Romualdez Marcos seal. It was only shortly before the end of the Marcos government when outside companies (again, Dance Theatre and Hariraya, with Manila Metropolis Ballet and Dance Concert Company in a joint "Festival Four" three-year annual series) were invited to perform at the CCP. For Dance Theatre and Hariraya, this was thirteen to fourteen years after 1969 and 1970 as the Festival Four ran from 1983-86.

After the 1986 EDSA Revolution, there was a concerted move to have other artists recognized and aided by the CCP. After many consultative meetings and assemblies, it had to confront the various voices and associations. After a final general meeting with all the artists, a special one was called just for the dance sector. This sought to address the ballet groups that were urging for either no single residency or for plural residency at the CCP. It was the Festival Four group that was called in for the meeting, and in the beginning the CCP declared that no help was forthcoming except to maintain Ballet Philippines.

But after three leaders of the Festival Four group walked out, the CCP's newly installed authorities relented and promised to provide partial subsidy and seasonal residency to other groups, *provided* that all the groups merge into one (as against the maintained permanent and unqualified residency of Ballet Philippines and its school). One member did not capitulate until after one year. That agreement made inevitable the consequent dissolution of the most active companies from the 1960s and 1970s.

Dance Theatre continued to plod on. In the same year that Philippine Ballet Theatre was formed (1987), Basilio resigned as director of Dance Theatre. The year before, the company's hold over the little subsidy from the National Parks Development Committee was cut off under the new Aquino administration; this after more than twelve years of performances at the Rizal Park. For a while, until 1989, Dance Theatre continued its residency at the UP with little maintenance, again under Layag Radaic's artistic and managerial direction.

To mark its twenty-first year, Dance Theatre restaged *Mir-i-nisa* anew, still by Borromeo and Layag Radaic. It wasn't as good as the 1969 version, but it saw the birth of a promising ballerina, Mylene Saldaña. Guests were from the newly formed Ballet Theatre, like Osias Barroso (previously of Dance Concert Company and now of Ballet Manila, Melanie Motus (previously of Hariraya Ballet), Noreen Ostrea (previously of Manila Metropolis Ballet and now of Memphis Chamber Ballet), and Katrina Santos (previously of Dance Theatre and now of Ballet Philippines). Some time after that, Layag Radaic gradually dissolved the company.

Dance Theatre's twenty-one-year history wasn't exactly as great as other ballet movements abroad, such as the twenty-year Ballets Russes. Its kind of artistic fare, limited by no consistent sponsorship except for intermittent help from Victor Puyat and Cesar Macuja, was more or less patterned after Diaghilevian vigor. Having worked with dancers such as Alexandra Danilova, Mocelyn Larkin, Mia Slavenska, Alicia Markova, Anton Dolin, Frederic Franklin, Michael Maule, Roman Jasinsky, and Leon Danielian, most of Dance Theatre's leaders came under the influence of teachers who were conscious of such classical and contemporary traditions; younger members also studied at the Royal Ballet School in London, heir to the Petipa and Diaghilev heritage.

They also followed up the earlier pioneering Filipino work of Adameit, Kane, and Orosa Goquingco, much like the Americana of Eugene Loring, Agnes de Mille, and Lew Christensen, or the English strain in de Valois, Tudor, Ashton and Rambett. Unfortunately their works were not always viewed at the prized CCP, nor did their dancers get as much national attention until they moved to Ballet Philippines or to the companies abroad.

The over-centralization of artistic patronage did not exactly reduce the creative output of dance groups outside the CCP at that time, but this did sideline their activities, and foreign tours were often far from reach; foreign embassies and cultural assistance bodies abetted this policy. Travel clearance from the central office of Malacañang Palace was also still required and arduously obtained (with many stories of "lost" papers) during the martial law years. Moreover, attractions at the Center also drained Dance Theatre of its own talents, although that is also a testament of the company's artistic capability.

Looking at the 1970s and 1980s, it is easy to see that it was generally unjust and inequitable in the dance scene. The end of the 1980s opened up the cultural policy to accommodate more groups, but at the start there were conditions that spelled the death of the above mentioned non-Center groups. Out of their ashes Philippine Ballet Theatre rose, but it is not the same company; Dance Theatre and the others had their own credible repertoire that inevitably got lost, save for what Ballet Theatre or the other groups absorbed.

The loss of these works is a reflection of the unjust situation that existed until the late 1980s, and these two decades of lost work should not be taken for granted by the country's cultural conscience. But those were also two decades that we may learn from in order to be fairer to future dance artists outside the more favored establishments. With the institution of the law on local autonomy, authority and finances have devolved to the provinces and municipalities. Should this apply to projects that deal with cultural empowerment, the arts would also flourish in the regions and would enable the safeguarding of their own resources and talents. The National Commission on Culture and the Arts (NCCA) must work towards making this happen on a wide scale and in an expeditious manner.

But the creativity of Dance Theatre and other non-CCP groups is still witnessed in Philippine dance today, such as in the dancing of artists like Macuja and Barroso, who are perhaps the most accomplished ballet artists in the Philippines today, and in the leadership and creative works done by former Dance Theatre dancers and choreographers, some of which are not only felt in Manila but also in the provinces and abroad, in places like Barcelona, Munich, Lubbock (Texas), Memphis, Wellington, Hong Kong and, for a time, in St. Petersburg. From Paris to St. Petersburg, London to New York, and back to the Philippines, ballet has become an authentic artistic form of expression for Filipinos. But artists should not rest on their laurels because their tradition-based art is perennially threatened in this world of commercialization and political motivations. A look at the decades of the 1960s to the 1980s has proven exactly that.

Ani
Cultural Center of the Philippines
1997

Notes

1. The demolition of Rizal Theater and the demise of Dance Theatre of late symbolize the passing of an age for Philippine Dance. Designed by Juan Nakpil, the theater was a classic of its time. In 1986, Dance Theatre celebrated its eighteenth anniversary on the very same stage in a tribute to Felicitas Layag Radaic hosted by former Dance Theatre ballerina Tina Santos; both were original members of the company.

2. Llacer now teaches in Singapore, while Gabriel, now in Irvine, California, was for a time ballet master for the Batdor company in Tel Aviv.

3. In 1970, the CCP Dance Company, then known as the Alice Reyes and Modern Dance Company, shared a twin bill for that year's commissions with Hariraya Ballet. After that Hariraya no longer had any such opportunities. In fact, Ballet Philippines became the sole resident dance company.

4. Worth mentioning are Basilio's *Crystal Concerto* and a *Canto to Canaletto* to Mozart, marking the fifteenth anniversary of the company, and *Salutations to Schubert*, which paid tribute to his mentors, all Philippine ballet pioneers: Leonor Orosa Goquingco, Rosalia Merino Santos, Remedios de Oteyza, and Elsie Uytiepo Torrejon. He also staged productions outside of the subscribed seasons, including *A Chair*, a twenty-minute solo for Macuja to Schubert, *Divine Anthology* to religious songs from around the world, etc. Periodically he staged numbers just to give breaks to young dancers on the Rizal Park stage.

5. Elejar's ballet to Maceda was reworked more lengthily into *Juru-Pakal* for Ballet Philippines in 1971. His Santos ballet, *Order for Masks*, was later absorbed by Philippine Ballet Theater.

6. Fabella realized himself more fully as a dancer (and company manager) in Ballet Philippines, and as director-choreographer of Manila Metropolis Ballet, which he shared with Elejar. He is the most Balanchinian in intuition and invention among Filipino choreographers, but unfortunately, he lost his most accessible instruments by way of these two companies.

Jose-Y-Marias: Philippine Dances with Colonial Casts

During the Spanish colonization of the Philippines (1565-1898), the converted natives called *indios* were given Christian names. Most common of these were Jose and Maria. Males were often named Jose Maria or Maria Jose, while females had names after popular saints, such as Maria Elena or Maria Clara. The former *santa* is a celebrated legend commemorated every May with a religious procession called the *Santacruzan*, or the ritual of the Holy Cross; the latter is the noted aide of St. Francis, and is also the name of the heroine in *Noli Me Tangere* by national hero Jose Rizal.[1] The Filipino, when provoked, can also exclaim the three personages of the Holy Family in quick succession: Jesus, Maria, Josef, or *susmariosep*.

My use of the names Jose and Maria for this essay's title can pertain to the characters in the ballets surveyed, the mood that they may invoke, or the mold that they are patterned after.

It is easy to deduce from the above process of naming how Spanish culture and the Roman Catholic religion were acculturated into the mainstream of Philippine life. The Muslim religion had come much earlier with a degree of dominance, but the governing sultanates gradually lost ground. Today the Muslims are a minority in Mindanao and Sulu archipelago; animism and some of its syncretic forms with acquired aspects of Catholicism are observed only in remote areas. Meanwhile, recent studies claim that religious rituals and practices have had symbolic or subliminal functions in the frustrations and actuations of a suppressed but rebellious people.[2]

It may also be pointed out how the acquired languages of Spanish, and later English, were used by Filipinos to articulate their pleas, protests, and propaganda. But these acquired languages couched native and patriotic sentiments, producing a kind of performative ambivalence, a subversive presence that was conveyed to both the colonized and the colonizer. This created "the more than one and other" that Homi Bhaba speaks of as a third space—the interstices or the in-between in social discourse.[3] For example, artistic forms like the zarzuela, vaudeville, and certain European dances (like *Voluntario* in Iloilo, about a guerilla fighter, and *Jota Moncadena*, with its figures of *desmayo* or *patay*, i.e., to faint or die) were translated or nationalized to express specific native sentiments or outright rebellious aspirations. Could these be examples of "the hybrid" that can in the long run contribute to some form of subversion? Do these undergird a protest to undermine past and present forms of colonization?

Colonialism, Accommodation, Resistance

Filipinos today take pride in having what they say is the most liberal press in Asia. But the flipside of that coin is the ability to be extremely and unreasonably patient—something that's questionable when the social circumstances call for more fire, more criticism. The "Asian-ness" of the Filipino has also made him consensual and open to compromise.

Historically, however, Filipinos were the first in Asia to fight for independence against Spain before the turn of the twentieth century. Unfortunately, the United States strategically intervened. Using the Cuban and Puerto Rican crises as an excuse, Commodore George Dewey sailed across the Pacific to supposedly clamp down on the Spaniards. Since the Filipinos had already declared their independence, the Americans decided to make them an enemy. The Philippine-American war ensued throughout what has been called the Period of the Commonwealth, when Filipinos struggled with armed encounters and massacres, propaganda and cross-country legislation, all of which required the American stamp of approval. Through political, economic, and cultural programs (such as the imposition of English in public instruction), the Filipinos were forced to accommodate the American way of life and governance. And up to the present day, many Filipinos still aspire to work or live in "the land of milk and honey" that is the USA because of this history of colonization. Millions are already there, making up the largest migrant Asian community.

Throughout this history of colonization, the importation of theatrical arts into the Philippines continued. Dances, even ballets, arrived with the circus and the vaudeville that were meant for the American soldiers, administrators, teachers, and missionaries. A Russian circus brought some "ballet beauties" while pseudo-orientalists danced in the manner of Maude Allan and Ruth St. Denis, who herself came with Ted Shawn as Denishawn in 1926. Earlier, a Loie Fuller imitator in Ada Delroy personified *She* from Sir Haggard's Indian-inspired novel. Expatriates from the Russian Revolution settled in Manila briefly to teach classical ballet. Anna Pavlova herself performed at the Manila Grand Opera House in 1922. A supposed member of her troupe, Lubov Adameit, stayed on to establish the most influential ballet school of the late 1920s. The famous Manila Carnival featured acrobats and clowns, buck-and-wing, Miss Philippines candidates, and local talents in staged shows and *comparzas*.

Prior to the American takeover, there were already the zarzuelas, operas, and staged European social dances in several Manila theaters. The Italian Maestro Appiani had his Compania Infantil de Baile performing there. Unlike the rest of Asia, the Philippines had no tradition of court dances so that Western social and theatrical fares easily took over the rustic and ritual dances of the colonized people. In the 1930s and before World War II (which devastated Manila, pounded to the ground by returning American forces), the European *ausdrukstanz* swept Manila's dance studios and the new Metropolitan Theater. The Viennese Kaethe Hauser and Trudl Dubsky (dancer of Gertrude Bodenweiser and a one-time choreographer for Camargo Society in London) taught expatriates and local talents modern dance. Both Hauser and Dubsky, along with their dancers influenced the theatrical productions well into the 1950s and 1960s. After them, there were greater opportunities to study in Europe and America, even Russia, while noted teachers and choreographers visited the Philippines periodically to stage their works in Manila.

The Filipino fascination with show business was consistent, allowing for the later ascendancy of the cinema. Some film stars even appeared on stage as well as in film; later, some even translated their popularity into political terms. The hyper-reality and propaganda that is quite characteristic of Philippine politics made it similar and even equal to cinematic action and mass support (formerly called the *bakya* crowd after the wooden clogs they used to wear). Pres. Joseph Ejercito Estrada exemplifies this effective transference.

During the American period and Japanese Occupation, the theater was also used to undermine the authority of the foreign invaders. Indigenized zarzuelas or vaudevilles (called bodabil) satirized the authorities. The translation or transformation of foreign forms, later couched in various regional languages, were hybrid presentations that overtly or subliminally subverted colonial administration.

Criticism in Dance Form

It took a long time for dance to begin taking a slant. The American tradition was largely about abstraction or entertainment. On the other hand, the folklore-based ballets of Anita Kane (born in New Zealand) and Leonor Orosa Goquingco romanticized the native stories and legends. But Orosa Goquingco also suggested "recalled dangers" in her *Noli Dance Suite* (based on Rizal's socially critical novel) by showing the uncompromising rebel Elias with Salome in moments of quiet, and the oppressed peasant woman Sisa in her moment of motherly martyrdom. Later, Corazon Generoso Iñigo rendered the same character Sisa as a suffering but strong woman who reminds society that fighting for freedom is their duty for their country. Iñigo based her rendition on a political play by Amelia Lapeña Bonifacio. Recently, Elias was rendered in dance by Agnes Locsin in a more complex and conflicted way, with a retrospective on his dying as social metaphor and his vision as metonym for the dawn to come; Dennis Marasigan wrote the resonant and elusive libretto.

There have been many more of these Rizal-inspired ballets. In New York, Reynaldo Alejandro staged his own versions of scenes from *Noli* and biographical depictions of the hero's life and relations. I myself was inspired by Rizal's and Ibarra's seemingly fated heroism and created *La Lampara* (The Lamp), a title that alludes to the story of the hero's mother herself punished with a long, hard trek to prison, about moths attracted to a scorching flame, and the pivotal lamp in Rizal's second novel *El Filibusterismo* (The Filibuster), which was meant (but failed) to signal the start of the people's rebellion. In the ballet's dreamlike, prognostic form, friends and foes are drawn into one incendiary personal and historical fate as sparked by a symbolic lamp that stood for Rizal's brief but brilliant life.

Gener Caringal has also rendered Andres Bonifacio's life and love, ascendancy, and betrayal in the ballet *Andres*, with a libretto by Lilia Quindoza Santiago. The height of irony here is that this less privileged hero falls into the hands of his own countrymen rather than those of the Spanish colonizers.

To take on more recent heroes, my own *Misa Filipina* took the contemporary figure of the martyred Benigno "Ninoy" Aquino, and in the ritual progress of the *Latin Mass* by Ryan Cayabyab (who incorporated Moslem tonality), I captured Aquino as the Man-in-White who was also Martial Bonifacio (Aquino's assumed name on board his flight home to Manila). The protagonist is killed in the *Gloria*, mourned over as a cloth-bound Christ in *Credo*, resurrected in *Sanctus*, and leads the self-flagellation in *Agnus Dei*. I end the ballet with an unseen Eucharist table for thirteen persons who open up with a gesture to invite all communicants.

Alice Reyes, on the other hand, has idealized the originary in the peasants who support the vengeance of the mulatto wife of the assassinated Governor General Bustamante in *Itim Asu* (Black She-Wolf). The protagonist then goes on to execute priests at the confessional (which was turned into a coffin and/or cut down phallus). Historically, priests themselves killed the governor at Malacañang Palace because of his liberal policies. Reyes's choreography was set against an ever-splitting boulder and a sky in conflagration. Another one of Reyes's socially critical ballets is *Amada* (a name that means "beloved"), which includes a syncretic ritual from animistic and Christian celebrations, and is based on a play by Nick Joaquin. Here, a submissive *señora* rebels against the dominance of her husband, and draws energy from the crude ritual of peasant women (or men *en travesti*) under the full moon. Reyes's rendition of this story in 1970 is one of the earliest feminist statements made in Philippine dance.

Two Demonstrations

What I really want to focus on are on two recent dance productions at the University of the Philippines College of Music. In 1994, the UP Dance Company staged a socio-religious statement with Benjamin Britten's *War Requiem*. This was seen at the World Dance Alliance festival in WUDAO '94 in Beijing. Two recent productions have been deconstructions of the ballet classics *Cinderella* (to Prokofiev) and the *Nutcracker* (Tchaikovsky, with a Filipino Christmas song as apotheosis). These were respectively entitled *Mariang Sinderela: Ang Bagong Bayani* (i.e., "the new hero," a slogan of the government to justify the migration of overseas contract workers who prop up the local economy), and *Cracked Nut: Maria Clara's Colonial Dream*.

Mariang Sinderela (1996) is a kind of vernacular, contemporary version of the original. Maria becomes a *japayuki*, a sobriquet for foreign entertainers in Japan. Most of these entertainers come from financially disadvantaged families, and with their lack of training and education, they are often exploited, sexually and otherwise. A few of these workers come home dead, as was the case with Maricris Sioson who inspired the ballet's deconstruction. Maria is three-times disadvantaged: by the ill treatment of her stepmother, the lack of opportunities at home, and the assault she suffers abroad. Made into the object of diversion by a nightclub's clients and a *yakuza* who fancies her, Maria is gang-raped and comes home in a coffin.

Although the choreographers, Joelle Jacinto and Angela Lawenko, rearranged sections of Prokofiev's music, they essentially kept the basic parts and structure of the original Cinderella story, including the fairies and the godmother. This godmother is in fact another exploiter, an agent who "sells" Maria's charms. Among the startling scenes are the dance of the showgirls with golden pairs of shoes or Cinderella's slippers multiplied, the rape of Maria by cravat-wielding men, and the last scene of a cortege of pallbearers.

A feminist has criticized the ballet for being tolerant of phallogocentric viewpoints; this critic would have wanted Maria to show enough strength to fight back and the other japayukis to rally together to support her. Perhaps the deconstruction, with my libretto, did miss out on an opportunity to support an outright feminist agenda or assert an empowering conclusion to the story. But it was also obvious that the critic failed to read the production notes closely. Here, it was clearly stated that the production meant to strongly reverse the escapist dimension of the fairy tale and stress the exploitation and violence that the japayukis suffer in the government-tolerated export entertainment industry. That it did not want to offer a solution was to emphasize the gravity and complexity of the still prevailing problems in this area.

In as much as it was only a deconstruction of an existing ballet classic, the critic also misdirected her question regarding the use of Prokofiev's music by objecting to it strongly. She also questioned the existence of the fairies that were in the original ballet text and music; in fact, the libretto wanted to show them as parody. It is true though, that the young choreographers had half the mind to prettify them—a clinging to ballet aesthetics so that the parody got neutralized or deflected. I can't help but agree that even if the exploitation and violence portrayed on stage are based on the geopolitical and economic reality in Asia, there were still escapist tendencies in the production.

But there is a problem too, with feminist criticism that misses out on the other factors that determine a production and ends up narrowly looking at it based on recognizable orientations. For example, the Western arguments for women cannot always be contextualized in a non-Western culture. For instance, mothers in general exert a major influence on their children in the Philippines and often hold the purse strings; they can even go to the extent of spoiling boys into growing up like their macho fathers. This is reflected in the dominance of female leadership in dance, as against the majority of male artistic directors in the West.

Moreover, men in dance experience discrimination in the macho Philippine society. They are not encouraged and supported (even banned by their fathers) to enter the dance profession. Most feminists also look down on male leadership in modern dance, stressing instead the women's liberation that has been equated with it. Rarely mentioned are the names Laban, Jooss, Weidman, Michio Ito, and Kazuo Ono in the feminist espousal of modern dance. Despite all these though, male leadership in modern dance has increased through the years.

Some feminist critics also seem to be lacking in sense of humor. This was obvious in some receptions to *Cracked Nut*, although the noted female choreographer Agnes Locsin who sat beside me laughed through most of it. There was a more resolute construction in *Cracked Nut* (1998). Again with my libretto, this was co-choreographed by Veronique Duma, Jesusa Noveno, and Desiree Peralejo. Like *Mariang Sinderela,* this ballet was also in two acts, starting with the Snow Scene, the fantasy of Americanized Filipinos. There was an unused alternative subtitle to *Cracked Nut*, "The Americanization of Maria Clara"; in the end though, this subtitle became "Maria Clara's Colonial Dream." Maria Clara is from the lowest class, even poorer than Mariang Sinderela, earning her keep as a laundry woman. She is easily lured to become an overseas contract worker, with a drunkard for a mother, a young and helpless sister, and her own dire straits. This situation though also makes her prey to materialism that is introduced in America by her Ninong Nick (godfather Nick), an allusion to both Drosselmeyer and Santa Claus.

The ballet journeys through the suite section of Tchaikovsky's *Act II: Spanish*, which is a kind of parody; the Russian film *White Nights* through a section with tap dancing; the Arabian in pseudo-orientalism situated in a Tokyo club; the Reedflutes as three doll-like girls who are easy preys of pedophilia; the Chinese who are a divertissement; the Waltz of the Flowers as a seductive dance of prostitutes (pam-pam) along with two transvestites; the pizzicato of the Sugarplum Fairy as Maria Clara's solo, which also shows her being sexually harassed by her own Ninong Nick (as Superman) in the *pas de deux*. Maria in America is exposed to the delights and dangers of a neo-colonized, globalized world. It is only in the end, to the strains of a Filipino Christmas carol in guitar arrangement (the whole ballet is done to guitar arrangement, an instrumentation familiar to Filipino ears), that Maria Clara's body and spirit are restored with the strengthened thoughts of home where she has a symbolic mother and the comfort of a young sister. The criticism of this *Cracked Nut* was more comprehensive in understanding and appreciating the ballet's stance against oppression. There were of course still reservations about the lack of an explicit solution in terms of women empowerment.

Both ballets, and the others which I have briefly surveyed, bring to the fore problems with the construction of stage dancing in a Philippine setting. In the rural areas, the ethnolinguistic groups continue to do their rituals and communal dances despite being threatened by Christian settlers, multinational corporations, and the government itself. In the urban centers, creating dances comes up against several barriers.

First of these is the fact that there is little of alternative dance in the Philippines. The conventional taste of the generally elitist theatergoer in dance, encompassed by the conservatives in dominant Catholicism, and the centrist governance (from public administration to cultural policies), has not allowed Filipino dancers and choreographers to seek and pursue more independent and plural/diversified creation. The realization of a broader, freer, and deeper Filipino artistic expression in dance today has been stifled by many things: 1) the force of the mainstream, which is often expressed in superficial discussions on art and society and in the proliferation of triviality in the "social whirl" that is media coverage as with Imelda Marcos's time; 2) the hegemonic cultural institutions with fixed ideas of performance "standards"; and 3) the espousal of "world-class" valuation (as in the high valuation of *Miss Saigon* and big classical ballets) against the emerging, original, even ethnic initiatives that are seen as minority or peripheral unless touted as tourist attractions.

Even "the past" has been often transmogrified into the marketable, fast-paced, and conveniently packaged folkloric panorama that has little room for anthropological appreciation or cultural contemplation. The solicited or subsidized arm of cultural anthropology is paid to serve tourism, while tourism itself does virtually nothing substantial for ethnological research. Nativism is being reversed to a certain extent through neo-ethnic or neo-Filipino presentations that receive general commendation. At times though, these also violate the ethos and customs of the cultural source in the act of restaging or choreography for the stage. Avant-gardism meanwhile is often "brought-in" by reputable foreigners who can afford to pose a challenge to us based on their international credentials and diplomatic support. This is slyly informed by the act of looking at the colonizer's superiority over the colonized indio's own attempts at difference, which only get cursory or momentary attention. A very popular newspaper can easily signal success or failure with a thumbs-up or thumbs-down critique or review a performance by watching it on video.

Ballet is still very much the dance form to live by. But after nearly seventy years of modern dance, there has been no Graham or Cunningham to insist on a revolutionary aesthetic formulation or technique, nor is there any consistent and substantial patronage that espouses innovation despite the Cultural Center of the Philippines, the National Commission for Culture and the Arts; there are no Rockefellers, Fords, Carnegies, or Mellons for the arts. The innovator in dance must first join the mainstream, often after foreign study or tour, to be recognized and supported. For example, with a cornucopia of so-called "baroque" influences there was never a chance for a new dance style or minimalism.

To the psyche of Filipinos, fusion, merging, and hybridity are more acceptable and are un-problematic. The neo-ethnic or neo-Filipino trend has succeeded to a certain extent in its focus on a native idea or movement mixed with a Western contemporary technique and production-packaging. Thus, even the UP Dance Company resorts to still referential deconstructions to attract a larger audience because freer forms are less acceptable. This acceptance of merged and fused forms is analogous to the linguistic accommodation Filipinos easily allowed into their lives from the "imperial" American English supplanting the earlier Spanish. In speech, ordinary Filipinos shift from whatever indigenous tongue they grew up with to the Tagalog-based National Language Filipino to English, and back. Dance education and promotion also reflect this cultural and administrative accommodation; Ballet Philippines started off as a modern dance company but later compromised and started prioritizing ballet technique and producing the ballet classics in order to attract an audience that could support the organization.

To many, the hybrid nature of dominant Philippine culture—slanted more towards the Western schools and styles—is considered "an advantage." Speaking English, for instance, opens doors for employment in multinational corporations and overseas jobs. Doing the ballet brings metropolitan, even international, recognition.

Otherwise, things can be as ephemeral as they can possibly be. Honors are being won in the acts of performance and not in choreography; Filipino performers are abroad reaping awards, while choreographers are more localized. Most of the time, the Filipino choreographer has had to adjust to the Western mode of creation and the Western market; he or she can hardly bring any of his own culture to the Western world. Meanwhile, the reverse still prevails, with Western choreographers creating reputations and dances in Manila.

To a certain extent, it's as if colonization has continued on our native grounds.

World Dance Alliance, Philadelphia, 1999 and
Asia Pacific Dance Research Society, Kuala Lumpur, 2000

Notes

1. Although largely a pacifist, Jose Rizal forged agitation into revolution through his works *Noli Me Tangere* and *El Filibusterismo,* something which Frantz Fanon calls "literature of combat."

2. See Reynaldo Ileto's *Pasyon and Revolution* and Vicente Rafael's *Contracting Colonialism* for consummate analyses of this phenomenon.

3. See Homi K. Bhabha's *The Location of Culture* for nuanced discussion.

Thinking of Philippine Dance in San Francisco

First, congratulations to the organizers of this great gathering who are concerned with the future of Philippine dance. It is an honor to be invited to join this distinguished body of dance leaders in California and a privilege to be one with all of you.

I've been asked to share a few thoughts that may create a buzz in our minds, a shake in our limbs, and a flutter in our hearts. Today, I speak of only three points that form my recommendation for how to sustain interest and create new directions in Philippine dance, or in dance in general. I am sure my colleagues from Manila—Ramon Obusan and Larry Gabao—share the same thoughts, and I court redundancy. But this repetitive assertion could still be a virtue as a means of emphasis, which even in choreography is a useful device.

First of all, I think there is a need for research. The importance of our roots cannot be underestimated. Our creation of dance needs to be rooted in an understanding of our culture, be this lived out in or recollected from the homeland, or transplanted/translated into Fil-American terms. It is important too that this recollection is not just born of nostalgia, nor an over-idealization of or extreme indulgence in prevailing notions of Philippine life because it is based on memory. These recollections need to be an analysis of what we've had (history), what we are (today), and what we aspire to be (a vision that is tied to that history and to today). The study of the past must not be a mere pastime but a passion, a reinforcement on the will to survive and make sense of art today, particularly in the context of a society where making art and creating texts mean having to assert and empower the self. This connection to the Philippines and examination of life/lives here or elsewhere in the world will be best achieved through research, which will back up your dancing and performance in the diaspora.

Secondly, education is of the utmost importance. The search and research for the past can only be fruitful if it is shared through education. Dance should be taught beyond steps and styles (which still need to be understood and mastered of course), and be realized (performed, among other things) within a social context. In the case of the Filipino diaspora in America, this context is the politics, economics, classes, sexualities, and racial differences in America, along with a home-culture in Asia. Dance, after all, is more than just a series of steps, a show of agility, or a spectacle. It is an enactment that is honest and efficacious all the time. Otherwise, success will be deceptive as it is only based on the praise and nostalgia of one's peers. Philippine dance in America must be a force to contend with in American life and land. In its subtlety and spectacle, dance must find and create meaning that will be useful in your assertion as Filipinos in American society.

Education is the most effective way of artistically and effectively capturing in scientific and systematic terms the ever-elusive phenomenon that is dance. Without education, dance may be perpetuated in performances that are bereft of substance and can mislead through so-called "bongga" spectacles or numerical success.

Lastly, it is important that dance be practiced with a consciousness of music's vitality. The fusion and function of music and dance have so far been neglected in the popular practice of dance. An unfortunate thing, particularly because the way music is arranged or rendered for dance may remove or distract from their mutual validity. As much as the tonality, structuring, and nuances of music determine the formulation and documentation of dance, there should also be an assiduous ethnomusicology in the research and revelation of dance.

I believe that with strengthened, solidified, and sustained research, education, and music appreciation, the performance aspect of dance will take care of itself. A performance will become authentic because of research and respected sources, while the staging will be a truthfully contextualized representation. Reception will be formed by the dance's meaning in your present lives, as well as in the lives of people who are being represented. Behind all these and within the performance will be the research, dance education, and music that have been strengthened. The performance then, becomes a kind of ritual that renews the spirit and strength of the art of dance, and of the people who make it.

Today, I have to remind myself that I am only here as a catalyst. The real work is yours. I challenge you to go out into this American world and assert yourselves. Like the writers Bienvenido Santos and N.V.M. Gonzalez, and the younger ones like Hagedorn, Rosca, and Francia, you have to wake this society up to your presence, your significance, your contribution. Remember that even in the Philippines, there has been a consolidation and tapering down of troupes. Where there were so many dance groups in the 1950s and 1960s, this number is so much less now. Many dancers have gone into research though, which is a good thing in itself; most live for the dance festivals where dancers converge and perform.

I also suggest that some of you go into theatrical dance where creativity rests in your individuality (something that's highly prized in American values), and where you may find and assert your identity. What Leonor Orosa Goquingco, Alice Reyes, and Agnes Locsin have achieved at home, you can very well do in America, what with the uniqueness and diversity of your Philippine—and now American—culture.

And then there's the realm of popular dance. Why not bring out the Filipino through this dance, just like what the Blacks and Latinos have done within American dance? Where are the Asian/Filipino elements in social dancing here? Why limit yourself to the tango and the rhumba? Why not the daling-daling or kuratsa?

Don't just follow instructions from books; make use of what you learn. Build up scholarly and compositional expertise. How many of you study choreographic modes and forms? Or know the mazurka in the West compared to the mazurka in Manila? Bring this scholarly and compositional bent into your work and in your teaching in schools and universities. Carmen Adevoso did this before; there is no reason not to do it now. In truth, dance practices should not be confined to performance and should be reinforced and perpetuated in dance scholarship and dance education. Where are the archival records of Philippine-dance-in-

America? Have there been efforts towards their retrieval? Have the pioneers of Philippine dance in America been interviewed and documented? Have you documented yourselves? What have you presented of yourself to Americans, fellow Asians, and Filipinos? How much collaboration do you do with each other? With others in a cross-cultural context? How much interaction do you have with fellow Asians? Have you compared our *pangalay* with the dancing of Indonesia and Malaysia?

Finally, how do you validate or valorize your performances here? What are your real and long-term goals for future generations? Is this pure nostalgia? How long can you sustain interest of the young ones in your art in the context of pervasive Western art and technology? How do you demonstrate the vitality of Philippine dance and culture to the younger generation, to those beyond the Filipino enclaves in America, to us "at home"? Secure sources from home, and inform those of us at home about what has been achieved here. That way we can keep a continued interest and involvement in what you do in the Philippine dance of the diaspora. Make your experiences public; get out there and be published. Be visible outside of your sphere. We need more of you out there, more of the Ubungens, Labayens, Jacksons, Tolentinos, Alejandros. Be visible beyond Barredo in *Giselle* or Salonga in *Miss Saigon*.

As the Good Book says, go out and multiply. Dare I say, even colonize?

US West Coast Seminar-Conference on Philippine Dance
San Francisco
1999

Bamboo Dancers: Dance Diaspora in Search of Economic Certainty and Artistic Integrity

"Frankly, that's your history and temper," he was telling Helen. "Spain's in the music. The good earth's in the bamboos."

Herb Lane in *The Bamboo Dancers* by N. V. M. Gonzalez

The epigraph is an observation made in Japan by an American character engaged to a Filipina writer, Helen, and overheard by the main protagonist Ernie Rama in N.V.M. Gonzalez's 1977 novel, *The Bamboo Dancers*. The dance referred to is the tinikling, which is ascribed to Leyte, and which imitates the tikling birds that prey on the rice fields; dancers hop in and out between two bamboo poles that are hit against each other in jota time.[1] Another literary reference to tinikling is in one of the poignant short stories of Bienvenido Santos, "The Day the Dancers Came." Here a Filipino exile in Chicago anticipates the coming of Filipino dancers with so much nostalgia and hope that he is eventually disappointed by the dancers' lack of interest in him. Again, the central dance in this story is the tinikling; again, it is situated abroad, outside the homeland. In Gonzalez's novel, references to the tinikling recur; he also mentions it in his autobiographical essays in *Work on the Mountain*. In his novel, the bamboos are also significant in a scene where Ernie Rama almost drowns while at sea riding a *bangka*, which is a light sea craft that is kept balanced and afloat by bamboo poles rigged to each side. Many read this scene as symbolic of the quite indeterminate character's redemption.

Ironically, it is the West-derived social dance called *cariñosa*, a courtship dance with the *hele-hele bago quiere* (acting coy yet caring) play of handkerchief and fan, which has long been named the national dance. But today, the tinikling is the best-known folk dance from the Philippines, and many think of it as the "national dance." With a presumed danger as spectacle, an increasing rhythmic clashing of the bamboos, and the agility and élan of the dancers hopping in and out of the poles, time has made tinikling the ubiquitous, albeit unproclaimed, national dance. That it is the only Philippine dance entered in the *International Encyclopedia of Dance* (1998) is testament to this.

This paper aims to do three things: 1) to summarize the areas from which dance in diaspora rests in and draws from the Philippines; 2) to observe general and specific problems that exist in these areas; and 3) to relate these problems to specific artistic, even literary, and social terms that may be observed in the situation of the Filipino dance artist in diaspora.

The Exportation of Philippine Folklore

In 1958, the Bayanihan (National) Philippine Folk Dance Company scored a global success at the Universal Exposition in Brussels. They brought the tinikling with them as their perennial climactic finale to a full evening Philippine panorama of dances. From Brussels, they were carted off to the West End and Broadway, appearing in the then much-coveted Ed Sullivan TV show. Other groups of the 1950s followed as successfully, from the Far Eastern University Folk Dance Troupe and the Baranggay Folk Dance Troupe, to today's Ramon Obusan Folkloric Group and the numerous school-based troupes throughout the Philippines. All these traveling presentations inevitably end with the frenetic tinikling.

Francisca Reyes Aquino (then Mrs. Tolentino) ascertained the tinikling's popularity when she did research in the 1920s with other ethnologists and anthropologists of the time, as espoused by the University of the Philippines and its president Jorge Bocobo. Aquino later formed a group called the UP Folk Song and Dance Club/Troupe, which toured the country to spread Philippine music and dances that had been threatened by the incursions of American jazz and racy social dances into the Philippines. After World War II, Aquino also formed the

Filipiniana group that entertained the American servicemen who stayed on.[2] Even more remarkably, it was Aquino who also brought folk dance into the educational system.

Since the 1950s, it has become fashionable to send folk dance groups for cultural or diplomatic "exchanges" worldwide. Many of these groups count on these forays abroad for homeland recognition (not unlike our choruses today that count on international competitions), and fights would ensue over the travel subsidies and seal of "officialhood." In the 1950s to the 1960s, these subsidies were awarded and coursed through the Music Promotion Foundation.[3]

Folklore shows became so famous that in the 1950s Steve Parker (then husband of Shirley MacLaine) presented Filipino dancers in Las Vegas wearing more hyped-up, show business fashion on the Strip. Dancers were drawn from both folk and ballet genres, which were mostly danced in Manila by the socially prominent students; it was for this reason that the Las Vegas presentation left in its wake controversies in the Philippines. A later consequence of this, along with similar folkloric shows, was that some dancers decided to stay in the United States, with those staying illegally living the risky life of *tago ng tago* or "T n T" (i.e., in hiding) until they were caught by US immigration. Some groups of dancers even became persona non grata to the US embassy in Manila.

Bite of the Ballet

At the same time that folk dancing became popular, girls from the better-off or middle-class families learned to dance ballet or to play the piano for their "social graces." Many of them became quite prominent, appearing in recitals at the Manila Grand Opera House or the Metropolitan Theatre. As a matter of fact, ballet came to Manila with the vaudeville and circus presentations at the turn of the century.[4]

Several teachers for these lessons may be mentioned, but the most important was Lubov "Luva" Adameit. One of the most enterprising of Adameit's pupils was Fely Franquelli, who traveled abroad as an artist. From her printed program, one can glean that she adopted her teacher's style of repertoire, exemplifying the exoticism and orientalism that was fashionable at that time. The writer Salvador P. Lopez, later president of the University of the Philippines, hailed her kind of performance at home.[5]

This orientalism pervaded all forms worldwide, from furnishings to fashion, from Art Noveau and to Art Deco (of which the Manila Metropolitan Theater is an architectural example). Many Western dancers came to typify this oriental vein, and arrived in Manila in the early 1900. American dancer Ruth St. Denis went into amateur anthropological research of the Far and South East, while the Canadian Maud Allan and her contemporaries made so many duplicates of the Middle Eastern Salome from the Bible.

One of them was Loie Fuller who became the toast of "electricity theater" in France and who was later made famous by fellow American Josephine Baker. In the 1900 universal exposition in Paris, the American Fuller built her own exclusive theater. At the same time, her home government demanded for expanded space to display its newfound colonial achievement after its 1898 victory over Spain that included Puerto Rico and the Philippines. It is known that the Philippines became part of that display, a first in the American global showcase of its colonization.

This exposure in and to Europe must have opened opportunities for Filipinos (and foreign expatriates in the Philippines) to seek further training outside of their country. In fact, this was just following the footsteps of the first Filipino ilustrados like Jose Rizal, the Luna brothers, writers Graciano Lopez Jaena, and Jose Ma. Panganiban prior to the Philippine Revolution of 1896. A number of them won prominence in scientific research (like Rizal), the arts (Juan Luna and Felix Resurreccion Hidalgo), and in political activism while arguing to be heard by the Spanish Cortes. Their propaganda movement centered very much on the publication of the *La Solidaridad*, and Rizal's two controversial novels, *Noli Me Tangere* and *El Filibusterismo*.[6]

In the first part of the twentieth century, a number of dancers from the Philippines sought out ballet teachers in Europe. Among them were de Oteyza, who went to Madrid and Paris for the prominent stars of the Ballets Russes, Anita Kane (an expatriate from New Zealand who grew up in the Philippines), who went for the British ballet system, and Manolo Rosado, who furthered what he began in Spanish dancing, later becoming a leading dancer in Europe and Mexico (as a modern dancer he also trained in Europe and the United States).

Following this group were their own and Adameit's other pupils, including those of Americans Ricardo and Roberta Cassell, from the 1950s on: in Europe, Maribel Aboitiz and Eddie Elejar who guested in Spain, Switzerland, and Hong Kong; Felicitas "Tita" Layag Radaic, Ruben Nieto, and Rose Borromeo, all in Spanish dance in the United States; Leonor Orosa Goquingco, Joji Felix Velarde, Sony Lopez Gonzalez, Benjamin Reyes, and wife Josefa Arnaldo. There was also Rosalia Merino Santos (in Europe with Mary Wigman and Harald Kreutzberg), following up her studies with the Viennese Trudl Dubsky in Manila, Adina Rigor Ferrer, Carmen Adevoso, Julie Borromeo, Tony Llacer, Israel Gabriel, Maureen Tiongco, Lydia Madarang Gaston, Vella Damian, Cesar Mendoza, and many more. Some of these dancers even gained professional experience abroad in "ethnic" dance productions, musicals on Broadway and on tour, some ballet companies, and later teaching in prominent schools. This trek to the West peaked in the 1950s and 1970s with ballet dancers like Tina Santos, Maniya Barredo, and Nicolas Pacana, who earned principal status, and in modern dance, Kristin Jackson, Manuel Molina, and Elizabeth Roxas.[7]

How were Filipinos cast in the West?

Well-noted in musical circles were the oriental roles essayed by Filipina divas such as Cho-Cho San in *Madame Butterfly*, the gypsy Carmen, the Middle Eastern Salome (with Fuentes as choice of Richard Strauss himself), and Lucia—all determined by vocal range and the traditional *emploi* expected from an Asian body. In musicals, Filipinos filled in as singers and dancers in *The King and I*, *Flower Drum Song*, and *South Pacific*, and of course there was *Miss Saigon* which featured a series of Filipinos starting with Lea Salonga, who later won a Laurence Olivier award in London and is doing extended runs on Broadway; she was also included in *Les Miserables*.

Some stereotyping (*emploi*) also prevailed in ballet, so that this restricted the casting of Asian dancers based on their Asian looks. The following have been essayed by Filipina dancers: Giselle, La Fille (Mal Gardee), Cho-Cho San, and to a limited extent Odette-Odile, a made-to-fit Juliet (by Thomas Pazik for Maniya Barredo, for example), and a completely new character in Shinyu, a Japanese ballet for Tina Santos by Michael Smuin of San Francisco Ballet. The ballets, such as those of Balanchine and Robbins, among others, didn't have stories and allowed for less stereotyping. Indeed, training in Western dance forms was empowering for Filipino dancers who were able to take on prized roles. (See the equivalent of this in English-learning in Lily Rose Roxas-Tope's *(Un)framing Southeast Asia: Nationalism and the Postcolonial Text in English in Singapore, Malaysia and Philippines*).[8]

Meanwhile, in the United States, Filipino folk dance groups became a common sight in Filipino communities, like that which was led by Bruna Seril and later Reynaldo Alejandro and Ching Valdez in New York. Today, Filipino dancers for all the dance forms—ballet, modern dance, jazz, and folk dance—are all over the United States, Canada, and South America.

Contemporary and Commercial Dance

The influx of popular dances such as jazz and the American social dances for the movies and later television was presaged by vaudeville, which was going strong as we entered the 1960s. By then, it was already being paired with alternate movie-showings at Clover Theater and Manila Grand Opera House, the two remaining vaudeville houses after World War II. From the 1960s onward, these "stage shows" were inevitably displaced by movies and television. During the heyday of the movie musicals, those from vaudeville found another home. By then, a number of them had been "discovered," coming from the lower-middle or even lower classes. Among the leading choreographers in the movies were Al Quinn (Alquin Pastrano) and Corazon Generoso Iñigo, who both worked for the three main movie-studio outfits: LVN, Sampaguita, and Premiere. Professional vaudeville dancers like Bayani Casimiro and partner Nieves Manuel (the "Fred Astaire and Ginger Rogers" of the Philippines), Dolphy and Chiquito, straddled this transition.[9]

Then in the 1950s, television became a major venue for entertainment. After the movie musicals with Pancho Magalona and Tita Duran, along with their younger counterparts like Nida Blanca and Nestor de Villa, TV musicals followed. Among those noted for doing choreography on TV were Julie Borromeo, Lito Calzado, Amelia Bonifacio, and Alice Reyes. Local productions of Broadway musicals were produced in prestigious auditoriums like those of the Far Eastern University, St. Paul's College, University of the Philippines, St. Joseph's College, Philamlife Building, and Rizal Theater.

A number of vaudeville artists also worked with the newer academically trained actors and directors, and there came to be created a greater mix of social classes in dance. The ballet dancers of Borromeo and Reyes from their respective companies also began to earn extra income from the musicals and television shows, while people in folk dance like Iñigo and Calzado also went into the more commercial genre and staged dances for the New Frontier Theater and the Araneta Coliseum.

What has become phenomenal of late, which truly picked up from the 1970s, is the new kind of "cultural dancers" (which vaudeville stalwarts like Katy de la Cruz, Ruben Tagalog, Pilita Corrales, Diomedes Maturan, and the music bands helped make famous in clubs and hotels in Asia). Today, they are there mainly to serve the needs of Japan; they have now been tagged as "talents" by the export entertainment industry, and in vernacular lingo these singers and dancers are also called "japayuki" (i.e., from Japan). These dancers' main aim is to be periodically employed in Japan for the limited period of six months (as regulated), and earn Japanese yen to help their families at home. Altruistically, it is a noble cause; artistically, it is shortsighted. In this type of commercialized dance, we can see the limited training dancers need in order to secure employment and income from abroad. The entrepreneurs in this business perpetuate a system where only the most minimal of competence is required. In the long run, this does not empower the talent based on her qualifications; it also doesn't assure survival through dance whether in Japan or elsewhere. The presumed gift of natural grace and musicality among Filipinos has always been spoken of, covering practically all areas of dance practice, and including that which deals with the exportation of entertainment. But how is this assumption used or channeled? How is a talent for Japan trained to be a performing artist?

There are two ways, both ending in a test of competence that will last for an hour or two, after which they are given the Artist Record Book (ARB). The talents gathered by the training center and supported by promoters undergo a short-term training program to master either of these two: a skills system where they memorize and demonstrate the syllabi of basic ballet and basic jazz, and a straightforward construction of a number of dances for "production testing." The skills system consists of two techniques that are used to put together a commercial production, with some folk elements to garnish and create a show. The straightforward construction, meanwhile, is judged according to a minimal technical ability, projection, musicality and deportment, along with some choreographic interest; this mode must generally produce a glamorous and marketable presentation.[10]

It is presumed though, that a dancer is competent in both these skills—something that is predetermined by the fact that the Japanese government will only deal with the Philippine government in its classifying talents as "performing artists." There is an aversion to any other name even if these dancers really do other work in Japan, like being a waiter or a guest relations officer (GRO).

But while Japan has become stricter with their rules, in the Philippines, the system continues to be open to abuses. The influence of the private training centers and promoters in the preparation, evaluation, and deployment of the talents continues to be pervasive; rumors about bribery from some of them for talents to make the grade have intermittently arisen, supposedly in collusion with some testing officers or Technical Education and Skill Development Authority (TESDA) personnel. Under the Department of Labor and Employment, TESDA now regulates the evaluation of talents and all other laborers who are deployed abroad, before the Philippine Overseas Employment Agency (POEA) finally clears everyone.

For the past decades, the number of dancers (and singers, musicians, and variety show talents like magicians) has reached millions. Although talents are only allowed six months to work in Japanese clubs and hotels, this number has not diminished and it looks like the demand for Filipino entertainers will go on indefinitely. It has become an accepted fact that much of the work of the singers and dancers labeled as "performing artists" involves them having "to sit" and entertain Japanese clients. Most of the clubs are too small to accommodate dancing, especially of a group; this has brought about the shady connotation of the word "japayuki." There have been scandalous incidents of talents being abused, most serious of which are those reports of suicide because of the many pressures of working in Japan, with the most famous case being that of Maricris Sioson who came home to the Philippines dead.[11]

Communities Abroad

What about the ordinary Filipinos who live abroad but are not there to sing or dance and just want to make a decent living? It has been mentioned that Filipinos are supposed to be innately musical and graceful. While I don't take this seriously because any people can have the potential to be such, we can all admit that most Filipinos love music and dance. Tribal cultures prove this in their rituals and celebrations where they chant and dance, albeit not necessarily with the kind of musicality and grace the Westerners define.

In metropolitan culture, there is the fusion of ethnic expression and Christian or Mohammedan practices, as well as of native and foreign elements. This is obvious in the contemporary popularity of modified, if not commodified, forms. Examples are the sinulog of Cebu and the ati-ati of Aklan that have been so urbanized, commercialized, and imitated.

These two very popular rituals (as promoted by both church and government) in the Visayas have influenced much of the national fiesta practices. The sinulog, which I have judged in staged competitions or pretend-rituals, has become so popular that generous prizes are being fought over, and even non-Visayans have joined the annual January competition in Cebu. Here, we see not just the conversion of the Cebuanos as legend and history state, but also of the Manobo, Bagobo, Maranaw, T'boli, and Tausug, as seen in the mix of movements and costumes in the presentations/representations. Most of the participants are Christians pretending to be part of these cultures. The sad result has been that much of the Cebuano sinulog has been diluted and now looks like an ethnic Mindanao festivity.[12]

A television weekly on Overseas Filipino Workers (OFW) is *Balitang Middle East* which, aside from the usual free phone calls between families, also has features on different events held by Filipinos elsewhere in the world. In the October 2003 broadcast that I saw, the show featured an *Anihan* (harvest) fiesta in Kuwait. There, they liberally staged the sinulog, ati-ati, kadayawan (of Davao), pintaflores (of San Carlos), hala-bira (of Iloilo), mascara (of Bacolod), and the Sayaw sa Obando (of Bulacan). The same program also showed a Catholic Mass in Abu Dhabi, and a bloodletting from donors in Dubai.

Whether we like it or not, Filipinos all over the world have unwittingly reversed the colonization of cultures! As a result, much can be said about the hybridity that has resulted, with some of the unglamorous "glamour of globalization," the alarming enforcement of unequal trade benefits between the developed and underdeveloped nations, and specifically the undermining or misrepresentation (even by Filipinos themselves) of the "authentic" (if there is such a thing) in the Filipino. Even if there are social, political, and economic problems that result in this mix-up, the global current is hard to contain with the prevalence of trade and travel, migration, information technology, cultural exchange, and tourism that feast on a people's folklore to boost the economy of countries. Meanwhile, the speed with which media works also gives us either a partial view of the global situation or too much of it with varying receptors that still have to be sorted through—to their own detriment. The comprehensiveness of the media, whether in print or in broadcast, is selective, and is only within a framework that its nature designs. The media's claim to truth is just a slice-of-life or is just edited or heightened to predetermine its reception.

In turn, the achievements of Filipino artists at home or abroad are conditioned by this nature and framing, and by the media practitioners' diligence (or lack thereof) in central or peripheral places. Furthermore, the cost of space and "timeliness" of the coverage often cause the imprecise or incomplete generalization or reduction of these artists' achievements.

Conclusion

In the same manner, this paper also only puts together some prominent features and factors, of the who-what-where-how-and-why in the diaspora of dance and dancers from the Philippines. Perhaps the first consolidation to be written, this paper has undoubtedly missed areas and aspects that are also scantily, superficially, and indiscriminately covered by the media, academe, and cultural institutions.[13]

There is a general lack of understanding of the performative nature of dance, and this can be gleaned from the already mentioned exhibition of Filipinos at the 1900 exposition in Paris where the United States first displayed its colonial habiliments. This became even more obvious in the 1904 St. Louis Exposition and in the expositions that followed it. Proud of its recent conquest and armed with the present's kind of ethnographic scholarship and showcasing, the US displayed to all and sundry the different Filipino ethnic groups in villages copied from the original in a distant and colder land. These groups showed their customs and rituals, music and dances, posed with their bodies for the cameras, in their clothes (or lack of it) and implements, all the time creating the impression of ethnographic variety and verity transplanted in time and space and now in changed dynamics and dimensions of performance because of the locale, climate, schedule, and the demands of both presenter and audience. (Playwright Floy Quintos has written on the effects on Filipinos sent to the Missouri exposition in his play with the ironic title *St. Louis Loves Dem Filipinos*.)

Those Filipinos were the "primitive" counterparts of the Filipino *pensionados* (subsidized scholars) in the United States, who acquired learning in English along with American forms of government and culture. Again, following the earlier sojourn of the ilustrados in Spain and the rest of Europe, the transfer and transformation of a people in this manner were a kind of performative metamorphosis in the new metaphysics and politics of living, new verbal and commercial currencies, to achieve some kind of dexterity to contend with the rest of the world.

Today the display of the Filipino body and its expressive abilities continue, not only in the United States but also in the more global setting, including home villages and tourist venues, in front of differing sets of criteria and cultures in a so-called clash of civilizations as embodied in thought and action, in more competitive sets of polarities or more contentions that had earlier been conditioned by precolonial, colonial, and now postcolonial experiences. With these, peoples bear their varying ethnic and national, ethical and class affiliations, in many shades of similarities and differences or even in misrepresentations and misunderstandings.

These are the characters and circumstances that spell the potential for actual conflicts in various parts of the world today—or even in one and the same place called country—that is now peopled by varying generations, classes, and ethnic and ideological identities which cohabit or collide with each other. These have created more rapid and more intermittent, if not sustained, problems between nations as well as within just one.

As the often-ignored players in this "global game," artists are poorly represented, even misunderstood (even fellow-artists misunderstanding each other), and are usually just given tokens of tribute. In general, they are marginal in the total social scheme, with some Filipinos having been relocated or dislocated to foreign lands because of disadvantages at home and supposed advantages abroad. What is even more frightening is that while the "serious" artists are more focused on artistic goals or on their integrity and knowledge enough to cope with the problems posed by living with other people(s), the fairly new but greater number of "performing artists" or japayuki generally come from the poorer and less educated sector and only aim for the economics of existence. Even if their aim is admirable—to improve their and their families' social situation—they generally only have a superficial understanding of the task they are faced with and of the implications of cultural displacement; they do not have a real artistic center through which they may become more creative and become more empowered by real commitment and competence. In effect, these Filipino "performing artists" are perennially endangered not only as artists, but also as persons.

This lack of center amid a world of clashing cultures is what Gonzalez had long implied in his novel. The first two conditions mentioned by Herb Lane are Hispanic music and the natural earth. The bamboos themselves suggest the clash of circumstances that keeps the people dancing in and out. Where the earlier performance of the tinikling by the folk was more graceful and in a much slower tempo, today the demand for climactic spectacle has made the dance more frenetic in its display of agility than of actual grace (in Gonzalez's acknowledged realistic world, of true and fructifying grace.)[14]

Relocating Philippine dance results in many areas of cultural concerns: 1) the adaptation to Western stages or spaces which may drastically change the look, nature, and purpose of dance, especially folk dance; 2) the role-playing or representation may involve various ways of appropriation (and appreciation) which may be positive or negative with regards to a specific culture; 3) the over-accommodation of foreign or extraneous elements and demands may not only change the form and function of the dance but also the artistry and social welfare of the dancers; and 4) the projection or representation that the nation-state may prioritize vis-à-vis the image and integrity of the people/artists and their cultural convictions may not always coincide, and may even perpetuate counter-productive forces in the practice of and living out the choreographic art. Examples of these concerns range from the "minor" case of the wearing of trunks beneath the men's bahag (g-string) in the '50s in order not to offend local and foreign sensibilities, to the major changes in temporal, spatial, and conceptual elements of dance and the culture it exemplifies because of the adopted staging and changed occasions. Even more widely and socially relevant is the urban representation of an ethnic culture that by relocation and promotion may violate the religious and social norms of a people.

The presentation of adopted urban dances like the ballet and modern dance may also unfairly put Filipino practitioners in an inferior light beside those who have practiced these dance forms through long traditions, under different cultural conventions and economic circumstances, and by different but expected physical and temperamental endowments. The time spent dancing abroad on tours, exhibitions, and employment may also deprive them of personal and interpersonal support; it may also alter their moral and political positions abroad and at home. An unmitigated desire for success or fame can also distract both artists and promoters from the essence of creativity in dance practice, making the image and projection the end and not the operational source and verity of artistic expression.

Doubtless, the exposure to other cultures, the adaptation or accommodation that leads to learning, the diplomatic advantages reaped by cultural exchange, and the economic returns, are beneficial to both artists and their country of origin. Widely acknowledged is how the OFWs prop up the Philippine economy through the remittances they send back home. But this can also lead to an unwitting, unguarded diminution (even denigration), and commodification of a cultural expression that may somehow undermine the very value of those advantages, if not of the total culture itself. It's as if natural and cultural entropy is courting social and human existence.

Moreover, there are two factors at home that don't help any: one is the exploitation by Filipino entrepreneurs of the japayukis and other overseas contract workers; another is the quite hegemonic cultural, political, and economic leadership in the Philippines that has encouraged a sense of superiority or inferiority among dance practitioners and an unhealthy practice of "political" positioning in the arts. This has resulted in an imbalance in overall support for dance artists nationwide; and both of these factors have undoubtedly stifled the survival and development of Filipino dancers.

And yet despite the state of Philippine cultural bureaucracy and system's inadequacies, Filipino icons or accomplishments abroad are easily trumpeted with our divas and dancers, along with a few scientists and scholars. This brings to mind a popular legend of a Malay named Enrique from the East who had joined Magellan's expedition back to the East, thus circling the globe. In as much as Magellan was killed by Lapu-Lapu in Mactan and Enrique survived, the latter is identified as the first man/Filipino (a nominal identity from King Felipe of Spain) to have done just that. Barring the difficulties in negotiating lands and oceans, are we simply proud of Enrique because he survived? He is assumed to have functioned as translator, but if we don't exactly know what Enrique accomplished, then we have yet to truly understand Enrique as exemplary. This is no different from our lack of understanding of the nature and meaning of a performing art like the dance and the dancer's job of work, effortful but ever in a flux, and always disappearing in its wake.

But here is one thing that's easy to understand: the contemporary tinikling continues to bring fame to Filipinos, as much as it is able to reflect the state of Filipino dancers in the diaspora. In Gonzalez's novel, the tinikling symbolizes the beaten traps between which the Filipino dancers dance to increasing tempo and, to a certain extent, to the point of redundancy and a simple superfluity of energy.

Philippine Studies Society
Quezon City
1993

Notes

1. The alternative instrument is a pair of wooden pestles used to pound rice in a wooden mortar. But the transportability of the lighter bamboos has made the bamboos popular. Dr. Jose Maceda says that dancing over two bamboos is also done by the Subanon and the Tausug in Southern Philippines. The Maranao also dance the singkil over beaten bamboo poles, often in two pairs that are crossed over, creating a cross-figure. These are beaten in 4/4 time.

2. I was also told by modern dancer Betty Jones (famous as partner of Jose Limon) that she performed in *Oklahoma* for the US servicemen in the Philippines after World War II, a production brought all the way from America.

3. The defunct MPF antedated the Cultural Center of the Philippines, established in 1969, and today's National Commission for Culture and the Arts. Its

chair was the soprano Jovita Fuentes, herself a diva with Isang Tapales and Mercedes Matias Santiago, all experienced in the European scene. Their students were to follow, some through musicals in Europe, Britain, Canada, and the United States.

4. Heretofore, under the Spanish and American regimes, social dances that were popularized came from Europe and the Americas. In a reverse effort, Francisca Reyes Aquino's research and performances were meant to neutralize this influence. After the heyday of the Spanish zarzuela (and its regionalization in several local languages including Tagalog), the vaudeville took over. Originally from Europe (in cabarets and music halls) but moving into an American variety, the vaudeville included skits, singing, dancing, juggling, acrobatics, even magic. Aside from the regular theaters, these acts were also seen at the annual Manila Carnival where the Miss Philippines was proclaimed. Many Filipinos became apprentices in this attractive cornucopia of forms both as amateurs and professionals.

5. Ethnographic discoveries brought about by colonialism influenced the artists early on, with Flaubert, Stendhal, T. E. Lawrence, and other specialists and adventurers. In dance, the Ballets Russes exported this exotic strain from Russia to Paris and the rest of Europe, as exemplified by the orientalism of Fokine and Bakst.

6. Marian Pastor Roces reevaluates the significance of the Filipino ilustrados in Europe in her discussion of Juan Luna and Felix Resurrecion Hidalgo.

7. Again, they were followed in the 1980s by Lisa Macuja in Russia, Anna Villadolid in Germany (which is more hospitable to Asian dancers than France and Britain), Franklin Bobadilla in The Netherlands, Irene Sabas in Belgium and later as teacher in Spain, and in the US by Enrico Labayen, Rebecca Rodriguez, Eloisa Enerio, and Hazel Sabas, among others.

8. In the 1960s, while in Manila, West Indies-inspired choreographer Katherine Dunham used Filipino dancers in lead parts. Earlier, in the 1950s, Alexandra Danilova, Frederic Franklin, and Mia Slavenska produced recitals with Filipino dancers as soloists.

9. One of the professional vaudeville artists was Isabel Rosario Cooper, anglicized into Elizabeth "Dimples" Cooper. She is famous as the first Filipina to have kissed in the movies. She was also famous as the mistress of Gen. Douglas MacArthur, Jr. Many others like her were given equivalents to American personalities, like Katy de la Cruz as the Carmen Miranda of the Philippines.

10. The ballet and jazz syllabi were commissioned by the Association of Concerned Artists in the Performing Arts of the Philippines (ACAPP) for the use of Technical Education and Skills Development Authority (TESDA). ACAPP also conducted workshops for trainers in dance and tested their competence; they were then accredited by TESDA. ACAPP also formulated the criteria and grading system to test the talents.

11. Locally, exploitation also exists in Filipino centers and through the promoters who deduct too much from the foreign income of the talents they helped, supposedly for their board and lodging, training, costuming, personal needs and travel, among other things. Talents are sometimes left with half their contracted income.

12. Furthermore, copies of the "sinulog formula" (as we judges call it) as first designed by Cebuano choreographers have been duplicated with thematic or ethnographic changes in Camiguin, Davao, San Carlos, and other cities. Cebu itself has forged sisterhood with cities abroad, drawing people from there to see the annual competition.

13. For instance, the NCCA has no data on or representation from the export entertainment industry. Even in the choice of eminent national awards for dance, the work in dance, where repertoire and performance are ever ephemeral (and achieved while young because of the art's exhausting nature), is not readily recognized or appreciated unlike in the more permanent arts.

14. Staging and stylization of folk dance has been made necessary by the proscenium perspective of Western theater. In Philippine practice, this has been carried far—if not too far—since the supposed advice of Broadway choreographer Agnes de Mille. How then do we judge this "folk" expression as folklore?

Are National Artistic Companies Necessary?

At first glance, the creation of national companies or groups for artists seems noble, for through it the sought-after and vaunted glory may be realized. Anything that's called "national" will be in the limelight, and artists and audiences will flock to support and rally behind it. After all, it will bear the seal of our nation, represent our people worldwide, and reap moral and financial support.

Such are the royal and/or national artistic companies in Scandinavia and Britain where several royal/national theaters, dance and musical companies are in existence. The creation of these groups stems from the monarchical traditions and policies of these countries, which certain Asian countries have taken on by taking from their own courtly traditions and bringing organizing practices into the academies through the national bureaucracy.

In the Philippines, we have no courtly or monarchical tradition. We perpetually grieve over our lack of classicism, which is both glorious and constricting. For good or bad, we are a diverse though still geographically and economically divided democratic society. Our own culture, which can only aspire for unity through a nationalist agenda, is so rich and deep in fruitful plurality that stems from the wide range of precolonial expression to colonial tradition.

It is therefore my conclusion that the current move to create national artistic companies—the two for dance (theatrical and folkloric) and those for drama, chorus, and orchestra—does not conform to our cultural history and creative tendencies. It has been reported that the Bayanihan is to be declared *the* company for folkloric dance through legislation. A decision such as this though needs to consider more than the easy dissolution of cultural groups and companies; it needs to consider why these companies break up. (Republic Act 8626 has long declared the Bayanihan national, sometime after this writing.)

All theater and dance companies in the Philippines and worldwide break up because of artistic impulse and originality, and I believe it's something that we need not always cry over. This is but a symptom of the creative dynamics of artistic organizations, the effect of the yin and yang, the positive and negative aspects as described by Nietzsche and embodied by Shiva. The pyramidal nature of these artist groups will, at some point in time, cramp the most creative leaders at the top. They become atrophied in isolation, purity or privilege. This was what happened in the much admired yet stunted peaks of ballet classicism in Russia.

It's also a well-known fact that the existence of a prestigious company does not prevent the creation of other groups, particularly when economics (although it is a much needed anchor) isn't what's at the core of the artists' or audience's organization. All the former company really has is an advantage, if at all. I believe it was France's own Andre Malraux who decentralized artistic centers in France, moving it away from Paris where dance was beginning to go backwards, even if the dancing was superb. Today, France has one of the most conducive atmospheres for creativity in the theatrical arts.

The creation of the national artist companies is also problematic in that these are restrictive and repressive. Prestige is given to few artists in these companies, and other artists are left with no choice but to work with the so-called "best" even when they may not be happy with the setup. This is one of the reasons why there is a lot of tension in theatrical organizations. In 1996, arts manager Rhoda Grauer seemed to address this problem. In a conference in Jakarta, Grauer asked why we often imitate the structure of the companies in the West when this may not fit our own social traditions and structures. An example of this, she says, are those centers that are inaccessible to the people.

In the Philippines, the years under the Marcos regime perpetuated a practice that eliminated agents for the classical arts, which did away with future Lozanos and Zuluetas, although Redentor Romero persists on his own. Our established entertainment agents are actually for commercial entertainers, specifically and in large number for the japayuki migration to Japan. This calls to mind what Conrado de Quiros also asked about our politicians: why are they all mostly old at the top? In the 1960s, we had the Guidotes and Morenos, the Borromeos and Reyeses. Today, we have so few Filipinos in their twenties gaining national prominence in the arts.

Why Not?

My paper for an international dance conference in August presents an example of the detrimental effect of having the folk arts subjected to state auspices or national flaunting. The famous folk choreographer Moiseyev exemplifies parallels worldwide, something that we court now at our traditional arts' risk. Moreover, see what happened when the Soviet state system collapsed, where not only the economy but also artistry fell. A recent reading on the scientific culture in Europe shows how the country had to operate within the courtesies or etiquette of a circle, a specific order or gentlemanly consensus, plus *sprezzatura* or "virtue" and *je ne sais quoi* understood by everyone. Even a Galileo needed the acceptance of such an order or attitude (which is not just about rules but also about appearance, perhaps the so-called presence in the performative) to prove himself in society. His contribution had to be "blackboxed" as a body of knowledge to be respected by his colleagues.

This is also why there are pockets of resistance in the artistic world to the proposal that national companies be established. Certain sectors are never consulted, and this raises the question: is the creation of these companies what the dance, theater, and music people want?

I suspect that this obsession with privileging the national is allied with such a tendency in the more private art of letters and the visual arts. In the 1960s, there was the obsession with the Great Filipino Novel (GFN) which, with the appearance of many good books by more good authors, suddenly didn't need to be named. To be ranked or compared, prizes are awarded in the visual arts; but this does not happen comfortably in the performing arts (although it is quite easy for the "packageable" films). Although there are dance competitions, these are more for individual performers or choreographers. In the folk arts, competitions are no longer favored because how can you rank a culture over another? In postmodern perspectives, how do you size up Halprin beside Balanchine, or Bausch beside Cunningham? They're just different in their own excellent ways.

I was tasked by a council for dance to prepare a response to the idea of national companies. They may have to refine my tone, but here goes the draft after a general consensus:

1. The setting up of a national dance company (ballet or folkloric) creates a hegemony that monopolizes influence and at the end homogenizes the aesthetics and practice of the dance;
2. A national dance company privileges one over, above, and against all others who exist in the rest of our diverse country and who may just as well contribute to our national culture in their respective and respectable ways;
3. A national dance company is counter-productive, namely, because it will provide the most bounty to one and deprive the rest equal opportunity and support and create a predetermined handicap for other artists who are then treated as second-class and less privileged. Besides, "unrivaled" companies may atrophy, which happens even to the best and well-endowed companies;
4. A national dance company is born out of an alien or colonial viewpoint, promoted by foreigners, or by our own authorities who wish to colonize our people and artists by their autocratic will and ways; and
5. A national dance company goes against the historic cry of artists who needed help after the EDSA Revolution. This was when one compromise-company was established for dance, which was saddled with many directors even then. The move to create this national dance company is against the call for reform. It is

but a move towards the perpetuation of the system where the privileged will be received once more by cutting off the rest; the system that exists on the arbitrary game of naming, promoting, and patronizing only "the best" is at the expense of "the rest." The creation of a national artistic company is nothing but an injustice and an injurious hegemonic move against the creative nature and future of Philippine dance and theater.

Manila Standard
1998

Fugitive Thoughts on Ethnicity and the Obsession with a National Art

The concept of "the national" is a modern one. It is both idealistic and pragmatic. Idealistic because the concept brings together the aspirations and ideals of peoples who finally agree to be unified as a group living in one land. Pragmatic because 1) it creates a structure for these people and their way of life in their act of living together; 2) it programs the land, its resources, and its possible uses; and 3) it serves in the interest of these people and land as it is the basis of resistance to foreign intervention.

This idea of nationhood inspires and propels a people to political, economic, and industrial development particularly when the atmosphere is conducive. Sometimes though, even a repressive atmosphere allows for people to be propelled as it stimulates cultural creativity. In the end, both contexts prove a people's psychological and artistic life, which allow the realization of oneness, of nationhood.

Ethnicity, on the other hand, asserts both a restricted identity and a more plural practice of identities. To the ethnic, his time and his place are his universe, given its own natural, social, and spiritual laws. He conceives his own beliefs about this life and the hereafter, about his own way of eking out a living, of dressing, of sheltering, of protecting himself and renewing his urge to be. Our geography has so imposed this reality on us; it is also a result of our various racial strains, including the various kinds of mestizos—Spanish, Sangley, etc. (see Teresita Ang See: *The Chinese in the Philippines*, 1990). This variety in racial roots is manifested in the varying loyalties and alliances in our society, something that has both enriched and undermined our proclamation and realization of nationhood.

Nationhood itself can also narrow our notion about life so that we lose sight of the reality of, and the wisdom from, ethnicity. Nationhood often focuses on periodicity and centrality within the restrictions of time and space, which causes it to lose sight of the vagrant yet eternal impulse of ethnicity. In turn, ethnic groups can feel so outside of the national movement that they can come in conflict with the so-called progressive aims of the technologically wise and nationally conscious man.

In terms of dance, it is very simplistic to say that all our ethnic dances make the Filipino. To start with, we haven't seen all these dances, nor may we see the end to the nuances and changes these dances may undergo. It would therefore be presumptuous to say that one understands these dances, for these dances are *not* even dances in the occidental sense. They are tied to rituals, of which dance is only part, and these rituals are so unconcerned with nationality and history. It is only us who view their paraphernalia as native rice and wine, sacrificial chickens, or carabaos.

Thus, even the respected researcher, National Artist Francisca Reyes Aquino, was wise to say that it's in the more Westernized mode of the cariñosa that we have a national dance, rather than in the singkil of the Maranaws or the tinikling of the Warays. Yet, she embraced all the possible dances she could see and recorded them lovingly no matter how tedious the process. It was the love of the whole that made her a Filipina, and not the easy identification and proclamation of this and that dance as *the* national dance, which could have simply detracted from our move towards nationhood.

I should think that this is the kind of love that choreographer Meredith Monk mentions in the September 1990 issue of *Dance Magazine*. It is an all-encompassing love that she expects of patrons and sponsors—their *wanting* for artists to be "there." It is a love that can cause us to feel for the great number of dances the Philippines has. In my own career as dancer, dance teacher, choreographer, and critic, I have also witnessed the lack of encompassing love in the dance field: ballet versus modern dance, folk versus theater, etc. The fact is, loving all these does not mean simple accommodation or convenient, even if inspired, compromise. Many mix them indiscriminately, proving ingenuity, but without really arriving at true integrity or creativity. A bit of this and a bit of that, and all we get is a choreographic *chopsuey*.

On the other hand, some artists are blamed for not being more encompassing or versatile. Recently, a composer was blamed for not creating music in a specific musical form and, because of her musical leadership, she was blamed for the death of that form. I believe that this same scale also measures artistic personages, and not just artistic forms. Personally, I don't classify artists as major or minor (two musical modes!), because I respect them for the integrity of the work they produce, whether lyric or epic, narrative or dramatic, programmatic or symphonic, character or classic. Each one's worth is his worth, and there are more factors to praise or blame than an artist's self. There's the society, and the opportunities it provides him or withholds from him. This can only lead to a history of personages and patronage, and not of actual achievements or works.

During the launching of the commemorative year of Francisca Reyes Aquino, we had the chance to witness the styles of the sua-sua, singkil, pandanggo sa ilaw and tinikling at various points in history—of Aquino's time and of updated researches. The young researcher can dismiss Aquino's recordings of these ethnic dances as simple and naïve. At the same time, this researcher can view the recent scholarship as more accurate and sophisticated (even if still more accumulative than intensive). It is so sophisticated that we get so carried away with its speed and spectacle—something that's far from the expressions of the folks themselves who created these dances. These are actually our own current expressions, and although I have no quarrel with that, it can be overdone and in effect empty the original forms of their intentions. In the end, it all just becomes dazzling and "packageable" entertainment.

As I viewed the Aquino recordings being danced, they had such a naïveté to them, which is in fact the very feeling you get when you see these dances done in situ by the people who created them. The very absence of speed and spectacle endowed these dances with a spellbinding Asiatic feel, showing the very dynamics and guise of the people who will never get to watch these performed in the theater.

This proves that those of us in the city court a danger when we believe we can deal with ethnic materials in our expeditious metropolitan ways (with our box-office, traffic, and theater schedule-regulated performances, for example). Indeed, we truly speak of the ethnic materials in our own way as Aquino dress them up with more than just costumes, and use a different floor, a different light, a different (two-hour) time span, a new space, and for new social purposes. This recreation is almost another kind of ritual that we city folks so hunger for in the hopes of replenishing our own exhausted imagination.

Yes, there is a need for truth in the portrayal of these ethnic works. And this need continues to grow. We court danger when we easily display our citified-nationalism and find comfort in, "This is it." The true folk dance lies among the people, and yet our national life has not done enough to keep these alive. There are so many so-called progressive and security forces that profess to make limited changes to the ethnic groups' ways of life. But we so easily display these for our scholarly interests, theatrical entertainment, and tourism promotions, even when we're so removed from them in terms of belief and economics that it is impossible for us to even help perpetuate the originals.

We regale our friends with how tedious, arduous, and even dangerous our sojourns to the provinces and hinterlands have been, but we leave the people there with even less opportunities to celebrate their rituals, songs and dances. Here in the city, we package our researches in sellable and photographable forms, comforted after a successful bout with what we "captured."

Fishing for inspiration and images from the folk should not rest easily on our conscience and on our very works of art. How often do we find folk-based ballets finally looking dated, eroded in appeal by the fast-changing taste of the city? Meanwhile the originals in the barrios and towns remain the same and nearly eternal—if not already lost. But how boring those originals could be for those in the city who are not involved in the rituals except as choreographers, scholars, and tour managers? Even the honest-to-goodness choreographer is trapped in the economy of the city that it's difficult to get away from the intricacies of transforming folkloric materials into choreographed dances. How, for instance, has modern dance not sufficiently dented the taste of the affluent class on whom the sponsorship of the dance theater depends? How has modern dance kept from truly reaching the young people in the Philippines, the way it already has in Europe by way of the former imperial opera houses? Our dance audience, especially in Metro Manila, is so conservative and self-protective of their acquired taste, the way that they were so politically during the Philippine Revolution.

A current example is the fact that despite the crippling cost of imported pointes shoes (which we still don't make, and in which no rich Filipino will invest), we still aesthetically prioritize the classical ballets that require these shoes. This is because this dance form is more sellable than modern dance or the "Filipino choreographies" and fills the till in the box-office. I have no quarrel with classical ballet in which I was trained, especially when danced beautifully, but this should not relegate Filipino works to second class. Artistically, Filipino works are not inferior; but in expenditure, publicity, and support they are made so, because of our own doing.

In the Netherlands, they have a small company in the small city called The Hague. It bears the country's name (as another company is called "national"), and this has lived on and off of staging non-classical ballets. It is also better recognized internationally (like the Taiwanese Cloud Gate company) even if the other national company still gets greater support and funding.

I believe our problem, to start with, is that we don't decide, confess, and insist on what our dance styles should be. We often opt for a compromise, as Martha Graham and those who preceded and followed her never did. In the same way that scholars abroad do not just collect data, but also decide on a focus so that they may go deeper into their research. Again, as Monk said, we perhaps lack an adventurous spirit; we are perhaps not curious enough, distrusting our intuition, and not wont to take risks in this business of art.

But artists are not the only ones to blame. It's also this big idea of a nation as partially and hegemonically conceived. Ethnolinguistic groups take care of their expression, with or without intervention. They celebrate birth, life, and death to no end. But as a nation, we're still short of obsessive concern (in the focused sense) for the arts. Yes, there are the CCP, the NCCA, and the other state institutions that concern themselves with culture. But the overall attitude is not obsessive, but discursive. It is in the field of science and business that being obsessive is a must, as it is imperative to success. This needs to also be true for the arts, as personified by an artist who is truly alive!

Then and only then will we be able to speak of a national art. Yes, there were arts in the past and there are those today, which are already national in manifestation. What I assert here is the need for the arts to be celebrated nationally. If the arts are provided with such, it will allow folk artists and other arts a chance at survival. At the very least, individual municipalities should initiate cultural plans, and at most, decentralize implementation of cultural policies. But when schools and hospitals are so badly provided for, why bother with the arts? Because the arts feed our consciousness and conscience. Without the arts, social consciousness and the spirit of service will suffer. The arts, ethnolinguistic and otherwise, dance and beyond, are not simply artifacts of our past and present, but are here to strengthen and serve society's spirit.

Terpsichore and Tourism: The Transmogrification of Philippine Folk Dance

There are two events in folk dance that are landmarks in the Philippine dance scene. Both fall within the umbrella of codification and stylization, after the discussion of which I will look into other processes that brought forth and sustained interest in folk dance.

Codification and Stylization. The first landmark event was in research, as done by one woman: Francisca Reyes Aquino, now National Artist in Dance. Aquino began the serious study of Philippine folk dances with the goal of documenting and saving them from foreign influences. In the 1920s and 1930s she was commissioned by the University of the Philippines to go out to the field in the company of composer Antonino Buenaventura and of photographer Ramon Tolentino. They coursed through the countryside as no one had done before, and for an unheard, perhaps taken-for-granted, cause.

Out of these trips Aquino was able to produce books, which at the end of her life and career came up to eight volumes; she was also involved in the writing of handbooks on foreign dances and other physical education subjects. She also formed the UP Folk Song and Dance Club, which brought national awareness to the folk culture's importance; this also reminded people of the possible extinction of Philippine dances. Aquino's later work with the Department of Education gave her direct access to schoolteachers, to whom she gave folk dance clinics, and who helped form the Philippine Folk Dance Society.

The second landmark event in the codification and stylization of folk dance was the 1958 triumph of the Bayanihan Philippine Dance Company at the Universal Exposition in Brussels. There were other and earlier foreign incursions, but this had the biggest delegation and it won accolades and the top prize. Other wonderful troupes were around then, such as the Far Eastern University Folk Dance Troupe, but they were not at the right place at the right time. The Bayanihan did have its own music and folk arts research center at the Philippine Women's University in Manila; it was also being headed then, as it is now, by National Artists Lucrecia Reyes Kasilag in music and Lucrecia Reyes Urtula in dance.

Thereafter, the Bayanihan, Filipinescas Dance Company, and several university-based troupes have gone through this mad scramble to become the "official delegation" of the Philippines in foreign festivals. The Bayanihan was the hegemonic one among them, and to date it is considered the premier folk dance company in the country. Second in rank but not in authenticity and artistry is the Ramon Obusan Folkloric Group. Many others groups have withered away.

Aside from school-based groups, it was also fashionable in the 1950s to the 1970s for folk dancers to perform in big restaurants, clubs, and hotels. That was one way by which the dancers and groups sustained themselves in membership and finances. Inevitably they had to cater to that kind of clientele. There and in the theaters, hundreds of Filipino dances had to be made palatable and digestible to its audience, which also means spectacular in bits and suites. This was where the folk dance program got the formula for success: begin with a tribal (or non-Christian dances of the ethnic minorities), follow with the Maria Clara (named after Jose Rizal's submissive heroine in his novel *Noli Me Tangere* and her typical costuming) or the Spanish and other European dances, and of Mindanao (made by various tribes connected to Islam and now beefed up with Lumad groups in Mindanao and Palawan), and then the usual finale of a Rural Suite (or lowland dances of the Christianized Filipinos), which often ends in the clashing of bamboos for the Tinikling in jota tempo.

Through the years, it has also become fashionable to stage the dances based on the Western aesthetics of the stage, or to go back to the more authentic renditions. Accusations have been hurled about how dances have been distorted—how a royal dance becomes questionable when danced in public by a Moslem princess, or how folkloric ballets are formed, or how they have been glossed up to fit Broadway's Winter Garden speed and delegation requirements.

Further Popularization and Commercialization. Having looked at the success of the above events, we can now look at our smaller achievements. There was a time when we also started sending these folk dances on floating expositions on board ships between islands and other Asian countries. Now no longer the fashion, we have continued to be involved in the actual "exporting" of dancers in the "entertainment industry" who do jazz, popular and folk dances abroad. They are called overseas contract workers (OCW), further classified into "cultural dancers or performers." Of late this has burgeoned into a big business, with promoters and agencies recruiting dancers from all over the country, and with dancers getting younger and younger. These agents get a big cut—sometimes half—of the dancers' fees or salaries. Although they are all around the world, Filipino dancers are mostly in Japan and they have been lumped together under the derogatory term "japayuki." The Philippine government regulates the dancers' migration to Japan as this is what the Japanese government requires; it is also said that this business is being infiltrated by the Asian mafia called "Yakuza." The bottom line is, for this profession it is money and not dance artistry or authenticity that is the most important and persuasive factor.

There has been a clamor for a more liberal handling of dancers' migration, one in particular that will be without artistic or diplomatic control and requirements. But these dancers are often exploited, as they are mostly untrained to begin with. They also leave the country quite ignorant of their economic and human rights. In a foreign land where they do not always understand the nuances and intricacies of the language and culture, they become the fast victims of exploitation by their employers. But the number of Filipino dancers who leave for abroad continues to increase because of the lack of work and the economic difficulties in the Philippines today.

Meanwhile, those who are required to audition to show their choreographic competence usually present Philippine folk dances in its commercialized form, far beyond the "stylized versions" of the aforementioned nationally recognized folk dance groups. Here, the market dictates the form and style of the dances, which are still viewed as "native" because of the charm and exoticism of the tribal or folkloric art.

But how folkloric are these dances exactly, when they are viewed on stage, and in hotels and clubs? There have been various degrees of adaptation involved in the staging as the dances are performed outside of their original habitat, and rituals end up being further ritualized on stage. As New York critic Deborah Jowitt recently and easily asked in Seoul, how are we to see these dances otherwise but in transplantations on stage?

Two basic and important factors need to be considered here. One, the groups or dancers must promote themselves, and they have to stage the dances and tour them into the universalized facilities of the theater, mostly with proscenium, stage-adapted costumes, artificial lights, and even taped music. There are the more cautious ones who "preserve the essence" of these dances. One reliable choreographer recently confessed that the climate abroad has now been about more authenticized performances, just like what the Asia Society has asked for. Too much stylization has relegated some groups out of the international touring league, or has relegated them to its fringes. We can see this in the inactive international life of the Russian Moisseyev Company. But with the entertainment industry's concern with commercialized art, the folkloric is really only an added spice to its fodder of dances that's being offered to club and hotel audiences.

Education and Scholarship. But within our very borders, beyond the concern with international festivals, performances, and migration, there has been a decline in the educational stress on the dance. Whereas most physical education teachers used to teach folk dance as second nature, many now do not know these dances anymore and students are not required to study any dance when there is no special school program.

Meanwhile, the emergence of dance contests has resulted in the staging of folk dances as spectacles. Spectacular as these dances may be on their own, the idea of spectacle is really about dazzling speed, sequencing, and sequins. This is proof of how even the communal rituals in the provinces are being commercialized. In a consumerist society, this is perhaps inevitable. Perhaps this is a kind of urban folk art, a transmogrification of the folkloric resources. Maybe it is similar to the so-called Hispanic dances that were Asianized in texture, technique and tempo, and the tribal dances that have begun to be rendered with Muslim restraint.

The *subli* in Batangas is an example of this. As the *sinulog* and the *ati-atihan* are performed to honor the Holy Child Jesus, the *subli* is danced to honor the Holy Cross. There are many versions of this ritual dance all over Batangas, varying in emphasis and nuances. But all are still centered on the Holy Cross—the women keep lofty elegance in their devotion and are often crowned with native hats. The men are earthy yet jaunty, often stooped as they rowdily click bamboo castanets with their hands.

But a more secularized version is that of Aquino's, as it is performed with "folk music" especially composed for it, and danced more flirtatiously and jubilantly by men and women. Of course there were also sexual undercurrents in the original, but it was still tightly bound to the ritual circumstance of the dance. Perhaps Aquino's recorded version has been distorted or popularized through time. Since most subli dancers now are not from Batangas, they have not observed the local ritual itself. They also don't live at a time when the saya and not the jeans were the regular standard outfits, so how can the feeling of the dance's form and essence be felt? These dancers' thinking have also already been Westernized, and their interests are on more mundane things. With their bodies sculpted by modern costuming, what can we expect?

Indeed, much has been lost, and there is the sinking feeling that dance has been violated. You mourn the distortion of movement, the casualness of the focus, the outright popularization of dance, as you think you are seeing another dance, even if it is dressed up in the right costumes, even if its name hasn't been changed. While the Philippines has no tradition of classicism or courtliness in its dances (there are only isolated cases such as the pangalay of Sulu), there is no real conscious effort at protecting these dances. Even serious Philippine dance scholarship is guilty of this. Whereas Aquino set out to preserve and conserve these dances, which she heroically virtually did alone in the beginning, under trying and limiting circumstances, doing the best she could in verbal notation, her followers have not grown in terms of depth and accuracy of scholarship.

Of course the video-film has come to the rescue. But it is not an analytic mode of recording. It must only be viewed with many considerations in mind, such as the recorder's selective processing, the technical qualifications of the instrument, its kind of space, with its processed colors, limited dimension, and the performers' own varying styles and abilities.

Philippine dance scholarship is largely unarmed with an accurate notation system because it is without the serious influence of semiotic and cultural studies. Anthropologists and ethnologists are patronizing but they are not equipped to deal with dance as well. Dancers themselves, while interested in dancing, are not interested in understanding dance. And then there are the tourism officials who are only bent on promoting but not respecting the culture of the Filipinos.

All of these point to one thing. With the currency of glamorized and globalized performances, cultural literacy and consciousness continue to be a long-term goal, one that remains to be seen.

Masyarakat Seni Pertunjukan Indonesia/
Indonesian Society for the Performing Arts
Mataram, Lombok
1995

The Role of Dance in Nation-Building: Is the Nation Dancing with Its People?

What is at stake is not just our souls but also our bodies.

—E. San Juan, Jr.[1]

A house on the hill is like an aerie, up in the clouds as it is, for people who move and dress like birds of the air. A house in the waters glints in the sun, for a people who sail with the wind and are as colorful as their faces and fans, their mats, swords, and sails. A bamboo house on solid ground is a comfort in the heat or rain, creaking and swaying in the quakes, but standing firm as those brown men who spanned centuries of elemental, economic, and imperial invasions.

In and by these houses were made the arts and crafts, rituals and dances that sustained the lives and concretized the cultures of the folks. These houses have been modified by the influx of influences, by the influences of interventions, by the interventions of disrespecting cultures.

Some of these houses, arts and crafts are "still there," but the lives that used to create them have changed. The establishments that ruled these lives abolished the essences and efficacies of these facts and artifacts. Today it is a great and grave task to rescue these from oblivion, to recall these as the racial memories of their folk, to relate them to development while at the same time guarding them against degeneration because of modern man.

How much of progress is healthy for the body and soul of man? How much of the health and wealth of man is for the environmental survival of his world? Why must we rescue the resources and artifices of man? Or, in this case, rescue man from himself?

The theme "The Role of Dance in Nation-Building" is an academic one. The Filipino people built this land long before there was a political concept of a nation. The institution and naming of the nation only came later. Now it is this nation's task to rescue the facts and artifacts of the Filipinos long before it was termed a nation. This must be done not only to preserve and assert the people's being, but also in order for this modern-day nation to give itself credit for acts that have warranted pride and privilege in global political, economic, and cultural contexts, and in the larger context of social history.

Our Filipino dances are there, indigenous or foreign-influenced, ready to be unearthed. They stem from the lives of the people, from their rites and relations, from their deprivations and celebrations, from their imagination and communication. That many have been lost is the fault of institutions that failed or refused to recognize their meaning, that ruled these out as forms, and that negated the very will and imagination of the people who made them. Currently, these institutions, even those in the so-called evolving nations, have not and still do not value the rhyme and reason behind many of the aged evidence of lives lived, of aspirations concretized, of rites that encapsulated and externalized a people's essences and meanings. This is what needs to be changed if we are to assert dance as a crucial cultural force in nation building, and this will mean taking clear steps towards this goal.

Researching and Rescuing Dance. One of the many tasks of a nation with regards to dance is to rescue and respect its peoples' dances. Preserving these dances will require not just ethnographic and anthropological proof; it also requires teaching the present about the wealth and wisdom of the past. The present is always threatened by a depletion of the imagination and the distortion of meaning, focused as it is on striving for novelty, imitating the alluring foreign craft, and competing for proof of progress. Only by respecting and rescuing the past, only by the renewal that comes with the recognition of it, only by the recognition that inspires recreation of our senses and essences, will mankind be made whole and wise.

Recognizing and rescuing these dances from the past will prove that this cultural form is as multifarious and munificent as the geography and culture of this nation. These dances do not only define but also, more importantly, *direct* the choreographic ideas and history of our people. This choreographic history will inculcate in the youth the past of our race, inspire our artists towards dynamic expression, and interest and inform the cultural inclinations and convictions of our society.

The problem is that society has lost its fondness for these dances. People sit back and relax in front of the TV and find ephemeral enjoyment in it, unthinkingly viewing it as art. Unlike other art forms, dance can only survive in performance, in rites, on stages, in fiestas, and in occasions. It can't be hung, put on a shelf or simply be heard. Dance is a total art that involves the body of man, his breath, shape and rhythm, his attitude, steps, and costume. Like the houses in which he lives, the dances of man have functions, whether physical, social, or expressional. Unlike houses (the making of which, according to the psychologist Havelock Ellis, happened simultaneously with and primary to dance making) dances are lived out like the brief breath of a moment, in the transience of a song, or the fleeting *now* in time.

Creating Dance Today. Another task that a nation needs to undertake toward building, sustaining, and renewing itself is to promote the creation of art. In dance, this simply means creating more dances. In preserving the past so that it may help us design the face of the future, we must reflect on the present.

Analyzing the present means asking, who am I? What am I doing, and what does it mean? How do I make life meaningful to myself? How can I communicate with others and contribute to the idea and the fact of a nation? Answering these questions will bring a consciousness of a nation, and a focused consciousness will direct us to the usefulness of our past toward our goals for the future.

Reflecting on the present entails the choreographing and recording of contemporary dances. Choreographing means making sense of events and tales that move us, of styles that matter to us, of matters that style us. It means looking at most of the dances that have been made, for example, in this century—a century that pretty soon will be history. Recording means looking at and documenting the dances of Leonor Orosa Goquingco, Anita Kane, Remedios de Oteyza, Ricardo Cassell, Eddie

Elejar, Tita Radaic, Alice Reyes, Julie Borromeo, Tony Fabella, Denisa Reyes, Agnes Locsin, to mention a few. It means looking at these lives that were lived and have become history, or are being lived and are still forging destinies.

A choreographer is a citizen who speaks by way of his art, in the act of moving.[2] Not to give him the chance to move is like infringing on, or depriving him of his right to speech or expression. It is no different from the crime of neglecting, repressing, or restricting the freedom of a citizen to practice his art. But to allow talent to go to waste can also be seen as a form of moral neglect, in the same way that it was immoral to have ignored Van Gogh and then to glorify him after his insufferable life. That is why the awarding of National Artist to the aged or the dead is such an anomaly; it's like practicing the art of painfully postponing recognition. (I suspect that for any recipient this awarding is always bittersweet.)

Already, the dances of our century's choreographers are lost. Many of our young no longer got the chance to see the achievements of thirty, even of twenty or just ten, years ago.[3] There was no technology then to record them, there was no notation expertise to hire (and to hire one is not even deemed important today), there was no concern beyond individual ambition and interest.

This loss is a reflection of the nation's general lack of concern for itself through culture. It is not concerned with seeing itself, and conserving its creative force and function. This institutional disregard for our past negates the idea of a nation apart from personal and national political maneuverings and economic ascendancy. Losing our dances from the past is a form of cultural betrayal that relegates us to the foot of history—a culturally impoverished, even depraved, nation.

It was not only criminal to have let Adameit or de Oteyza die poor, or to have allowed Kane (of foreign blood but with such national ballets like *Maria Makiling, Mutya ng Dagat, Inulan sa Pista*, etc.) to leave and fend for herself as an old migrant to America; it is also now a crime to allow the works of Orosa Goquingco and her contemporaries like Rosalia Merino Santos, Corazon Generoso Iñigo, and Manolo Rosado to slip into obscurity. A choreographer is nothing outside his or her works, and a work has to be *there* in the art of dance.

The losses and gaps in any cultural image or historical preservation are an eternal injustice to the imagination of a people. In his speech on history in Berkeley, Greil Marcus[4] (author of *Lipstick Traces: A Secret History of the 20th Century*) said that even the writing of history can be injurious or unjust. He said,

> history is finally a matter of accountability: a good historian can bring all of us up on trial. We are all accountable to what we have seen and done, to what shaped us, to what made our place and time. In a good history, we are not permitted to get it wrong, so far as it can be known what is right. A good historian will challenge *us* when *we* forget, when *we* elide, when *we* invent: the historian will have the documents, and we will have to face them.

In the present time of global politics, ideological battles, and media hype, it is wise to heed him further. To wit:

> It's commonplace that history is written by the powerful; it's more to the point to say that power writes history. Events that do not change into power or that take place outside of the normal circuits in which power is exchanged, outside of the institutional distribution and control of social goods [which otherwise he calls "circuit of significance" or "circuit of institutional significance"]—such events, in certain ways, do not make history at all. They are resistant to history, because history does not know how to account for them; and history resists them, because it can get away with it.

It is reason enough to distrust an institution, even that which we call our government, for giving out a partial or incomplete history. This has happened many times in dance. In this age of mass media, partial histories are the rule rather than the exception. Meanwhile, accessibility to history is only there for the influential, those who have the money to pay for media, or even just the bits and pieces of information which historians and critics choose.

Today we avoid the term "new society," but the need to make new a nation, continues to be true. A nation should always be new or contemporary, confessing about its present problems and sources of pride, while recognizing and keeping alive its heritage. Just like a conscious human being or artist, it creates from recollection and projection. At the same time, the nation is a contemporaneous bridge between resources from the past and its possible results in the future; and it is on that bridge that the artist paces back and forth, ever critical and ever creative, conscious of history, and armed with humility so that he can record, reflect on and refashion the past with humor or honor.[5]

There is no prescription for an artist. His palette, so to speak, is of various colors and shades, his tones of various pitches and harmonies, his words of various rhymes and reasons, and his movements of various styles and psyches. The artist is free. He has all of life to explore, all of history to attend to, all of subjects to deal with, all of love and hate to inspire him. But by being in *a* situation, in *a* sphere of time, of period, of place, he is undoubtedly bound even when he only sits and waits. In the end, this artist can only be a Filipino, and he is accountable to that. His freedom only lies in his creation of himself and his culture, in the act of creating the picture, the literary text, music, and dance that stem from his existence. The artist creates from that which lies deep within him, which is broadly related to his people and feels the pulse, resources, and needs of his society.

Recreating Dance. Our dance roots may be used in various ways toward varying ends. The Eastern Africans had their Beni Ngoma to express their political will. The Chinese had their acrobatic opera to display their ancient extravagance. Americans used jazz to confess about their glamorized repression in exhibition. We Filipinos have our own confused mixed bayanihan bag of tribal-cum-regional-cum-pseudo-European-cum-Moslem-Malay choreography. So many have contributed to this rich confusion, this embarrassment of riches. But more contributions are needed.

Some forty to fifty years since the Francisca Reyes Tolentino (later Aquino) researches, we have yet to fully make sense of these documented dances beyond its functioning as tourist displays, as export products for diplomacy, or as exhibition material for physical education classes. There have of course been major efforts, but in the context of our wealth of resources, these are exceptionally limited.

Of late, it has become tiring to flaunt these dances as diversity in unity or unity in diversity, or as the many faces of the Filipino, or as the choreographic panorama of our social equity-in-dance. Certainly we have not really refashioned these dances (except to "Broadway them up" which has also ceased to be fashionable in today's traditional dance presentations) in order to make them truly functional in our lives. At this point, they are but ready entertainment, a tourist attraction, or a token proof of cultural hoarding.

This is all we can make of the present function of dance because of two reasons. First, and again with exceptions, our scholarly studies and critical approaches to these dances are predominantly superficial, patronizing, and/or purely for appreciation's sake. We costume and recostume these dances to make them appealing, we lighten them up to look exotic (if not prettified), and we hike up their prices to make them exportable.[6] Frankly, this is the kind of choreographic wealth that I've seen from one Filipino dance troupe to another.

Secondly, and more importantly, the actual folks who do or who used to do these dances do not have the food, clothing, and shelter to live properly—the life necessities that are also essential for these dances to be lived out in rites and rituals. The actual folks who created these dances do not get a cent from those of us who "stole" these dances for stage display and diplomatic boats.[7] As San Juan says, "What is at stake is not just our souls but also our bodies." In dance, it is the body that speaks.

The conscience of our institutions is stunted by ignorance and in their lack of concern. The consciousness of the folks who made these dances is stunted by hunger and endangered by distress, destruction, and deprivation. Even the contemporary choreographers who are closer to the centers of power that be, the dancers who decorate institutional functions, the artists who get honorific awards; they also can't find that liberating space within which they may realize their dancing.

The People, the Artists. The artists are workers. They explore and imagine, study and plan, but it is *the* work that they focus on, the one thing they are intent on succeeding in. They live for it, love for it, hate for it, fear for it, hope for it, some even die for it. The so-called soul of a nation is there, not up in the air but in the lives of the people. Particularly for the artist, the soul of the nation is in their work and in their sharing this with society. The nation is there in the totality of the artists' efforts, in the preservation of their works, in the performance and sharing of their music and dances.

The Filipino is there in the harmonies, even in the contradictions and dissonances of the expression. It is in the minor and major modes, in the flow and contrast, in the skin and in the soul of art, in the highs and lows of the people's cultural history. The people—the artists—continue to make and build this nation through their work. But are the nation and its institutions keeping up with the works of its people? I think they are not. Institutions are never enough and are also never abreast of the creativity of the people. They have never been adequate in sustaining cultural creativity. Even history itself never gives due recognition to the work that has been done.

This shouldn't stop us from building that nation through the creation of art. To build is to continue to create art. It is to make art a part of life, to work towards making more food and houses, to have bodies that will dance and dwelling places to dance in. To build is to protect the past, and to recreate it for present usefulness and meaning. To build is to create the future from out of the significance of the past[8] and our imaginations.

The institutional and governmental stand on art and dance needs to be immediately changed. Social recognition of the importance and urgency of these cultural tasks and functions is imperative. Society and its institutions need to help the artists create, be they in the tribes, in the regions, in the cities, or in the centers. This act in itself is an act of building social relationships and rituals, centers of convictions, of poetry, of dance. If it's any consolation, support for the arts gives new meaning to the act of governing, the value of which will be documented in history.

Notes

1. "Masks of the Filipino," *National Midweek*, June 7, 1989, 19-22.

2. Moving is one mode of expression that perpetually projects into the future. A step forward is both a pose and a fall from balance to imbalance; it has the look of equipoise because of the energy or life of a push forward, which leads to a suspended movement of imbalance and which has to be directed forward or aimed toward a goal: a projection of the self beyond the moving body. I tell my dance class, "Your soul is out there," perhaps in the same way that astral projection is done in the psychic sphere. Thus, the moving-dancer ever aspires for the visual and virtual future. As a dance is never exactly the same when danced by another body or in another time, the very moving presence of a dancer is an arc between past and future; it is only possible and visible from the balance of what was to the balance of what's to be. As a symbol, the dance exemplifies this past-present-future of life and of a culture.

3. See my paper for the National Conference on the Arts of the Presidential Commission on Culture and the Arts, May 1989, National Arts Center, Makiling: "The Ever-Threatened Art of the Dance, or the Move into the 21st Century."

4. Greil Marcus, "History Outside of History," *Harper's Magazine*, December 1988 (Vol. 277, no. 1663), pp. 21-24.

5. See note 2.

6. There is a concerned sector in popular entertainment that has for a while been reexamining its conscience. It is a minority beside the business of cultural dancers or singers which has long been dominated by the export-industry/contract-worker mentality.

Some members of the board of auditioners, with the most lenient of hearts, do their best to help out by creating criteria and setting it out four to five times a week from four to five hours. This is to flush out the adequate and potentially adequate from the very inadequate. And they do get death threats when slightly strict. The "best advice" is to let everyone pass; for the ready dollars waiting at the doorstep, even if the poor "dancer" can't dance.

The government has set up a process through which talents may be accredited based on whether they can actually sing or dance. Otherwise, without the "blue-card" they can't travel. But out there in Japanese "new" geisha culture, for example, "the girls" are expected to entertain in the Japanese cultural way: through singing or dancing, as well as to dance with, sip drinks, and sit with the clients. When the function becomes mainly the latter, this is a mockery of what the auditioners try to do because much of what will and does happen has nothing to do with the talents' competence as singers or dancers. But the new Japanese bargirl culture—which we

Filipinos wish to serve for the yen or dollar to send back home to a sick father or mother, an unemployed sister or brother or child—can't make a distinction between those who sit and those who sing and dance. To the Japanese, they are all entertainers. Ask Prime Minister Uno.

The aforementioned entertainment sector with a conscience has presented a graphic history of the kind of entertainment we have sent to Southeast Asia and elsewhere in the past. During the time of veterans like Katy de la Cruz and Pilita Corrales, artists had to have done the ropes. But the idea of an artist has changed drastically in the past thirty years. First, they are the super or ever-new movie and TV stars who marry, separate, and re-marry, living in and out of relationships. Expectedly affluent or at least glamorous, these are the lives the media wastes its space and airtime on. The sponsors will pay for the scandalous; in fact in our culture, the scandalous gets results. The Japanese themselves picked up the "see-through" shows we devised in the 1960s and 1970s, and these conveniently fitted into their new entertainment culture.

The media loves gossip and intrigue in entertainment and politics, and with so much noise one has to make a scene or create an exposé to be heard. Bureaucrats have to be propositioned by way of letters to the editor, radio calls, or TV shows for them to act on age-old pleas or emergencies. Cabinet and congressional members are perennially busy posturing in their own halls, rallies, cocktails, and TV talk shows. They are mostly adept showmen, jugglers (of their alliances), and charlatans. With the Middle Eastern and Japanese macho complexes abroad, it is easy to fall into this kind of showmanship, high or low, in entertainment or into prostitution, or in government by bribery.

In defense, the legitimate artists in popular entertainment are concerned and are terrified. This profligacy, cheapness, and meanness (playing it out with the Yakuza, for one) can easily lead to the self-destruction of the business in due course. There are many more competing entertainers who never pass the auditions but still go as language students, fiancées or brides, or LAs ("look-alikes"), and are therefore illegal and easily trapped into compromising situations. Already, Yugoslavia is threatening to bar Filipino "pilgrims" to Medjugorje who jump off in Italy to become maids. (This was written before the political and racial break up there.)

Our idea of success has been pegged to the dollar, to either having studied or worked aboard, and to coming home as a balikbayan (a *bayani* for being "stateside" or with dollar or yen) with the radio, stereo, video, and what-have-you. Our idea of art has been brought so low to the depths from which theater-artists of the past have had to extricate themselves through history.

Our media comparatively devotes little time and space for the more serious but no less enjoyable arts and less scandalous artists. If they do, many do nothing but name-drop. On the other hand, the government can build a whole edifice and office to serve the "entertainment industry" (a manpower bureau), particularly for export.

The government respects and is beholden to this export industry that supports the economy, brings in the dollars, provides employment, and then simply ignores the moral risk our men and women take to serve the industry. The ignorant *provincianos* are the easiest victims. In the end, it is who and what brings in the money—the solvency—that counts.

The alternative to making good and proper art (and I do not mean moral art) is doing art for the cause of jobs, the cause of tourism, the cause of education, the cause of happiness—all virtually ignored or afforded a tokenism in cultural support.

7. I believe that dance never stays exactly the same because bodies change and occasions are refashioned. However, as much as we wish to keep the past "authentic," the conditions of our lives change. Even bodies change generally, and even size and casting determine the style or manner of movement. But as long as people dance—held fast by a living tradition and doing well in the present occasions—the dance is an authentic expression. Often enough, though, the conditions are changed by forces that subvert the independence of the society, economy, or imagination. This is where the inauthentic expression comes in, and where the betrayal becomes a dirge for anthropologists and historians, and for the very people who made the dance.

8. Martha Graham says that "The past is not dead; it is not even past. People live on inner time; the moment in which a decisive thought or feeling takes place may be any time. Timeless feelings are common to all of us." From "Frontier of the Mind: Martha Graham at 95," interview by Marian Horosko. *Dance Magazine*, May 1989, pp. 50-57.

Graham sculptor set-designer Isamu Noguchi also spoke of "timeless time" in dance on stage. "Frontier of Design: Isamu Noguchi, 1904-1988," Martha Ullman West, *Dance Magazine*, May 1989, pp. 58-60.

Stage/State-Managing: Ethnicity and Identity in Dance

In 1958, the Bayanihan Philippine (now National) Dance Company scored a singular success at the Brussels Universal Exposition. Fairly new (as a Philippine Women's University group) after being a neophyte in international festivals in Pakistan and Japan, the success in Europe brought the Bayanihan to the United States, where they conquered even national television and Broadway. Today, this success continues, albeit for some groups, it goes unnoticed or undocumented. While there were other folk dance groups during its time like the Baranggay at the Philippine Normal College (now University), it was the Far Eastern University Folk Dance Troupe that also fired up audiences abroad, particularly in France's Theatre des Nations in 1957, and in Spain where they won top prizes in Mallorca and Caceres. My own first experiences of these two famous groups were in their series of homecoming performances in Bacolod City, Negros Occidental.

In my career as dance writer, I have witnessed the rising and waning of many other Philippine folk dance groups. Were these groups solely determined by artistic production? What is theatrically artistic about folk dancing? Were there other cultural factors that somehow decided the fate of folk dance groups, including the late Filipinescas Dance Company of the National Artist Leonor Orosa Goquingco, and the many other school and office-based troupes that flourished in the 1960s regionally and nationally? What were the economic and political contexts of these groups, their creation, and their survival? More importantly, what relationship did these groups have in relation to the cultural policies of the state?

The Rise and Fall of Dances in the Philippines

David Maybury-Lewis of The Millennium TV series on ethnic culture distinguishes between state and nation. Referring to the rise of nationalism, he says that a nation is a people, so that a state may in fact host nations. Focusing on the ethnic (which he still proudly calls the tribal) cultures, Mabury-Lewis asserts that many tribes—especially those marginalized, like in his own American (USA, Canada, and the South) continent—are discriminated against if not ignored outright by the hegemonic state which represents the majority of voices and implementations.* He also argues for the federal scheme exemplified by the Iroquois Indians (of various groupings) who formed it in 1771. But the political power of the White Americans ultimately ignored their presence and argument, and even negated whatever agreements were forged between the Iroquois federation and the dominant white majority in the United States.

At home, Philippine folk dances were threatened by the influx of foreign ones during the American period (1898-1945). Some of these dances were not of the white Americans, but were social dances from the Caribbean and South America including those from the black communities. To generalize about these dances as coming from white America is to simplify their origin. Alerted by the threat of losing our folk dances, National Artist Francisca Reyes Aquino (earlier Tolentino) braved the hardship and danger of the hinterlands to record hundreds of dances, including those Spanish-derived, to her dying day. Scholarship of this kind was done earlier by missionaries, later teachers, even officials, of both Spain and the United States with their own agenda—to convert, to conquer, to fulfill McKinley's doctrine of Manifest Destiny. Still, this type of scholarship exemplifies the zeal that had, in their own estimation, the welfare of the peoples of the Philippines in mind.

This kind of zeal for scholarship was what Dean Worcester had. His anthropological interest was exemplified in the "benevolent exercise"

* Jonathan Ree's book on the deaf and the dumb and their language, *I See a Voice*, also mentions the claim of the deaf and dumb community as a nation.

that was demonstrated by the St. Louis World's Fair in 1904. Familiar as we are with the procedure and result of this exercise, I will not dwell on the exhibition out in a northern environment. (Playwright Floy Quintos has already written a play, *St. Louis Loves Dem Filipinos*, which tackles the sad experiences of the Filipino tribes in and after the fair.)

But are Filipinos in the metropolis portrayed any better? I come to the representation of the Filipinos in the metropolis in contemporary dance theater, including its manifestation in ballet and modern dance. According to Joann Kealiinohomoku, ballet is a kind of folkloric expression of our time. The most popular dance among audiences, ballet finds its roots in the court of France (styled after the spectacles of Italy), which integrated the courtly ethics and behavior of the period. This is still evident in the ballet steps that were drawn from rustic practice but as with *danse d'ecole* have been refined. Now, strictly codified, dance steps have been modified by migrations from country to country, masters to masters, dancers to dancers. Its own subjects shifted from the Olympian personifications to the folkloric spirits that inspired Romanticism, from the hegemonic classicism of the French Marius Petipa in the court of Russia to today's pluralism in many urban centers.

Modern dance, on the other hand, rebelled against the strictures of classical ballet into a new technical and expressive medium, and revealed itself as something that is representative of the middle class and its economic and aesthetic values. Having grown out of the spectacle and vulgarities of the popular vaudeville in the 1960s, its techniques and aesthetics were undermined by more proletarian sentiments in urban Manhattan where artists lived at an economic disadvantage to many migrant of different origins. Earlier, in the Depression of the 1930s, a leftist orientation in dance emerged, long presaged by Isadora Duncan herself who sympathized with Russia and even married a Russian poet, Ysenin.

The Philippine experience of modern dance came from Europe in the *Ausdrukstanz* expressionism style. After World War II, with intimations of the orientalism of the Denishawn that visited in 1926, the American branch came to dominate the scene with studies of Filipinos in the United States and the visits of American choreographers to Ballet

Philippines of the CCP. Using essentially the same acquired techniques, Philippine modern dance carved its own Filipino identity through themes (folkloric and historical, iconic and musical), steps and gestures, and syncretic accommodation of modern and postmodern formulations, plus some influences from Asian styles.

As with other parts of the world, ballet in the Philippines catered to the taste of the upper and middle classes, partly because of its clean and elegant classical aesthetics, codified into a teachable academic setting. Ballet schools proliferated and impresarios for local and foreign groups convinced the public of the hegemonic ascendancy of classical dance or ballet. This is why despite the fact that modern dance merged and mixed easily with folk styles, the works of the Austrians Kaethe Hauser and Trudl Dubsky (mostly pre-World War II), Manolo Rosado and Rosalia Merino Santos disappeared from the scene.

In 1969, Alice Reyes came back from scholarships in the United States—and at exactly the right time! Reyes had a Bayanihan background, and with the Bayanihan's musical director then sitting as artistic director of the CCP, she launched the Alice Reyes and Modern Dance Company there in 1970. Earlier groups that aspired to reside in the center, like Hariraya Ballet (first called Hariraya Dance Company) and Dance Theatre Philippines, lost out to Reyes, and these groups' contributions to the inaugural and 1970 seasons of the CCP did not gain them any more favors. In the mid-1970s, meanwhile, the Folk Arts Theater with Teodoro Hilado accommodated the short-lived Ballet Federation of the Philippines.

With the call for reforms after the EDSA Revolution of 1986, dance groups outside of the CCPDC or Ballet Philippines asked for concessions from the center. What happened was that they were made to merge into Philippine Ballet Theatre—which they said was an expediency, partly because lack of funding. The two oldest groups from 1968 therefore diverted efforts. Dance Theatre continued its existence even after it lost its Ballet at the (Rizal) Park aid from the National Parks Development Committee. Briefly helped by the University of the Philippines, it consequently closed shop altogether.

In folk dance and in the late nineties, the Bayanihan was legislated into a national dance company. The CCP itself gave a small subsidy and periodic performances for the Ramon Obusan Folkloric Group.

Representing "Us"

Despite all these groups that exist, the Bayanihan National Dance Company and Ballet Philippines (BP) are still the two most favored. Because of their prestige and the belief that they will better project the Philippines abroad, these two groups have also had more frequent access to travel grants. BP refers to itself as the flagship company—and true enough, only BP and the Bayanihan are sent to most festivals abroad. They mostly fill even ASEAN projects and affairs, and create the image of the so-called Filipino identity in folklore and dance theater, nationally and internationally. The question here is simple: is that representation of Filipino identity and nationality only true and real as created by these companies?

Does the Bayanihan's (and all other folk dance groups') panoramic format and representational staging of the folk arts exemplify our regions? Are the lfugao or Maranaw allowed their opinion or voice about an exhibition of their dances in Manila and abroad? In this day and age, should there not be a much more actual and intensive representation of our ethnic folk dances, like how the Balinese or Javanese in Indonesia have always done it?

For more than half a century, since the days of the UP Folk Song and Dance Club and the post-war Filipiniana of Francisca Reyes Aquino, we have perpetuated our folk expressions as anthology, giving superficial "glimpses" of various dances such as what the first compendium title of the Bayanihan in Brussels did, and limiting the appreciation of those dances' styles and essence, in the form of suites and spectacles. Where and how do the citified personnel represent the tribes in the repertoire?

I have mentioned the St. Louis World Fair, but there have also been Filipino expositions at the Smithsonian Institute in Washington, DC that use indigenous participants for its folklore projects, about which much has been written. One basic problem of these expositions is the tension between the intent of presenters and the roles and performances of the indigenous participants who are invited to exemplify their culture on fixed time and in the showcase setting.

The NCCA itself courted the dangers of projecting the Filipino's regional diversity in compendium form. In the year 2000, under the chairmanship of Jaime C. Laya, it staged the *Dayaw* showcase in the *Sambayan Festival* at the Rizal Park grounds. The project meant bringing to Manila tribes from North to South, lodging them in hotels, and bringing them to the open-air venue to show their rites, music, dances. and crafts based on the scheduled show time released to the general public.

Wasn't that just a short-term version of the St. Louis World's Fair, this time in our own land? Wasn't it simply a copy of an oppressive colonial experience?

In the end, no matter how good Ballet Philippines is, with the existence of established groups like Philippine Ballet Theatre and Ballet Manila which have both toured abroad, why is it the group that's preeminently entitled to project the Philippine image in creative dance worldwide? And how do these groups function when their prominence has not encouraged the growth and survival of alternative ensembles that are the plural laboratories of experimentation and the enunciators of other views about and voices of dance?

Whose Identity?

On the levels of the municipal and provincial, and on to the national, how are cultural expressions proclaimed as official? How did the old sense of nation as people (and nations as peoples within one country) become what the state now proclaims it to be? How have ethnic expressions survived and changed in the context of a globalized perspective and projection? While these expressions have always been here, how has it changed in light of being utilized to promote national identity-in-diversity? More importantly, how has it survived its change in cause and reason, which in recent times have exploded into political assertion and even warfare?

How has colonization abetted these movements towards integration and divisions thereafter?

Given the situations I have cited thus far, more specific questions need to be asked and answered.

How are the "ethnic representatives" of the country chosen for international venues or presentation? Are the State's selections done through narrow umpiring, in order that the hegemony's chosen image or identity is the one that's projected? In which case, where are the voices of the tribes in this representation? Who is representing them? Where are they when non-tribes end up being the "representatives"?

How enlightening is the "colorful, varied, extensive" and hybridized mix of styles and traditions from within the country itself? Now, how is the growth of art from these grassroots sources opened and pluralized, even in the urban setting, alongside the more supported and protected mainstream groups?

How is the tension between the roles of presenters and participants resolved in exhibitions of ethnic/regional cultures, such as what we see in the "best foot forward" mentality or the "bongga" Wow Philippines! tourist promotions? What happens to an ethnic culture that has been internationalized by tours? How far should cultural curating go in the exhibition of the tribes and regions, which only has as goal impressing an audience in the capital or abroad?

How does the centralization of arts administration consequently marginalize small and less prestigious groups that are outside the circle of prominence that the bigger groups belong to? Isn't this proof of how the Filipino concept of comradeship in difference doesn't always produce the spirit of the bayanihan, and instead can also bring to the fore the compadre or clique mentality?

Is Philippine identity and ethnicity in dance today truly comprehensive and integrative of our dance practice, even when seen abroad?

When the St. Louis World's Fair came to be in 1904, the United States projected its sweeping potency by displaying a variety of conquered identities and ethnicities. That variety or diversity perhaps proved America's benevolence towards the so-called primitives. But that was both an ethnographic and political display, perhaps proving the United States's manifest will dated 1898.

In the end, it is these last questions that need urgent answers. Is the colonizer's orientation being imitated by the colonized? As a child of that hegemonic will to improve our image to the rest world, have we fallen into the colonizer's space? Is the image of the Philippines just that which is being perpetuated by the State, given all its biases and hegemonic practices? Or is the State being truthful to the realities and instrumentalities of culture?

Kolkata
2004/2005

Creativity in the Face of Globalization: The Best Defense Is Difference

What will we dig up about our culture several hundred years from now? Accustomed as we are to the idea of historical artifacts, we will most probably say pottery and jewelry, furniture and high-rise buildings. We will say that we are as advanced in culture as the rest of the world. But we forget what Claire Dane has said: there will be bodies without heads, hands, and legs as representations of what Filipino culture is. Hopefully though, there will be busts, books, and computer discs to show we had our heads on our shoulders. The question now is, where will our hands and legs be? Without these, how do we prove that we had our dances?

Too often, education pertains to what goes into our heads, and not to the rest of the body. When we set up archives, we think of pots and pans and not of the perishable necessities like clothes that keep our bodies warm. Clothes also dictate our positions and movements, and if it isn't seen as something that's important enough to document, what more gestures and steps that disappear the moment they are done?

Where is dance in our archives? How do we preserve dance?

Sadly, this isn't being problematized at all. We live in our bodies and move around in it, but our intellectual institutions forget the joyful and painful, or just the daily experiences that our bodies allow us. We neglect dance as a mode of cognition and recognition, as a manifestation of a person's mental state and spiritual expression. We often omit this art form in our books on philosophy and psychology. (This is reminiscent of Foucault and his assertions that we talk about sexuality medically and morally in order to escape confronting it phenomenologically.)

Where has dance gone? It is only being dance now—a futureless action. Even film cannot capture this physical phenomenon; all it can do is recapture it. How then do we come to understand dance? Only by watching and/or doing, after which it is gone.

What makes up dance? The body, of course, and by what course the body takes through time and within space. Dance is made up by the body's rhythmic flow, its accents, its starts and stops. It is created by its adornments, through make up, costumes, and music, by the story that's being told, and the mood that's being made. We need thought and residual feelings for dance to be created. Imagistic, temporal, kinesthetic, phenomenological thoughts, along with thematic and referential thought.

I would like to limit myself to one thought that needs much processing. One that makes a dance memorable and distinctive. Where did the choreography come from?

Simple enough, it comes from the people. This is what we call folk dance—coming either from play or work, for ritual or socialization. This is the type of dance that can't be detached from their way of life, their social system, and beliefs. These dances are intricately connected to their music and crafts, their history and storytelling.

Yet how often do we simplify these dances in our performances, making of it a show, catering to the wiles and wails of the cosmopolites. I believe that we currently have a crisis in the proliferation of dance troupes that do steps rather than styles and adduce rather than educe a cultural enactment. We stage our dances as if they were set on a Broadway stage, and the whole system of life that the dance represents is changed in the representation. In the end, we do not *inform* but *reform* a cultural expression. The representation then enters the possibility of illegitimacy and becomes a commodification of a way of life.

This is proof that often, cultural appropriation does not empower the people who made the dances. Instead, they are a way to better other peoples' reputations in Manila or abroad. Nothing goes back to the tribal choreographers. Also, as the exigencies of the commercial or festival stage dictate the way a dance will be performed, the dance becomes situated in a new technical environment and its whole context is changed.

But we've been so successful at these dance festivals and commercial dance performances, that since Brussels in 1958 we have not questioned its premises, its effects, the prestige it gives, and its possible directions. In the last Philippine International Dance Festival and Conference, Antony Shay read his paper, "Choreographic Politics: The State Folk Ensemble, Representation and Power" and raised questions about the success of what has been considered the exemplary staging of the Moiseyev Russian Folk Company. The latter company has been copies by many, the way our Bayanihan Dance Company has a Mexican version. But often, all these folk dance groups do, particular those of ours, is present a cornucopia of rituals and swift suites of socials. It is for this reason that the dances of the people have become indistinguishable and have ceased to be a source of knowledge. Instead, it is all about entertainment. Success can indeed blind us to the original causes we fought for. And it can go to our heads, enough for us to practice choreographic over-intention. Personally, I have been delighted by this success, but in light of anthropological studies, I feel guilty about this happiness.

Another type of dance that begs discussion in light of archival work is that which is meant for the theater. Here, creation is dependent on the individual artist who may draw from his or her racial and social context. Often enough, at the core of theatrical dance is our colonial experience, and not our local courtly tradition (of which we don't have much). We have the ballet, modern dance, and jazz, not to mention the vaudeville, musicals, and operas.

In theatrical dance, originality has not been wanting. There have been the likes of Leonor Orosa Goquingco and her body of work which culminated in *Filipinescas: Philippine Life, Legend and Lore in Dance*, the Dance Theatre Philippines days of Borromeo, Radaic, Elejar, and company, Ballet Philippines from Alice Reyes to today, and a number of school-based groups or presentations. Today we are experiencing a second wave of choreographers who are more strongly steeped in their cultural roots. (I don't use here the term "national" roots, as this is often questionable because it is possibly tied to a political agenda such as what has been happening in the ASEAN conglomerations.) Choreographers and dancers

Agnes Locsin and Denisa Reyes have gone beyond the superficial putting on of ethnic guise and gestures that prevailed in former times.

We can't always blame the earlier choreographers for their lack of originality. Access to travel, research centers, etc., has not always been available or comprehensive. Up to the 1970s and 1980s, it was easier to listen to Tchaikovsky than to Kasilag, or to Messaien than to Maceda. The accessibility of things Western, along with the dearth of materials on and lack of experience in an Asian environment, posed the danger of technical and choreographic uniformity at that time, something that was even called in the West as supermarket choreography.

The present combination of what's Western and what's Filipino has both positive and negative sides. On the one hand, dancing is a very peripatetic profession, allowing dancers to move abroad and find better-paying jobs. Elsewhere, roles can be fashionably Asian; for a time, there was the various stagings of *Madame Butterfly*, as there are now for *Miss Saigon* (preceded by *Lakme*, *Kismet*, *King and I*, *Flower Drum Song*, etc.). These have made us proud of our Maniya Barredo, Anna Villadolid, and Lea Salonga (earlier, Cely Carillo, Maureen Tiongco, Evelyn Mandac, not to speak of our older opera divas). And while not as celebrated, there are the Filipino singers and dancers in Japan who prop up our economy by bringing home the yen to help stabilize the peso.

Sadly, these much-praised opportunities take our artists away from the country and their artistic contributions are used to gain international prestige rather than be a testament of local productivity. In compositional terms, ballets can begin to look the same—homogenized in technique, style, and perspective. Keeping up with the Joneses is the accepted term for the need to gain "world-class" adulation for one's talent. Versatility is most prized as simply dexterity in juggling idioms. We end up wowing other countries without really creating a name for the Philippines as a distinct culture.

In this age of globalization where almost everything becomes merchandise, there is a great need to preserve our identity in dance. And the best way to do this is to insist on difference. What makes a Filipino work "Filipino" is that which is uniquely ours, whether in folkloric or theatrical terms. This insistence is tied to the system—the choreographers, the dancers, and the economy—that rules them. How much are they guarded and provided for so that they may insist on creating what they want?

Obviously, the lure of dollars from abroad has robbed us of even our serious dancers who have turned to the japayuki category and the japayuki type of presentation they must conform to. Even the training that's provided them is such that they are not qualified for a future as a professional performer that will gain them the respect and remuneration they deserve elsewhere and at home. This is why it's surprising that we easily claim that Manila is—or we aim to make Manila—the cultural capital of Asia, when in fact our training and creative practices have lagged behind. What we think of as "advanced" have been with us since in the 1950s and 1960s.

Of course there have been efforts that promote non-Western forms and aspects in performance. There are organizations like the Asia Society, which now insists on sponsoring "authentic" presentations (sometimes down to the costume materials). Postmodern site-specific productions that are often staged abroad which are in fact the background of our traditional art making are also being done now. There are choreographers like Merce Cunningham and Robert Wilson who have adopted the oriental sense of time in their presentations, from the simple simultaneity of movement and music to the hours-long performances in Brooklyn. And then there are those young artists who have demolished and deconstructed old forms to revitalize and review them.

The sad thing is, in the end, we still prioritize the need to fit into the Western stage and its production values because we would like to be certain of selling ourselves. How often have we heard artists talk as if they are dealing with the IMF or World Bank, about foreign investment and the "racket" of simultaneously earning from several assignments? How come we believe that it is truly the economists who run our lives and sell our creations? This belief is pervasive enough, for one autistic scientist (in Oliver Sacks' *An Anthropology on Mars*, 1995) to insist that our world be mainly carried out by the creative sector and geniuses; otherwise "the whole world would be taken over by the accountants." The fact is, we end up succumbing to the more general and global forms of expression because we *find the need to*, even at the risk of losing our difference—our currency for identification and recognition.

I have three final points to make about Philippine dance in the context of globalization. First, after nearly seventy years since Francisca Reyes Aquino started her dance research in UP, the systematic documentation of our ethnic or folk dance has not been perceptively broadened, with the exceptions of Ramon Obusan and Ligaya Fernando Amilbangsa. Despite the advancements in technical assistance for sound and visual recordings, analysis has not been taken advantage of. There are remarkable experts in research in Obusan and Amilbangsa, but they are not being systematically assisted; they are not even in the academe. Notice too, how UP does not have a folk arts center (whereas PWU established one in the '50s), and how our UP Filipiniana group does not have a fixed research component.

Second, whereas our creative output in choreography has been striking, our exploration of dance technique has mostly been tied to importations and foreign influences. Proof of this is our lack of local technical equivalents to the various dance vocabularies and theories that exist: from the philosophical (like Humphrey's fall and recovery that traces the so-called arc between two deaths, or Asiatic posture and composure in Cunningham's creative processes and productions) to the psychological (like Graham's contraction and release as muscular and emotional states of being), and the ethnic-styled vocabulary (like Jack Cole's techniques and choreography). There's the breadth of release technique, the therapy of somatic rehabilitation, the agility of martial methods (which are also mental orientations), the systems of Feldenkrais, Alexander, Bartenieff, Ideokinesis, Rolfing, Pilates, etc., which have largely only been applied abroad. Asian martial arts and yoga have not been integrated into our local dance training, although Steven Patrick Fernandez is that lone horse in having started with the use of the *pangalay* as a training system for the Integrated Performing Arts Guild in Iligan. Our teaching of dance has not brought any particular method about—perhaps out of subservience to colonial mentality.*

Lastly, our sociology of dance has, for the most part, been historical. We do not discuss dance in terms of politics and economics, nor in terms of class, race (the Chinese aspects in dance for example), gender, projection, reception, commodity, etc., because of our conciliatory nature. We have refused to confront issues of legitimacy, equity, and culpability in our cultural leadership (look at how easily we succumbed to Imelda, for example). We have conveniently ignored the injustices—artistic, economic, and otherwise—in our cultural activities.

All of these point to one very simple question: notwithstanding the great reputation we've created for ourselves in dance and other cultural forms, are we really and honestly dancing our dance?

* The 1998 emergence of a Philippine ballet syllabus proves that we are beginning to think concretely of dance from show to science; this was spearheaded by Felicitas Layag Radaic, Vella Damian, and Noordin Jumalon.

How Is Dance

Moving into the Twenty-First Century: The Ever-Threatened Art of the Dance

The eyes have lost the ability to measure themselves in the mirror of the past.

—Walter Sorell, *Looking Back in Wonder*

What the scientists have learned is that every event is unique; its own occurrence distinguishes it from all other events. For that reason, each event not only claims a place all its own in the world but cannot be said to share an objective reality with any other phenomenon. Its subjective occurrence, in turn, is not the result of a particular initial set of conditions. Rather, it owes its occurrence to the entire labyrinth of all past subjective occurrences whose collective configuration gave rise to its own particular unfolding.

—Entropy, A New World View
Jerry Rifkin with Ted Howard

La danse, madame, c'est une question morale. (The dance, madam, is a moral question.)

—George Balanchine

Dance only has the present. Strictly, it has no past or future. It is only in the now. Everything else was or will be another dance.

Dance is a verb more than a noun. Its essence is performance, as ephemeral as a whiff of a scent or the taste of something sweet or salty. Everything else about dance is recollection, an evocation of what was, or an idealization of what will be. The reality of dance is always fleeting, and no film or act of notation can capture its every dimension, its dynamics or virtuality (Langer). Dance can't be cupped in a hand, can't be stilled by an eye, and can't be captured in the mind. Dance can only be done by the act of dancing. "You can't sit down and think about dancing, you have to get up and dance," said Balanchine. He continued, "I am not interested in later on. I don't have any later on. We all live in the same time forever."

Thus, it is always academic, apologetic, or adulatory to speak about dance. Even to speak about its present is temporal, as this present is always threatened by one of its essential elements—time. Today's step will be yesterday's achievement. A dancer's career is only as good as his or her persistent presence. Tomorrow there will be new Noverres, Fokines and Isadoras, or de Oteyzas and Orosas to upset or even offset today's good work. Unlike the other more permanent arts, dance can't truly be viewed in perspective because this perspective always changes. Dance is different from every seat it is viewed from; and it can't strictly be evaluated or remembered.

Unlike most arts, dance suffers as the fashions of the times change. For example, Fokine's explosive and revolutionary orientalia like *Scheherazade*, *Coq d'Or*, or *Firebird* looks dated today. How are we to speak of their values and effects as conditioned by the abstractions of Balanchine and the revived classicism of Petipa today? Agnes de Mille's historic Americana in *Rodeo* (or *Carousel* and *Oklahoma*) is no longer a triumph to swear by. Yet it remains proof of the existence of American ballet in the face of Russian bias early in the century, the origins that Eugene Loring's *Billy the Kid* and Jerome Robbins' *Fancy Free* enjoy when they are present.

Even the ballet classics are not spared of changes. The Russians flaunt their so-called Petipa classics—about six survive out of some sixty masterpieces—when in fact these have mostly been Sovietized as technical feats and war horses with which to wow the people. The Frenchman-in-St.Petersburg held the fort for fifty years in virtual dictatorship as ballet master, but a power struggle finally banned him from going backstage. An awkward tribute to him meant laurels offered at the wings and not before the public's eyes. Today though he has once again become the master.

What about our own classics? How meaningful are Anita Kane's *Maria Makiling* (1939) and Leonor Orosa's *Noli Dance Suite* (1956) to those of us in the present? Even *Itim Asu* by Alice Reyes, which was staged more recently and was hailed as a landmark by Alfredo Roces in 1970, is underappreciated and not written about now. Today, I would rank Reyes's *Amada* higher (a reworked graduation piece from the Sarah Lawrence days but with new music by Lucrecia Kasilag), while many more are of lesser stature (not to say that they are less beautiful), including my own favorite *Bungkos Suite* and the new and relevant *Mga Babae*. Ironically, this modern dance choreographer now has more revived works in the ballet mold.[1]

Judging dance is a risky business. When people like me attempt to do it, we risk perjury. But I would rather write than be silent. Besides this is a risk that critics and historians have to take. Otherwise the dances will just disappear, undocumented as a record of social history or as history reflected in dance. Today's newspapers, conditioned as these are by advertising space, political verbosity, or some other more persuasive influence, can't even do plain and simple cataloguing. Then there is the irresponsible criticism that's created by bias (which can still prove invaluable when checked for consistencies/inconsistencies, e.g., John Martin who was initially against Balanchine), narrow coverage (for Metro Manila or *pang*-CCP *lang*), or of having the wrong seat in the house.

What is a pressing concern now is to have comprehensive information on the dances of today, both in the center and the fringes. We need a ballet or dance archive to document not only the dancing but also the music and the designs that have been done in the past fifty years of ballet in the country and through the centuries by our ethnic artists. Works need to be documented in photographs, films and writings, including in notation. Critics need to look into the thought processes of choreographers and come out with oral histories or published notebooks (e.g., Graham's and Cunningham's). Choreographers need to be more open to talking about their kinetic art and how they create out of idiosyncrasy or perversity, as against the false sense of mystique about their silent art, or the plain lack of verbal competence.

Much has been done for Philippine dance, both in the folkloric and theatrical fields. Reputations have been built and international accolades have been won by our folk dance troupes. Researches have grown in number, even if not extensive because of lack of funds or lack of expertise. Many cry in despair over the difficulty of rescuing our ethnic dances, but they do not wish to learn the more exact art of movement notation and still depend on verbose or ambiguous words. Folk dances are mainly aimed at public display more than for social expression; the advancements in economy and industry, of politics and media, have eroded the practice and meaning of a rite or a way of life of a people. Even the urban middle classes, who have varied regional roots, easily change under the influence of advanced media technique and content.

Bienvenido F. Nebres has seriously sounded the call to science to be more rational than relational (*Chronicle*, April 3, 1989); the failure to be such in the past has placed our sciences many years behind the rest of the world. At the same time, the art of ballet in China has grown by leaps and bounds in technique, because of a more systematized, organized, and subsidized way of ballet instruction; recently China has even rediscovered two ancient movement notation systems. Our own scholars based in Indonesia have also returned to the Philippines to say that Indonesia has become more accomplished in utilizing its classic and folkloric forms into contemporary expression (in its strictest sense we do not have a classic dance; at most, there's the pangalay and some other southern styles.)

But regardless of these, we are proud of the achievements of the Bayanihan company and its folk arts center, of the Folk Arts Theater and its contribution of folk festivals and workshop programs, of the Folk Dance Society, of the public school system and its inculcation of the folk dance since the time of Francisca Reyes Tolentino (later Aquino), of the different folk dance groups in the universities, of the individual efforts of regional physical education teachers, and of specialists like Ramon Obusan and Ligaya Fernando Amilbangsa whose concern over our folk arts has been life consuming. They are the few heroes who have plugged their fingers into the widening holes of our threatened cultural walls.

This is not to say that all external influences have been bad. We have improved our health and well-being because of it, realized our exploitation because of the worldwide liberation movements, compared and proven our worth in the various national venues of international arts. We have in turn influenced a few political, technological (if not always with our own capital outlay), and cultural fields because of our initiative, intelligence, and inventiveness. Our national efforts are essential to us, but they are also essential to the promotion of peace and progress of mankind. In the field of dance, my criticism teacher Jack Anderson once said that the greater the number and the wider the range of people working creatively, the greater the possibilities for artistic growth.

And that, after all, is what it's all about. Dance and all art are a continuum, something that never stops growing and changing, something that comes from inside and out, something that will either flourish or die, depending on the air it has to breathe. This is why as an artist, one has to be aware not only of one's field and region but also of the varying political and social forces of the East and West.[2] That is also why I truly believe that new music must be heard, and that with new Filipino music the originality and significance of Philippine choreography will be achieved.

But our annual dance commissions have had such a bad record in the past twenty years. Why is this? How many original ballets with original Filipino music have survived, and who determines their survival? Is it right to ask whose works are perpetuated? And who failed to do their homework—composer or choreographer or designer—as with disappointing productions such as *Mir-i-nisa* and *Gabriela*?

I raise these questions because I am most concerned with choreographers at this point. They design the image and create the impact of Philippine ballet or modern dance. Often enough, our society and media would rather focus on the star dancers who revel in foreign classics, at the expense of the choreographers who create these dances. The latter is behind the scenes, but they are the ones who create Philippine dance iconography and echo the pulse and spirit of the times. Serious choreographers are paid very little—even less than star-dancers—and they are so few to demand better pay.

The choreographic gift belongs only to a few dancers, and in the Philippines, these few ones have to preserve dance in the task of choreography despite the lack of time and space, the lack of materials like danceable libretto and Philippine music, and in the face of the little funding for new ballets. Especially when a choreographer is young, he has to ask that he be given time for his rehearsals and he be given talents for his cast. He may have to cope with the ego of soloists and designers, or with undisciplined fresh talents with whom he often has to put up just so he can start his career.

Choreographers have to be dancers, training for which takes some five to ten years, before they can properly study the craft of choreography in compositional workshops. Very few schools, if at all, teach the rudiments of choreography—studies that focus on the elements of dance and their manipulation, and not on poses and steps. Choreographers have to prove themselves to their well-known predecessors, who hog positions, programs, and press releases. They have to live on so little, or compromise by dancing with Vilma or Alma. It is no wonder that so few survive. Choreographers are an ever-threatened lot.

But then there are even less critics who will take time to present an objective picture of the world of dance, or who would take time out to see or write about a choreographer from Bohol or Butuan. Critics, too, are paid measly sums. Even out there in the provinces they do not exactly encourage local talents, and they'd rather have a "named" dancer for their shows in the same way that we insure a full house in Metro Manila by importing a foreign star or an acclaimed balikbayan.[3]

I had written about this problem of lost works by our local choreographers in 1977 for the Ballet Federation of the Philippines annual. I argued then, as I do now, "For a Live Archive," and following is an extensive quote from that paper:

> Where are the ballets of Trudl Dubsky, Totoy de Oteyza, and Anita M. Kane? We are giving awards this year to Dubsky and Manolo Rosado, but how truly can the younger dancers appreciate the older dancers' contributions? With the closing show of Filipinescas Dance Company, Leonor Orosa Goquingco's *Life, Legend and Lore* can no longer be seen. Even recent works like Eddie Elejar's *Gates of Hell*, Julie Borromeo's *Zagalas de Manila*, and Basilio's *The Rebels* are no longer available after the old DTP's demise.

This is so because ballets' lives are tied with the companies that produced them and with the respective director's artistic taste. Within this system, companies become guardians of national art treasures—our classics—and of artistic tastes (the choreographies encouraged) that make up a country's tradition of dance theater. Because of the obsessive vision of Ninette de Valois and the choreographic gifts of Frederick Ashton, the English Ballet evolved out of the Russian roots provided by Petipa and Diaghilev. Because of Lincoln Kirstein and George Balanchine's insistence (through the New York City Ballet and its antecedents) there came to be an identifiable class of American dancers, even while "folklorists" as Agnes de Mille and Eugene Loring were doing their American ballets.

The problem of preserving ballets in the Philippines is complicated by other factors. One is the public demand for novelty—a taste set by Diaghilev and a very strong Filipino trait. It is often heard that people have seen enough of the CCP Dance Company doing mostly the same things. But that is how a repertory is preserved. Dancers, too, may complain out of boredom, but if they realize what service they are doing for the future, they might value more each repetition. However, this places a responsibility in the hands of the director to shift ballets around so that each repetition could be approached with a fresh outlook.

How many of our dancers today know the names in Philippine ballet and modern dance that I've mentioned above? I myself have not seen Goquingco's *Noli Dance Suite*. Some dancers have never heard of Pacita Madrigal and Benny Villanueva (Reyes) who were our first Giselle and Albrecht, much less of Elisa Robles who was our first Maria Makiling. Not even perhaps of Mary Anne Garcia and Nini Gener who were our first Mir-i-nisa. Some have not seen Tina Santos's or Ester Rimpos's performances even if these were not long ago; nor have many seen the founders of present companies like Inday Gaston Mañosa, Julie Borromeo, Tita Radaic, and Alice Reyes. No ballet of Elejar or Fabella exists in the Ballet Philippines repertory.

After seven years as artistic director and two to three years as ballet master for Dance Theatre Philippines, I recently noted in DTP's *Mir-i-nisa* souvenir program more than forty of my works. But I doubt whether five percent of that will survive.

Who and what are the significant names and titles in Philippine dance today and yesterday? With many misses and a restriction in time and in coverage, I attempted a checklist survey. This still lacks validity, but here is the result distributed to sixteen from the CCP Summer Dance Workshop, UP College of Music dance majors, and the company of Philippine Ballet Theater.

Those who scored 15 and up are: Ballet Philippines, CCP Summer Dance Workshop (when the questionnaire was administered), Nonoy Froilan, Agnes Locsin, Lisa Macuja, Alice Reyes, and Edna Vida.

These scored 10 and up: Ballet Federation of the Philippines, Maniya Barredo, Basilio, Bayanihan Philippine Dance Company, Julie Borromeo, *Camille* ballet, Dance Theatre Philippines, Sonia Domingo, Eddie Elejar, Tony Fabella, Filipiniana Dance Company of UP, Inday Gaston Mañosa, Hariraya Dance/Ballet Company, Hotlegs, Corazon Generoso Iñigo, Nes Jardin, Noordin Jumalon, Lucrecia Kasilag, *Limang Dipa* ballet, Manila Metropolis Ballet, Metropolitan Dance Theatre, Brando Miranda, Manuel Molina, *Mosque Baroque* ballet, Douglas Nierras, Nicolas Pacaña, *Pas de Quatre*, Luther Perez, Power dance, Tita Radaic, Denisa Reyes, Hazel Sabas, Tina Santos, Cecile Sicangco, Anna Villadolid, Steve Villaruz, Norman Walker, Margot Fonteyn, Natalia Makarova, Fred Astaire, Anna Pavlova, Rodolf Nureyev, and Alvin Ailey American Dance Theater.

Among those that didn't even scored a point are: Ligaya Fernando Amilbangsa, Paz Cielo Belmonte, Elizabeth Guash, Kaethe Hauser, Alfredo Lozano, Cristina Matias (a Miss Philippines, too), Cesar Mendoza, Greta Monserrat, *Noli Dance Suite*, Phlippine Revue—Las Vegas, *Seven-and-a-Half* ballet, *Siklo* ballet, Maureen Tiongco, *Young Person's Pleasure* ballet, Trudl Dubsky Zipper, and Rafael Zulueta, along with many many others.

In her book *State of War*, Ninotchka Rosca emphasized that we are a country of beginnings. We always tear down the achievements of those ahead of us, or those ahead eat up their children. We are slow to give recognition (National Artists are all very old) to the young ones due to the shadows of the Titans. I know of one choreographer who condemns those who closely follows her footsteps, accusing them of copying, which, after all, is a high form of flattery.[4] We don't allow others to continue our work or companies in the way that those who follow may wish to run things or reveal themselves to be worthy of taking on that position. We tie them to our apron strings. What we lack is trust.

But companies can only live on and survive by being open to change and by being independent from their founders. Moving into the twenty-first century means keeping a clear and concrete memory of our beginnings through the preservation of our small and more scaled classics, and in keeping alive our racial or folkloric memories. But we need to move on the way dancing always does. This also means we must cope with changes in time, space, and dynamics.

But what time and space can we work with? The traffic is always heavy, inter-island transportation is decrepit or disastrous, diplomatic and political moves are tardy, foreign loans are fought for but are left unallocated or misspent, ecological and anthropological concerns are reactive rather than active. In the field of culture, research is lagging behind in both expertise and funding; recognition too, is late and even reviews of performances happen long after a show has closed.[5]

Way back in 1976, an article of mine, "State of Philippine Dance Today," was published in New York. I started with martial law and the shutting down of newspapers at a time when *Sunday Times Magazine* had Tina Santos on its cover. Since then I've written on the state of Philippine dance many times, for conferences and publications (including an entry in the *Oxford Concise Dictionary of the Ballet*). Frankly, I was a bit peeved at the subject assigned me for this conference. I confessed to Ramon Obusan that if at this point people still don't know what the state of Philippine dance is today, they certainly didn't care then and don't care now. This is like repeating oneself again and again; it's like boring oneself.

But like the ballet repertory I harped about earlier, I conceded by fulfilling my assignment. This time, I am not keeping to factual enumeration and instead have raised some concerns. Perhaps like my inability to keep up with developments in the other arts, you haven't been able to keep in step with the advances in Philippine dance.

I've mentioned some of the grave concerns I have, especially about the survival of our own folk dances and classics, and I've pointed a finger at narrow-minded leadership in dance. But the young ones are equally to blame, as they are not always brave enough to take up the cudgels for better leadership and are not as single-minded in their devotion to dance—as both a business and as an art—as the now older ones were during their youth.

How many of you saw a folk dance performance or a ballet in 1988? Perhaps you still quote Nick Joaquin and Pura Kalaw Ledesma on heroic achievements in Philippine choreography thirty to forty years ago. Many more folkloric troupes and ballet groups have been encouraged to flourish today. Many more young people take up dancing and aim to make it their life and profession.

How many are aware of their dance history and the tradition that has been built for them? How will they balance tradition and change? Many dancers are more concerned about virtuosity or what the superstars do in films than with the integrity of a classic or choreography. As they are excited by the progress of their art, they must also keep their heritage in their hearts:[6]

> They had the manner of trees and the manner of waves
> That accept the wind and the rain,
> Accept the night and the sun,
> And in the midst of change they do not change.
> They were good lads.
>
> George Seferis, from *The Argonauts*

How young were Aquino, Orosa, de Oteyza and Merino when they started researching or producing—without those cultural centers, subsidies, and grants? How old were Elejar, Radaic, and Borromeo when they founded Dance Theatre? Or Alice Reyes when she built her own company, now Ballet Philippines? And they were not even paid to be presidents or directors.

How much more encouraging are we now in molding more creative talents in and out of centers, theaters and schools? How much and how far can the government or private sector sustain regional efforts? How much funded autonomy can we give them? How quick are we to respond to the needs of this art that revolves around the young (in gymnastics, for example, look at what happened to Bea Lucero)? How restrictive is our bureaucracy as far as experimentation and research projects are concerned, at a time when it would rather fund a popular effort such as a conference like this?

I have already stated facts to be proud of. Since the Bayanihan's thirtieth anniversary, other dance groups have celebrated their own decades of productivity and continuity. Already, festivals and arts councils have devolved to the provinces. There are many reasons to be optimistic, as much as there are reasons to insist on a change in dance leadership in the country. And there remains a growing list of concerns, as more dances are done and more dancers dance.

There are things to be glad about. For me, it is that occasional choreographer who surprises with an outstanding craft and a considerable concept. Craftsmanship has definitely improved on the older modes of presentation that have become boring.[7] Artistic integrity is not always sacrificed for commercial gain or sex appeal, and one can never tell when or from where the next genius of Philippine dance will come.

So, on with the dance!

President's Commission for Culture and the Arts
Los Baños
1989

Notes

1. The current favorite choreographer is Denisa Reyes, about whom I invariably rave. Yet I feel there is an amount of injustice here, because all out focus is given to only one person. There are so many others who have suffered and continue to suffer neglect, like Tony Fabella who's a Mozart of movement, a Mark Morris in wit. Indeed, his predominant purism is not favorable in the current social involvement in the arts. His craft, like Denisa's, is sure, but it is Bergsonian, unlike Denisa's more categorical and overt statements. All dance is of course Bergsonian, but content or concept does not determine the total or final impression a dance creates.

2. That is why I have to be at least aware of what happens in the other arts than mine—and how difficult that becomes when one grows older and has to earn a living, and when there is a proliferation of movements and practitioners. When I

was writing as a young critic (N.V.M. Gonzalez and Consorcio Borje were my editors), I dared write on all the arts—about some of which I feel like an ignoramus today. At least I have to periodically dip into my old field of literary studies, sip the surface of its critical and creative productions, and sense and be moved by language because dance is also a language. At the very least, I may find incidental or characteristic echoes there to reinforce my own choreographic statements.

3. When I did the dance-drama *Ang Babaylan* for Iloilo last year, I also conducted a choreographic workshop because I thought that next time they should use a local talent who is steeped in the regional culture. Fortunately, I'm from the region and familiar with its myths and history.

4. Martha Graham in her *Notebooks* says: "I am a thief—and I am not ashamed. I steal from the best wherever it happens to me—Plato—Picasso—Bertram Ross. I am a thief—and I glory in it—I steal from the present and from the glorious past and I stand in the dark of the future as a glorious and joyous thief ... I steal and I treasure it for all time—not as a possession but as a heritage and as a legacy ..." Like Prometheus, she has gifted mankind.

5. "Today the Philippines is in a sad state, in shambles, as marked by widespread and crushing poverty, remaining weak in agriculture and industry, threatened by diminishing natural resources in the face of a too rapid population growth, and paralyzed by continuous currency devaluation and increasing price inflation, as a direct result of foreign domination and exploitation of its national patrimony, its internal market, and its foreign trade for several decades.

"The economic despair being suffered by more than 3 million of our people is not an accident. Rather, it is the consequence of inordinate exploitation by greedy and powerful human beings, both foreign and Filipino, who took advantage of us, and our carelessness and our innocence." From "Building a People, Building a Nation," by Leticia R. Shahani at the 1989 Educators' Congress (DECS), Baguio City, Ap. 10 1989, *Starweek*, Ap. 23, 1989, 10-11 and Ap. 30, 1989, 6-7.

6. "Our people, particularly the young generations, do not even know what really happened in the Revolution of 1896 or in the war against the Americans after we defeated Spain. The *La Revolution Filipina* of Mabini is not even translated and made available to the people... a vital document for us to complete our historical consciousness." Shahani, *op. cit.*

7. Even Balanchine, Robbins and de Mille worked in commercial settings. For one, it develops quick reflexes. In my time, we danced for Pilita Corrales or Lyn Madrigal—but we never gave up the serious but impoverished side of the dance profession. Choreographers depend on bodies and souls available: there are plenty of that sent—even sold—to foreign lands! If much of our economy is afloat because of the maids and other manpower abroad, it might just be that our artistic fame or choreographic investment can come by way of (foreign earnings in) Japan!

What upsets me—confessed in this added note in the twenty-first century—is the proliferation of step-filled choreographies, seemingly formulaic and measured by "the mile" in extended, propulsive music, coming out redundant in superfluities.

The Quest for Filipino Choreography

There is a gap between how Filipinos in general like their ballets to be and what foreigners expect of Philippine ballet. More often than not, Filipinos pack the house when the bill is a full-length nineteenth century ballet classic (as most foreigners would too, in their own countries) especially when it has foreign guest artists. But when a Filipino company goes abroad, the demand is the other way around: what sells are the ballets by Filipinos.

Last July, Dance Concert Company left for Guam for its first foreign commitment, and they brought with them a ballet repertoire with works by Eric V. Cruz (adapting some international-style pieces of his into quasi-Filipino molds), Felicitas L. Radaic's now inimitable *Oy, Akin Yan*! (a comic *pas de trios*), and Basilio's *Mosque Baroque* (a section from *Tropical Tapestry*, albeit to Vivaldi). Founded some eleven years ago, the main body of Dance Concert Company's repertoire is international, even if Russian and Filipino in ardor. But it had to *look* instantaneously Filipino in Guam.

When the CCP Dance Company tours abroad as Ballet Philippines, it invariably brings along Alice Reyes's *Amada* and Gener Caringal's *Ang Sultan*, both to the music of Lucrecia R. Kasilag. Even if they include ballets by foreign choreographers who are famous internationally, the company gets more acclaim for its Filipino-made ballets.

Dance Theatre Philippines also gets more attention because of ballets made by Filipinos. Based on their experiences though, both the Filipino ballet and the non-regional style are well received, as with Radaic's *Tanan* and *The Prey*.

What is a Filipino ballet? What does it look like? What *is* Filipino? This last question no one really has an answer to; it is likely to be answered with "It is this and that." But we need to look at the things that might define a Filipino ballet. Does it matter who makes it? What is its shape, vocabulary, and significance?

Did Madam Luva Adameit achieve it by dressing up her dancers in Maria Clara gowns and by putting cariñosa and *planting rice* on pointes? Is Leonor Orosa Goquingco the first truly Filipino choreographer with her *Trend: Return to Native, Noli Dance Suite*, and *Filipinescas: Life, Legend and Lone in Dance?* How do her *Firebird* (Stravinsky) and *The Clowns* (Meyerbeer) fit in? What about the Spanish expatriate, the late Remedios de Oteyza, who lived most of her life here? How do we place her Tchaikovsky and Grieg concertos in Philippine ballet history? What about Anita M. Kane's *Maria Makiling*, the Asian-looking *La Mer* (Debussy) and *Mah-jong*, not to mention Paul Szilard's attempts at mixing folk dancing and ballet during his time? Will we regard the international styles of Manolo Rosado and Luis Layag as non-Filipino?

Or have we gone beyond the nationalistic period in Philippine ballet? How come the CCP Dance Company's current season is dominated by Western ballets? What has changed its point-of-view? Why did Dance Concert Company resort to dressing up *Haunted Ballroom* and *Minkusiana* in Philippine clothes for its performances in Guam? Does Basilio's *Tropical Tapestry*, supposedly a Philippine suite, suffer because it uses the music of the Spanish Joaquin Rodrigo or the Italian Antonio Vivaldi? How do we consider the lovely *Juliet and Her Romeo* (Shostakovitch) and the Japanese *Gates of Hell* (Varese) by Eddie Elejar beside his *Kapingangan* (Kasilag) and *Juru-Pakal* (Jose Maceda)? What about Tony Fabella's adept command of Western formalism and his use of folkloric subjects and steps?

The Fountainheads

Western theatrical dancing, be it ballet or modern dance, took root in Manila in the 1920s and the 1930s. That was when Kay Williams, Katrina Makarova, Luva Adameit, Kaethe Hauser, Trudl Dubsky-Zipper,

Olga Dontsoff, Vladimir Bolsky, and Anita M. Kane established their studios here. Even then, there must have been an indication of the kind of devoted following that a Remedios de Oteyza, a Leonor Orosa Goquingco, a Rosalia Merino Santos, a Corazon Generoso Iñigo enjoyed later, and there must have been a formulation of some schools of thought.

I can only speak with some knowledge about the three senior choreographers, de Oteyza, Orosa Goquingco, and Generoso Iñigo.

De Oteyza was of truly classical persuasion, if not always of the standard Coralli and Petipa-Ivanov works, then of the so-called neoclassical mold. Together with Inday Gaston-Mañosa she churned out typical Filipino stories such as *Ibong-Adarna* (Rodolfo Cornejo), and they both encouraged Reynaldo G. Alejandro and Roberto Caballero to produce their *Sari-Manok* for the Hariraya Dance Company. But de Oteyza was always international in style whether dealing with Tchaikovsky in *Design and Variations* or Cornejo in *Spectrum*.

During her last years, she worked for the CCP Dance Company, and she must have infused the company with her classical ballet leanings. Whereas during his years as director, Eddie Elejar was more willing to absorb the modern dance pieces of distinction, Oteyza was uncompromising about her ballet aesthetics. Surprisingly, today the leader of modern dance in Manila, Alice Reyes, is more consistently producing the ballet classics of the nineteenth century, in contrast to how Ballet Rambert turned turned things the other way around.

A great admirer of George Balanchine, the master of neoclassicism in the world today, de Oteyza says that even if she also produced the classics (as Sony Lopez Gonzalez has done, too), she never went in the direction of the British Royal Ballet which adopted the classic full-length and story-ballet structure.

On the other hand, de Oteyza's contemporary Leonor Orosa Goquingco espoused the merging of folkloric dancing and subject with ballet vocabulary and theater. Her folkloric ballets are unique in that they proved to be one of the most innovative impulses in Philippine dance history. In fact, it was this work of hers that prompted me to start writing dance essays. Orosa Goquingco's inquiring mind has brought about the *Noli Dance Suite* and *Filipinescas*, which are sadly lost to the young dancers of today. Frequently compared to Agnes de Mille of America for her originality, Orosa Goquingco has actually established a school of thought in Philippine choreography that insists on native resources and on deep feeling. Having trained in both drama and dance, Orosa Goquingco believes in their integration into a theatrical whole.

Meanwhile, there was also Corazon Generoso Iñigo who, I believe, is underrated in most dance discussions. Perhaps because for a while she went into commercial productions while going commercial did not in any way diminish Balanchine's and Jerome Robbins's reputation in America. And Alice Reyes, Luis Layag, Tony Fabella, and Gener Caringal have also done this with much ease, perhaps because Generoso Iñigo had earlier allowed for craftsmanship to be at their fingertips.

Generoso Iñigo was first introduced to modern dance through Trudl Dubsky Zipper, a Viennese dancer who worked in the West European school of Mary Wigman, et al. At the same time, Generoso Iñigo carried on with her ballet training (with Ricardo Cassell) and steeped herself in folk dancing that brought her to the leadership of the Far Eastern University Folk Dance Troupe, the University of the East Dance Company, and now the Filipiniana Dance Company at the University of the Philippines. She never stopped studying and continued with Alice Reyes and the string of guest teachers and choreographers at the Cultural Center's dance workshops and school.

Her choreographic works combine a number of styles and vocabulary—folk dance, modern dance, and ballet—although they are not always classified as major works, except perhaps *Sisa* (Kasilag) for the CCP Dance Company. I believe this is because her work has been mainly in the context of schools where production work is restricted and classified as non-professional. Therefore, the significance of Generoso Iñigo's works has not been truly acknowledged. It is hoped though that it may be recovered in the years to come.

The Influence of Alice Reyes and the CCP

Like Generoso Iñigo, Alice Reyes brings into her work her folk dance, ballet, and modern dance background. She can produce straight formal works like *Company* (to Bach), or mood-pieces like *Bungkos, Chischester Psalms* (to Bernstein), and *Carmina Burana* (to Orff), and story ballets like *Amada* (to Kasilag) and *Itim Asu* (to Buenaventura), which are both literature-based. In all these works, Reyes's craftsmanship is always sure and her theatricalism is always effective. Many of those who worked with Reyes learned to take command of structure and texture, particularly in the modern dance form. Her musicality has in turn made her "students" more sensitive to the music they work with. Reyes is also unsparing in her editing of dances, sometimes to the point of changing the choreographer's intent—even if it's Balanchine.

Eddie Elejar and Tony Fabella are two choreographers who worked closely with Reyes and took much from her. They both, however, had solid training and experience in ballet and have the advantage of doing choreographies on pointes as well as on bare feet. Although it might not exactly be fair to compare a version of Elejar's *Juliet and Her Romeo* danced on flats by Alice Reyes, and another version of it recently danced on pointes by Irma Bringas Aguado, it must be said that I found greater sublimity in Juliet's dancing on pointes. (In most versions of *Romeo and Juliet* to Prokofiev, only the heroine and her friends dance on pointes.) I also consider Elejar's *Gates of Hell* produced for Dance Theatre Philippines (with Robin Haig and later inherited by Nini Gener), and his modern dance piece *Kapinangan* (to Kasilag) as two of his major works. The former was produced before Elejar's collaboration with Reyes at the CCP; the latter when he was already working with Reyes. Another of Elejar's works, *Rigodon Sketches* (to Pajaro) for the CCP, is I think worthy of mention.

In the first three ballets, Elejar uses the corps de ballet in the Greek manner. And in *Juliet and Her Romeo* he also uses an objective (Fellini-like) physical setting, with his main characters coming out stark and most pitiably at the mercy of Fate because of this backdrop. Elejar also does repetitions of steps in these ballets, along with an obviously deliberate and controlled structure.

Meanwhile, Tony Fabella, Elejar's contemporary, is a master craftsman with ready physical wit. He is fond of surprising twists in relationships with which to end some of his ballets. To enrich his work, Fabella draws allusions to known situations, stories or ballets, and whenever he manages it he turns out the most perfect workmanship hereabouts in works endowed with gusty life. His underwater kingdom from *Prince of the Pagodas* (to Britten), *Changes* (to Bach) and *Batuque* (to Fernandez and Revueltas) exemplify these virtues. His latest work *Entrances, Exits* (to Mozart) retains his surprising wit, unrestrained invention, and rhythmic vitality. His artistic direction of the Manila Metropolis Ballet enriched the Philippine ballet scene.

Other than Elejar and Fabella, there are other choreographers influenced by Reyes who are worth mentioning. Gener Caringal has produced two distinguished works for the CCP, *Ang Sultan* (to Kasilag) and the first part of *Rites of Spring* (to Stravinsky). In the former work, Caringal works uses formalism to tell a touching story; in the latter, with energy and ingenuity he is able to send across a primal and compelling emotion as performed by the University of the East Dance Company, of which he was director. A ballet master to Reyes, Caringal choreographs with muscled and musical forcefulness. Like Reyes, his craftsmanship is always sure.

Luis Layag, on the other hand, was also a member of the CCP Dance Company and further grew as a choreographer there. But Layag started creating choreographies before the company was formed. For Dance Theatre Philippines, he composed an avant-garde piece to the music of Felix Padilla, Jr., *Take Four*. Layag took this same choreographic attitude to the CCP, if not taking more care of formal structure and enlarging his vocabulary. All these (including his having danced with Anita M. Kane's Pamana Ballet) Layag honed when he did several musical shows such as the *West Side Story*, *Cabaret*, and *the Survival of St. Joan*, along with a number of choral concerts which won him awards. He was remarkable in his solo in *The Fugitive* (Fukushima) that was revived in Germany, and in *Transept* (Robert Helps) with Yvonne de los Reyes as the violated and catalyzing factor. Layag's last ballet in Manila was *They Came Jorkin In* (Lennon, McCartney, Rifkin), which was a ballet for straight dancing; in Germany, he has choreographed in places like Heidelberg and Wuppertal, and he has done the same for television in Cologne.

Layag had an unusual choreographic imagination that's always reveling in the experimental and in the extraordinary (to the end, he worked for and praised Pina Bausch). These characteristics may be seen in various aspects of his work and in all aspects of production—the movement, the costumes, the scenic and lighting designs—seemingly in the manner of Alwin Nikolais before Layag even saw his works. All these Layag visualized as a whole before the rehearsal work is done. I wonder what he would have come up with were he given greater opportunities in Germany, or had he come home to work under better conditions. His death in 1979 was a loss to Philippine ballet.

Basilio, meanwhile, was also an apprentice in craftsmanship at the CCP like Layag; and like the latter, Basilio also started choreography elsewhere, specifically in Iloilo where he set up the Central Philippine University Student Ballet in the sixties. There, Basilio created and acted under the inspiration of both Orosa-Goquingco and Balanchine. Examples of his works then are *Bailes Fil-Hispano,* a stylization of the actual textures of some social dances, and *Bach Ballabile*, an abstract work. Although he did not find growth while at the CCP (where he did *The Resurrection of Lazarus* to Messaien), he learned a lot from Alice Reyes there. But it was in Dance Theatre Philippines that he found his real ground, starting with *The Rebels* (the Prodigal Son story, to Janacek) and *The Elements* (to Bach). He did pieces to Carole King, Yvonne Wright, and Kasilag (*Fantasia Filipina*). His *Tropical Tapestry*, begun with *Mindanao: Mosque Baroque* (Vivaldi), was inspired by Balanchine's aesthetics and utilized the Asian use of hands, feet, and properties. Later, Basilio added *Luzon: La Adoracion* (to Rodrigo), inspired by *Pandanggo sa Ilaw*, and *Visayas: Los Pintados* (to Barber, later revised to Federizon, on Malakas and Maganda).

For his Movement Manila, Basilio did emotional pieces like *Royal Sonnets* (to Faure and Shakespeare) and *Perjured Hearts* (to Tchaikovsky). Abstracted characters were the Dark Lady, the Lord, and the Poet in the former ballet and Peter, Antonina, and von Meck in the latter. His *Between Sky and Sea* (to Mahler), inspired by Thomas Mann's *A Death in Venice*, expressed basic and profound emotions which transformed his characters into elemental forces—the sky (ideal), the sea (passion), and Man (the ground on which the first two have their battle)—almost equivalent to the Filipino legend of the conflict between the sky and the sea. And then there's Basilio's work *An Odyssey* (to Yvonne Wright and sung by Stevie Wonder), a solo on suicide.

Today, Basilio is working on Bartok's *Third Piano Concerto*, called *Testament* and centered on the feeling of alienation, but with hope. Here, he is reminded of de Oteyza's choreographic method; at the same time he keeps an emotional core to hold the structure together. Like Orosa Goquingco and Alejandro, Basilio is also inspired by Rizaliana and has scenes that may be danced to composers Cornejo and Dadap; the latter has already been done as *La Lampara* for the CCP Dance Company.

Orosa Goquingco's Disciples

Eric V. Cruz and Reynaldo G. Alejandro were dancers of Leonor Orosa Goquingco and are her true children. Cruz has kept Orosa Goquingco's deep emotionalism and broad theatricalism, although he has also produced a neo-classical piece *Visions in Blue* (Vivaldi), which is one of his best. His *Carmen* and *Medea* are histrionically powerful vehicles for his prima, Vella C. Damian. Distilled forms of these emotional dances are found in Cruz's other works such as the Bolshoi-derived *Spartacus* (recently retitled *Ang Katipunero* and about Andres Bonifacio and his wife Gregoria, but still to Khachaturian), and the light *Meditation* (to Massenet).

His more ethnic numbers though, are less inspired. Cruz's 1976 version of *Mir-i-nisa* (to Pajaro) was not ideally worked out and did not have enough of the production requirements (the spectacle of sets, the number of dancers, etc.). His latest *Cañao* (to Kasilag) also didn't predominantly agree with its music's texture and needed to be worked out further as "a homage to divinity." Meanwhile, Cruz's reworking of de Oteyza's *Haunted Ballroom* (to Dohnanyi, 1973) into *Ang Pagbabalik* improved the dance's credibility without losing its phantasmagoric effects. But the structure and characterization remain weak, either for lack of clarity or unnecessary length. Cruz was more effective in reconstructing the *grand pas* from *Paquita* and *Don Quixote*.

I believe that Cruz has yet to make a Philippine ballet that would be testament to and use to the full his years with Filipinescas and his background in classical ballet.

And then there's Reynaldo G. Alejandro, an even truer product of Orosa Goquingco. More than anyone, it is Alejandro who has carried on her vision, as modified by his own imagination. His works in New York, other than for the folkloric Philippine Dance Company based there, are inspired by the same preoccupations with Rizal, with Philippine motifs, and with Philippine literature, all of which are seen as original works. I myself have rehearsed under Alejandro in a number about Rizal, Leonor Rivera, and Henry Kipping (this never went into performance). While Alejandro's works belong to modern dance, they also use some folk steps and gestures and are sustained by characteristically Filipino sentiments.

Three Women

I sensed these same sentiments when I ran a rehearsal of Julie Borromeo's *Zagalas de Manila*, which would've been easy to judge as just another abstract ballet that's no different from those in international repertoires. But the kinds of relationships, gestures, and material things (fans and scarves) that Borromeo put into the dance, together with Julio Nakpil's turn-of-the-century music, compels the viewer to understand the dance through characteristic Filipino feelings. In spectacular lifts, the manner is gentler; flirtations too, are less forward. This couldn't be otherwise, of course, given the Maria Clara-inspired costumes. Borromeo was also deeply emotional in *Babae at Lalake* (to Tapales), rendering the story of the first man and woman in a stark and sensual way as no other dance has done. To more popular music, Borromeo kept this same starkness and sensuality in *Bamboo Fantasy* (Mangione), even if without a specific story in mind.

Today, Borromeo has done so much for jazz that she has become peripheral to the ballet mainstream. But after her new and happy version of *Zagalas* for Dance Theatre Philippines, she should involve herself more regularly in ballet productions.

After establishing Dance Theatre Philippines with Borromeo and Elejar, Felicitas Layag Radaic found her choreographic breadth and scope in the company. Her first work there was what is now a classic pas de trios, *Oy, Akin Yan!* which is a constant hit with any public. Layag Radaic followed this work with *Tanan* (also to Juan Silos, Jr.), a comedy that has been found to be effective, both here and abroad. Even if short, *Tanan* is a local equivalent of *La Fille Mal Gardee*, a ballet that is not far from our folk experiences. Unlike the Petipa classics which have princes and princesses, *La Fille Mal Gardee*, along with the Bournonville classics like *Napoli* and *La Sylphide*, are in rustic settings. They are thus the closest in Western repertoire to our lives, and to Orosa Goquingco ballets. Layag Radaic's other Filipino genre ballet is *Nan-Pangkat*, set among the Igorots (like Borromeo's own ballet to the same music by Angel Peña called *Kalingan*) with its basic structure, and sculptural and atmospheric rendition. This story of the brave, his betrothed, and an enemy, ends with the brave's burial derived from a customary practice. A highlight of the ballet is the pas de deux, a form in which Radaic easily succeeds.

Other than these, Layag Radaic has also produced *The Prey* (to Abejo), which is about a woman and a group of humanoids; the woman is deceived by a sympathizer who turns out to be an agent of the group. Layag Radaic has also done ballets for pure dancing like *Rondo* (to Abejo) and *Sinfonia* (to Bizet), and some of them have lovely moments.

Together, Borromeo and Radaic choreographed *Mir-i-nisa* (to Pajaro) in 1969 for the inauguration of the Cultural Center of the Philippines. I don't think a ballet of that scale and setting has been produced again, with its spectacular ceremonies and underwater scenes. The nearest to it was Elejar's shorter work, *Juru-Pakal.*

Along with Reyes, Borromeo, and Layag Radaic, Effie Nañas completes the quartet of Manila's female choreographers. She did her apprenticeship in the recitals of her school, but I believe Nañas learned more when she was faced with choreographic challenges at the CCP, Reyes, and the host of guest choreographers there. This, coupled by a remarkable memory for the steps and structures of some classical pieces, assured Nañas her solid craftsmanship. Together with Layag, she mainly does imagistic choreography, portraying the visually unusual and often approaching dance in terms of pure pictures and pure rhythms. Nañas is, however, less bold in approach and does prettier dances than Layag. Her *Images* (to Santos) created striking pictures as I thought only a Layag could, while her *Variations d'Amour* (to Francaix) had Nañas's particular feminine touch. How far she still has to develop is a happy prospects to watch for.

Further Questions on "Filipino-ness"

How are these choreographers Filipino? Is it in their subject matter and references, their vocabulary and structure? What becomes of them when they do numbers called concerto, variations, and such non-ethnic forms? How much of Petipa or Ivanov, of Balanchine, of Ashton, do these Filipino choreographers take on? Or of Graham, of Cunningham, of Taylor? What happens when they treat or render Filipino music in the "abstract" way, and when they deal with Western music in either a quasi-Filipino or an international manner? In the face of a growing demand for the ballet classics of the nineteenth century, how do these choreographers function, and how are they to be supported artistically and financially?

When the British ballet was established on the Russian base of Diaghilev's tastes and of Petipa masterpieces, there were leaders like Marie Rambert and Ninette de Valois who unconditionally encouraged British talents. De Valois was herself one of those. The choreographic genius of Frederick Ashton started in his days with Rambert, and flowered with the Royal Ballet. Andreé Howard and Antony Tudor were equally significant, until the latter found his true opportunities in America. Among the next generation of choreographers were Kenneth MacMillan and John Cranko, who first found scope in the Continent. Today, there are no new British choreographers of their stature, but there are promising ones in sight, especially at the Sadler's Wells Royal Ballet and in the modern dance companies which are beginning to proliferate.

Only one or two choreographers are allowed to find their scope within a dance company; in the CCP only three can be accommodated at a time for their stay to be fruitful. In the first phase there were Reyes, Elejar, and Fabella; later Caringal and Nañas joined the force. Dance

Concert Company basically has only one choreographer in Cruz, a unique opportunity that allows the company to be truly owned by one person that can shape it according to his knowledge and tastes. Like Cruz, Borromeo directs her own personal company to her own liking, while Generoso Iñigo commands the Filipiniana Dance Company at the University of the Philippines, where she exercises her creative will and imagination as choreographer and pedagogue. Elejar and Fabella are today very fecund as choreographers through their Manila Metropolis Ballet. Dance Theatre Philippines is Layag-Radaic and Basilio's choreographic ground and its existence assures the creative lives of these two.

Indeed, all these choreographers will survive as long as their companies do. A large consortium will limit its leadership, end in a stalemate, or break up because of too many cooks. If it survives at all, a company that allows for a great number of choreographers to work together has to have immense scope and finances to do so. The American Ballet Theatre was first conceived with that as goal (with a classical wing, an Anglo-Saxon wing, a Black wing, etc.), and if it has realized itself that way, it is only because it was given time to do so through several generations, and only after years of hits and misses. At any given moment most companies, even with the stature and size of the Royal Ballet in London, still only employ two to three choreographers at the most; the rest come in periodically as guest choreographers.

There has been a move to organize what has been described as "a classical ballet company" and for this to be rooted in the nineteenth century classics. Ideal as that may sound, and fulfilling as this may be for the dancer who aspires to mature in a ballet of this scope (with a few prima ballerinas at the top), this is really only half of the picture. A company such as this must nurture one or two Filipino choreographers in its fold at the same time. Otherwise, it will simply be a museum of dance even if, as in Russia, it is well attended by the populace.

I believe that true experimentation and the apprenticeship of new choreographers happen only in small groups. It is on these grounds that they will find themselves and from which the Philippines will draw its geniuses in choreography—something that is not found in every generation). Big companies may be justified as well, as that is where the Corallis, Petipas, Bournonvilles, Balanchines, Ashton, MacMillans, Crankos, and Neumeiers find their real growth and scope as dancers and choreographers. Of course this is usually at the expense of others, as the company's pyramid will not allow many geniuses to be born. These next geniuses though, always find their apprenticeship in the smaller groups.

There is therefore a need to financially support and promote the welfare of small companies. In America, there are companies like the Martha Graham, the Alvin Ailey, the Jose Limon, the Joffrey, and the Eliot Feld that survive within the popular plurality of New York, and within the scheme of a national touring program and national endowment. In the Philippines, we are a long way off from a time when regionalism in the arts will be supported, as in Canada, the United States (taking the form of civic and city ballets in San Francisco, Texas, Philadelphia, Pittsburgh, Cleveland, Boston, Atlanta, etc.), in Germany, in the Netherlands, in Great Britain, and in the Soviet Russia. And yet, Metro Manila dance companies need assistance *now* as far as finances and programming performances, festivals, or tours are concerned. These are imperative to these companies' existence, as it will help its choreographers and dancers to find their scope and fulfillment within the group.

More than the dancers who find it easier to move from one company to the next, choreographers are born, and grow and fulfill themselves, within the context of their permanent companies. They are also dependent on their dancers who are their instruments for the realization of their ballets—the works of art that are later claimed by the nation as part of its cultural treasury.

Final Thoughts

The heart of Philippine dance's future lies in the hands of the Filipino choreographers. They are the Ashtons and the MacMillans who have made British ballet what it is, the Crankos and the Neumeiers who have made and still make German ballet what it is, the van Dantzigs, van Manens, and Kylians of the Netherlands, the de Milles, Lorings,

Rudors, Balanchines, Robbins, Grahams, of American ballet. Their stature in these comparisons may be disproportionate, but that is not the point.

The classics are there to meet the demands of the audience to whom they are popular (like the Beethovens, Bachs, and Brahms, or the Chopins and Liszts for the general musical audiences), and locally these classics are needed by dancers to grow in and mature technically and artistically. These dances are the staples of ballet companies' repertoires, and they may be rendered in a manner that is "Filipino" (as the Russians do it the "Russian way" or the British do it their way). We are of course, a long way from that, and much needs to be learned towards that long, imitative, and "authentic" way of doing it.

In its Merce Cunningham issue last February, *Ballet News* carried a well thought out editorial:

> For the moment, things look safe, even a bit flat, without much innovation, a reliance on the past, a constant aim of appealing to the widest possible market, a kind of treading water with a wait-and-see attitude. Of course, a time for reconsidering older values is welcome at intervals—after abstraction, why not a renewed respect for form and order?

The mandate for the future will be to preserve and coddle these art forms, not allowing them to be used merely for seeking new audiences, or dragging them down to a low common denominator. Other observers have noted a neutralization, a standardization of the arts, just as we find in easily digestible fast food. Dance will have to take care of this creeping trend, since basically, movies and theater have already succumbed. The creative element appears in dire straits; choreography is having a hard time of it. The dance audience often seems more appreciative of a spectacular jump or lift by a big star than in the work of art itself. Individual styles are beginning to disappear. The 1980s hopefully will not turn into a time of bread and circuses, while the essence of the art—its all important standards and taste—flounders. We cannot be at the mercy of promoters, the subscription syndrome, the manipulators. Too much is at stake.

Philippine ballet will always make its mark through Filipino choreographers doing their own ballets, reflecting their own needs (artistic, psychological, economic, social) and their own training levels, craftsmanship, and points-of-view. The need to encourage the Filipino choreographer to create is crucial, as it has to be done *now*, with the new ones nurtured and the older ones given the opportunities to go farther in their work. Filipino choreographers need not match the dimension of the classics, nor of the foreign contemporary works; they simply have to reflect the present-day, or *their* vision of the future.

It is therefore criminal to neglect this heart of Philippine ballet's present life and future.

I speak of the need to come to terms with the folkloric researchers and the folkloric experience, which can only result in an enrichment of the international ballet tradition, in the same way that character dancing has augmented the classical style's substance and references, the Asian heritage is still a mine of resources for the Asian choreographers of ballet. The Asian psyche, confronted as it is by Western values and productivity standards, can only give birth to an outlook or an orientation that should in the far future bring about a more original contribution to the world of dance—even for that *one* world's survival.

It is modern dance that easily lends itself to the adaptation of ethnic resources, and there lies the strength of the style and creative approach to it in the Asian context. It offers the best chance at the anticipated contribution to dance that has yet to be discovered or has yet to evolve. Ballet's architectural and symphonic approach will emphasize the ornamental and imagistic resources of the Asian dance, arts, and tradition. It will also have to come to terms with Asian sound, not nearly in the traditional form, but more so in the contemporary composers' usage and stylization. Perhaps the dancers' future lies there in the composers' and choreographers' quest for the same goals and aspiration for some original idea and unexplored dimension.

Thus, the interaction between the two must be greatly encouraged; otherwise Philippine dance will remain imitative of Western archetypes. It needs an outside impetus (the Western repertoire is still an inner source for the choreographer), in the same way that Petipa produced his best with Tchaikovsky, and Diaghilev with Stravinsky and his other musical and artistic collaborators. Because in order for dance to renew itself, it must interact with something outside it.

Way back during the time of Adameit, she saw the need to use the Philippine imagination in creating an original production. This was the same thinking pursued by Leonor Orosa-Goquingco. Several of their students followed their footsteps, even Reynaldo G. Alejandro in America. This same thinking remains to enrich this tradition or school further, for future choreographers to sift through the best means, the best patterns, and the best syntheses. Koestler's definition of the creative act works even for dance. Creativity and originality come out of interaction, of confrontation, of crisis, of dialectics; it comes between the sky and the sea, heaven and earth, the male and female, the dark and the bright, the East and the West, the real and the ideal, the old and the new, perhaps, of the good and evil.

As talent is numerous and genius so rare, the only chance a country can take for its cultural future is to encourage as many of the willing and of the able, and create the climate for such geniuses to grow. There is no other way. After all, even science cannot predict its own creative giants.

Evening Express
Manila
1980-81

Princess Aurora or Maria Makiling and the Myth of Choreographic Success

Who will rule the Philippine kingdom of dance? Princess Aurora or Maria Makiling? Before the war, composer Ramon Tapales in collaboration with Anita M. Kane composed a full-length evening ballet on the story of Maria Makiling. Unfortunately, the score for the ballet is lost and, except in the memories of the dancers and witnesses then, the dance leaves no evidence of existence.

The legend of Maria Makiling, however, remains, what with the foundations of the National Arts Center on the mountain that bears her name. She prevails as a spirit that inspires the creation of art in the country today. Maria Makiling is still worshipped, feared, or loved, as tales of her comings and goings persist in the highlands, stories which the lowlanders seem to take as truth out of belief or wariness.

Meanwhile, the dance theater in Metro Manila has shifted to other legends. The legendary ladies of the international ballet repertory—such as Giselle, Odette, and Aurora—brought to life on stage by previous generations are once again dominating the ballet scene.

These three heroines typify the culmination of the Romantic and Classical periods of ballet and how these evoke the grandeur and perhaps define the forms of the art. Modern times have, however, extended the range of the art, particularly through the inspired efforts of Serge Diaghilev and his choreographers, from Fokine to Balanchine. Diaghilev's period injected a new impetus into ballet that produced the collaboration among several artists, including those in the musical and visual arts. Despite the fact that Diaghilev subsequently harked back to the grandeur of the deified classicism of ballet in his revival of the *Sleeping Beauty*—a legendary financial disaster in London—his distinct contribution remains to be that which we can call modern ballet, then, and even now, if with modifications.[1]

In Diaghilev's time, another revolution in dance was happening with the leadership of Isadora Duncan. Her influences were not confined to the art but were also obvious in terms of lifestyle. She was an utterly free being, if limited by circumstance. There were other legendary women like Loie Fuller and Ruth St. Denis who were fascinated with the oriental tradition, but the Divine Isadora was the crowning glory of that rebellion. Ironically, she left no school of thought; instead, it is the thought of her that continues to inspire many of today's dances as both ballet and modern dance choreographers create them.

Other influential and isolated changes, to list indiscriminately, were brought in by the Russian Kasyan Goleizovsky. The latter has been credited with having influenced Balanchine, the German painter Oskar Schlemmer, Jean Borlin of Ballet Suedois, perhaps the Japanese Michio Ito, and Leonide Massine through his symphonic ballets that gained universal acceptance only today. Meanwhile, through Trudl Dubsky (Mrs. Zipper) and subsequently Manolo Rosado, Manila witnessed the Central European school of modern dance that was led in Germany by the articulate Mary Wigman. Perhaps through Alice Reyes, because of her studies with Hanva Holm, a Wigman disciple, this school has become influential in the Philippines. However, it is more easily noted by critics that Reyes stems from the Martha Graham, although her studies with that school were not direct. Graham, too, took much from Asian dance tradition, not only in ideas but also in technique. Between ballet and modern dance, I still think that the latter has the greater flexibility and range to absorb inspiration from Asian dance forms. Its tradition of freedom opens it to diverse influences and a merging does not create a problem with style. Musically, too, the range is almost limitless, like movement in a Merce Cunningham event that may be I-Ching "determined."

If dance in the Philippines seems to worship both foreign and domestic gods, both Princess Aurora of the royal court and Maria Makiling of the mountains, this is also true in general terms in our total social life and government, from cottage industries to the multi-million media. Elsewhere I've pointed out that the rustic ballets of Bournonville are closer to our lives and to Orosa Goquingco ballets than the courtly kingdoms of Petipa. Apparently, we can never stop speaking in English or Taglish (and from my region we speak Ilongish, which Metro Manila commentators often forget), and we rave over Bergman at the same time that we do over Brocka, if not always on the same level.

There is no equivalent, however, to Tchaikovsky in local ballet music literature, and the area has yet to be explored. It is a field that I think is richer, and where I do not expect a quasi-Tchaikovsky or a quasi-Stravinsky, instead it will be a new ground altogether, and become the Philippines's distinct contribution to the world of dance. But the musical field has not done enough work on its own grounds. There is, aside from the success of nostalgia and popular music, little appreciation of contemporary Philippine music. How often do orchestras play them? Once a year in a CCP gala maybe, or in commissions that hardly get repeated. Or maybe in those back-patting medley combinations that the public easily applauds to, and which are favorites of patronizing guest conductors. Perhaps when music gets some visual aid through dance, that audience will come to accept Philippine contemporary music.

But often enough, choreographers (albeit with little musical education) for the CCP annual commissions complain about how the music composed for the occasion is not danceable or uninspiring. Sometimes the choreographer and the composer do not even have a fair chance at talking about the ballet at all. Like when I did *La Lampara* by Jerry Dadap, he had an altogether abstract concept into which I fitted a specific story—that of Rizal's external and internal last hours. However, I thought it worked well. The CCP list of composers is extensive, with the two Buenaventuras, the three de Leons, Pajaro, Dadap, Santos, and a lot of Kasilag, to mention only those who have composed for dance more than once.

The subjects range from the legends (*Juru-Pakal*, *Kapinangan*, *Tales of the Manuvu*, *Rama*, *Hari*, and others), history (*Itim Asu*, *Rajah Sulayman*, *La Lampara*), Philippine fiction (*Amada*, *Anak-Bulan*, *Sisa*), what I'd simply lump as local color or evocation (from *Semana Santa* and *Ang Sultan* to *Baile de Ayer* and *Recuerdos*), and more universal themes with indigenous designs and motifs. To foreign music, the CCP has produced a Maranaw scene (Colgrass), the Philippine-titled ballets by Edna Vida (Fanshawe and Tariverdiev), and even Jan Stripling's *Ties of Life* (Carr and Walton), which was Philippine-inspired.

Hariraya Dance Company once produced the *Legend of Sari-Manok* to Bayani de Leon, and recently the Dance Concert Company started dressing up their Katchaturian and Dohnanyi ballets in Philippine costumes and gave them local color. They even went so far as substituting a Molina for a Massenet, and producing the original *Cañao* to a Kasilag and a new version of *Mir-i-nisa* of Pajaro. As I mentioned before, I look forward to Eric V. Cruz producing a ballet that stems from his working with Leonor Orosa Goquingco, as Reynaldo G. Alejandro is doing in America, if with his own original mind.

From Dance Theatre Philippines, Julie Borromeo has produced two versions of *Zagalas de Manila* (Nakpil), an Igorot ballet (Peña), and a legend of the first man and woman (Tapales). Eddie Elejar first used Jose Maceda for his *Katakata Sin Rajah Indarapatra* which he extended at the CCP in *Juru-Pakal*. Recently, he gave DTP *Masks* to music by Ramon P. Santos, a sophisticated ballet inspired by Virginia Moreno's poem *Order for Masks*.

Except for my *La Lampara* and a not very successful Kasilag piece, my Philippine inspired ballets for Dance Theatre Philippines have been done to Western composers. *My Tropical Tapestry* had, sectionally, Luzon with Rodrigo, Visayas with Barber, and Mindanao with Vivaldi, odd as that may seem. My latest *Id* to Debussy was inspired visually by both the surreal painter Paul Delvaux and the aboriginal Pintados of the Visayas, and the theme was universal. (When we speak of Debussy, do we say he is universal or French? And if we don't know the term impressionism, what would we think of his music?)

In Tony Fabella's latest *Limang Dipa*, set to the music by and as collected by Ryan Cayabyab, how universal or Filipino were the elements of music, words, ballet, and modern dance vocabulary alongside Fabella's own interpretation of subjects as *tsismis, bakya ni Neneng, kutsero*, love, and crowd? Fabella, who has not always stuck to local color, has choreographed most to Filipino-composed music, second to Alice Reyes.

Going back to a previous generation, would we consider the late Remedios de Oteyza, a Spanish expatriate with her penchant for ballets set to standard Western music, finally irrelevant to the mainstream of Philippine dance? What about the original impulse of Leonor Orosa Goquingco to use Philippine themes and motifs, styles, and stories in her ballets? As she's Filipina, do we judge her as more successful or meaningful? What about the early stylization of Luva Adameit and Paul Szilard themselves?

And because I recognize my drive to abstraction to be similar to de Oteyza's processes (and the Balanchines I've seen), and my drive to find a dramatic core (a unifying factor and not always a narrative structure) as akin to Orosa Goquingco, what can be made out of my ballet that's trying to merge both in *Testament* to Bartok which has, by the way, a section on alienation? Whose alienation? From what and why? Do the social issues we live for or against matter a lot to a choreographer and his creation of dances? Does he truly care about reflecting them? And how? How clearly? How bluntly? What happens to his vocabulary? His structure? Is this possible in the nonverbal dance?

Edru Abraham once asked me why no one has done a ballet like Kurt Jooss's *Green Table* in the Philippines. Curiously enough, I am planning a ballet about men going off to war; on the other hand, I've also done ballets to Biblical stories of the Prodigal Son and Lazarus. William Morgan also recently did *Herodias* with the characters Herod, Salome, and John the Baptist. The question now is, do our works now make both of us Hebrew choreographers?

If I had wanted to do a ballet about Macbeth as it is about power, would that have any relevance to our life today? If I do a motif-ballet using Moslem moves and props to Vivaldi, is that formal exercise meaningful or empty? An English friend who was to see this work had great reservations, but they was broken down soon after watching the ballet. As he knew Vivaldi and not Rodrigo, he had fewer questions about the latter used for the Luzon section. And in my *Between Sky and Sea* (Mahler) based on Thomas Mann's *A Death in Venice*, last performed in 1975, I recently recognized the Philippine legend about the fight between the sky and the sea, which had the earth and man caught in the crossfire. Can the audience spot this similarity or sameness?

When we ask questions like these, are we preconditioned by what we think art or dance should be? Undoubtedly, the Filipinos do not dance ballet in exactly the way Westerners or even the Japanese and Chinese do. Although we also think that we should dance based on the art's universal standards, but are these standard Russian? English? American? French? In the end, we do things our way, in the same way that we speak our very own kind of English. Of course there are those who say we should not speak English anymore. Incidentally, while seated beside Alex Dacanay of WHO magazine at a concert at the Heritage Galleries, he confessed his guilt about writing in English and not in Tagalog. I remarked that we Visayans, don't have as much guilt, if at all, because we were forced to be trilingual at an early age.

I view a Fonteyn, a Nureyev, a Makarova, or a Morishita, all contemporary legends in the dance, as dancers first and English, Russian, or Japanese second—when there is a need to be proud of them as such. That's what we do with our Maniya and Tina. But elsewhere, they are first dancers and get hired as such. And they possibly dance as Princess Aurora. If we improve their lot at home, perhaps we can persuade them to come back and dance as Maria Makiling.[2]

I believe that choreographers make ballets as they will, taken up by their obsessions (including that with success), inspired by a musical, visual or literary collaboration (conditioned by their social and geographic connection), powered or limited by their technical and experiential background, and given liberty by their confidence in their craft, by the trust of their board of directors, by the receptivity of their dancers and their audiences, and by the economy that will allow their art—any art—to survive. This is not simply a question of the choreographer and the society. It is a question of whether this society is with and for him or not? It is only then that he can perhaps say thank you and celebrate his society's folklore and fantasies, fairness and fame. And more likely, he will make a ballet about Maria Makiling, instead of copying a Princess Aurora. But that's the big ballet—the dance of life—that has yet to be put on stage.

Dance Philippines
1983

Notes

1. How often do we trust ignorance more than intelligence, the digest more than the original, the clap-trap more than the subtle, the small talk more than the book, the word-of-mouth more than the actual show, even the record or the videotape for the performance. This comment has nothing to do with looking down on simple forms, or ethnic styles which are sometimes more esoteric in their purity, as it is a looking down on our laziness born out of convenience or our fondness for surface elegance and fads in the so-called age of adolescence. There are fashions in theatrical dance, too. For example, for a time folk dance had to be a la Moiseyev or the Bayanihan; now it's the Asia Society's insistence on authenticity of everything down to the costume materials. Then it was one-act ballets, now it's the three-acts that are in fashion.

2. Once I wrote on the dance as a peripatetic profession. Dancers are indomitable travelers, perhaps because their job is a lot about steps. A bit more settled are the choreographers who basically find their fulfillment and instrument of success in one company. Still, they've usually been through a lot of migrations. The grand old man Petipa traveled widely until he settled down in St. Petersburg to rule the ballet kingdom there for about half century. So did Bournonville who gained cosmopolitanism before he settled down in his home country, Denmark.

Fokine was an expatriate, and after his time with Diaghilev, he worked worldwide. Balanchine escaped Russia through a pretext, traveled with Diaghilev's Ballets Russes, tried settling down in London but was refused and finally established his hegemony in New York. American Ballet Theatre was founded by an American who was trained by a Russian, and ABT is now in the hands of a Russian, Baryshnikov. De Valois is Irish who worked with Diaghilev, established the English school, and made famous the so-called British ballet. Rambert in London is Polish. Lifar in Paris is Russian. Today, Neumeier in Germany is American.

John Cranko, who made famous the Stuttgart Ballet today, was a South African trained in England and, gaining fame after the French Noverre in Germany.

Jiri Kylian, whom I consider one of the best choreographers in the world today, is a Czech exile who trained in London, danced in Stuttgart, and now directs a Dutch company composed of American, Australian, and Dutch dancers.

The strong foundation of ballet in the Philippines was established by another expatriate, Luva Adameit, and her students included a Spaniard, de Oteyza. Anita Kane is a New Zealander who has now settled in California. Trudl Dubsky was Austrian who worked briefly in London, and then worked with her husband Dr. Zipper in Manila, and retired in Los Angeles where she lived until she died.

As an interview in the magazine *Dance Australia* put it, ballet is always a story about some group touring and someone choosing to be left behind.

Dancing to One's Own Tune

Ethnicity has surfaced in the general consciousness of the Filipino, which is not surprising if one considers the fact of our great variety of ethnic identities (close to two hundred, based on strict linguistic groupings) that have woven a national tapestry that is of varying colors and strands. Before, this variety in ethnicity was not very clear to most Filipinos. The colors were hazy and could be dismissed by hasty generalizations and superficial scholarship. Of late, the racial origin and aboriginal artifacts of Filipinos have been reexamined and have been thrown under clearer light so that a more honest, credible, and coherent picture can now be seen.

The tantalizing details of this composite image of the Filipino have urged folklorists to unearth more regional dances, and have inspired theatre artists to base their themes and vocabularies on these cultural revelations and identities. This quest for a national picture has been going on for generations, but it's only now that results have been truly appraised, and their researchers or authors more widely recognized.

For example, National Artist in Dance Leonor Orosa Goquingco pioneered in utilizing folkloric and indigenous materials in her dance theater from the 1930s to the 1970s. There were also foreigners who used Filipino and oriental stories and characters, like Orosa Goquingco's own teacher Luva Adameit, and her contemporaries like Anita Kane and Paul Szilard.

The Folk-Field

Today, there is an increasing collection of folk and ethnic materials from the people, and festivals, workshops, and seminars are conducted nationwide to disseminate this variety that makes up what is considered to be the common heritage of the people. This was done in the 1970s and 1980s by the Folk Arts Theatre with its various artistic directors for music, dance, the visual and useful arts, etc. Today, the performing arts and regional art councils of the Cultural Center of the Philippines are carrying it on.

The Cultural Center of the Philippines needs to be mentioned at this point as the national source of endowments of grants, programs, and recognition in the country. Through the annual *Pangalay* festival of folk dance groups at the Center, Manila is able to get a glimpse of the prodigious folk dance activities from all over the country. This activity also dates back to the annual national folk festivals at the Folk Arts Theatre coordinated by the Philippine Folk Dance Society. Elsewhere, regions and provinces have initiated research projects and festivities on their own. Every September, for example, there is the *Kaamulan* festival in Cotabato that gathers various tribes or ethnic groups in Mindanao. Choreographer-anthropologist Ramon Obusan has in the past been involved in organizing this big festivity in the south. Another researcher-dancer, Ligaya Fernando Amilbangsa, has been specializing on the Jolo archipelago with its varied Tausug, Samal, and Bajaw culture.

What remains to be done in this field is to bring local scholarship to international standards. Philippines folkloric scholarship in dance tends to be insular and over-protective of its parochial roots and achievements. With the lack of an adequate notation system (mostly just *aide-memoires*), researchers cannot truly dialogue with their counterparts in the other areas of the world. Sadly lacking is a regular and sustained, as well as an intensive and all-encompassing, system that can fund researchers. There are virtually no private grants for this kind of work.

Theatricalizing Dance

Lately, Philippine theater has enjoyed a number of choreographic works inspired by native resources. The interest is not just based on images, as it has mostly been in the past. Thanks to more assiduous scholarship, the significance of native materials is being given broader understanding and deeper analysis. I have already cited the work of Orosa Goquingco.

Another is of Rosalia Merino Santos who is well known for a modern ballet that's based on a fictional and folkloric legend written by a national writer-researcher, Alejandro Roces. Santos has also done sketches based on legendary and contemporary Philippine life.

Still another scholar worth mentioning is Corazon Generoso Iñigo who has for many years directed commercial, folkloric, and modern dance groups in various venues and institutions. Today, she is the most senior scholar who's still active in the profession. Based on literary and historical sources, she created the notable works *Sisa* (1978, based on a character in the national hero Dr. Jose Rizal's novel *Noli Me Tangere*), and to an extent *Gabriela* (1989, based on the life of a northern heroine, much idolized by the feminists).

Sometimes, the inspirations for the work are more famous than the creators of the dance. The so-called Rizaliana materials covering the life and works of the national hero (his two novels, *Noli* and *El Filibusterismo*, and his poetic and dramatic works) has inspired numerous films, plays, and dances. Recently, the Bayanihan Philippine Dance Company referred to Rizal's life in a suite *Leonor Remembered*, choreographed by National Artist in Dance Lucrecia Reyes Urtula. Orosa Goquingco herself had created the *Noli Dance Suite* (1956) which captured key scenes from the first novel of social criticism. Her own dancer (and now dance and culinary author) Reynaldo Alejandro covered many fictional Rizal characters (Sisa, Maria Clara, Salome, and Elias) as well as historical characters (the hero, Josephine Bracken, Leonor Rivera), and poetic allusions ("The Flowers of Heidelberg") in his works since his days in Manila and in his *Sayaw Silanganan* series in New York in the 1980s. Even the Chinese artistic director of the Central Ballet of China, Li Cheng Xiang, did *Farewell, Maria Clara* for Philippine Ballet Theatre in 1990.

Nineteen ninety-one is the centenary of Rizal's second novel, *El Filibusterismo*. For the occasion, Philippine Ballet Theatre is reviving Basilio's *La Lampara* (1980, music by Jerry Dadap, first staged for Ballet Philippines). Flowing like a film in a stream of dream and reality, it is based on the Jose Rizal's last hours before execution by the Spaniards. The lamp symbolizes different things, all of which have to do with Rizal's life. The dying of the lamp is the end to his life, the way a moth is attracted to the flame; it is also about the ideals he wrote in his last poem, *Mi Ultimo Adios*, which was smuggled out in an oil lamp. The lamp in his novel was also supposed to signal a revolution.

Historical events have also been used by Alice Reyes, director emeritus of Ballet Philippines, in her *Itim Asu* (the symbolic name of the vengeful wife of a Spanish governor general who was assassinated by the priests, done in 1970) and *Raja Sulayman* (the Moslem defender of Manila against the Spaniards, done in 1975). *Itim Asu* is one of Reyes's more significant works.

Meanwhile, in *Misa Filipina* (1984), Basilio situated the martyrdom of Ninoy Aquino in the structure of the Roman Catholic Mass to stand for a contemporaneous Christ. He also worked with playwright-director Eduard Defensor on the figure of the native shaman and his religious and revolutionary role in Philippine society in *Ang Babaylan* (1988).

Other Themes

Mythic or legendary stories have also been rendered by Eddie Elejar since the 1960s and 1970s in *Katakataka sin Rajah Indarapatra* (1968) that was later lengthened and reworked into *Juru-Pakal* (1971), about the Maguindanao figures of the brothers Indarapatra and Sulayman. Elejar also did *Kapinangan* (1972), an excerpted tale from an epic that he had also been dealt with in an earlier work, the operatic *Gintong Salakot* (Golden Native Hat, 1969) by Lucrecia Kasilag and Jose Lardizabal. There were also Alice Reyes's own rock-opera ballets *Tales of the Manuvu* (1987), based on the beliefs of an ethnic group, and the Asian-based *Rama, Hari* (1980).

It is inevitable for the Philippine legend on the first man and woman, *Malakas at Maganda*, be rendered in dance. Orosa Goquingco, Julie Borromeo, Alice Reyes, Basilio, and many unrecognized others have dealt with these primary mythical characters. Mythic elements are also found in Agnes Locsin's *Dabaw*, both a contemporaneous picture of her hometown in the South and the native belief in the eclipse as an event in which the sun is swallowed by a monster, with the ensuing darkness allowing evil to happen. Recently, Locsin's contemporary Hazel Sabas choreographed *Daragang Magayon*, about the enchantress of Mayon Volcano—the Philippines's perfect cone—in a total theatrical production with a feminist slant. Another legendary lady of the mountain is Maria Makiling, whose person has been turned into ballets since 1939 by Anita Kane, and later by Effie Nañas and Sabas herself. Denisa Reyes, now artistic director of Ballet Philippines, was involved in the creation of a scripted legend in the engrossing dance-drama *Diablos* (1989), which alludes to present-day problems and power play; this was produced by the Philippine Educational Theatre Association (PETA).

Customary life and rituals are also replete in modern ballets. Denisa Reyes herself transformed a ritual dance of fire in *For the Gods* (1985) to suggest the continuance of life as very much a woman's function. She has also created pictures of Filipino life in *One-ton Pinay*, *Made in the Philippines*, and *Asong Ulol* (crazy dog). Her *Siete Dolores* (1988) recreated the sorrows of the revered and prophetic Virgin Mary in contemporized situations that was written for her by Nicanor Tiongson.

More distant but appealing in its rawness is the use of ethnic motifs and movements by Agnes Locsin in *Igorot* (1989), *Bagobo* (1990), *Moslem* (1990) and *Moriones*. They are generally abstracted, although one of them has a more concrete situation. *Bagobo* arouses primal fear in a cannibalistic ritual sacrifice of the *baganis* (warriors).

Basilio, on the other hand, has dealt with exotic and rural references in his *Tropical Tapestry* (1975 through 1983) with the Visayan tattoo, dancing of lights, and Maranao inspiration; *Cavatina* (1986), which was on Hispanic culture; *Sa Baybayon* (1986) on life by the Visayan sea with Indonesian touches; *Id* (1981) and *Muling Pagsilang* (1986), both with Visayan touches, the latter about a woman's succession after her husband's killing); *Itawis* (1980) a drama turned into dance with dialogue, about a tortured ethnic woman; and *Ritual Bonds* (1990), which culminated in a Filipino carnival.

Meanwhile, rural is the setting of Felicitas Layag Radaic's comic *Tanan* (1968), a Filipino capsule of *La Fille Mal Gardée*; and *Tubig*! (1979). Urban but still set during the Spanish period is Julie Borromeo's *Zagalas de Manila* (1968), which is about the grace of young ladies then. Tony Fabella is closer to the present time in *Limang Dipa* (1981), with the thick crowd in Manila's streets, and *Six Popular Songs* (1986), which mixed the current with ethnic motifs. *Pinoy Talaga* (Truly Filipino, 1989) and *Beautiful Girls* (1990) were both on beauty contests as culturally derived form the religious Santacruzan procession. Way back in 1971, he also juxtaposed a prison scene with a pious procession in *Semana Santa* (Holy Week). All of these Fabella rendered with urban gloss.

Edna Vida has also dealt with religion in her abstract *Pagsamba* (1976) which was set to an African *Sanctus* recording, and an urban scene in *Ensalada* (1981) in a street scene like Fabella's. Provincial choreographers have dealt with many religious and regional rituals as well, like Jess de Paz in Leyte and Cris Barrera in Iloilo. Delia Villacastin in Cebu and Steven Patrick Fernandez in Iligan have transformed folkloric materials into dance-dramas, too.

Recently, rituals and persecution in the regions—and urban transitions and corruption—have been the themes of the newly launched choreographic arm of the Philippine Educational Theatre Association, the Dance Theatre Collective. Choreographers were Jack Yabut, Raul Alfonso, Maribel Legarda, Jojo Atienza, and a collective piece in *Ina ng Poonbato* (1991, mother of a god-stone), which refers to the exploding Mt. Pinatubo, its spirit, and that of the people living around it.

Several literary works have also been translated into dance, some of them mixing legendary and historical data. There's Alice Reyes's redoubtable Spanish woman *Amada* (1990), based on a Nick Joaquin story. Radaic has also translated another Joaquin story into dance in *May Day Eve* (1971), while Lydia Madarang Gaston did the same for *Anak-Bulan* (1976, moon's child). Another story of the past is *Mir-i-nisa*, which was based on a story by Jose Garcia Villa and choreographed by Borromeo and Radaic (1969 and 1989 versions), and Eric Cruz (1978). There was also Gener Caringal's unfailing success with *Ang Sultan* (1973), and his pseudo-ethnic *The Tribe* (1988), *Vinta* (1989), and *The Offering* (1990).

For a Total Picture, and a Future

The Cultural Center of the Philippines has commissioned many projects in the past, which have produced bodies of native works. Yet, these have largely been neglected by Ballet Philippines, except for those favored by its past directors. Where before the company was not the sole executor of those commissions, after 1970, Ballet Philippines hardly bothered with those pieces except to heap them up as prestigious documentation. Today, Ballet Philippines is still the much-favored dance theater institution so that its choreographers get more opportunities to create dances and spread their influence in Manila and the provinces. Meanwhile, the creative output of Filipino choreographers in the five-year Philippine Ballet Theatre has been limited by its ambitious accommodation of so many foreign and native works each season. In the end, many works that are collected and invested in are not preserved or revived in order to build a truly Filipino repertoire.

After the demise or relegation to minor status of smaller, albeit as creative, dance companies after 1986, the Cultural Center of the Philippines's encouragement and support of provincial dance and dance-drama groups is a welcome development. The CCP has also started to support performances, not just in Metropolitan Manila, but in regional tours as well. The CCP's encouraging moves are as welcome as the enterprising new groups are. This is creativity waiting to happen.

Recently, for example, Manila saw the experimental works of Enrico Labayen who just came back from some twenty years of dancing in the United States. Aside from his overrated multigravitational pieces, he has come up with truly interesting and relevant works, minimalist, gravitational or danced-out. In 1991, there were *Songs: Sa Isip, sa Salita at sa Gawa?*; *Icarus Eternally, Damned the Dupe of Time …*; and *Etchings* with Myra Beltran. In such a short time, he has created an impact on Philippine dance that could only be equaled by Alice Reyes's first modern dance concert in 1970. He has also come at a time when there is a need to sustain the creative drive of such dancers like Beltran, Joanne Ko, Tina Fargas, and Sofia Zobel, who have just left Ballet Philippines.

Another new group is Jojo Lucila's Chameleons. It still has to truly stir up the scene in terms of originality or relevance, but its choreographic intent is serious, with a Filipino orientation and dedicated dancers. I have already mentioned de Paz and Barrera, Villacastin and Fernandez who have long been creating dances in the provinces. A provincial boy who has made good in Manila is Douglas Nierras. For the most part, his popular group Powerdance has been the most creative in modern jazz as far as output is concerned. Nierras's performances are also always important.

Mention must also be made of works done in the more universal subjects and style. Most of the choreographers mentioned have created a large body of works as a Philippine collection. Some of these are truly outstanding, including Alice Reyes's modern pieces like *Carmina Burana*, *Chichester Psalms* and *Carmen*, and her *The Nutcracker* (in Philippine setting), *Romeo and Juliet*, and to a certain extent, *Cinderella*. There have also been Eddie Elejar's *Juliet and Her Romeo*, and *Masks*; Tony Fabella's *Three Tchaikovsky Waltzes*, *A Dance Offering*, *Love Like the Moon*, and the modern *Ang Kasal* (translated *Les Noces* and set in the Philippines); Basilio's *Id*, *Tchaikovsky Fantasy*, *Testament* (to Bartok's third piano concerto), *Sweet Warfare*, and *Awit* (a multimedia performance with a very Asian mood and motif set to avant-garde music by Ramón Santos); Eric Cruz's *Visions in Blue* and *Carmen*; Denisa Reyes's *Te Deum*, *Muybridge Frames*, *Love Lies Bleeding*, and *Desert Passages*: and Edna Vida's *Vision of Fire*. Many of these and many unmentioned others are now relegated to the past, as most Philippine repertoires have been.

It is unfortunate that much of the seminal works in Philippine dance are now unknown to younger dancers and audiences. Some dancers do not even recognize senior figures and icons who are National Artists in Dance, as my informal survey proved. As the lives of the works created depend on the survival of the companies that produced them (in folk dance, of the communities that made them), or the directors that ruled these companies, many repertoires have withered away undocumented. Therefore, current repertoires are insufficient in showing the total creative output of Philippine dance. The planned encyclopedia on the Philippine arts from the Cultural Center of the Philippines should help relieve this lopsided impression. But the problem remains. One can only trust the inherent creativity of Filipino choreographers and the encouragement of plurality in the dance scene, because it is both these factors that would complete the tapestry of the multifarious nature and texture of Philippine dance and culture.

As the Philippine economy has been trailing behind its Southeast Asian neighbors, it is easy to have a pessimistic view of culture. Only artists with their own resources, their own enterprise, abetted by the few souls sympathetic to the arts, have for the most part created and lauded Philippine dance theater and folk dance research as national achievements. As the artistic director of the CCP, Dr. Nicanor Tiongson has urged that there may be an aesthetic of poverty but not a poverty of aesthetics in a setting of economic deprivation and social dislocation. With the dedication, aspiration for excellence, motivation for originality, inspiration from research, awareness of social and historical dimensions, and geographic and cross-cultural consciousness, Tiongson says that there should still be an even greater creative future for Philippine dance.

Such awareness and determination was explicit in the 1991 International Dance Conference of the Asia Pacific Dance Alliance (now World Dance Alliance-Asia Pacific) in Manila. It was set to mediate exchanges among more than a thousand dance educators and administrators, dancers and choreographers, researchers and theater technicians, but in the end, it simply proved that dance is very much alive in the Philippines. So did the concurrent Festival of Dance Academies and the First Manila Contemporary Dance Festival. Here, some foreign delegates and young dancers from around the world were present, which allowed the Filipino dance artists a view of the rest of the world. This exposure led them to realize that they are not alone in working hard towards preserving and promoting their art. Because like the rest of the world, the Filipino artist is just finding—and dancing—to its very own tune.

Performing Arts
Singapore
1991

The East-West in My Blood: Endo/Exogamy in Choreographic Creation

It may be our minds that govern us, our souls that guide us, but it is our bodies in which our histories are written, in which our stories are embedded.

—Sharon Sloan and Steve Fiffer

Taking off on a barge to take them through the Pasig River in Manila, President Joseph "Erap" Estrada abandoned his office and residence in Malacañang Palace in January 2001. But legal minds and politicians spend time disputing this act of abandonment because Estrada did not write out a letter of registration.

Up in the Baguio City mountain residence for Philippine presidents and on National Hero Jose Rizal Day in December 2002, President Gloria Macapagal Arroyo appeared on television to announce that she would not run for president in 2004. But doubting Thomases refused to believe her. Perhaps she should have inscribed her declaration in paper or in stone.

These are two examples that illustrate how, for a long time now, our perceptions and intellections are locked in verbal discourse and dispute. Many of our historians trust only written laws and documentation, and for a while, the book was the icon and document-of-life. We owe much to the behavioral sciences for the validation of psychological and physical expression. But these had to be sifted through and encoded in the print medium to be made worthy and trustworthy.

My area of concern is my generation's choreographic production, most of which happened in the mid-1960s to the present, a time span short of half-a-century. At that time, our works typified the emerging recognition of the Filipino choreographer in 1) their métier as art, 2) their subject matter in the national and international realm, and as a consequence, 3) their having proved themselves as artists in Asia and the rest of the world. Increasingly, the globalization of today has become foreboding condition to reckon with.

All these are now considered problematic in light of a discussion about colonial and postcolonial assertions of identity and emancipation. How have these efforts served the national cause and culture? Were the national and international subjects/repertoires complementing or undermining each other? How did work in the area of dance at this time differ from the work by their predecessors? In what way did these predecessors presage my generation's endeavors? Did we continue or change a trend or tradition? Did we work at asserting a national identity and both a creative and social liberation?

My focus is mainly on my own choreographic productions. This is partly because I am most familiar with their artistic motivation and social circumstances of these works, and partly because I am at this more reflective point in my career when I want to do Philippine cultural assessments. That my dances raise questions about identity and emancipation make it but part of this general project of analyzing Philippine culture.

I will contextualize my works alongside a few sample works by my own peers and predecessors. In some way, therefore, I speak of and for my generation: our aesthetic inclinations, our social situation and concerns (including production and preservation), and the structures in and by which we argued for our creative efforts as demonstrated by specific contributions.

Lastly, this also aims to prove that the generation of choreographers I belong to, and all choreographers in general, do speak in the language of movement and its structural and stylistic means. Consequently, even matters identified as "foreign" may be claimed as autochthonous, perhaps by adaptation, allusion, symbolization, and other devices.

Historical Background: Contextualizing the Choreographer

My background is provincial. I grew up in Western Visayas (mid-Philippines mostly made up of islands), which in my youth was far from the capital in Luzon (northern Philippines). Thus, visits to the center that was Manila was limited because of the expensive ferry and air services.

My own island of Negros is very much dominated by the rich few or landed hacienderos who own capital and hold on to political leadership. The majority here are poor peasants or laborers, with some middle class. Many of the rich carry foreign surnames (Spanish, French, some English) and control the high cultural productions. The second and third are either *sacadas* (lowly paid seasonal workers) who cut sugarcane for milling or are laborers in factories. The latter social classes are, at best, occasional spectators, mainly of low-priced movies or of their own humble rural fiestas for Christmas or Holy Week (which in towns are often sumptuous and facilitated by more affluent hermano/hermana mayors). Both of my grandfathers were farmers and my father was a laborer who bettered his position in one of the sugar mills of an industrialist based in Metro Manila.

In the urban centers, these cultural festivals and theatrical presentations are only possible with the patronage of the government or of the affluent, or both. As most festivals are tied to celebrations of patron saints, the Catholic Church is very much involved. Often enough, the church also wields political and economic influence. Add to the government, the affluent, and the Church to today's big business and mass media, and we get a complete picture of the influential factors that lead to and deal with cultural productions.

Putting personal relationships to the fore, a monopoly in business and politics more often than not results in hegemonic cultural leadership in the Philippines. Nothing is deemed a success unless the effort is deemed "official" or is tagged as such by the powerful. Focus is on the center, the space of governance and dispensation, and the marginal only gains credence when it is somehow "certified" by this kind of patronage and approval.

One eminent example of this is the building and setting up of the Cultural Center of the Philippines. It was a project of then First Lady Imelda Romualdez Marcos who became the Metro Manila governor at that time. At the CCP's inauguration in 1969, some foreign seal of approval was deemed important, and California Governor Ronald Reagan, who became US president, was invited. Today, despite the institution of the National Commission for Culture and the Arts (NCCA), the CCP still rises on the reclaimed land of Manila Bay as the foremost venue for artistic productions and exhibitions. Even within the structure of the NCCA, it is an administrative determinant.

My Peers and I

My generation aspired for this cultural landmark that is the Cultural Center of the Philippines. Before it was established, auditoriums were owned and/or controlled by private entities like universities or business enterprises. Before World War II, there was the Manila Metropolitan Theater. It was destroyed, but many years after the CCP was established, Mrs. Marcos managed to restore it. But it gradually fell into debt so that it is now moribund and foreclosed, decaying as an art-deco monument like some historic theaters on Broadway and the West End.

Meanwhile, my predecessors and my generation all looked up to the CCP as indeed the cultural center that will not only house artists (the residency is limited to a few by reason of space and funding—and choice) but will also prop up our artistic reputation at home and abroad. The provinces could prove themselves worthy of national recognition by having an invitation to do a presentation there. This is like being given a seal of professionalism (something that is also practiced in Repertory Philippines, although the latter is not as respected among the more nationalistic circles). Sometimes even those who aren't really great performers or productions worthy of national recognition get a semblance of this seal of professionalism just by appearing at the CCP. It's as if they are now of "world class" standing, to use current jargon.

Claims to professionalism in dance are varied and sometimes even distorted. Several pioneer teachers who learned from expatriates like Lubov Adameit and her contemporaries—if they did not study abroad themselves—created some kind of professional name through companies from the 1950s. Strictly, it was the New Zealand-born Anita Kane who first paid dancers regularly in Panama Heritage Ballet in the mid-1960s. Later, Hariraya (Festival) Ballet was sustained by subsidy for a year or two. Dance Theatre Philippines, founded with the help of the Danish Poul Gnatt who started the Royal New Zealand Ballet, paid dancers weekly through lecture-demonstrations in schools and television shows.

Today there are three groups that claim the seal of professionalism: Ballet Philippines, which was founded by Alice Reyes and Eddie Elejar, Philippine Ballet Theatre, which came from a consortium of earlier companies, and Ballet Manila, which now has its own two theaters. The first two are resident companies at the CCP—all year-round for Ballet Philippines, and seasonally for three productions a year for Philippine Ballet Theater. Two other resident companies in dance are the Bayanihan Philippine National Dance Company and the Ramon Obusan Folkloric Group. They perform regularly at the CCP but are not professional in terms of remuneration.

Many groups may have created their own reputations but their activities remain marginal or less prominent when measured beside the resident companies at the CCP. This is one reason why the rise of new or alternative dance or avant-gardism is not favorable in the Philippine setting. There exist bigger organizations that dictate what is to be seen as tasteful or correct.

Regardless, my generation from the 1960s aspired to create a Filipino identity in dance. We were inspired by the example of National Artist Leonor Orosa Goquingco whose exemplary work from the 1930s culminated in the full-length evening presentation, the *Filipinescas: Philippine Life, Legend and Lore in Dance*. There were also some important works from Kane who used native themes such as the legend-based Mariang Makiling and commissioned music from Filipino composers as well.

Here is a limited listing of exceptional works from my peers: Alice Reyes's history-based *Itim Asu* (Black She-Wolf) about political vengeance, and the ritualistic *Amada* (Beloved) that captures the primitivism and feminism during the Spanish times; Eddie Elejar's two epic *Katakata Sin*

Rajah Indarapatra, which was later turned into *Juru-Pakal* (Magical Sword) and *Kapinangan*, which is about the unfaithful wife of a legendary datu; Antonio Fabella's *Semana Santa* (Holy Week), which juxtaposes a religious street procession and a rape in a jail, and *Siklo* (Cycle), which has cosmic and ecological depiction; Gener Caringal's *Ang Sultan* (The Sultan), and *Andres*, which focuses on the life of the revolutionary hero Andres Bonifacio; Julie Borromeo with *Zagalas de Manila* (Young Ladies of Manila), set to Fil-Hispano music by Nakpil, and *Kalingan*, which exemplified a highland courtship and rivalry; Felicitas Layag Radaic's *Tanan* (Elopement), set in a rural setting and *May Day Eve*, which is based on a superstition among the Fil-Hispano aristocracy; my own *La Lampara* (The Lamp), which captures the last hours of the National Hero Jose Rizal with reference to his novel *El Filibusterismo*, and *Misa Filipina* (*Philippine Mass*), which provides biblical and historical parallels.

There are many others who continue to follow this pursuit, with the prominent ones being Agnes Locsin who captures ethnic stories and styles, and Denisa Reyes who lives out her personal myth, including the Filipino-American in her works. A most promising artist is Alden Lugnasin, whose ethnicity is not simply tied to nativism but aspires for contemporary relevance. In the United States, we may include Reynaldo Alejandro, Kristin Jackson, Enrico Labayen, Pearl Ubungen, and Alvin Tolentino in Canada.

These expressions and articulations have been possible because of the expanded perspectives brought on by anthropological research, especially from folkloric and historical sources. Better exposure to ethnic music and its instrumentation has also been a factor in this growth, as contemporary composers availed of this music to create new sounds and recreate the newly found worlds that were just strange and inaccessible before. Designers for dance also became more attuned to these studies and started pursuing their work with greater fidelity to details in Philippine and Asian crafts, ritual pieces, and practices. These researches and compositions have also become more available in recordings, whereas before these were only heard from commissions performed in concert halls. Earlier too, the quality of recordings restricted its usefulness. Today, both the commissioning and performing of music remain expensive, whereas in the 1960s to 1980s many of our performances were done to canned music composed by foreigners. Some composers though, like Hovahness, Takemitsu, and Part, lent themselves to the native atmosphere and styles, but many others were still more "universal" or "classical" in orientation and ornamentation.

The fact that the Philippines is predominantly a Christian country and most of those in my generation were Christian did not make our efforts strange to ourselves or our audience. Our Western-based educational system (from Spain to the United States, with brief spells from England and Japan) has lent to the development of international taste. Thus, to choreograph to the music of Bach or Mozart, Shostakovitch or Stravinsky is not altogether strange in our country.

I would like to cite as an example here my own work, *Tropical Tapestry*, and how it evolved. Strangely enough, the urge to be indigenous came when I was training in Europe and the United States. A friend asked me to dance in San Francisco, and I borrowed the first accessible recording: a Vivaldi. At that moment, too, I was inspired by the aesthetics of Balanchine, but because I was in a foreign land, I also found the need to assert an identity that was distinctly Filipino. I practiced a solo, but in the end did not perform it. Back home, I worked on this sonata for an ensemble. These were the beginnings of *Tropical Tapestry*.

Based on the limited knowledge I had of the so-called "Muslim dance" of Filipino folk dance groups, I adapted a style and a costuming that was "sort-of-Southern-Philippines." I then imposed these on Balanchine choreographic aesthetics and the Vivaldi sonata. This became one of my most performed works; in Aberdeen, Scotland it was even hailed as the marriage of the East and West. For a second performance of it in Scotland, I added a new section called "Adoracion," inspired by the folk dance *pandanggo sa ilaw* (from Mindoro which uses lit drinking glasses on the hands and head) and set to guitar music by Joaquin Rodrigo.

Much later, I added a third section to the dance based on the legend of the first Man and Woman in the Philippines who supposedly came out from bamboo, but for which I used a tree branch. I did this section to the music of young Filipino composer Ruben Federizon, and costumed my dancers in painted unitards to simulate the famous tattoos of the Visayan Filipinos of pre-Hispanic times.

In the end, I finally named these sections after the three basic regions of the Philippines: Luzon, Visayas, and Mindanao, and called the ballet *Tropical Tapestry*.

Misa Filipina, another one of my works, started off when I was asked to choreograph a Mass for the international tour of the University of the Philippines Concert Chorus. Luckily, I was able to watch a performance of the Ramon Obusan Folkloric Group that depicted all the *kwaresma* (Holy Week) rites that happen in the Philippines. From there, I took images, properties, and practices that I could include into the Latin Mass with music by Ryan Cayabyab.

Later, when it was staged by Dance Theatre Philippines, *Misa Filipina* was already a fuller dance. I studied the order and text of the Mass, and incorporated a historical event that happened in 1983: the assassination of Senator Benigno "Ninoy" Aquino in the last years of the Ferdinand Marcos government. Meanwhile, the composer Cayabyab had just come from Morocco, and he infused his Mass with some Moslem sounds and created a Moslem atmosphere. I, in turn, juxtaposed the historical protagonist (Marcial Bonifacio, the pseudonym of Aquino in the flight manifest) with the biblical one of Christ. In *Misa Filipina,* this hero is assassinated by being impaled by a flagstaff (equivalent to the shooting/crucifixion), and Marcial becomes the more universal Christ-figure without the historical costuming, who presides over a suggested Eucharist at the end.

One of our performances was held at the Manila Cathedral, in the presence of Cardinal Jaime Sin and Mrs. Aquino, who had yet to be persuaded to run as president. A critic felt that the Mass came out as a primal ritual expression of the Filipino.

A third example I wish to bring forth is my feeling of alienation from the hegemonic political and cultural situation in the Philippines. When I was doing my studies in movement notation in London, a friend made me listen to a concerto of Bela Bartok, an avid folk-music researcher. Its adagio seemed to fit my feeling of dejection and rejection. I thus started with this movement, fleshed out as a solo for a female dancer, depicting a struggle to rise on pointes after several drops of the head and torso. It was also minimalist, but trying in the attempts to balance. The first movement starts off with a full cast and a brave soloist who jetted off and an aerial soloist who will be lifted above the throng to prepare for the paucity and difficulty of the adagio. The last movement showed more symmetry and harmony, with groups of men and women flourishing in the speed and lifts, to end with the female protagonist lifted by the throng, still reaching out to the world at large.

Some Conclusions

As evident from these examples, my generation had to do with the limitations of circumstances so that we created works that were testament to our creative copings. Sometimes we would be commissioned to choreograph to a new music by a Filipino composer—something that used to be done annually by the CCP, and later on unfortunately made exclusive to one dance company, and then stopped altogether in the 1980s. But even with foreign music, we managed to do works that expressed both our national and personal sentiments, as media for both artistic liberation and Filipino freedom. We were able to "indigenize" foreign music through native subjects, like in the case of my work in *Id* for Dance Theatre Philippines, a balletic depiction of the Visayan pintados to the music of Debussy, or in my *The Resurrection of Lazarus* to Messaien which made allusions to the Filipino style of having a wake for the dead and the Vietnam War that was ongoing at that time, with emphasis on the humanity of the Miracle Worker before his own death and resurrection. Agnes Locsin and Gener Caringal, meanwhile, have both used the method of adapting foreign workers in their works that are obviously Filipino. Locsin did this in her work *Bagobo*, depicting an ethnic group performing a cannibalistic ritual; Caringal in his *Vinta*, which is a southern Philippine sailboat. Many others use foreign music for personal and national depictions.

An unrealized project from the 1960s was a *Macbeth* set to Fiser's music, which was intended to bring out the parallelisms to the Marcos's conjugal dictatorship. But the frequent guestings of foreign choreographers in Ballet Philippines did not allow that to be done. This was what ultimately made me decide to quit the company.

Most of us were also trained in Western choreographic forms partly because much of the music we listened to then was recorded in the West. On the other hand, a choreographer like Martha Graham has been analyzed for her debts to Asia. Since the fad of orientalism in dance gained ground, choreographers like Michel Fokine, Ruth St. Denis, and company aspired for an amount of ethnological authenticity. The Polish-Russian pioneer of ballet in Manila, Lubov Adameit, followed this leaning, and who knows how much this influenced Leonor Orosa Goquingco who became her assistant. No one is really outside the trends and traditions of his craft, his society, his national and global context.

But more exposure to indigenous dance, musical forms and styles opened our eyes, and we attempted to adapt or absorb these in our works, to both foreign and Filipino music. With anthropological and ethnological researchers who introduced us to the life, rituals, stories, and crafts of non-Christian Filipinos, this just became easier to do. Still, Catholic rituals remained in our lives, in the town fiestas, in street processions, and in the now flourishing town-and-country competitions. It is here that some merge Western worship with indigenous dance and production styles. A danger is that some provincial celebrations and competitions are also unconsciously adapting television and spectacular club devices, modifying their own structures and styles.

Our choreographic literacy is tied to the increasingly global perspective and situation we live in. We also have to "sell" our productions beside products of technology and the media. We have to speak the language of the market, of tourism, and of the so-called "international dance" festivals we participate in. Yet the idea that to be really global is to be local still persists. But in art, we do not sell a product from one mold to begin with; we are not creating a "plastic culture." Culture after all, is more than the external; it is, more importantly, the carving out of the internal towards exposition and communication.

And so we expose our selves. Confusingly, if not in contradiction, for these selves have been formed by both native and foreign factors. In many ways, this idea has hindered the emergence of one identity, the so-called Filipino one. Of course the important question here is whether there is only one of this identity, and if yes, is it hegemonic?

We are products of our history. At this point in time, new avenues are being opened. These are more possibilities for future choreographers. My own generation has lived most of our prime lives, especially in an art like dance that depends so much on the body, on the strength of youth, on the adventurous spirit of the imagination as it is tied to the body as medium. Much of our creations were products of the latter half of the twentieth century and of our reflections on our predecessors. Indeed, we ventured, and our productions are documents of that period. Some of us were pioneering and forward-looking, but most of us were also limited by the opportunities that were restricted to the chosen few. Those in positions of privilege had access not only to support but also to bodies of information and knowledge, as well as to opportunities that have not always been open to everybody.

The validity of our work is conditioned by those times, as some of us were more often than not performing at the open-air Rizal Park or Puerta Real, rather than in the more talked-about and hallowed halls of the CCP. Except on rare occasions, the media didn't really bother to cover those popular and often rained-out grounds of the 1970s to the 1990s. Even to this day, critics for the broadsheets have not reviewed performances of Myra Beltran's Dance Forum in her studio-theater, and the E-Dance of 2002 has more or less dissipated because of lack of attention, except for a fluke of support from the NCCA. This favoritism in media is not surprising when one considers its coddling of the favored or the reverse, the favored coddling the media. Critics are wanting, partly because of the aforementioned reason and partly because they are so badly paid for their time and expertise. No discourse in dance emerges except in academic quarters like that of the University of the Philippines (Art Studies, Dance Programs, etc.). Every time I am asked to help deliberate on the National Artists, the UP Chancellors' Awards, or any of the such awards, the more I get to realize how little of dance's nature people actually understand. If only our modes of questioning and answering could bring into our works a depth that may lead to our enlightenment about our creative roles. If only we realize that our roles are in our wants and wishes, our past, present and future, the local and global worlds—all of which we are enamored with.

Dance is discourse in body-form, in movement and styles of movement, in various modes of expression like the folkloric and the theatrical, the classical and the contemporary, the street and the stage. The dance is a means to exemplify and express an idea through gestures and style that most often works within a tradition. At the same time charting new grounds (like feminism, deconstructing a story, postcolonial assertion, etc.) is remote in the Philippines due to lack of plurality in patronage and subsidy, and the dearth of study and research.

Beyond dance, my generation had spoken about all these and the historical sites in which we may practice. However the future will judge us. Our works are documents in movements, the most immediate means with which we may express our selves and our time. Creating dance is a way of identifying ourselves, of freeing our obsessions, expressing our concerns. As social beings, we speak not only in our own voice but also echo the situations in which we live, some more eloquently than others, some with the limiting or liberating structures of our time. Once done, dance is a document and a movement with form. Unfortunately, this document disappears with the body, with the occasion. Like the ephemeral phenomenon of the fiesta, it has to be celebrated and sustained again and again, out of remembrance and respect, and out of trust that dance will say something of and to our lives and history.

To understand dance perhaps means stepping into another avenue, the one that functions as the frontier grounds of our social sciences. To understand dance is to understand a kind of "speaking" and a kind of stylized act that stems from both mind and body that, when put together, actually works. It is also a combination of a complex form of knowing and concretizing that should move us toward the realization that we are ourselves artists and Filipinos.

Association for Asian Studies, New York, 2003 and
World Dance Alliance-Asia Pacific, Taipei, 2004

Teaching Dance

Approaches to Teaching Dance

Dance has both technical and theoretical components, which are both important if we are to understand dance in general, and the proper approach to teaching it in particular.

The technical component of dance pertains to the actual training of a dancer in a mode, movement, or technique (for example, ballet, modern dance, or jazz). This is also concerned with the ways in which a repertoire of dances may be acquired in any of these styles of dance. The technical aspect of dance also includes the study of traditional styles, a school of thought in a system, and a compositional approach, such as what the *Natya Shastra* prescribes in the East or the musical forms or dramatic structures in the West. Intricately connected to this is the practical understanding of the allied arts, which may mean technical experience through collaborations with musicians and designers or through involvement in a theatrical presentation or art installation.

The theoretical component of dance is concerned with the understanding of dance in its historical and social contexts and their aesthetic and semiotic aspects. As with technical training, this theoretical umbrella includes the understanding of the art's affinity with its allies in music, design, and theater. Notions about representation and reception, expression and abstraction, form, content and style, are the varied concerns of dance theory. Embodiment through the body or person—his/her color and shape, sex and gender, place in economics and politics—is now something that also concerns dance.

May I briefly add that in between technical and theoretical studies and their common concerns, there are also studies that deal with anatomy, movement notation, and movement analysis. Anatomy can lead to kinesiology and corporeal embodiment, while movement notation and analysis focus on the recording, reconstruction, and kinesthetic understanding that can underlie anthropological analysis. In colleges that are given more financial support, computers are used in relation to movement notation and analysis, choreography, research, and documentation.

This paper was brought about by my concern for the Humanities and Art Studies, and I would like to focus on the theoretical aspects of teaching dance. But before I do so, I would like to emphasize that it is essential that a teacher or student experience dance in terms of movement and compositional devices. These can be included in theoretical instruction.[1] The medium of dance is the body so that it can only be understood from *within* through movement in terms of time and space. Even a dance critic who is not a dancer should have some experience with movement to truly appreciate and enunciate the nature of dance.

And yet, dance can also be experienced from another perspective. You can appreciate dance from the more removed but involved position of a spectator or scholar. Through our kinesthetic, visual, and auditory senses, we may have a vicarious dance experience and study dance through various lenses.

History and Anthropology. A historical perspective about dance is imperative. Studies may still be started with Curt Sach's classic *World History of Dance*,[2] although we have now moved far from this approach. If anything, this historical study should be amplified and deepened by anthropological studies. Anthropology and ethnology in particular have not only concerned themselves with the older or heretofore so-called "primitive" and "tribal" dance; they have also dealt with the cultural in a contemporary setting. Contemporary may mean those dances that are "old" but are still performed, and the "new" that may show traditional roots, multicultural influences, and those that arise from today's vernacular setting. Here, we view dance as a social phenomenon, not just through its linear, diachronic development, but also through a synchronic or synoptic analysis.

Aesthetics and Semiotics. Dance may also be studied based on its formal or aesthetic qualities and semiotic characteristics. What does a movement mean? How does a movement create meaning? Does this movement have a technique, code, school, and tradition? When is a movement altogether new and innovative? How does the movement or the whole dance come out in spatial and temporal designs? How are the movements and sections structured? Does this structure relate to musical forms or to a particular mood? To a narrative form or theme? Does its form veer towards a realistic or abstract fleshing out? Toward an emotional or formal end? Even by way of a cellular articulation as a metaphor?[3] In the broadest of terms, what kind of narrative or temporal telling, psychic or spiritual content and underpinning, and formal values are brought out through the dance? And what racial, sexual, social, economic, ideological forces, allusions, and accretions are suggested or emphasized by it? How do all the elements cohere and come up to prove a point? How does a dance as a whole make sense? How does it make sense in relation to its allied or collaborative arts, its ideological source, its social and economic situation, and its historical tradition? For example, what choreographic or folkloric tradition does a dance invoke, elaborate on, transform, or transcend? Is it by any means contemporaneously multicultural or postmodern? Does it raise an aesthetic or social issue or bring about a cultural understanding—or misunderstanding?

Movement as Text and Metaphor. Today, dance is also being seriously studied for its movements' qualities (movement and spatial analysis from Ray Birdwhistell to Rudolf von Laban, Warren Lamb to Edward and Stuart Hall, Virgilio Enriquez to Prospero Covar), and by "reading" it as a choreographic and social text. In Labanalysis, you chart out the energies, shapes, spatial and temporal dimensions of dance, which has led to a serious reading and writing on dance as a kinesthetic and visual text that can reveal psychological, ideological, and social purposes.[4] Dance can now be viewed from both its initiator-spectator aspects, both as a maker's intention and an audience's reception, both as an aesthetic realization and a social expression.

The question that is important here is this: in its reception, what code operates in a dance's communicative process? What attendant factors condition its choreographic "success"? Is there a problem with its embodiment or economics, its sexual or political color? The one main problem of dance is obviously its ephemeral nature. Its interpretation is also tied down to the human body that, for a time, was considered a sinful instrument. The body deemed low in Cartesian thought[5] was in operation for a long time, while today the fashionable somatic studies on the body reveal its own "wisdom" in charting the survival and wellbeing of man.

For a long time too, scholars did not take dance seriously. It had no respectable verbal or intellectual text, no scoring or documentary system. It was considered trivial or unimportant by virtue of its ephemeral yet physical manifestation. Now, with the aid of movement notation systems (Benesh, Laban, Eschol-Wachman, etc.), video documentation, and computer-generated choreographic plans, dance study may be backed-up by textual or contextual references. Dance appreciation can be contextualized in choreographic or formal reasoning, as well as sociological backgrounds. Even as dance remains a phenomenological experience—done by dancers and viewed with the eyes, ears and kinesthetic sense—it has gained keener and broader significance with the aid of analytical, historical, social, and semiological approaches. A few of these are: 1) Formal and Aesthetic Study, 2) Semiological Study, 3) Phenomenological Study, 4) Historical Study, and 5) Social/Cultural/Anthropological Study.

When I was young, I wasn't able to notice many facets or defects in dance performances. When I trained in dance, I began to see the subtleties and nuances, traditions and derivations that I formerly missed. When I studied movement notation, I was forced to see even more clearly and exactly the spatial and temporal aspects of dance; I had to record, read, or stage a text in the most faithful way I could. But there were still the bare bones of dance—movements themselves.

It was when I learned to choreograph that I began to see the textual and structural patterning, and symbolical and developmental devices, as well as gain some intuitive insight into what works and what doesn't in dance. Now, I also look at dance as a social phenomenon and form of expression, something that may be reckoned with in a cultural context where it may function as a form of recollection, reflection, or rebellion.

Watching dance is now more demanding, as it has become a responsibility. There is a need to see it in its totality, with its shapes and dynamics in time and space, and the historical and social determiners and receptors that are its context. Dance has become more than just a physical education requirement (the way by which it got into the academe) or a preoccupation exclusive to professional dancers. It is now a mode of study, an art and science. Dance is now a serious part of the academic world, and it can undoubtedly enrich the knowledge and wisdom, research and relevance in that world.

University of the Philippines and Commission on Higher Education
Quezon City
1997/1998

Notes

1. Smith-Autard, Jacqueline M. 1994. *The Art of Dance in Education*. London: A and C Black.

2. Sachs, Curt. 1937. *World History of Dance*. New York: W. W. Norton. Numerous histories of dance have been written since; unfortunately, most mainly cover the West or approach dance from a Western point of view.

3. Foster, Susan Leigh. 1986. *Reading Dance: Bodies and Subjects in Contemporary American Dance*. Berkeley: University of California. This is one of the first books to view dance using a structuralist and post-structuralist approach.

4. Ness, Sally Ann. 1992. *Body, Movement, and Culture—Kinesthetic and Visual Symbolism in a Philippine Community*. This contemporary anthropological study is backed by expertise in Labanalysis to chart and understand movement or dance; significantly, it deals with the three types of *sinulog* in Cebu.

5. See the following readings: Adshead, Janet, ed. 1989. *Choreography: Principles and Practice*. Surrey: National Centre for Dance, University of Surrey. Best, David. 1978. *Philosophy and Human Movement*. London: George Allen and Unwin. Sheets, Maxine. *The Phenomenology of Dance*. Madison and Milwaukee: University of Wisconsin. Sheets-Johnstone, Maxine, ed., 1984. *Illuminating Dance: Philosophical Explorations*. Lewisburg: Bucknell University. Sparshott, Francis. 1988. *Off The Ground: First Steps of Philosophical Consideration of the Dance*. Princeton: Princeton University.

Basic aesthetic/ philosophical readings should include: Suzanne K. Langer. 1957. *Problems of Arts*. New York: Charles Scribner's Sons. Her "The Dynamic Image: Some Philosophical Reflections on Dance" is essential. This is also found in

Cobbet Steinberg, ed. 1980. *The Dance Anthology* New York: New American Library. This collection also has Paul Valery's "The Philosophy of the Dance." Both essays are in No. 33-34 (Spring-Summer 1976) of *Salmagundi*, published by Skidmore College. Both are also in Roger Copeland and Marshall Cohen, eds. 1983. *What Is Dance?* Oxford: Oxford University Press. This is a notable collection of dance readings, the philosophical section including Sparshott's "Why Philosophy Neglects the Dance" that first came out in *Dance Research Journal*, 15:1 (Fall 1982), which also includes Monroe C. Beardsley's "What is Going on in a Dance?" Copeland and Cohen's book also has "Virtual Powers" by Langer from *Feeling and Form* (1953. New York: Charles Scribner's Sons) and Selma Jeanne Cohen's "Dance as an Art of Imitation." Cohen should be further consulted with "A prolegomenon to an Aesthetics of Dance" in Nadel, Myron Howard and Constance Gwen Nadel, eds. 1970. *The Dance Experience—Readings in Dance Appreciation*. New York: Praeger Publishers. And Cohen's full book, *Next Week, Swan Lake: Reflections on Dance and Dancers*. 1982. Middletown: Wesleyan University.

Perceiving dance is also keenly observed by critic Marcia Siegel in her books *At the Vanishing Point* (1973. New York: Saturday Review Press) and *Watching the Dance Go By* (1977: Boston: Houghton Mifflin).

Basic understanding of dance forms should be found in Humphrey, Doris. 1959. *The Art of Making Dances*. New York: Grove Press. Horst, Louis and Carroll Russell. 1967. *Modern Dance Forms in Relation to the Other Modern Arts*. Adshead, Janet, ed. 1988. *Dance Analysis: Theory and Practice*. London: Dance Books.

Basic anthropological readings are: Peterson Royce, Anya. 1980. *The Anthropology of Dance*. Bloomington: Indiana University. Lange, Roderyk. 1975. *The Nature of Dance—An Anthropological Perspective*. London: Macdonald and Evans. Basic selections are in Spencer, Paul, ed. 1985. *Society and the Dance*. Cambridge: Cambridge University. A popular reading is Jonas, Gerald. 1992. *Dancing: The Pleasure, Power and Art of Movement*. New York: Harry N. Abrams. This volume is enhanced by accompanying video-films for each chapter. My specific favorites are the above-mentioned Ness book and T. O. Ranger. 1975. *Dance and Society in Eastern Africa, 1890-1970*. London: Heinemann. Books of Victor Turner and Clifford Greetz should also be relevant readings.

The two volumes of *Dance Research Annual* XIV and XV (1983 and 1985): *Dance As Cultural Heritage*, edited by Betty True Jones. New York: Congress on Research in Dance. And Gere, David, ed. 1995. *Looking Out: Perspectives on Dance and Criticism in a Multicultural World*. New York: Schirmer Books. This relates criticism to anthropology. This was earlier raised in a 1989 Dance Critics Association Conference that came out in Ross, Janice and Stephen Corbett Steinberg, eds. 1990. *On the Edge: Challenges to American Dance*. San Francisco: Dance Critics Association.

The ethnological approach is used in Orosa Goquingco, Leonor. 1980. *Dances of the Emerald Isles*. Fernando Amilbangsa, Ligaya. 1983. *Pangalay: Traditional Dances and Related Folk Artist Expressions*. Makati: Filipinas Foundation. Historical is Alejandro, Reynaldo. 1978. *Philippine Dance*. Quezon City: Vera-Reyes.

The ethnological volumes I and II of Tiongson, Nicanor, ed. 1994. *CCP Encyclopedia of Philippine Art*. Manila: Cultural Center of the Philippines are basic references with Volume V: *Dance*. Historical articles in Volume V are illustrated in film: in the *Tuklas Sining* series *Sayaw*, which provides an overview of ethnic dance in the Spanish, American, and present-day periods.

Bringing the Body Back to the Academe

For a while now, teachers of dance have been upset by the marginalization of dance in the educational system. Although there have been some changes in sight, these do not measure up to the kind of focus given to dance in former times.

There was a time when the dance curriculum in schools stressed the importance of teaching dance fundamentals and the focus on folk dances. Perhaps this was due to the influence of Francisca Reyes Aquino, who had fought for both the cause of preserving Philippine folk dances, and the need to teach it as the dances of our people. Unfortunately, we no longer have an Aquino today, and most are interested in just showing (sometimes in overstaged spectaculars) our dances, instead of teaching and preserving them.

It is not surprising then that we are at a point when our folk dances are being taught simplistically. In fact, the study of folk dances is not just about the knowledge of its steps but also of fitness, physical and psychological coordination, and social adaptation. It is also relating to and knowing about music, costuming and crafts, and the very customs of our people. It is as much a form of physical education as it is a total form of cultural education. It trains both the mind and body, both the aptitude and attitude, in both the arts and civics. It is history as written through the body, anthropology as social science through art.

Of late, the teaching of dance has been compromised by other curricular concerns. The arts, especially the performing arts, require training and performance and need to be given the time and space to take place, to happen. Dance, after all, is a kind of laboratory discipline, and its exercise and experimentation, its molding and unfolding occur over a period of time.

Dancing is an education of the body, be it the throat and diaphragm for singing, the arms and feet for gesturing, the head to lead, or the body to bend. The education of the body takes more than just a stone or wood to sculpt with. The body is made up of various coordinated parts; it is made up of a total person who will step out and sway, with a mind that will conceptualize and execute or actualize an idea. The body needs time to get accustomed to this doing and going that is dance.

It may also take a deeper knowing. The body has a genetic past, an archeological root and a biological inheritance. It is also equipped with its social conditions, which sometimes it may need to overcome. The body is more than the body; it is a sensitive instrument to feel the world with, which Mabel Todd describes as "a thinking body through which perception, reception and expression and expression take place." The body can also have repressed functions that may need to be unbound and released. It may need physiological, psychological, and social functions to be activated (or reactivated), and be fully restored. Dancing and choreography can retrain the body and mind into a kind of aesthetic, psychic, and social balance, all of which entail time.

Creative dance employs a lot of improvisation in a classroom setting. These are compositional devices that explore and exploit both body and imagination; these are processes that are challenging or restorative, inventive and innovative.

But our educational system hardly gives enough attention to these kinds of processes, and is stuck in the rut of teaching dance in the "physical education" kind of way. To begin with, an understanding of time, space, and dynamics in dance are basic to its creative processing. These can in turn be translated into personal and social dimensions, and can even go into the depths of emotion so that an individual can externalize his or her very own experiences or problems, beliefs and convictions to be communicated to others.

Dance works with music and the other arts, and even for social and therapeutic concerns. This collaborative relationship can extend into both creative productions and the understanding of scholarly and ameliorative ends. With the other arts, it can relate to new music or installation art, dramatic techniques and forms or cinematic or video art, through which new modes of expression may be found.

A problem for teachers of dance is the sustainability of respect for their art or subject in the academe. There is still strong emphasis on the verbal disciplines (the left-brain) that, in spite of newly found wisdom of somatic studies and techniques, the body is still considered lowly, if not actually sinful. This intellectual or moralistic Puritanism regards the body as less than the mind (stuck in Cartesian duality), and the art and teaching of dance as less than other tasks and disciplines (as reflected in unit and load evaluation).

While the Indians with their yoga, *chakras*, and *kundalini* have no problem with both interior and exterior dimensions, and the Chinese with their T'ai Chi Chuan and other restorative martial arts gain mental and physical balance, we Filipinos have been so Westernized in our educational models that we are still distrustful of the wisdom the body brings. We have also not been able to keep up with new developments in West-initiated somatic or physical education studies by Feldenkrais, Ideokinesis, Laban-Barteniff, Alexander Technique, Rolfing, Skinner Releasing, and Pilates among others, so that we are left behind.

But going back to the body is in fact the first step towards basic cultural education. Recognizing our Filipino body acknowledges its looks and actuations, with the Filipino cultural identity and history at the base of our ethnic sources and consequent acculturations. We also need to talk about dance in its phenomenological and choreological dimensions, its anthropological and semiotic aspects, its notation system and movement analysis. We cannot continue to isolate dance from politics and economics, which give the scientific circles in the academe more reason not to have anything to do with the subject. We have somehow isolated dance from life (even in our little understanding of the body's biological and chemical makeup) that it is no wonder that dancers and teachers always have to justify dance in the context of overall curricular and pedagogical concerns.

Dance is more than dancing. It is all of life. And that is enough reason to make it a crucial concern of education.

University of the Philippines Faculty Conference
Quezon City
1998

Codifying and Undoing: What Is *The* Filipino Dance? (Or Choreography Is Not Enough)

My recent private readings have been thought-provoking. Peter Berger of the 1960s and Randy Martin of the 1990s made me change my perspective for this talk today. Berger raises the problem of what shapes who and who shapes what via the investigative thrust of a social science. Sociology can be disturbing, even disenchanting, in its curiosity to know: "No passion is without its dangers." (Peter L. Berger, 1963, p. 24) It can also be controversial in the "debunkings" it does as a result of scientific inquiry. Martin, on the other hand, speaks of dance and politics and examines practice and theory, body and idea, agency and history, and how dance contributes to our conjugal consciousness of the two—how dance as politics or the politics of dance will make us understand epistemology and society.

Berger and Martin were the stimulants, as much as Prospero Covar was in his *Larangan* (1998), which kept me on solid ground. These three provided texts and contexts in and by which we ought to understand dance and its place in society. Dance study has been amiss in contextualizing itself in the broad field of culture. Meanwhile, the academe has been remiss in its dismissal of bodily and kinesthetic concerns, biased as it still is for logocentric or linguistic approaches. The agency of the body—ephemeral in its actualization and, according to Langer, virtual in its powers—is not respected in the academe either out of puritan tradition or ignorance of its phenomenological or cultural reality, or as Martin insists, because of its political effects.

What Is "National"?

The issues I will raise are few, some incidental, some crucial. One, when we speak of Filipino dance, who defines it and what is its marked domain? What is included and what is excluded? For instance, when people speak of "the green book" *Philippine National Dances* (1946) of Francisca Reyes Aquino (then Tolentino), they also mean "the national dances." Did she really mean to discriminate against the folk dances in her subsequent and even more extensive books? Was her use of "national" then less exclusive than our understanding of it now?

I suppose that what made the dances "national" then was the recognition awarded based on the time it took her to compile the green book; and if we view it as such, then I don't think we can be nailed to or stay static with that category of more than half a century ago. For example, the declared national dance cariñosa has been outpaced by the popularity of the tinikling as the Filipino dance. In fact it must be said, unfairly as it may be, that tinikling is the only Philippine dance included in the *International Encyclopedia of Dance* (1998). We wish for Aquino to be alive today so that she could expound on the green book, and perhaps include more "national" dances from recent perspectives.

What authority declares a dance or a dance company "national"? Are a majority of teachers consulted? Do contests and tourist promotions make a dance or company national? Because the sinulog or the ati-atihan are popular, are they more national than other communal or ritual events? It is claimed by Patrick Alcedo that the ati-atihan used to be called ati-ati, and the suffix Tagalized the word to make it national in currency and projection. Who makes a company national? By legislation? Has the Bayanihan achieved it lately by its frequent official representations in the national and global communities? What about those that are marginal(ized) or have passed away, like that of the Far Eastern University, which was just as good and famous as the Bayanihan in the 1950s but did not have the influence to bring its name around?

Who are the dancers who are deemed "national"? The prominent cosmopolites who do the *Pagdiwata*, or the Tagbanwa who themselves do not get to go on stage, much less go abroad, or even get to be in glossy brochures? Who is included and excluded as "national" dance companies? How is a dance "upgraded" from "ethnic" to "folk" in our peculiar local usage? How do we see the difference between what is the majority from the minority, what is central from the peripheral? In fact, the terms "world class" and sometimes, "contemporary" discriminate against what exist in the regions or what has always been there by calling them "primal," "tribal," "primitive" because they are not seen in Metro Manila.

Codifying to Preserve and Privilege

From the issues of the national and the processes of nationalization, I come to that of codification. Code can pertain to several aspects of dance: 1) the steps and gestures, which are the voluntary phonetics of movement; 2) the choreographic structure, which includes the grammar and syntax of a danced phrase, or a modular scheme such as the classical pas de deux or the saludo before and after a dance, the musical sequence (ABA, etc.) or frame; and 3) the style of a dance, which rests not just on its rhetoric of movement but also on the social conventions of roles and gender, of genre and purpose, by which we can identify and classify.

It is an important task to conserve cultural heritage. It is a heroic work of scholars and cultural workers. But it can also be loaded with discrimination. What has been codified gets the academic nod and respectability that other dances are unable to obtain. For example, because ballet is well-codified, it has persisted through centuries as a technique with a distinct set of aesthetics. However, today there has been a lot of debunking of the ballet as representative of our contemporary society and democracy, and it has been criticized for being Eurocentric and elitist, although anthropologist Joann Kealiinohomoku has also called it "a form of ethnic dance." Ballet has also been tagged as sexist and still prevalently racist. Moreover the hierarchical structure of dance companies has of late also been deemed inequitable.

Meanwhile, when modern dance finally received its respectable status, postmodern dance demolished its choreographic bases and technical flourishes, much in the same way that modern dance had earlier taken shots at the frozen formalism and fripperies of the ballet. Postmodern dance draws motivations and images from the people, such as pedestrian gestures, steps, and situations. Modern dance itself has been so codified that one can speak of a spiral as something that's like a *pirouette*, see a leap that's like a *jete*—it has become stultified and needs some breaking up.

This is because codification has a way of making elite—even commodifying—its product through an established educational system. Before, dance was mostly in the physical education departments, from which American universities have departed and we haven't. Strict codification is scholarly but it can also solidify study enough to exclude new modes of perception and appreciation.

The use of movement notation, only one of the many systems that I know of, may also limit the teaching of dance to what has been set between covers. The issue of authenticity is raised: what or which is *the* real dance? That which has been notated on stage or that which is out in the field? When we add the medium of the film to movement notation, do we get to see just an aspect of the temporal setting rendered on a two-dimensional surface? The space is circumscribed because the camera selects (or pre-edits) the angle and area, as we assume the rest (by a peripheral sight for example) or confess not to know. In a set choreography, who is to say which tempo or accent is right? Which version do we officialize, Urtula's or Obusan's? If a dancer were nursing an injured foot, was he/she going to step to the other side instead? This is important in copyrighted ballet, and might be ritually required in a specific society, and in this sense it becomes a question of trust: who can trust the video? The cameraman/woman? The dancer?

Here in the Philippines, we haven't taken major steps in learning nonverbal notation, and we are still puzzled when a film is taken too near or too far, left to right, right to left, etc. We are also being confronted with computer technology that can generate lifelike forms and can design and document a choreography or research. Any technical means of recording or codification pegs us to its orientation—visual, aural kinesthetic, proxemic, etc.—or its economic and global prerequisites. A code posits assumptions into which a dance may or may not fit. There is always something more to it. Can we see beyond a code of steps into a code of culture or a strategy of manipulation? Lately I have started to question the suitability of the very useful means of Labanalysis, because it is sometimes also used to judge the energies of the Asiatic bodies and genres, something that might downgrade the nature and style of Asian codes and modes of performance.

So where does this question find folk dances which are so far unrecorded or uncodified? They may even disappear soon with the invasion of hydroelectrification, quarrying, and mining, and of a Christian and linguistic majority. Popular as they may be to a particular group of people, they are not national or may not lead to profitable tourism or electoral agenda.

Toward New Perspectives

When we identify or classify a dance—into ritual, occupational, recreational, martial, imitative, etc.—we sort of simplify or essentialize a kinesthetic practice or privilege a viewpoint. When new research on the *subli* came out, for example, people were confused about which were first recorded and which were later discoveries. When Sally Ness wrote on the sinulog, she described three kinds; but when we go to Cebu, we conveniently see only one, the sinulog contest, very much a new "folk" practice, institutionalized and prioritized above the two others. When I myself went to a buklog in Dipolog, it was not under the same circumstance that Obusan captured on film for one of the Cultural Center's *Sayaw* series; instead it was replete with a fiesta atmosphere, political speeches, and promotional appurtenances. This did not negate the choreographic aspects of the ritual, but it was not done exactly because of the need of the Subanon and their religiosity.

More intent focus needs to be given a specific dance or event. Most of our research is accumulative rather than introspective or cumulative on an area. We like to gather a collection of dances to flaunt our repertoire, rather than do an intensified or a specific area of study. Variety has become the current cosmopolitan spice of life, and it has become easier, not to mention more colorful, to just catch dance between book covers, or finish it on stage with a flourish after an hour or two.

Certainly there is a lack or even a loss of details, a neglect of the background, and a simplification of complications, alongside the act of ignoring the need for close analysis of choreographic texts, structures, and effects, and the scant attention that's given to the culturally important context. We often want the "understanding" of dance to be easy, accessible, and popular, and we think we are able to do this by having a great variety of dances in our repertoire and by staging these fleetingly in the act of doing and seeing.

The meager funding for dance studies also keeps it from being more intensive and extensive compared to other artifacts and social processes, or even when situated within synchronic parallels and analyses. Instead, we do a lot without truly knowing the subject or "Other" (so-called *lumad* or cultural minority) who make the music and dance themselves; nor do we know the the reasons and occasions for these. Instead, we begin to dance these with fanciful facility in all sorts of situations or celebrations to come up with a suitable suite or synthesis. By doing so, do we represent or misrepresent the autochthonous dance and dancer? I, as researcher, get all the credit when I speak on their behalf, while they remain in their *sitio* or barrio as the acknowledged or unacknowledged "author" of the dance. The rest of the world perceives the *Tagbanwa* as a Bayanihan member, or it is "quoted" as *the* Filipino dance in a coffee-table book, brochure, or TV-magazine.

Undoubtedly, our "advanced" lives place us in a position that allows us to see and seek all these from a different perspective, one that perhaps more total and integrative. But we can also wrest a dance out of its source or culture and misrepresent it. Claims to authenticity are always hard to settle, if they can be settled at all. Undoubtedly, we appropriate knowledge and we use it for our academic advantage and performative ends. But we need to ask ourselves the question: are our means and motives always nonviolative of the people's own practice and "property" (which to them is ancestral *not* legal, cultural *not* promotional)?

This is why we need to know much, much more about the dances of the Filipinos, enough to admit that the more we know the less we can claim total and terminal understanding. Who is to finally say that this or that is *the* Filipino dance?

Today's focus on and invocation of the past—even by redrawing its parameters and reexamining its implications based on new information, insights, and techniques—is a useful exercise that may be used to find a weighty counterpart for today and find the spirit to launch a future tomorrow.

University of the Philippines/*Furthering Francisca Forum*
Quezon City
1999

Dance Teacher as Scholar

Culture cannot possibly survive without the teacher. Rizal was a teacher just like his mother, who not only taught him how to read, among other lessons. Motherhood, in fact, involves teaching a child his or her first habits, which will equip him or her for life. When we speak of Mother Earth, we speak of the more natural and cosmic dimension of nurturing.

Fathers are also teachers. When we speak of imitating them, we mean father-image learning. For good or for ill, children can truly be their parents' own, not only in genes but also in social behavior.

Grandparents, uncles and aunts, brothers and sisters, cousins and peers are also instruments of teaching. In the very close family and societal system of Filipinos, these folks exert influence on a person for life.

We are never wanting of teachers. Perhaps those who make the most impact upon the child as authority figures outside the home are the teachers whom he or she meets in school. It sometimes happens that children defer more easily to the authority of their teachers than their parents. Teachers often and ideally embody intelligence and integrity, making them fine role models. (Consequently, when teachers fall short of such ideals, their pupils are disappointed and disillusioned.)

The Dance Teacher

The teacher of dance is sometimes taken for granted and unfairly deprived of respect in the academic circle. Because his or her subject is the body, the dance teacher's work is often not seen as academic by those who ought to be his or her colleagues, and therefore, equals.

This bias against the body is partly religious in origin. Paulinian theology harps on the body as a sinful instrument and of the flesh as metaphor for carnal desire. Whereas Christ used the body—and the blood—as sacramental symbols, culminating in the communion, which should make us think twice about the so-called sinfulness (or sanctity) of the body. He also used it as a metaphor for the Church. But sometimes the accusation against the dance teacher is justified. Why? Because the dance or physical education teachers themselves do not realize and assert their strengths and intelligence. They are ill-equipped, not truly schooled in their subject and forced to do their task because no one else wants to do it. There are so many seminars and workshops held all over the country for them, yet they attend without exerting any effort to learn, contenting themselves with handouts and a certificate of attendance.

What does a dance or PE teacher know? He or she ought to know that the body has its own intelligence. We speak of body language, which perhaps is language derived from a place other than conscious thought. These are spontaneous reflexes and movements that hark back to the psycho-physical consciousness of the evolutionary man. The body contains centuries of programmed intelligence that we need only to be conscious of and reexamine in order realize and evaluate their potential.

That's why the study of psychology, anatomy, and kinesiology involve the understanding of the nervous system. (This is so stressed in Margaret N.H. Doubler's book *Dance: A Creative Experience*. She was the first to lead a dance degree program in the United States.) Motive is never removed from motion, and their combination results in manifested emotion. Or dance.

Martha Graham spoke of blood memory. She essentially meant her creative life and career in modern dance. She meant not only the performance but also the psyche—perhaps even the racial memory—behind her performance and profession. She was not only thinking of her familial and professional ties but also of the total tradition of dancing (and she learned from, among others, Asian sources)—even if she consciously departed from tradition in order to bring us a new mode or technique of dancing via her rich collection of creative works.

She also spoke of muscle memory—how technique is learned by the body through the years, and how it finally becomes internalized so that it becomes both automatic and artistic instrumentation. An externally applied technique becomes an inculcation, an expressional mode from within. This is when freedom truly comes, Graham claimed. In the discipline of dancing, the artistic formulation and expression are harnessed and released. Her own breathing technique of contraction-and-release exemplifies how the dance artist takes in then expels, that is, expresses.

Today, Graham is highly respected in the intellectual world. Recently, a psychologist studied the factors behind and the phases undergone by the gifted Howard Gardner in his book *Creating Minds*, set her beside Freud and Einstein, Stravinsky and Picasso, T. S. Eliot and Ghandi. Her own autobiography *Blood Memory* is worthy of close attention.

How often do we identify people by the way they move, from the body language of acquaintances to that of other races or nationalities? We distinguish between the body language of Asians and Americans, or the English and the Italians. Indeed we "read" much in and of life through the body. (Read Birdwhistell, Morris, Feldenkrais, Edward Hall, Shawn on Delsarte, of course Darwin, and the simpler *Body Code* by Warren Lamb and Elizabeth Watson.)

Mathematically and linguistically oriented academics sometimes fail to acknowledge the depth of meaning and wisdom we derive from the body, to the point that we often fear grammatical fault more than postural fault. But how incompetent, unhealthy, and dangerous the body is when it is not properly carried. It is even injurious to the vital organs and the nervous system.

There is so much to learn about and from the body that can make our lives safer, wiser, and happier. It is best to heed its reflexes and rhythm; to do so results in a gainful, graceful, fuller life.

Managing one's body as an organic whole can be related to society. The biological cannot be separated from the psychological because both automatic and motivated functions are controlled by the same nervous system. When we speak of both sciences, we relate the internal and external factors. And a keen observer of these sciences is a teacher.

Maker as Teacher

Compositionally, dance as art combines spatial and temporal elements. But this is realized only through the physical interaction of dancers or the interaction between themselves and the space around, their movements modulated by tempo and rhythm. Thus dancing—or choreographing—is a physical and social realization. As bodies and temperaments vary, the dance maker has to orchestrate not only compositionally but also socially. Very often the dance teacher has to do this for his group, or in his community.

Choreographers or makers of dance inevitably have to teach their artwork. Unlike composers and conductors, playwrights and directors in the performing arts, dance makers have to teach not only the structure and style of their dances but also the scale and details, from figures to gestures. It is such an intimate art that it can't possibly be taught in the original by any form of notation, although notation may be available for reproducing dances.

Moreover, inasmuch as a dance often deals with a theme, the dance maker has to relate with other forms of art—literature, music, design, technological arts—and even with the social and physical sciences. He or she also has to produce, and this means dealing not only with dancers but also with space or stage personnel (from janitors to technical directors), promoters (from ticket distributors to publicity personnel), the public, and other out-of-studio personalities and authorities. Long after a performance, if it remains socially relevant or meaningful (to critics, readers, historians, and later dancers), then he or she inevitably repeats the production procedure.

The Dance Researcher

The dance teacher may also do clinical (as in a studio or school, with the aid of medical and psychological scientists), social, statistical, and field research. This means relating to an even wider circle than just the artists and the audience. He or she has to survey, analyze, synthesize, and communicate. In the administrative set-up of a school, he or she is a little manager responsible for an area or sector.

Thus the dance teacher has his or her degree of effect in society—among students, colleagues, superiors, artists, audiences, and the greater community, near or far. Should he or she be really creative, the teacher contributes something significant to society. His or her vision, enterprise, or creative work can even transform an aspect of society, or society as a whole.

As in the case of National Artists in dance like Francisca Reyes Aquino, Leonor Orosa Goquingco, and Lucrecia Reyes Urtula, we often think of them as teachers first before we regard them as great artists. After all, their art can only be realized through instruction, through the molding of dancers, through the study of cultural trends and traditions. They have also effected changes in society so that they are catalysts in Philippine society—for which they are recognized. One helped preserve our folk arts and disseminated them through the educational system, another explored national themes that veered from foreign orientation. Still another further popularized our folk arts, projecting Philippine culture to the rest of the world.

Less nationally recognized but regionally renowned researchers like Juan Miel, Jose Balcena, Petronila Suarez, Corazon Generoso Iñigo, Libertad Villanueva Fajardo, Teresita Pascua Ines, Teresita Pil, Jovita Sison Friese, Ligaya Fernando Amilbangsa, and Ramon Obusan are also perceived as teachers first, and only tangentially as artists. Dancing always involves teaching—the unavoidable manner by which the art is passed on through the generations and survives the centuries. Teachers are inevitable factors of existence.

With their expertise in body knowledge and body language, and in the cultural dynamics and manifestations of the art of dance; with their unavoidable social relations in their teaching, creating and administering; with their study and research, which exert influence on their colleagues and communities—dance teachers are truly catalysts, and society has reaped many benefits from them. The degrees vary but the rewards are certainly there. We just need to be more conscious and assertive about them.

Often enough, the knowledge and creativity of dance teachers are not well recognized except on special occasions such as shows and fiestas. Often enough their other academic colleagues leagues do not understand that dance is more than dancing (often dancers do not understand this too), that it has cognitive and conceptual content and relevance.

Often enough the dance teachers themselves underestimate their own importance so that they do not rank their work at par with linguistically and mathematically linked subjects and disciplines; thus, they are not regarded highly and make do with the low pay. In their own academic circle, they do not publish much; nor do they produce journals that may open up possibilities for them professionally. Even their librarians do not care to include dance books in their collections, even if their college offers degrees in dance.

Dance teachers may so underestimate themselves to the extent that they stop growing and learning in their own field; they stop asking questions and lose the urge to engage in academic pursuits.

Should they be more clear and emphatic about their intellectual and creative contributions, their personal and social roles, the dance or PE teachers could justifiably assert themselves as true scholars and catalysts in society.

Manila Chronicle
1995

Dance Degree?

While in Iloilo last October, I received a request to know more about the dance degree program in Diliman.

The diploma in creative performing musical arts (DCPMA) at the UP College of Music is a four-year academic program that balances both theoretical and practical preparation in the performing arts. Among the major emphases is dance, instituted under the deanship of Ramón Santos in 1981. Earlier, consultations were made with professionals like Eddie Elejar, Tita Radaic, and myself.

At the same time, a two-year diploma certificate and a four-year bachelor's program were instituted at the College of Human Kinetics (then called the Institute of Sports, Physical Education and Recreation). But these have now been dissolved.

Nothing much is heard, too, of the dance degree at the Philippine Women's University, which began offering the degree much earlier than UP, and has graduated Ballet Philippines dancers such as Florence Perez and Edna Vida. There is also emphasis on dance in the physical education and master's programs of the Philippine Normal University.

So far, the performance emphasis is obvious only at the UP College of Music. Student dancers have daily technique classes (ballet and/or modern dance), as well as classes in Filipino folk and ethnic dances, and Asian dance. They undergo two semesters of dance composition courses, and four on dance notation (Benesh system).

They are also exposed to music—voice, piano, or other Asian instruments, and musical ensembles. They listen to hundreds of hours of music repertoires in their five-days-per-week music theory class (two semesters) and history and elective requirements. Sometimes they have eurhythmics.

They also take theater courses in stagecraft and management with the Theater Department. They must graduate with a production recital, with restaged or original choreographies.

Dance theories are explored in dance history, criticism, pedagogy, and dance and society, as well as in classes in human anatomy. General education courses in languages and the social sciences make up the rest of their academic curriculum.

As most young students already dance with Ballet Philippines, Philippine Ballet Theater, Metropolitan Dance Theater, or Powerdance, it takes them a long time to graduate. So far, there are only a few dance degree holders.

Among the most distinguished is Hazel Sabas, now artistic director of Lubbock Ballet in Texas. She took her master's degree at the Tisch School of the Arts of New York University without having to complete a bachelor's degree. This was because of her four-year diploma program and her long experience of dancing with Dance Theatre Philippines and Ballet Philippines.

Now on the faculty but still dancing with Ballet Philippines is the program's newest graduate, Christine Maranan Novales. Also teaching is Sonia Domingo, who is the current organizer in the Philippines for the Royal Academy of Dancing, which conducts seminars and ballet examinations for children, majors, and teachers worldwide. A student of Ruth French (a dancer of Anna Pavlova) in London, and dancer of the now defunct Dance Theatre and Ballet Federation of the Philippines, Domingo now runs her own newly inaugurated Dance Centre-Philippines off of West Avenue, on Villegas and Moore Sts., San Francisco del Monte.

Among the distinguished faculty in the past were Elejar and Radaic themselves, Tony Fabella, Ester Rimpos (the prima ballerina of Ballet Philippines for fifteen years), and Agnes Locsin (current artistic director of Ballet Philippines II). Guest teachers have included the American Joan Laag in jazz, Malaysian Marion D' Cruz in modern dance and

Malaysian dance, and the Indonesian maestro Wisnusubruto Sunardi. Master classes have been taught by Ricardo Cassell, Tina Santos, Mary Anne Santamaria, and Ligaya Fernando Amilbangsa.

Distinguished "dropouts" include Anna Villadolid of the National Ballet in Munich, Rebecca Rodriguez of Cincinnati Ballet, Sophia Radaic of Royal New Zealand Ballet, Eloisa Enerio of Ballet Pacifica, and Ernest Mandap of Claude Brumachon's company in France.

This January, a three-week dance workshop in technique and dance composition with Gerri Houlihan will be held, a first for the program. Houlihan is on the faculty of the New World School of the Arts in Miami and of the historic and most prestigious American Dance Festival (started by Martha Graham, Doris Humphrey, Hanya Holm, etc.) in Durham, North Carolina. After her stint in the Julliard School of Music, Houlihan danced with the companies of Paul Sanasardo and Lar Lubovitch in New York. In Boston, she conducted the Boston Dance Project, and was one of the five finalists in the first international choreographic competition of the Boston Ballet.

Sponsored by the USIS, Rockefeller Foundation, UP President's Committee on Culture and Arts, UP College of Music, and UP Dance Company, Houlihan comes under the auspices of ADF directors Charles and Stephanie Reinhart.

The UP figures prominently in the history of dance in the Philippines, especially with the research of National Artist Francisca Reyes Aquino from the '20s. Together with National Artist Antonino Buenaventura and her husband Ramon Tolentino, Reyes Aquino was appointed by then UP president Jorge Bocobo to do field research in folk dance.

The result of the project is history of still unmatched dimensions. Aside from her early book on Filipino dances and games (with Petrona Ramos), Reyes Aquino published "the green book" of *National Folk Dances* (New York, 1946), and the six-volume *Philippine Folk Dances*. She also authored or coauthored other books on folk dances and physical education, including the sought-after reference *Fundamental Dance Steps and Music*.

No one has yet matched her dedication to the dance, which continued while she was with the Bureau of Public Schools. Her influence on the Philippine folk dance movement is immeasurable.

Other notable dancers who have been involved in dance at the state university in Manila/Diliman include the pioneer Austrian modern dance teacher Trudl Dubsky Zipper, the visiting Russians Olga Dontsoff and Vladimir Bolsky, and Anita Kane, who choreographed the first Filipino full-length ballet, *Mariang Makiling*, with composer Ramon Tapales.

The College of Human Kinetics program enjoyed the presence of Remedios Villanueva Piñon, Corazon Generoso Iñigo, and Leilani Gonzalo. Iñigo brought prestige to the UP Filipiniana Dance Company in France by winning gold prizes in dance and music. She also provided guidance to the prize-winning Far Eastern University Folk Dance Troupe and the University of the East Dance Company.

The UP Dance Company in the College of Music is today co-directed by Basilio and Sonia Domingo. It has performed at the Hong Kong International Festival of Dance Academies in 1990, and lately in Aparri, Tuguegarao, and Isabela. It has participated in the Cultural Center's Balletfests and the National Commission on Culture and Arts's Manila Contemporary Dance Festivals. Its members (mainly dance majors in the college) contribute to the choreographic output of the company. From the past resident company of the college, Dance Theatre Philippines, the UP Dance Company has inherited some works, while to the Ballet Philippines repertoire, it contributed Agnes Locsin's *Muslim*, premiered by the UPDC in Hong Kong.

Admission to the dance program is by audition. Students are also placed according to their musical competence. Their dancing—with at least three full years of preparatory training—is the main criterion. A number have come from the Philippine High School for the Arts at the National Arts Center in Los Baños. Some who have partly completed that dance program (dance minors or those simply interested to study dance) have had further studies in London's Laban Center and the University of Surrey, as in the case of Paul Morales and Zenaida Halili.

What do dance majors do after they graduate?

Naturally, they still dance, even as some already perform with BP, PBT, etc. Parents insist they complete a degree, and the dance program can only broaden their perspective on their art and its relation to music, theater, and scientific and general education.

While in college, some already start to choreograph, as required in their dance composition and recital courses. They also often perform on campus and at other UP-related events, like the old UP-Philamlife auditorium seasons in Manila, with the *Romeo and Juliet* opera in February and with the British Council in March.

They will, of course teach, and this is most important because teaching practice prepares them for a future beyond their short performing years. The degree program permits them to know dance from the educational perspective, and to realize their mission to perpetuate their art.

They will also be more aware of the dance traditions (Philippine, Asian, world, and various dance forms), and see where they situate themselves in their profession, in our society, in the rest of the world. They will not simply dance; they will dance in dialogue. They will listen much to its music, produce dances themselves, and therefore know, to the fullest possible extent, what their art and life in dance are all about.

[Since this essay was written, the UP College of Music has instituted a 5-year Bachelor of Music, major in dance, degree. Cited personalities have moved on, assumed even more prestigious posts.]

Reading, Writing

Reading Performances

Performance means that which is played out on or offstage.

To Stanislavksy, it is an authentic-looking illusion that represents reality. To Brecht, it is illusion undermined to underline a reality. He called the process alienation or estrangement, achieved by disorienting the actor and the audience to raise the play into an issue, an agent for social change. Grotowski asked, "How should one live?"

Of late, the performance of our judges and legislators has come to be controversial. You begin to question the laws they proclaim (which they themselves contravene) and the interests they mean to protect. As state performers, they are always in view of the public and the press. They have the whole nation, sometimes even the world, to review them.

On the other hand, how have our artists realized or failed their art and themselves? Ineptitude is an easy answer. But brilliance and virtuosity can also lead them away from truth and the realization of the self. In the political sense, an artist may betray his or her moral position and the people's will. Our astute actor or premier danseur was Ferdinand Marcos.

In postmodern times, performance is no longer an avenue for self-indulgence. Action is not a means but the very mode of being, of validation. The somatic process the actor, dancer, or musician undergoes undercuts preconceived thinking for a more honest reaction. Both in the artistic and political sense, performance is a form of spontaneous realization and social signification.

Today, reading has come to apply not only to a book or verbal text, but it also means understanding in the performing arts and in social situations. And reading is no longer unilateral; the very notion of universality has been eroded by the plurality of experience and the ambivalence/diversity of methods and meanings. Absolutism is out of fashion.

Postcolonial peoples have experienced the world differently (painfully) from that of the privileged colonialists. Politicians and economists (including those in our country) must open themselves to many testimonies and viewpoints. The world of performance can no longer be simply read as good and bad, black and white. Ballet Philippines recently showed a French work in postmodern aesthetics. Critics read it from old classical and revered modern art values. Today's theater does not just deal with its elements but even with the very problem of how to view a performance—that is, reading. And spectators have to be better equipped or have to do more: do they have the proper spectacles with which to see?

John Berger writes about how seeing precedes thinking or the use of words. How, after a time, words themselves become doctrines.

The theater directors I named questioned traditional theater productions, considering how somatic understanding should precede even the study of a text, or how interaction clarifies character (in a play) and the process of acting out and receiving a performance.

In social terms, we should trust action more than protestation. Our legislators, judges, and executives are often lost in their pronouncements—delivering laws and services with so much delay. They lose the will (to be true to themselves) and to do (good for us). They may be brilliant performers, but they deliver a lousy performance.

It is important to read performances in the best way possible—including that which has *not* been done, or in history, that which has been left unwritten.

Manila Standard
1996

Reading and Writing about Dance

A metaphor for life is smoke: *Lumabay-labay nga daw asu, asu pa lamang/ Ang tanan ng butang sa kalibutan* (Passing like smoke, [are] all things in the world). This Visayan ditty reminds me that of all the arts, and because of its ephemeral nature, dance is the one that is most often compared to life. In fact, to Havelock Ellis, "It is life itself."

What do we see when we watch dance? First, we see the body inscribing itself in time and space, its physicality immediate, appealing to our senses, expressing an inner and outer energy. For a long time now, dance has been marginalized in academic discussions. This is for various reasons, one of which is the fact that dance is a nonverbal kind of discourse or telling, although today there are a number of dances that use words for punctuation as parallel or counter-text, or are accompanied by the words of a song. Dance also didn't have real documentary evidence except in dates, titles, and names. Today, we have the videofilm, movement notation, and Labanalysis or effort-shape graphing. Dance research can now be backed up by hard facts.

Generally though, there has also been a puritanical and/or intellectual bias against the body. There was a time when the body had to be hidden and certain words were unacceptable: "legs" had to be called "limbs," "breasts" termed as "bosom." Today's fashion flaunts the body, reveals a body language, and changes the vocabulary and syntax of choreography.[1] In religion, dancing Christian Africans now feel much like David and Merriam during the Biblical times. In psychology and physical therapy, movement notation now includes the recording of the physical behavior of patients.

The current studies on dance have reinforced the importance of body writing not only as choreographic text but also as cultural and historical writing. Postmodernism, feminism, multiculturalism, and gender studies have all opened up our perspectives on dance beyond the established orientation toward techniques, styles, and choreographic traditions. There have also been a lot of transfusions between styles so that the rebellion of modern dance against ballet has lost force in the present. Learning from the vernacular language of street-dancing is also a new development, one that's beyond the ritual and stylized adaptations of Katherine Dunham or the Philippine choreographers.

More and more critics have gained technical training through dance classes, Labanalysis, multicultural exposures, anthropology, and semiotics. Imperious objectivity is no longer the trend in dance writing.[2]

Watching a dance/body is no longer taken for granted. We now have a greater understanding of time and space. The technique of dance is now viewed from its physics, kinesiology and anatomical definitions and improvisational processing. A dance system or style is better understood from both its exemplification and its transformation. These corporeal and stylistic structurings have become factors in viewing dance as perceivable reality despite its ephemeral nature.

In contrast, there is the making of dance with the use of new technology. For quite a while Merce Cunningham utilized the computer with its life-form to set his dance compositions. He was also the first one to work on choreography from chance and its simultaneity (not complementarity) with music. Just as the stick, the quill, the pen, and the typewriter have modified the look and structure of writing, cybernetics is also changing today's choreography.

In Hong Kong, I recently witnessed choreography being done through the computer. Everything was being done on the machine, from designing a set, choosing music, the color of the floor, and the defiance of gravity. Will this be tomorrow's dance? The way TV is to today's theater performance?[3]

Just a few years ago, dance was closely evaluated based on its choreographic text. This was a departure from the impressionistic and personal approach of the first credible critics among the Romanticists, Theophile Gautier. Already, we can compare Paul Valery's writing on dance with D. H. Lawrence's on the Hopi Indian snake dance or Suzanne Langer's "virtual image" with *being* danced.[4] Traditionally, the choreographic text may be a style or school, a system established by a guru or dance master like Petipa or Balanchine. These basically deal with time and space, with dynamics and conceptual framework or means for cohesion, what shapes, scales and areas of space we see, what movement-ideas or linkages (*enchainements*) or juxtapositions the creator of dance dwells on, what auditory enhancements or parallels (music, silence, or drumming—essential to African dance or to our subli), what phrasing or accentuating are used or played with, what energies are underlined (in modern dance, jazz, folk dance) or hidden (in ballet, even tap-dance), what improvisationary device is used, etc. How are shapes and spaces harmonized or made oppositional? How is an area made central or peripheral? Do these shapes, spaces and energies conform to a musical, theatrical, ritual, or narrative tradition? Do they come from contemporary derivations, and if so, what are these? These are all compositional concerns.

In terms of other production values, the designs—from costuming to lighting—need to be considered. Is the show meant to be spectacular or anti-spectacular? Where is the authenticity or innovativeness of its designs, from its steps to conceptualization? For what kind of space is the show intended? (Remember Hazel Sabas and Ramón Santos's *Daragang Magayon* at the CCP's loading dock.) Do these production values adhere to a cultural framework—old or new, East or West, traditional or iconoclastic, gender-based or gender bending, etc.?

In terms of its overall cultural context, how much do you know of a people's history and tradition, folklore, and religion? Today, much writing is concerned with a people's colonial experience, and with social and gender biases. Are you judging from absolutes or relative to a cultural complex, evolving standard or multicultural expression?[5] (In the Philippines most patrons expect that Filipinos prove classical competence in ballet—they're too rear-guarded to admit deconstruction. There is also talk about a one-company hegemony in ballet, which deprives the audience of a choice and gives dancers no choice at all.)

All of the above considerations where writing about dance is concerned will be apparent in the writer's language. Marge Enriquez says she wants to be "readable" and is not writing for dancers but for the general reader (notwithstanding the many kinds of readers). Enriquez also writes for a widely circulated newspaper that dictates the language she must write in. Perhaps because of my age and academic leanings, I tend to be more conservative or old-fashioned where language is concerned. I've also never been trendy. I wish, though, for new and many more critics. Some of my students in dance criticism may one day serve that function, hopefully in the near future.

Of course an understanding of the "language" of dance—its currencies and schools, its technical and critical changes—is a must for someone who wants to write about dance. In the 1960s, dance writing tended to be descriptive because of the prevailing anti-spectacular and nonlinear approach to dance, and because of all the above-mentioned aspects. I am receptive enough to new works and schooled enough for the classical. I'm no expert though, as I consider myself a general practitioner.

I have also shifted from doing straight reviews to writing columns, which are quite different from each other. In some way, writing a review is easier because it is mainly reactive. I used to have enough space to give larger underpinnings to my criticism, which is mainly true about writing for journals. The latter kind of writing also takes more time, and you can go into explanations about how things are, not only in dance but also in music, theater, economics, politics, etc.

But whatever kind of dance-writing you may find yourself in, remember that it is only a parallel text to choreographic writing. This is not even like a parallel translation in literature; in dance, you use language to describe and evaluate a nonverbal medium that, as John Blacking insists, is very, very different.[6] To compensate, be descriptive about the body and what it does to make the writing more concrete. Of course, you're not always allowed much space for this if you're writing for a newspaper.

Dancers and audiences have different expectations of a critical essay. Dancers wish to be praised, while audiences want to be informed. Critics read other critics to confirm their own opinions. In our cultural milieu, it is hard to be truly critical, that it begs the question: should the critic wear a mask? There was a time when even *The London Times* left its reviews unsigned. As many local critics are/were also known as dance practitioners, how does the public receive their assertions? I believe local readers expect critics to be experts in the field, and yet the situation also leaves room for doubt. As a dancer, my colleagues often sought my opinion about their dancing, perhaps because I was not a threat to them as many of them were better than me. As one of the founders of Philippine Ballet Theatre, I've had to resign as one of its artistic council members. Having been a member of most of the professional dance companies, I feel qualified to be critical of them and their dancing. On the whole, we keep a collegial attitude with regards each other.

In my 1994 conference paper in Malaysia, "A Critic in an Asian Context," I harped on the critical tradition of Filipinos—from the political (our Propaganda period) to the theatrical (the zarzuela, for instance) and today's newspaper tradition. Yet as Asians we are generally more conciliatory than confrontational (except in *kanto*-encounters and sometimes in congressional and sports situations).

When I was asked to formulate the criteria for the last UP Chancellor's Awards, I listed the following for dance:

1. Originality of work or an innovative deconstruction or (a worthy) reconstruction of a standard work, hopefully relevant to Philippine life;
2. Choreography explores the basic elements of time, space, shape, and energy, i.e., inventive in movement-terms (visual, rhythmic, kinesthetic);
3. Work deals with a concept or story with incisiveness, relevance, wit, humor, or pathos (emotions);
4. When possible, the accompanying music and designs are native or innovative (Filipino, tradition-based or forward-looking); and

5. Level of performance is competent to outstanding; which means: a) done with considerable technique that is clear and strong; b) an expressive or nuanced rendition—in feeling or in musicality; c) competent in staging, including costuming, lighting and other designs, and utilization of performance.

I may not always speak of all these in my dance-writing, but they are the general things I consider whenever I write about dance. You can ask more of dance and add to these criteria.[7] After all, we all view dance in different ways, and you may view dance and see what I myself haven't.

Notes

1. Body contact, called contact-improvisation, has now reformed our making and seeing of dance. See Cynthia Novack, *Sharing the Dance: Contact Improvisation and American Culture*. (1990, Wisconsin University Press) Also see Susan Leigh Foster's (ed.) *Corporealities*. (1996, Routledge) Aikido influenced the initiator of contact improvisation, Steve Paxton.

2. See Sally Ann Ness's *Body, Movement and Culture: Kinesthetic and Visual Symbolism in a Philippine Community*, which is about the *sinulog* of Cebu. (1992, University of Pennsylvania Press).

3. See William Smith's (ed.) *Dance and Technology I: Moving Toward the Future* and *Dance and Technology III: Transcending Boundaries*. (1992, 1995, Fullhouse Publishing, Ohio)

4. See Leslie Satin's "Being Danced Again: Meredith Monk, Reclaiming the Girlchild" in Gay Morris' (ed.) *Moving Words: Re-writing Dance*. (1996, Routledge)

5. See Christy Adair's *Women and Dance: Sylphs and Sirens* (1992, New York University Press) and Ramsay Burt's *The Male Dancer, Bodies, Spectacle, Sexualities* (1995, Routledge) on gender: Judith Lynne Hanna's *Dance, Sex and Gender* (1988, University of Chicago Press) on sex in general. Or Chapter 8: "Community—The Body Politic" in White, Friedman and Levinson's *Poor Dancer's Almanac* (1993, Duke University Press): Karla Jay and Allen Young's (eds.) *Lavender Culture* (1978, Jove/ HBJ Book); and the significant *Looking Out: Perspectives on Dance and Criticism in a Multicultural World* edited by David Gere (1995, Schirmer Books). On the colonized, exoticized dance and body, see Marta Savigliano's *Tango and the Political Economy of Passion*. (1995, Westview Press, Boulder)

6. See his "Movement, dance, music and the Vanda girls initiation" in Paul Spencer's (ed.) *Society and the Dance*. (1985, Cambridge University Press)

7. As further reading, see Ellen Goellner and Jacqueline Shea Murphy's (eds.) *Bodies of the Text: Dance as Theory, Literature as Dance*. (1994, Rutgers University Press). An essential for today's critic is the writing of Edwin Denby; see his compiled *Dance Writing*, edited by Robert Cornfield and William Mackay. (1986, Alfred Knopf.) My other favorite critics are Marcia Siegel, Deborah Jowitt and the controversial Arlene Croce of the *New Yorker*. Resil Mojares delivered a landmark paper, "Remembering the Body, Notes on Philippine Dance History" at the 1997 NCCA Dance Committee national conference in Cebu.

Notating Art and Life

A system of notation is a sign of a developed culture. It is a culture where information and knowledge are systematized, not only to keep order but also to refine and understand what has been systematized by analysis.

Systems of notation involve the use of numbers, the emergence of scripts, the scoring of music, the plotting out in graphs, and lately, the recording of movements. These aid in study, documentation, and preservation. Certain methods and mystiques keep each system consistent and compelling. Each system establishes its own influences, sometimes linked to political, economic, and cultural hegemonies.

Allied to these notation systems are the technological tools we now have in preservation and documentation. Sound and visual reproductions and recordings have enabled works of art to be transported beyond the means they were originally intended and rendered. Packaging them has become a business that goes beyond scholarly and archival intentions.

These reproductions are so attractive and alive that they sometimes replace the original media. Some people would rather listen to a recording at home (records, tapes, compact discs) than attend a live concert. With video recordings, some people no longer patronize movie houses—which can be so dirty. At home, you can stop and pause what you are watching and raid the cupboard or refrigerator at leisure.

Because of these sophistications at the fingertips of the audience, sometimes a work of art is no longer viewed or heard consistently or with the necessary concentration. Where you open your eyes and ears as much as you can in a theater, at home you trust the machine to rewind a process if you miss a segment while answering the phone. Sound is amplified and balanced, and colors are reproduced and mixed in filmic saturation. Inauthentic factors creep in.

The more personal styles can prevail over the more generic manner of notation systems. Close-ups and cutting out of other bodies and properties refocus your attention, whereas in the theater you look at the total picture of moving and living. In master copies, faults are edited out and a recording or film ejects any contretemps.

On the other hand, a notation system records only the essentials of music or dance. It does not "color" a performance even if tempo, directions and qualities are indicated. These indications are often conventions universalized in an art form, like the dominantly Italian directions in music.

A first dance notation seminar-workshop was recently held by the Dance Committee of the Presidential Commission on Culture and Arts. Although there is still strong resistance from those brought up in the old word-based movement notation, the workshop gathered an enthusiastic bunch of dance students and teachers who took to the new systems "like water."

In two days they were able to read the basics of the Benesh system, and in another two that of Labanotation. This was surprising to the instructors, who often experienced slower absorption. Those who attended were from all the different regions of the country. Their aptitude and application were remarkable, from the young to the old.

It was suggested that a society or committee for dance researchers be established, primarily to assure the survival of our folk dances threatened by time and modernization. By its composition, initiatives will come from the provinces and not just from Metro Manila. Membership will be maintained by submitting a research on a dance, a tradition, a method of instruction, etc., annually, and not by fees. Money will instead be solicited from sympathetic sources. After all dancers, teachers, and researchers are not paid enough and often not at all for their scholarly pursuits.

It is heartening that the first workshop on movement notation had such a positive response. Educatior authorities who have spent so much on physical education and other allied aspects of movement—dance, sports, play, etc.—should wise up to this late, late move toward "literacy" in the most universal means of communication—movement.

Notation is a recording of time, space, and energy. These are the materials of life. Notating movement—that may be transformed into dance, performance art, sports or play, or observed in the sick and handicapped in clinical movement notation—is, therefore, a veritable recording of life's basic manifestations.

The Manila Times
1990

Semiotic Stretching

Either he has overestimated his wit or he has in fact lost his wisdom. Much has been said about ambiguity in art. This is one source of its richness and resonance. A work of art can justifiably be contradictory within an accepted framework or prepared context. We call this paradox, where we see a truth in its opposite yet verifiable sense.

Should it say one thing and mean another (irony), then what you have is wit worthy of serious consideration. But as it happens in the real world, this double entendre may not be acceptable. It may fit one occasion but not another, especially in times of crisis when clarity and forthrightness are the necessary strategies.

Lack of real wit is a problem of one "presidentiable." He is not sharp enough to distinguish what he may mean. He comes out like the very jokes he invokes. He may be the most sincere one among them all, but he does not know how to "operationalize" his communication but by blatant "me-and-all-my-goodness" or simplified intention.

Lately, I spotted an anthropological reference on how sense of humor becomes a means of coping for the underprivileged (mentally or monetarily?). We are world-famous for our sense of humor; it is indeed a means of survival for the common *tao*. In general, this confirms our underdog status; we laugh and laugh hard over our misfortunes. It's a kind of smiling martyrdom.

Wit and wry humor have been the advantages of President Fidel V. Ramos. It shows his intelligence. But it also displays his contrivance, from rolling up his sleeves to inordinately traveling abroad.

His incompetence in dancing (First Lady Ming Ramos, who is a Physical Education major, should have taught him rhythm) was echoed by the awkward footfalls at Cha-cha in Congress and countered by the opposition with the more vociferous lambada. (Miriam Defensor-Santiago twitted the president's dance as the twist.) All these have caused a general political confusion—including in the president's own Lakas Party—and economic repercussions.

In an exam in Dance and Society, I asked for comments on communication/receptivity, such as why Princess Diana still came out clear and popular despite her disjointed personal life. Because her more public life never deflected from her (often-denigrated) goal, including her put-down of Prince Charles as possible king.

Whereas President Ramos has overextended his witticism to the point of being capricious—his declared anointing of one of the four Ds (one of them even more vaguely alluded to), his own "graduation" after 1998, his tolerant "neutrality" over the call for Charter change (including the extension of time limit for himself and the legislators), his statements abroad countered by his own men at home. How do you expect people to take these contradictions in real-life situations?

In art you deal with contextually initiated connoisseurs; in life you address a more plural mass ranging from common people to the business and ecclesiastical hierarchies. Life may imitate art, but that can be a dangerous game because you don't deal with metonymies or metaphors but with the very mouths and muscles of men and women. Politicians can only go so far as to play around with their witticisms; the people can soon wise up to these to the point of leading rallies or revolutions.

Manila Standard
1997

On Knowing and Taking Sides

While the war between Iraq and Iran was going on, it seemed natural to side with the former, knowing that the latter was ruled by a fundamentalist bigot.

You might even have heard of Iraq's chemical assault, which was not only illegal but also genocidal, but you pretty much closed your eyes to it, as you hated the Iranian leader more. When Rushdie's novel became controversial, as part of the literati you easily sided with the author without having read the book, it being unavailable in your country, with most liberated press.

But last week, this mad Saddam overcame Kuwait, where you might have a relative or friend working for this country's and his or her family's sake. Suddenly, you were shocked by the fact that this man was just as cruel as the late Iranian imam.

In this world of changing colors and moving fences (the breaking down of the Berlin Wall, the ethnic movement for autonomy in the USSR and even in your own country, other wars and foreign interventions in civil wars), do you really know whose side you're on? (See Schweid's "Shifting Alliances in Mideast," in the August 13 issue of *The Manila Times*.)

Do we know enough of what happened in Kuwait despite the hundreds of laborers we have there? Do we also know that several Filipinos died of brutality in Japan while we were freeing Fumio Mizuno in Negros, which was well covered by the media and the militia? Do we know enough of what Yellow, Red, and Black are for us to speak ill or well so easily of such political and racial colors?

Why does our government take such a cautious stance about the Kuwait invasion, even with the UN, US, USSR, and Arabian sanctions? Does our president know enough of what happens around the world, tried as her government is by the domestic aftermath of the July 16 quake? How will she and we cope with the next oil crisis? With the Filipinos still in and returning from Kuwait?

We often divide the world simply into Black and White, North and South, East and West, Us and Others.

We may even change sides, only to find ourselves caught in another new hegemony, determinism, or cycle. The arts have even been used and abused to perpetuate power or push a specific agenda. Yet it is not always that simple, because as recent scholarship shows, even the supposedly notorious Catherine de Medici had her own good intentions about her genetically weak children or for her dear, dear France in a religious war.

Moving from the professional realm of the arts to the media, you are expected by colleagues to wave the flag for them. Even critics who used to pick on you expect you now to be kind to them—as artists.

But the world and the arts are always enlarging their spheres or shifting their borders, and history periodically calls everyone to judgment. As a critic you are expected to see from a larger perspective. Can you inevitably be so cruel by taking sides? Or by being so surely right? It is hard to say. But History's moving hand urges you to mark its moments, so to speak. Last week, the Young Critics Circle marked its formation in the Ateneo. CCP President Ma. Teresa Roxas warned against the critics' overweening stance, although she mostly noted this in dance. (I don't think that critics have so much potency, especially in this country. Each is only one voice although multiplied in print which, if good, is also multiplied in photocopies by the artists and their agents.)

National Artist Francisco Arcellana said that it is a critic's job to write well as in any writing—and to owe it to no one! Criticism to him is an exercise in consciousness (about art), a meditation on art—which is life aware of itself.

To structuralists like Soledad Reyes, art making is a system of production (after Foucault, et al.) and criticism is an examination of the text, which can have many meanings—from the author, for the audience, and by the code or signals used. A work is no longer sanctified as idealized by the Romanticists or authors who petulantly nursed their "genius."

As a citizen or critic, writer or whore (e.g., pro-or anti-Bases) you are always asked to take a stance, make a choice. Often enough you do not know the whole issue at all, and the stand is either narrow-minded or meaningless.

Since starting *Dance of Life*, I've had to see more and be moved more. More than my easygoing self was willing to take. The more I see, the more I seem to know less! But the very act of writing week by week has shown me how to take life, helped by the tracks of words to keep me on the way, and even byways.

The Manila Times
1990

Hydra Head: Choreography to Criticism

I have sometimes wondered what Tiresias would have been like to dance with.

—Mary Catherine Bateson

Critique and emancipation are two ends of the same piece of string.

—Simon Critchley

Appreciation may even require the connoisseur (*sahrdaya*, the qualified spectator) to forsake his individual point of view, and annihilate the distance between his way of looking at the art-object and its phenomenological objectivity in an intentional space.

—Kalidas Bhattacharya in Pabitra Kumar Roy

Half the home of the dance is the place to rehearse in—the artists' private domain. The other half is the stage or ground for performance that is exposed to the public. In between sits or stands the critic, who is supposed to be informed by both private and public spaces and manifestations of dance. He or she is assumed to have insight into the creative processes of all those collaborating in the artistic formulation and expression, and into the process by which society appreciates dance from outside the context of creation and production. This takes into consideration what Wolfgang Iser says of the "gaps" to be filled in between.

Both ends of the spectrum actually have traditions about motives and styles, techniques and signification. These traditions sum up the aesthetics and history of dance, its modes of signaling and symbolizing, its means of acquiring meaning from both the dispensing and receiving ends.

The critic therefore has to have all these in his/her equipment to be able to speak of dance. He or she is a kind of physician presiding over the state of health, the clarity or obscurity of symbols and symptoms, the perspicacity of artists, and the relevance of dance in society.

Put in between these private, closely creative and openly receptive, public fronts, the critic takes on a hydra head to justly view and join these extremes; moreover, he or she must do so from both past and present perspectives.

This paper attempts to describe the position and problem of a critic, to delineate the function of criticism in artistic understanding and, in greater measure today, to link or contextualize art in its process and its social environment.

It puts across two points: the first pertains to how cultural and anthropological studies need to be adapted by critics in order to have an in-depth, comprehensive and just view of dance; the second considers how the contemporary media have served and yet dis-served the arts in their coverage, which was perhaps once fair but is now so selective (if not reductive) as practiced by a restricted community of communicators who are often ruled by popularization and market forces that determine what they make of "fame" or "success." And how this in fact, by media's mechanical means, leads to the mechanization of arts promotion and appreciation.

Furthermore, this critical cogitation or weighing, especially when written down, happens in reflection after a performance, taking stock of a dance's elements and manifestations in that "vanished point" (a term after Marcia Siegel), when you think about your feelings about a dance.

Anthropology and Aesthetics

In Seoul in 1995, an American critic in my panel argued with my plea that critics should know much more about an imported/exported performance, and what possible processing this had undergone. She claimed that that performance is (perhaps) the only way for a critic in her territorial location to know about that kind of dancing.

On the other hand, Marcia Siegel has suggested how an outsider like her considers together the lexicon, orchestration, structural elements, and performance practice in/behind a dance. She summed this up in a visit to Manila and articulated them in a 1990 Los Angeles conference on multiculturalism. (A term which filmmaker Kumar Shahani dislikes.)

I myself have raised issues about how folk art is represented by the people (even in the same country) other than those who created it. This is a delicate question because appropriators (whom I've often seen in several Philippine dance troupes) can dress up, perform, and relocate a dance, transforming it from ritual to entertainment. (Lest we forget, entertainment involves some kind of ritual if of a secular kind.) Beyond aesthetics, I am concerned about ethnic representation and empowerment.

As a critic, I myself see how difficult it is to see a traditional dance without knowing that tradition firsthand. Remoteness—in time, space, and access, including degrees of sacredness and secularity—may stem from existential and psychological reasons.

But there is no excuse to escape anthropological awareness in order to do justice to a performance. Even transformed dance can only be rightly viewed knowing where it came from and where it has so far gone. In the proliferation of so-called fusion or hybridity, it is truly hard to be judicious when you don't know where the dance is from, where you yourself (viewer/critic) have been, and where both of you are heading.

Look at this example of an Italian in a Spanish flotilla, led by an alienated Portuguese in 1521:

> In order that your most illustrious Lordship may know the ceremonies that these people use in consecrating the swine, they first sound those large gongs. Then three large dishes are brought in; two with roses and cakes of rice and millet, baked and wrapped in leaves, and roast fish; the other with cloth of Cambaia and two standards made of palm-tree cloth. One bit of cloth of Cambaia is spread on the ground. Then two very old women come, each of whom has a bamboo trumpet in her hand. When they stepped upon the cloth they made obeisance to the sun. Then they wrap the cloths about themselves. One of them puts a kerchief with two horns on her forehead, and takes another kerchief on her hands, and dancing and blowing upon her trumpet,

> she thereby calls out to the sun. The other takes one of the standards and dances and blows on her trumpet. They dance and call out thus for a little space, saying many things between themselves to the sun. She with the kerchief takes the other standard, and lets the kerchief drop, and both blowing on their trumpets for a long time, dance about the bound hog. She with the horns always speaks covertly to the sun, and the other answers her. A cup of wine is presented to her of the horns, and she dancing and repeating certain words, while the other answers her, and making pretense four or five times of drinking the wine, sprinkles it upon the heart of the hog. Then she immediately begins to dance again. A lance is given to the same woman. She shaking it and repeating certain words, while both of them continue to dance, and making motions four or five times of thrusting the lance through the heart of the hog, with a sudden and quick stroke, thrust it through from one side to the other. The wound is quickly stopped with grass. The one has killed the hog, taking in her mouth a lighted torch, which has been lighted through that ceremony, extinguishes it. The other one dipping the end of her trumpet in the blood of the hog, goes around making with blood with her finger first the foreheads of their husbands, and then the other; but they never came to us. Then they divert themselves and go to eat the contents of the dishes, and they invite only women.

That was Antonio Pigafetta, chronicler of Fernao de Magalhaes e Mesqita (Fernando Magallanes/Ferdinand Magellan) at the so-called "discovery" of the Philippines. Some legends have cropped up that in fact it was a Malay (claimed as the baptized Enrique, captured from an earlier expedition eastward) who first circumnavigated the globe, not Magellan who was killed in Mactan off Cebu in central Philippines.

For me that is a pretty good description of dance in its time. It has the protagonists, properties, and setting. But it lacks detail about the generically described "dancing" so that we have to fill in much of which we are not sure.

Today, an anthropological/ethnological eye can't be avoided for a critic's viewpoint. Otherwise, even his or her supposed encyclopedic knowledge of dance will remain partial, parochial, or Eurocentric. All of us who have been systematically educated by our colonial masters—to both blame and praise—have been trained on well-articulated aesthetics from the West-end.

Today, anthropology brings our feet back to the ground where the actuality of dance is as real as the body dancing. That body is whole because it is a thinking (Mabel Todd's) and conceptualizing body. It lives geographically and historically, expressing itself within society, a society undergirded by a belief system, a system of codes and regulations, of the said and unsaid, the gaps or "no-thing" Iser speaks of in interpretation, and of the deciphering Vicente Rafael speaks of in translating.

Therefore, how demanding critical reading and writing have become. Both processes have to deal with the idea of beauty in dance (philosophically) and the beauty of the moving body (and bodies that may no longer be prescribed by stereotyping, or dead bodies that had inscribed a dance's shape and style). Both have to deal with the artist(s) and the audience, the processes by which they create and imagine, carrying on or transmuting a tradition in a modernized society.

It is no longer as easy as before to say what is beautiful and why. One must also deal with *how* through time and space: how the old is still beautiful and relevant, and how the new is meaningful for both past and present, from the private and the public perspectives, in multicultural/ transcultural settings.

Eastern Aesthetics

In aesthetics, often enough we are swamped with Western viewpoints and contexts.

A 1982 issue of *Dance Research Journal* (of CORD) juxtaposed two arguments about what the material of dance is. Monroe Beardsley's "What's Going on in Dance" stood for motions becoming "movings" (including the pauses), of volitional and expressive movements—yet not for utilitarian ends.

In the wake of postmodern dance, Noel Carroll and Sally Banes argued against the need for (superfluity of) expressiveness. In light of the fact that the '60s postmodern dance did not require "the intensified way" or obvious expressiveness, Carroll and Banes discussed the significance of framing, contextualizing (of event), and using ordinary movements as ordinary movements in Yvonne Rainer and her peers. They even brought out the use of "refraining" in action and "studied omission." All these in the context of anti-illusion, of anti-tradition, of polemical (not always as "saying," as Beardsley insists) postmodernism in demystifying movements, exemplified then by Jasper Johns and his colleagues in the visual arts.

To Indian filmmaker Kumar Shahani, this framing is based on an individual vision, beyond a cultural framework. In his case, a film may be set or shot in India, but the work is rooted in the individual artist making it. (See later anthropologist Jesus Peralta's perspective.)

Then you come upon Rabindranath Tagore's own idea of man as "the angel of surplus." To him, this is the overflowing in an integrated personality—personality being a character of creative imagination. Moreover, Tagore's idea of beauty (the sensible) is also moral (the supersensible). Thus, he invades and involves the territory of freedom and transcendence, which to him are a priori in creative expression and experience. This freedom is aesthetically transcendent because it goes beyond the factual, natural, and necessary.

To Tagore, art is felt in subjectivity, exemplified by the *rasas*. Again, these rasas are tied to the Maya, where appearance and imagery themselves lead and are instrumental to freedom, to knowing the true world. He invokes the Aristotelian catharsis, in that Tagore's appreciation of art involves the subjectivity of consciousness. He somewhat sums all these up as "existential anthropology."

Again, an important Indian view of art points to the role of the *sahrdaya*, the informed, qualified, or ideal spectator. This is articulated by Kalidas Bhattacharya (again as summed up by Pabitra Kumar Roy, as he does Tagore, Coomaraswamy, Sri Aurobindo and Krishachandra Bhattacharyya; I owe Roy this digest of mine). His qualification also involves freedom from expediency and utility. As described by Roy, to him this freedom is "existential perspective that underlies the aesthetic response."

A respondent, like in Iser's active move to "fill" gaps, is described as in "a free disposition to be filled in by richer contents of freedom in cognitive and conative senses." This freedom is still tied to some form of order and not just the "impression of feeling"; yet this opens to "new possibilities of feeling" or "unknown modes of being" (from Wordsworth).

While the artist's freedom can cut him loose from natural roots and what is called "natural freedom," the *sahrdaya* "combines acute sensitivity and formidable technical understanding with warm and generous susceptibility" or what Tagore may call empathy. These Eastern viewpoints about art do not always jive with Western attitudes.

Anthropologist Jesus Peralta explains the difference between community-based art and more individualized art. The first is posited on societal equilibrium, between all state coordinates, like that between the indigenous and the colonial. Not that communal arts do not undergo change; they do, but again attain (a word suggesting Tagore's "achievement" as the art of creative imagination) a phase of equilibrium. In these phases and contexts, an art value is "explicit only in specific area of relevance" which, again, may suggest Tagore's specificity of aesthetic experience.

Coming to the arts after colonization, Peralta explains how a church- or officially sanctioned art practice became secularized after an edict of Charles III in 1785. From genre to portraiture, art practice gained more individuation. After the academic, prize-winning successes of Juan Luna and Felix Resurrecion Hidalgo in Europe, impressionism influenced Filipino artists, from Fernando Amorsolo and Fabian de la Rosa to modernists like Edades.

But Peralta poses the problem of how this more individual art is based on "alien value." While church-related art was sanctioned by officials, they still or went on to serve the religious feelings of native inhabitants, transforming indigenous belief systems to colonial Christian discipleship and sacraments.

The same issue confronts us today when dealing with the more folkloric arts and the more current arts which arise from different motivations, ways of processing, and methods of dissemination (i.e., marketing). (A relevant study on beauty as power among Tausug gays in southern Philippines also points out this confusion, contradictions, and accommodation. See Mark Johnson, 1997, and related comments from Fenella Cannell, 1999.)

Media and Mass Orientation

The more mercantile use of the arts can be glimpsed at in the coverage of these by the media today.

It is quite easy to say that dance comes from a community, and we laud this as folklore or heritage. Some are even of sacred lineage or usage and therefore revered. Much can't always be qualified, and may only perhaps be justly described in anthropological or psychological terms.

But first I must say that the term "mass" does not exactly match the use of the term "community" in the old and more restricted way. "Mass" is a product of a modern way of life—its economy, politics, and culture. It has popular (or populist) applications, determined not only by traditional class structures but also very much by political agitation and marketing strategies—both manipulating ranks and affiliations.

"Community" once had a more specific geographical application, from villages to sectors of urban conglomeration.

Both terms are often loosely used as one and the same, without much distinction, so that writer and reader, powers-that-be, the fourth estate (the press), and the economic (and professional) classes down the line suffer misrepresentation or careless use, misuse, even abuse.

We are of course grateful (sometimes sycophantically) to the modern media for giving us more access to the arts. They have popularized art acquaintance, appreciation, and promotion. Travel and technologies have even pluralized these further. By the media, criticism has defined and refined itself and its functions, also broadening and deepening our consciousness. From listening and seeing to studying and teaching, traditional and electronic media have been overwhelmingly helpful.

But I fear that the media has been so valued that it has priced itself so high, becoming too self consciously aware of its power. (That power is so beneficial when made to expose or espouse the cause of the disadvantaged and the abused, and those who suffer disasters in many parts of the world.) In the more commodified function, the media has also come to be an amateur impresario or unreliable curator for the arts.

Popularization can turn out to be reductionism, and coverage biased or based on uninformed selectivity. Media's own "formalist" packaging or ratings-orientation can condition the kind of coverage they do. And in the past, media members have also used the arts to lend themselves prestige and respectability, after all, the media also hanker for status—and revenues.

Now, the media market (by for-sale mediation) food, fashion, fitness, religion and scandals, products as contest awards, even news, by their graphic voyeurism. Politicians take advantage of these. In the Philippines, they welcome radio calls at five or six in the morning for them to respond to "issues of the day" to boost their media mileage and voting popularity. Radio and television shows also depend on "text messages" or e-mail (which even CNN solicits) from any Tom, Dick, or Harry—whose opinions are more likely to be unqualified than qualified—to upgrade their ratings.

In the Philippines, where the broadcast media used to volunteer to cover performances, they now ask you to choreograph and appear for "exposure-value." In print media, there are less and less critics on the arts, and their writings are often accompanied by big, colorful pictures—the better to cut down on text—or are simply about the glittering cocktails that mark an opening. A recent forum exposed the fact that feature writers on the arts practice "envelopmental journalism" (popularized during the Marcos government), so that to be covered, you have to "augment" their newspapers' standard fees.

I have a five-point guessing game about critics/dance writers in Metro Manila, depending on how many right answers you can come up with. Guess who these are: 1) a self-referential critic, 2) a sister who lauds sister, 3) a critic with an eye for only one dance company, 4) a magazine editor who is in the board of a company that always lands the cover, and 5) a tough critic, but not when it comes to her own media-patronized solo performances. To top it all, a self-proclaimed national dance company recently closed its season with a clothing brand-sponsored concert; to show what's beneath those "costumes," the dancers dropped their signature jeans to show off their signature undies.

With this kind of artist-market-related production, what kind of art or writing could you expect?

While the late critic Leonides Benesa is respected and anthologized, today, criticism in the Philippines is so suspect. Certainly, writers here are so badly compensated that they have to juggle several jobs (and be hydra-heads economically) to survive. Yet some of the privileged few also enjoy the perks of airlines and hotels, of affluent boards of trustees, of hand-delivered press releases (and sometimes gifts), so that their taste comes with a price tag and their self-importance becomes way out of line.

The coddling of mainstream artists and the neglect of alternative artists in Manila are so flagrant. The idea of "who's who" has gone haywire—not based on worth but on connections, not based on what you can do but who you know—a cultural situation in the Philippines that is not only seen in politics but in the coverage of the arts, even other fields.

Moreover, the very speed by which the media wants to cover the arts and the ephemerality of its focus (on currency, what's "hot" today) go against the more deliberative and concerted processes of art-making. Perhaps the (over)value of the byline has given much potency to the writer's ego and curatorial influence. From what I know, the old *London Times* never used to carry a critic's byline. The later empowerment by acknowledging the writer by name was necessary to give him or her both independence and self-respect. But from current practice, some writers have been so commodified by what they espouse, if not blatantly sell. One's opinions lose credibility when the self has lost its balance and priorities. Yet newspapers and the broadcast media tolerate, if not encourage, this obvious (if still restricted) trend, which only spells doom for the tradition of criticism in the long run. At no point has criticism in the Philippine media gone so low, if not yet rock bottom.

Conclusions

The pledge of anthropologists to be both observers and participants should exemplify to media men and women (whose culture page used to be called women's page) as well as art aficionados the serious and influential scope of their coverage and patronage. For much-read trivia (especially in film coverage), many media practitioners in Manila pose to be both outsiders and insiders, i.e., as gossips rather than real followers of the arts. This kind of double-face or hydra-head is powerful fence-sitting, so different from what I have argued from the anthropological stance.

The hydra head and arms of the modern media can be used deliberately or indiscriminately to reduce life and art to a popularity (or superficiality) contest. Their advanced technologies can turn them into supermachines (earlier exemplified by media hero—who was also social critic—Charles Chaplin) and supermerchandise that have to keep on running and selling.

I have been a longtime critic for the arts in the Philippines (since the 60s), and I now regretfully turn against my own job in confessing some of these current anomalies. But perhaps criticism (or the media) has to turn around on itself to see itself, to be hydra-headed in an honest sense, in a much more complex world where "honesty is the best policy," to be like Tiresias and see both sides of the coin.

World Dance Alliance-Asia Pacific
Kuala Lumpur 2005

Indigenous Scholarship for Informed Criticism

> The past should be altered by the present as much as the present is directed by the past.
>
> —T. S. Eliot

The Filipino critic is still caught in a cultural bind because of his historical background. Among his Southeast Asian brothers, he has had such prolonged general subservience under two Western masters (three, counting the British). Many of his artifacts were either too fragile to survive time, or suppressed and destroyed by his colonialists.

Or these colonial masters were skillful enough to transform the animistic and ancestral spirits and objects of veneration—the diwata and anito—into Europeanized saints, without exactly obliterating the indigenous penchant for and process of ritualization. Today there is a prevailing veneration of the Virgin Mary in many of her guises, the Christ Child in the Santo Niño, and many occupation- and festival-linked saints.

On the other hand, to this day and even in their threatened marginal state, some of these indigenous practices have persisted and have somehow been rescued from oblivion. Scholars trained under colonial education and experience have redirected their attention from the former preoccupation with the signs of hegemonic Western civilization to local and national culture, literature, and arts.

The Situation

My own teacher in Romantic English poetry, Dr. Damiana Eugenio, has for years been assiduously scrounging for materials for her volumes of folklore and traditional literature of Filipinos. Cultural anthropologist

E. Arsenio Manuel has devoted his life to documenting the life and achievements of his countrymen from centuries back. He has long departed from the heretofore-unquestioned theory on migrational waves (Otley Beyer and company), which claims that the country was peopled by Philippineasian or "Austronesians, or a great Mongoloid or Asian. For there is no such thing as Malay race." (See Arnold Azurin's *Reinventing the Filipino*.)

My own colleague Ramon Obusan has devotedly continued the pioneering work of National Artist Francisca Reyes (Tolentino) Aquino by collecting numerous dances from the countryside and hinterlands of the thousand-plus islands of the Philippines. Like her, he runs the danger of being swamped by the data so that, although as an anthropologist he has a broader and deeper background, he may simply succumb to accumulation and suffer largely unprocessed data. Inasmuch as he also directs a dance company, he can be enticed by prestige-giving presentation than by conscientious study and preservation. He rightly acknowledges the fact that a living folk art does undergo changes through time, but primarily these should rest and come from the "owners" (the provenance) of the dances and rituals than from the certified "appropriators" (inheritors) who are modern-day choreographers (such as what Martha Graham claimed about herself—a professional, creative thief for the theater).

As Manuel himself commented, that was the limitation in Aquino's and Candido Bartolome's studies of the folk games: "These pioneers were more interested in their performance rather than in their distribution and prehistory so that often the ethnic identification of the games is not indicated, and much less are they compared to similar ones inside and outside the country." (See Mauro Garcia's *Readings in Philippine Prehistory*.) Understandably, that was the limitation of the general scholarship of the time, such which later-day researchers like Jose Maceda in music have remedied.

So largely is the real scholarship in Philippine dance impoverished that even in academic circles, the preparation and provision for it are not only timorous but stingy, not only innocently uninformed but also insistently insular. There is a great deal of praise for the amount of collected dances than for the depth of understanding of a few, for the impact of restaging or "recreating" than for authentication and contextualizing. In practice, these dances are for the most part given token acknowledgment as signs of regional or provincial pride rather than as living cultural artifacts beyond the success of folk dance groups in national and global projections.

In the midst of these colonial and postcolonial conditions, the dance critic is ill-equipped to deal with indigenous expression. Brought up under the Western system of thinking, he conveniently falls under the spell of accessible Western forms and processes, rather than be well-armed with Eastern insights and information. Especially in dance where ethnological research is scarce, lacking in means and methods, the critic is trapped in superficial knowledge of his own choreographic culture. Because of the prevailing "acquisitive" inclination in the field to collect without thorough understanding, there has been no outstanding ethnological study of Philippine dances. As already said, these dances are consequently showcased by the Christianized majority rather than by the tribes themselves who are politically and economically marginalized. From these performances, the critic inevitably gets an approximation or interpretation of these dances. Both from the supposed scholar and from the spectacular stage, he gets perhaps all-too-sifted information.

A Further Advance

One recent endeavor to somehow remedy this situation was undertaken by the last artistic director of the Cultural Center of the Philippines, Dr. Nicanor Tiongson. With his leadership he gathered together sets of artists and scholars to undertake the following:

1. file video-documentation of Philippine rituals and practices, complemented by photographs;
2. edit and package video-films and monographs that anthologize these Philippine practices, primarily for educational purposes;
3. publish periodicals of anthologized regional Philippine literature, with general culture somehow covered on the side;

4. publish the ten-volume *CCP Encyclopedia of Philippine Art* that consolidates ethnological entries in two volumes, and specific procedures and personalities in the seven arts of architecture, dance, music, theatre, visual arts, film and literature in the others.

The last succeeds the ten-volume *Filipino Heritage* (1977-78) released sixteen years earlier and considered the most reliable encyclopedic publication in Philippine culture of its time.

All of these efforts aim: 1) to temper the predominance of Western bias, procedure, and provision in historical, ethnological, and critical scholarship; 2) to present in a broader perspective the cause, form, function, and effect of cultural practices, including that of calling attention to the paucity or inadequacy of studies in several fields; and 3) to recognize the contributions of personalities and groups in the functioning and building up of national culture, even if they are drawn from specific ethnolinguistic areas.

This monumental contribution only initiates a more concerted and general effort to gather information on Philippine culture. In the field of dance, with the slimmest volume in the set, there is so much more to be done and the result simply shows the grave lack of dance scholars (and critics) in the Philippines.

Present State

Unfortunately there are too few Tiongsons around to spearhead this kind of scholarly thoroughness. Himself a critic, historian, and playwright, he is of course highly aware of the importance of research and scholarship. Tiongson understands that creative work and critical study must be paired with research and documentation. The latter can incite creative output from the artists, and critical writing becomes reliable with informative data. Moreover, both become truly relevant in the context of social conventions and traditions.

However, serious scholarship in dance remains erratic in the Philippines because of a lack of consistent support and respectable methodology. While critical writing, especially for the newspapers, is also a kind of scholarship—a scholarship in a hurry, and consequently a historical document—it still needs to be informed by the past (colonial and precolonial), and not just keep apace with the present fashions. Criticism becomes trustworthy with awareness of tradition. In assessing today, it becomes meaningful and believable with the background of yesterday.

As a Tagalog saying puts it, "Ang hindi marunong lumingon sa pinangalingan ay hindi darating sa paruruonan." (He who does not know how to look back cannot arrive at his destination.) To contemporize the analogy, in order to drive safely, you have to have the reflecting mirrors to see what's behind you.

The development of research is handicapped by many factors: 1) most educational approaches are just for dance instruction, with hardly any emphasis on dance history and ethnology; 2) tenacious fidelity to past procedures hinders the improvement of systems of study;* 3) video-film has become an all-too-convenient means of documentation, stealing the critic's attention away from the analytic process of movement notation (so far there are only two *trained* notators—in Laban and in Benesh—in the whole country of sixty-plus million; 4) the emphasis on restaged performances (and contests) has drawn attention away from authentication, from the very originators of the dance (in the countryside) to its appropriators (in nationally recognized dance groups); 5) cultural policies are still much centered in Manila so that focus and funds are still far removed from the folk of the provinces where dance and music are still essential to ritual or social practices than just to theatrical attendance. Today, even centralized educational policies have marginalized dance

---

* "Each generation, like each individual, brings to the contemplation of art its own categories of appreciation, makes its own demands upon art, and has its own uses for art. 'Pure' artistic appreciation is to my thinking only an ideal, when not merely a figment, and must be, so long as the appreciation of art is an affair of limited and transient human beings existing in space and time. Both artist and audience are limited. There is for each time, for each artist, a kind of alloy required to make the metal workable into art; and each generation prefers its own alloy to any other. Hence, each new master of criticism performs a useful service merely by the fact that his errors are of different kind from the last; and the longer the sequence of critics we have, the greater amount of correction is possible." T. S. Eliot on "The Use of Poetry and the Use of Criticism," 1993.

and cultural instruction as fringe factors to the development of the citizenry and to their academic and cultural life.

As for the critic, with the paucity of scholarly studies in dance, the dance critic is still not fully and freely informed of his cultural roots, and therefore not comprehensively and incisively equipped to deal with dance expressions in national and global perspectives.

Kide, Seoul
1995

Who Writes the World Dance History?

To answer the question directly, the world dance history has been written by Westerners. With the triumph of the Western script and the success of the Gutenberg press, it became inevitable that the Westerners would dominate in publishing. Moreover, with the present hegemony of the English language, world history is mostly written and marketed in the tongue of the global powers. My own personal education was nurtured in English so that it has also taken over not only my hand but also my heart.

Let me begin with the venerable Curt Sachs (1937), translated by Bessie Schoenberg. He gave us a sweep of the expert musicological and anthropological perspectives of his time. Today, we find his method inadequate, but he also laid the groundwork on which the future of world dance history should be written. No matter how wanting his work is by today's standards, he did open our eyes to the diverse range and aspects of looking at and experiencing dance.

Janet Adshead Lansdale and June Layson (1983 and 1994) present a wider perspective, not only examining the aspects and forms of dance, but also linking it with various intellectual and societal studies. The two authors humbly call their book *Dance History: An Introduction*. Yet one wishes that its sample readings had acknowledged a wider range of dance practice, especially from Asia and the Pacific. Fortunately, Paul Spencer (1985) provides a larger spectrum, but his purpose is to serve a more specific (sociological, ethnological) perspective rather than historical.

Although we now realize that we can't get further from the mainly Western and theatrical emphases of Mary Clarke and Clement Crisp, when their *The History of Dance* (1981) came out, I eagerly looked forward to it. They did give all of twenty-six pages (some as full-page illustrations) to "Eastern Dance." To my disappointment, the book never mentioned the Philippines. Before the book came out and while in London, I gave Ms. Clarke a copy of Reynaldo Alejandro's book (1978, which I edited and updated). But she never made any reference to our islands.

Mike Davis and Fernau Hall's picture book on the world of dance (1973), at least, devotes five paragraphs on the Bayanihan and one full page to a reduced yet centered photograph of Singkil with dancers Linda Anido, Eddie Elejar, and Lita Ramos. Arnold Haskell's now antique *Ballet Annual* reviewed with photographs the Bayanihan appearance in London.

These popular historians of dance still carry on a "colonizing gaze" so that they always prioritize and emphasize the Western forms and practitioners. To most of them, dance in the East is mainly of the court or the folk so that later achievements and changes in Asian dance (including the theatrical) have not gone beyond the various rituals and wayangs, kabuki, etc. Understandably, other than a few anthropologists (who could be consulted), these popular authors do not travel to Asia extensively so that they are largely ignorant of what's happening here. (One exception is critic Jochen Schmidt of Germany. He has made possible special Asian issues of *Ballett International-Tanz Aktuell.*)

But how we in the Philippines (and the rest of Asia) depend on these sample texts for our undergraduate courses! Do we have any choice? On Philippine dance, Alejandro (1978) and Leonor Orosa Goquingco (1980) are useful. But these are not always accessible because they are either out of print or expensive as coffee-table books. One has to seek them out in the few libraries we have, if they are there at all.

Recognition

Speaking of periodicals, the so-called journalistic "bible" of the dance world, *Dance Magazine* of New York, has limited input on the Asia-Pacific scene, and, for the most part, prioritizes theatrical dance. In fact, its annual award, which has been given out since 1954, has never honored any Asian practitioner. Last year, 1997, it did honor Hernando Cortez (a Filipino-American) and his Dancers Responding to AIDS, but only because of the group's special concern and not for Cortez's own artistic merits. Moreover, Cortez has spent his life and career in the United States.

Dance Australia's first editor used to welcome news from Asia, but since my correspondence with the magazine ended a long time ago, I have lost track of the magazine's coverage. Another big English dance press is of course in England. Unless Asian dancers travel to the West, they are not interested in news from this side of the world, except from Australia and New Zealand, and occasionally, the former Commonwealth countries.

Serious historical research and critical dance and theater journals from the West are also way beyond the means of most Asian academicians and students. Consequently, they are hardly referred to or seen. Membership in dance societies (with publication privileges) is also priced with the Western income in mind. (Just look at how WDA's *Channels* is processed at the most economical means, paying no editorial or writing fees.) More recently, Jack Anderson unearthed (again) such names as Michio Ito, Uday Shankar, and a few more in *Art Without Boundaries* (1997), and Sally Banes featured Sada Yacco in *Dancing Women* (1998). Though they should be commended for acknowledging the importance of these dancers, their attention might perhaps be attributed again to the fact that these dancers have appeared in the West. In fact, these dancers are cited for their significance in the Western context. Otherwise, they'd be blotted out like all the other "modern dancers" who lived and are living in the East.

Asian/Philippine Problems

Dance histories have been written in the East, but many of these are not readable to Western writers or even for colonized Asians like me. Catalogues of Asian publications (even from the English-speaking India, etc.) are hardly available to us and the rest of the world. The Association of Southeast Asian Nations (ASEAN) monographs on the dances of member countries are hardly heard of and barely available. (An ASEAN project on dance instruction on three dancers per member country has been processed for video-films and textual, musical documentation, but these are not yet available.)

The new and handsome *Kasaysayan* (1998), a ten-volume set on Philippine history, only solicited two pages on Philippine dance. In contrast, Japan Foundation's profile on Philippine dance, together with all the other arts and education, in *Contemporary Philippine Culture* (1998), the text on dance occupied ten of its 230 pages.

Indeed, we ourselves fail to contribute scholarship on Philippine or Asian dance. With the rich and diverse repertoire of our people and the history of theatrical dance that spans over a century (since the zarzuela, opera, musicals, and Maestro Appiani's troupe in the Spanish times), we still turn to the authority of Pigafetta or Fr. Colin to tell us about our ritual dances, or we are happy with few sketchy articles in popular magazines. Of course, most Filipino writers in general are not paid for their research publications. Or they are paid a small lump sum for their output, and they lose their rights to it. Most are also not paid royalties, as sales are hardly monitored.

When we called for articles for the *Cultural Center of the Philippines Encyclopedia Of Philippine Art* (1994), we had a hard time getting writers for dance who were not only reliable (which meant they could meet deadlines), but also possessed comprehensive background knowledge and few biases. Volume V on dance ended up as the slimmest volume in the set of ten. (This encyclopedia is now available in CD-ROM).

We love to regale ourselves and our guests with enactments of so many dances. But no serious writer aside from Alejandro, Orosa Goquingco, or Ligaya Fernando Amilbangsa has emerged to focus more attention on choreography. (A musicologist, Elena Rivera Mirano, has presented a comprehensive view of the dance *subli* of Batangas.)

The lack of local enthusiasm for movement notation (Benesh and Laban have been introduced by two practitioners here) proves further how illiterate the Philippine dance world is. There is hardly any interest in or concern for exactness, for broad usefulness (for international exchange and scholarship), for analytic study, and for a real sense of history.

Final Questions

When the *International Encyclopedia of Dance* came out this year, I was unhappy about the fact that there was a merely token attempt to gain a broader input on the Philippines. Local experts were never consulted. Again, at the cost that the six-volume set is sold, it will hardly be available to Asian readers and students of dance. I myself will have to save all of my net income at the university for five months to afford a complete set.

So, who writes Philippine dance history? So far, in the last twenty years, only one has done a book on it comprehensively, and it needs to be enlarged and updated.

Who writes the dance history of the world? Mostly Westerners, who in turn write mostly about themselves and from their own colonial world map and perspective.

World Dance Alliance-Philippines/*Korean Journal of Dance Studies*
Manila/Seoul
1998/1999

Writing on the Margins

For a long time I have grieved over the absence of writing on the rise of new talents. By new I don't mean just the young but also the not-so-young who may have found their own artistic identities later in life in what Peter Brook calls "the rough" in theater.

In the world of dance, such vibrant talent was embodied at the turn of the twentieth century by Isadora Duncan and company, including a cabaret queen in France, Loie Fuller, who moved like a George Melies film with all her lights, her skirt-and-sleeves-that-are-wings-that-are-flowers-that-are-flames, etc. Their tribe cleared the air and stage for what in the '60s also came to be called New Dance. At Judson Church in New York, they "destroyed" the dance to renew it.

Thus, it is disheartening to find that such an artist as Myra Beltran is not even seen and written about by two of our leading dailies' writers on dance, especially when one of them is just a kilometer or so away from where Beltran holds fort on West Avenue.

When the Asia and Europe Foundations and Goethe Institute-Singapore held a Dance Forum last January, they sought out non-mainstream artists. Success—as Jaime C. Laya calls and hails the "successful financial group" in his new book—was not the aim, but sincere efforts to find and make dances in our time.

And so they invited Paul Morales, Liza Fernandez (who had just won the UP Gawad Chancellor for choreography), playwright-dancer Jay Cruz, and Jay Loyola of Palawan, along with old fogeys like Tibo Fernandez of Iligan, Cora Iñigo, and me. They held workshops and we window-shopped when free. Otherwise, they can be expected to keep the company of well-known names like Denise and Edna, Eddie and

Tony, Gener and Douglas. Which is not to say that Denise essentialized the *Ramayana* in making *Realizing Rama.*

As I said earlier, writers on dance have neglected not only young bodies but also not-so-young bodies. After all, talent is not bound by age. Talent manifests itself in one's ability to make up new things from what one feels strongly about. New because freshly thought of, and this includes old things seen in a new light. To have talent is to confront and cross swords with whatever aesthetics and cultural attitudes are raised and exhibited.

In dance (or other art forms), to remedy the neglect is to attend performances and to be happy or unhappy with what the tyros of choreography do. They can either disappoint or reward you. As a critic, you are mining for potential, for the hidden, even scarce, lode.

But beyond the act of mining, you can help them age and heat up their lodes to be gems in less than a lifetime.

Because they are people, they may respond with anger or gladness. Perhaps this will help them find themselves. Specifically, themselves as artists.

But what do our papers seem more interested in? They feature, for example, my student Liza and a splash of photos of *Don Quixote* or another set of trophies and medals of my friend Shirley. Nothing wrong with these, but it will also be good if they allot some space to the less famous females and fellows.

By seeing fresh talents, you train your eyes to view dance with more sophistication instead of limiting yourself to what you're comfortable with, as when you put on dark glasses the under glare of the sun. Some of us are now so comfortable in tinted airconditioned cars or FXs. Consequently, we miss out on how the young ones (and rejuvenated ones in their 40s and 50s) remake the dance, or any art form for that matter.

You might have heard of the superstylist Arlene Croce of the *New Yorker*. She must have provoked the book *The Crisis of Criticism* after refusing to see the not-so-Balanchine (Croce's god) ballet of Bill T. Jones about AIDS. Calling the work "victim art," she said she could only sympathize with the ill per se, but not with them in a piece as performers. One of the most witty, incisive, and provocative writers on dance—and I myself rave over her pointedness and style—she consequently lost her prime and prized post in New York's respected if not revered periodical. (A side note: from my experiences in the local scene, critics can lose their assignment because of a sudden change in editor. This has happened to me three times.)

It is not enough for a critic to criticize well. You must somehow also have a great heart. Love artists, even if you have to bite them sometimes. Tell them those are "love bites."

We also seem to neglect seeing the old for what it is or was. For example, in folk dance, much of what we see is staged and romanticized for commercial purposes.

Although real for what they are *now*—as what is exhibited of the tagged and prized material culture in the Cameroon Grass-fields—their roots and province have been buried under spectacle and success. (For example, I again heard at "Magandang Gabi Bayan" that the singkil is a courtship dance.)

There was an obvious contrast in 1998 when we had an international folklore/folkdance festival. While those from abroad danced their folk dances in the manner of native dancers, we did ours with all the flourish (*bongga*), the purpose of which, it seemed, was to set our best foot forward. When I watched a Kaliwat co-production of *Mindasilang* in Davao in 2000, it looked "provincial" to some but authentic to me; however, when it got to Manila as NCCA's best choice from Mindanao, I was blinded by the gold costumes and fanfare in the finale, and it lost its edge as a result of toning down and trimming of the presentation's arguments on the problems among the *lumad*, *moro*, and *kristiano*. Perhaps such changes were undertaken to suit Manila's sophisticated audience. How far have we gone from Francisca Reyes Aquino to the Bayanihan and its contemporaries? We may say the Bayanihan is true to what it wishes to project to itself. But to the respective cultures displayed and professed abroad, how true?

When the December 2000 *Dayaw* was staged at the Luneta by the NCCA, did you have the uncanny feeling it was like the St. Louis Exposition? A kind of endo-colonialism, where we use "the other" among us to display a kind of bureaucratic aesthetics?

How do we find again what we had found? Do we continue to ask questions about what we have done to our dances? Or just trust what the Bayanihan or Ramon Obusan says is our people's artistic expression? Do we even bother to go and see how the real Ifugao or Maranao do it? (Which is also a question of funding, and in our political situation, of connection, as in how to get there.) How true is Metro Manila's truth?

Thus, even in the realm of traditional arts, we must never stop inquiring. We must interrogate even that which is encased in glass and considered "hallowed research." When was the research undertaken? On the basis of whose assumptions? Beyer's, Fox's, Jocano's, Peralta's, or Magos'?

Last month I was pressed to go to the Subanon conference in Zamboanga, but then again, I didn't. There was an ethnomusicology conference in Diliman, a transferred/relocated discussion on the musics of Asia. Which one could be truer?

Both. One pertains to what the folks themselves do. The other has to do with how we performers and scholars play and talk about it. None is actually false—except by way of obvious errors and erasures. Both rest on how we value them, their distinctions and differences. The work of the critic is so broad and so immediate, and for so cheap a fee or no fee at all.

In my semiotics class, I always start with John Berger's ideas in *Ways of Seeing*, in order to clear (or heal) the very act of seeing. Much of what Isadora Duncan and the "terpsichores in sneakers" (Sally Banes) did twice in the twentieth century was to sweep the ground anew. Inasmuch as there are more practitioners and performers now—what with our population explosion and migrations—we have to do much more for so little material rewards. There are more greenhouses and larger farms, and the systems to set beds, plow, plant, nurture, prune, water, etc. are more complex and time-consuming.

It doesn't matter what specific field, the same (small) privilege and responsibility hold. Go to know. Look to see. Listen to hear. What's the buzz? What's the pitch? How's how?

Yet so few are critics actually writing and publishing or being published. (Newspapers don't employ deputy critics, so that when a presentation is missed, it is not reviewed. Our papers are no longer reliable as sources of research.)

And how nearsighted are the ones who have the means and power to speak! Some aren't even out in the sun and already they are behind dark glasses and tinted car windows, with tainted views about Philippine arts and culture.

University of the Philippines/Young Critics' Circle
Quezon City
2002

Who Is Dance

Bayanihan the Beloved

A byword here and abroad since its historic 1958 debut in Brussels, the Bayanihan is the company that is most identifiably Filipino. Encyclopedists like Koegler (German), Wilson (English), and Grigorivich et al. (Russian) include the Bayanihan in their dictionaries. Those of you who weren't around then can't imagine how jubilant the country was over the 1958 triumph.

After more than twenty-five years, the Bayanihan remains a beloved company welding amateurism and professional expertise; the former refers to the dancers who have changed from generation to generation (as in the fortunate Anido and Ramos who have been immortalized in a Ladro sculpture), and the latter to the artistic and administrative staff in charge of the Bayanihan Folk Arts Center.

Under the Columbia Artists, the Bayanihan scored its tenth world tour recently, celebrating their homecoming with their *Pagbati* presentation at the Cultural Center from April 6-8. Their amateurism and expertise, their research and theatricalism, have helped sustain and intensify the Bayanihan charm.

To quote Vilma R. Santiago-Felipe in the April 8 issue of *Bulletin Today*, "So, this is what Bayanihan is today!" And what will it be tomorrow?

Today, it has remained essentially the same since its post-Brussels homecoming. *Flight of the Idaw* keeps the Mountain Province suite with its bold warriors, serpentine *banga*-bearing maidens, and its stamping, hopping dancer-musicians—all in their red skirts or G-strings, feathers and beads. A play on crescendo, it includes the indispensable war dance washed in dramatic red and green light, the bouncing or gliding line of women balancing pots, a swooping blanket-cloaked suitor pursuing an exotic and dexterous maiden (with more pots on her head, ten to be exact), and a nuptial ceremony.

Imagine all of them turning from brassy primitives to polished Christians in *Aires de Verbena.* Guitars, singing (aptly in Spanish), capiz-shell bulbs, and elaborate arches set the stage for black-and-white Maria Clara-gowned *zagalas* and baro-and-salakot-clad *zagales*. Other attractions include a *paseo* (one maid, several swains), a green shawl to reify a Spanish innuendo, tambourines, and noisy Latin or bamboo castanets. Add to these the novelty of ribbons, and what you have seems like a scene from Ashton's *La Fille Mal Gardee*; add the urgent *zapateados*, or the whirl of *Polkabal*, and you have a panorama of Spanish Philippines with its pretty, prepossessing women and adorable, adoring men.

Muslim Mosaic, another such cornucopia of colors and sounds, is set in the Philippine South. It is flirtation based on male bravado and female coy assurance—a kris-flashing prince and a (red) fan-expert-princess dressed in gold (from her sarimanok headdress to her delicate shoes), together with a troupe of fan dancers walking through bamboo traps like gods on turbulent but festive waters. Add to these a gliding, running solo paced and laced a la Loie Fuller, the awesome *pag-alay* on two hoisted bamboo poles with vinta-effect, and you have another play on crescendo, from the languid to the frenzied.

Cut again to familiar and unfamiliar regions, the display of variations in *Halinhinan,* and you get another multicolored mosaic. Opening with a bang like *Flight*, it has men in red and purple pants and coconut shells in maglalatik, yellow and black patadyong-clothed girls who are literally chicks in *itik-itik*, a deliberately slow-paced *dugso* with Bukidnon maidens in fan-like headdresses, geometric-patterned gowns, and ankle bells, and a gambol of T'boli guys and gals, ending with the now signature *pandanggo sa ilaw*, which turns into *oasioas*, itself turning into fireflies by a skillful blackout.

Bayanihan typifies any troupe's ending, complete with a bahay kubo built on stage; an occupational suite on the rice culture; a bench scene accompanied by the quietly spectacular *binasuan* made more dexterous by a slow-tumbling dancer; a *musikong bumbong* (sounds like a name for ever-adolescent musicians); a paced-up *bulaklakan*, *kuratsa*, and *subli* (subservient men, indeed, as one theorized), and the finale of all finales, tinikling, the trap-filled bird dance elevated to a symbol by N. V. M. Gonzales or suggestive of our skillful maneuvers regarding international debts today.

The Bayanihan remains the beloved. With the most meaningful name for any dance group and unwavering excellence in stagecraft—pacing, blocking, costuming, lighting, parallel, or crisscrossing storylines—the Bayanihan Philippine Dance Company remains as spectacular and endearing as ever. It always promises and delivers a broad spectrum of sheer dance delight. Expertise is always evident as already acknowledged, but this is well balanced by the authentic charm of youthful dancers that charm the world wherever they go, on and offstage. They are the real magic that moves us.

Long after the international taste shifted to authentic importations (as that demanded by the Asia Society in the United States), the Bayanihan has remained durable and appealing. Now, after more than twenty-five years, perhaps it needs to review, modify, or amplify its scope of presentations. We still need its time-tested success, but I certainly agree with Santiago-Felipe that we can't keep loving it for all the same reasons—its broad, broad way or folkloric smorgasbord for all men. As Bayanihan the beloved, it gets all my devoted admiration, but like a long-standing affair, ours must deepen into a marriage. For this to happen, it needs to evolve more willfully, perhaps in terms of a more decolonized style of presentation, if not artistic direction. The Bayanihan needs and deserves to be venturesome again.

Arts Monthly/Cultural Center of the Philippines
1984

Women of the Dance

The quest for a better life for themselves and their families has led many women to seek employment opportunities abroad. It is sad to see these women leave their homes and schools—the very core of our social ties and institutions—in order to find better ways to support their families. It is easy to understand their migration—there are so many to feed, so few (low-paying) jobs available, and so much poverty and danger in the countryside from which they come.

Today our women (and men) are our best merchandise to sell—as so obviously seen in the japayuki—in order to prop up our sagging finances. The finances may be propped up, but not always the families, the emotional security of the spouses and children left behind, and the happiness of our people in general. Our men and women abroad, in their labor for the future, end up sacrificing their today.

Fortunately, in the world of dance in the Philippines, there are outstanding women who have chosen to stay home. Perhaps they are and were never as hard up as our teachers-turned-domestic helpers, or teenagers-turned-japayuki dancers. Certainly, these extraordinary women do not aspire for riches, for they remain here, uplifting the art of dance at home and assuring the future of the art here in the country.

Some of our first extraordinary women in dance were Francisca Reyes Aquino and her numerous followers in folk dance. In theatrical dance, there were Remedios "Totoy" de Oteyza and Leonor Orosa Goquingco. The first group exemplified assiduous research and restoration of the dances of our people. The second group exemplified classicism and Filipinism, respectively. Their colleagues, like Anita Kane, Rosalia Merino Santos, Fe Sala Villarica, etc., shared their respective idealism, including a specific modernism (Santos, Carmen Adevoso, with Manolo Rosado).

Of the current practitioners, Corazon Generoso Iñigo continues to hold the fort at the University of the Philippines, Tita Layag Radaic in her school at St. Theresa's College, and Julie Borromeo and Vella Damian in their studios at home. Unlike a number of dancers who have enriched themselves through our export-entertainment industry, these special women are like sacerdotal ladies of the art of dance. Iñigo has led three university folk dance groups that have won accolades and awards abroad. Intangible aspirations like prestige—not material possessions like cars and condominiums—have been fuel for her drive for excellence. She was also in popular entertainment, the cinema, and worked for the Araneta enterprises, but she remained a teacher in the main. Now still a teacher at the College of Human Kinetics in Diliman, she periodically leads a fourth group, the UP Filipiniana alumni group, in festivities abroad.

Radaic has also spearheaded some trips abroad with her Dance Theatre Philippines, against great odds at one time. Her group was classified "junior" and therefore harder to "sell," but it also provided "senior" companies, including those abroad, with dancers. The group also survived by frugal management, trust in each other, and her very own indomitable will. Now she has lost her company of twenty-one years, without anyone's tears but her own. She continues to train dancers.

The same fate met Damian's Dance Concert Company. One of the most respected teachers of ballet in the country, she also raised a number of distinctive dancers, including her nephew Augustus, who danced with Maurice Bejart and Yvonne Cutaran of Les Grands Ballets Canadiens. She and Radaic continue to teach in their private schools, and are still involved in the consortium company called Philippine Ballet Theatre. Damian also has musical projects on the side; Radaic now has pointe-shoes to further serve the dance.

Borromeo still runs her Dance Arts Studio in Mandaluyong, one of the oldest surviving schools in the country and thus deserving some citation. In both ballet and jazz, she has not only developed dancers but also aficionados for dance. Sometimes she goes to Singapore to choreograph or produce, together with her expatriate sister Rose. Recently she organized the Alliance of Committed Artists in the Performing Arts of the Philippines, choosing members with national stature. Its first project is to help upgrade the technical level of trainers in our entertainment industry in cooperation with the government.

A fifth figure is Alice Reyes. Although now long settled in the United States, she had helped found one enduring company, Ballet Philippines. It was her vision, initially shared with cofounder Eddie Elejar, which sustained the company and its school, both celebrating their silver anniversary this season. She is, of course, well known as a choreographer of remarkable achievements. After the two sisters' (Edna and Denisa) terms, the company is now in the good hands of Agnes Locsin from Davao.

These five senior women—three of whom I once called "the mad women of Manila"—have definitely shaped the direction of our theatrical dance, as much as the "five mothers"—Orosa Goquingco, de Oteyza, Kane, Santos, and Villarica—did in their own time. Except for Reyes, they have all stayed in the country and continue to pledge their labor to their art. Some have won token recognition, but never riches. But beyond any measure and reward, it has been much through their leadership that our art of theatrical dance has prevailed and progressed.

In comparison, our men in dance have also continued to do their share, though some of their great moments were also tied to the women they worked with. Without denigrating their own achievements, these men were served by women. They were like sisters, mothers, wives who more than tended to artistic gardens. It was they who hunted for funding and sought avenues to ensure stable operations in various dance endeavors. Except for one, these women even selflessly helped men outside of their own school or company's interest. I believe that the still-to-be-written history of dance will do better justice to them.

These women's "home" has been the dance itself. Like beautiful but hard-working Cinderellas, they tended their art's hearth with their life's dedication.

Immediate followers have come and gone, with no one matching these five women's practice and resolve. Much younger ones are coming up, like those in the Association of Ballet Academies in the Philippines and those with the Royal Academy of Dancing system. They seem to be conscientious teachers, more than just ambitious dancers or get-rich-quick entertainers. Hopefully they can be spared the arduous hurdles their seniors had to *jete* over.

Any art has its high and low moments, its rise and decline. I believe that, despite the lack of institutional support (except for one), the golden days of our theatrical dance took place during the time of Iñigo, Radaic, Borromeo, Damian, and Reyes, and theirs was a glorious period in our dance history. Theirs was a most trying but tantalizing time.

Manila Chronicle
1994

Note

Since this was written, much more have happened. For example, Iñigo became artistic director of the Cultural Center of the Philippines; Radaic and Damian worked out a Philippine ballet syllabus with Noordin Jumalon. Jumalon's teacher Villarica received her ballet school with its Queen City Chamber Ballet in Cebu.

Leonor, My Penpal

These days you have textmates, chatmates, and e-mail pals. In my younger days, our circle of virtual friendships was smaller, partly because it involved more effort. We had to write with a pen and paper, then mail the letter at the post office. We had less access to addresses, and we had to wait for weeks to get an answer. Enduring the passage of time while waiting for a letter in the mail was a powerful lesson in patience.

Today one can quickly make friends via the Internet. And get married more quickly too, perhaps at risk. E-mail is composed by just "thinking aloud," and texts sent and passed from person to person are made to sound knowledgeable, witty, or funny—sometimes at other people's expense. These methods of communication can make you sound better and attractive than who and what you really are.

One day, entering the lobby of the CCP, National Artist Leonor Orosa Goquingco handed me a letter. It was photocopied—*xeroxed*, in Filipino lingo. It was a copy of a letter I sent her many years ago. Leonor then greeted me as *penpal*.

Yes, Leonor was my penpal. Chatting with my mother back in Negros as she worked at her sewing machine, I got to know that she and Leonor went to the same high school in Bacolod. Leonor was the valedictorian of her class. (Later, she would be *summa cum laude* in St. Scholastica.)

I first knew of her through the newspapers as one of Manila's foremost choreographers, directors, and producers of dance. Her own sister Rosalinda Orosa was a critic for *Manila Chronicle*, while Morli Dharam was a critic for *The Manila Times*. Leonor soon followed suit and started writing for the papers too. I began writing long after Leonor did. I was motivated to be like them in *Negros Clarion* of Angel Lobaton.

When I was teaching literature in Iloilo—my first job—I once asked my penpal to get me tickets to performances of Margot Fonteyn and the rest of London's Royal Ballet at the Rizal Theater (now demolished, which I think is truly unfortunate) by architect Nakpil.

Last year, with Bien Lumbera, I curated the NCCA-CCP's *Luwas* exhibition on national artists, where one of the three in dance was Leonor, and one of the three in architecture was Nakpil.

When I moved to Quezon City to do graduate work in comparative literature in UP, I was in the Morato area, the neighborhood of Leonor. When I had freer weekends, I used to visit Leonor on Timog, and our talks lasted into lunch, even dinner. Those days brought dance history to life.

At the time, I helped myself through school by writing reviews weekly for the *Weekly Nation*. My editors were NVM Gonzalez and Consorcio Borje. I was a "nodding acquaintance" of Baby Orosa and Morli Dharam, too. As for Leonor, we became pals in the field of letters, and not just postal-wise.

What got me interested in Leonor as dance artist was her Filipino ballets. She was not just a choreographer, but she was identifiably a Filipino choreographer.

When I did my dance productions in Iloilo in the '60s, I was motivated to create such Filipino ballets. When I joined Dance Theatre Philippines (DTP) in the late '60s, my colleagues Eddie Elejar, Tita Radaic, Julie Borromeo, and Luis Layag were similarly inspired. DTP, which helped get Ballet Philippines going in 1970, was one of the first professional ballet companies to set a full Filipino ballet repertoire. We felt we were carrying her torch. Thus, we also became pals in choreography and dance production.

It seems that today's dancers have more opportunities to enjoy the limelight and more access to the local and international stage. Often, their careers become solely their own. They flit from studio to studio, company to company, even in and out of the country.

Often their sense of rootedness lands them in a smaller circle—sometimes a hegemonic one. Often, they lose sight of dance from a nationwide perspective, focusing only on the so-called "national" name, as in a dominant group or project. Artistic success in Metro Manila can lead to a loosening of provincial ties, and I don't mean just going to the provinces to visit and dance. What I mean is the sense of belonging and giving to the provinces, and even the whole country.

This we somehow had with Leonor's achievements, her Filipino ballets like *Return to Native*, *Noli Dance Suite*, and *Filipinescas*, and her books. She had a commitment to dance not just as art but as a people's expression.

May I offer a humble acronymic verse to Leonor today:

L – evitate body and mind,
E – lucidate us to find
O – ver the ground of our soul
N – ative steps and songs to call
O – ur hearts to claim ascendance,
R – eturnings by way of dance
O – nward as we remember
R – ivers of dreams forever,
O – rdered in Art's heated forge.
S – uchness as suchness enforced—
A – wake by Leonor's own love.

Quezon City
1994

The Dancing Dolls Are Still

Prior to her Araw ng Maynila Award in dance in 1974, Remedios de Oteyza, known to friends and colleagues as Totoy and to dancers and pupils as Teacher, requested me to write a profile of her for the City of Manila Commission on the Arts.

Sitting it out for hours over dinner at Leila's by Rizal Theater in Makati on April 28, 1977, with both of our bony frames shivering due to the air-conditioning, de Oteyza revealed the genesis not only of her life but also of her choreographic process.

She spoke of her dancing dolls, visions of which she would see in her mind's eye when she was inspired. From the corps de ballet to the exacting lifts and twists of the soloists, the dolls would dance the figures and patterns for her. They were already in costume, giving her a preview of the abstract ballets for which she was famous.

De Oteyza was born in Manila on June 7, 1920 to Carlos de Oteyza of Madrid and Manuela Alvarez of Manila. She lived in Manila until the age of three. In Spain, at the age of eight, she started taking ballet lessons, and upon her return to Manila, she continued her studies with Madam Luva Adameit.

A Dancing Career

In Spain again before the revolution, she progressed soon enough to join the corps de ballet in Paris, but had to resign because of a weak constitution. She was back in Manila at the onset of World War II and was unable to pursue her training in Europe. During the war years, she studied and danced with Paul Szilard at the Metropolitan Theater.

When Alicia Markova and Anton Dolin visited and toured the Philippines after the war, she furthered her studies with the famous couple. This she also did with Mia Slavenska when the ballerina came with Frederic Franklin and Alexandra Danilova.

Encouraged to return to Europe, she continued her training with Markova and Dolin and danced with them in Livepool. Dolin refers to her in the Philippine section of his biography of Markova (*Alicia Markova: Her Life and Art*, New York: Hermitage, 1953). While in Europe, she also trained with the best teachers in Paris: Olga Preobrajenska. Lubov Egorova, Leo Staats, Jeanne and Nelly Schwarz, George Balanchine, and later, Sulamith Messerer.

In September of 1947, de Oteyza founded her school, Classic Ballet Academy, on Buencamino, San Miguel. It was later moved to San Rafael, fronting Plaza Liga Anti-Imperialista and Malacañang Palace. September 1977 marked the thirtieth anniversary of her teaching career.

Choreographic Metier

Once, the Marquis de Cuevas asked de Oteyza to choreograph for his company. She was unable to leave because of the travel ban during the Quirino administration. (A telegram exists to substantiate this claim.) Prior to this, she took annual trips to Europe and lived with her sisters who are also artists. Thus, she was personally spared of the ballet ban in the fifties.

De Oteyza, a great admirer of Balanchine, was famous for her abstract neoclassical ballets, like her two ballet concertos to Edvard Grieg and Peter I. Tchaikovsky, *Symphonic Variations* (Cesar Franck), *Theme and Variations* (Tchaikovsky), and *Masquerade Suite* (Katchaturian). Her only known story ballets are *Haunted Ballroom* (Dohnanyi) and *Ibong Adana* (Rodolfo Cornejo); the latter was done in collaboration with Inday Gaston Mañosa.

She made her debut as a choreographer at the age of twelve, putting on an Egyptian suite to Grieg for a contest during a Manila Carnival. She won first prize. Her attachment to piano music was due to the influence of her mother, a concert pianist who graduated in Barcelona at the age of fourteen, playing the same piano concerto de Oteyza was to choreograph to. Her mother also made her debut as a singer at the age of sixteen in *Madam Butterfly* at La Scala.

Manuela encouraged all her children to explore the arts, and they did. De Oteyza had three sisters, Lourdes, Maitos, and Charo, and a brother Antonio, a businessman who is also a musician. (Lourdes and Charo lived in Paris, Maitos in Makati, and Antonio in Iloilo.) Their father was a journalist-turned-businessman.

Her Artistic Progeny

In turn, de Oteyza encouraged and molded numerous dance artists and ballet masters. She was proud of such luminaries as Maribel Aboitiz and Maniya Barredo, whom she had coached.

Even more so, she was proud of those who carried on the tradition of the ballet through their teaching and choreography. Among the countless who trained with her are Inday Gaston Mañosa, Joji Felix Velarde, Sony Lopez Gonzalez, Lydia Madarang Gaston, Pinky Mendoza Puno, Bonnie Weinstein Calagopi, Vella C. Damian, Carmina Gutierrez, Eric V. Cruz, and Basilio.

De Oteyza headed as artistic director the eldest of surviving ballet groups, the Hariraya Ballet Company. Earlier, she set up the Manila Ballet Company. With Inday Gaston Mañosa, she co-directed Ballet and Dance Centre in Makati, Hariraya's official school. She also choreographed for the CCP Dance Company for the Philippine Music and Dance Festival. During the First National Ballet Festival in 1976, de Oteyza was cited by the First Lady Mrs. Imelda Romualdez Marcos for having "unreservedly sustained the classical tradition in dance, deeply inculcating its inner and outward beauty, its moral and aesthetic order."

Among the last works of de Oteyza were the revival of her Tschaikovsky concerto, which was done together with Rene Dimacali's *Carmen* in 1976 at the Cultural Center, the choreography for the opera *La Gioconda* in 1977, and *Prelude* (Antonino Buenaventura) for the Philippine Music and Dance Festival.

De Oteyza's Hariraya Ballet Campany had very much reduced activities in the last few years. However, she was greatly encouraged and assisted by her devoted pupil, dancer and colleague, Inday Gaston Mañosa. For years the latter assured de Oteyza continuity in her artistic life, and she kept her spirits up by teaching. Among her last ballerinas were Maiqui and Mia Mañosa, Rita Garica, Gina Katigbak, and Marina Corpus. Nida Onglengco, Jun Dalit, and Conrad Tiolengco consistently served her as instruments for her imagination and craftsmanship. She also devoted her last teaching days to the CCP Dance School, contributing greatly as an active adviser and providing equilibrium to the Ballet Federation of the Philippines.

Eric V. Cruz and Vella C. Damian wanted to pay tribute to her and her contemporaries. There is now a plan to do an all-de Oteyza program called *Legacy*. Rene Dimacali of Bacolod and Iloilo has planned a benefit concert for her, while someone is thinking of initiating a Luva Adameit Cup for Pedagogy with de Oteyza as the first recipient to mark her thirty years of teaching.

De Oteyza died on June 25, 1978 at the age of fifty-eight. Gaston Mañosa aptly said that before her death, de Oteyza's life came full circle. Once more she was able to work with her former dancers like Eddie Elejar—and, to my great fortune, myself—in *La Gioconda*, Effie Nañas in *Prelude*, and Maniya Barredo in preparation for *Giselle* in Manila. Vella C. Damian consistently sought her advice, while she found a colleague in Alice Reyes.

Cool Classicism and Warm Humor

When I was new in Manila, I went to de Oteyza armed with a letter of introduction from my teacher in Bacolod, Pancho Uytiepo. She took me in immediately as a scholar, but because of ill health, my study was postponed. I didn't get back to my studies until much later. When I came back, I was greatly impressed by her cool classicism while conducting a class, which contrasted greatly with the irrepressible and unquenchable sense of humor by which she is remembered by colleagues, students, and friends. Sony Lopez Gonzalez tells of how de Oteyza once jumped over a wall to enter her class, and how she would herd her pupils to a double bill at the Manila Grand Opera House on Avenida.

But in the her heart of hearts is pure discipline of which I wrote, interspersed with lines from Jean Genet in 1966:

SACRE DU PRINTEMPS

With Matisse's balance, purity and serenity,
She tents the tenterhooks of young graces.

Young girls (she herself was young)
would come to be lynched.
Here: Arms do not make, but flower
gesticularias;
Feet do not go, but travel eternity–
Proust-history of beautiful
Tired breaths, body rain and Petipa and
Ivanov.

Young girls (they no longer are young)
would come to be im-
prisoned, gracefully,
tortured, measuredly, and executed,
finally,
by arabesques, accents and pirouettes.
"They were the surprise packages of vagrant
children for whom the world is imprisoned
in a magic lattice."

Eloquence come silently silent,
sliced by her wand-weave
of "toes as hard and agile"
(ribbon bound, as pink
as Chinese hierarchic feet),
and mad memories of Markova.

Razors and flowers
come, cut, come, as freedom
fenced in by ancient grace-*barres*.

The dolls are no more, but, through her dedication, inspiration, and actual progeny, the art to which de Oteyza devoted her life goes on.

Ballet Federation of the Philippines
1978

Corazon Generoso Iñigo: Contributor to Philippine Culture

Folk dance revival peaked in the late '50s to the '60s, with several troupes winning global accolades. The best among them at the start were the Bayanihan and the FEU Folk Dance Troupe. Two highly regarded choreographers were at the helm of these troupes: Lucrecia Reyes Urtula and Corazon Generoso Iñigo.

As a provinciano in Bacolod, I saw them respectively in "Glimpses of Philippine Culture" and "Portrait of a Filipino." The Bayanihan lived up to its name—colorful and gregarious. The FEU Troupe had a distinctive choreographic style.

I got to read about their successes in Brussels and Paris. FEU performed at Theatre des Nations—receiving raves and, as Eddie Elejar said, an invitation to the United States. The group also won two first prizes, in Caceres and Palma de Mallorca Festivals. Even after Iñigo left FEU, the life of the troupe went on under various directors and was respected by such luminaries as Alejandro Roces and Sarah Joaquin.

When Iñigo moved to the UE Dance Company, I met her casually as she had my sister as a member. The group always bested other participants at the UAAP spectacular openings at the Rizal Memorial Stadium. They toured Asia with the Philippine Presidential Lines, and the stint included the Osaka World's Fair. They also inaugurated the new UE Theater with Iñigo's *Lam-ang*. For this modern ballet, she collaborated with writer Mig Enriquez and composer Jerry Dadap. It was one of the first Filipino epics to be translated into modern dance.

Moreover, UE then produced the most promising male dancers—many became members of Ballet Philippines. Among them were Manuel

Molina (our most dynamic and charismatic danseur), Gener Caringal (now PBT's artistic director), Brando Miranda (premier danseur for Royal New Zealand Ballet), and Nonoy Froilan (premier danseur of Ballet Philippines).

I did not know much of Iñigo; I only saw her now and then taking dance classes at Julie Borromeo's studio or at the CCP Dance School. I also saw some of her choreographic contributions to UP or BP, like *Baile de Ayer*, where she collaborated with Rodolfo Cornejo and Rolando Tinio, *Gabriela Silang* with Eliseo Pajaro, and *Gabriela* with Joey Ayala.

When she moved to UP, she took charge of the Filipiniana Dance Troupe, training the dancers in folk and modern dance. While on tour in Europe—among several other tours—they won two gold awards in Dijon. According to Anton Juan, it was the first time the festival gave such honors to one group. In Diliman, she also had dancers like Froilan (from UE), Douglas Nierras, and Nestor Jardin.

After seeing her most important work, *Sisa*, in UP, Alice Reyes once more invited Iñigo to stage it for BP, with herself in the title role. In collaboration with Amelia Lapeña Bonifacio, Lucrecia Kasilag, and Tony Mabesa, Iñigo scored another success at the annual CCP Music Festival. Under Mabesa's direction, the work was rich in form and dimension, integrating dance, chant, designs, Kasilag's music, and the Rizal and Lapeña Bonifacio narrative.

Much, much later, I got to know Iñigo better through the CCP and the NCCA. When I edited the Dance Volume of the *CCP Encyclopedia of Philippine Art*, she contributed the most entries after me. Her writing there is as thorough as her choreographic and now-legendary directorial efforts.

I can see how former dancers who are now colleagues and leaders in their own right continue to defer to her. One is the noted *taray* in the dance scene today, the prize-winning Douglas Nierras.

From my research, I also got to know about Iñigo's work in popular media as choreographer-director at the New Frontier Theater and later, at the Araneta Coliseum in the J. Amado Araneta multicultural productions. Her father Jose Generoso was a wartime showman like Avellana, Poe, Estrella, Roque, and the Salvadors. He worked for UP

President Jorge Bocobo, at around the time National Artist Francisca Reyes Aquino started her pioneering research in Philippine folk dances. As a child, she was exposed to a lot of music and dancing.

Iñigo also danced and choreographed for movies for production outfits like the Sampaguita, LVN, and Premier. Among the practitioners in the popular entertainment today—including dance artists working abroad—and you will find several former dancers of Iñigo, from FEU, UE, and UP to New Frontier and Araneta Coliseum. They range from one of the best ballet teachers in Vella Damian and the jazz maestro Douglas Nierras, to CCP's artistic director Nestor Jardin, and the entertainment industry's Bella de Mayuga. She has exerted the most influence in the field of dance without building a hegemony.

As a professor in UP College of Human Kinetics, she once fought with me on the issue of separate dance degree programs in the university. She must have [sort of] hated me. But later she also took the dance majors from the College of Music in dance composition and folk dance. Once she even took an overload by teaching in the College itself. And we also worked together for a research project on the dances of Mindanao.

Earlier, she had also done this kind of work in Luzon and Mindanao, when she taught at PWU in Davao.

In summary, Iñigo has danced, taught, and choreographed ballet, modern dance, jazz, and folk dance. She has directed numerous dancers, and disseminated dance in the educational system through four universities. She has written on dance and directed projects for the ASEAN, Council International of Festivals of Folklore (CIOFF), CCP, and NCCA—where she was the chair of the Dance Committee. On the other hand, she had made contributions to popular entertainment—in theater and cinema—including Technical Education and Skills Development Authority (TESDA) for the standardization of dancers' skills for trainers abroad. In recognition of her work, the CCP has made her a trustee, council member, and a centennial awardee. The City of Manila, UP (where she became a resident artist), PWU in Davao, and Sigma Delta have also honored her. When she retired from UP, I staged the first series of "Bravo/Bravi" presentations in her honor, and FEU, UE, UP,

Lyceum, Ballet Philippines, Powerdance and those in the entertainment industry also paid tribute to her.

As fellow choreographer-director Eddie Elejar said, Iñigo has long deserved the National Artist award—which is late by ten to fifteen years. Although from a rival company of the Bayanihan in his time, Elejar acknowledges her choreographic gifts and leadership, and the awards she helped win for the groups she led abroad. UP colleagues Antonio Mabesa and Anton Juan acknowledge the same dedication and creativity.

Iñigo continues to be productive, as she was active in NCCA endeavors, such as the last commemorative production of *UP Naming Mahal* directed by Tony Mabesa, and the gala and ritual opening for the thirtieth anniversary of the CCP. She has conducted workshops on dance nationally (the last in Iloilo, teaching some 300 teachers single-handedly) and internationally.

Among her peers—and those ahead of her—she has sustained and still sustains the longest creative output in dance—as dancer, teacher, scholar, choreographer, director, and leader in the most varied style, techniques, and modes of dance advocacy, education, and production.

Three Mad Women of Manila

"All dancers are godmothers (to the dance)."

—Arlene Croce

Fairy godmothers must be madwomen; they always espouse the cause of the oddballs of society. Three such madwomen are famous in Manila. They are all at once crazy enough to take up the cause of dance—its helter-skelter financial and executive production. They have long been responsible for the glittering nights of the ballet in this country.

The most senior among them is the most classically trained, even in terms of academic education. After graduating from the University of the Philippines, she pursued her master of arts at the University of Madrid. Having mastered a Latin tongue, she is well read in the history and literature of Spain and the Philippines. Above all, her madness about dance urged her to go beyond pure intellect to the more physical world of the theater. She immersed herself in the discipline of dance, became a prima ballerina of her teacher's company, the Anita M. Kane Ballet, and earned her full Royal Academy of Dancing qualifications to the advanced level in London—and all this time she was also raising a young child. That child is now the dancer Sophia Radaic of the Royal New Zealand Ballet.

Tita (Felicitas Layag) Radaic established the R.A.D. syllabi in the Philippines and now runs her school of dance at the St. Theresa's College in Quezon City. She also manages Dance Theatre Philippines (which she established with Julie Borromeo and Eddie Elejar in 1968), now based in the UP College of Music and going strong, with its thirteen-year old Ballet at the (Rizal) Park and its performances in the different

UP campuses. She has also taken the company to Great Britain twice, and twice, too, to Hong Kong.

The second trained to be a pianist at the University of Sto. Tomas but never managed to do her graduation recital. Recital stage fright dogged her as the dance concert stage exalted her. She started dancing late, but once her teacher Remedios (Totoy) de Oteyza, a pioneer in dance, recognized her passion and potential for dance, she granted the budding dancer a scholarship to her old school on San Rafael, fronting Malacañang Palace. The student, Vella C. Damian, became one of the ballerinas of Hariraya Dance Company. She went on to America and trained in George Balanchine's school in New York, and in Robert Joffrey's. She said she was so innocent then, she went to church everyday. She got to teach underprivileged children in the United States, and she toured the country with Mara's folk-inspired dance troupe as the heroine. Upon returning home, she was told that de Oteyza's company would enter the portals of the new Cultural Center of the Philippines.

Vella ended up founding her own company with Eric V. Cruz and Exequiel Banzali, the Dance Concert Company. She became its ballerina and ballet mistress, and lately, choreographer. She has brought the company to Guam and around the country.

The third and the youngest went to a school run by the Americans, Maryknoll College in Quezon City, where she earned her foreign service degree. Since she was a child, she was already fully involved in dance. The daughter of Mr. Folk Dancer—Ricardo Reyes, a member of the Bayanihan company—it seemed only natural for her not to pursue a diplomatic career, though a diplomat of sorts she was. Her company, Ballet Philippines of the CCP, is the most well-traveled dance theater company hereabouts, and it earned merits for Filipino dancing wherever it went.

Alice Reyes returned to Manila after a full dance education at Sarah Lawrence College as one of the protégés of Hanya Holm. She made waves with her personal company's debut at the Center. This was followed by a summer workshop she conducted with Eddie Elejar and her company members (concurrently members of DTP and the University of the East Dance Troupe), which led to the establishment of the CCP Dance Workshop and Company, now the Ballet Philippines.

Tita Radaic, Vella Damian, and Alice Reyes are distinctly individual personalities, but they are all devoted to the same art of dance. They have delivered the most memorable performances as Giselle or Sugarplum Fairy, Carmen or Azucena (two operatic heroines), and Amada or Itim Asu (Reyes's own heroines), respectively. Tita, whose sign is Cancer, is very tenacious in her beliefs and is most creative when challenged. A small woman, she can never keep still although she always projects the composure of European ballerinas; she incessantly regales you with her ideas and expects to convince everyone to side with her on any issue. She may be small but her vision is large. She's an indefatigable dreamer.

Vella is more down-to-earth, and she exudes an Indian or Polynesian kind of sultriness. When not dancing, she devotes her time to raising orchids, crocheting intricate patterns, knitting, and weaving. Her sign is Scorpio, but being clingy, she could very well be a Cancer, which makes such a faithful friend. When she plans, she does so calmly but with determination. She speaks vociferously (often with a sharp sense of humor) about what she believes in. She says that she used to fight other people's battles, but now she has stripped herself and her life of much complication and simply focuses her energies on running her school by her home and her company. A dogged and systematic teacher of dance, she has concocted her own syllabi, which she disseminates to collaborative colleagues in the dance training field. She is also a lecturer in dance at the University of the Philippines.

Alice is even more down-to-earth than Vella, a model for Gaugain. A Libran, her seductiveness is almost unconscious. Perhaps, she inherited this from her father's terpsichorean élan. She also possesses the most womanly looks, one reason why this writer once thought of her as the faithful Alcestis in a ballet that has never been realized. Nothing detracts her from her motivation, and she pursues her own vision regardless of what everyone else is doing. Her independence of mind has ensured her success. Interestingly, she is as skillful in collaborations in theatrical dance. Throughout her career, she has chosen her collaborators well that she can be absent and still run an operation. If Tita leads by always keeping tabs on all developments down to the smallest details, and Vella by tirelessly taking on numerous functions (administering, teaching, rehearsing, dancing, and choreographing), Alice takes charge by trusting her tried-and-tested henchmen, which allows her to sit back and enjoy life and art. Exhibiting confident nonchalance, nothing seems to daunt her. But she has also been known to cry, or be sympathetic, especially when she appreciates a talent.

Their tastes vary. Tita has cosmopolitan balletic preferences. Even if she accommodates modern dancing, she prefers ballet—both classical and contemporary. As a dancer, she was distinctly classical. Vella is exclusive to ballet, but she herself was most distinguished as a dramatic dancer, as Carmen or Medea. Alice was a modern dancer par excellence, but she expanded her choreographic range to ballet and is the sole Filipino choreographer to have done full-blown recreations of the classics—*Giselle, The Nutcracker, Cinderella* and the more contemporary *Romeo and Juliet.* Her best works remain in the modern dance vein and are, coincidentally, about three women: *Amada, Itim Asu*, and *Carmen*. She has also influenced a great number of choreographers, both friends and detractors.

Tita has encouraged many talented dancers and has produced international names from the small foundry of her dance studio: Irene Sabas in Belgium, Sophia Radaic in New Zealand, Anna Villadolid and Mary Anne Santamaria in Germany, Lisa Macuja in Russia, Eloisa Enerio in Canada, Mitto Castillo in England, and Victor Madrona in Hong Kong. Although she gave up choreography too soon, her valuable work lives on in the esoteric *The Prey* and the comic *Tanan,* and the underwater act of *Mir-i-nisa*. She brought recognition to Luis Layag and Basilio as choreographers.

Vella has lately taken a serious hand at choreography. Influenced by her close collaborator Eric Cruz, she remains well known as the longest-lasting ballerina among her contemporaries, and as the mentor of lovely dancers—Marivic Mapili Vela, Myra Beltran (now of the People's Theater Resident Ballet in then Yugoslavia), and lately, Yvonne Cutaran. Her nephew Augustus Damian became a soloist in a German company after only a year with Ballet Philippines.

These days, Tita focuses primarily on teaching, aside from making sure the management side of Dance Theatre runs smoothly. She is now on a big campaign for new studios in Diliman. Vella has lately taken on even more functions (including being a gourmet), but still finds time for her plants and handicrafts. Alice has remarried and is often away. This season, she delegated artistic direction to her sister Denisa (assisted by still another sister, Edna). She is luckier now in love and enjoying motherhood.

These three women are still as madly in love with dance, their common obsession. The life of theatrical dance in the Philippines owes much to their untiring and inspired efforts. There are more women who devote themselves to dance today—Cora Iñigo, Inday Gaston Mañosa, Julie Borromeo, Lydia Madarang Gaston of Bacolod, Fe Sala Villarica of Cebu, etc.—but in the context of longevity, of distinction (extending to the dancers they have produced), of courage, of resolutions, and of grace—which they exude on and off stage—Tita, Vella, and Alice take the biggest slices of the cake.

Their respective schools and the companies they head—Dance Theatre Philippines, Dance Concert Company, and Ballet Philippines of the CCP, respectively—are leaders in the field of dance in the country and are responsible for the most consistent and commendable artistic enterprises. They each have their unique interests and preoccupations in the field, but they share the same single-mindedness of vision. They have surpassed the male leaders in the business and art of dance production.

Writing poetry in English and Spanish, caring for orchids and handicrafts, and mastering antiques and diplomatic social grace—these are other pursuits of Tita, Vella, and Alice. The first is a widow with a ballerina daughter, the second is single, and the third is happily married and lives in California—these three madwomen of Manila have lived life to the fullest. They have enriched the artistic life and culture of this country by their teaching and directing, by their dreaming and perhaps scheming, by the essences of their ever female, ever fatal personalities. All in the name of dance.

Arts Quarterly/Cultural Center of the Philippines
1986

The Ballerinas of Manila

To be a ballerina is to be in the forefront of a dance company. It was in Russia that this significance arose in the usage of the term. Previously, it simply meant a dancer.

Today, to be considered a ballerina requires a facility and an aura from the title-holder. And to be *prima* ballerina means a great deal of authority and responsibility. There are so few of them in key cities of the world, and only one or two are conferred the title *prima* ballerina *assoluta*. An Ulanova at one time, a Fonteyn at another.

In America, the term does not really carry much value, except for dancers of the old school, or dancers from Europe. Americans have come to use the terms "principal dancer," "soloist," "demi-soloist," and "corps de ballet." Such an old word as *coryphée* is almost meaningless, even if it is still found in books written as late as the sixties.

In Manila, the term "ballerina" has value, perhaps due to the fact that the Spanish language remains in use. But since most dancers in the Philippines go to the United States, not Europe, the term is hardly used in the program notes' vitae. Only senior dancers would care to claim the title for themselves.

Vella Damian is *prima* ballerina of Dance Concert Company, while Irene Sabas of Dance Theatre Philippines would probably settle for principal dancer. Felicitas L. Radaic, when she dances, would appreciate the use of the hallowed term, especially as she is the last of her generation to keep on with the pioneering work of performing in Manila. Alice Reyes of the Cultural Center of the Philippines Dance Company (called Ballet Philippines abroad) has frequently been called a *danseuse*, which is hardly used to designate a modern dancer in America. She is, of course, with Effie Nañas and Ester Rimpos, the principal dancer of the company she directs.

This essay was originally conceived as a description of the ballerinas I've seen and heard of in Manila. I then thought it useful to examine the currency of the Italian term to indicate the change in the evaluation of the dancers in Manila today.

Joji Felix

I saw a Filipino ballerina for the first time at fourteen, when I witnessed my first ballet performance in a Bacolod cinema house. (It could have been the one where Markova and Dolin danced immediately after the war.) It was during the tour of the de Oteyza company. Looking at the cast-list now, I am delighted to have come to know the dancers as friends when I became a dancer myself later: Lydia Madarang, Inday Gaston, Eddie Elejar, etc.

But the most unforgettable figure in my first encounter of ballet as a performing art was Joji Felix, dancing a brief piece, *Prayer*. I was stunned by the delicacy of her dancing and her beautiful line. I remember her statuesque stance very well because she got on the cover of *Hiligaynon* (I was an avid reader of Ilonggo novels by Magdalena Jalandoni, Clodualdo del Mundo in translation, etc.—a literary exercise I regret abandoning), her full figure in miniature. I vaguely remember the other numbers in the program, but the lyrical moment of her dance lingers in mind, albeit impressionistically.

How unfortunate that I didn't get the chance to see other ballerinas perform at that time (I came to the Metropolitan Manila much later), like Felicitas Layag Radaic, Maureen Tiongco, Elizabeth Guasch, and others.

Puertollano and Aboitiz

The next ballerina who had me spellbound was Lulu Puertollano, and that was before she left for the United States. It was her farewell performance at the Far Eastern University auditorium. Again, Elejar was there to serve as partner. Again, I vaguely remember the full extent of the program, but what I can't forget was the simplicity of style, her balance, and her dark beauty. She was a gentle rose then, so feminine, and among the Philippine ballerinas, I thought she was the most Filipina. Her performance affected me deeply, rippling through time as a cherished memory.

The most striking of ballerinas then was Maribel Aboitiz. It was then, too, that I came to realize the stature of Elejar, as he was at the peak of his performing ability. For one thing, his partnership with Aboitiz remains unequalled even after Tina Santos came into the picture. (Tina danced with more partners than Maribel.)

Maribel was unparalleled in temperament onstage. I never saw her in full-length ballets (such as *Giselle* and *Swan Lake*, which she did), but on the occasions I witnessed when she exhibited the full range of her showmanship (the grand pas de deux from *Don Quixote*, *The Sleeping Beauty*, *The Black Swan*, and the second act of *Swan Lake*), she always brought the house down. In performance, she never hesitated and always plunged headlong into any role. I remember her as a bright and technical ballerina, and perhaps she was the only one who could have claimed the title *prima* ballerina in her time. She was a diamond amid other gems. It is a regret that she stopped and left for Spain soon after her marriage.

DTP Ballerinas

I came to know Felicitas L. Radaic only after the birth of Dance Theatre Philippines, which came after she was the leading ballerina of Anita M. Kane's company. I don't think DTP showed the full range of her abilities, because even if Julie Borromeo did *Zagalas de Manila* with Tita (and Tina Santos and herself) and *Kalingan* (as a mountain maiden in a dramatic vignette), Tita never had the chance to grow in or reclaim her roles in the Kane company.

It was therefore a startling surprise that she danced very well during Odon Sabarre's farewell performance in 1977. Doing the Peasant pas de deux from *Giselle* with Sabarre, Tita found a role she was most at home in, showing off a true absorption of the classical style, and the femininity and simplicity of her personality. She evoked a world that is already missing in the contemporary atmosphere of the dancing in the Philippines—the ideal and traditional.

Julie Borromeo is most memorable as a dramatic ballerina, giving all of herself to her roles. She was a bit of a ham in comedy, but watching her in such ballets as her *Babae at Lalake* (i.e., Woman and Man—note the order in Philippine usage), I was moved to write a poetic commentary for the program notes. She was also lovely in her own *Zagalas de Manila.* I did not see her in Poul Gnatt's *The Miraculous Mandarin* (I saw Puertollano instead), and missed her classical parts during her time with Cassell or Kane.

Before I come to the reigning ballerinas today, may I just mention that I got to see Greta Montserrat and Serafina Guinto once, in separate performances, the former during her Pamana Ballet days (again, with Elejar), and the latter during her period with Anita M. Kane (although I never saw the company as such).

Tina Santos

I came to admire Tina Santos during our DTP days together. Even if Borromeo and Radaic were around, she actually was the unacknowledged *prima* of the group. Not that she was always better than the two, but that she was most popular with the dancers and the public. Part of it was because of her versatility, as she could turn from one dance style to another. Moreover, she was so adaptable that she even took part in the corps de ballet during tours. The experience must have prepared her for the rigors of her Harkness Ballet days. Tina was endearing in the pas de deux from *Flower Festival at Genzano* (restaged by Poul Gnatt) and deliciously young in *Zagalas de Manila.* She was always convincingly comic in *Tanan* and *Oy, Akin Yan*! And quite striking in the *Black Swan* pas de deux during her farewell performance before she left for America.

When she joined the Alice Reyes and Modern Dance Company (later known as the CCP Dance Company), in her brief part as the *tadtarin* in *Amada*, she almost overshadowed the role of the heroine. She remains unequalled as the Moslem bride in *At a Maranaw Gathering.*

Tina has always thought out her parts before going on stage. She is possessed with artistic sincerity that has brought her to the forefront as a performing artist. Her *Shinju* and *Moves* with the San Francisco Ballet further demonstrated this conscious artistry in her. Yet her instinctive nature is a glowing effervescence that pervades her work. She always radiates an aura that puts her a way above her contemporaries.

In 1978, she did *Cinderella* for the Ballet Federation of the Philippines, and she showed off the progress she had made since she last came home in 1976. I don't think she had the time to truly explore the nature of Cinderella's character and the dimension of the ballet (she and Gary Wahl hardly worked with the company together), but given ample time and more performances, I believe she would have infused the ballet with sheer majesty.

Maniya Barredo

This brings us to Philippines's other *prima*, Maniya Barredo. Another special person in Philippine ballet, she used to be the technical trump card of the Hariraya Ballet Company, and was thought to have lost that depth that Borromeo claims Maniya had when she started as a pupil of hers. She came to be a ballerina of Les Grands Ballets Canadiens and represented that company in Cuba for the international festival there in 1977. Today she guests for them and other companies while reigning as a ballerina with the Atlanta Ballet.

I did not see her when she returned to Manila in 1974, but when she came again in 1977, this time with Burton Taylor, all of Manila came to see her. No one has ever before sold out the house with an unscheduled performance, and to think it was held at the ungodly hour of eleven in the morning.

Her *Giselle* with Taylor was witnessed by Fonteyn, a Russian cultural minister, and the President and Mrs. Ferdinand E. Marcos. It was a distinguished Giselle as no other Filipina or foreign ballerina had pulled off. Her essentially appealing nature (which belies the steel determinations beneath) fused with the role seamlessly. During her last performance of the ballet, she brought out the balance and the assurance that she invariably showed during her gala performances (pas de deux from *Don Quixote*, *The Nutcracker*, and *Swan Lake*). After every performance, it seemed like the public would not let her go. She had that command over herself, over her art, and over her audience that made every performance soar (even if there may have been be less balance here and there). Maniya approached her work with simplicity and innocence, a striking contrast to her wild abandon in dancing.

Three in the CCP

Alice Reyes leads the dancers now performing in Manila regularly. She heads her company, which also has Effie Nañas and Ester Rimpos as its ballerinas. Technically, the term ballerina does not suit Reyes because she is a modern dancer, but this by no means reduces her significance as a dancer.

Alice's assets are her long limbs, flow of movement, and dark beauty. Through the years, she has sharpened her command of her part as Amada in her ballet with the same title. She is, I believe, irreplaceable in it already, although I wish Tina Santos had tried it, too. I even found her more suited as the Governor's wife in her *Itim Asu*, a Clytemnestra role (although not against her husband). Here no one could be like her: the wifeliness at the beginning, the painful sorrow at the middle, and the willfulness at the end.

Only to a certain extent does Ester Rimpos equal Alice's performance of Norman Walker's *A Season of Flight*, for Alice is more bird-like and womanly. (Rimpos is herself bird-like, but in a more balletic way.) She also fulfilled Walker's *Songs of a Wayfarer* as the woman-ideal-tree, and, I am told (I've never seen her in it), a perfect Juliet in Elejar's *Juliet and Her Romeo*. She does not always perform Tamiris's Negro Spirituals adequately anymore, but when she does, she is the absolute. Recently, she has lost much of the edge of her work. Her *Lonely Hearts Band* embarrassingly showed her lack of clarity and appeal. Only her innate flow helped her control her longish solo. But then, her last performance in *Amada* that I saw rectified this impression for me.

Of the other ballerinas in Reyes's company, Effie Nañas has the bravura and radiance that brighten up the image of the company. Handicapped by not too perfect feet, she however carries herself with such elegance and appeal that her personality comes through even to the galleries.

Recently, she seems to have paid less attention to her line that this creditable virtue exploited by Totoy de Oteyza for her company is almost absent in her present-day work. She is apparently aware of linear value, because she exhibits it fully in her choreography for other dancers, but then she should reclaim this as a dancer for herself.

Always, Effie dances with a flourish, but by no means the cheap kind that others do. She is always on tempo, even if sometimes mechanically, and when Reyes gives her a lyrical part, she recalls the loveliness of the water section in Hariraya Ballet Company's *The Elements*. She can be a jewel when she wants to be, especially given her unquestionable discipline and confidence in dancing.

I must confess that Ester Rimpos is a favorite. She is so musical that her play with tempo and musical coloring adds a heightened flavor to her dancing. She is the only one I know who noticeably brings this into her work. Others bring in feeling, others brio, others elegance, but Ester, quiet as her person is, appeals by bringing out the succulent tang caused by a perfect blending of music and movement.

Ester could be technically sure and intensely dramatic (she's a dark beauty too), but what she always crowns her dancing with is an ardor that comes out of the union of movement and musical rhythm. Thus, she is the most concise and precise dancer we know, and therefore the most purely poetic. I'll have none of the rah-rah that some people wrongly look for in her. For me, she is the crowning glory of Philippine ballet today. And she is none too aware of it as a person, too!

The Final Pas de Quatre

Vella Damian is also a favorite. Because she started dancing later in life, she can't match the younger dancers in neatness and lines, but she always manages to bring out character, even in the most classical parts (as in *Paquita* or *Don Quixote*). Again, like Aboitiz, she is full of temperament and determination. She could be made to work ceaselessly, despite her heavy teaching and coaching.

Even if she carries the abandon of Petipa, Vella is still best remembered for her dramatic sincerity. This is nowhere more visible than in her *Carmen*, for it was made as a full role for her by Eric Cruz. How much the ballet itself owes to her portrayal and her insight into the character will be obvious when another dancer takes over the part.

She is also musical and vital enough that she always delights me when she performs. Today, like the rest of her company, there is the tendency to overplay, which falsifies the performance a bit, but with her experience and intelligence, she could very well hold back the reins and make form, not indulgence, prevail on stage. Still, it is this very vigor that shines through Vella's dancing. Like no one in the Philippines today, she is the image of fire.

Of the younger dancers, I must confess that Irene Sabas is a favorite. Not that I think she made a consummate performance in *Coppelia* (as Swanilda) in 1978, for Irene still has a long way to go. But she did show off a kind of elegance that other dancers in Manila lack. That elegance is not the playing-up-to-the-galleries type, but the kind that reminds me of Fonteyn—so transparent but not elicited conscientiously. She compensates for it in her work (I am sure she's not aware that she is compensating) with such depth and nuance, surprising even those who make dances for her. She always falls into a pose or pulse that endows a movement with serenity and sincerity. (The other dancer, although still inexperienced, who strikes me in the same way is Anna Villadolid, and they both have the same physical handicaps, too.) Doubtlessly, she is instinctively musical like Ester Rimpos.

Working with Irene has always been an inspired experience for me as choreographer because not only does she have that long concentration and quick adaptation, but we *both* also always immerse ourselves in an undistracted flow that is characteristic of her dancing.

Another ballerina who has charmed me is Loulie Dalupan. You may say she has been typecast in sultry and dramatic parts, but she truly plays these parts flawlessly. She brings into her work a complete sincerity and skillful application that can only prove the authenticity of her performance. She is competent, if not distinguished, when taking on other parts. Still her personality and vigor are quite arresting. I must say, however, that I'd still want to see her in classical parts. Why not Myrtha?

A last favorite in this final pas de quatre of ballerinas is Marivic Mapili of Dance Concert Company. She has the line, the profundity, the musicality, the technical capability, and the wisdom to bring all these together. It is a regret that she had to stop dancing for a while because of marriage, but she has gone back recently. Another dark beauty, she evokes the spiritual qualities of dancing which only romantic ballerinas bring about. I often regret seeing her in overly dramatic parts, because she is best seen in truly classical roles—delicate, light, long, and restrained—where I believe she is the only true successor of Ester Rimpos. Her last *Swan Lake* (Act II) had brought her dancing to another level and I could only wish for the continuance of such progress.

These are, to me, the ballerinas in Manila today. They are the city's treasures—worthy of adoration and deserving of more honors than the country gives. They have carried on the roles of the late Totoy de Oteyza, Pacita Madrigal, Chloe Cruz, and Leonor Orosa. They have brought the art of dancing further heights by simply dancing. In a country where dancers are not paid enough and in a city where the periodicals do not give adequate coverage of the arts and the artists, it is a wonder that they still persevere.

It is certainly their devotion to the dance, unwavering and absolute, that has allowed them to become the half-divine women we call ballerinas.

Note

This unpublished essay was written in the seventies. Thus, the roles referred to were those reviewed at that time.

Tina Santos Is Thoughtfulness Supreme

What a spate of happy returns!

Manuel Molina and Gloria dela Casa with the Ballet de Caracas. Franklin Bobadilla and Irene Sabas with Dance Theatre Philippines. Noel Velasco visiting with Sarah Caldwell, Rowena Arrieta after a Moscow success, and Joseph Esmilla on the Metropolitan and Rizal Park stages. And, finally, Tina Santos. On vacation, but teaching at the University of the Philippines, and for both the Elejar-Fabella Makati studio and Dance Theatre Philippines.

In my review of the Caracas company (AM, vol. II, no. 7), I made known my delight in Manuel and Gloria's charm and competence, dedication and dynamism. I was fortunate enough to work on a program billed "Salute to Stravinsky" last August with Franklin and Irene (and her partner David Campos Cantero)—he with his unassailable professionalism and she with her growing assurance.

Albeit briefly, I got to chat with Noel, heard Rowena at Paco Park, saw Joseph on television, and lastly, renewed my friendship and professional collaboration with Tina.

After her injury from the *Swan Lake* affair with the CCP Dance Company in 1979, which was no one's fault (but, for one, the hard floor that injures dancers for life, often left without remedy like our lack of caution about asbestos-lined water pipes), Tina went back to the United States, forever regretting what could have been another high point in her career.

In an interview, she told me that earlier she had been coaching—and paying for it by the hour—with Penelope Lagios Johnson, one of San Francisco's famous Odette-Odiles, and with Madam Sulamith

Messerer, before she flew to Manila. She even ultimately sacrificed her place in the San Francisco Ballet for that very engagement, as Michael Smuin was not ready to release her around that time.

She went back to dancing in Denver with Fernand Nault, but an infection of her toes kept her off her pointes once more. A film of the short, short *Poeme* that her husband Gary Wahl made for her and Tomm Ruud (her partner during that Jerome Robbins's *Moves* performance that injured her earlier) showed the progress she was having at that time. Reconciling herself to these signs, Tina settled down to teach in the Palo Alto area for the Pacific Dance Center. And what a marvelous teacher she has become. I've always believed Tina to be a natural. The basic requirement has always been there: the enthusiasm to share and encourage.

Even as a performer, Tina was not one to stand still and let other dancers engage in their wild attempts. If she recognized a fault, she analyzed it and offered suggestions. Tina was not the type of guest artist who focused solely on herself.

Today her classes are punctuated by remarks like "So much better," "Very good," even "Bravo." The emphasis is on the positive. It's also the positive side of one's personality and performance that she wants to elicit and bring out.

Tina nurtures, but not at the expense of precision. Musically, the movements must be exact, with breadth and brio. The path of a limb or pattern must be direct, open, and clear. Placement must rule despite the freedom of the shoulders and arms and the height of the legs. The weight or center must always be felt. The feet must articulate, accentuate, if need be, and sharpen or speed up without cheating.

A class for Tina is a performance. In England, people who teach say they *take* a class. And with Tina, she does take it. In tenor of voice, in verve of body, in clarity of mind and spirit, Tina draws out and gives it all. She does not withhold trade secrets; nor does the fire of her passion ever burn out. She is spontaneous in pointing out faults or showering with praise, but her goal is never to discourage or spoil.

With such radiant awareness, nothing escapes Tina's attention. She makes it a point to memorize everyone's name from the very first lesson. When I watched her DTP and UP classes, I saw that she was consistently the same despite differences in class-levels and aims. As a teacher, Tina breeds artists. Not the fuzzy and daydreaming ones, but those who are truly clear-minded and dedicated.

Tina is a teacher by example. Her standards are high, and her students can clearly see that she herself embodies the discipline and hard work that she expects of them. She is a very good dancer who works with unwavering passion. Though a master herself, she's always ready and willing to learn from others that she hasn't stopped growing and has embraced the shift in her career. Her perception is not clouded by illusions about her own merits or limitations. Versatile as she was as a dancer, she now deals with dance in all its fullness—rhythm, clarity, articulacy, liveliness. Sometimes I think, fair as she is, she has the depth of soul that we associate with blacks. She revels in vigor and talent, recognizing these traits even in the most unlikely individuals, telling them, "You are like me." She has a certain way with boys, a chummy concern for them.

A thoughtful teacher in class, Tina does her homework and prepares her classes. She has a notebook brimming with combinations. It's computerized in the primitive balletic way, I must say. She attributes her insights to her teachers like David Howard, Perry Brunson, Hector Zaraspe, Lew Christensen, Richard Gibson, and Tatiana Grantzeva, and to her husband Gary Wahl's own analytic mind and physical facility. (Gary is now studying microprocessors technology and is one of the top four in his class.) She does not fail to attribute learning from her local teachers like Joji Felix Velarde and Eddie Elejar.

The only other Filipino I know who probably matches her zest and zeal in teaching is El Gabriel, who is himself a noted teacher in Los Angeles. They exude the same charm, the same positive outlook, and the same enormous capacity to share. When El was ballet master for Dance Theatre Philippines, he and Tony Llacer brought the company to a remarkable level of performing prowess and confidence.

When Tina made her farewell performance at the Meralco Theater in 1970, I wrote about her versatility, style, and incandescence, echoing Abraham Florendo's *Daily Mirror* accolade, "Like a magnet, she draws all attention to herself, transfigured, incandescent." Anthony Morli of *The Manila Times* tagged her earlier as "lithe, limber, lollapalooza"; another critic called her "the Philippines' First Lady danseuse."

Writing about Tina's *Cinderella* in 1978, I wrote: "As a dancer, Tina gave a home report that showed greater ease and fluidity in her dancing, and the serenity and assurance of her self-delineation. Her leaps were split and sharp as arrows, and her arms were lively and free as they were richly decorative."

"Tina Santos and Gary Wahl's coming added depth and dimension to our understanding of dancing, its technical base and expressive range. Their example off and on stage shall sustain our young dancers' hopes, and inspire them and balletomanes in the art of dance. Thus is the widening influence of our accomplished dancers from abroad; for Tina it is a continuing involvement in the state and future of her art, the ballet, in her homeland."

Tina is Toughness, Inspiration, Naturalness, and Articulacy, all required by the art of dance. Without these, one can dance perhaps, but not truly—not with excitement or inner fire.

Again, a regret. Like Manuel and Gloria, Franklin and Irene, and the rest of our best performing artists, Tina is leaving this home for another. Some, after their experience abroad as in the case of my colleague, the late Luis Layag, never even had a chance to make a national contribution, however brief. Like our talented technicians and ambitious laborers, many of our artists also hope to find their place and seek recognition abroad; thus, they spend the peak of their artistry outside the country of their roots. They will continue to do so. Even those who have pioneered to little credit at home.

Sometimes at the expense of those who have stuck it out here, these "foreign" Filipinos reduce the former's stature or importance by their prestigious credits and careers in foreign lands. The result is psychic alienation right here. Incentives are restricted or limited to a particular orientation or image. Even "foreignness" is inbred.

But with artists like Tina, it is quite different. As she projects a future of "coming home," she does not contemplate "elimination." She asks, what can I do beside my teachers, partners, co-dancers, and the up-and-coming young ones? Knowledgeable and talented as she is, she considers the potential of collaboration, not domination. She remains a Filipino, through and through.

As shown by her fidelity to her husband, her attachment to her parents and family, her concern over the Filipino dancers, and her generosity both on and off stage—in class, as a colleague, as a human being—Tina is thoughtfulness supreme.

Arts Monthly, Cultural Center of the Philippines
1982

Ester Rimpos:
An Appreciation of a Philippine-Made Ballerina

Did you see Ester Rimpos in *Swan Lake, The Sleeping Beauty, Don Quixote,* and *Giselle*, all in two years' time, all debuts? Did anyone sit up and notice, that is, write a notice? Does this prima ballerina of ours have to compete for attention against foreign stars, in matinees, unaccompanied by an orchestra?

That this musically magical ballerina, admittedly one of my favorites, has to appear under the shade of gala nights and gala stars is a fault of our ballet-goers who only buy importations of ballets, ballerinas, and billings. This is a sad, sad state of affairs.

The dancers of Fonteyn's generation who started under wartime conditions that isolated Britain from the Ballets Russes and the baby ballerinas were lucky. Lucky were the choreographers who began on the minuscule stage of Mercury Theater. Lucky were the early Petipa classics that did not compete with the video-films of a Bolshoi or a present-day Royal Ballet.

I myself missed Ester's *Beauty*, as I was off to Hong Kong then. I thought *Don Quixote* wasn't her sort of thing, but I should have gone anyway. Immediately after my return from London in 1980, I hankered to see her in *Swan Lake* by Armin Wild, again with gala stars (Morishita and Bujones) on gala nights. About the matinee I wrote for *Business Day*:

> As alternates ... Ester Rimpos and Nonoy Froilan commendably essayed the Siegfried and Odette-Odile parts. Were there no foreign stars, they would have been credited more, and that afternoon's audience tried to give them their due, overpowering the canned applause.

> In fact, in Philippine dance history Rimpos and Froilan's performances deserve greater significance. Froilan gave a convincing portrayal, Rimpos understood well the lyrical limpidity of the White Swan and the open seductiveness of the Black; it was her admirable artistry that welded the two. (Aug. 27, 1980)

Last February, I saw her in her debut in *Giselle*, in a matinee, and I thought she captured the spirit of the second act better than Morishita did. There was the feel for Robert Medina (Albrecht), her defense of him, as much as the subjection to Edna Vida's (Myrtha) command. There was the unaccustomed obedience at her initiation (in Act 1, Giselle is quite a foolhardy peasant girl, falling in love with an unknown migrant), and the falling under the spell of the night (Hecate-Diana's?). There also was the musicality that invariably invested her gestures and steps with clarifying rhythm.

Ester needs to work out the more realistic characterization in Act I, to interact with her Albrecht more sensitively, credibly, precisely, and not to overplay the mad scene—which was so subtly, so smoothly played on a delicate string by Morishita. But I was told Ester etched a better Act I on her final matinee.

I've always admired Ester's dancing, but I wasn't fully aware of why—aside from her fine feet and unstrained line—until lately. In 1978 I saw her do Balanchine's *Pas de Dix*, and what she made out of the rubato in her solo brought about such enchantment! Last March she did again Norman Walker's *Song of a Wayfarer*, and where formerly she had to stand comparison with the femaleness of Alice Reyes, she did it this time around with a womanliness that she has never sacrificed all these years to bravura. A dark dream (not the whiteness of La Belle Dame Sans Merci), she captured the soft mysteriousness and magnetism of the Bride with the clarity and pulse of her dancing. She and Froilan (the wayfarer) danced the ballet as though for the first time, fresh as the dew we chance to catch early in the morning, clear as the dream we still taste in our mouth upon waking.

The first time I saw Ester, she was a young girl attempting her Sugarplum Fairy at the Army and Navy Club for Anita M. Kane's production. In that cramped place, made more so by the bustle of children on stage, she and John Ting looked valiant, giving the production a legible lift. When she joined the CCP Dance Company, I was still a member, and that gave me a closer look at her gifts. We were partners in the late Luis Layag's *Positive-Negative* (music by Fellagara).

A small dancer, she is gifted with lovely limbs, a compact figure, a pair of a somewhat upraised shoulders, and a fairly attractive face. Best seen on pointes, giving her a regal look, Ester articulates her feet to the precise shape of delicacy and to the right rhythm of musicality. She adapts herself well to the modern dance idiom, today endowing her roles with the right maturity, but perhaps she looks a bit small and less commanding here. But for very feminine parts, Ester becomes the part naturally, classical or modern.

Ester is a purely Philippine-trained dancer. This does not exclude Ricardo Cassell and Kane who were her first local mentors, because it seemed both foreigners adapted to the local physique and temperament. After Kane left, Ester studied under Eddie Elejar in ballet and Alice Reyes in modern dance, and through the years, she worked with various visiting teachers at the Center, including the late Remedios de Oteyza and her associate Inday Gaston Mañosa, as well as Tony Llacer. I believe a dancer does not simply take on the various instructions she gets; the best one refines what she learns and adapts them to her innate gifts. Those innate gifts are uniquely hers—they define her presence, when sharply honed, they create for her a style all her own.

A review of mine of a Gener Caringal ballet in 1980 described her for Business Day:

> The name is Ester Rimpos and the quality exquisite. This was how our own country's prima ballerina—a title she now deserves—moved in Gener, Caringal's *Recuerdos* ... She danced with the style and sensitivity that could make her our own cherished Fonteyn soon. It was to Restie Umali's commissioned music that she evoked the noble period of the women that inhabited the supposed historical (Rizal's time) fantasy. (Nov. 19, 1980)

Ester achieved her style locally, and it is a tribute to her artistry that she has truly become the ballerina she is today, without the flourish of geographical ganglia in her bio-data, and without the ompa-pa of colonial galas.

See you again at Ester's matinees!

Arts Monthly/Cultural Center of the Philippines
1982

The Prestige (and Pity) of Losing Our Beautiful Ballerinas

Dance Theatre Philippines—soon on its sixteenth year—has had the honor and misfortune of losing its best dancers to the best companies. Since 1970, it has fielded out scholars and soloists to the far corners of the world.

A most recent case was that of founder Felicitas L. Radaic's own daughter, Sophia, who left to join the Royal New Zealand Ballet in January. But the trend was set way back in the '70s when the majority then, led by Tina Santos and Eddie Elejar, made up the new Alice Reyes and Dance Company, now Ballet Philippines. (It must not however be forgotten that this came about soon after DTP temporarily disbanded after *Mir-i-nisa,* which was produced for the CCP's inauguration.) After the ARDC debut, Santos herself left for New York. She became a soloist with Harkness Ballet and later a principal dancer with the San Francisco Ballet. Santos was the most enticing of DTP ballerinas, perhaps to be matched later only by Anna Villadolid's subtle attraction.

After Santos, the trend of leave-taking for foreign shores did not pick up immediately. But the next to go was Luis Layag, who stayed on in Heidelberg after a German grant because of the choreographic opportunities available to him. He later moved to Wuppertal to join Pina Bausch's company and choreographed some productions for television in Cologne. The third was Mitto Castillo, who, in 1975, led DTP on a trip to a festival in Great Britain. After guesting in Germany, he landed in Northern Ballet Theater (NBT) in Manchester. He has now retired, but is a lifelong member of NBT's Friends. After another festival in Britain, Irene Sabas followed in 1979. Already at home in a foreign land because she had previously spent two years at the Royal Ballet School (RBS) as a British Council scholar, Sabas soon ended up in a

German company in Hagen. After another two years, in 1983, she joined the Royal Ballet of Flanders based in Antwerp. Sabas was our first Swanilda in the Philippines when the Ballet Federation premiered *Coppelia* in 1978.

To follow Sabas at the RBS was Sophia Radaic. Also a British Council scholar, she came home and spent a little more than a year with DTP, gained so much performance confidence, and then left for New Zealand. In that short time, she premiered Gary Wahl's *Poeme* in Manila, Felicitas L. Radaic's *La Innamorata* (Chopin), Lucy Layag de los Reyes's *Chopin a la Moog*, and Basilio's *Tchaikovsky Fantasy* and *Bouquet from Britain*. She danced in the grand pas de deux from *Don Quixote* with Nonoy Froilan, *The Sleeping Beauty* with Rupert Acuña and Jonathan Terry, *Swan Lake* Act II with Terry, and *The Nutcracker* with Terry and Augustus Damian.

Anna Villadolid spent two fruitful seasons with DTP, where she gained soloist status from the start. In 1982, she entered the International Ballet Competition in Jackson with Enrico Labayen as partner and made it as finalist. There she was offered a Heinz Bosl scholarship to Munich by Konstanze Vernon, a member of the jury. After another summer in New York, she left for Munich in September 1983 and joined the National Theater's ballet in January 1984.

Villadolid played principal parts in Eddie Elejar's *Masks* (R. Santos, inspired by Virginia Moreno's poem), Tony Fabella's *Limang Dipa* (Cayabyab) and *Love Like the Moon* ... (Massenet), Layag de los Reyes's *Bach in Blue*, and Basilio's *Ode to Boticelli* (Reinecke) and *Tchaikovsky Fantasy*. She premiered Balanchine's *Tchaikovsky Pas de Deux*, restaged by Labayen for DTP. With the Manila Metropolis Ballet, she capped her Manila appearances with *Giselle*, a remarkable debut. In New York, she danced with the New York State Ballet (Eglevsky's) in Balanchine's *Serenade*. From Munich she writes that she has renewed her English training by working with the theater's new artistic director, Ronald Hynd.

Prior to Villadolid's new career, Lisa Macuja and Mary Anne Santamaria entered the legendary Leningrad Choreographic School, the academic base of the Kirov Ballet. Soon to wind up their two-year scholarship from the USSR Ministry of Culture and Dance Theater, both merited choice parts in the school's performances. During her first year, Macuja earned a laureate for her work as a representative foreign ballet student. This was awarded to her in a special ceremony in Moscow. Last Christmas, Macuja made her debut as Masha-Sugarplum Fairy, both at the school and at the Kirov Theater. In the Vainonen version, the usual *The Nutcracker* grand pas de deux involves a Prince and four cavaliers, and the regal fairy is also Masha the girl (our Clara) in the first act.

Like Macuja, Santamaria herself has essayed solo parts in divertissements. She has done Nikiya from La *Bayade're*, and has always distinguished herself in character roles. Both dance regularly in the school's scheduled participations at the hallowed Kirov Theater.

Macuja has the distinction of going through the ranks of DTP. She did not qualify for a 1978 trip to Hong Kong but learned fast enough to join that of 1979 to Britain. A return to Hong Kong in 1980 earned her solo parts in Julie Borromeo's *Zagalas de Manila* (Nakpil) and in Basilio's *Testament* (Bartok), which marked the rise of her career, even if earlier she had essayed after Villadolid the La Zagala role in his "La Adoration" (Rodrigo) from *Tropical Tapestry*. The second show of DTP at the Meralco Theater in 1981 gave her the formidable Flora in *Ode to Boticelli*, and she ended that season again with *Testament* and the premiere of Balanchine's *Tarantella* with Labayen. A second season brought her together with Franklin Bobadilla from Amsterdam in Elejar's *Once Upon a Village* (Arnold) and Basilio's *Paean to Pavlova* (Poulenc), completed as a quartet by Sabas and David Campos Cantero. Basilio challenged her further by creating a twenty-minute solo, *A Chair* (Schubert), especially for her. She has also premiered the de Oteyza part in his *Salutations* (Schubert), Michael Hennesey's A *Moment, A Memory* (Debussy-Tomita), and she danced the role of Maria in Radaic's *Tanan* (Silos) before she left for Leningrad. Winter and summer breaks brought her back for debuts as Taglioni in Robin Haig's *Pas de Quatre* (Pugni) and Aurora in *The Sleeping Beauty* grand pas de deux with Terry.

Santamaria has danced choice parts in DTP's repertory: Robin Haig's *Triptych* (Mozart) and *Pas de Quatre,* Borromeo's *Zagalas de Manila,* Radaic's *Tanan* and *Nan-Pangkat* (Peña), the title role in William Morgan's *Herodias* (R. Strauss), Gener Caringal's *Vermilion Scarf* (The Beatles), Basilio's *Testament* as the alienated protagonist, *Salutations as* Merino Santos, *Sweet*

Warfare (Stravinsky) as femme fatale, and La Dama and Sultana in his *Tropical Tapestry*.

Of all DTP dancers, Radaic has the most elegant style enhanced by her regal stature. Physically handicapped in allegro, she nevertheless has an elegant air and an impeccable musicality that make her dancing subtly eloquent—not obvious to those who look for the obvious. She grows in portrayal of the same roles, so that by the time the viewer sees them again, it's as if they are new or renewed, powered and polished by fresh inspiration.

Villadolid is lyricism personified, and a lambent light that radiates from within exudes true intensity, quite the opposite of easy flamboyance. When she dances, she is as though thinking and living it moment by moment, as though feeling or making up every step from her consciousness. When approaching a role, she visibly expands and deepens the range of her awareness that the effect blows the viewer's mind into an intimated inner galaxy of intuitions. She radiates pure rapture. She is a *rara avis*.

Macuja is another natural talent. Not exactly complete with natural endowments for dance—like perfect feet, although she has of all four the highest extensions—she has a natural and infectious verve in allegro that even Villadolid has to strive to match. She moves the broadest of the four, opening up spaces around her with her wind of positive confidence. Élan personified, even when injured, she sometimes needs a bit more restraint, which on occasion she has shown (as in Taglioni, a lyrical and defined role, or *A Chair*, a range of expressions). Any coach or choreographer can trust her to sustain a part to its climactic end.

Santamaria is also unfailingly reliable. Working with her is a rewarding task. She has remarkable extensions and flexibility, which she uses to advantage. Not exactly in the pure classical mold, she is however very adaptable and attuned to more modern pieces. Because of her bones, her face has a certain set expression, but she completes a performance with a versatility not often recognized. She could be intense or playful, coloring any role with a certain sensuality, the mark of her personal charm.

Other dancers from DTP have also come and gone: Victor Madrona, now in Hong Kong; Ricardo Ella, a "permanent" guest artist from Dance Concert Company, in Australia; and Eloisa Enerio, who just left for the United States. A previous batch was led by Loulie Dalupan, who soon freelanced and then left for the US; Emillie Rigonan, Malou Rivera, and Hazel Sabas, who joined Ballet Philippines when DTP again went moribund; and Juliet Molina, who, after studying in Philadelphia, joined BP, which she has now left for a lay mission.

An older batch of dancers included Elejar and Fabella themselves who founded the Manila Metropolis Ballet after establishing Ballet Philippines and its school; Cecile Santos, Joy Coronel, and Nini Gener (who was a Mir-i-nisa with Mary Anne Garcia), who are now living in the US; Irma Bringas (now Mrs. Aguado); and Manuel Molina, who premiered Radaic's *May Day Eve* (Pajaro) and Basilio's *The Rebels* (Janacek) in 1971.

Now a resident ballet company at the College of Music, University of the Philippines, DTP is now made up of younger dancers, like Regina Debuque and Veronica Restituto, Jonathan Terry and Roberto Clemente, all of them below twenty. Like their seniors, they are all made to upgrade their technical standards by entering the international Royal Academy of Dancing graded examinations, and to develop their performing talents on the Rizal Park stage (Ballet at the Park series of the National Parks Development Committee, arranged by Teodoro F. Valencia and coordinated by the Metro Manila Symphony Foundation).

There are others who have lived their lives as dancers with DTP, tutored by teachers and coaches like Poul Gnatt, Tita Radaic, Julie Borromeo, Eddie Elejar, El Gabriel, Tony Llacer, Basilio, Luis Layag, Loulie Dalupan, Tina Santos, Gerard Sibbritt, Robin Haig, Deirdre Watts, David Blair, and Alfred Rodrigues. Some of the latter were inspired to make ballets for these dancers, emphasizing the collaborative nature of ballet and pursuing such collaborations in DTP's repertory. Ballet as a performing art is produced by talent and teaching, by courting chance and confronting challenges, by rigorous study and faith in mystery.

Arts Monthly
1984

A Diva of Dance

We met when she was twelve. Tita Radaic, her teacher, asked me to choreograph for her preteen and teenage pupils at St. Theresa's College in Quezon City. They were a choice crop that rarely came a tutor's way. And there were two who were to be top of the crop. One was Lisa Macuja, the other Anna Villadolid.

Since the Bavarian National Ballet is coming in June, let me focus on Villadolid. She is one of the company's prima ballerinas. The two other famous ones are the Canadian Evelyn Hart and the Russian (Kirov Ballet) Elena Pankova.

The mid-year visit marks the local premiere of John Cranko's *Romeo and Juliet* from June 20 to 22, with Villadolid dancing as Juliet. It will be followed by two nights of a mixed bill. This visit is a collaborative effort of the company and the Cultural Center, with the involvement of its resident ballet companies, Ballet Philippines and Philippine Ballet Theater.

Because of costs, we haven't had performances by foreign companies in the Philippines in a long, long time, especially a company of such prestige as this one from Munich. Several ballet companies go to Asia but they often ignore us. Although the Bavarian troupe is visiting the Philippines for the first time, another member, aside from Villadolid, is not new to this country. Former American Ballet Theatre (ABT) danseur Wes Chapman has guested twice in Manila, performing in *Swan Lake* and *Don Quixote*. He expresses classical dancing with lucid purity without sacrificing characterization.

But back to my earlier story. I worked with the young girl Anna for the first time in 1976. At their age, she and her peers had just mastered some specific steps that, if put together, could produce a dance piece in the classical style. They were not capable of virtuosity, but they could manage to execute poses and phrases that lent visual life to the music of Lanchbery. It was called *Gemima*, later renamed as *Petit Pas*.

At their age, the girls were probably mulling over the possibility of pursuing ballet seriously. From ages eight to ten, they had to struggle to turn out their hips, to rise and run on pointes, and to perpetually round their arms in the traditional royal manner. They were nurtured and cultured creatures whom Alice Villadolid called "Radaic's butterflies."

By then Radaic would have already indoctrinated them on the rigid rules and exquisiteness of ballet. Their bodies would have internalized a bit of the dance's language. Anna was one of those girls who early on showed that she had her own unique style and identity as a dancer. Her lyricism was just in its budding stage, something National Artist Leonor Goquingco would later rave about in writing, "Anna [is] now the most lyrical Filipino ballerina."

But what of the sleek and silken movement coupled with pink and painful blisters? The young girls would have built an athlete's stamina expressed in grace and fragility. Like most serious ballet teachers, Radaic was rightly ruthless about this paradoxical combination, knowing that only the hardy would survive and become the beautiful ballerinas they wished to be.

With the irregular academic load combined with rigorous training from either six or eight in the morning until ten in the evening, a routine that spans eight to ten years, shouldn't dancers be awarded degrees? Dancers are doomed to a lifetime of training no matter how famous they are. The mirror is there to take cognizance of one's imperfections (in body, technique, and interpretation) in order to aspire for what should appear on stage as perfection.

And they are ever at the beck and call of their ballet masters and directors, expected to be obedient to death as they train, yet they are paid so poorly, especially here in the Philippines. For their discipline and pain they can easily be candidates for saintliness or madness. Today Anna Villadolid would complain of increasing pain that comes with "aging" (and she is only thirty years old, mind you).

At a young age, Anna already had something special about her to be chosen from among the rest and placed centrally as a gem. There were the subtle turns or inclinations of the head that gave her poses nuance, the delicacy of arms that belied bony points and the trim torso that made her look like a leaf. Moreover she executed her steps with clarity and resilience. She revealed movement in musical terms. She would more than follow instructions; she infused them with her personality and perception, lending grace to the choreographer's conception. But she could be inscrutable, listening to you like a stony sphinx. That is, until she dances a passage out for you.

Anna is not even extraordinarily endowed—no high extensions, no exquisite feet. She is feminine but not sensual. Anna is short and slight by Western standards. She lacks the scale required of most Balanchine dancers. But she always had the feeling for line. She is more in the mold of older ballerinas like the Danish Margrethe Schanne, and English Margot Fonteyn. She has their singing, spiritual style. (Later on Anna was one of three ballerinas in Sir Frederick Ashton's spare and pellucid *Symphonic Variations* at the Birmingham Royal Ballet; it was originally made for Fonteyn, Moira Shearer, and Pamela May. She also danced Schanne's *La Sylphide*, the ballerina's trademark in the Boumonville repertoire.)

But today Anna can be steel-like. Her work exhibits angularity in poses and phrasing. She can also be seductive (and subtly flirtatious even in romantic roles like the Sylphide), as she showed once in a pas de deux for a Ballet Philippines gala.

Back then, I did not get to work often with Anna. First she had to be an apprentice with Dance Theatre Philippines, dancing under fairly inclement weather at the Rizal Park. Her seniors included Loulie Dalupan, Irene Sabas, and Emellie Rigonan. They typified a dancing range: dramatic, dramatic-lyric, and lyric. She must have thought of them as models. She also had her peers in Sophia Radaic, Hazel Sabas, and Lisa Macuja. DTP also had guest artists like Marivic Mapili, Gina Katigbak, and Heidi Domingo, who were exemplary. They have all made their mark in dance, here and abroad.

For Irene Sabas, I created the sultana in *Mosque Baroque* to the music of Vivaldi, for Katigbak the alienated protagonist in *Testament* to a piano concerto by Bartok, for Radaic the initiate in *Id* to Debussy's *Nocturnes* (with Anna and Mary Anne Santamaria as soloists). Anna and Lisa Macuja were the symmetrical pair in *Testament.*

Especially for Anna, I created *Ode to Botticelli*, which was inspired by the painter's "Primavera" and "Annunciation," to a harp concerto by Reinecke. She was both Virgin and Spring, attended to by three male angels. Lisa Macuja herself had a brisk duet with Raul Sauz, like Mercury and a nymph. Inspired by Tchaikovsky's life (before seeing Ken Russel's *Music Lovers*), I also gave her Antonina, the Russian composer's distressed wife in my *Tchaikovsky Fantasy*, to Sophia Radaic's Madam Von Meck and Augustus Damian's Tchaikovsky.

During my term as artistic director of DTP, guest choreographers Eddie Elejar and Tony Fabella had the first choice in casting and they invariably picked Anna. Elejar had her in *Masks* to the dramatic poem of Virginia Moreno and music by Ramón Santos. Fabella had her as the girl in the crowd in *Limang Dipa* to the music of Ryan Cayabyab, and in the extended pas de deux, *Love Like the Moon* ... to Massenet. This duet was later acquired by the Manila Metropolis Ballet (MMB).

After leaving DTP due to some controversy, Anna danced with MMB and blossomed there in *Giselle* and in excerpts from classics like *Swan Lake* and *Raymonda.* It was also around that time that she was offered a scholarship to the Heinz Bosl Foundation in Munich. Konstanze Vernon, one of the judges at the 1982 Jackson Ballet Competition and her current artistic director, spotted her there.

She went to Munich in 1983, and within months she became a member of the Munich company. Her stellar debut was phenomenal in Fokine's *Spectre de la Rose*—one prolonged pas de deux originated by Tamara Karsavina and Vaslav Nijinsky. She was hailed as "star of the week."

Shortly after that, she danced Giselle, Princess Aurora in *The Sleeping Beauty*, the Sylphide, Juliet, and the modern *Undine* of Shilling. She was a guest dancer in ballets in Berlin and Leipzig, and of the Birmingham

Royal Ballet, dancing the works of Ashton, Peter Wright, and David Bintley. She also guested in Manila—in *Swan Lake* with BP and in *La Sylphide* with PBT.

Her latest Juliet with Chapman as Romeo caused a critic to speak of her "huge aura," her "clever use" of Prokofiev's music, her realizing "all the possibilities of Juliet's character," and her acting that "makes it movingly clear that the poison which she drinks is not one of death but of love."

Another wrote of the performance: "Everyone says, 'She is an artist'. Truthfully so but she is more a person with an enormously rich heart. She simply has the instinctive knowledge about these existential yearnings, tenderness, fears and conflicts. And how she lets these shine totally without vanity, with this honesty, and immense simplicity—the word Art can only describe half of it."

Of her earlier Juliet here, in Alice Reyes's version, I wrote: "With glass-like vulnerability, Anna Villadolid—for all her ardor and abandon—invests the role with tragic inevitability: Her partnership with Nonoy Froilan as Romeo is love-committed, not surrendered. Clear-minded, she stirs him to the course that resolute love like hers deems serious and without question."

Of her *La Sylphide* here, I also said, "With Villadolid you do not speak of dancing but of inhabiting a role, not of portraying but of living."

Of her musicality, London's principal critic John Percival spoke of her as "a revelation so full of energy, so exact and with a highly individual but entirely convincing way of relating to the music, dancing to its phrases rather than the notes."

Of the three Giselles in Munich last year, she was the most hailed. Manuel Brug wrote, "One believes her most as the frolicsome girl as well as the fluid, somnambular transparent spirit. Her mad scene is magnificent. There was nothing theatrical, superficial about it."

And late last year her Lise in Ashton's *La Fille Mal Gardee* reaped her more praises. One said, "Villadolid had fleet footwork and was musical as always," while another added, "Anna Villadolid is, a heavenly, innocent

Lise, who, together with her teasing Colas, Mark Pace, also displayed fantastic dancing."

Today Anna is no longer the girl I knew. But back then she already showed that dancing is richness not to be flaunted but to be felt and understood—the soul, the movements, and structure coalesce in the dancing, in our perceiving and intuiting it with her. Like all great art, we experience and live her art with her. As in *La Sylphide*, she "[dances] with a most concentrated expressive intent" and the "gift of simplicity." No wonder the girl has become our dance diva.

Manila Chronicle
1995

Lisa Macuja: A Partner in Our Ballet

In Stirling, Scotland, the youngest member of the contingent of Dance Theatre Philippines to the Aberdeen Festival was Lisa Macuja. As one of the adolescent girls in the school recitals of Tita (Felicitas) Layag Radaic, she was, like any girl her age, struggling with awkwardness, yet she possessed a looseness that, if religiously strengthened and centered, is an asset in ballet.

For an entrance or exit in my "La Adoracion" (a ballet inspired by pandanggo sa ilaw to the music of Spanish composer Joaquin Rodrigo), she struck an arabesque that just stood out for its poise and balance. (Arabesque generally means two things: the ornate abstract Arabic design, often round as a rose stained-glass in a cathedral; or the most extended ballet position with legs and arms open and afloat in space.) The teenage Lisa was cause for admiration and envy, what with her skills in the balancing aesthetics of ballet—keeping a glass with a lit candle on the head, performing pirouettes on pointes, ease in partnering, etc. Who knew that decades later, Lisa was to bring her own company Ballet Manila to the Aberdeen Festival?

Entrances and exits, of which there are many in any performance, emerge periodically in the professional life of Lisa. To me that sustained pose in Britain (where I moonlighted as stage director while on break from study at the Benesh Institute) in 1979 was an early boost in her ballet career, marking her as different. And true enough, as her career progressed, Lisa would prove to be a cut above the rest.

It took another year (1980) after my return home, now as artistic director, that I had further occasions to work with Dance Theatre. Lisa was still in the corps de ballet, as background to senior members and guest artists. But if I remember correctly, she soon did older roles, like the comedic *tindera* Aling Tale in Radaic's ballet *Tanan*! (This is a local and capsule version of *La Fille Mal Gardee*, which later Lisa did as the lead *Pilya*, adapted by William Morgan.) Already, she was that versatile.

And reliable, too. She was already studying at the Vaganova Institute in Leningrad when she came home for a break. Dance Theatre had a performance at Puerta Real in Intramuros, curated by Zenas Reyes Lozada. We were also doing a Mozart ballet on pointes of mine when one of the girls stubbed her toe in the garden before the preliminary run. The ballet called *Crystal Concerto* (for the fifteenth anniversary of the company) was also longer because I added a fourth movement, *Canto to Canaletto*. Given the repertoire, it was difficult to fill the girl's part. But Lisa did just that. She only had that one run to mark and copy the corps de ballet before performing the rest of the evening. Minor as the part was, she had to keep her eyes and ears extra alert that night!

To date, dancer-decorator Rupert Acuña marvels at Lisa's twenty-minute solo which I did for her. (Earlier, Australian Michael Hennesy choreographed a shorter one which we first called *For Lisa*, and later, *A Moment, A Memory*.) It was set to a suite of Schubert called *Moment Musical* which I called *A Chair*. It was about a girl expecting a visitor (possibly a suitor) and going through varied moods—first eager, then disappointed, then heavy-hearted, etc. Capturing a range of moods required great technical and histrionic abilities. Lisa was not simply competent in her performance; she was extraordinary.

Lisa can always be trusted to complete any task with distinction. This was the case upon her graduation in Leningrad. I went to see her and Mary Anne Santamaria, our other Dance Theatre scholar. Over there, teachers/coaches had to fight for their own students' slots in the graduation recital in the Kirov Theatre. It was a great surprise that her teacher Tatiana Udalenkova entrusted to her the grand (wedding) pas de deux from *Don Quixote* (with partner Bakhit Smagulov), one of the most sought-after showpieces. Again, it was a foreshadowing of things to come.

Later, as member of the Kirov (now called St. Petersburg again) Ballet and caught in the complicated net of casting schedules (an apt metaphor because once, Lisa literally had to extricate herself from a net of a set on stage!), she did *Don Quixote* in full. This time she was paired with Farouk Ruzimatov, one of the pyrotechnical stars of the ballet company today. Also in Kirov, one of her most classical roles (in the same class as *The Sleeping Beauty*) was the girl-ballerina Masha (Maria, called Clara in the West) in the Hoffmann-based Vainonen *The Nutcracker* ballet.

During her stint with the Kirov Ballet, Lisa was a public favorite. Known to express their admiration vociferously, balletomanes openly lauded and cheered for Lisa in the theater. At performances as a pupil and on her graduation, she was awaited by admirers with flowers by the stage door. I witnessed her fans crowding late into the night to see her.

After two more years in Leningrad, Lisa decided to come home, again at a fortuitous time. Sony Lopez Gonzalez had just staged Act II of *Giselle* with Toni Lopez and Rupert Acuña at the Metropolitan Theater. To celebrate Lisa's homecoming, we negotiated for a repeat, this time with herself and Nonoy Froilan as the leads. I set up the rest of the program, including Lisa's and Froilan's *Le Corsaire* grand pas de deux. Thus began their long partnership.

Soon after, Ma. Teresa Escoda Roxas and Nicanor Tiongson invited her to be their first and only resident artist in dance at the Cultural Center. She was to dance with Ballet Philippines as such—not exactly as its member. There she once more danced in the definitive classical ballets, including the Morgan adaptation of *La Fille* which historically ushered in romantic vernacularism (folk elements) in the ballet repertory. She also toured many provinces with Froilan and the company. Not surprisingly, she became the personification of the ballerina in the country.

In her pre-Leningrad days, she created original parts in ballets by Eddie Elejar, Tony Fabella, and myself. In Elejar's *Once Upon a Village* and my *Paean to Pavlova*, she danced alongside my friend Franklin Bobadilla, one of our first dancers to be soloist in Germany and The Netherlands. In the latter piece, she also danced alongside Irene Sabas and David Campos Cantero, who then were soloists in Belgium. For my *Testament*, which was set to the third piano concerto of Bartok, I cast her in a soaring entrance and in a double pas de deux with Anna Villadolid and their partners. Originally created for Gina Katigbak and Mary Anne Santamaria, it had a lyric double-duet that ushered the ballet to its coda. She and Anna then were nascent ballerinas.

I also worked with her in preparation for Jackson (Mississippi), where one of the most (if not the most) prestigious ballet competitions in the world today is held. We prepared the *Giselle* and *Don Quixote* duets, as well as a contemporary piece of mine set to the last movement of a Kasilag concerto.

When we got there, she and her non-competing partner Froilan were adopted by the Cuban coach Laura Alonso, daughter of the legendary Alicia Alonso. She had them rehearse with Cuban candidates Anna Lobe and Jose Manuel Carreno, so that they forged friendships. At the competition, Lisa was a public and media favorite, getting a colored spread in *Christian Science Monitor*. (Today, Carreno—who won the grand prix over a gold medalist in Paris and Moscow—is now a star of American Ballet Theater in New York.)

And that Cuban collaboration was not to be the last. Lisa did her first full-length *Swan Lake* in Cuba, followed by her first *Romeo and Juliet* in New Zealand. She guested in Singapore with our most virtuosic of male danseurs, the Cebuano Nicolas Pacana. She also went back to Russia to guest with several companies, including a partnership in *Giselle* with one of Russia's (later of London's Royal Ballet) superstars, Irek Mukhamedov.

Prior to the Jackson competition, she garnered the silver prize at the first Asia Pacific International Ballet Competition in Tokyo. Later, she earned another prize in Moscow during a Diaghilev Festival. These experiences inspire her today to urge dancers to join international competitions and to support them in such endeavors.

After spending a few years with the CCP/Ballet Philippines, Lisa was invited to join Philippine Ballet Theatre. Once more she did the classics, but she also increased her contemporary repertoire from local and international ballet masters and choreographers, including the most famous one from Russia, George Balanchine.

Following the examples of earlier dance leaders like Radaic, Elejar, Julie Borromeo (Dance Theatre), and Alice Reyes (Ballet Philippines), Lisa herself wanted to found her own company. She collaborated with Eric V. Cruz who was also a founder of Ballet Theatre (and earlier of Dance Concert Company with Vella Damian). They started their seasons at the GSIS Theater, staging the classics and commissioning works from Jean Paul Comelin, David Campos, Hazel Sabas, and others. Today at her two theaters, Star and Aliwan, she works closely with partner Osias Barroso (earlier of DCC and PBT), not only in productions but also in training the members and scholars of Ballet Manila.

With Ballet Manila (BM) and by consensus, she earned the title "people's ballerina" by virtue of her extended provincial tours. Before her, Radaic's teacher Anita Kane was the pioneer in this enterprise. Her Kane company had involved Radaic and Borromeo themselves, Lucio Sandoval, Tony Llacer, El Gabriel, Marcelino Garcia, Serafina Guinto, etc. Later called Pamana Ballet (with Elejar, Greta Monserrat, and Ruben Nieto as leads, along with Effie Nañas, Ester Rimpos, Radaic's sister and brother Lucy and Luis Layag, even Lino Brocka), her company popularized ballet in the country. They traveled by air, land, and water (including traveling by *bangka*) throughout the Philippines. Kane's own student, Fe Sala Villarica of Cebu, followed the example by touring the Visayas and Mindanao with such dancers like Mario Recto, Nicolas Pacana, and Noordin Jumalon.

When Radaic honored Kane by bringing her back to Manila, it was Lisa and Vivencio Samblaceno (also Dance Theatre, and now of Royal New Zealand Ballet) who performed *Giselle* at the Meralco Theater.

This example of Kane must have also inspired Lisa's teacher Radaic to institute the Ballet at the (Rizal) Park, which lasted for over twelve years. With the support of Teodoro Valencia, the free presentations at the Luneta developed both dance artists and a dance following. At a time when alternative dance was hardly seen outside of the Cultural Center, Ballet at the Park nurtured choreographers and teachers who are now in the forefront of our dance education and production. Lisa is one of them. Today, she periodically revives ballet at Rizal Park in order to achieve the same aims.

At her own two venues in Star City, with the support of her husband Fred Elizalde and the Ballet Manila office, Lisa ably balances the classical and the popular. I have said enough of the first in the company's productions. At Aliwan itself, especially during the Christmas season, BM cooks up a variety presentation that fills the theater to full capacity. There you see Lisa and her ballet dancers performing with acrobats and trapeze artists, clowns and fire-eaters, whom we generally export as dollar-earners.

Some have been critical of this commercial venture, but it certainly addresses the demands of the mass audience, and it is a great opportunity for our variety artists to be seen and to earn. Lisa has learned to live with this criticism. After all, you may say that the presentation follows the tradition of the circus in Russia itself. Among the first to bring ballet to the Philippines were members of an imperial Russian circus. In the early days of the CCP and Meralco Theater, there were Russian visiting contingents whose members performed as circus, folk dance, and ballet artists.

To amplify our artistic debts to Russians, let me just say that several so-called "white Russians" exiled after the Revolution migrated to Manila, where they taught dance. A foremost example was Lubov Adameit, supposedly Polish-Russian and a dancer of Anna Pavlova, who became one of our earliest ballet teachers and trained Leonor Orosa, Remedios de Oteyza, Rosalia Merino, Conchita and Luisa "Inday" Gaston, Joji Felix, Maribel Aboitiz, etc.

Lisa has proven that there is ballet-life after such predecessors. Now inculcating the Vaganova technique, establishing and touring locally and internationally with her Ballet Manila, she is indeed a national partner in Philippine ballet.

Which leads me to ay that another quality of Lisa—aside from reliability, versatility, and virtuosity—is her venturesomeness. Not afraid to take risks, she is willing to put her reputation at stake, clashing with elitist perceptions and persuasions. Thus, she makes her art accessible to people other than those in private ballet schools' and other companies' enclaves. She serves not only herself and her art but also several young charges and artists who work with her. Recently, she and Barroso participated in, and in effect, supported a local ballet competition by sending a representative. (Let me just say, as an aside, that the competition was initiated by the National Music Competition for Young Artists and was criticized for including dance—as if a ballet were not a musical art. What then do we make of Adam, Delibes, Tchaikovsky, Glazounov, Prokofiev, Stravinsky, Pajaro, Kasilag, Santos, etc.?)

Only those who have the narrowest of vision and aims can ignore what Lisa has done for dance in the Philippines. She herself defends the purity of classicism, but she has opened not only her eyes but her company's operation to include contemporary dance and variety productions, which reach a wider audience and give periodic employment in this field. She has broadened the business strategies of her art, and in that way has also empowered her artists economically.

Perhaps Lisa has taken to heart what she learned in her student and early professional days from the Soviets, who honored contributors to culture as "people's artists." Lisa is one such artist. Like our pioneers before her, she has made ballet an art for and of the people, bypassing the insistence on purism and chauvinism that sometimes threatens the very motivation, ground, and operation of such a composite (and even political) art as ballet.

2005

Three Graces at the Home and Heart of Philippine Ballet

The three graces I am referring to exemplify the image of dance in the Philippines, its progress and problems. A few quotes:

"Nowhere was Vida more an attractive and assertive yet giving woman than in this [bedroom] scene. Edna Vida was the woman we all could imagine Carmen to be, earthy and reckless, but with tantalizing eyes and arms and a warm womb … Carmen, the existentialist." (*Arts Monthly*, 1984)

"The central woman, the bride [in *Songs of a Wayfarer*], was played by Sicangco with virginal pensiveness that she truly looked like a woman to aspire for. Different from Reyes and Rimpos' earthier womanliness, Sicangco was translucent and near-transcendental." (*Arts Monthly*, May 1984)

"That crystalline look [in *Coppelia*] was brought by Toni Lopez Gonzalez. She kept a composedly centered presence and translucent tone that excited in doing without a put-on elegance. Her moves were seamless, her persona classically crowned." (*Arts Monthly*, 1984)

Succeeding the two phenomenal and stellar names in the firmament of Philippine ballet—Maniya Barredo and Tina Santos—is a new crop of dancers full of promise like the recently hailed corps of Baryshnikov in America. Nowadays you can fill the house with the mere mention of the names Anna Villadolid or Manuel Molina. Whereas the homegrown talents of an earlier period like Ester Rimpos, Effie Nañas, or Vella Damian were eclipsed by visiting foreign stars, now a Lisa Macuja or a Rey Dizon can stir up the media and the populace.

With the participation of Toni Lopez Gonzalez at the Varna and the New York competitions (making it to the top five in the second), the assumption of Cecile Sicangco of the role of Princess Aurora in *The Sleeping Beauty*, and the latest portrayal of Edna Vida in *Carmen*, her sister's successful ballet, the company of Ballet Philippines at the Cultural Center has come up with its own Philippine-made stars who are finding a sizeable following.

Hope for Philippine Dance 1: Edna Vida

Edna gained noticed in Armin Wild's *Firebird* (which I haven't seen and which, from what I've heard, was received both positively and negatively in 1979). She became a figure of controversy, making it to the pages of *Sunday Special* (now defunct) this year, when she assumed associate directorship of Ballet Philippines. This more or less prompted me to interview Edna for this article, which has been extended to include two other principal ballerinas, Cecile and Toni. The first interview with Edna was in May, before the company left for the American Dance Festival in June. The interview with Cecile was in August after the festival, and the one with Toni was in November of the current 1984-85 season.

Q: What are your responsibilities as associate director?

A: I take care of the company members. I monitor their attendance, make sure they keep fit, and manage their schedule of both rehearsals and casting for tours and restaged pieces. I do not cast for the programs of the season. I also act as rehearsal mistress, directly dealing with the dancers from day to day.

Q: How do you fit yourself in as a dancer with those directorial functions?

A: As a choreographer, I have no problems. But as dancer, I have to consider the welfare of my co-dancers and set a good example myself. Because it's a difficult role, I also never ask to be cast in any ballet.

Q: Have there been others who tried out your function as associate director?

A: Yes, two. But these didn't work out. One of them refused the job.

Q: As associate director, what are your goals?

A: I foresee a time when our dancers will attain star caliber, meeting international standards. Perhaps in five years' time. Stars are born, not made, but I see among the young ones so much dedication, and I even learn from them. I also wish to be more democratic in dealing with the dancers, to show more concern over their welfare, for I recognize their dedication. I also wish to give more leeway to senior members, in recognition of their work.

Q: As choreographer, what are your plans?

A: I am to restage *Vision of Fire* for the current season. I will make some changes. I accept the criticism of Alice. I also wish to do a ballet danced on pointes.

Q: Now that you have assumed a position of authority, what do you do as a dancer?

A: Aside from running the rehearsals, I observe a lot from the sidelines. When I'm not on, I consider the audience's response for my own motivation. My two years of dancing helped me realize the worth of dancing, something I didn't understand deeply before. Motherhood has also helped me. There was a physical change. The responsibility of motherhood made me quit smoking and drinking. I had to eat the right food when I was pregnant with Mica (Michaela Vida Froilan). As a wife and fellow-dancer, I watched Nonoy grow as a dancer—his discipline, humility, and patience. As I've said, I learned a lot from watching the young dancers, how much they work to be good.

Q: What are your favorite roles?

A: Well, my first big one, *Firebird*. Soorphanaka in *Rama*. It was really fun doing *Hari*. *Itim Asu* I first did in Indonesia; its dramatic element was a challenge. *Sisa* by Cora Iñigo I had to do in Russia, and the character's deep loss demanded mature acting. And Lilac Fairy in Luminita Dumitrescu's *SB*, which was a technical test.

Q: While your generation of dancers has increasingly been drawn to dance abroad, why have you stayed home?

A: I think there is now an audience for our own dancers. We're developing that audience—this is our function. I get good roles at home, something that will take time to happen abroad. My own two-month experience being on my own in New York revealed these to me, and I chose to be back with my own colleagues and people.

Still quite overshadowed by the prestige of her elder sister Alice as choreographer, it needs to be stressed that Edna is exciting to watch mature. Of her works, *Mutya ng Pasig* (Abelardo) and *Vision of Fire* (Federizon) were brought by Ballet Philippines to the American Dance Festival, a choice that was made by Charles Reinhart, Edna explained. She has also done the Christmas spectacular *Peter Pan* with its full-evening demands, the "vernacular" *Ensalada* set to songs by Ryan Cayabyab and his arrangements, *Gardenia* to the music of Tariverdiev, *Pagsamba* to Fanshawe's African *Mass* (the earliest listed of her works, from 1976), and *Isaiah* to Lord, this writer's favorite piece of hers. (*Vida AM*, vol. II, no. 5, p. 6.) The last was concise, forceful, and deep. It was as good as her sister Denisa Reyes's *Photography, A Gentleman's Honor* (to Class), and what ADF called *Muybridge* (a less universal name, to Obispo's music)—but in a different way, more Eastern and emotional.

As associate director, choreographer, ballet mistress, and dancer, Edna's task is, indeed, immense—something not to be envied, despite the prerogatives. She handles and avoids criticism by keeping a low profile. She has enough work to do and too little time outside of the theater and rehearsal hall at the Center. The little time she has left is for her family. One cannot help but acknowledge and admire the energy, patience, and talent she pours into her responsibilities.

Love for Dancing 2: Cecile Sicangco

Cecile Sicangco hails from Bacolod. She started ballet with Mellie Hofileña Hojilla at the age of five, and moved on to the school of Lydia Madarang Gaston at eight, where she stayed for five years. Hofileña

Hojilla is the sister of Manila Metropolitan Theater's Rene Hofileña, and was a senior dancer in Elsie and Pancho Uytiepo's school in Bacolod. I started partnering work with her in class. She also trained further in Manila. Madarang Gaston was a dancer with Remedios de Oteyza and nearly became a member of the Ballet Russe de Monte Carlo in New York, but she married and became mother to BP's Lydlyd Gaston, now of Baltimore Ballet. Of Cecile's classmate in Bacolod, Baltimore's *Evening Sun* wrote, "Her dance—Leslie-Jane Pessemier's *Les Chansons*—was brought alive by Lydlyd Gaston, whose sinewy body breathed life into the choreography as she bared her soul as a dancer through her changing emotions of desire, longing, regret, loss. Gaston is a beautiful dancer, a gift from the Philippines to Baltimore."

When she moved on to Manila after the first summer dance workshop at the Center, Cecile studied ballet with Eddie Elejar and modern dance with Alice Reyes and Tony Fabella. She danced with the company from 1973 to 1976, and again moved on to New York at Joffrey's Ballet Center. There she studied with Meredith Baylis and Peter Nelson. She also studied with David Howard, Larry Rhodes, and Douglas Wassell. She credits Wassell for much of her improvement; he was with Les Grands Ballets Canadiens, and had taught at the Harkness and Howard schools, and New York University. She also credits much to Norman Walker—whom she had as a teacher in Manila—for a sense of discipline, and William Morgan, for a real understanding of how the body works and more.

Like Edna, Cecile left dancing for one and a half years to study ophthalmology in New York. Fortunately, brother Toto (Eduardo), the designer, asked her a life-defining question: "What do you do best?"

Q: Why did you stop dancing?

A: I evaluated my chances in the showbiz jungle that was New York, and I realized the chances of Asians doing well there. But stopping made me realize what I wanted to do most, and it was dancing.

Q: Are you, like Edna, from a family of artists, too?

A: My grandmother, Dolores Rodrigues, was a singer and my grandfather, Homero Sicangco, was a pianist. My mother, Gloria Varela, was a voice graduate from the University of Santo Tomas, and of piano from St. Scholastica College. My father, Jose Sicangco, is a businessman. My brother, Toto, is a stage designer for operas and musicals; he has done productions in San Francisco, Texas, and Lincoln Center in New York.

Q: Aside from the training background you have mentioned, how do you keep on improving as a dancer?

A: I watch a lot of videotapes on dance, and I learn from them. I also watch tapes of my own performances. Lately, I have also been challenged by principal roles. Princess Aurora in 1983 had high standards that had to be met, and it required a lot of stamina, especially in Act II. And I've also done *Don Quixote*, and this 1984 season, I am doing Swanilda in *Coppelia.*

Q: What other choice roles have you had?

A: I had a role in Brando Miranda's *The Awakening* and played the bride in Walker's *Songs of A Wayfarer.*

Q: How long have you been with the company?

A: Before New York, three years. After New York, since 1980. I was made principal dancer in 1983.

Q: How do you regard the administration of the company?

A: I think it is very fair. I don't mind the alternation of roles, because it gives me time to rest and also learn from my alternates. I even do corps-work on tours due to the limited personnel. And I like doing new roles, exploring other characters.

Q: You have been taking trips abroad for how long, and why do you come back?

A: I go for summer work abroad. But I come back. I'm happy to stay and work in Manila. I watch the younger dancers of the company, and they are a talented bunch. It would be a pity if, because of financial difficulties we are all undergoing these days, all that talent will go to waste.

Indeed, Cecile's own talent is riding on a high crest. Increasingly, she is getting more challenging roles and she is now ready for them. The pace of her growth has been steady, and in a dancing career, that kind of pace assures her of a stable durability and an exciting development to watch. She has the strength and the sparkle for extrovert characters, but in *Songs* of Walker, she also exhibited an ideal quality in contrast to the earthier interpretations of Reyes and Rimpos. She has a lot of roles and years to look forward to, and with her prime concentration on dance, hers will be a long and colorful career to judge Philippine ballet by.

The Faith to Dance 3: Toni Lopez Gonzalez

Perhaps the youngest to be made a principal dancer in Ballet Philippines (BP) and the one with a record of five seasons with the company, Toni Lopez Gonzalez went on to be one of the five finalists in the last (and first) New York Ballet Competition in 1984. Earlier, she joined the competition in Varna while nursing an injury. Today, at nineteen and on her sixth and final season with BP, she looks forward to a career in America by mid-1985. Like her close-contemporaries Lisa Macuja and Anna Villadolid, she is seeking new and broader experiences which Philippine ballet at present can't provide.

The cost of American-made pointes-shoes alone at P800 a pair (as of this writing) can set back Philippine ballet by a few years. Marikina is not interested in producing these shoes. The technical standards so far attained by dancers can be undermined as a result of the limited availability of these crafted (what I'd like to call) "musical instruments." This is just one obvious indication of the state of dance as an art in the Philippines, which has led to the exodus of our best talents. Aside from our women, including Irene Sabas, Elizabeth Roxas, Maiqui and Mia Mañosa, Tina Escoda, Myra Beltran, Gina Mariano, Lydlyd Gaston, Gia Montinola, Maricar Drilon, Becky Rodriguez, Sophia Radaic, Mary Anne Santamaria, etc., we have also lost our much sought-after men, including the late Luis Layag, Manuel Molina, Rey Dizon, Franklin Bobadilla, Mitto Castillo, Maxie Luna, Enrico Labayen, William Miller, Javier Picardo, Victor Madrona, Cesar Ongkingko, Benjie Toledo,

Augustus Damian, Ricardo Ella, etc. At the start of the seventies, we lost Lulu Puertollano, Tina Santos, and Maniya Barredo.

Toni also feels that there is not enough tutorial expertise to go around, something that pulls back or delays the development of young dancers. Moreover, our audiences for the dance are still colonial in mindset, more interested in the foreign guest artists than our own talents. The current state of dance in the country, further aggravated by the current financial crunch, discourages the young from taking their art seriously. The progress of Philippine ballet might just "go to waste," she said.

Q: Are there artists in your family, like in Cecile's?

A: My mother was a dancer and she was also a piano major. She is cousin to the Kabayaos, the musical family.

Q: How early did you start dancing?

A: At about three. But I only really started taking dance seriously at twelve, when I joined Ballet Philippines as a company scholar. Then it was only two years ago when I came to decide to make it my career.

Q: How did you arrive at that decision?

A: Well, I sort of realized that I was "destined to dance," so to speak. I realized that this is my talent, the gift I am to live by. Even when I don't perform well, I came to realize the significance of my work, why it didn't work well, and what I ought to do after. My own growth here at home had built my confidence to enable me to decide I have this gift and that I can make it. I also love to travel, which company work provides.

Q: Who are the teachers who helped you most develop this confidence?

A: My mom, to start with. Then Nanette Glushak (formerly soloist with American Ballet Theater) in New York, who helped me use the correct muscles, taught me the right use of the feet.

Q: What are your favorite roles that had helped you extend yourself?

A: *Romeo and Juliet.* Primarily I love the music, and then the story, with which the music fuses very well. I love the acting. I also enjoy dancing *Les Sylphides* and the Bournonville even if they are hard. I like Walker's *At Summer's End.*

Q: How about your modern work? How do you shift, from the classic to the modern?

A: Edna says I must have the same attack for both. I prefer doing classical work.

Q: How did the competitions serve you? What benefits do you get out of competing?

A: In Varna I worked hard. I was working to my limit then, and I was inspired by the other competing artists. But before the competition, I realized I must first compete with myself.

Q: How did you find the New York competition?

A: It was more gregarious. We were between seventeen and twenty-three in age, and *we* were like one company. We got to know each other. We even helped each other out.

Q: What did you dance there with your partner Michael Foster? (Foster, formerly of American Ballet Theater, is now with Houston Ballet.)

A: Michael was a good partner; we first met at the ABT scholarship program one summer. In the first round, we did the *Les Sylphides* pas de deux. My solo was the valse. In the second round, we did the white act pas de deux of *La Bayadere.* In the third, from *Gaite Parisienne,* while I did Edna's *Mutya* solo. In the fourth and final round, we did Igor Youskevitch's *La Fille Mal Gardee* pas de deux.

Q: How much time did you have to prepare? Who were the judges?

A: We only had two weeks to prepare all that, and we had limited time for rehearsals at the Harkness school. We had classes in the mornings and allocated rehearsal time in the afternoons. The judges, headed by Violette Verdy, had representatives from

Japan, Denmark, Venezuela, the USA, etc. There were seven or eight judges.

Q: How do you size up your opportunities abroad?

A: I'd like to start with a small company, and work my way up to the bigger ones. I believe there are lots of opportunities there, and I have this inner drive to work harder. I have been strengthened by my training here and abroad. I also know what it takes out there. And I have this faith. This idea that I was destined to dance, given this gift to use.

Q: What roles do you look forward to? And what else do you expect?

A: Another *Romeo and Juliet*, and *Giselle*. I think I'd find the first act the most challenging. Of course, the second act requires a lot in terms of technique. I also wish to make some guest appearances. I admire a lot the work of Maniya Barredo. Considering her small size and her local background, she made it. She gives me a lot of inspiration.

Here are three ballerinas of Ballet Philippines, which is about to end its fifteenth season. The first is also a talented choreographer, eager to meet more challenges and presently working hard daily as a taskmaster of the company. The second, like the first, had the experience of giving up dance and finding it again, valuing it the more and enjoying the liveliness of dancing. The third looks forward to a next stage in her career abroad. The youngest, she has perhaps the most time and opportunities open to her as a dancer, as seen in her achievements in international competitions.

As I mentioned at the beginning of this essay, all three exemplify the image of the dance in the Philippines, its progress and problems. Toni prefers to stay home, but she feels her potential can only be fully realized abroad, where there are more facilities and opportunities. Edna and Cecile have come home, finding meaning in "domestic work." Given the present-day economy, companies are now forced to capitalize more on available talents and venues of local companies other than BP. The dancers are ready to confront the challenges—the financial, training, and leadership problems of the theatrical art as well as the great demands of the profession—but their needs also need to be met. After all, the dancers are the ones who sweat it out in classes, rehearsals, workshops, daily and nightly, on and off stage. Behind the illusion of the beauty of ballet dancing, there is the diurnal work that should allow them to reap artistic, occupational, and economic rewards. Laymen may not realize it, but the daily grind—the tough, relentless training—is what makes possible the breadth and depth of beauty that dance uniquely and dynamically provides.

Let me end by saying thanks for the hope, love, and faith of Edna, Cecile, and Toni.

Arts Monthly
1985

Lead Us Dancing into the Nineties

As the new decade rolls in, two new directors make their presence felt in the Philippine dance scene.

Given the recent national and international events, we can only view the coming decade with suspense, even apprehension. No longer predictable, economic trends worldwide prevent safe and sound projections. Political maneuverings and alignments are similarly fluid and uncertain. Nature itself hasn't been motherly, perhaps because her exploitative human children have been insatiable and have thus gravely upset her balance. But neither director seems daunted. The young Denisa Reyes says that she's here to stay, ready to contribute something to the scene and to look beyond one company's goals. On the other hand, the more senior Eddie Elejar is quick to observe that, in the 1950s when import controls were imposed on the Philippine economy, there were no tights available from abroad so dancers had to knit their own. Perhaps we might even have to make our own pointes-shoes; so prohibitive are their prices at the current exchange rate.

Both Reyes and Elejar are not exactly new hands at dance directing. Reyes was acting director of Ballet Philippines (BP) in its 1985-86 season. Recently appointed artistic director of BP, she takes over the task of her sister Alice (now titled Artistic Director Emeritus)—not the passing of the torch from sister to sister, she says, but from artist to artist.

Elejar was, in fact, a co-founder and co-director of BP in 1970. He was also a founder-officer of Dance Theatre Philippines (DTP) (with Julie Borromeo and Tita Layag Radaic), and later established, with choreographer Tony Fabella (another DTP and BP alumnus), the Manila Metropolis Ballet. (Like Alice Reyes, they were both leading dancers with the Bayanihan Philippine Dance Company.) Recently, Elejar was appointed artistic director of Philippine Ballet Theater.

The New Reyes of Ballet Philippines

Denisa was a member of BP—first called the Alice Reyes and Modern Dance Company, and later the Cultural Center of the Philippines Dance Company—until she went for further studies at the State University of New York. A very literate artist, she pursued many years of enrichment in the United States. This international background, she feels, is unique to the new breed of dance leaders—from herself, associate Cecile Sicangco, and BP-II artistic director Agnes Locsin, to the recently returned Enrico Labayen and Hazel Sabas.

In the US, Denisa became a member of the Asakawalker Dance Company (of Takako Asakawa and David Hatch Walker, former members of the Martha Graham Dance Company, who did a production for BP in 1975) and the 5 by 2 Plus Dance Company. She also guested with the Hannah Kahn Dance Company.

As choreographer, she did a number of acclaimed productions in the very plural atmosphere of New York. At the Clark Center's Young Choreographers series, she did *Ifugao* (from her seminal *Arem* of 1975 in Manila) in 1978. She produced three concerts, in 1981 at PS 122, in 1982 in Chicago, and in 1984 at the Larry Richardson Dance Gallery with a Neo-Filipino theme.

In these presentations, she choreographed works that established her identity: *One-ton Pinay, Public Places/Private Hearts, Made in the Philippines,* and *For the Gods*. Most of these she later restaged in Manila.

In Manila between 1983 and 1985, she premiered *Muybridge/Frames*, set to the music of Fabian Obispo (formerly *Photography* when first set to Philip Glass), *Firebird*, and *Te Deum*. A home-based Neo-Filipino in 1987 brought in more seminal works in *Cock vs. Cock*, *Balimbingan*, and *Hula*, initiating collaboration with theatrical and visual artists like Agnes Arellano and Nonon Padilla. The years 1988 and 1989 came with more significant works in *Siete Dolores* (again to the music of Obispo, with libretto by Nicanor Tiongson) and *Diablos* (for PETA). Both works have powerful meaning and impact, although the latter comes out more whole and focused in artistry.

In 1990, she took over the helm of BP. Because the plans were, however, earlier laid out by Alice Reyes, she is mainly the implementer of a previously conceptualized season. But with another Neo-Filipino in November, she came up with a deeply felt and suspiciously autobiographical yet universal theme in *Desert Passages* (to Arvo Part's tantalizing music), and an amusing and words-spiced *Asong Ulol Atbp.*, with the Picasso-like design of Santi Bose.

Denisa has come a long way. Still shuttling between her home base in Los Angeles and Manila, she is determined to achieve something for Philippine dance in her own way. She is open to cooperative ventures with her colleagues both within and outside of the company.

She plans to go into producing works relevant to the times—like making the Neo-Filipino format part of the BP season, juxtaposing experimental works with the ballet classics, and moving forward with neoclassical dance. She hopes to acquire some foreign works in this vein (Kylian, Van Manen, etc.), and is conceptualizing a Nijinsky festival where she may invite choreographers like Tony Fabella to contribute *Les Noces* (originally by Nijinsky's sister, Bronislava Nijinska).

She also wishes she could acquire some modern dance classics, such as those by Kurt Jooss and Martha Graham, even as she confesses a partiality for Paul Taylor. She is also open to working on collaborative experiments with some young PBT choreographers.

Denisa is greatly encouraged by the positive attitude of the BP dancers, their discipline, and their persistent hankering for more rehearsals. Some of them would even cry, just to be rehearsed or coached. She is proud of the dancers' commitment to their art. She has high hopes for the young ones and contemplates a choreographic future for the older dancers. She believes what they are is a breed of thinking dancers, asking how and why this or that is done.

Looking back, Denisa thinks there has been a renaissance in Philippine dance. Much has been done through the years and much has been achieved. Her own works have been hailed abroad, and our dancers have been appreciated internationally.

But there are problems. Money is one. However, she feels it is available both from private funding and from the sustained support of the Cultural Center. She is encouraged by the enthusiasm of BP's present chairman, Ernesto Escaler. She feels that the trustees only need to see the amount of work the company is doing, to pinpoint needs, and to set up committees that may work on different areas.

Even if she wishes to recruit more members into the company, there is not enough funding to do so. Although she wishes to produce new works, the company has to come up with the means to finance them. She believes that if only other artists and groups were more understanding of the needs of dance companies, they would go out of their way to lend assistance.

In terms of training, BP needs rehearsal space, regular ballet masters, even good pianists for classes. (Because they are paid so little, we do not have full-time dance pianists.) She is happy with the ballet work at present provided by Leon Koning and Enrico Labayen, the Graham training from Agnes Locsin, and the Limon technique from Hazel Sabas.

She is convinced that the Filipino body is a flexible instrument that can accommodate different techniques and styles. She believes that the discipline of ballet should be combined with the naturalness of modern dance. In fact, this kind of mix is somehow the Filipino identity, a "fruit salad" of sorts, which she believes is most certainly a good thing.

In the international context, the call is for good Filipino works. These works realize Filipino creativity and represent Filipino identity. She is envious of the kind of easy identity which Thai and Indonesian choreographers project. Especially in Indonesia, dance is a way of life, even a religion. This is also what Denisa dreams for the Philippines.

Elejar's New Domain

On the other side of town, in Pasig, Philippine Ballet Theater is hosted by the Meralco Theater. After it was launched in 1986 (soon after the EDSA phenomenon) and granted some subsidy by the Cultural Center, PBT based itself in the private studio of Inday Gaston Mañosa in Makati. But the lease soon expired so that PBT had to find another place. With the aid of Manolo Lopez, it was given studio space in Meralco. (When the studio floor had to be reset in 1990, PBT was also hosted for a while by Julie Borromeo in her Dance Arts Studio in Mandaluyong.)

PBT is a pool of resources in terms of talents. It had its unplanned beginning in 1984 with the "Festival Four" encouraged by Lucrecia Kasilag at the CCP. In 1986, with "Sayaw Sining" at the Metropolitan Theater, it was welcomed by Conchita Sunico and Chinggay Diaz Lagdameo. Existing as the Hariraya Ballet Company, Dance Theatre Philippines, Dance Concert Company, and Manila Metropolis Ballet, through many years they were also given performing opportunities in the Puerta Real Evenings. DTP itself realized the "Ballet at the (Rizal) Park" monthly for twelve years, through the joint efforts of Teodoro F. Valencia and Tita Layag Radaic.

Today PBT has an Artistic Council composed of Borromeo, Radaic, Elejar, Eric Cruz, Vella Damian, Tony Fabella, Sony Lopez Gonzalez, and Inday Gaston Mañosa, with National Artist Leonor Orosa-Goquingco and Basilio as additional founding members. Mañosa and Borromeo were PBT's first directors.

This year (1991), Elejar assumes the directorship of DTP, assisted by Gloria Angara as president and Mita B. Rufino as executive director. Elejar's background is perhaps the most durable in the ballet field. Starting young with Ricardo Cassell, he trained in the atmosphere of professionalism that Cassell initiated with his Studio Dance Group in the 1950s. That group produced other reputable male dancers like Benjamin Villanueva Reyes, Tony Llacer, and El Gabriel. While working with Pacita Madrigal, Cassell staged the first production of *Giselle* in the Philippines in 1950.

When dancing for another teacher-director was considered taboo, Elejar dared to dance with several. It was not only a way to realize himself as an artist (at a time when performances were few and far between) but also to help groups form themselves, sometimes at the cost of having his own hand bitten by those he generously fed.

Thus, he danced for Remedios de Oteyza's Manila Ballet Academy as well as for Sony Lopez Gonzalez and Joji Felix Felarde's Ballet Arts, in productions of *Giselle* and *Swan Lake* in 1961 and 1962. In these productions, he danced with the beautiful Maribel Aboitiz (with whom he was partnered in several grand pas de deux in a tour of Spain and Switzerland, long before any Filipino—except for Manolo Rosado, Villanueva Reyes, and his wife Josefa Arnaldo—was heard to have joined foreign companies). Elejar also danced for Anita Kane's Pamana Ballet, which toured the Philippines quite extensively for its time. Elejar's ballerina was Greta Montserrat, and dancing with him were Ester Rimpos and Luis Layag. The impresario was Jose Limlengco.

In 1968, with Borromeo and Radaic, he formed Dance Theatre Philippines, a company launched with a production by the Danish Poul Gnatt, but later focusing on Filipino ballets. Among these were his own *Katakata sin Rajah Indarapatra* (to the music of Jose Maceda) and an adaptation of the Japanese film *Gates of Hell*. He was also artistic director for the *Mir-i-nisa* production that helped inaugurate the Cultural Center, DTP having been personally chosen by the late composer Eliseo M. Pajaro.

With Alice Reyes, Elejar later formed the CCP Dance Company, now Ballet Philippines. In taking over the direction of the four-year-old PBT, he feels that all the groupings and regroupings realize the dreams of our pioneer ballet teachers, despite their own narrow self-protectiveness in the past. Now in PBT (for a time he was in the ad hoc company of the Ballet Federation of the Philippines, from 1976-78), teachers and students of today have come together. Perhaps it was fate that brought them in one company.

Already a true professional in the earlier stages of his career, Elejar considers his new status a meaningful "autumn" of his life.

He wishes to bring in more coaching into the delineation of roles. He feels that this has been neglected, and dancers are left to learn their roles by themselves. While dancers today are better trained because of foreign teachers coming in and out, and local teachers keeping up with the standards worldwide, Elejar sees the added need of closely coaching them. Like athletes—Elejar was a swimmer in UP—dancers also need looking after, and they would certainly do better with more hands-on coaching. Elejar feels that they need to move more broadly, cover space, and expand gestures. He yearns for beautiful *ports de bras* (carriage of the arms), as typified then by Tina Santos and now by Maiqui Mañosa. But all these will take time to achieve.

Furthermore, Elejar thinks some of our dancers still have a very academic approach to movement, which seems to show that their training has restricted rather than liberated them. More importantly, he believes we still have to realize an identifiably Filipino style in ballet. He wishes to achieve such a style in PBT. He believes that style has so far eluded us, although our dance teachers have always been aspiring for it.

Like Denisa Reyes, Elejar thinks that we have dancers whose progress has fulfilled and gone beyond our expectations. They have a healthy attitude toward work, like Osias Barroso who thinks out his roles. (For example, Barroso essayed the roles of both father Mang Basyo and son Kardo in Radaic's *Tanan* recently, and Sol Fernandez did a moving Dr. Coppelius in 1989.) He sees good prospects for Melanie Motus, Noreen Ostrea, and Mylene Saldaña. And of course, PBT has an asset in the versatile Lisa Macuja who leads the company.

With these dancers, Elejar finds reason for the merger of small companies into a mother company. Beyond groups that have earlier collaborated in Metro Manila, he looks forward to involvement from schools and groups so that they can be professional in their work.

With a more centralized funding system, keeping dancers as professionals and producing ballets should be more practicable. This will even make possible what PBT seems to have planned without really planning—to end its season annually with Filipino works. This has now become a tradition.

Elejar has so far contributed his *Rigodon* (1989), which might be described as a kind of revision of his old *Rigodon Sketches* in BP, to that tradition. In BP, he was mainly responsible for the early staging of ballet classics. He created ten original works for BP, among them *Juru-Pakal, Kapinangan, Misang Pilipino, Juliet and Her Romeo, Jewels, Who's the Clown*, and *Swan of Tuonela*. This tradition will continue in the 1991 season of PBT.

PBT has been commissioned to do a ballet version of *Dalagang Bukid*. This will be completed along with the first Philippine production of *La Sylphide* and the premiere of Thomas Pazik's *Madam Butterfly* ballet.

Elejar is worried, however, that 1991 may not bring enough people to the theater because of the economic crunch. CCP's own public relations man Mag Hatol Cruz confessed in *Manila Bulletin* (December 30, 1990) that cost-cutting measures may have a deleterious effect on theater attendance. While Malacañang, in Memorandum Order no. 24, has ordered austerity program, it is inevitable for the cost of production to rise. Theater is strapped for money, for this is not the time to increase ticket prices.

But Elejar also remembers that during the Pacific War, Filipino artists were widely patronized by the public in the downtown cinema houses of Manila. Drama-theater flourished, and the Metropolitan Theater was quite busy. In the 1950s, during the Import Control days, dancers knitted their own tights and found means to extend the life of their pointes-shoes. Necessity is the mother of ingenuity, so Elejar does not sound too pessimistic about the year 1991.

The ingenuity of both Elejar and Reyes will be tested in 1991. Since both their careers have flourished and continue to grow as a result of their intense creativity, they may certainly find the means to sustain the art of dance that have eluded bureaucrats and technocrats. The two are happy that they have trustees who are out-and-out lovers of dance. They are bound to exhaust all means to give the art life and sustenance.

Though tough times lie ahead, dance is still assured of unwavering originality of impulse and productivity in the hands of such diehards as Elejar, Reyes, and their respective trustees and artists.

Kultura
1991

Skirting an Issue*

How does a boy get to dance? With a few exceptions, boys are not encouraged to get into professional dance training and performing. In our macho culture, fathers generally object to their sons dancing. Were it not for my mother's tolerance and love for the arts, I would not have gotten into dance.

Some teachers of dance in formal schools or dance studios invite boys to join their schoolmates or sisters in taking dance lessons. One example is Vella Damian. She is one of the few teachers who encourage boys to start dancing at a young age. Through a scholarship program, Tita Radaic also used to get boys from public high schools, and for a good time Dance Theatre Philippines and Ballet at the Park survived with a few of them as the company's backbone.

In general, males start dancing seriously when they are older, unlike many female dancers who begin training in childhood. Even groups like the largely amateur Bayanihan or Baranggay recruit beginners who are already in college, dividing their time between school and after-school or weekend training. At the University of the East, male students in the troupe are exempted from military training. In the past many of them became part of the strong male contingent of Ballet Philippines, among them Manuel Molina, Gener Caringal, Nonoy Froilan, Brando Miranda, Mario Esperanza, etc. In UP, male dancers get certain honorarial privileges or are enrolled in a dance degree program—but again there are so few of them. Most men only get into full-time dancing after college, like

* A paper in honor of Mr. Eddie Elejar, danseur noble, dance teacher, choreographer, and director.

Tony Fabella, or drop out of school altogether. It is remarkable how they manage to dance well, especially in ballet where training is expected to start in childhood. A few even manage to join companies abroad and/or become solo dancers—Molina, Mitto Castillo, Nicolas Pacaña, Victor Madrona, Augustus Damian, Vivencio Samblaceno, Jun Mabaquiao, etc.

The Necessity of Men

Dance schools and companies seek boys out of necessity. In general, girls who dance are supported by their parents. They are provided transportation, and their costumes and pointe-shoes paid for. When they are older and train abroad, some parents are able to cover their board, lodging, and medical expenses. In our social system, men are expected to fend for themselves financially at the age of twenty-one. The continuous financial support of families for daughters does not, in general, apply to sons.

But at the start of their life in dance, men have some advantages over women. A school or company will often give them tuition scholarships, perhaps even living allowance, however small, to supplement the support they get from their parents and to cover the cost of transportation and meals. They may also be provided practice clothes and shoes. (Unless they are foreigners and full members, they do not usually have the privilege of being lodged in company-paid apartments.)

They also get paid for performances ahead of the women and might even be paid more out of consideration for their living needs or marital obligations. Men who choreograph are occasionally compensated for commissioned works (at a minimum rate). Their greater mobility and social freedom also allow them to get additional fees for dancing on television or trade shows, teaching or choreographing for schools or banks, or—if they are additionally gifted with such talent—designing sets and costumes (as is the case with Arturo and Eric Cruz, Rupert Acuña, and Victor Ursabia).

The male dancer is indispensable as a partner to the ballerina. Ballet has always had this "balance" of male and female aspects in dancing, even at the time when male dancers were dispensed with and women had to dress up *en travesti* to take on the role of men, as in the original *Coppelia*. When the women took over the lead during the Romantic Period of ballet (after an all-male period when men dressed up as women in the court ballets), they were dominant in the ballerina-hegemony, to the ballet's final disadvantage. It took Serge Diaghilev starting with Vaslav Nijinsky to redress the imbalance.

Social Provision and Recognition

Most male dancers in the Philippines come from the lower class. More affluent families will not tolerate their sons getting into "the lesser professions." But by dancing these men from the lower classes get to break down certain social barriers and discrimination. Because they partner daughters from more affluent families, they get to hobnob with those they would normally not interact with in social—even diplomatic—functions they would normally not be invited to attend. As long as they serve this need, they are tolerated, even extolled and additionally compensated. The exceptional male dancers get to head dance companies (although most dance schools and companies are still dominated by females—including those masquerading as artistic associates or executive directors), so that they may even move in the same circles as socialites and politicians.

But once they leave these functions—as partners to ballerinas or director-choreographers to companies—they revert to their class status. Their many years of dancing do not enrich them or give them political clout. It must be said that female dancers do not get rich either, but if they are from influential families to begin with, they can easily take on crucial positions as trustees or producers.

Thus, to a degree, dancing has given men from the lower class a certain degree of social mobility and recognition. If they are equipped with some form of academic education, as is the case of Nestor Jardin, they may even enjoy high administrative functions. But this is exceptional, considering how most dancers without such background revert to survival status, as is the case of Manuel Molina.

The Continuing Influence of Men

Male dancers who invest their lives in the art usually venture into dance-related professions such as teaching, coaching, choreographing, and directing. Except for directing, these jobs may not earn them enough money to keep financially afloat. For example, Froilan has to go into videography to supplement his teaching income. Our most senior danseur, Eddie Elejar, continues to humbly serve his young charges in Quezon City, together with Fabella and Luther Perez. He does not have the added influence in social functions or fundraising events that should come with his past achievements. He is not included in the much-anticipated centennial awards for artists even if he helped found three professional dance companies—the early Dance Theatre Philippines, Ballet Philippines, and Philippine Ballet Theatre, plus the Quezon City Performing Arts Development Center serving the disadvantaged youth—and was part of a triumphant tour of the Bayanihan in New York as lead dancer (unlike Bayanihan's Lito Atienza who became a politician). Our first best-known male folk dancers (both acknowledged as "Mr. Folk Dancer"), Ricardo Reyes and Lucio Sandoval, withered away in quite obscure jobs. Unlike dancers in Russia or Britain, they did not get state or royal titles with emoluments; in fact, there is still no National Artist in dance who is male.

Some male dancers continue to exert national influence. One example is Ramon Obusan, by virtue of his phenomenal achievements in research and dance presentation. But Obusan's projects are largely self-financed. His recognitions from national institutions are a result of their own need of him. But what will happen to his collection and documentation when he is no longer as active and aggressive as he is today?

Remaining Status with Reservations

An issue that has been skirted all along is that the male dancer is not truly recognized and remunerated for his service to the arts and society. Moreover, in his practice of an art that is sometimes deemed less important than the more permanent and quantifiable forms, such as painting and writing, his significance has still to be duly, fully appreciated. Again, how many writers and visual artists are National Artists, compared with the few dancers, none of them male?

The sexual and social discrimination against male dancers, the taunting they get especially while still young, and the all-too-temporary generous provision for them in their prime have not made dancing a justly viable and respectable profession for men. (Nor does it ensure compensation, considering the early retirement of a male dancer, especially in ballet.) What other men in Philippine society strive for—economic independence or affluence, and social standing or influence—which most of society still expects of men—are still generally far from the male dancer's reach, or if somehow reached, grudgingly given to them.

The issue of man's economic and social stability, despite all the accolades given him, has not been and is still not gained by or granted to our men dancers in just measure.

World Dance Alliance-Philippines/*Dance in Revolution, Revolution in Dance*
Manila
1999

The Male Dancers and Society

Rafael Zulueta da Costa throws us back to a cherished past. His welcome series on music, opera, dance, and drama in "Footfalls Echo in the Memory" in *Manila Chronicle* enlightens the young and old about the long history of our cultural life, its vitality existing long before the Marcos and post-Marcos years. Many artists have been obscured not only by the popular arts but also by partisanship of cultural leaders, politicians, and bureaucrats "in charge" of culture and the arts.

Zulueta's own impresario work made it possible for us to enjoy and learn from the artistry of Filipino and international artists. In dance, he gave us great stars like Fonteyn, Vyroubova and Daydee, Greco, and I believe, a few more Spanish dance virtuosi. His appreciation of Filipino dance artists came quite late, and he seemed more invested in paying tribute to them than extending managerial help. I understand, of course, that to espouse the cause of local dance in his time was to make the most feeble of sounds in the face of an overwhelming amount of attention bestowed upon foreign visitors.

With his third series, "Tides of Ballet in the Philippines" (June 11, 1989), he kindly acknowledged the efforts of male dancers in the development of our ballet. They are often neglected, given the preferred management and media espousal of the ballerinas.

Zulueta himself missed out on the contribution of Nonoy Froilan who, after his beginnings with Julie Borromeo and Tony Llacer, sustained the longest premier danseurship in Ballet Philippines. Froilan has his limitations, but at this point in time he has contributed more to Philippine ballet than most of the ballerinas he has partnered, whatever glories the latter might have gained for themselves in the international field. Perhaps, he is only rivaled by Ester Rimpos—a locally trained ballerina whose astounding contributions have yet to be fully acknowledged—and by such enduring danseurship as Elejar's or Villanueva Reyes's in the US-West Coast.

Because Mr. Zulueta made mention of these two premier danseurs and myself in the same breath, I was prompted to write this rejoinder. I felt both flattered and uneasy because I am certainly not in the same league as these two danseurs. They are my superiors—Elejar was one of my teachers, and Villanueva was an acquaintance I sought out in the USA and during his brief visit here with his wife Josefa Arnaldo.

Though not their equal, the following should also be acknowledged: El Gabriel, Tony Llacer, Cesar Mendoza, Jamin Alcoriza, Marcelino Garcia, Mario Recto, even Al Quinn and Jun Dalit. It can be said that Manolo Rosado and Ruben Nieto are a class all their own. Of course one must mention composer Pajaro, playwright Montano, and two Mr. Folk Dancers, Ricardo Reyes and Lucio Sandoval, who danced for Anita Kane.

Froilan, mentioned previously, has partnered several prima ballerinas, including Robin Haig, Yoko Morishita, Maniya Barredo, and the younger Anna Villadolid and Lisa Macuja. One cannot neglect Rimpos and Cecile Sicangco. For him, Norman Walker created *Songs of Wayfarer* (a much more superior work than Maurice Bejart's European fancifulness) and Jean Deroc cast him in *King David* in Switzerland.

Manuel Molina is a modern danseur, a Dionysian magnet who is endangered today by ego-tripping and pricing himself outside the range of the local market. But he has also been a favorite of Walker (*Season of Flight*), Elejar (*Juliet and Her Romeo*), Alice Reyes (*Rajah Sulayman*, etc.), and Basilio (*The Rebels*, a cyclic Prodigal Son ballet). He went on to join the Harkness Ballet, the Ballet Nuevo Mundo de Caracas, where he was a star, partnering prima ballerina Zhandra Rodriguez, and later, Ballets Jazz de Montreal, which visited Manila without him. He is perhaps our most magnificent modern dancer, but today even Walker regrets his neglect of his art.

Of my colleagues, I would also rank high Franklin Bobadilla, who is my junior yet possesses superlative technique in leaps and turns. Before our Rey Dizon and Conrad Dy-Liacco came into the scene, his double-cabrioles were as amazing. In Heidelberg, he took the title role of *Pinocchio*, and in Amsterdam (Scapino Ballet) he was in many a featured part in the busiest of Dutch ballet companies. His last performance in Manila had him dancing with the soloists of Royal Ballet of Flanders, Irene Sabas and David Campos Cantero, and Lisa Macuja in my *Paean to Pavlova.* Elejar specially choreographed a whole ballet that centered on him in that season of Dance Theatre Philippines. Bobadilla's colleague in Heildelberg and later a dancer with the now guru of German Dance, Pina Bausch in Wuppertal, is Luis Layag, also a unique dancer. Also a choreographer, he made pieces in Heidelberg and for television in Cologne for a director-friend of mine. With Bobadilla and Mitto Castillo (who danced in Britain with the Northern Ballet Theater in Manchester), Layag was among the first to establish the reputation of Filipino dancers in Europe.

Then there's Tony Fabella whose rhythm is impeccable. He was a great Puck and Tommy for Alice Reyes. Odon and Tommy Sabarre were virtuosi. The latter could have been a danseur noble; he was lost in the MV Dona Paz tragedy. Eric Cruz had his protégé in Rupert Acuña as Don Jose, Armand, and Spartacus—all passionate and noble heroes. After Molina and Castillo, I had my own Sultan (*Mosque Baroque*) and Tadzio (*A Death in Venice*, retitled *Between Sky* and *Sea*) in Joseph Rañola, and Tchaikovsky (*Fantasy*) and martyr (*Misa Filipina*) in Jonathan Terry, both brief in their dancing careers.

Today, we still have the marvelous Nicolas Pacaña leading the Atlanta Ballet. He was hardly touched by Manila because he was trained by Fe Sala Villarica in Cebu. Briefly, he took classes with Llacer and myself in Manila and at the Cultural Center of the Philippines before his years with companies in Hawaii, the US West Coast, Boston, and Atlanta. With Villanueva Reyes, he was the first to attain the highest rank in the Western companies, and he did it all by himself. Having done most of the classical roles, Pacaña still keeps a low profile, coming home belatedly to thrill his hometown enthusiasts.

Rey Dizon now leads Les Grands Ballet Canadiens, where Maniya Barredo was once a ballerina and where our young Yvonne Cutaran dances. (Tina Escoda of American Ballet Theater used to be there too.) Essentially a modern dancer—in ballet or modern dance proper—Dizon now dances classical roles in Montreal: Albrecht, Franz, Colas, etc. He is a dynamic dancer whose muscular projection is tantalizing, making up for his quite wan expression. He was once the toast of London (landing on the cover of *Dance and Dancers*), and he occasionally stirs up the New York scene.

Brando Miranda now leads the Royal New Zealand Ballet. Director Harry Haythorne came to audition (which I had arranged) and Miranda was an immediate choice. Together with Vivencio Samblaceno who is now in the corps de ballet, Miranda alternated with China's Ou Lu as Romeo when Lisa Macuja was there last year to dance Juliet. Previously, Ricardo Ella was leading the RNZB in many a modern ballet but also did Albrecht in *Giselle*. Ella is now a demisoloist with the Australian Ballet.

Also abroad is Augustus Damian. He is with Bejart's Ballet of the 20th Century, which has moved from Brussels to Lausanne. Damian trained with his aunt Vella and danced with Dance Concert Company, Ballet Philippines, and with two German companies before joining Bejart. Of course Bejart shows off his male dancers more than his females, so Damian can have much going for him.

Maxie Luna is also doing well with Alvin Ailey's American Dance Theater in New York, where our own Elizabeth Roxas also shines. A recent issue of *Dance Magazine* took notice of him. We have not heard much from Robert Medina, but for a while he was doing well in New York or Frankfurt. So is Enrico Labayen with the Eglevsky Ballet. And even more so, Andre Reyes (the son of Benny Villanueva Reyes) with San Francisco Ballet, where Tina Santos and Becky Rodriguez danced.

We have more male dancers working in Asian cities. One of them is Victor Madrona, who has stayed long with the Hong Kong Ballet; three other Filipinos have now left. The Hong Kong Ballet director occasionally comes to Manila to audition men. Madrona was the late

Anton Dolin's choice for a gala in Paris. In Singapore, we have Mario Esperanza, Ric Culalic, and Donato Ferrer.

The role of the male dancer is often rated second to the ballerina's. There was a time, however, when the male dancer reigned supreme. In fact, since King Louis XIV and the glory of Gaetan (pere) and Auguste (fils) Vestris, Dupre, Duport, to St. Leon (choreographer of *Coppelia*), male dancers were the stars. Romantic ballet changed all that and the ballerina took over. Sometimes a phenomenal danseur like Nijinsky, even the character dancer Massine, would rise to restore the male dancer's glory. Nureyev and Baryshnikov did and continue to do it for us today, although there are also great male dancers like Dowell in England, the late Bosl of Germany, and Villella and Cragun of the US (the latter dancing in Germany), who are less seen worldwide.

The lack of male dancers is cause for grief, and it seems this lack greatly stems from social neglect and ostracism. Since ballet has been identified as a ballerina's realm since the Romantic period, there is an easy tendency to consider dancing a woman's profession.

What father, therefore, would encourage a son to dance? Given that dancing took a long time to be a professional career locally, what security would a male dancer have? His capability to be the head of the family would be questioned.

A female in our society can long remain with her family without earning a substantial income. The added burden of buying dance supplies like pointes shoes could still be remedied by her family. But a male is expected to be responsible for his keep soon after he finishes college, or even after high school, if he does not go to college. This is especially true if he goes into the unstable and sexually ambiguous world of dancing.

Often enough, our own dance teachers and directors do not realize this difference. Most likely a female will be encouraged to dance while a male will be discouraged, not only by his family but also by his peers and the rest of society.

Luckily, the man who go into dancing seriously has the tenacity and the dedication to overcome all these obstacles. He has more liberty to live outside of his family (as a prodigal son, he may have to work while training to dance), and he works hard to master dance techniques (not dancing on pointes but jumping high and lifting ballerinas) in two or three years to be able to dance passably. The moral support of his fellow female dancers and sympathetic ballet masters is of great influence.

Usually, the male dancer does not have the social or economic advantage the female dancers have. Thus, even if a male dancer rises to the top, in our kind of social structure and appropriation, he is admired onstage but not exactly respected in society. There are no influential parents to push for him, and the glamour and women's magazines would rather have the *mestizas* or the macho men on their covers. Still we wonder why there are not enough male dancers around.

Despite these disadvantages, we have an Osias Barros with Philippine Ballet Theater, or Dy-Liacco, Jun Mabacluiao, and Edmund Gaerlan with Ballet Philippines. With the rest of their colleagues, they continue to bear the brunt of espousing the cause of male dancers, balancing the sexual appeal of roles in ballet, working with less of a spotlight than the women dancers—when all of their seniors or peers have found better wages and appreciation in foreign lands. For the interesting fact is the majority of our dancers abroad in the field of serious dance are men.

Manila Chronicle
1989

The Young Manuel Molina

Manuel Molina III was one of the founding members of the CCP Dance Company, then established as the Alice Reyes and Modern Dance Company. At that time, he was a young man who, like the rest of us—Jose Antonio, Gener Caringal, Tony Fabella, Luis Layag, and myself—was eager to train in modern dance with Alice and in ballet with Eddie Elejar. The women were Tina Santos and her sister Cecile, Nini Gener, Irma Bringas, Joy Coronel, Delia Javier (all of Dance Theatre Philippines), Menchu de Jesus of the Bayanihan, and Tessie Reyes of the UE Dance Company.

Manuel and Gener, too, were members of the UE Dance Company, directed by Corazon G. Iñigo, and of Dance Theatre Philippines, starting with Eliseo M. Pajaro's ballet *Mir-i-nisa*, choreographed by Julie Borromeo and Felicitas L. Radaic, which helped inaugurate the Cultural Center of the Philippines in 1969.

February 1970 was marked by Alice's success, highlighted by Lucrecia R. Kasilag's *Amada*, with the part of Don Rafael that Manuel was to inherit from Elejar in London in 1972. Another Quijano de Manila-based ballet Manuel did was Radaic-Pajaro's *May Day Eve* (as Montiya, opposite Irma Bringas's Agueda) for DTP in 1971.

Indeed, many wanted to choreograph for Manuel. It was with DTP that he assumed his first major role in the Radaic ballet and, at the same time, in my *The Rebels* (Janacek) as the Prodigal Son. I was also eager to pair him with Cecile Santos (the Harlot), something I was unable to do in an earlier project—my *The Diurnal and the Dream* (Webern) for the first Summer Dance Workshop at the Center in 1970—because of the latter's injury, although I was grateful Alice took over her part. Had that number been longer and with a less balanced cast (with Menchu and Tony), it could have been his first central part. Other significant performances were in his own short piece, *Nightmare* (Stravinsky), which he danced with Irma, or in Luis Layag's *Positive-Negative* (Fellagara), which he and I danced with Radaic and Lydia M. Gaston for that same workshop concert. It must also be noted that Manuel had a very good part in Alice's short finale *7* (Hendrix-Zeppelin) in her company's debut in 1970, and she has always remarked on his dynamism and charisma.

Soon after, everyone was casting Manuel. Eddie made *Juliet and Her Romeo* (Shostakovitch) for him and Alice, and he was Elejar's Indarapatra (with Ed de Guzman as his brother Sulayman) in *Juru-Pakal* (Maceda), Datu Sumakwel in *Kapinangan* (Kasilag), and Prince Desire in his staging of Aurora's *Wedding* (1972). Alice designed the cameo role of the Governor General Bustamante in *Itim Asu* (Alfredo Buenaventura) for him, and the late Remedios de Oteyza featured him in *Spectrum* (Cornejo) with Effie Nañas in 1973. Finally, Norman Walker chose him as a lead in *Season of Flight* (Constant) in 1972, opposite Alice, a part in which he has remained the definitive. Soon after, Norman arranged a scholarship for him at the Harkness School.

Manuel also danced with unexpected distinction in Tony Llacer's *In the Beginning* (Villalobos) for DTP; Fabella's *Semana Santa* (R. de Leon) as the leader of the gang; Undersea from *Prince of the Pagodas* (Britten); Rosalia Merino Santos's *Halina't Maglaro* (Kasilag); Elejar's *Jewels* (Hindemith) as Sapphire, with Nini Gener and Tommy Sabarre; Miro Zolan's *Young Person's Pleasure* (Britten); Layag's Coffee with Nini in *The Nutcracker*; and Reyes's *Punch* (Nyro), *At A Maranaw Gathering* (Colgrass), *Company* (Bach), and her rock opera-ballets *Jesus Christ Superstar* and *Tommy* (as the bully Cousin Kevin who was called "Cain Resurrected") by a critic, among several others.

Manuel left Manila for New York in 1973 for his advanced studies, sponsored by the JDR III Fund, and subsequently joined the Harkness Ballet. I next saw him in Paris with the company in the summer of 1974, dancing a small part in Todd Bolender's *Souvenirs*. He was progressing very well, but soon after, the company disbanded. He joined Vicente Nebrada's group in Venezuela—although he was liked by Alvin Ailey in

New York and by the Netherlands Darts Theater in The Hague, and today stays there with Ballet Nuevo Mundo's directors and principals, Zhandra Rodriguez and Dale Talley. He never fails to earn superlative reviews from critics worldwide.

But I fondly remember Manuel most as a co-dancer, with DTP and CCPDC, as the central protagonist in my first major ballet in Manila, *The Rebels* (where he had no rest for quarter of an hour that I supplied him with honey to keep his energy up), as Eddie's inimitable Romeo to Alice's Juliet, as the heroic Bustamante in *Itim Asu*, as Norman's unrivalled sinewy image in *Season of Flight*—in summary as the unique and magnetic dancer who essayed his parts with exactitude, excitement, and ecstasy.

Yes, Manuel is a dancer of the ecstatic kind, Dionysian in appeal and zeal. He has always been an intuitive, musical, and muscled dancer, with a prominent face—unmistakable and expressive—and a sturdy build. Articulate and expansive, he has now matured in technique and depth by virtue of his training in foreign lands. Yet I believe he remains the same: a dynamic dancer to marvel at.

Arts Monthly
1982

My Friend Franklin, Ballet's Bobadilla

Unknown to most, Franklin Bobadilla's dancing for Dance Theatre Philippines last August was his farewell performance. He last performed in Manila seven years ago.

My friend Franklin left the Philippines to join the State Opera Ballet in Heidelberg in 1975. He was endorsed by our colleague Luis Layag. Luis and I were together in Germany the previous year, enjoying grants from the German International Theater Institute as arranged by the Goethe Institut. Luis stayed behind in Germany (I left for a John D. Rockefeller III Fund grant in the United States) to join the company in Heidelberg. The three of us danced together for the Alice Reyes and Modern Dance Company, which has gone by the names CCP Dance Workshop Company and CCP Dance Company, and is now called Ballet Philippines.

We took turns severing ties with the CCP and worked together several times for the Rizal Park performances arranged by Dance Theatre Philippines. Luis had his own independent outlet through musical stage productions, and in one of them, *The Survival of St. Joan*, Franklin danced for him.

Franklin and I formed the Movement Men together with Mitto Castillo and Eli Jacinto, with the blessings of Tony Llacer. At various times, we performed with Rene Hofileña, Ronnie Leonardo, Armand Angeles, Don Marasigan, Tony Salamat, and other Dance Arts Studio dancers. But Franklin and I were constant coworkers.

Through the courtesy of Inday Gaston Mañosa, I conducted fundraising classes (at one peso per class!) at her old Goldcrest Studio before it burned down. It was a way for Franklin and me to keep in shape and to pay for a few costumes and occasional lunches at Sulo restaurant. It was the only morning professional class in town, in the tradition of DTP's former morning classes with El Gabriel and Tony Llacer. Among our steady patrons were Yvonne de los Reyes, Vella Damian, Nini Gener, Rory Laico, Lulu Fernandez, Lelu Fidelino Barredo, and occasionally, Jun Dalit and Conrad Tiolengco, whom we considered "members." It was there that Nicolas Pacaña, now of Boston Ballet and who has recently signed up with Atlanta Ballet, took several classes before he left for the United States. After my return in 1975, I continued the classes at Vella Damian's studio on Mayon Street, Quezon City. To this day, this project has been carried on by William Morgan on West Avenue. Among our patrons then were Eddie Elejar, Rupert Acuña, the Sabarre brothers, Tita Radaic, and Josette Salang.

Movement Men was active enough to produce my *Royal Sonnets*, set to Gabriel Faure, with a few lines read from Shakespeare. This we premiered at Rizal Park and repeated for Lelu Barredo's Malabon studio, with Nini Gener as the Dark Lady, Jun Dalit as The Lord, myself as William, and Roy Alvarez as the reader. (A section of this was first presented at the Philamlife Auditorium, with Noemi Estrella as the Dark Lady.) We set a short *Fugue for Four* to William Boyce, later acquired by Dance Concert Company. This number we did almost everywhere—at the Rizal Park, in Quezon City, in Malabon. We also produced *Between Sky and Sea*—set to the music of Gustav Mahler and inspired by Thomas Mann's *A Death in Venice*, with Mitto as the Sky (Tadzio) and Rene as Man (Aschenbach)—jointly with Dance Arts Studio. This was also later acquired by DTP, a success at the 1975 Aberdeen Festival in Scotland, with Joseph Ranola as The Sky and Mitto as Man. We joined affairs like a Dance Revolution at the Meralco Theater. When more women started appearing with the group, I renamed it Movement Manila, as in the Second National Ballet Festival at the Folk Arts Theater.

So that was what Franklin and I were doing before he left for abroad, although he was gone before all of that happened. When he was accepted in Heidelberg even without an audition, Alice was kind enough to bring him along on her company's trip to Germany.

In Heidelberg, Franklin danced in the artistic director's ballets. Dragutin Boldin liked him well enough to cast him as alternate for his *Pinocchio* (music by Laszlo Kovari). There he also danced in Boldin's *Well-Tempered Klavier*, *Scheherazade* and *Les Noces*, and Luis's numbers, like *Back to Bach*.

After a stint in that idyllic city where I visited him and Luis in 1975, Franklin moved to Amsterdam, which he now considers home.

He joined Scapino Ballet in 1976 and made very good his years of dancing in Armando Navarro's full-evening works like *The Nutcracker* (where he danced a Bronislava Nijinska "Tea"), *Coppelia*, and *Cinderella*. Guest choreographers like Charles Czarny, Kathy Gosschalk, Hans van Marten, and others used him, too, but he especially found personal success in Eric Hampton's *P.G. (Peer Gynt) Suite* set to Edward Grieg, and in David Morse's *The Kites* to Jacques Ibert.

In these two pieces, he was noticed by the press and public. Ex-Bayanihan dancer Ricardo Tuazon raved over his solo in *P. G. Suite*, and I personally found him matching the virtuosity of the Japanese Hiroshi Okazaki in *Kites*. Even as a new member of Scapino, the Dutch press noted him to have "especially excelled."

Thus, it was no surprise that during DTP's "Salute to Stravinsky" program at the Meralco Theater last August, critic and National Artist Leonor Orosa Goquingco thought he stood out among the guest artists. For his dancing as The Young Man in Eddie Elejar's *Once Upon a Village* (music by Malcolm Arnold), he merited Goquingco's unabashed praise. She elaborated in *Times Journal*, saying, "Franklin Bobadilla was smoothly competent in both his dancing and his miming in the rewarding role of the young man." Rosalinda L. Orosa echoed this in *Daily Express*, "Franklin Bobadilla danced with a neat and engagingly spirited style."

During that concert, he also danced in Basilio's *Paean to Pavlova* (Poulenc) with Lisa Macuja, Irene Sabas, and David Campos Cantero, and *Testament* (Béla Bartok) with the rest of the company. As artistic director, I was very proud to have given him the venue for his farewell from the stage.

Characteristically unassuming, Franklin did not want to announce that the performances were to be his formal farewell.

Meanwhile, even if he was given the option to renew his contract with Netherlands's third major ballet company, he decided to follow his studies in library science and in Dutch instruction. He had earlier been a graduate student at the University of the Philippines. All the time he was dancing in Manila, he was studying Communication Arts at the Ateneo de Manila University. Books and memorabilia are Frank's enduring love. With his stable income in Amsterdam, he has acquired a small collection of choice works, particularly by those of his favorites. He also keeps up-to-date his personal clippings, long begun in Manila. He is also a most constant correspondent. His particular fondness for ballerinas Olga Spessiva and Elaine Field—perhaps out of great sympathy for stresses in their personal lives and careers that landed them in asylums for some time—led him to track down records on them. He introduced me to the theater museum collection in Amsterdam and the dance archive in The Hague. When I visited him in Germany, we sought out museums near Heidelberg. We visited the Jose Rizal marker in Heidelberg and walked often the Philosophenweg, which we imagined to be one of Rizal's haunts. Franklin should have been born among the ever-walking English romantic writers.

Coincidentally, we were among the first two to know about our colleague Luis's illness in Wuppertal in 1979, immediately after Wuppertal Dance Theater's tour of Asia. We both went to visit him in that city, but we were no longer allowed to see him, as he was gravely ill. It was Franklin who discovered what was perhaps Luis's last note; it was scribbled on a page of a German magazine and addressed to me. It was around that time I decided to do a ballet to honor Luis. Honoring my late sister, Edna, too, DTP produced it as *Domain of Peace* (music by Alan Hovahness) last November.

These things I share in common with Franklin as well as Luis began in 1970 at the first CCP Summer Dance Workshop. Teaching then was fielded out, but mainly handled by Alice in modern dance and Eddie in ballet. Looking back at the souvenir program, I realized that I was personally challenged by the young Bacolod group of Lydia M. Gaston (with her daughter Lydlyd, Cecile Sicangco, and Balin Roig) and by Franklin's skill. I featured him in my brief *Games*, set to Handel.

Soon after, all three of us danced together in Eddie's *Jewels* (Hindemith), Tony Fabella's *Noche Buena* (Kasilag), and Alice's *The Emperor's New Clothes* (Milhaud). In the last, Franklin was featured as the jester.

A workshop scholarship concert brought us together again in ballets by Yvonne de los Reyes Hernandez, in Eddie's long-titled but short, short polka set to Shostakovitch and his *Juru-Pakal* (Maceda), a ballet attempting an admixture of Asian theater styles. During another summer we were together in Miro Zolan's *Young Person's Pleasure* (Britten) where Franklin was one of Zolan's favorites. That summer, too, I produced my theater-piece, *The Resurrection of Lazarus* (Messaien) and Franklin was in that, too.

Considered a technical wizard, noted for his sustained elevation, clear beats, and sure pirouettes, Franklin was given choice part. Luis specially choreographed for him the "Tea" solo in the CCP's first *The Nutcracker* (Act 11), and later Norman Walker rechoreographed the part for him in another version. Eddie made him the colt in *Trio Con Brio* (Pajaro) to Effie Nañas's mare and Manuel Molina's stallion, and the "Hop o' Thumb" in the CCP's first *Aurora's Wedding*. Tony featured him as a goldfish with Florence Perez in his "The Kingdom Under the Sea" from *The Prince of the Pagodas* (Britten) and in his *Ang Konsiyerto* (Rubio). Alfred Rodriguez chose him as The Boy in a Mask in his *Souvenir* (Tchaikovsky). The late Remedios de Oteyza choreographed for both of us "Tea" from *The Nutcracker* for the Rizal Park with Hariraya Ballet Company, and his solo part in her *Bolero* (Ravel) for the Manila Symphony Orchestra Corps de Ballet. Alice made him Enrico Labayen's rival for Irma Bringas in *Dugso* (Santos), and Tony's alternate in *Tommy* as Tommy.

Other than these, he also danced in Alice's *Chichester Psalms* (Bernstein), *Untitled* (Dello Joio), *Company* (Bach), and *Itim Asu* (Buenaventura); Eddie's *Who's the Clown?* (Ibert), *Kapinangan* (Kasilag), and *Misang Pilipino* (Kasilag); Cora Iñigo's *Baile de Ayer* (Cornejo); Tita Radaic's *Tanan* (Silos); Denise Garcia's *The Last Flower* (Stravinsky); Muñeca Aponte's *Symphony* (Mendelssohn); and Norma Walker's *Season of Flight* (Constant) and *Songs of a Wayfarer* (Mahler), all with the CCP Dance Company.

Franklin went on his first foreign trip with the company in 1974, around Asia and Australia. Breaking loose for a season, he rejoined them in Germany in 1975.

Thus, Franklin's life has been very colorful. He has danced in both ballet and modern dance idioms, for national and international choreographers and directors, to various kinds of music, and in different places. While with Scapino, he toured not only the Netherlands but also the rest of the continent.

His training has also been quite diverse. Locally, he started briefly with Anita M. Kane at five, continued with Benny Villanueva Reyes, and after a long hiatus retrained at seventeen with Joji Felix Velarde, Eddie Elejar, and Cesar Mendoza. Other than at the CCP, he also studied with Edgar Valdez. In spite of his perpetual apology for his slow learning of steps, Franklin has always had the respect of his directors and the admiration of his peers.

I can imagine him now, poring over his collection in his small but warm place on Jacob van Lennepstraat in Amsterdam, occasionally entertaining friends from his CCP or Movement Men days—and, now, Scapino days—and indulging them with his choice recipes. I can imagine him either nostalgically watching an Ingrid Bergman, Grace Kelly, or Audrey Hepburn movie (his Philippine favorite is Barbara Perez), or striving anew with a reacquired study, library science.

His last interview by Bert Pasquin (*Times Journal*, August 6) reveals more about Franklin. He urged young people to dance if they wished yet still encouraged them to pursue a formal course. Franklin was finally described by Bert in this manner: "At thirty-two, Franklin obviously still carries a passion for dance which indicates he will last for a few more years. The inspiration, definitely, is not about to dry up."

Arts Monthly
1983

The Man Nonoy and the Froilan Image

The child is not the father of the man. Except for the facial resemblance and the natal data, the prankster in Calbiga and the danseur in Manila are quite different from each other in character and achievements.

Keeping the naughty and notorious boy under control was quite an ordeal. But Amparo Froilan had the strength to steer him toward the proper use of courage and initiative. In fact, for her guidance, the man later was to pay tribute to her by choreographing *For Amparo*.

But the boy could not be faulted easily for his ways, having grown up virtually without a father—the man was never around. Also, his mother bravely coped with her own mother's (Nonoy Froilan's grandmother Macaria) unwavering disapproval. Mother and son had to live with Nonoy's grandaunt.

Meanwhile, Amparo and Fidel Cabujat lived separately. It was only some three hours before Fidel died that they were married. Amparo gathered courage and finally ,decided to wed the man she loved.

Thus, Nonoy Froilan became a legitimate child at the last minute. But it was too late to change his name. Too late to enjoy the riches of the Cabujats, which was wasted away through the years. But such things did not matter anymore, for Nonoy had by then carved out his own identity and worked independently for his achievements.

The Nonoy Froilan we know today is the danseur. But he insists, "The man is the essential thing." While the last homage to him by Ballet Philippines in its final 1992-93 program, "Dance Classics: A Tribute to Nonoy Froilan," was a fitting climax to his twenty-year career as dance artist of the company and as the Philippines's *premier danseur*, Nonoy is not someone to rest on his laurels. He says he has just turned a page and is set on another course, "Let's just say it's like eating the same food for the last twenty years, and I want to try something else."[1]

As he sets off, he does not have the little securities of a dancer's charmed yet monkish life. "I'm back to zero,"[2] he says. He leaves behind the bastion of ballet at the Cultural Center's basement rehearsal hall, where professionalism in dance was established by co-directors Alice Reyes and Eddie Elejar. It was there that unsalaried members of the first company (the Alice Reyes and Modern Dance Company) helped establish the company's reputation and reliability. It was there that sponsors and subscribers provided support for dance. It was there that Nonoy found regular working hours, built up his repertory, and could expect regular pay. The pay wasn't enough to support a wife and two children, so that until his retirement, he pleaded for society's fuller support of the dance artist.

But the pay was better and more regular than at the University of the East, where he was a student enjoying tuition scholarship and meal allowance. It was better than the haphazard income from dancing for television, erratic musical comedy productions, and vagrant ballet performances in those days.

Still he looks back with gratitude at his days with Julie Borromeo's Dance Arts Studio, where he was nurtured in dance technique and his personal needs attended to by his dance master Tony Llacer, who took care of two other protégés, Mitto Castillo and Enrico Labayen. (Both earned their enviable dance spots abroad, the latter now directing his own Lab Projekt.)

Modest returns for regular work were better than even his glittering days with the Karilagan International under the late Conchita Sunico, patron and producer of fashion shows and musicals (at Top of the Hilton, in theaters, and on international tours.) Were Nonoy a more frivolous man, he would have fancied the world of fashion and high society until it would be too late for him to become a serious dancer. He was much simpler and wiser, determined to be what he wanted most: a danseur. Tony Llacer taught him well.

As a dancer, he did not start young. He was in college when he plunged into regular training and performing. First, it was at the University of the East, where he apprenticed himself under Corazon Generoso Iñigo and danced with already established names like Gener Caringal and Manuel Molina. It seemed he was too late for ballet when his cousin Tommy Sabarre steered him to Dance Arts Studio in Mandaluyong, where he properly became a ballet student. Tony Llacer, who trained in New York, taught in Los Angeles, and appeared in musicals and Hollywood movies, was a ballet master for Dance Theatre Philippines and at the time choreographer for Sunico's Karingan outfit. He saw to it that Nonoy developed a technique to speak of. He also saw to it that when he brought Nonoy to Ballet Philippines, where he was guest teaching, Nonoy would be noticed. In fact, he was noticed not only as a dancer but also as a young man by a young woman (Edna Vida) as well.

Nonoy was already quite experienced, even if not very polished, when he joined Ballet Philippines. He had danced in many recitals and benefits (including the one for the scholarship to New York of another cousin, Odon Sabarre), on television locally and in Hong Kong and on various stages for fashion modeling and musicals here and abroad. As a kid, he also danced in school. He even danced for groups above his level and had won prizes and acclaim.

Nonoy is not a stranger to acclaim. Not only does he have the stature, but he also has the face to make him a hero, even prince and king. In fact, he assumed these royal roles in the ballet classics (*Swan Lake*, *The Sleeping Beauty*, *The Nutcracker*), in Alice Reyes's *Rama Hari*, and Jean Deroc's *Roi David* in Switzerland. In *Giselle* he was Duke Albrecht, in *Rajah Sulayman* a tribal lord, in *Amada* an ilustrado in Don Rafael, in *Itim Asu* a governor general, and in *Songs of a Wayfarer* a universal lover or Werther.

He led a charmed life. Choreographers were inspired to give or carve out new roles for him. He explains, "I was just at the night place at the right time."

He had to work his way up, especially when he started assuming the roles of Eddie Elejar and Manuel Molina in Ballet Philippines early on. He knew he wasn't always ready, but there was no stopping him from rehearsing lengthily. Pain did not daunt him. Except for an injury that kept him away from the studio for a while, nothing could make him take a break. He danced through pain, even fever, when he could bear it. He "pushed those muscles"—his own advice to young dancers.

"You should go on that stage because you like to do it. Money should be secondary. Discipline, *'yan ang gusto kong i-emphasize sa kanila.* Are you there because your mom *e hinila ka rito*? No, you have to want it, you have to want to dance."

Obsessed as he was with working, he had equanimity. "Everyday whatever was given to me, I took it. I didn't plan. *Nang bigyan ako ng kape ni Alice* with sugar, I drank it with all my heart. I did not foresee myself twenty years after. I just took it day after day."[3]

An easy, natural charisma and dogged dedication spelled out Nonoy's heroic grace and premier position. These both got him to partner our best ballerinas, like Alice Reyes, Ester Rimpos, and Effie Nañas earlier on, and later, Edna Vida, Cecile Sicangco, Anna Villadolid, Tony Lopez Gonzalez, and Lisa Macuja.

Reyes was the director who dared him slip into Molina's unforgettable part in Norman Walker's *Season of Flight.* She also created for him the roles of Rama, Romeo, Don Jose in *Carmen*, and Prince Charming in *Cinderella*, at the same time that she bestowed on him Elejar's Don Rafael in *Amada*, Molina's Bustamante in *Itim Asu*, and principal parts in contemporary ballet classics. To Rimpos and Nañas he was Prince Siegfried, Prince Florimund, or Nutcracker Prince. To Vida's *Firebird*, he was Prince Ivan.

In real life, Edna was the young lady who eyed the new young man brought in by Llacer. Although he had other girlfriends, when he saw Edna he immediately said that this was her, his wife-to-be. Today they have two children, Mica, ten, and Rafael Jr., four, a spitting image of his father. Nonoy and Edna have always been supportive of each other. When she decided to give up her full-time commitment to dance, she started writing again and painting to supplement their income. Their differences complement each other.

Edna says, "What a contrast we made. As I trudged the swamps of self-importance, he skidded with the freedom of selflessness. It brought him stardom for two decades while I, sister of Alice Reyes, equipped with high extensions, merely gained insight. The two of us coming from different poles met, and we took off on an interesting journey. The contrast remains. He thrives on simplicity, while I wallow in complication. I make all sorts of detours, while Nonoy walks in a single direction pursuing his goal steadfastly even as he stumbles."[4]

He enhanced even the younger ballerinas. He paired with Toni Lopez Gonzalez in romantic and comedic roles, the last being their hilarious but harmonious partnering in *The Taming of the Shrew*, which Edna choreographed. (She has also choreographed A *Midsummer Night's Dream* for him and Sophia Zobel.) Nonoy also partnered Toni at the Varna ballet competition, where she placed as a semifinalist.

Lisa Macuja he partnered at the Jackson, Mississippi, ballet competition, where she also placed as a semifinalist. They danced together in several seasons of Ballet Philippines and in a number of provincial tours. Lisa never dreamed of the partnership. It all started on her return from the Kirov Ballet in 1986, when she staged a homecoming at the Metropolitan Theater with Act II of *Giselle* and the *grand pas de deux* from *Le Corsaire*.

Cecile Sicangco was a regular partner in Ballet Philippines, and their last bride and wayfarer during "Dance Classics" was one of the best realizations of the Norman Walker modern dance classic. Reviewing the performance for *Manila Chronicle*, I wrote: "It was a wonderful metaphor for Froilan's own attainment of his dancing ideal. It was both an Apollonian and Bacchic distinction, classical and modern. He was a modern *babaylan* in ballet dancer's guise in a modern ritual of our theater-going, showcasing dance at its most exacting and noble, the image from which younger dancers drew their own image-making."

"Froilan's humility in person and at work was echoed by the Wayfarer's submission to his dream and suffering. Indeed, Froilan long suffered for his art, not just physically, not just economically, but also in his almost solitary, lonely hoisting of the pennant of his art. For twenty years, he was to proclaim dancing's virility and integrity on stage and off stage to his colleagues, society, and country."[5]

He feels privileged to have partnered Anna Villadolid, whom he considers his most lyrical ballerina. He is awed by her sensitivity. His *Giselle* with her is unforgettable.

But what is truly memorable is his dancing with Yoko Morishita. She already had an international reputation (gold medalist in Varna, dancing with Rudolf Nureyev and Fernando Bujones, Japan's prima ballerina), and he could only defer to her. But they found instant rapport, aided by Morishita's own simplicity and ability to attune herself to her partners. "She doesn't compete with her partner. The less she did, the more appealing and beautiful she looked onstage."[6]

Somehow she must have influenced his artistry, putting technique second to expressiveness without compromising the total delivery. She typifies the fullness in artistry that Nonoy was to see, share, and imbibe. When he did *Giselle* with her at thirty-one, he felt it was his "rebirth again as a classical dancer" and more—"everything, being actor, a dancer." The respect must have been mutual, because Morishita honored Nonoy by dancing in the tribute program to him last March.

Nonoy had also partnered the lovely Australian Robin Haig, once of the Royal Ballet, and the dynamic Muñeca Aponte. A rare and supreme achievement for a Filipino danseur was to partner (along with John Meehan and Kelvin Coe, premier danseurs of Australian Ballet) Margot Fonteyn in *Dahil sa Iyo*, a paean to the *prima ballerina assoluta's* glory.

When he danced with her, he said to himself, "My God, I can't believe I'm holding the body of England's prima ballerina. God, there was something divine about her. She was beautiful even at her late age. I could have fallen in love with her if she were younger."[7]

For the obscure little boy from Calbiga, Samar, these experiences were unimaginable. But the man the boy became simply worked to deliver what was expected, then worked even harder to exceed expectations. "*Walang inaantok ako, masakit ang likod ko*. I'm still going to go there, even if I have fever, [even] if I'm not 100 percent [well] …."[8]

The fact that he has highest stature achieved by a male dancer in the country does not go to Nonoy's head. The image of the premier danseur and his glorified roles do not affect him personally. He has no ego problem, and he takes all his parts as responsibilities, his duty for the time being.

Was he ever conscious he was constructing the image of a male dancer in our society? Did he feel he had to defend or embellish it? His answer is no. "I don't want to consider myself a hero," he says. Although he didn't intend to be a hero, he became one anyway, simply working at the ballet *barre*, on the modern dance floor, or for a choice role, with unquestioning concentration and application.

No one has had a longer and richer career as a male dancer than Nonoy. In Philippine and international repertory, no one had danced such a fine string of roles, those in classical ballet contrasting with the ones in modern dance.

Ballet Philippines, other companies he danced for, like Dance Theatre Philippines, and ballerinas he has partnered are only too grateful to have danced with Nonoy. They will not find as princely a Philippine danseur, as seemly, supportive, and humble, as Nonoy had been—at least not anytime soon.

The audience has its own illusions about this Philippine prince of the dance, a hero of our time in the field. (Nonoy has also portrayed ill-begotten characters as in Anton Juan's *Yerma*, or even Reyes's Don Jose in *Carmen*. But Don Jose is still admirable, in the same way that the deceptive Duke Albrecht takes our heart at the end of *Giselle*.)

For the past twenty or more years, we have built our idea of what ballet is, what its characters are like, their vigor, grace, and charm, through Nonoy's dancing and portraying. We explicitly claim for him what he had intuitively lived as a hero on stage. The heroic stance, however, he disclaims offstage.

Today Nonoy is no longer just a dancer. These days, he is often found teaching and coaching. He was already rehearsal master and had started choreographing when he was still dancing the principal parts in

Ballet Philippines. Among his works, aside from *For Amparo*, are *Danzas*, *One Afternoon, Iba't Ibang Salita,* and *For Marla.*

These days too, Nonoy is busy about town. Since he formed the Contemporario Ethnico Filipino with Jojo Lucila, he has been traveling from Mandaluyong to Manila to Quezon City. The company had its debut last January at Tanghalang Aurelio Tolentino, and he and Lucila are planning to take the group to Europe on a tour.

He is also running off to Samar to help stage a comedia or zarzuela in Calbiga's town plaza. He has finally found time to contribute directly to the affairs of his hometown. The town had much earlier honored the naughty dancing boy, and again the danseur whom Manila also honored with the *Patnubay ng Sining at Kalinangan* in 1983.

What excites him even more these days are his video-film projects. He distinguished himself by filming the choreography of Denisa Reyes in *Cock vs. Cock*, staged for "Neo-Filipino" last November. It was part of the tribute program for him last March. For two weekends he was honored with the dancing of his past ballerinas—Sicangco, Lopez Gonzalez, Macuja, and Morishita.

Some weeks afterward, Nonoy was persuaded to dance Norman Walker's *Summer's End* to Chopin, partnering Lopez Gonzalez. It was somehow a fitting finale, as it celebrated the Araw ng Sayaw '93 or the International Dance Day at the Araneta Coliseum, under the auspices of the National Dance Committee of the National Commission on Culture and Arts and of the Dance Committee of the International Theater Institute.

But video-filming is the present-day obsession of Nonoy. When he documented the making of Agnes Locsin's ballet *Encantada*, his work won first prize in a competition sponsored by the Cultural Center. He has also documented the graduation composition of Christine Maranan and Cherish Garcia, *Children's Credo*, an environmentally inclined ballet based on Sedfrey Ordoñez's poem and Leo Quinitio's original music, which premiered at the College of Music, University of the Philippines.

He is even contemplating some bit-part acting on stage or on film.

To Nonoy, the coming days are largely unscripted. But they will certainly be filled with activity. Having said that what he does he wants to do best, it seems inevitable that we will soon hear about Nonoy doing well in one or two new fields.

Nonoy has no illusions about himself. He also makes no apologies. "I have absolutely no regrets about my dancing career."[9] He adds, "I sweated it out here. I persevered even if dancers hardly ever get what is due them. I am a homegrown artist who did his homework."[10] He knows what he has (or had) to do—as artist, husband, father. He has not failed himself, his colleagues, his loved ones. He has the discipline and the endurance instilled by dance, the agility and elegance imparted by his art. Both are sure to keep Nonoy Froilan essentially the man and artist we know him to be.

Kultura
1993

Notes

1. Pablo A. Tariman. "Nonoy Froilan Bows Out," *Manila Chronicle*, March 7, 1993. p. 44.

2. Susan A. de Guzman. "Nonoy Froilan's Turning Point," *Philippine Daily Inquirer*, March 7, 1993, p. 19.

3. Oral history interview by Anamarie Tirol, December 21, 1992.

4. Edna Vida. "Married to Prince Charming;" *Philippine Star*, March 18, 1993, p. 28.

5. Basilio Esteban S. Villaruz. "After Him, Who?" *Manila Chronicle*, April 4, 1993, p. 35.

6. Tariman. "Sorry," *Manila Chronicle*, March 14, 1993.

7. Tariman. March 7, 1993, p. 44.

8. Oral history interview, December 21, 1992.

9. De Guzman.

10. Tariman, March 14, 1993.

Rupert Acuña: Male Dancer Exemplary

It has been fifty years since Trudl Dubsky (Mrs. Herbert Zipper) founded what was perhaps the first formal dance-theater troupe in the Philippines, Ballet Moderne. Within this span of time, we've witnessed the rise and fall and rise (to ape Don McDonagh's phrase) of dance troupes—including Cassell's Studio Dance Group, de Oteyza's brief Manila Ballet Company, Anita M. Kane's Pamana Ballet, which was antedated by a company with her own personal name, and the folk dance groups that arose out of the fifties. Meanwhile the last Ballet Russe-named company was holding its ground in America, and the sixties became the period of real flowering of the regional ballets in America, supported by the media, and of the municipal companies in Germany, supported by their governments. Bridging that time and ours were the births of two aesthetically contrasting companies, the Hariraya Dance (later Ballet) Company and the Dance Theatre Philippines. (See my "In-Counter: Dance Theatre Philippines and Hariraya Dance Company" in *Philippine Cultural Arts*, Vol. II, Easter issue, 1971.) It was a colorful if brief period of rivalry and a "stealing" of a dancer that harked back to the stirring controversies in international ballet history. Both helped start the first years of the Cultural Center.

Alice Reyes and Modern Dance Company came in 1970, and from workshop-company of the CCP to today's Ballet Philippines, it gained unmitigated ascendancy. Serving the two gods of classicism and modernism, Reyes has, to this day, ably balanced the varying persuasions. (See Selina Jeanne Cohen's *The Modern Dance: Seven Statements of Beliefs*, Wesleyan University Press, 1965, one of the best of its kind.) At around the same time, Dance Concert Company entered the scene with its all-classical tenet—a departure from DTP, where classical training is paramount yet the repertoire of contemporary-styled ballets is wider. Except for the Choreographic Concepts Concert of works by Filipinos, even more true to the classical tradition were the productions of the Ballet Federation that harked back to Russian and British examples. All these considered, it might still be fair to ask, what has been the function of the male dancer? How did he come about? Why did he persist? What kind of support did he get?

In a culture that puts much responsibility on the shoulders of the man to support a family, how could a male dancer be encouraged or manage to survive? Moreover, with a so-called macho complex, how does he maintain his image, or prevail on society to recognize his profession? How do dancers like Rupert Acuña, whose father strongly objected to his dancing and who could pursue his passion only after his father's death, come about? For myself, it was by sheer will and waiting, training as well as studying in college, which finally gave me the financial independence to be able to dance. Younger men do dance these days, but financial obligations catch up with them so that they either thrust themselves into commercial entertainment—with its own brand of glamour—or leave for abroad. Unlike their female counterparts who may remain much longer under the aegis of their parents, these men may ultimately stop dancing and find an "honest-to-goodness" job acceptable to their family.

The above-mentioned companies did support male dancers, some of whom grew to be principal dancers, but we have also arrived at a present situation where our better male dancers—Manuel Molina, Luis Layag, Franklin Bobadilla, Enrico Labayen, Nicolas Pacaña, Mitto Castillo, Rey Dizon, Ricardo Ella, Victor Madrona, and a number of now almost forgotten ones after the famous Benny Villanueva Reyes, like Cesar Mendoza and Jamin Alcoriza—have opted for foreign rewards. We are not only losing our ballerinas to better opportunities abroad, we are also losing the few superb male dancers we have.

What have the past fifty years done for the male dancer? (Before the reign of ballerinas, the first professionals in the court ballets of old were men.) Coming unpredictably into the profession by sheer liking or male camaraderie, male dancers serve the art until their dancing years—shorter than that of women—run out. By then, it may be too late for them to find other more rewarding opportunities. Unlike the situation in some countries which have adopted this art of Italian, French and now international heritage, where dancers may be supported to retrain in another profession where earlier, they were supported by the state to train and then to dance, the Filipino male dancer hardly knows where he's going. Thus, the late start and the early disenchantment. Unless they are truly sympathetic to their juniors—whose future they already foresee—it seems unjust to expect them to serve their art in a mentor's capacity. It is that very capacity that has kept this art of theatrical dance alive from country to country, through its four centuries.

One male dancer who may soon give up dancing completely is Rupert Acuña. His story and appended interview may not answer all the questions but it should be of real interest to concerned balletomanes, and his life considered a significant example of a male career in dance.

Making a Decade with Rupert Acuña

Considered tall in the profession among local male dancers, broad-shouldered and pigeon-breasted, Rupert Acuña strikes a riveting presence on stage whether as Don Jose to Vella Damian's Carmen, Siegfried to Marivic Mapili's Odette, or Lover to Sophia Radaic's Beloved in *La Innamorata*, a new ballet by Felicitas L. Radaic to the music of Chopin. Tenderly or vengefully intense, as the case may be, his eyes are set on a handsomely shaped face that first impressed the magnetic Manuel Molina. Rupert, to speak of him as a colleague, has caught the eye of many an attractive and accomplished ballerina with his manly bearing and skillful partnering.

Like most male dancers in this country, Rupert came late into dancing. Although his mother, Alita de los Santos, born in Bago City in Negros Occidental, was a dancer of Ricardo Cassell, Rupert's father, Emiliano Acuña from Cabugao in Ilocos Sur, objected to his dancing. From an early age, perhaps as far back as when he was five, he had watched his mother teach and had always been drawn to dancing. He believes that he took his dramatic flair from his mother who, he describes, was one of the most promising in Manila in her time but stopped dancing when marriage came into her life.

It was at twenty-three, considered very late in the profession, that he started training. But then we are reminded of such dancers as Francisco Moncion of the early New York City Ballet who went to dancing after a degree in engineering. Moreover, Rupert had been trained as an athlete. He was a volleyball player (later to be the coach of a St. Joseph College team) that Eric V. Cruz discovered him. He, too, was Cruz's student in interior design at the University of the Philippines.

It all started informally, with Cruz giving classes for a group of amateur adults. He went on to be a principal dancer for Cruz's Dance Concert Company and partner Vella Damian, Marivic Mapili, and Heidi Domingo; and to be "permanent guest artist" with Dance Theatre Philippines, and dance with Irene Sabas, Mary Anne Santamaria, and Sophia Radaic. Thus, he is a reliable source of information about what ballet is like outside of the Cultural Center. He may even have guested more broadly locally than Nonoy Froilan as he was freer to dance in Bacolod, Iloilo, Tacloban, or Cagayan de Oro. It is no exaggeration to say that he has been the principal dancer, if only as guest, of organizations like Dance Theatre Philippines, Hariraya Ballet Company, and the Ballet Federation of the Philippines. With Dance Theatre, he traveled to Britain and to Hong Kong, and with Dance Concert to Guam and many provinces.

Rupert has seen ballerinas come and go—Sabas to a career in Europe, Mapili to marriage, or Domingo to medicine. He has served as an example to younger dancers like Ricardo Ella, now in Australia, Cesar Ongkingko and Victor Madrona, now in Hong Kong, and those who hold the local fort like Luther Perez and Augustus Damian. Imagine, too, the ballets he has danced in and what memories he has of them.

His debut was in November of 1974 at the Cultural Center, dancing the pas de deux in *Masquerade* (Katchaturian) by Cruz, after Remedios de Oteyza, and partnering Mapili in what used to be Nini Mendoza's gently expressive vehicle. A coup was made with the ballet *Carmen*, which has undergone various versions.

A first, Cruz and Rene Dimacali attempt in Bacolod gave him the toreador Escamillo. Separate versions came about, with his dancing Don Jose for both Cruz and Dimacali opposite Mary Mae Asencio in Bacolod in 1975. His dancing with Damian for Cruz's versions has made him the definitive Don Jose, and he has never failed audiences with his deeply felt histrionics in the same way that the ballet has made Damian a dramatic ballerina as Carmen. He describes their dancing together like making love, each of them drawing fire from each other.

The partnership progressed to Cruz's reconstructions of the grand finales from *Paquita* and *Don Quixote* with a full corps de ballet. Both were featured during the National Ballet Festivals in the seventies and in a round of theatres in Manila and the provinces. Again they danced together in Cruz's *Haunted Ballroom* (later retitled as *Ang Pagbabalik*, to the music of Dohnanyi), a free adaptation of de Oteyza's original which was made for Damian and Cruz.

Throughout this time, he had also been forging a partnership, a most cherished one, with Mapili. Where Damian challenged his dynamism and dramatic gifts, Mapili plucked at the subtlest chords and complemented him with a harmonious line to make what may be considered among the rarest and most intuitive partnerships in local dance history. Rupert describes it as competitive but sensible and sympathetic. Cruz created for them his pas de deux from *Spartacus* (later retitled *Ang Katipunero*, set to Katchaturian) and another pas de deux from *Le Corsaire*. (Felicitas Radaic cast them in her *Nan-Pangkat* [Peña] of 1980). Aside from their *Paquita* and *La Bayadere*, their partnership found another culmination in *Swan Lake* Act II, restaged for DCC by William Morgan.

Two other Dance Concert ballerinas he partnered are Gina Katigbak in Cruz's *Carmen* and *La Gitana*, she as Micaela and Azucena, respectively, and Heidi Domingo in *Don Quixote*, *La Bayadere* and Cruz's *Mir-i-nisa*. Katigbak inspired him with her expressiveness; Domingo, being unfailingly reliable, made for a most comfortable partner.

With Dance Theatre, he first found partnership with Irene Sabas in Julie Borromeo's *Zagalas de Manila*, Basilio's *Mosque Baroque*, Radaic's *The Prey*, and Robin Haig's Adagio from *Triptych*. In the last, he has also partnered Sophia Radaic and Mary Anne Santamaria. The young Radaic he partnered in *The Nutcracker* pas de deux, Gary Wahl's *Poeme*, and the elder Radaic's new *La Innamorata*, matching her elegance with virile chivalry. He considers her versatile and the most serious of his ballerinas. He partnered Santamaria, now in Leningrad, in Basilio's *Testament* and *Mosque Baroque*.

Worthy of mention is the one time he partnered with the senior Radaic in the *Les Sylphides* pas de deux, where he found a real feel of romanticism with her. In three Cruz ballets, he danced with Teresita Carrion in the elegiac "Meditation" from *Thais*, with Shirley Halili in *Minkusiana* (or *Las Festejadas*), and with Myra Beltran (and Katigbak) in *The Interior Castle*.

A significant partnership would have been forged with Maniya Barredo in 1981 in The Shades act of *La Bayadere* and the finale of *Paquita*. After a period of intensive rehearsals, a dreaded fall cancelled the plans. Press releases and photographs had already been sent out that it also became a public disappointment. Cesar Ongkingko and Augustus Damian valiantly took over his parts.

Tired from the repetitious efforts in a rehearsal, Rupert lost control. He fell and his knee ligaments tore. It was a critical point in his dancing career. It was to determine whether he was to dance again or not. Two months of therapy did not remedy the problem. He had to be operated on. For the sake of dance, orthopedic surgeon Dr. Antonio Rivera volunteered to do it for free. For six weeks he was in a cast, after which he had to undergo further rehabilitative therapy.

It took three months more before he started retraining. Was he going to dance as he used to? How much weight could the left leg take? Will the knee take the stress of turns and jumps? He also had to adjust psychologically, given the anxiety of dancing with a less-than-perfect knee. He grew uncertain of his abilities as a dancer. Was it going to be worth it all?

In our first interview, I told Rupert about Gary Chryst's recovery from a torn Achilles tendon, and how it affected his attitude toward dancing once more with the Joffrey Ballet. After a trying period of retraining mainly with Maggie Black, Chryst realized that now there was more to life than dancing. While he missed the cloistered life of dancers, life revealed its full scope and sensibilities to him. Somehow Rupert feels the same.

Not only because his dancing prowess has been altered and he has to be more dependent on his right leg (although this may be a factor), Rupert has also found a job that offers more security than dancing. His present work challenges him and his background in interior design is being put to good use. Even if he has no long-term plans, he feels that there are many avenues open to him in designing, such as for windows, stages, or homes. He has also found a personal relationship that he can no longer neglect. It has even changed his nightlife; now he spends more time at home attending to the needs and interests they share.

Dancing no longer holds its old and overwhelming attraction. Where before he was willing to suffer the deprivations that the training and rehearsal hours entailed and the little monetary compensation it gave, today not even the excitement of performances and the necessity of and pleasure from partnering prestigious ballerinas are able to outweigh the inconveniences and demands. "Now I want to get rich," he says.

Rupert dances with such passion and energy. In *Le Corsaire*, he wildly shot through the air at considerable heights. Then new as a performer, he gave his all with a verve that awed the audience and with an innocence that made him ignore the quite ruinous Liepa-like arched back at the peak of a leap. As Don Jose, after a handsome introduction during the capture of Carmen, he was the personification of intensity throughout—in a solo of longing with a rose, in a complete giving-in-to-love pas de deux, and in a final unflinching revenge that ended with acute remorse after he had killed the heroine. As Siegfried, he was unquestionably noble, solicitous over Odette's fears and needs, ever ready to shield or support her, making her more a woman than she ever was. In *Paquita* and *Don Quixote*, he had the fiery flair, in *A Haunted Ballroom* the desperate, if exaggerated, ardor, in *Testament* the right abstraction but with rabid feeling, in *Zagalas* the subdued masculinity of a Filipino in flimsy *barong* showing off his maiden, and in *Poeme* the unexaggerated strength and sensitivity solicited by its coach Tina Santos.

Cruz, in *Spartacus* or *Ang Katipunero* pas de deux, exploited his raw arabesques and leaps as much as his partnering prowess and poignancy. Radaic, in *La Innamorata*, did the same; though his performance was somewhat robbed of technical abandon because of injury, he managed to paint his role with the pathos matched or countered by Sophia Radaic's radiant sensuality or pitiless rejection. Without a doubt, Rupert is an artist of sensibility, full of warm charm, impetuous magnetism, and innate nobility. Sometimes wanting in precise polish because of his late and irregular training, Rupert nevertheless balances these out with his unique kind of dancing.

Comments on Philippine Ballet

In a concluding interview during a lunch off from his office in Makati, Rupert made thoughtful remarks on the following queries.

Q: What do you think of Philippine ballet today? What keeps it going?

A: Foremost is the dedicated work of present-day directors and teachers. They have improved dancing in the local scene, and that improvement is encouraging. Moreover, the great interest in dance abroad stimulates and inspires our own dancing. It helps people become more aware of what ballet is about.

Q: What sort of ballets should be encouraged?

A: Story ballets specially. Not necessarily long ones. The full-length classics are important as they are musts for dancers; they signify watermarks in their careers. Eric Cruz is perhaps the best in story ballets, as in his adaptations of the operas. The neo-classics are enjoyable to do. I'm not too fond of modern dance, perhaps because it's not in me; there's no urge in me to try the style.

Q: How many dance companies should we have?

A: Even if there were a national company there should be smaller companies. They should all be subsidized. Smaller companies can tour the provinces. The question about a national company is: who should direct it?

Q: What advice do you have for the male dancers today, especially those just going into ballet? As a senior dancer, how do you feel toward them?

A: For along time I had to be an example to some of them, and I've even encouraged the young. I'm concerned about the lack of male dancers today. However, it is encouraging to see the non-gay image of such dancers as Baryshnikov, Godunov, and our very own Froilan; this helps combat the prejudice against the male dancers. I consider my dancing days a unique experience that nothing else can replace. It is both physical and spiritual. Ballet is a mixture of poetry, music, and the theater arts. It is an experience of its own kind. It involves sacrifices, especially financial, which is why I think a dancer must finish a degree. It is something to fall back on later. In my case, I had to take on extra jobs while dancing full time. Although I wish the situation were better, I still feel that all the sacrifices were worth it, for they allowed me to experience the challenges and peaks that come with the life and art of dance.

Arts Monthly
1983

The Question of Identity

> Here we are, here is the Filipino identity, individualized for each one of us, but it is here as clearly as in the individuals of the more homogeneously cultural groups of the world. Perhaps we are more interesting for the fact that this Filipino identity is so varied. We can honestly believe this until the systematic move of universal education, there comes a more or less balanced state of culture in the country, and then our identity may be comfortably, if less colorfully, asserted. But sufficient is our Filipino identity today. Tomorrow will take care of itself.
>
> —Pura Santillan Castrence, *As I See It*

Time and again, the arts have been called upon to provide expressions of the indigenous self. The contemporaneity of our present day art is much maligned. We must, it is urged, have an ethnic approach. Present-day art is charged with having no Filipino spirit. Filipino art must reflect the so-called Filipino.

The confusion lies in the fact that we do not know that we do not know what a Filipino is. Or, sometimes we are not honest, for honesty offends. We refuse to see that we, as a people, are divided. We do not have so much a self as we have many selves within one self. This process of definition is not arrived at by analysis. It is arrived at by living. In living, there are such factors as time and space.

We have many selves for many times. These selves are related. Our present self is a modification of our older and other selves. All these selves are equally valid according to their times. It is not so much a matter of faith or of betrayal as it is of the desire for self-preservation.

We have faith because we believe that we can live and live more fully with faith. We have found out that betrayal, in the long run, destroys us.

Tradition is like our fathers—because of them, we are. At the same time, we are ourselves. We can never be completely unique. Neither can we be completely like our fathers. Yet it is said that we live in the ideational values of our fathers as they did in their fathers'. Man is Janus-faced. He looks at the past (a sense of history); he looks at the future (foresight). Where the past and the future coexist—that is the present. Tradition is always in the making. Our today will be the tradition of our children. We do not so much betray our past as we live our present.

The culture of a people depends upon their time and place. To judge them according to our time and place is unjust. Their responsibility rests upon how they lived, how they made use of what they had. Society is divided into classes. Each class has its own principles and things to live by. The distinction comes from the different faces of men (and even of a man) in the same time cycles. Thus, all forms of art, the highly and less developed, are reflections of the refined and the common (not meant derogatorily), of the sophisticated and the simple, selves. Both exist simultaneously—ever changing, each influencing the other but still retaining that distinction between the "refined" and the "common." They both serve their purposes, social or aesthetic, for their own class which originated or adopted (due to the influence of one class on the other) and transformed them.

Maybe only in a truly socialistic society will we be able to find a common self. But human psychology never allows such absoluteness to happen. The quest for the Filipino soul is, in a sense, utopian. Humanity changes. Therefore, his final self can only be reached when he stops changing—when he, in short, becomes extinct.

We would like to believe, for instance, that the true self of a Roman is reflected in Virgil's *Aeneid*. But, as T. S. Eliot has pointed out, the *Aeneid* has truly, in all senses, become a classic because the language and the history of the *Aeneid* no longer change. And this reflects just one of kind of Roman. The other kind is not recognized because it is, on the one hand, not deemed admirable, and on the other, not couched in a distinctive form.

What we want to see is the best Roman. An ordinary citizen who is as much a Filipino as Rizal. But we admire Rizal because he really lived and found significance in that living. We ourselves find meaning in his life because he has relevance to our time, and he is relevant to us only *because he was relevant in his time.*

Finally, the obsession to define ourselves sometimes stems not so much from our desire to know ourselves as from our desire *to show* something of ourselves. We want to create figments of our greatness as an excuse for our littleness. To compare ourselves with other people exposes our weaknesses, and we fail to relate the sociological facts to the historical frame of our present-day mentality. We often compensate for our cramped houses with the sumptuousness laid out on our tables, as if to appease the little gods who are our guests. Our much-brought-up-rather-than-seen merits are often the other side of our apologies. We are a young nation and we have not realized our potentialities. With all due respect to our heroes, we can say that we have yet to show our mettle. We have a long way to go. (But how tragic it would be if we realize that Rizal is greater than we can ever be!)

The quest itself is both noble and ridiculous. We can just imagine how the future generation may deem us foolish as to overindulge ourselves in such matter with great confusion. However, we cannot live without ideals. Or we think we have faith. It infuses our existence with a sense of purpose, as sense of direction, which binds man to man. Ours is an age of comedy. We are all fools. By being such, we preserve our well-being. By being fools, we do not suffer the fate of Lear. Like the fool, we must be wary of exclusiveness. Snobbery results in a quixotic neo-scholasticism, Dr. William Overholt of Boston University tells us. Like the fool, we must communicate to avoid the threat of social disintegration. To see a part as the whole is an illusion. A fragmented mind is the cause of social dissolution.

Who or what is the Filipino: Rizal or Bonifacio? The Filipino is a mythical hero. We are looking for a culture-hero. We shall discover someday to our consternation that this hero is, just like all of us, "with a thousand faces." Yet the quest must go on, but not in platitudes. The advice of Antonio J. Molina is to compose and let us see. According to Nick Joaquin, the need is to write than to define. Let us stop talking about the "Filipino soul"—let us strive to live it.

Comment
1964

Note

Much has transpired in the forty-year span of existence between 1964 and 2005: the traffic of journeys and studies, the trajectories of thoughts and choreographic/pedagogical concretization. These crossings from the margins (mainly Iloilo) to Metro Manila, of borders within and without one's homeland, have buffeted and beatified one's life.

Coming back by chance to this 1964 brief essay for F. Sionil Jose and Alberto Benipayo's P. E.N. *Comment,* I was reminded of how the comings and goings from the core of one's belief, made of our of essence and potential, are embodied in one body of many parts—anatomical, intellectual, material and spiritual, foreign, and familiar.

All these make me, and my thoughts and productions in, on, and out of dance.

Afterword:
Letter to a Young Dancer/Choreographer, Living and Working in the Philippines, 2005

Dear young colleague in dance,

You have in your hands a most precious gift—a book that is testament to one person's commitment and unconditional love to the art form that is DANCE.

In its pages are documented the work of those who have come before you, who paved the way for you, who toiled with their bodies, hearts and minds, that you may enjoy what it is now you enjoy, as a Filipino dance artist.

It is probably more usual these days to lament your very precarious position as a dancer, living and working in the Philippines, where the tides of market forces and globalization seem to occlude all importance and value of the art form, and you are still quite noble to pursue it at this point in the 21st century, I do not discount that.

However, I would like you to reach beyond time and place, and track your legacy as a dance artist, to trace the line beyond your immediate mentors and colleagues, to those who have formed them to who and what you know them now, because in your body is inscribed all the bodies of all who came before you.

In your body is written the many hours of work and experimentation, the many trials and errors of dedicated dancers and teachers who broke barriers in this country, who sustained dance with love so that others could learn its craft, pass it on and imbue it with their indomitable spirits. It is those indomitable spirits that have kept dance alive in this country.

It is no complex thing to understand history, the pages of dance history written in this book. You only have to look at your own *experience.*

"Historical enquiry," according to Husbands, is not to be cut off from personal experience, nor is it to be locked into personal experience. It is fundamentally a way of relating the internal, the personal to the external, the public."

Ultimately, understanding history is no different from your work in the studio—each step you take and try to understand and perfect is "imbued with centuries of tradition and change." And where, when you are material for a choreographer's vision, you participate in a choreographic strategy that inevitably "rests on an acceptance or rejection of the strategies of others, whether formed years ago or yesterday," as is often said. (See Alexandra Carter, *The Routledge Dance Studies Reader*. London: Routledge, 1998.)

At the risk of running irrelevant and out of fashion in this so-called postmodern world, you perhaps dip yourself in the many styles, inclinations, articulations of those around you, here or in the predominant dance tradition of the West (Europe or the United States), but I believe that in order to make this tradition alive, to make it yours, and perhaps enable you to eventually contribute to the body of work that dance is, you have to understand whence it is coming from in your *context.*

What is of primary importance is that you know dance from your context, the *Philippine context.*

"How many are aware of their dance history and the tradition that has been built for them?" "Steve" Villaruz asks, and thus, "how will they [you] balance tradition and change?"

Yes, how would you stem the tides of change if you do not know yet what ground you stand on? I know this by experience. Listen:

As a young dancer, out and alone in the American mid-west pursuing a dance degree, I had the benefit of correspondence from Steve, then in England for his studies. The act of writing down my experience and having it resound through someone else, a respected voice in Philippine dance and who was still furthering his understanding of the art also in a foreign country, guided me, strengthened me, to understand the art-form in my context.

Those were the days when cell phones and the Internet did not exist, when a phone call was prohibitively expensive, and a handwritten letter in your mailbox was all you had to remind you of your tradition, your ties, to make you tearfully remember where you came from, and the struggle you belonged to.

Amidst the conflicting atmosphere of dance in the late 70's, early 80's, when dancers—in New York City, at that time—considered the use of prohibitive drugs to mask the true search for their soul in dance, I could only be thankful for this correspondence and for the steadfastness, the anchor it gave me as a dancer.

I did not have the benefit of history then and I wished I did.

I did not know yet that the dance environment I had come into, so different from what I had been exposed to, or maybe different from the "illusions" I had been taught (as I told myself one day), was really a result of the forces of history, dance history. And that all around me, dancers were pushing classicism to its limit, wondering if more speed, more height or more virtuosity was the key to the advancement of the form. No one around me considered that this point of view could just be a dominant one and that there might eventually evolve other articulations, other processes, other points of view just as valid, just as original, and that different types of bodies would articulate such differing points of view.

I was content to suffer in my "aloneness," thinking this kind of isolation was a by-product of being an "artist"—that brooding, suffering and insufferable kind, the image of which is thrust upon you as a sign of "brilliance" and "dedication to the art."

I could not see it then but later, I began to see from concrete and painful experiences that I had a Philippine passport, brown skin, and like all other dancers from my generation who had gone abroad, was an OCW. The practice of the art was not really as "universal" as I had been taught it was. As a matter of fact, its practice had the nuances of race, prejudice, politics and aesthetics. Predominantly, dance companies inclined toward certain "trends," certain unsaid notions of beauty, and this you sensed and ultimately, internalized, subtly conforming to those notions of beauty, thinking to yourself, perhaps even convincing yourself, that this is the way the art is, this one way, this one process, this "universal aesthetic." My young, zealous, but sheltered mind could not see that this "one way" was merely a dominant way, imposed on the entire body of dance as the privileged way, excluding other diverse articulations, which are just as beautiful. Who really is to say what constitutes "beauty"? When one thinks about it, what is the truth of beauty anyway?

Despite this, I centered on my intuition which told me another thing: I sensed that I had all the impulses and articulations of a Philippine/ Filipino body, and that this was actually a *strength*, a thing of beauty. I had a memory and a value system that was different, though this I had not yet articulated. I did not yet have the means, the conscious know-how of expressing in a bodily way my precise context as a dancer born and proudly made in my country. I did not yet know who could articulate it for me.

Another "lack" that I realized in those encounters with other cultures is that dancing had more meaning in the "collective" spirit of dance which I grew up in, where colleagues and teachers worked for the same goal of furthering dance in this country and that this collective spirit was very much part of why I loved dance in the first place. I could not take myself seriously as a "specially gifted" dancer apart from everyone. Instead, my enthusiasm lay in what I sensed and what I know now—the determination of the identity of the Filipino in dance, to take active part in the shaping of history.

At that time, my colleagues and I were aware that our every step, every effort, was making Philippine dance history. We were bigger than ourselves, and therefore, dancing to the best of our abilities. This sense of one's place in dance history was an aspect of the passion for the art that was not fully articulated to me at that time, which at this point in Philippine dance in the 21st century, has taken new and inspired meaning.

Now, twenty-five years hence, and as I go through the pages of Steve's panoramic view of forty-five years of Philippine dance, I am humbled by the realization of my small contribution to it. I am humbled by the many contributions of my teachers and mentors, of the struggles they faced, and of how they generously gave of themselves. I am humbled by those who came before my teachers and whose lonesome efforts must have been a pitch in the dark at that time.

I see clearly that my struggles to form myself as a dancer and to dance all that was given me to the best of my understanding and ability, locates my body as the site of self-determination in dance in the Philippines.

In essence, my young body, and for that matter our bodies, are not merely sites for struggle—overcoming physical limitation is not the essence of everyday work—but the medium for the search for form, meaning and process, toward determination and thus, identity, as a Filipino dance artist. I now know that history converges in the ever-present body of the dancer. And as Steve says, we "sail in two streams" as we speak and manifest "the language and body-politic of Philippine Dance" or alternately, the "body-politic of the Filipinos."

How alone you must think you are sometimes! It does not have to be.

Silence, and therefore isolation, as a dance artist is a symptom of the way the art has been touted as an art of "privilege." I discovered this as I awakened to myself, as a woman and an artist: I realized that I need not suffer that "silence" in an already "silent" art-form.

How easier it was to stretch through time and connect myself to the *babaylan* (loosely translated as "shamanic") tradition of women to which we all belong as Filipino artists. Connecting to these medicinal women, the first performers of our tribe, described by poet Marjorie Evasco as women whose "scarred bodies ... showed the marks, signs and symbols" of their tribe's history, meant that I was given the chance to connect *bodily* to history. The stories the women told, their "art," which were generously and anonymously shared, bound the community in a whole and thus, offered me a blueprint of how to be an artist in my culture. I felt less alone as a dance artist. I was connected.

Finding my voice, I discovered that in the search for articulation in one's community ends the imposed silence of the dancer. In the dismantling of the notion of "privilege" in art and the melding of one's desires with that of the community at large, with real-blooded people in general, ends the "silence" of the dancer. To want to connect through the bodies of history into the one body of your culture prepares you to accept and understand all diverse articulations, and eventually become articulate yourself.

Steve's book wonderfully puts in perspective the conflicts (i.e., my very own) of the young dancer at that time; it weaves the myriad of forces surrounding my training and my coming to fruition as a performer. It also frames the deep concerns of dance artists of a specific period of time, and any physical exploration can be seen within that frame. As we go forward in ever-renewed definitions of our art-form, we have to understand the nature of those artistic concerns, summarized by Steve with the declaration, "we have to assert our own style and sensibility. These may not altogether exclude all foreign ideas and techniques because in life everything is utilized by transformation if not outright imitation, but creatively these should be processed and made anew."

The trajectories of Philippine dance history are wonderfully present and illuminated in this forty-five year account. Ostensibly, "history is a shifting discourse constructed by historians and … from the existence of the past no one reading is entailed: change the gaze, shift the perspective and new readings appear." [quoting K. Jenkins, *Rethinking Dance History*, London: Routledge, 2004:13].

The "gaze" of history I had as a young dancer, culled from dance magazines and some dance books, tantalizing in some respects, did not allow me the perspective to see myself in my culture vis-a-vis that of the West, which was writing most of the history I was reading—"the history written by the powerful."

With this compilation of essays, a "shift in perspective" occurs for all Filipino dance artists. This new "reading" of Philippine dance is another aspect of self-determination in dance, another way of "owning the dance." What an effective deconstruction of the concept of "privilege" in dance, what a generous template for all whose voice in dance wish to be heard.

The lone and original oppositor to hegemony, Steve resists it even more by defining the nature of that resistance at the most basic level—the level of the creator: "I am not interested so much in explaining the choreographer's creative process—as much as in clarifying the possible counter-tensions between the two factors that determine the kind and quality of his craft."

With this, he liberates all the choreographers of my generation, those who are currently working independently, away from the hegemonic center which he so resists. This he does, not for personal benefit but of real concern and knowledge for the workings of the art, and of the distinctness of our culture.

This is an inspiration for my generation of choreographers, an urging to search for our unique choreographic language, to clarify to ourselves and embrace the counter-tensions in which we work, while also constantly reminding ourselves that this should then always lead us to listen, to understand and appreciate the gestation of each choreographic voice.

What a comforting thought for a starting choreographer to think that regardless one's humble estimation of one's contribution, it will have resonance.

Steve illustrates this inclusive attitude when he says: "Personally, I don't classify artists as major or minor, because I respect them for the integrity of the work produced ... each one's worth is his worth, and there are more factors to praise or blame than an artist's self [for] this can only lead to a history of personages and patronage, and not of actual achievements or works."

"Actual achievement or works" as the worth of an artist—this is likewise an inspiration for the more "senior" independent choreographers working in the independent dance scene. We are now more confident and assured that each of our ventures into the unknown, each resistance to indifference, each critique of our own "success," will be embraced by an inclusive dance community, and that now, we can enjoy the process of our work and not have to resist our own colleagues.

We are now confident that there exists an unsaid code that respects each incursion into new terrain, as yet another step, another weave, another thread in the fabric of Philippine dance. This has taken a long time to build, and painstakingly—sometimes hazardously! Steve critiques those who "easily display our citified nationalism and finding comfort in 'this is it'."

As I confront the vastness of this historical account, I can only hope that we have the intellectual and physical stamina to track each voice as Steve has done for the past forty-five years—"cultural literacy is still a long-term aim, washed under the glamorization and globalization of 'so-successful' performing," he adds—and that we become as magnanimous and big of heart as he is.

His admonition that "we are perhaps not so adventurous, not curious enough, not trusting of our intuition and not taking risks in this business of art" is one voice that will forever haunt our choreographic careers towards the hoped-for flourishing of our art form.

The question of whether it would be better to put energies and ever-scarce resources of this country to cultivating one major national dance company, and as the argument goes, one espousing the Filipino cause, the Filipino identity in the international circuit, enabling Philippine dance to reach the "international standard," obliquely questions our existence and espousal of an "independent dance community." The answer to that question is many-sided and multi-dimensional. Steve quotes theologian and critic Nathan A. Scoot, Jr. on this important point: "If there is no large efflorescence of activity, of the sort that becomes possible when a host of significant artists of minor scope are exploring the possibilities of a particular medium, then we do not have a sense of that medium's possessing vivaciousness and richness of interest." And he cites his criticism teacher, Jack Anderson, who says, "the greater the number and the wider the range of people working creatively, the greater the possibilities for artistic growth. And that, after all, is what it's all about ..."

This is the intelligence behind an independent dance movement, whose "radical" label does not mean a lack of an appreciation for the tradition, nor whose "personalistic" sojourns signify a negation for "nationalistic" aspirings, but rather, a dance movement that is independent hinges on a sense that the transformation of our inherited dance tradition, both local and western, is to be done "not self-consciously by the generic and indefinable filter we name "Filipino," but by *each individual artist making his free choice* ..." Undoubtedly, Steve stresses this when he claims that "true experimentation and the apprenticeship of new choreographers happen only in smaller groups."

It is no wonder, forty-five years of tracking Philippine dance still finds Steve in the midst of this post-colonial era of Philippine dance. That is testament to his honest critique of himself, and integrity as historian and critic, and also as choreographer, because in the 21st century choreography is essentially a critical practice. This is choreography not just of immediate bodies, but of dancing bodies through the years. It is a framework, like any choreography, that Steve has dreamt, conceptualized, recorded on paper, and then, left to the universe to realize, and if I may say so, is unfolding gracefully as choreography at this point.

It is the strength of the independent dance scene to have Steve as a towering intellectual figure to help us define, contextualize our work, and I will always be forever personally grateful to him for embracing my initial choreographic ventures and appreciating the facts of my personal struggle.

Maybe he sensed that since all of us are "products of history," I was intent on defining it myself. Or that maybe his concept of a dance globe must somehow include my awkward steps to definition, or that I struggled with such conviction about my feelings that the form I came up with might convey something, in some small way, of our life as a nation. Or maybe with some humor, he concluded that art is a way of life, and proceeds anyway with or without intervention, so might as well witness/enjoy someone else's unfolding.

Most probably, he sought to resist the "overall attitude of being only discursive, and not obsessive" about the art, trekking a beaten path to alternative performing spaces, obliquely critiquing premature discussions of a notion of national art when such "obsession" did not exist.

Like the one who says the emperor does not wear any clothes, Steve reminds us that the superficial manner by which we approach our dance tradition does not truly take into account the lives of the people from which it is derived and that intellectual and artistic integrity must moor us away from this inclinations for ready entertainment.

What enables such a person to teach continuously, to choreograph, to engage in unpopular initiatives in behalf of the art, to acknowledge unselfishly the contributions of others, to praise but admonish, to recognize yet critique, to acknowledge and yet to challenge? It must be LOVE, unconditional love for dance as an art form. One who loves the art form and cares deeply for it has the right to lament its commodification, the undermining of its value, the lack of appreciation of its power. Terpsichore, the muse of Dance, moves in such a person's heart. Steve's commitment to the dance demands a kind of love "that is all-encompassing, ... a love that can cause us to feel for the just too formidable store and variety of dances the Philippines has." He attributes the dichotomies that some dance makers impose on the art form as a "lack of encompassing love in the dance field: ballet versus modern, etc.," but quickly qualifies such "encompassing love" by saying, that "loving all ... does not mean easy accommodation or convenient, even inspired, compromise."

Jean George Noverre, pioneering choreographer of the 16th century, perceives dance as an art of self-erasure. Perhaps, it is the nature of the art that its true servants are necessarily self-effacing. Steve remarks: "It is not enough to be good or great. You have to somehow also be a great heart."

So, my young colleague in dance, as you might by now surmise, history trudges on whether or not you are aware of your place in it. How much more complete if you had this whole world of Philippine dance history come alive for you!

How much more wide and imaginative would your work be, your curiosity for other things spurring its eventual forming? How much you would be imbued by the spirit of your teachers, the more important thing to absorb rather than seemingly repetitive instructions or corrections? In the end, it is your concept of things, of your body and how it relates to other bodies that allow you to blossom as an artist.

You must be awake to the fact that your ever-present body does not erase the past, or history. In truth, as critic Andre Lepecki explains, "the past is not that which vanishes at every second that passes, but rather that which presents itself in the present as a forceful absence." So, dear colleague, much as you are younger and think yourself "inconsequential" because of it, still, in your dancing body is inscribed all the signs, references, lines of force, defining the ground on where dance, Philippine dance, stands. Your body and all dancing bodies in this country carry the memory of the forming of its culture, and signify its imagination and therefore, identity.

In the age of globalization, where we must guard against mere framing of dancing bodies as "exotic" products, we need to look at our individual and collective pasts with empathy, insight and deep involvement.

We must inculcate in ourselves a deep desire to re-negotiate our artistic identity within our rich and plural resource. A lucid view of history enables us for this task; a sincere understanding prevents us from cloaking it with false sentiment and nostalgia, and offers us the insights by which to keep these traditions truly alive, resonant. Because with the many things besetting us as a country, still, the important thing to do, as Steve says, is to make more art, "to build more, to continue—to make art a part of life, ... to make institutional, governmental, societal recognition, important and urgent." We must have the passion and commitment to act, to build, to "stop talking about the Filipino soul and instead, strive to live it."

In the course of reading this compilation of essays, I often wondered about the function of the critic and the historian in Philippine society. Writer Lawrence Durrell says that "we really write to the dead or the unborn." If so, then the writing of history must be truly a lonely task, and Steve's work of forty-five years, a form of psychic endurance for a seemingly quixotic and maybe, thankless task in a country given only to valuing the "material evidence of its culture" and not, its dances.

Perhaps, it was an inner necessity that compelled Steve to write through forty-five years of Philippine dance. Perhaps ultimately, he was not concerned with his collection's readership; writing the history of Philippine dance just had to be done. I feel he wanted to remedy or correct in his own way, the institutional unconcern which cause the loss of the dances of the century's choreographers, believing it to be a "cultural betrayal that sits at the foot of history like an impoverished, even depraved, nation."

As he straddled past and future, creating this dialogue with bodies before him with the aim of laying the groundwork for the future, I am honored and humbled that he has laid the tracks for all of us.

Our recognition now of the value of his work and the content of what he is saying only means we are ready to elevate our art-form to the discipline that it is, of both theory and practice to its forming, in a dynamic, exuberant exchange of energy. Our recognition of his work also means we are willing to assert the value and power of dance in our society.

So dear artist, you must humbly go and do your work everyday, knowing that the conditions you find yourself in, the conditions of embodiment in which you struggle to create your own presence, only means you anchor the dance in your historical and material body and thus, create the history that your body dances.

Always remember, that the history you dance is always on the verge of its own withdrawal. This is why it becomes history, and thus, you must never forget all those little steps that someone else took for you, that you may dance and realize your soul in the present. "Because of them, we are. At the same time, we are ourselves. We can never be completely unique. Neither can we be completely like our fathers" (and mothers), as Steve remarks.

It might seem overwhelming, this "weight" of history thrust on you. But no, you must *dance*, you must be light-footed, tread lightly on the "burden" of history. Your work, art is about *play*. We must play and communicate, "we are all fools ... by being fools, we do not suffer the fate of Lear. Like the fool, we must be wary of exclusiveness. Like the fool, we must communicate to avoid the threat of social disintegration."

Finally, to see your part, to find your place in the whole, it is both your birthright and your responsibility. As your older colleague in dance, with the knowledge and experience I have thus acquired, the only real task for me is to find the magnanimity by which to watch and wait for you to find your place. This is the example of Steve's work. This is what has been reinforced in me from reading his work: that I have to usher you, yes, but also that I have to let you go. I have to let you find and define your place in history, in the tradition of a true and wise mentor.

We are both inextricably bound to history. As you have "all of life to explore, all of history to attend to, all of subjects to deal with, all of loves and hates to inspire" you, you are still in a specific time or period of place and, you are definitely bound. "Even [those] who sit and wait. [We] can only be a Filipino. [We are all] is accountable."

At the end of this book, Steve comes full circle by going back to an essay he wrote in 1964: "I was reminded of how goings out of and comings back to a core of one's belief: made out of essentials and potentials—are embodied in one body of many parts, anatomical and intellectual, material and spiritual, foreign and familiar." He says, "all make me, and my thoughts and productions in, on and out of dance. Parasitic, prodigal and poised as a pirouette on a still point."

Thank you, Steve, for bringing us back to the core of our beliefs, for reminding us of the essentials, and opening to us our potentials. You have been that still point on which we have pirouetted, sometimes awkwardly, sometimes brilliantly. As we make another turn toward an ever-renewed vision of dance, may your work always remind us of how great we can become, as a people, as a nation, dancing and poised for anything.

Young dancer, please allow me:

Thank you, Steve, from the bottom of my heart.

Always,

Myra (Beltran)

General Bibliography

Abad, Gémino R. 1989. "Exchange: No Deadline for Language," *The Manila Chronicle Magazine*, April 30, pp. 21-22.

______________. 1990. "Language and Words: The Space Between," *UP Newsletter*, February 14, p. 4.

Adair, Christy. 1992. *Women and Dance Sylphs and Sirens*. New York: New York University Press.

Adshead Landsdale, Janet and June Layson, eds. 1994. *Dance History. An Introduction*. London: Routledge.

Adshead, Janet and June Layson, eds. 1986. *Dance History*. London: Dance Books.

Adshead, Janet, ed. 1987. *Choreography: Principles and Practice*. Surrey: National Resource Centre for Dance.

______________, ed. 1988. *Dance Analysis: Theory and Practice*. London: Dance Books.

Aitchison, Jean. 1981. *Language Change: Progress or Decay*. London: Fontana.

Albright, Ann Cooper. 1997. *Choreographing Difference*. Hanover: Wesleyan University Press.

Alcedo, Patrick. 1999. "From Ritual to Nation: Performing Politics and Power in the Philippines." In 1998 *Philippine International Dance Conference: Dance in Revolution, Revolution in Dance*, ed. Basilio Esteban S. Villaruz. Manila: World Dance Alliance Philippines, 4-6.

Alderson, Evan. 1997. "Ballet as Ideology: *Giselle*, Act II." In *Meaning in Motion*. Edited by Jane C. Desmond. Durham: Duke University Press.

Alejandro, Reynaldo. 1978. *Philippine Dance: Mainstream and Crosscurrents*. Quezon City: Vera-Reyes Inc.

Alejandro, Reynaldo and Amanda Abad Santos Gana. 2002. *Sayaw: Philippine Dances*. Manila: National Bookstores Inc.-Anvil Publishing.

Alejandro, Reynaldo. G. 1978. *Philippine Dance, Mainstream and Cross-currents*. Quezon City: Vera-Reyes.

Alexander, Jeffrey C. and Steven Seidman, eds. 1990. *Culture and Society: Contemporary Debates*. Cambridge: Cambridge University.

Algeranoff, H. 1956. *My Years with Pavlova*. London: William Heinemann, Ltd.

Amilbangsa, Ligaya Fernando. 1983. *Pangalay: Traditional Dances and Related Folk Artistic Expressions*. Makati: Filipinas Foundation.

Anderson, Jack. 1974. *A History of Dance*. New York: Newsweek Books.

______________. 1987. *Art Without Boundaries*. Iowa: University of Iowa Press.

Aquino, Francisca Reyes. 1950-76. *Philippine Folk Dances*. 6 vols. Quezon City: Kayumanggi Press.

Arandez, Presperidad and Lucrecia Reyes Urtula. 1992. *Sayaw: An Essay on the Spanish Influence on Philippine Dance*. Manila: Cultural Center of the Philippines.

Arjuna. 1990. "Asian Diary: Anti-English Brigade," *The Manila Times*, May 20, p. 4.

Armstrong, Lucile. 1985. *A Wisdom on Folk Dance*. West Yorkshire: Springfield Books Ltd.

Arriola, Fe Maria and Onib Ohnedo, eds. 1993. *The Body Book*. Manila: GCF Books.

Art and Confrontation, The Arts in An Age of Change. Greenwich, Connecticut: New York Graphic Society Ltd., n.d.

Arts in Society. 1975. Vol. 11, no. 3. *The Arts in the Post-industrial Society*. Madison, Wisconsin: Research and Statewide Programs in the Arts, University of Wisconsin Extension.

Ashcroft, Bill, Gareth Griffiths, and Helen Tiffin, eds. 1995. *The Post-Colonial Studies Reader*. London: Routledge.

Atayde, Juan. 1982. "The Theaters of Manila," *Philippine Studies*, Vol. 30: 1st Quarter, pp. 70-91. In original Spanish and in translation by Conception Rosales and Doreen Fernandez.

Atkins, G. Douglas and Laura Morrow, eds. 1989. *Contemporary Literary Theory*. Amherst: University of Massachusetts.

Azurin, Arnold Molina. 1990. "Anthropologist E. Arsenio Manuel Wants to Correct a 'Great Error' in History," *The Manila Times* (28 October), B-9.

_______________. 1993. *Reinventing the Filipino: Sense of Being and Becoming*. Quezon City: University of the Philippines Press.

Balce, Ma. Nerissa. 1988. "Folk Dance Research Today," *Kultura* 1:1, 52-56. A forum with Lucrecia Reyes Urtula, Ramon Obusan and Ligaya Fernando Amilbangsa.

"Balitang (News) Middle East." 2003. ABS-CBN ANC, October.

Bañas, Raymondo C. 1975. *Pilipino Music and Theater*. Quezon City. Manlapaz Publishing Co.

Banes, Sally. 1980. *Terpsichore in Sneakers*. Boston: Houghton Mifflin Company.

_______________. 1994. *Writing Dance in the Age of Postmodernism*. Hanover: Wesleyan University Press and University Press of New England.

_______________. *Dancing Women*. London: Routledge.

Bar, Ramsay. 1995. *The Male Dancer*. London: Routledge.

Barba, Eugenio and Nicola Savarese. 1991. *A Dictionary of Theatre Anthropology: The Secret Art of the Performer*. London and New York: Routledge.

Barclay, Raoul. 2003. "They Have a Traditional Hatred for the Coast Dwellers." In *The American Colonial State in the Philippines*, eds. Julian Go and Anne Foster. Durham: Duke University Press.

Bartolome, Candido. 1936. *Philippine Recreational Games.* Manila: University of the Philippines.

Barucha, Rustom. 1990. *Theater and the World. Performance and Politics of Culture*. London: Routledge.

Basilio, ed. 1972. *Sayaw Silanganan ng 1976-77: The Philippine Annual and Guide to the National Ballet Festival.* Manila: Folk Arts Theater.

Bautista, Teresa. 1978. "Concerts Collage: A Former Presence Felt," *Sayaw Silanganan*, May, p. 4

Bayanihan. 1987. Manila: Bayanihan Folk Arts Center.

Benesh, Rudolf and Joan. 1977. *Reading Dance, The Birth of Choreology*. London: Souvenir Press.

Benjamin, Andrew and Peter Osborne, eds. 1991. *Thinking Art: Beyond Traditional Aesthetics*. London: Institute of Contemporary Art.

Bentley, Eric. 1972. *Theater of War, Comments on 32 Occasions*. New York: The Viking Press.

Berger, John. 1972. *Ways of Seeing*. London: Penguin and British Broadcasting Corporation.

Berger, Maurice, ed. 1998. *The Critics of Criticism*. New York: The New Press.

Berger, Peter. 1963. *Invitation to Sociology*. New York: Doubleday.

Best, David. 1978. *Philosophy and Human Movement*. London: George Allen and Unwin.

Bhabha, Homi. 1994. *The Location of Culture*. London: Routledge.

Bharucha, Rustom. 1990. *Theatre and the World: Performance and the Politics of Culture*. London: Routledge.

________________. 1995. *Chandralekha: Woman, Dance and Resistance*. New Delhi: India.

Blacking, John. 1976. *How Musical Is Man?* London: Faber and Faber.

Blair, Emma and James Robertson, eds. 1903-1909. *The Philippine Islands,* 1493-1898. Vols. I-V. Cleveland: Arthur H. Clark.

Boas, Franziska. 1944. *The Function of Dance in Human Society*. New York: Dance Horizons republication of the Boas School.

________________, ed. 1972. *The Function of Dance in Human Society*. New York: Dance Horizons.

Bocobo Olivera, Celia. 1972. *History of Physical Education in the Philippines*. Quezon City: University of the Philippines.

Bornoff Nicholas. 1992. *Pink Samurai: An Erotic Exploration of Japanese Society*. London: Grafton.

Borromeo-Roche, Julie, Tita Radaic and Tony Fabella. N.d. "Performing Artist Syllabus: Ballet." A Manual. Mandaluyong: Association of Concerned Artists in the Performing Arts Philippines.

Brady, Joan. 1982. *The Unmaking of a Dancer*. New York: Harper and Row Publishers.

Bremmer, Jan and Heman Roodenburg, eds. 1991. *A Cultural History of Gesture*. Ithaca: Cornell University Press.

Brook, Peter. 1968. *The Empty Space*. Middlesex: Penguin Books.

Buenaventura, Cristina Laconico. 1994. *Theater in Manila: 1846-1946.* Manila: De la Salle University.

Burt, Ramsay. 1995. *The Male Dancer: Bodies, Spectacle, Sexualities*. London: Routledge.

Carter, Alexandra, ed. 1998. *The Routledge Dance Studies Reader*. London: Routledge.

Carter, Alexandra. "Destabilising the Discipline: Critical Debates about History and their Impact on the Study of Dance," in *Rethinking Dance History: A Reader*. London: Routledge.

Carter, Alexandra. "Making History: A General Introduction" in *Rethinking Dance History: A Reader*. London: Routledge.

Casey, Betty. 1981. *International Folkdancing USA*. New York: Doubleday and Company. With Philippine dances, 219-31.

Chew, Gerald. 2002. "Taking to the Stage: Asian Theatre Comes of Age." *Theatre Arts Magazine* (Singapore). September-October.

Chua Soo Pong. 1989. "Cultural Pluralism in Dance: The Changing Scene in Singapore." *Performing Arts* 5 (July), pp. 52-54.

_______________. 1992. "The Symbolic Construction of Singapore Community in Dance: Studies of the Asean Dance Festival Choreographers." *Performing Arts 7* (July), pp. 50-52.

_______________. 1993. "Southeast Asian Performing Arts: Issues of Cultural Identity." *SPAFA Journal*. Vol. 3, no. 2 (May-August), 26-36.

Clarke, Mary and Clement Crisp. 1981. *The History of Dance*. London: Orbis Publishing Ltd.

Clifford, James and George Marcus, eds. 1986. *Writing Culture: The Poetics and Politics of Ethnography Berkeley/Los Angeles: University of California Press*.

Cohen, Selma Jeanne, ed. 1965 *The Modern Dance—Seven Statements of Belief*. Middletown: Wesleyan University Press.

_______________. 1982. *Next Week, Swan Lake—Reflections on Dance and Dances*. Middletown: Wesleyan University Press.

Cohen, Selma Jeanne, George Dorris, et al., 1998. *International Encyclopedia of Dance*. 6 vols. Oxford: Oxford University Press.

Contemporary Assessor Accreditation Procedure Manual. n.d. Taguig: Technical Education and Skills Development Authority.

Contemporary Philippine Culture: Selected Papers on Arts an Education. 1998. Manila: The Japan Foundation.

Copeland, Roger and Marshall Cohen, eds. 1983. *What is Dance? Readings in Theory and Criticism*. Oxford: Oxford University Press.

Cordero-Fernando, Gilda. 1978. *Turn of the Century*. Quezon City: GCF Books.

Cordillera Ethnic Dances: A Manual for Teachers. 1994. Trinidad: ALA Printing Press.

Coronel, Patricia Borromeo. n.d. Performing Arts Syllabus: Basic Jazz. Mandaluyong: Association of Concerned Artists in the Performing Arts-Philippines.

Corpuz, Rina. 1996. "Constructing Women, Constructing Dance: Reading Dancing Women in 'Mariang Sinderela' and the Politics of Dance Production." Unpublished paper for the Department of Art Studies, University of the Philippines.

Corrigan, Robert W. 1965. *Theater in the Twentieth Century*. New York: Grove Press.

Cortes, Joseph. 1990. "Why Nationalist Awareness Is Lacking Among Filipinos," *The Manila Times*, June 10, pp. 1, 3.

Covar, Prospero R. 1998. *Larangan*. Manila: National Commission for Culture and the Arts/Sampaguita Press.

"The Creative Force Behind Filipinescas." 1970. *The Filipinescas Story*, 1960-70, September 18, A pamphlet on the Filipinescas Dance Company.

Crisp, Clement and Mary Clarke. 1974. *Making a Ballet*. London: Studio Vista.

Croce, Arlene. *Going to the Dance*. 1986. New York: Alfred A. Knopf.

Cummins, Paul, 1992. *Dachan Song: The 20th Century Odyssey of Herbert Zipper*. New York: Peter Lang.

Cunningham, Merce. 1968. *Changes: Notes on Choreography*. New York and Frankfurt-am-Main: Something Else Press.

Cunningham, Merce and Jaqueline Lesschaeve. *The Dancer and the Dance*. 1985. New York: Marion Boyars.

Current, Richard Nelson and Marcia Ewing Current. 1997. *Loie Fuller*. Boston: Northwestern University Press.

Daly, Ann. 1997. "Classical Ballet: A Discourse of Difference." In *Meaning in Motion*. Edited by Jane C. Desmond. Durham: Duke University Press.

"Dance Criticism in Asia Today" in *Japan Asia Dance Event*. 1993. Conference proceedings with papers by Susan Street (Australia), Basilio Esteban S. Villaruz (Philippines), Daryl Ries (Hong Kong), Sheryl Dare (Hawaii, USA), and notes by Hakudai Yamano (Japan). Tokyo.

Dance Education and Training in Britain. 1980. London: Calouste Gulbenkian Foundation.

Daniel, Yvonne. 1995. *Rhumba: Dance and Social Change in Contemporary Cuba*. Bloomington: Indiana University Press.

Datoc, Salud C. 1995. "Folk Dance Movement in the Philippines." *International Academic Conference in Dance*. Malborg Kim, ed. Seoul: Yong-ku Park.

Davis, Con and Ronald Schleifer. 1991. *Criticism and Culture: The Role of Critique in Modern Literary Theory*. London: Longman.

De los Reyes, Angelo J. and Alma M. 1987. *Ethnologies of Major Tribes:* lgorot. Baguio: Cordillera School Group and Syner Aide Consultancies.

De Villa, Maricor. 1982. "DTP Dancers Used to Dislike Raising Their Legs on Stage," *Philippine Panorama*, January 24, pp. 16-19.

Dell, Cecily. 1970. *A Primer for Movement Description*. New York: Dance Notation Bureau.

Demetrio, Francisco R., ed. 1972. *Dialogue for Development*, Papers from the First National Congress of Philippine Folklore and Other Scholars. Cagayan de Oro: Xavier University, 1975.

_______________, ed. 1975. *Dialogues for Development: First National Congress of Philippine Folklore*. Cagayan de Oro: Xavier University.

_______________. 1978. *Myths and Symbols*. Quezon City: National Bookstore.

_______________. 1991. *Encyclopedia for Philippine Folk Beliefs and Customs*. 2 vols. Cagayan de Oro: Xavier University.

Demetrio, Francisco, Gilda Cordero Fernando, Fernando Zialcita, and Roberto Feleo. 1991. *The Soul Book*. Manila: GCF Books.

Desmond, Jane, ed. 1997. *Meaning in Motion: New Cultural Studies of Dance*. Durham: Duke University Press.

Diamond, Elin, ed. 1996. *Performance and Cultural Politics*. London: Routledge.

Diwa: Buhay, Ritwal at Sining. 1988. Manila: Cultural Center of the Philippines.

Doherty, Thomas, ed. 1993. *Post-Modemism—A Reader*. New York: Columbia University.

Dolin, Anton. 1953. *Alicia Makarova, Her Life and Art*. New York: Hermitage.

_______________. 1960. *Autobiography*. London: Oldboume Book Co., Inc. pp. 179-89.

Dormiendo, Justiniano. 1981. "Dance Theatre Philippines Turns 13 and Luckier No Matter the High Cost of Ballet Shoes," *Philippine Panorama*, September 13, pp. 33-35.

During, Simon. ed. 1993. *The Cultural Studies Reader*. London: Routledge.

Eliot. T.S. 1953. *Selected Prose*. Middlesex: Penguin Books.

Enriquez, Virgilio. 1994. *From Colonial to Liberation Psychology: The Philippine Experience*. Manila: De la Salle University Press.

Epskamp, Kees. 1992. *Learning by Performing Arts: From Indigenous to Endogenous Cultural Development*. The Hague: Centre for the Study of Education in Developing Countries.

Eugenio, Damiana. 1987. *Awit at Corrido: Philippine Metrical Romances*. Quezon City: University of the Philippines.

_______________. 1989. *Philippine Folk Literature: The Folk Tales*. Quezon City: University of the Philippines.

_______________. 1993. *Philippine Folk Literature: The Myths*. Quezon City: University of the Philippines.

Ewen, Stuart. 1988. *All Consuming Images. The Politics of Style in Contemporary Culture*. Basic Books.

Ewing, William A. 1994. *The Body: Photowork of the Human Form*. London: Thames and Hudson Ltd.

Fajardo, Liberad V. 1961, 1964, 1975. *Visayan Folk Dances*. Vols. I-III. Manila: Kayumanggi Press.

Fajardo, Libertad V. 1987. *Visayan Folk Dances*. 3 vols. Manila: Solidaridad Publishing.

Fallows, James. 1987. "A Damaged Culture," *The Atlantic*, November; *Philippine Daily Globe*, January 4, 5, 6, 1988.

Farnell, Brenda M. 1994. "Ethnographic and the Moving Body." *Man: Journal of the Royal Anthropological Institute*. Vol. 29, no. 4 (December).

Fernandez, Doreen G. 1978. *The Iloilo Zarzuela*. Quezon City: Ateneo University.

Fernando Amilbangsa, Ligaya. 1983. *Pangalay—Traditional Dances and Related Folk Artistic Expressions*. Makati: Filipinas Foundation and Ministry of Muslim Affairs.

Fernando Amilbangsa, Ligaya. 1989. "Diffusion of Traditional Dance in the Philippines." *Performing Arts* (Singapore) 5, 39-41.

Fohrbeck, Karla and Andreas J. Wiesand. 1980. *The Social Status of the Artist in The Federal Republic of Germany*. Bonn: Inter Nationes.

Foster, Susan Leigh. 1986. *Reading Dancing; Bodies and Subjects in Contemporary American Dance*. Berkeley: University of California Press.

_______________, ed. 1995. *Choreographing History*. Bloomington and Indianapolis: Indiana University Press.

_______________. 1996. "The Ballerina's Phallic Pointe." In *Corporealities*. Edited by Susan Leigh Foster. London: Routledge.

________________. 2002. *Dances that Describe Themselves*. Middletown: Wesleyan University Press.

Fox, Robert. 1982. *Tagbanwa: Religion and Society*. Manila: National Museum.

Fraleigh, Sondra Horton. 1987. *Dance and the Lived Body*. Pennsylvania: University of Pittsburgh.

Francis, David. 1913. *The Universal Exposition of 1904*. St. Louis: The Louisiana Purchase Exposition Company.

Francisco, Juan. 1971. *The Philippines and India*. Manila: National Bookstore.

Franko, Mark. 1995. *Dancing Modernism/Performing Politics*. Bloomington: Indiana University Press.

Franks, A. H. 1963. *Social Dance, A Short History*. London: Routlege and Kegan Paul.

Gainor, J. Ellen, ed. 1995. *Imperialism and Theater*. London/New York: Routledge.

Galbraith, John Kenneth. 1979. *The New Industrial State*. New York: The New American Library.

Gamboa, Alcantara, Ruby. 1994. *Ritwal: Sayaw-Awit sa Lumang Makati*. Manila: Rex Bookstore.

Garafola, Lynn. 1989. *Diaghilev's Ballet Russes*. New York, Oxford: Oxford University Press.

Garcia, Mauro, ed. 1979. *Readings in Philippine Prehistory*. Manila: Filipiniana Book Guild.

Garelick, Rhonda. 1995. "Electric Salome: Loie Fuller at the Exposition Universelle of 1900." In *Imperialism and Theater*, ed. J. Ellen Gainor. London: Routledge, 85-103.

Gere, David, ed. 1995. *Looking Out: Perspectives on Dance and Criticism in a Multicultural World*. New York: Schirmer Books (Simon and Schuster Macmillan) and Prentice Hall International.

Gibson, A. Boyce. 1972. *Muse and Thinker*. Middlesex: Penguin Books Ltd.

Gloria, Heidi. 1987. *The Bagobos: Their Ethnohistory and Acculturation*. Quezon City: New Day.

Go,Julian. 2003. "Introduction: Global Perspectives on the US Colonial State in the Philippines." In *The American Colonial State in the Philippines,* eds. Julian Go and Anne Foster. Durham: Duke University Press, 1-42.

Go, Julian and Anne Foster, eds. 2003. *The American Colonial State in the Philippines*. Durham: Duke University Press.

Goellner, Elen and Jacqueline Shea Murphy, eds. 1995. *Bodies Text: Dance as Theory, Literature as Dance*. New Brunswick: Rutgers University Press.

Goldberg, Marianne. 1997. "Homogenized Ballerina's." In *Meaning in Motion*. Edited by Jane C. Desmond. Durham: Duke University Press

Goldberger, Paul. 1990. "Wren, St. Paul's and Politics," *International Herald Tribune*, May 5-6, p. 9.

Gonzalez, N.V.M. 1965. "In the World," *Weekly Nation*, October 15, 80.

_______________. "Goquingco," *Philippine Panorama*, April 25, 10-11.

_______________. 1977. *The Bamboo Dancers.* Manila: Republic Book Supply.

_______________. 1995. *Work on the Mountains*. Quezon City: University of the Philippines Press.

Goquingco, Leonor Orosa. 1977. "My Memories of Madame Adameit," *Philippine Panorama*, May 1, 32-33.

_______________. 1980. *The Dances of the Emerald Isles*. Quezon City: University of the Philippines Press.

Gordon, Suzanne. 1983. *Off Balance: The Real World of Ballet*. New York: McGraw-Hill Book Company.

Graham, Martha. 1973. *The Notebooks of Martha Graham*. New York: Harcourt Brace Jovanovich.

Gray, Judith. 1989. *Dance Instruction: Science Applied to the Art of Movement.* Champaign: Human Kinetics Books.

Gruen, John. 1975. *The Private World of Ballet.* New York: Viking Press.

Guerrero, Marietta, trans. 1990. *From Revolution to a Second Colonization: The Philippines under Spain and the United States.* Manila: National Historical Institute.

Gutierrez, Lydia C. 1959. "Twenty-Five-Year Old Ballet School," *The Sunday Times Magazine* April 12, 18-21.

Guzman, Arnel de. 1996. *Goddesses of the Lust Triangle: An Excursion into Manila's Erotic Dance Industry.* Manila: The Media Gallery.

Hall, Fernau and Mike Davis. 1972. *The World of Ballet and Dance.* London: Hamlyn Publishing Group Ltd.

Hall, Stuart, ed. 1997. *Representation: Cultural Representation and Signifying Practice.* London: The Open University and Sage Publiations.

Hanna, Judith Lynne. 1979. *To Dance Is Human—A Theory of Non-Verbal Communication.* Austin: University of Texas.

______________. 1983. *The Performer-Audience Connection: Emotion to Metaphor in Dance and Society.* Austin: University of Texas Press.

______________. 1988. *Dance, Sex and Gender: Signs of Identity, Dominance, Defiance and Desire.* Chicago: University of Chicago Press.

Harris, Marvin. 1978. *Cannibals and Kings. The Origins of Cultures.* Glasgow: Fontana and Collins.

Hartendorp, A.V.H. 1930. Editorial on Art and the Metropolitan Theater Company. *Philippine Magazine,* March, 633.

______________. 1932. "The Metropolitan Theater," *Philippine Magazine,* January.

______________. 1938. "Philippine Cross-Section, 1904," *Philippine Magazine,* January, 14-16, 58-60.

______________. 1939. "The Manila Ballet Moderne," *Philippine Magazine,* November, 449-50.

______________. 1940. "The Manila Ballet Moderne for 1940," *Philippine Magazine,* December, 273, 472-84.

______________. 1941. "The Manila Ballet Moderne," *Philippine Magazine,* October, 412-13.

Hawkes, Terence. 1977. *Structuralism and Semiotics.* London: Methuen.

H'Doubler, Margaret N. 1966. *Dance, A Creative Art Experience.* Madison: University of Wisconsin Press.

Hedberg, Augustin. 1992. *Faith under Fire and the Revolutions in Eastern Europe.* Princeton: Sturges Publishing.

Hila, Antonio. 2003. "Music as a Tool for Pacification." Paper for the 2003 Sangandaan Conference, University of the Philippines, Quezon City, July 7-11.

"History of the Met," *Pagdiriwang, A Festival of the Performing Arts.* 1980. Manila Metropolitan Theater.

Hoopes, Ned E. and Richard Peck, eds. 1966. *Edge of Awareness: 25 Contemporary Essays.* New York: Den Publishing Co., Inc.

Horst, Louis. n.d. *Modern Dance Forms in Relation to the Other Modern Arts.* San Francisco: Impulse Publications, 1961 and New York: Dance Horizons.

______________. n.d. *Pre-Classic Dance Forms.* New York: The Dance Observer, 1937, 1940, 1968 and New York: Dance Horizons.

Hosillos, Lucila V. 1992. *Hiligaynon Literature: Texts and Contexts.* Quezon City: Aqua-Land Enterprises.

Humphrey, Doris. 1959. *The Art of Making Dances.* New York: Grove Press.

Ileto, Reynaldo Clemena. 1979. *Pasyon and Revolution: Popular Movements in the Philippines.* 1840-1910. Quezon City: Ateneo de Manila University Press.

Ingles, Raul R. 1965. "Fifty Years with the Times: Latest Ballet Steps Danced by Nijinsky," *The Manila Times,* January 12.

Jacinto, Joel. 1999. "Translating Tradition: An Applied Approach to Philippine Dance in America." In 1998 *Philippine International Dance Conference: Dance in Revolution, Revolution in Dance*, ed. Basilio Esteban S. Villaruz. Manila: World Dance Alliance Philippines, 52-55.

Jameson, Fredric and Masao Miyoshi, eds. 1998. *The Cultures of Globalization*. Durham: Duke University Press.

Jardin, Nestor. 1996. "Contemporary Dance in the Philippines." *Ballett International/Tanz Aktuell*, 11 (November).

Joaquin, Nick. 1977. "Julie Borromeo's Jet Set Dancers" in *Nora Aunor and Other Profiles*. Manila: National Bookstore.

______________. 1994. *La Orosa: The Dance-Drama That Is Leonor Goquingco*, Manila: Anvil Publishing and National Commission for Culture and Arts.

Jocano, F. Landa. 1968. *Sulod Society*. Quezon City: University of the Philippines.

Joel, Lydia. 1990. "Discovering Catherine de'Medici," *Dance Magazine*, April and May.

Jordan, Stephanie. 2000. *Moving Music*. London: Dance Books.

Jose, F. Sionil, ed. 1987. *A Filipino Agenda for the 21st Century*. Manila: Solidaridad Publishing House.

Jowitt, Deborah. 1977. *Dance Beat, Selected Views and Reviews*. New York and Basel: Marcel Dekker, Inc.

______________. 1988. *Time and the Dancing Image*. Berkeley, Los Angeles: University of California Press.

Kaeliinohomoku, Jo Ann. 1983. "An Anthropologist Looks at Ballet as a Form of Ethnic Dance" Ed. Roger Copeland and Marshall Cohen. *What Is Dance?* Oxford/New York: Oxford University Press.

Karnow, Stanley. 1989. *In Our Image: America's Empire in the Philippines*. New York: Random House.

Karp, Ivan and Steven D. Lavine. 1991. *Exhibiting Cultures: The Poetics and Politics of Museum Display*. Washington, D.C.: Smithsonian Institute.

Kasaysayan: The Story of the Filipino People. 1998. 10 vols. Manila: Asia Publishing Company Ltd.

Kendall, Elizabeth. 1983. "A Possible Grace," in Roger Copeland and Marshall Cohen eds., *What Is Dance? Reading in Theory and Criticism.* New York: Oxford University Press.

Kim, Malborg, ed. 1995. *International Dance Conference on Dance: The Challenge and the Meaning in Dance.* Seoul: Kide '95 and FEEL C and A.

Kim Tae-Won. 1993. "Brief Notes on My Viewpoint of Dance Criticism." Unpublished manuscript submitted to the International Dance Critics Conference of the American Dance Festival, Durham, North Carolina.

Kipling Brown, Ann and Monica Parker. 1984. *Dance Notation for Beginners* (Labanotation and Benesh Movement Notation). London: Dance Books.

Kirstein, Lincoln. 1969. *Dance: A Short History of Classic Theatrical Dancing.* New York: Dance Horizons.

______________. 1983. *Ballet: Bias and Belief.* New York: St. Martin's Press.

Knaster, Mirka. 1996. *Discovering the Body's Wisdom.* New York: Bantam Books.

Koegler, Horst. 1982. *The Concise Oxford Dictionary of Ballet.* London: Oxford University Press.

Laban, Rudolf and F. C. Lawrence. 1947. *Effort.* London: Macdonald and Evans.

Laban, Rudolf. 1988. *The Mastery of Movement.* Plymouth: Northcote House.

Laconico Buenaventura, Cristina. 1979. "The Theaters of Manila: 1846-1896," *Philippine Studies,* Vol. 27, 1st Quarter, 5-37.

______________. 1994. *The Theater in Manila: 1846-1946.* Manila De La Salle University Press.

Lamb, Warren and Elizabeth Watson. 1987. *Body Code: The Meaning in Movement.* Princeton: Princeton Book Company.

Lange, Roderyk. 1975. *The Nature of Dance: An Anthropological Perspective.* London: Macdonald and Evans Ltd.

_______________, ed. 1986. *Dance Studies* vol. 9 (Laban's System of Movement Notation). Jersey, Channel Islands: Centre for Dance Studies.

Langer, Suzanne. 1957. *Problems of Art.* New York: Charles Scribner's Sons.

Larson, Leonard A. 1976. *Foundations of Physical Activity.* New York: Macmillan Publishing Company.

Laurel, P. Kwan. 1989. "In Whatever Language, Keep Writing," *The Manila Chronicle*, Feb. 19, p. 12.

Layton, Robert. 1997. *An Introduction to Theory in Anthropology.* Cambridge: Cambridge University Press.

Leigh Foster, Susan. 1986. *Reading Dance—Bodies and Subjects in Contemporary American Dance.* Berkeley: University of California.

Lepecki, Andre. "Maniacally Charged Presence," in *body.con.text: The Yearbook of Ballet International/tanz aktuell 1999*, Berlin: Friedrich Berlin Verlag.

Logarta, Lita Torralba. 1986. "The Battle of the Ballerinas," *Mr and Ms*, July 1, 1986, pp. 29-32, 60-61; July 8, 1986, pp. 28-30, 40.

MacClancy, Jeremy, ed. 1977. *Contesting Art: Art, Politics and Identity in the Modern World.* Oxford/New York: Berg.

MacClancy. Jeremy. Ed. 2002. *Exotic No More: Anthropology on the Front Line.* Chicago: University of Chicago Press.

Maceda, José. 1981. *A Manual of a Field Music Research with Special Reference to Southeast Asia.* Quezon City: College of Music, University of the Philippines.

_______________. 1998. *Gongs and Bamboos: A Panorama of Philippine Instruments.* Quezon City: University of the Philippines Press.

Madel, Myron Howard and Constance Hadal, eds. 1970. *The Dance Experience*. New York: Praeger.

Mails, Thomas. 1978/98. *Sundancing: The Great Sioux Piercing Ritual.* Tulsa: Council Oak Books.

Malay, Paulina Carolina. 1958. "The Zarzuela," *Weekly Women's Magazine*, February 28, 12-23, 29.

Maletic, Vera. 1987. *Body-Space-Expression: The Development of Rudolf Laban's Movement and Dance Concepts*. Berlin: Mouton de Gruyter.

"The Manila Carnival," *Philippine Magazine*. 1939. February, 66-67.

Manila, Quijano de. 1961. "Dance of the Cross," *Philippines Free Press*, April 1. On Leonor Orosa Goquingco and the Filipinescas Dance Company.

______________. 1997. "The Ballet Dancer and the Refugee." In *Reportage on Love*. Manila: National Bookstore.

Manuel, E. Arsenio. 1985. *Guide for the Studies of Philippine Folklore*. Quezon City: Philippine Folk Society.

Marasigan, Dennis. 1998. "Current Philippine Cultural Policy" in *Contemporary Philippine Culture*. Makati: Japan Foundation.

Marcus, George E. and Michael M.J. Fischer. 1986. *Anthropology as Cultural Critique.* Chicago and London: University of Chicago Press.

Marcuse, Herbert. 1968. *One Dimensional Man*. London: Sphere Books Ltd.

Martin, Randy. 1998. *Critical Moves: Dance Studies in Theory and Politics*. Durham: Duke University Press.

"Masters of Musical Performance and the Ballet," *The Times* (London). 1979. November 16. An obituary supplement that included Federico Elizalde Sr.

Maybury-Lewis, David. 1992. *Millennium: Tribal Wisdom and the Modern World*. New York: Viking Penguin.

Maynard, John. 1929. "Impressions of the Manila Vaudeville Stage," *Philippine Magazine*, October 1929, 264-265, November 1929, 332-333.

Mazo, Joseph. 1974. *Dance Is a Contact Sport*. New York: Saturday Review Press and E. P. Dutton and Company. (On New York City Ballet)

McD. Wallace, Carol, Don McDonagh, Jean L. Druesedow, Laurence Libin and Constance Old. 1986. *Dance, A Very Social History*. New York: Metropolitan Museum of Art-Rizzoli.

McDonagh, Don. 1970. *The Rise and Fall and Rise of Modern Dance*. New York: New American Library.

McFee, Graham. 1992. *Understanding Dance*. London: Routledge.

McGuiness-Scott, Julia. 1986. *Movement Study and Benesh Movement Notation*. London: Oxford University.

McMullen, Roy. 1969. *Art, Affluence and Alienation, The Fine Arts Today*. New York: The New American Library.

Mead, Margaret. 1928. *Coming of Age in Samoa*. New York: Morrow.

Mendez-Ventura, Sylvia. 1989. "Exchange: Filipino Is Tagalog in a Hurry," *The Manila Chronicle on Sunday*, April 23, p.17.

Menez, Herminia. 1996. *Explorations in Philippine Folklore*. Quezon City: Ateneo de Manila University Press.

Menon, Sadanand. "'Passport, Please!' Border Crossings in the Invented Homelands of Dance", *Global and Local Dance in Performance,* Kuala Lumpur: The Cultural Centre, University of Malaya.

Mercado, Leonardo N. 1977. *Applied Filipino Philosophy*. Tacloban City: Divine Word University Publications.

"The Metropolitan Reborn," *People*. 1978. October 15, 5.

Miel, Juan C. 1979. *Samar Folk Dances*. Catbalogan: Government of Samar.

Millado, Chris. 2003. "Wandering Stages, Wondering Nation: Postcoloniality and Performance in Philippine Diaspora." Paper for 2003 Sangandaan Conference, University of the Philippines, Quezon City, July 7-11.

Minihan, Janet. 1977. *The Nationalization of Culture: The Development of State Subsidies to the Arts in Great Britain*. London: Hamish Hamilton.

Mirano, Elena Rivera. 1989. *Subli*. Manila: Cultural Center of the Philippines.

Mirano, Elena Rivera, Neal Oshima, and Basilio Esteban S. Villaruz. 1989. *Subli: Isang Sayaw sa Apat Na Tinig/One Dance in Four Voices*. Manila: Cultural Center of the Philippines.

Mitchell, Don. 2000. *Cultural Geography*. Malden: Blackwell Publishers Inc.

Miyoshi, Masao and H. D. Harootunian, eds. 2003. *Learning Places: The Afterlives of Area Studies*. Durham: Duke University Press.

Mojares, Resil B. 1985. *Theatre in Society, Society in Theater*. Quezon City: Ateneo de Manila University.

______________. 2003. "The Formation of Filipino Nationality Under US Colonial Rule." Keynote address for 2003 Sangandaan Conference, University of the Philippines, Quezon City, July 7-11.

Monahan, James. 1976. *The Nature of Ballet*. London: Pitman Publishing.

Morelos, Trining Alvarez. 1958. "The Golden Years of the Visayan Theater," *Weekly Women's Magazine*, February 28, 34-35.

Moreno, J. 1995. *Philippine Costume*. Manila: J. Moreno Foundation.

Morli, Anthony. 1968. "Art and Life: Splendid Company," *The Manila Times*, July 20, p. 15-A.

Morris, Gay, ed. 1996. *Moving Words; Re-writing Dance*. London: Routledge.

Mulders, Niels. 1997. *Inside Philippine Society*. Quezon City: New Day Publishers.

Mura, David. 1996. *Where the Body Meets Memory: An Odyssey of Race, Sexuality and Identity*. New York: Doubleday (Anchor Books).

Nadel, Myron Howard and Constance Gwen Nadel, eds. 1970. *The Dance Experience: Readings in Dance Appreciation*. New York: Praeger Publishers.

Nebres, Bienvenido. 1989. "The Demands of a Science Culture," *The Manila Chronicle*, April 3, p. 4.

________________. 1992. *Body, Movement and Culture: Kinesthetic and Visual Symbolism in a Philippine Community*. Philadelphia. University of Pennsylvania Press.

________________. 2003. *Where Asia Smiles: An Ethnography of Philippine Tourism*, Philadelphia: University of Pennsylvania Press.

Nettleford, Rex. 1985. *Dance Jamaica: Cultural Definition and Artistic Discovery*. New York: Grove Press.

Newman, Barbara. 2003. *Grace under Pressure*. New York: Limelight Editions.

Nograles-Lumbera, Cynthia and Teresita Go Maceda, eds. 1977. *Rediscovery, Essays in Philippine Life and Culture*. Quezon City: Ateneo de Manila University and National Book Store Inc.

Nor, Mohd Anis Md., ed. 2000. *Asian Dance: Voice of the Millennium*. Kuala Lumpur: Asia Pacific Dance Research Society of World Dance Alliance of Asia Pacific and Cultural Centre of University of Malaya.

Novack, Cynthia. 1990. *Sharing the Dance: Contact Improvisation and American Culture*. Madison: University of Wisconsin Press.

Noverre, Jean George, trans by Cyril W. Beaumont. 1966. *Letters on Dancing and Ballets*. New York: Dance Horizons.

Obusan, Ramon and Basilio Esteban Villaruz. 1992. *Sayaw: An Essay on Philippine Ethic Dance*. Manila: Cultural Center of the Philippines.

Obusan, Ramon. 1993. *Philippine Folk Dances*. Malolos: Mico Records.

Olivar, Celia Bocobo. 1972. *History of Physical Education in the Philippines*. Quezon City: University of the Philippines Press.

Opiniano, Jeremiah. 2003. "A 'New' Migration Chapter." *Intersect* 18 (January 2003), 29-32.

Orosa, Rosalinda L. 1975. "The Filipino as Seen Through the Dance," in H. C. Santaromana, ed., *Sinaglahi*. Quezon City: Writers Union of the Philippines.

______________. 1980. "Leonor Orosa Goquingco: Her Pyrrich Victory," *Above the Throng*. Quezon City: Heritage Publishing House.

Ou Jian-ping. 1993. "Dance Criticism in China Today." Unpublished manuscript. Beijing.

Overseas Performing Artists Testing and Certification System-An Executive Summary. 2001. Taguig: Technical Education and Skills Development Authority.

Palma-Beltran, Ruby. 1999. "Dance as Gender and Empowerment Issue." In *1998 Philippine International Dance Conference*." *Dance in Revolution, Revolution in Dance*, ed. Basilio Esteban Villaruz. Manila: World Dance Alliance-Philippines, 125-128.

Palmer, Winthrop. 1978. *Theatrical Dancing in America*. South Brunswick and New York: A. S. Barnes and Company.

Pangan, Augusto. 1966. *Philippine Folk Dances and Songs,* Manila: Bureau of Public Schools.

______________. 1979. "A Descriptive Study on Philippine Vaudeville," MA thesis, Quezon City: Ateneo de Manila University.

Paredes, Amante F. 1953. "Ballet for the Millions," *Freedom*, January 26, 14-21.

Pascua Ines, Teresita. 1973. *Ilocano Folk Dances.* Manila: National Bookstore.

Pastor Races, Marian. 1991. *Sinaunang Habi: Philippine Ancestral Weave.* Manila: Nikki Coseteng-Communication Technologies.

______________. 2002. "Hidalgo and Luna: Vexed Modernity." in *Zero In: Private Art/Public Lives.* Metro Manila: Ateneo Art Gallery, Ayala Museum and Eugenio Lopez Foundation, 7-35.

Pei, Mario. 1966. *The Story of Language*. New York: New American Library.

Peterson Royce, Anya. 1977. *The Anthropology of Dance*. Bloomington: Indiana University.

Pfeiffer, William. 1975. *Music in the Philippines*. Dumaguete: Silliman Music Foundation.

"Philippine Baranggay Folk Dance Troupe—4 Decades of Showcasing Philippine Culture." 1989. A souvenir program. Manila: Philippine Baranggay Folk Dance Troupe.

Philippine Entertainment Exporters and Promotions Association (PEEPA). 1998-99. A handbook.

Philippine Folk Dances and Songs. 1966. Manila: Department of Education-Bureau of Printing.

Pieper, Josef. 1965. *Leisure, The Basic of Culture*. London: Fontana Library.

Piñon, Remedios V. 1976. "The Start and Stars of Ballet in the Philippines," in *The First National Ballet Festival*. Manila: Folk Arts Theater.

Poblador, Liberato C. 1948. "They Laughed as He Sallied Forth," *The Evening News Saturday Magazine*, June 26, 16-17.

Pops, Martin Leonard, ed. 1976. *Salmagundi: Dance*. No. 33-34, Spring-Summer.

Portrait of Mr. B. 1984. New York: Ballet Society-Viking Press.

Postman, Neil. 1992. *Technology. The Surrender of Culture to Technology*. New York: Alfred A. Knopf.

Quindoza Santiago, Lilia. 1988. "The Language Question—On Filipino: Another View," *Philippine Collegian*, February 2, pp. 6-7.

Quintos, Floy C. 1980. "Limelight—Conching Sunico," *Women's Home Companion*, October 29, 42-43.

Quirino, Ricardo. 2003. "A Taste of Honey—The American Era in the Philippines." Paper for 2003 Sangandaan Conference. University of the Philippines, Quezon City, July 7-11.

Radaic, Felicitas L. 1978. "Ten Years on Toe-Dancing to the Grassroots," *Sayaw Silanganan*, December, pp. 16-19.

_____________. 1985. "Dance Journeys to the Altar," *Philippine Panorama*, April 28, pp. 4-5.

_____________. 1985. "Dance Theatre Philippines and Ballet Both Come of Age," *Karats*, February, pp. 3-4.

Rafael, Vicente. 1988. "Contracting Colonialism: Translation and Christian Conversion" in *Tagalog Society under Early Spanish Rule*. Quezon City: Ateneo de Manila University Press.

_____________, ed. 1995. *Discrepant Histories: Translocal Essays on Filipino Culture*. Manila: Anvil Publishing.

_____________. 2000. *White Love.* Durham: Duke University Press.

Ranger, T.O. 1975. *Dance and Society in Eastern Africa, 1890-1970: The Beni Ngoma*. London: Heinemann Educational Books.

Redfern, Betty. 1983. *Dance, Art and Aesthetics*. London: Dance Books.

Redfern, H.G. 1973. *Concepts of Modern Educational Dance*. London: Henry Kimpton Publishers.

Ree, Jonathan, 1999. *I See a Voice: Deafness, Language and the Senses—A Philosophical History*. New York: Henry Hol and Company.

Revilla, Ines. 1951. "Ballet in Manila," *The Philippine Quarterly*, Vol. 1, No. 1, July, 58-60.

Riantiarno, N. 1991. "Prospects of Contemporary Indonesian Theatre." *Performing Arts* 6 (July), pp. 36-38.

Rimpos, Ester. 1984. "Philippine Dance Today: An Admixture of Eastern and Western Influences," *Performing Arts* (Singapore) 1, 3-8.

Roces, Alejandro R. 1980. *Fiesta*. Quezon City: Vera Reyes, Inc.

Roces, Alfredo R., ed. 1977-78. *Filipino Heritage: The Making of a Nation*. Vols. I-X. Manila: Lahing Pilipino.

Rogers, Frederick Rand, ed. 1980. *Dance: A Basic Educational Technique*. New York: Dance Horizons.

Rogosin, Elinor. 1980. *The Dance Makers—Conversations with American Choreographers*. New York: Walker and Company. (Shawn, Weidman, Graham, Hawkins, Cunningham, Nikolais, Lewitsky, Ailey, Tetley, Tharp, Clifford and Feld)

Romualdez, Beatriz. 1968. "With Dance Theatre Philippines Ballet Goes Professional," *Sunday Times Magazine*, August 25, pp. 28-29.

Rosaldo, Michelle Z. 1980. *Knowledge and Passion: Ilongot Notions of Self and Social Life*. New York: Cambridge University.

Rosario, Elaine del. 1976. "Leonor Orosa Goquingco, Mother of Philippine Theatre Dance," *Commemorative Folio on National Artists*. Manila: Cultural Center of the Philippines.

Ross, Janice and Stephen Cobbett Steinberg, eds. 1990. *On the Edge: Challenges to American Dance*. Proceedings of the 1989 Dance Critics Association Conference. Dance Critics Association.

Roszack, Theodore. 1972. *Where the Wasteland Ends, Politics and Transcendence in Post-industrial Society*. New York: Doubleday and Co., Inc.

Roxas Tope, Lily Rose. 1998. *(Un)Framing Southeast Asia: Nationalism and the Postcolonial Text in English in Singapore, Malaysia and Philippines*. Quezon City: University of the Philippines Press.

Royce, Anya Peterson. 1977. *The Anthropology of Dance*. Bloomington and London: Indiana University Press.

Russell, Elizabeth. 1983. "Gertrud Bodenweiser, The Story of a Style," *Dance Australia*. No. 12, June-August, 52-53.

Rydell, Robert. 1984. *All the World's A Fair: Vision of Empire at American International Expositions, 1876-1916*. Chicago: University of Chicago Press.

Sachs, Curt. 1937. *World History of the Dance*. New York: W. W. Norton and Co., Inc.

Said, Edward. 1991. *The World, The Text and The Critic*. London: Vintage.

_______________. 1993. *Culture and Imperialism*. New York: Alfred A. Knopf.

_______________. 1995. *Orientalism*. London: Penguin Books.

Santos, Bienvenido. 1962. "The Day the Dancers Came." In PEN *Short Stories,* ed. Francisco Arcellana. Manila: International PEN-Philippine Chapter/Regal Printing, 185-199.

Sarkar Munsi, Urmimala, ed. 2005. *Time and Space in Asian Context: Contemporary Dance in Asia*. Kolkata: World Dance Alliance-West Bengal.

Savigliano, Marta. 1995. *Tango and the Political Economy of Passion*. Boulder: Westview Press.

Schechner, Richard. 1988. *Performance Theory*. New York/London: Routledge.

Schechner, Richard and Willa Appel, eds. 1990. *By Means of Performance: Intercultural Studies of Theatre and Ritual.* Cambridge: Cambridge University.

Schlundt, Christena L. 1962. *The Professional Appearances of Ruth St. Denis and Ted Shawn, A Chronology and an Index 1906-1932*. New York Public Library.

Scott, William Henry. 1982. *Cracks in the Parchment Curtain*. Quezon City: New Day Publishers.

_______________. 1984. *Prehispanic Source Material for the Study of Philippine History.* Quezon City: New Day.

_______________. 1987. *Chips*. Quezon City: New Day Publishers.

_______________. 1995. *Barangay: 16th Century Philippine Culture and Society*. Quezon City: Ateneo de Manila University.

Senate Committee on Education, Arts, Culture and on Social Justice, Welfare and Development. 1988. "A Moral Recovery Program: Building a People, Building a Nation." May 9.

_______________. 1990. "Cebu Revolts Against 'Filipino'," *Focus: Chronicle Magazine*, June 3, pp. 9, 15.

Shay, Antony. 2002. *Choreographic Politics-State Folk Dance Companies, Representation and Power*. Middleton: Wesleyan University Press.

Sheets, Maxine. 1966. *The Phenomenology of Dance*. Madison/Milwaukee: University of Wisconsin Press.

_______________. ed. 1984. *Illuminating Dance—Philosophical Explorations*. Lewisburg: Bucknell University.

Siegel, Marcia, ed. 1969. *Dancer's Notes*. New York: Dance Perspectives (issue 38). (Hoving, Moore, Nagrin, Redlich, Louis, Litz, Charlip and Dunn)

_______________. 1968 and 1973. *At the Vanishing Point—A Critic Looks at Dance*. New York: Saturday Review Press.

_______________. 1977. *Watching the Dance Go By*. Boston: Hough Mifflin Company.

_______________. 1981. *The Shapes of Change: Images of American Dance*. New York: Houghton Mifflin Company and Discuss Books/Avon Books.

Sietereales, Erlinda N. 1973. "The Folk Dance Revived," National Artists Folio. Manila: Cultural Center of the Philippines. On Francisca Reyes Aquino.

Sinfield, Alan. 1994. *Cultural Politics: Queer Reading*. London: Routledge.

Sison Friese, Jovita. 1980. *Philippine Folk Dances from Pangasinan*. New York: Vintage Press.

Smith, W. David. 1974. *Stretching Their Bodies: The History of Physical Education*. London: David and Charles.

Smith-Autard, Jacqueline M. 1994. *The Art of Dance in Education*. London: A and C Black.

______________. 1996. *Dance Composition*. London: A and C Black.

Sorell, Walter, ed. 1966. *The Dance Has Many Faces*. New York and London: Columbia University Press.

______________. "Notes from the Zurich Diary: East/West," *Dance Scope*, Vol. 15, no. 2, pp. 28-36.

______________. 1971. *The Dancer's Image—Points and Counterpoints*. New York and London: Columbia University Press.

______________. 1986. *Looking Back in Wonder, Diary of a Dance Critic*. New York: Columbia University Press.

A Sound of Tambours, An ASEAN Tapestry. 1991. Manila: Bayanihan Folk Arts Center.

Spencer, Paul, ed. 1985. *Society and the Dance: The Social Anthropology of Process and Performance*. Cambridge: Cambridge University Press.

Steinberg, Cobbett, ed. 1980. *The Dance Anthology*. New York: New American Library.

Stier, Theodore. n.d. *With Pavlova Around the World*. London: Hurst and Blackett Ltd.

Suarez, Petronila S. 1971. *A Collection of Heretofore Unpublished Folk Dances from the Province of Iloilo*. Iloilo: Central Philippine University.

Sy, Elsie. 1975. "Dance Theatre Philippines—A Hit in Scotland and Britain," *MOD* September 12, pp. 48-49.

Tariman, Pablo A. 1980. "Leonor Orosa Goquingco and the World of Dance," *Celebrity*, September 30, 16-18.

Taylor, Harold. 1965. "The Arts in America," *Dance Magazine*. November, 35-39, 90.

Taylor, Jim and Ceci Taylor. 1995. *Psychology of Dance*. Champaign: Human Kinetics Books.

Tenorio, Vyvyan. 1980. "Philippine Dance" in The 5th Festival of Asian Arts. Hong Kong: Urban Council, pp.172-77.

The Manila Times, from October 12, 1898 to July 9, 1902.

Thomas, Helen. 1995. *Dance Modernity and Culture: Explorations in the Sociology of Dance*. London: Routledge.

Tinggal, Zainal Abbiddin, ed. 1998. *The Dances of ASEAN*. Brunei Darussalam: Association of Southeast Asian Naitons.

Tiongson, Nicanor G. 1976. "Save the Metropolitan Theater!" *Mr. and Ms.*, September 14, 12-13.

________________. 1989. "Philippine Dance and the Task of Nation-Building: or Giselle in the Forest of Smokey Mountain," *Kultura* 2:3, 39-45.

________________, ed. 1991. *Tuklas Sining: Essays on the Philippine Arts*. Manila: Cultural Center of the Philippines.

________________. 1994. *CCP Encyclopedia of Philippine Art*. Vols. I-X. Manila: Cultural Center of the Philippines.

________________, ed. 1994. *CCP Encyclopedia of Philippine Art*. Vol. V: Dance, edited by Villaruz, Basilio Esteban S. 1990. "Sailing in Two Streams: The Language and Body-Politics of Philippine Dance." *The Fifth Hong Kong International Dance Conference*. Vol. II. Hong Kong: Hong Kong Academy for Performing Arts.

________________, ed. 1994. *The CCP Encyclopedia of Philippine Art*. (Vol. V: Dance, edited by Basilio Esteban S. Villaruz). Manila: Cultural Center of the Philippines.

________________. 1982. *Kasaysayan ng Komedya so Pilipinas: 1766-1982*. Manila: De la Salle University.

Todd, Mabel Elsworth. 1972. *The Thinking Body*. New York: Dance Horizons.

Tolentino, Francisca Reyes and Petrona Ramos. 1927. *Philippine Folk Dances and Games*. New York: Silver Burdett.

Tolentino, Fransisca Reyes. 1946. *Philippine National Dances*. New York: Silver Burdett. 1990, Quezon City: Kayumanggi Press.

Tolentino, Francisca Reyes. 1990. *Philippine National Dances*. New York: Silver Burdett, 1946. Quezon City: Kayumanggi Press.

Torre, Visitacion R. de la. 1976. "The Metropolitan Theater, Waiting for a Curtain Call," *Philippine Panorama*, September 15.

Traditional and Transformation in Asian and Pacific Dance. 1991. Conference papers for the 1991 Manila International Dance Conference, July 15-20, 1991. Manila: Cultural Centre of the Philippines.

Traynor, Gladys. 1936. "The Dance as Expression," *Philippine Magazine*, March, 129.

Trimillos, Ricardo D. 1985. "The Changing Context of Philippine Dance Performance." *Dance As Cultural Heritage*, vol. II, Betty True Jones, ed. New York: Congress on Research in Dance.

_______________. 1984. "Contemporary Dance in the Philippines." *The Aesthetics and Cultural Significance of Modern Dance*. Durham: American Dance Festival.

Turner, Margery J. 1971. *Approaches to Nonliteral Choreography*. Pittsburgh: University of Pittsburgh Press.

Turner, Victor and Edward Brunner, eds. 1986. *The Anthropology of Experience*. Urbana/Chicago: University of Illinois Press.

Tuyl, Marian Van. 1969. *Anthology of "Impulse," Annual of Contemporary Dance 1951-66*. S.F. Impulse Publications, 1969. New York: Dance Horizons, n.d.

Urtula, Lucrecia Reyes. 1981. *The First Philippine Folk Festival*. Manila: Folk Arts Theater.

Urtula, Lucrecia Reyes and Prosperidad Arandez. 1992. *Sayaw: An Essay on the Spanish Influence in Philippine Dance*. Manila: Cultural Center of the Philippines.

Valois, Ninette de. 1959. *Come Dance with Me, A Memoire 1898-1956*. London: Hamish Hamilton.

Van Tuyl, Marian. 1987. *Anthology of Impulse*. San Francisco: Impulse Publications, 1969 and New York: Dance Horizons, n.d.

Van Zile, Judy, ed. 1976. *Dance in Africa, Asia and the Pacific: Selected Readings.* New York: MSS Information Corporation.

Vega, Patricia Calzo. 1998. "Mixednuts." *Philippine Collegian.* December 3.

Verene, Donald P., ed. 1970. *Man and Culture, A Philosophical Anthology.* New York: Dell Publishing Co., Inc.

Vergara, Bonito. 1995. *Displaying Filipinos: Photography and Colonization in Early 20th Century Philippines.* Quezon City: University of the Philippines Press.

______________. 2003. "Colonialism and the Meaning of the Philippine Nation at the Louisiana Purchase Exposition." Paper for 2003 Sangandaan Conference, University of the Philippines, Quezon City, July 7-11.

Vida, Edna. 2002. "What Moves the Three Major Ballet Companies?" In *Sanghaya* 2002, ed. Bienvenido Lumbrera. Manila: National Commission for Culture and the Arts.

Vidad, Rudy and Doreen Fernandez. 1981. *In Performance.* Quezon City: Vera-Reyes Inc.

Villaruz, Basilio Esteban S. "The Quest for Filipino Choreography," *The Evening Express*, December 24, 31, 1980, January 7, 14, 21, 28, 1981.

______________. "Twice a Step-Child: Cinderella Fits Satin Slippers-Dance in the Philippines during the American Regime." Unpublished paper for the Diamond Jubilee Lectures, University of the Philippines.

______________. 1971. "In-Counter: Dance Theatre Philippines and Hadraya Dance Company," *Philippine Cultural.* Arts, Vol. II (Holy Week, 1971), pp. 8-9, 12-13, 19, 37.

______________. 1977. "The State of Dance in the Philippines Today," *Eddy About Dance* (New York), Winter, pp. 31-38.

______________, ed. 1977. *Sayaw Silanganan ng 1976-77.* Manila: Ballet Federation of the Philippines and Folk Arts Theater.

______________. 1978. "A Turning Point for the Filipino Dancer and His Dancing," *Sayaw Silanganan*, December.

______________. 1978. "Keeping the Philippine Ballet Tradition," *Sayaw Silanganan*, July, 6-8.

______________. 1978. "The Dancing Dolls are Still, But Only for Totoy," *Sayaw Silanganan*, July, 4-5. On Remedios de Oteyza.

______________. 1982. "An Odyssey into Authenticity: A Choreographer and His Society," *The Diliman Review* (University of the Philippines), January-February, pp. 47-51.

______________. 1982. "Ballet in the Philippines," *Islands*, Vol. 1, No. 1, December, 25-26.

______________. 1983. "Twice A Step-Child, or Cinderella Fits Satin Slippers: Dance in the Philippines during the American Regime." Unpublished paper for the Diamond Jubilee Lecture Series, Division of Humanities, College of Arts and Sciences, University of the Philippines, Quezon City, October 3.

______________. 1985. "A Wondrous, Dangerous Direction in Philippine Dance," *Sunday Pahayagang Malaya*, September 15, 3-5.

______________. 1989. "Philippine Dance Theatre Scene: Meeting a New Age in Asia in Dance Theatre Terms." *Performing Arts* (Singapore) 5, 34-38.

______________. 1989. "The Ever-Threatened Art of the Dance, or The Move into the Twenty-First Century." Unpublished manuscript read for the 1989 National Conference on the Arts of the Presidential Commission on Culture and Arts, Mt. Makiling. Los Baños. Laguna.

______________. 1989. "The Philippine Dance Theater Scene: Meeting a New Age in Asia in Dance Theatre Terms." *Performing Arts* (Singapore). No. 5 (July 1989), pp. 34-38.

______________. 1989. *Sayaw, An Essay on Philippine Dance*. Manila: Cultural Center of the Philippines. This special monograph comes with a video-documentation, directed by Ramon Obusan, scripted by Villaruz.

______________. 1990. "Catalabutte's Equivocal Calls to Manila: The French-Filipino Connection in Dance." Unpublished paper for the French Studies Lecture Series III and the Foundation Montaigne, Ateneo de Manila University, February 8.

______________. 1990. "Sailing in Two Streams: The Language and Body-Politics of Philippine Dance." *5th Hong Kong International Dance Conference*, Vol. II. Hong Kong: Hong Kong Academy of Performing Arts.

______________. 1991. "High Hopes for 'Habi'," *Manila Chronicle*, August 24-30, 24.

______________. 1991. "Identities in Festivity," *Manila Chronicle*, July 27-August 2, 34-35.

______________. 1991. "Lead Us Dancing into the Nineties: Denisa Reyes and Eddie Elejar," *Kultura* 4:1, 38-43.

______________. 1991. "Rizaliana and the Hispanic heritage in Contemporary Philippine Dance." Unpublished conference paper at the 14th Annual Conference of the Society of Dance History Scholars, February 8-10, Miami, Florida, USA.

______________. 1992. "Dance in the Philippines 1991: Dancing One's Own Tune." *Performing Arts* (Singapore), No. 7 (July 1992), pp. 11-12.

______________. 1993. "Philippine Dance Criticism: Who, Whence, Where." *Jade '93 Proceeding.* Tokyo: Jade '93.

______________. 1994. "Bodabil Dancing." In CCP *Encyclopedia of Philippine Art,* ed. Nicanor Tiongson. Manila: Cultural Center of the Philippines. V: 72-73.

______________. 1994. *Sayaw: An Essay on the American Colonial and Contemporary Traditions in Philippine Dance.* Manila: Cultural Center of the Philippines.

______________. 1995. "Indigenous Scholarship for Informed Criticism and a Philippine Bibliography." *International Academic Conference in Dance.* Malborg Kim, ed. Seaul: Yong-ku park.

______________. 1995. "Terpsichore and Tourism: The Transmogrification of Philippine Folk Dance." Paper read for Masyarakat Seni Pertunjukan Indonesia (Indonesian Society for the Performing Arts, Mataram, Lombok, Indonesia.

______________. 1996. "Multicultural Faces and National Imaging: Appropriating and Appreciating Philippine Folk Dance." Paper read at the Indonesian Dance Festival, Jakarta.

______________. 1996. "Philippine Folklore and Modernism." *Ballett International/Tanz Aktuell*, 11 (November 1996).

______________. 1997. "Ballet in the Non-Western Society: Dance Theatre Philippines-A Pirouette Off-Center." In *Ani* 24: *The Performing Arts and Literature*, ed. Basilio Esteban S. Villaruz. Manila: Cultural Center of the Philippines, 11-17.

______________. 1977. "The State of Dance in the Philippines Today," *Eddy About Dance*, Winter, No. 9, pp. 31-38.

______________. 1980-81. "The Quest for Filipino Choreography." *Evening Express*. December 24, 1980:8-9; December 31, 1980:8; January 7, 1981: 8; January 14,1981: 8; January 21,1981: 9; January 28, 1981: 8.

______________. 1983. "Crystallizing a Dance Company" in Celebration: Crystal Concerto souvenir program, April 9-10.

______________. 1983. "Princess Aurora or Maria Makiling and the Myth of Choreographic Success," *Dance Philippines*, October, pp. 6-8.

______________. 1983. "Revivals and Discoveries," *Arts Monthly*, April, pp. 22-23.

______________. 1983. "The Dance From Four Corners," *Dance Philippines*, July 1983, pp. 12-14; August 1983, pp. 9-10.

______________. 1985. "A Wondrous, Dangerous Direction in Philippine Dance," *Sunday Magazine—Malaya*, September 15, pp. 3-5.

______________. 1985. "Are Dances Forever? Looking Back and Forward," *Arts Monthly*, January, p. 17-19.

______________. 1986. "A Historical Note: Salvaged Dances" in 18th Anniversary Concert—*A Tribute to Tita Radaic* souvenir program, July 18.

______________. 1986. "Looking at the Dance," *New Day Magazine*, May 19, pp. 16-17.

______________. 1986. "Reforms, Recognition and Reconciliation in Dance," *Sunday Magazine—Malaya*, August 3, p. 6.

______________. 1987. "There's Less Cheer on the Ballet Front, but Hope Shines Through," *Sunday Magazine—Malaya*, November 8, pp. 10-11.

______________. 1988. "In Praise of Those Who Slipped Away," *Sunday Malaya*, July 31, p. 10.

______________. 1988. "Into the Cherished China Year" in 20th Anniversary Celebration: Giselle souvenir program, January 9-10.

______________. 1989. *Sayaw: An Essay on Philippine Dance*. Manila: Cultural Center of the Philippines.

______________. 1989. "The Philippine Dance Theatre Scene: Meeting a New Age in Asia in Dance Theatre Terms." *Performing Arts* (Singapore): 5.

______________. 1994. "A Critic in an Asian Cultural Context." Printed proceeding from "Tari '94" (Persidangan Dan Festival Tari Antarabangsa/International Conference and Dance Festival) 13-20 July 1994, Kuala Lumpur: Ministry of Culture, Arts and Tourism.

______________. 1994. *Sayaw: An Essay on the American Colonial and Contemporary Tradition in Philippine Dance*. Manila: Cultural Center of the Philippines.

______________. 1998. "A Brief on Philippine Dance Today" in *Contemporary Philippine Culture*. Makati: Japan Foundation.

______________. 1998. "The Philippine Music-Theater" in *Compendium of the Humanities. Musical Arts,* ed. Corazon Dioquino. Taguig: National Research Council of the Philippines.

______________. 1998. "Controversial Bill to Name 'National' Folk Dance Company in the Philippines." *Dance Magazine*, August. P. 32.

______________. 1998. "Philippines." In Zainall Abiddin Tinggal, gen. ed. *The Dances of ASEAN*. Brunei Darussalam: Asia Printers/ASEAN Committee on Culture and Information.

______________. 1998. "A Brief on Philippine Dance Today." *Contemporary Philippine Culture*. Manila: Japan Foundation-Manila.

______________. 1998. "Who Writes the World Dance History?" *The Korean Journal of Dance Studies*. Vol. 2. Fall, pp. 127-37.

______________. 1999. "Ballet Bias: Social Clash and Compromise." In 1998 *Philippine International Dance Conference: Dance in Revolution, Revolution in Dance,* ed. Basilio Esteban S. Villaruz. Manila: World Dance Alliance-Philippines, 46-51.

______________. 1999. "Sayaw sa Kawayan." Seminar paper. Taguig: National Research Council of the Philippines.

______________. 2001. "Wanted: Vision to Lead the Feet." In *Sanghoya* 2001, ed. Bienvenido Lumbrera. Manila: National Commission for Culture and the Arts, 40-43.

______________. 2002. "Promoting from the Center: an Asian Critic's View, a Philippine Experience." Keynote address. Dusseldorf: World Dance Alliance, August.

______________. 2001. "Dance: Wanted Vision to Lead the Feet." *Sanhaya 2001*. Manila: National Commission for Culture and the Arts. 40-43.

______________. 2002. "Promoting from the Center: An Asian Critic's View, A Philippine Experience." A keynote-speech delivered at the Global Dance assembly: World Dance Alliance, August 2002, Dusseldorf.

_______________. 2003. "Thinking on, Dancing to Dance: Dance Education in thc Philippines" in 2003 *International Theater Institute Asian Dance Conference*. Tokyo: Japan Centre of International Theater Institute.

Villaruz, Basilio Esteban S., and Agerico V. Cruz. 1986. "Philippine Dance: Tradition and Trends," Country Report of the Philippines, SPAFA Workshop for Choreographers and Dancers for the Younger Generation, Bogor, West Java, Indonesia.

Villaruz, Basilio Esteban S., and Ramon Obusa. 1992. *Sayaw: An Essay on Philippine Ethnic Dance*. Manila: Cultural Center of the Philippines.

Wazir Jahan Karim, ed. 1995. *Male and Female in Developing Southeast Asia*. Oxford: Berg Publishers.

Whitehead, Alfred North. 1949. *The Aims of Education*. New York: The New American Library.

Whitehead, Alfred North. 1955. *Adventures of Ideas*. New York: The New American Library.

Wigman, Mary. 1966. *The Language of Dance*. Trans. by Walter Sorell. Middletown: Wesleyan University Press.

Wigman, Mary. 1996. *The Language of Dance*. Middletown: Wesleyan University Press.

Wu Ji Mei and Gao Chua Lin. 1987. *Coordination Method Dance Notation*. Trans. Huang Yue Hua. Shanghai: Shanghai Literature and Art Publishing House.

Wulff, Helena. 1998. *Ballet Across Borders: Career and Culture in the World of Dancers*. Oxford: Berg Publishers.

Ylanan, Regino R. and Carmen Wilson Ylanan. 1974. *The History and Development of Physical Education and Sports in the Philippines*. Quezon City: University of the Philippines Press.

Young, Allen and Karla Jay, eds. 1979. *Lavender Culture*. New York: First Jove/HBJ Books.

Yousof, Ghulam-Sarwar. 1994. *Dictionary of Traditional South-East Asian Theatre*. Kuala Lumpur: Oxford University Press.

Yu, Doreen. 1990. *Ballet Philippines: Twenty Years of Dance*. Manila: CCP Dance Foundation.

Zaide, Gregorio, ed. 1990. *Documentary Sources of Philippine History*. Vols. I-X II. Manila: National Bookstore.

"Zipper to Wield Baton in MSO's Beethoven Concert," *Philippine Daily Express*, July 15, 28, 1977.

1991 Manila International Dance Conference Papers, 15-20 July 1991. Manila: CCP.

The Author

A dance and theater critic, choreographer and choreologist (movement notator), Basilio Esteban S. Villaruz is a professor in University of the Philippines. He helped set its College of Music dance degree program and UP Dance Company. He has had associations with Dance Theatre Philippines (dancer, choreographer, director), Ballet Philippines, Philippine Ballet Theater and founder of Movement men/Manila.

A contributor to organizations like the Cultural Center of the Philippines, National Commission for Culture and the Arts, and World Dance Alliance, Villaruz has been awarded grants in Asia, Europe, Britain, and United States, and cited for national and international productions and publications, lately from Congress on Research in Dance (CORD).